P9-CKR-764

I Chose Canada

Also by

Joseph R. Smallwood

Coaker of Newfoundland
The New Newfoundland
The Book of Newfoundland, 4 vols. (Editor)
Stories of Newfoundland (with L. E. F. English)
Handbook, Gazetteer and Almanac of Newfoundland
The Peril and the Glory
To You With Affection (pamphlet)

I Chose Canada

The Memoirs of the Honourable Joseph R.
"Joey" Smallwood

Macmillan of Canada / Toronto

ISBN 0-7705-1064-7

Printed in Canada
for The Macmillan Company of Canada Limited
70 Bond Street, Toronto M5B 1X3

To

my great-great-great-great-grandfathers
Captain Charles Smallwood, John Jamieson, Captain David Lawson

and

my great-great-great-grandfathers
Charles Smallwood, Laurence Brown, William Lawson

and

my great-great-grandfathers
Captain Joseph Smallwood, John Gamberg, John Brown,
George Cooper

and

my great-grandfathers
James Smallwood, John Cooper, Anthony Devanna,
Charles Gamberg

and

my grandfathers
David Smallwood, Michael Devanna

and

Charles William Smallwood and Mary (Minnie) Devanna,
my father and mother

and to

my wife, Clara, and our three children, Ramsay, William, Clara

and

our eleven grandchildren, Josephine, Lorraine, Dale, Joseph,
Jane, Ramsay, William, Robert, Tanya, Bruce, Douglas

and

our two great-grandchildren, Natasha and Tonya

All of them covering a span of 273 years

Contents

Illustrations

Every effort has been made to trace the copyright holders for these photographs, but the publishers will be pleased to know of any errors or omissions so that they may be rectified in future printings.

Acknowledgements

This book couldn't have been written without the help that I received, and I acknowledge gratefully the cooperation of J. Robert Mutch, who may be Canada's ablest genealogist, Wendel Kielly, and Mrs. Ira Brown in Prince Edward Island; my daughter Clara Russell and her daughter Dale in Newfoundland. John A. Nolan, James R. Thoms, Wally Millman, Elmer Harris, Albert B. Perlin, all of St. John's, rallied to my call for help, as did Dr. G. Alain Frecker, Gordon F. Pushie, Kenneth Duggan, Dr. Ray Barrett, Bruce Woodland, and Vice-President M. O. Morgan of Memorial University. My relative, Paul Smallwood, The Old Rectory, Stanford, near Ashford in Kent, was very kind and helpful, as were also several members of his family. The Hon. John W. Pickersgill and the Hon. John Turner gave help from Ottawa. Premier Frank Moores of Newfoundland, Premier Richard Hatfield of New Brunswick, and Premier Alexander Campbell of Prince Edward Island didn't hesitate to help. Bertrand Smallwood of St. Petersburg and Toronto, William D. Mulholland of Montreal, Air Canada, Eastern Provincial Airways, and the C.N.R. were unstinting in their response to my requests for assistance.

Daniel Hay, curator and librarian of the Library and Museum of Whitehaven, Cumberland County, England, the Scottish Ancestry Society of Edinburgh, the Public Records Office of London, Magistrate Geoffrey Smallwood of Hanley, Staffordshire, the Rev. Father Howard Docherty of London, the Irish Genealogical Society of London, all came to the rescue. John F. Gamberg, my cousin in Corner Brook, and the Rev. Charles G. Greene, Parish Priest at the Basilica, St. John's, gave me invaluable help in my genealogical research. Garry Callahan was especially helpful.

The public libraries and public archives in St. John's, Montreal, Ottawa, New York, Baltimore, Md., Richmond, Va., Washington, D.C., St. Petersburg, and Clearwater, Fla., and in London, Chester, Dublin, and the Channel Islands rendered valuable assistance. Prentice Price of Richmond, Va., unearthed and gave me needed information. Mrs. Dorothy Johannsen and Mrs. Frances Nordbye of Clearwater and Largo, Florida, gave loyal and indefatigable assistance. The book owes more than I'd like to admit to Kenneth McVey of the Macmillan Company of Canada.

Above all, I acknowledge gratefully the inspiration, loyalty, and support that the Newfoundland people have given to make my exciting career, and this book, possible.

I Chose Canada

Strait of Belle Isle
Hare Bay
Roddickton
73
Port-au-Choix
Port Saunders
River of Ponds
GULF OF ST. LAWRENCE
LONG RANGE MOUNTAINS
Daniel's Harbour
Portland Creek
White Bay
Fleur de Lys
Parson's Pond
Cow Head
St. Paul's
Baie Verte
BURLINGTON PEN.
Rocky Harbour
Norris Point
Trout River
South Brook
Bay of Islands
Deer Lake
Sandy Lake
Sheffield Lake
Lark Harbour
Cox's Cove
Howley
Botwood
TRANS-CANADA HIGHWAY
Grand Lake
Badger
Corner Brook
Grand Falls
Buchans
Long Point
Lourdes
PORT-AU-PORT PENINSULA
Mainland
Cape St. George
Point-au-Mal
Red Indian Lake
Stephenville
BARACHOIS POND PARK
ANNIEOPSQUOTCH MTS
1
St. George's Bay
Meelpaeg Lake
Victoria Lake
Round Pond
Long Pond
ANGUILLE MTS
Cape Anguille
South Branch
Doyles
St. Alban's
Red Rocks
Grand Bruit
Pushthrough
Gaultois
Cape Ray
Port-aux-Basques
Rose Blanche
Burgeo
Ramea
Cape La Hune
François
Hermitage Bay
Pass Island
Harbour Breton
CABOT STRAIT
Grand Bank
Fortune
MIQUELON (FRANCE)
L'ANGLADE (FRANCE)
ST. PIERRE (FRANCE)
St. Lawrence
Point-au-

NEWFOUNDLAND
ATLANTIC
OCEAN
Hebron
Nain
Hopedale
Indian Harbour
Michikamau Lake
LABRADOR
Cartwright
Churchill Falls
Labrador City
Wabush
Hamilton River
Goose Bay
Battle Harbour
NEWFOUNDLAND
QUEBEC
NEWFOUNDLAND
St. John's
CAPE BRETON I.
0 100 200
MILES
FOGO I.
Ragged Hbr
Carmanville
Lumsden
Cape Freels
Gander Bay
Wesleyville
Indian Bay
Bonavista Bay
Hare Bay
St. Brendan's
Burnside
Salvage
Bonavista
Catalina
Port
Kerley's Harbour
Trinity
Grate's Cove
Trinity Bay
Clarenville
RANDOM
Hants Hbr
Bay de Verde
Heart's Content
Conception Bay
Pouch Cove
Carbonear
Torbay
Spaniard's Bay
BELL I.
ST. JOHN'S
Topsail
Harbour Buffett
Holyrood
Whitbourne
Bay Bulls
Witless Bay
Placentia
Colinet
Salmonier
LaManche
Aquaforte
Ferryland
Renews
Branch
Biscay Bay
St. Mary's Bay
Cape Race
St. Shott's
Trepassey
0 20 40 60 80
MILES

"I'm warning you fellows – if I hear any more foolish talk I'll cut you adrift!"

The Chronicle-Herald (Halifax)

Preface

I was born in 1900.

What a year that was! The world seemed to stagger from the impact of conflict, for ten countries were ravaged by bloody war. Colonialist and anti-colonialist (as we call them now) shed blood in eleven other countries. Revolution of one kind or another burst out in still another eleven lands. Elsewhere, convulsive disorders, mutiny, rioting, atrocities, nationalistic demonstrations, famine, plague, and civil commotion of almost every kind overspread the face of most of the earth. In the year of my birth, much of mankind, civilized and "un"-civilized, was lacerated by bloody disorder.

Nineteen hundred was a remarkable year, one of the best or one of the worst to be born in; a typical twentieth-century year, too, as it turned out, heralding unmistakably the seven decades to follow. Without anyone's knowledge, the world was exploding into universal revolution, a mighty rushing, a chain-reaction of titanic explosion, the Götterdämmerung of the ages. The revolution engulfed all of Europe and the Near and Middle East, all of Asia, all of Africa, all of South America and Central America and the Caribbean, all the world except perhaps North America and Australia and New Zealand.

Even a quick look at the outline of events bears this out:

1900

1. In South Africa: war
2. In China: war
3. In Manchuria: war
4. In the Philippines: war
5. In the Ashanti (now partly Ghana): war
6. In Dahomey: war
7. In Colombia: war
8. In Abyssinia (Ethiopia): religious war
9. In Albania: border war
10. In Algeria: war

These were the formal, admitted, "honourable" wars. But fighting was going on in a lot of other places:

1. Fighting in French Equatorial Africa
2. Fighting in Guinea
3. Fighting in Kenya
4. Fighting in Liberia
5. Fighting in Madagascar
6. Fighting in Morocco
7. Fighting in Nigeria
8. Fighting in Nyasaland
9. Fighting in Somaliland
10. Fighting in the Sudan
11. Fighting in Arabia

Most of this fighting was with the English and with the French.

And even that is not all, for my birth-year was a year of revolution in nearly a dozen lands:

1. Revolution in Borneo
2. Revolution in Panama
3. Revolution in Colombia
4. Revolution in Uganda
5. Revolution in Argentina
6. Revolution in Martinique
7. Revolution in Venezuela
8. Revolution in Sierra Leone
9. Revolution in Rhodesia
10. Revolution in San Domingo
11. Revolution in the French Congo*

In addition to these full-fledged revolutions, there were riotous disorders in the world:

Revolutionary disorders in Spain
Anti-Semitic rioting in Germany
A reign of terror against Romanians in Bulgaria

Many terrible atrocities in the Congo; many villages burned down, much slaughter of natives for refusing to work at the rubber plantations: *700 natives had their hands cut off.*

*There have been 84 wars in my lifetime, and 210 revolutions. Nine kings, four queens, and two princes have been assassinated, as have been also 16 Presidents, 18 Premiers, 6 Ministers, and 2 Governors.

In Turkey, the Young Turks demanded an end of the Sultan's reign. There was some fighting.

Russia mobilized the East Siberian Army for operations in China. The reserves were called out.

There were Jewish riots in Odessa. Count Leo Tolstoy wrote the Czar, appealing against religious persecutions.

In China, the German Ambassador was assassinated.

Japan mobilized its troops, in view of the situation in China.

King Humbert of Italy was assassinated.

Great Britain annexed the Tonga Islands in May and the Orange Free State in September.

In Ireland, a great nationalist demonstration was held in Phoenix Park.

In India, terrible famine and plague mutilated a large portion of the land.

But not everything that happened in 1900 was bad. In Great Britain, a law was passed to forbid the employment of children underground in the mines. That was good. Astonishingly late, but good.

In the United States, labourers working on the new Cornell Dam at Croton, New York, went on strike for $1.50 a day. They were getting $1.25 a day! Not for another fourteen years was Henry Ford to startle North America and Europe by paying labourers $5 a day.

In Newfoundland, 1,500 miners at Bell Island went on strike for an increase of two and one-half cents in their ten-cents-an-hour pay. The strike lasted for many weeks, and several of the strike leaders were jailed in St. John's. That was good and bad—I think they gained one cent an hour.

In Great Britain, the Labour Party was founded—and that changed history.

Winston Churchill was first elected an M.P. Bad news for Adolf Hitler, who was then eleven years old.

In Germany, the first flight by the Zeppelin airship was made. It was not until 1903 that Orville Wright flew the first heavier-than-air engine-driven airplane.

In the United States, William Jennings Bryan was nominated for the second time to be the Democratic Party's candidate for president. After his third defeat, he was said to "lack sanction"—the gentlest term yet coined for electoral defeat.

In Newfoundland, 4,000 men in sealing ships at the Icefields took 350,000 seals worth $600,000. They were happily ignorant of the uproar that their trade was to stir up around the world in the 1970s.

In Newfoundland, Sir Robert Bond was elected Liberal Prime Minister. Though I'm a Liberal, realism forces me to say that his election might have been bad for Newfoundland's development. If Sir Robert G. Reid, who died in 1908, can read this he will laugh, sardonically.

Sir Frederick B. T. Carter, one of the two Newfoundland Fathers of Confederation, a former Prime Minister, died at the age of eighty. I am glad that he and I were alive in the same year, though in different parts of it. I'm glad, too, that we had a family relationship through marriage. (The other Father, Sir Ambrose Shea, died in 1905.)

The Dominion of Canada had seven provinces. Its population was 5,371,000 in 1901—a lot less than Ontario's today.

The United States, a second-class power, had forty-five states. Its population was 76,000,000 in 1901.

Newfoundland's population was 220,984 in 1901. It had taken us 400 years to get that far, but at least we could have taken ironic satisfaction from the fact that, largely in consequence of our poverty, a lot of England's West Country merchants, two and three centuries before, had founded their family fortunes in Newfoundland.

All of these and other things happened in 1900, but before my birth. I was born on December 24, Christmas Eve, so don't blame me for any of it.

Most of the revolutionaries were my contemporaries in 1900. By name and age, they were Alexander Graham Bell, 53; Thomas A. Edison, 53; James Kier Hardie, 44; Theodor Herzl, 40; David Lloyd George, 37; Henry Ford, 37; Sun Yat-sen, 34; Nikolai Lenin, 30; Wilbur and Orville Wright, 33 and 29; Mohandas Gandhi, 31; Guglielmo Marconi, 26; Albert Einstein, 21; Joseph Stalin, 21; Leon Trotsky, 21; Mustapha Kemal Ataturk, 19; Angelo Giuseppe Roncalli (later Pope John XXIII), 19; Eamon De Valera, 18; Franklin D. Roosevelt, 18; Benito Mussolini, 17; David Ben-Gurion, 14; Marcus Garvey, 13; Adolf Hitler, 11; Antonio de Oliveira Salazar, 11; Michael Collins, 10; Jomo Kenyatta, 9 (?); Josip Broz Tito, 9; Francisco Bahomonde Franco, 8; Mao Tse tung, 7; and Chou En-lai, 2.

I am not, of course, one of that remarkable crew, probably the most potent lot of revolutionaries ever to be in the world at one time. But a cabin boy, perhaps?

If I had been born five years earlier, I would have been a contemporary of Friedrich Engels, Karl Marx's partner; four years earlier, I would have been a contemporary of Harriet Beecher Stowe. Three years earlier, I would have been a contemporary of Newfoundland's first Prime Minister, Philip Francis Little, who took office in 1855. Two years earlier and my life would have overlapped the lives of Gladstone and Bismarck, and I would have been contemporaneous with the arrival at Port-aux-Basques of the first trans-Newfoundland railway train.

Human slavery still disgraced some parts of our earth in 1900. I have discussed the matter with the Anti-Slavery Society in London, and they did not disagree strongly with my guess of 10,000,000 human slaves in that year. They reminded me gently that an accurate figure would be very difficult to get, because by 1900 slavers and slave-owners, and the governments of slave countries, were well enough aware of the bad name that slavery had earned to make them more secretive than they had been. After all, 1900 was only thirty-nine years after the United States had plunged into a bloodbath largely over the same thing. And even today as I write, there are still nearly a million human slaves in thirty-eight countries of the world!

The Commonwealth of Australia didn't get born until the next year, 1901; New Zealand, not until 1907. Marconi did not receive that first generative wireless signal across the Atlantic to St. John's until December 2, 1901, almost a year after I was born. Queen Victoria was in her sixtieth year on the throne.

But it was only the third day after I was born that Carry Nation carried out her first big raid on a saloon, that of John L. Sullivan, in the Carey Hotel at Wichita, Kansas. She smashed everything in sight that she could lay her axe on.

Yes, an "interesting" world it was in 1900, with "imperialist aggression" at its peak, the "white man's burden" vigorously advertised, and the virtues of Christianity and democracy conferred upon inferior peoples whether they liked it or not. And often at considerable profit, too.

There were two billion of us in the world in 1900; there are almost four billion of us now. Billions have died, but billions have been born, for as Alfred Lord Tennyson so incontestably said:

Every moment dies a man,
Every moment one is born.

I have known half a dozen worlds since 1900 and lived a dozen lives, all of them stimulating, to say the least!

It really *is* exciting to be living in a time of universal revolution.

1

Light of Day in Gambo

There is nothing like a start, and being born, however pessimistic one may become in later years, is undoubtedly a start.

William McFee

Every one believes in his youth that the world really began with him, and that all merely exists for his sake.

Goethe

I was born on Christmas Eve 1900, in the tiny outport village of Gambo.

In that year, Newfoundland's population of 220,000 lived in 1,359 hamlets and villages separated one from the other by a mile or two or ten of empty coastline reaching thus along 6,000 miles of mostly rough coastal shore, and almost totally unconnected by road. In the whole country, there were not three settlements out of sight and sound of the Atlantic Ocean, I doubt that there was even one. The population of the only city, St. John's, was 29,594. The next largest place in the country, Harbour Grace, had 5,184 people. Hundreds of the settlements contained fewer than 20 families. There were 83 medical doctors, 93 policemen, 789 teachers, 500 miles of roads, no paving, not one public library, and only four places in the country served by central water and sewer systems, and they were only partially served: St. John's, Placentia, Harbour Grace, and Carbonear. The only way to get into or out of 90 per cent of the places was by sea. The illiteracy rate was a blighting 40 per cent and for a quarter of a century longer hovered over the Island, a dark cloud.

You would wonder why that handful of people of English, Irish, and Scottish descent did not demand better. Perhaps it was that, except in quite recent times, poor people weren't conscious of their own poverty. Today's rising tide of expectation is very much the result of airplane travel, movies, television, and all the other very modern means of quick and massive communication and mass movement of people. It used to be said that half the world did not know how the other half lived. The have-nots just did not know what a marvellous world was owned and enjoyed by the haves, and they couldn't envy what they didn't know. Certainly that was true, with a vengeance, in Newfoundland.

Nearly three-quarters of the Newfoundland people were directly engaged in the fisheries, and fisheries then overwhelmingly meant codfisheries: catching the fish, curing them with salt and sun, and packing and shipping salt-dried cod. The cod were shipped in sailing vessels across the Atlantic to Greece, Malta, Italy, Spain, and Portugal; and to the West Indies and Brazil in the South Atlantic. These were poor countries, incapable of paying a price for the cod that would allow Newfoundlanders to have a much better standard of living than they had themselves, if as good. And yet for 400 years, Newfoundlanders followed the codfisheries and lived the always perilous, perpetually poor life that was the requital of that trade.

Scores of years after Newfoundlanders first settled on the Island, other settlers from Europe made feeble clearings in the forest on the mainland of what is now Canada and cultivated half-acre by half-acre, seeding between the stumps. By 1900, they had coaxed millions of acres into smiling green meadows and prosperous fields, with their barns and stone dwellings and livestock and local roads and post offices, and a degree of material prosperity that Newfoundland had never known, had never imagined, in all its generations.

Newfoundlanders cultivated, too; but at the end of the first 400 years of toil, they had no productive meadows, almost no local or any other roads, precious few substantial houses, and no standard of material prosperity anywhere near that known in any other part of North America. For during those four centuries, their cultivation was of the unquiet, infuriate North Atlantic Ocean. They toiled as no farmers ever toiled in North America, risking death daily, and all the toil and danger had not won an acre for them or earned them much more, for most of the time, than unending scarcity on land and on sea and in the home.

The Newfoundland into which I was born might have been on another planet, in another age, so remote was it from the wide world outside. And Gambo, like every outport, was as remote from the rest of Newfoundland as Newfoundland was from the outside world. Gambo was not a typical Newfoundland settlement in any case, for it was not a fishing settlement. Twelve hundred of the 1,359 settlements in the country lived wholly by means of the fishery, but Gambo, Dark Cove, and Middle Brook got their living almost entirely from cutting saw-logs and then processing the logs into lumber in the big mill. In the 1860s, very good spruce and pine trees grew there, down to the very backyards of the houses, and my grandfather David Smallwood was the first to operate a sawmill in Gambo or anywhere else in Bonavista Bay for that matter. It was a mill driven by water-wheel, and it burned down. David replaced it with a steam-driven mill, the first in Newfoundland. One of his early acts in

Gambo was to select from the primeval forest a tall "suant" pine flagpole that he had decided to contribute to Harbour Grace's new Masonic Lodge, of which he had become a charter member in 1867, the year of Canada's birth. I was the grateful Master of that very Lodge 100 years later, in 1967, and enjoyed immensely the distinction of being installed in office by the Grand Master Mason (Scottish Constitution) Lord Bruce, who came from Scotland especially for the purpose. So met Gambo and the direct descendant of King Robert the Bruce. Proud? Oh, yes.

Gambo's population was 107 men, women, and children. Dark Cove's was 171 and Middle Brook's, 215. Mint Brook brought the total to 618 souls—virtually a Newfoundland metropolis, but a forlorn metropolis of small, mostly crude one-storey houses, rough log-cabins, or even tar-paper shacks. These settlements today are quite up-to-date villages with "all modern conveniences", snuggled inextricably together at the head of Freshwater Bay, which itself lies well up into Bonavista Bay; but in 1900, they were four separate communities. It was a poor place then, and is now, for inshore fishing. Cod just didn't come in adequate numbers that far up into the bay. There were, nevertheless, three or four small boats that fished daily out of Gambo, and there were two or three Labrador schooners as well. These thirty- to forty-ton sailing schooners, with five or six men on each of them, would sail off in the spring to the distant shore of Labrador. They formed a tiny part of the Labrador fishing fleet of 700 or 800 schooners based in their little harbours along the north-east coast of the Island. Newfoundlanders had a name for the fishermen in them—"floaters"—to distinguish them from the "stationers". Floaters fished from schooners and lived on board, while stationers lived on shore.

The new transinsular railway passed through Gambo, reinforcing its status of metropolis on the Newfoundland scale. As the railway followed its corkscrew pioneering trail across Newfoundland, through country much of which had never previously been travelled except by the aboriginal Beothucks or the more recent Micmac Indians, it touched the shoreline at only one point in the 253 miles between Port Blandford on the east coast and Humbermouth on the west coast of the Island. Gambo was the lucky place. The building of this primitive, narrow-gauge railway with its spindly rails 500 miles and more across the empty interior of an island whose population was only slightly more than 220,000 souls was a miracle of political and economic courage, if not of engineering performance.

My father, Charles William Smallwood, had only one trained skill, that of lumber surveyor. He too had been born in Gambo, as were a couple of his brothers, when my grandfather David operated the sawmill in the 1860s; but like me, he spent only a short time there after his birth. When he married in 1900 and found himself with a wife to support, he sought and got a job at the one trade he knew from the new owners of the sawmill enterprise in Gambo, at a salary that I suppose wouldn't exceed $40 a month. Thus it came about that I was born in Gambo. For more than a century, the Smallwoods have been connected with the history and life of the community. Of the approximately 500 voters there were in the combined Gambo community in 1946, when I stood for election to the National Convention, more than 490 voted for me. They voted in much the same proportions in every subsequent election when I was a candidate.

I was the first-born of 13 children—a family of 7 girls and 6 boys: Marie, Ida, Isabel, Sadie, Alice, Dot, and Maxine; and Dave, Charlie, Alex, Reg, and Gus. The children kept coming along through the first 24 years of my life. Maxine, the last of our brood, also was born on Christmas Eve, in 1924. All 13 of us have had good health and energy, and all 13 of us married. Twelve of us have had children, 10 of us have had grandchildren, and 3 of us have had great-grandchildren: 62 children, 118 grandchildren, 5 great-grandchildren—a total, with the 13 of us, of 198. The only member of our family who had no children was my sister Sadie. She died in 1965. In the 72 years since I was born, there have been nine deaths in our family, not counting our two parents: one of the original 13, and 8 children or grandchildren. Nine in a total of 198 in the 72 years. It may not be a record, but it surely doesn't fall far short.

My mother was twenty years old and a Roman Catholic when I was born. She was only nominally a Roman Catholic, and she had been married to my father, a Methodist, in the Methodist Church in St. John's earlier that year. She often told me of her religious life as a girl growing up in a Roman Catholic family—the usual large family—in the 1880s and 1890s in St. John's. For some reason, she hated going to Mass, and often she was almost literally driven there with her father and mother walking behind her. She skipped Mass every chance she got, though I have never understood why. She never in her life seemed to have any ill-feeling toward the church into which she had been born, and often she repeated for me in Latin some words of the Mass that she still remembered. Three of her sisters married Protestants; but unlike her, they held on to their faith and made every effort to procure the conversion of their husbands. They did all finally succeed. Uncle Jim Scott, an Anglican, converted on or near his deathbed; and the others too, perhaps to please their much-worried wives, agreed before their end to convert.

I have said that my father was a Methodist. But he was only nominally so. He had been christened in the Methodist Church in St. John's, and insofar as he had any religious experience at all, it was in the Methodist Church. This only meant that he went to Methodist Sunday School on any Sundays when he couldn't avoid going, and to Methodist Church when he was driven. His indifference as a Protestant was much the same as my mother's as a Roman Catholic. Neither of them was a bit interested in religion when they married and for a good many years afterward. My father never to his death showed any interest whatever in religion. I cannot say that he was a Protestant, but only that he was the usual anti-Roman Catholic of the times. My mother eventually became deeply religious, but I will come to that.

The people of Gambo took the young St. John's bride, my mother, to their hearts, and her closest friend was a young married woman named Mary Broderick (née White, of St. Brendan's). She had been married about the same time as my parents, and her first child, a boy, came along seven days before I did. Each of the new mothers had a new baby carriage (I think Grandfather Smallwood sent ours to Gambo), and it was their delight to show off their babies (and the baby carriages) along the single, muddy, rocky street there was in Gambo. Mary Broderick named her boy James, and Jim is still flourishing in Gambo. Years afterward on a visit to Gambo, quite by accident, I ran into Mrs. Broderick, and my heart was warmed by her delight when she discovered who I was.

I was a very tiny baby, and I had bow-legs that had to be straightened later by laced boots reaching to my knees. I had to wear them for several years, until I was four or five years old. These special boots were made by hand in my uncle Fred's boot and shoe factory in St. John's. For the first few years, my mother lived in mortal fear that I was a dummy, for I didn't speak a word until I was nearly three. Some of my friends say that I have made up adequately for it since.

It was my grandfather David who chose my names. The Rt. Hon. Joseph Chamberlain, Her Majesty's Principal Secretary of State for the Colonies (known more briefly to his admirers as Joe), was in the eyes of romantic millions in Britain and the Colonies a great statesman, an illustrious Empire man, and a pre-eminent imperialist. My grandfather David admired him greatly, and he admired "Bobs" even more. This was Field Marshal Lord Roberts. Lord Roberts was believed by every patriotic British subject to be the most eminent soldier in the world. After forty years in India, he was, when I was born, Commander-in-Chief of the British Army in South Africa, where the Boer War was providing the lucky culminating springboard for young Winston Churchill's first election to Parliament.

And so I was named Joseph Roberts, but of course I still had to be christened. There was no clergyman in Gambo. Nearly all of the people were Irish Roman Catholics, and they were visited at intervals by a priest.

The leading citizen of Gambo was an ardent Roman Catholic, and he was scandalized to discover that the wife of one of his important employees was a Roman Catholic married to a Protestant in a Protestant church.* So one day, when I was only a few weeks old and the Roman Catholic priest happened to be in Gambo, this man came along by the house; knowing my father was away, he poked his head in through the open window and told my mother urgently that now was her chance to get the baby baptised. My mother declined firmly.

Protestant clergymen had rarely—if ever—visited Gambo, but one arrived just at the right moment. This was the celebrated Welsh-born Newfoundlander, the Rev. Charles Lench. Mr. Lench was the Methodist minister at Bird Island Cove (now called Elliston) in Trinity Bay, and he became one of the most popular preachers, lecturers, and pamphleteers of the century in Newfoundland. He used to break into song during his sermons, and his sweet singing appealed enormously to his congregations. He was very tall, had no eyebrows, and wore a villainously ill-fitting wig. The Methodists had decided to build a larger church in Elliston, and their minister came to Gambo to buy the lumber for it. His arrival was timely, and my mother got him to christen her child. He baptised me and entered me on the Methodist records at Elliston. Years later, when I was in politics, I

*His grandson became a member of my Cabinet. I never knew a more tolerant Christian gentleman.

used to enjoy pointing out that I could thus count myself a Trinity Bay man as well as a Bonavista Bay man.

I got to know Mr. Lench when I grew up and found him to be one of the most attractive personalities I ever knew. His son Bert was a poet with ambitions to be a novelist: he confided to me that he wanted to write the Great Newfoundland Novel. But he was gassed in the First World War and died, as a result, in the 1920s. His early death perhaps deprived Newfoundland of a novelist and poet of authentic style. Another son was Thomas, the architect. He designed many new schools during my time as Premier, and I always had a certain secret pleasure as I performed the official act of opening them—the outward joy of opening another new school, and the inward satisfaction of sharing the joy with Parson Lench's son.

I often listened to my mother's tales of her life in Gambo, which lasted less than two years: of the usual "characters", the escapades of the young crowd, the wild fights at the dances, and all the other simple but colourful incidents of life in a Newfoundland outport, especially an Irish outport, in the early days of this century. One of the Devine brothers of King's Cove worked as timekeeper in the sawmill where my father was the lumber surveyor, and he used to chronicle the principal humorous events of the settlement in verse. Maurice Devine and Patrick K. Devine, two of his brothers, were celebrated editors and authors throughout the early years of my life in St. John's. P. K. was a good friend to me, as was his son Lou and his grandson, the lawyer John H. Devine.

As a boy, I used to listen delightedly to stories that my grandfather David told me about life in Gambo in the 1860s, when the settlement couldn't have been more than twenty years old. There was a small number of Indians, Micmacs, living at Gambo. They made their living mainly as guides to hunters going upcountry after caribou and other game, and doing odd jobs around the settlement. One of them was Jim Joe. He liked to be given a drink of rum and expected payment in that form for any small service he gave. A man intending to go upcountry without a guide asked Jim Joe what the weather was going to be like. He offered no payment for the advice and so Jim Joe, looking solemnly at the sky, replied, "Him may rain, him may snow—me don't know."

2

John Barleycorn Won This Round

Bacchus hath drowned more men than Neptune.

Thomas Fuller

O God, that men should put an enemy in their mouths to steal away their brains!

William Shakespeare

There are more old drunkards than old doctors.

French proverb

My grandfather David came to Newfoundland from Charlottetown, Prince Edward Island, in 1861. He was accompanied by his cousin, Fred Stagman, and they came as passengers on a sailing vessel loaded with hay and vegetables for sale in St. John's. The very day he landed in St. John's, he found a job and a wife for himself. He had heard of a big construction job in the West End of the city, the building of St. Patrick's Church on Patrick Street, and to it he went straightaway from the schooner and asked for a job as a carpenter. He got it at once and was told he could start work the next day.

As he strolled back eastward on Water Street, gazing into the shop windows, he came to a millinery shop (where women's hats and bonnets, and ribbons, were processed in a back room and displayed for sale in the shop). He peered in and was struck by the sight of a very pretty girl inside. He went into the shop, and the girl, who was two or three years younger than himself, asked him, "Yes, sir, what do you want?" "I want you, if I can get you," he smiled. And he did, for they were married a few months later. Julia Cooper owned and managed the shop, and was doing a fairly brisk trade, for she was an energetic and ambitious young woman and possessed a strong love of money that lasted throughout her life.

To his first job in St. John's my grandfather took with him his tool chest filled with a number and variety of carpenter's tools, the like of which the other carpenters on the job had never seen. It was all that my grandfather had to his name, apart from his skill as a carpenter, for his five years' apprenticeship with a carpenter in Charlottetown. His father, my great-grandfather James, following the practice of the times, got that carpenter in Charlottetown to agree that David on his sixteenth birthday should be articled in writing to him for five years. This meant that on his twenty-first birthday he would graduate as a full-fledged journeyman carpenter. Throughout the five years, he would live with his employer and receive in payment, besides his room and board, perhaps $10 or $15 a year to start, with a small amount added each succeeding year. It was barely enough to keep him in clothes and to enable him to buy his set of tools, piece by piece.

Father Crook, an Irish priest stationed in St. John's, showed considerable interest in the young Prince Edward Island carpenter. Often while David worked on the building of St. Patrick's Church, Father Crook sat on a bench and watched him. "I never saw anyone who could drive nails like you!" the priest exclaimed. David, fun-loving then as ever afterward, got one off on Father Crook. "Father, what happens when this church is finished?" "It'll be consecrated, of course," the priest told him. "You mean everything in it will be consecrated?" David asked. "Yes, everything in it." "All the stone, and wood, and everything in it?", he persisted. "Yes, everything in it," Father Crook repeated. Then came the punch-line: "Smallwood, too?"

His work on St. Patrick's Church was the only wage work that my grandfather ever did, for very soon after, he set up business as a small-time building contractor and built a number of structures in the city and nearby. One of them was pointed out to me by my father when I was a very small boy; it was the big barn on Cowan's Farm on the Topsail Road. I remember looking at it with wonder, for it was certainly the largest farm building anywhere to be seen in Newfoundland at that time. In later years, over half of the barn was removed, but I believe part of it stands to this day. And there is still in St. John's at least one substantial dwelling that my grandfather built. It is on Maxse Street, and he built it more than 100 years ago for a fellow Prince Edward Islander, Sir Joseph Little, Judge of the Supreme Court and brother of Newfoundland's first Prime Minister, Philip Francis Little.

I have mentioned my grandfather's love of fun and jokes. More than once he told me the story of his joke with Bishop Howley. Bishop Howley was the first native-born Newfoundlander to become a bishop, and he was a great Newfoundland historian, an ardent public admirer of Sir Robert Bond; and I was delighted, in my studies of Confederation, to discover that Howley had been a strong Confederate in his day. My grandfather was in business on Water Street at the time, and in chatting with Bishop Howley one day, he remarked innocently, "I suppose, my Lord, that pretty well every family has its black sheep?" The bishop agreed, and cited a few instances. "Yes, my Lord," remarked my grandfather, by way of corroboration, "and we have a black sheep in our family, too." "Is that so?" the bishop asked guardedly. "Yes, indeed, I have a cousin who is a Roman Catholic priest." If Bishop Howley laughed as heartily when he heard this from my grandfather as my grandfather did when he told me the story, then truly he must have had more of a sense of fun than most bishops have.

My grandfather loved horses dearly, and he kept one or two throughout most of his life in St. John's. Indeed, one of the sights of St. John's was that of my grandmother Julia dressed in her silks and satins being driven in a stylish rig by a coachman along Water Street. She was a very proud woman, and she liked to cut that kind of dash. David's most famous horse was the stallion General Gordon that he imported from Canada; it was the fastest horse that had ever been seen in Newfoundland up to that time and for many years after.

It was only two or three years after he arrived in St. John's that my grandfather went to Gambo to establish the first sawmill in Bonavista Bay. A few years later, he moved to Greenspond, where he became an important merchant.

The most serious flaw in my grandfather's character was one that made him less of a businessman than he needed to be to make money, but it was indispensable if he was to be a decent Christian gentleman. He was endlessly, patiently generous; as the saying goes, he would give you his heart. One famous winter and spring, when David and his family were living in Greenspond, the entire northeastern third of Newfoundland's coast was frozen in. The ice blockade barred every harbour from Baccalieu to the Strait of Belle Isle and far beyond. Food supplies began to run out all along the coast, and there was no early prospect of replacement. Soon people were rationing themselves, and then they began to be without food. To make matters worse, the spring break-up was very late in coming. Rarely in our 500-year history has there been such a desperate predicament. Since David had a large family, he had put into his home about twenty wooden barrels of flour to last through the late fall, winter, and spring until navigation opened again. The flour was in a storehouse attached to the dwelling. As people came to him in distress, my grandfather gave them small supplies of flour from his own home stock. Men or women would come along pleading for help as the spring advanced, and he would tell them to come back that night and bring a bag of some sort. He would then slip into the storehouse and extract some flour from a barrel. One by one the barrels emptied, but he filled them with sawdust to fool Julia. She would never have allowed it for a moment, and it is not difficult to imagine her fury when she discovered the deception. They were then down to his last remaining barrel of flour. She raged at him, accused him of trying to starve the family to death, and made life as miserable for him as she was capable of doing. I may say that her capability was considerable. His answer only maddened her the more. "Don't fret, my dear, the Lord will provide," to which she replied, "You and the Lord! You'll starve us to death before you're finished." David only repeated patiently, "The Lord will provide." Every day he climbed to the highest point on Greenspond Island, the better to gaze out to sea over that wide expanse of ice for the hoped-for vessel. His neighbours shook their heads as they saw him go daily to his lookout. And then Greenspond sprang alive with wild excitement as the word flashed around that a vessel was coming. And a vessel did come, and she was loaded with foodstuffs. As her skipper stepped onto the wharf, my grandfather asked him how he had managed to get through. "I don't know, Mr. Smallwood," the man replied. "All I know is that the ice opened before me and closed behind me, and here I am." And there he was indeed, loaded to the gunnels with barrels of pork and beef and flour, bags of peas and beans, tubs of margarine, puncheons of molasses, chests of tea, and all the rest of the outport Newfoundlanders' rough diet of those days. The vast expanse of ice stretching out thirty miles from the shore was still there. Of course, my grandfather always considered the explanation to be quite simple: the Lord had truly provided.

He had that kind of simple faith, undeviatingly held. That winter was the coldest in remembered Newfoundland history. Most people just kept the wood piled into their stoves to keep the house warm and never poked their noses outdoors, except to get fresh supplies of water or to do other absolutely necessary chores. I don't know why, but one day my grandfather set out with a companion to walk over the bay ice from Pool's Island to his home in Greenspond. He had his gun slung over one shoulder, and his shot-bag and powder-horn over the other. He was wrapped up as warmly as a man could be then and wore long, fur-lined mittens reaching to his elbows. The two of them went through the ice at a point where it was only an inch thick or less. With his heavy load of gun, powder-horn, and shot-bag and his heavy clothes, my grandfather began to sink. He wriggled out of his gun and let the shot-bag and powder-horn go, and then hauled the mittens off and struck out to get to the surface. But he came up underneath the ice. A glimmer of light showed him where he had fallen in, and he struck for the place. As he grasped the broken edge of the ice, it gave way beneath him, and he realized that he would have to be extremely careful. When he was in a spot where the ice was thick enough to hold him, he did not have the strength to get himself up out of the water onto the ice. He prayed desperately in words that he repeated to me so many times, "Oh God, save me!" And then, as he used to tell it, it was just like someone grasping him by the ankles and physically thrusting him up onto the ice. He lay for a moment to get his breath, and then he remembered his companion, who was still struggling in the water. My grandfather stretched out on his stomach and, cautioning his friend not to haul him into the water with him, reached out gingerly and allowed the man to clasp his two hands; then he wriggled backward on the ice until they were both safe.

His friend was almost completely exhausted and wanted just to lie down and be left alone. Clouting and booting him, my grandfather got him up and moving, and made him trot ahead of him toward Greenspond. They hadn't far to go then, but by the time they reached shore, their clothes were frozen like boards on them. When at last they staggered into my grandfather's house, these had to be cut off them with a knife. My grandmother gathered all the pots and pans she could crowd on the old-fashioned kitchen stove and started to heat lots of water for them. While they soaked themselves in the hot water in another room, Julia prepared the sure and certain stimulant in such a case, hot ginger tea. My grandfather drank a vast quantity of it—sixteen or eighteen scalding hot cups. Never afterward, to his death, was he able to drink or eat anything hot, but doubless the ginger tea saved his life and that of his friend as well.

In the 1880s, my grandfather returned to St. John's from Greenspond to look around for a new enterprise. He heard of a prosperous boot and shoe business that was available; its owner, a Nova Scotian named Archibald, was a personal friend of my grandfather. He showed David the latest balance sheet of the business, offered to sell it on a plan of installment payments, and gave an option of two weeks. My grandfather then started to look for a money man who would be interested in putting up the first sizable downpayment in return for a partnership. The man with whom he negotiated was the only person that I ever heard my grandfather condemn or even speak harshly about in all the years that I knew him. And the man in question was famous, for he was the Hon. Moses Monroe.

Moses Monroe was indeed a money man. He had built the famous Rope Walk in St. John's, was interested in other enterprises, and took an active part in municipal affairs. He was also the uncle of one of Newfoundland's prime ministers, Walter S. Monroe. As my grandfather told me the story, Moses Monroe appeared to be deeply interested in the proposed deal, but failed to act on it up to and immediately beyond the expiry date of the option. And then, to my grandfather's lasting disgust, Moses Monroe stepped in and personally purchased the business. Thus began the famous Newfoundland firm of Parker and Monroe, who are now by far the largest footwear merchants in the province. They used to have a large boot and shoe factory as well, but that became one of the first casualties of Confederation.

Perhaps because he was angry, David was all the more determined to go into the boot and shoe business, and he never stopped until he had built one that was in its day the largest of its kind in the country. He specialized in the manufacture of leather fishermen's boots. They were made mostly by hand and in three styles: one came well above the ankles, the other came up to the knees, and the third pretty well to the thighs. It was then that my grandfather had a chance to show his real flair; he was undoubtedly the pioneer in advertising and commercial public relations in Newfoundland. He did everything in the book to make the name and fame of Smallwood's boots known to the entire population throughout the Island.

Once he arranged to have one of his smartest skilled workmen blacken his face and hands to make himself look as much like a Negro as possible (I don't think there was even one black person living in Newfoundland at the time). The workman took his tools into the front display window of the shop and proceeded calmly but swiftly with the making of fishermen's boots, exactly as though he were at his own workbench in the factory. "No matter what happens outside on the street," David enjoined, "don't look up. Don't look out at anyone. Just pretend that you don't know that there is anyone on the sidewalk. Remember now, this is a very important part of it!" So the blind was drawn, the tools and the workman installed in the window, the work started, and the blind raised. Inside an hour, that section of Water Street was blocked from sidewalk to sidewalk, and the crowd continued to grow as the word spread through the town that a black man was working down at Smallwood's, and you could see him at work in the window. The best-known policeman in St John's then, and for years afterward in fact, was Sergeant Long. After trying, without success, to get the crowd to disperse, he finally pushed his way into the shop and expostulated vehemently with my grandfather. David managed to look surprised and said, "Surely you're not suggesting that I am in any way responsible for a crowd gathering on the street?" Now his foresight paid off. If the workman in the window had looked up and smiled or grinned, or otherwise acknowledged the crowd outside, it could have been a different story. In any event, it was a clever way of advertising Smallwood's boots.

He employed a Frenchman who called himself Count deCourcy. I don't know if he actually was a count, but my grandfather found him quite useful to write doggerel verse about Smallwood's boots. These verses were printed on cards and distributed in large quantities, and they came to be very well known. I remember one:

> Smallwood's Boots are the best of leather,
> Smallwood's Boots they suit all weather,
> Smallwood's Boots they are so grand,
> They are the best in Newfoundland!

I don't know just where these lines fit in, but they were part of it too:

> Smallwood's Boots for lads and lasses,
> Smallwood's Boots—They suit all classes.

It wasn't great poetry, I reluctantly admit, but it constituted magnificent advertising in Newfoundland during the 1880s and 1890s.

Over the front door of his shop on Water Street, David hung a huge boot made of planks strapped together with iron bands. Down the leg of the boot on each side were the words, "Buy Your Boots At", and then along the length of the foot on either side, "Smallwood's". I remember seeing that boot many times.

David practised countless stunts to advertise his boots. I remember once talking to John Batt in Openhall, on the south side of Bonavista Bay. He was then seventy-six or seventy-seven, and he told me of being in his tiny field years before, mowing his hay with a hand-operated scythe. Suddenly a voice hailed him. He looked up and saw a stranger leaning over the fence. The stranger was David, and they got talking, and the upshot was that my grandfather (who had been born and raised on a farm) climbed over the fence and took a turn at cutting the grass. John Batt told me that never in his long life had he seen a man who could swing a scythe like that. Then he told me about one of his earliest recollections: he and the other young fellows in Openhall would go looking for patches of smooth mud into which they could press the heels of their leather boots; when they lifted them carefully away, a clear print was left in the mud from an iron casting nailed to the heel of the boot, spelling in a semi-circle the name Smallwood.

My grandfather's greatest advertising stunt was performed in the Narrows, the entrance to St. John's Harbour. The cliffs rise vertically from the water on both sides of the Narrows, and nearly every fisherman in Newfoundland used to pass between them by schooner at least twice every year. My grandfather saw here a marvellous opportunity to advertise his boots. He had a hole drilled horizontally into the face of the cliff, and into this hole he had installed a stout iron bar four or five inches in diameter and twelve or fifteen feet long. This was wedged tightly in place, and from it a huge boot was suspended by two stout chains. The boot was made of three-inch planks powerfully banded together with iron strapping. It was painted black on both sides, and in luminous paint—so that they could be read by day or night—were printed the same words as those on the boot hanging over the front door of his shop. That boot remained there for years and years. It was the first view of St. John's for everyone coming into the city and his last view as he left. Finally, a terrible storm blew and twisted the boot about until the chains broke and it fell into the sea. I have often wondered why it was not replaced. Perhaps it was because of the invention of the rubber boot, which doomed Smallwood's fishermen's boots to extinction. The rubber boots were very light in weight and flexible, and did not need half the attention that leather boots required. They were also cheaper, being mass produced in American and European factories.

And the question of caring for leather boots brings to mind another tale. The boots had to be greased to keep the leather supple; if they weren't greased, they'd dry out and crack and become leaky. One fisherman came in to see David in the fall and registered a complaint. "Mr. Smallwood," (or as many northern fishermen said it, "Smallood"—I have myself been so addressed by fishermen in Bonavista Bay) "Mr. Smallwood, I has a complaint to make." "Is that so, my son?" my grandfather asked solicitiously. "What is it?" "It is that pair of boots you sold me last spring, you mind?" My grandfather probably didn't remember, but he nodded and said:

"Yes, what about them?" "They fell off me feet!" exclaimed the fisherman. "They just fell off me feet, sir." My grandfather said, "Of course they did—you smothered them in grease and they rotted off your feet." "No, no, sir," protested the fisherman, "I did not put ar a bit of grease on them!" "Exactly," my grandfather said triumphantly, "and that's where the trouble came in." The story did not end there, with my grandfather using his quicker wit to defraud the fisherman. He would in fact trade the boots for a pair of new ones, and the fisherman would go off happy.

He was a wonderfully popular man, David Smallwood, with scarcely an enemy in all the world. All day long, particularly in the spring and in the fall when fishermen arrived—and thousands came to St. John's and visited the shop to buy their boots—he would stand in the middle of the floor to greet the fishermen or to be greeted by them by name. His beard grew down over his chest, and a patriarchal figure he must have looked. But his manner was invariably genial, and he had always a free, joking word for every fisherman. For his customers' part, it never occurred to them on entering the shop to go to one of the clerks to be served. They went straight to David Smallwood himself, who after greeting them and learning what they wanted would call a clerk over, introduce the fisherman, and give directions for him to receive every attention. Even after David ceased to own the business, the new owner, his oldest son Fred, was wise enough to ask his father to continue working for the firm in this capacity, as the official greeter of Newfoundland. Subsequently, my grandfather grew to be too old even for so pleasant a work, and Fred then gave him a pension for life.

My only conscious recollection of my grandfather is of that part of his life when he was a retired pensioner. He played a great part in shaping me, though he never did succeed throughout his life in converting me to be a Confederate, our Newfoundland term for one who believes in Confederation with Canada. He was himself an ardent Confederate, and he used to bemoan the fact that his native Prince Edward Island had been so slow to enter the new Canadian Confederation. And he used to tell me earnestly that it was a great pity indeed that Newfoundland had not entered in 1869. "How much better off we'd be today if we'd gone in with Canada," he would say feelingly to me. I remember it now, but at the time his words had little impact on me. He fought for Confederation in that famous '69 General Election, when Charles Fox Bennett, the leader of the Anti-Confederate Party, raged through the country with rum and lies to frighten the fishermen into voting against the union. The Confederate Party had its Confederate flag, and the Anti-Confederates had theirs. Many an election battle was fought to raise or tear down a flag. In Greenspond, my grandfather proudly flew his Confederate flag from the flagpole in front of his house; and when a crowd came to tear it down, he stood at the foot of the pole, axe in hand, and dared anyone to come near. No one challenged him, and the flag continued to fly.

David Smallwood, I judge, must have been one of the most remarkable athletes of his day in Newfoundland. He stood perhaps five feet four inches tall and weighed about 150 pounds. He was a great walker, runner, and jumper. Once, after he had become a Water Street merchant and manufacturer, he went down to the annual regatta on the shore of Quidi Vidi Lake near St. John's. This regatta, perhaps the oldest event of its kind still operating anywhere in Canada (it has been running continually since about 1828), attracted the whole population of the city and many from the nearby outports. David stood for a while watching the best high jumpers of the city competing for the highest jump of the day; and after they had notched the pole up slowly inch by inch and it was clear that one jumper in particular led all the others, David asked mildly if anyone could get in on this. They replied laughingly that anyone could, so my grandfather took off his coat and vest, collar and tie, and tied his braces about his waist. There was a laugh all around from the crowd when he directed them to raise the pole another inch, but he went over it without touching it; then he told them to raise it another inch and flew over it again.

Captain Abram Kean, the greatest sealing captain in Newfoundland's history, the man who brought more than a million seals to shore, was himself a Bonavista Bay man who had been born on a small island not far from Greenspond. He knew my grandfather well and told me of another of David's feats: eighteen empty molasses puncheons had been placed side by side, and my grandfather had jumped into the first one, from that into the second, and so on in and out of all eighteen puncheons.

There was another occasion when he showed his remarkable ability as a jumper. He was down on his own wharf in Greenspond awaiting the arrival of his schooner, *The Fanny S,* which was due in from St. John's with a load of provisions and fishery supplies. His wife, Julia, had been up to St. John's on a visit and was expected back on this schooner. There was the usual crowd on the wharf as the schooner made her way into the harbour, but a shout of laughter went up as the schooner, instead of tying onto David's own wharf, for some reason tied onto the near-side of the next wharf. "You won't see the Missus for a while yet, Mr. Smallwood," called out one of his neighbours, and there was another laugh. My grandfather said nothing but climbed down onto the deck of a schooner by his own wharf, stood on the rail nearest his own schooner, and in a standing jump crossed the twenty-one-and-a-half-foot stretch of water between and landed on the deck of *The Funny S,* just inside her rail! This jump became as celebrated in Bonavista Bay in its time as Mark Twain's celebrated Jumping Frog in its day.

David truly had remarkable stamina. Even in the last year of his life, as he approached ninety, he went for a daily walk downhill from his home on upper Springdale Street to the two shoe shops on Water Street at the lower level of the town; then, after a rest, he walked all the way upgrade to his house again, a distance of at least a mile each way.

The most distinctive physical features of David Smallwood's face were his kindly, humorous, eloquent eyes separated by a nose that was too big for his face—almost a proverbially Semitic nose. "The Smallwood nose," he called it, and he never looked at a grandchild or great-grandchild for the first time without remarking with satisfaction that yes, sure enough, the child had the Smallwood nose.

I revered my grandfather David. He was ahead of his time in most ways. In another milieu or time, he might have been a great politician, or a minister of the Gospel, or even a great athlete.

Businessman he was never cut out to be, if this means careful building of a business enterprise with a view always to making money and holding onto it. He was the promoter, the enthusiast, the idea man, and what he always lacked was the thing he needed most: a loyal partner who would give the business the kind of careful balance-sheet devotion that David was incapable of giving.

As I have mentioned, my grandfather David's family was a large one. He used to be pleased when someone asked him how many children he had, for it gave him another chance to say, "Well, figure it for yourself: I have eleven sons and each one of them has a sister!" My father, Charles William, was his third son.

A Cabinet colleague told me that the first time he got drunk he was twelve years old. I didn't tell him that my father had been drunk at least once before he was twelve. He had to be carried home by his chums, who dumped him in his doorway, rang the bell, and ran. I read with understanding Upton Sinclair's account of his alcoholic father.

Excessive drinking, even alcoholism, has been pretty widespread, though not universal, in our family. It ruined the careers, if not the lives, of several of my uncles as well as my father's. I think that my father's case was the worst, and in my early years, his drinking was a secret shame that I lived with. I had a violent fear of drinking. I not only shrank from touching any kind of alcoholic drink myself, but ardently advocated temperance for all others; and not only temperance, but absolute prohibition by law. It took a good many years, until I was well into my forties, before my fear was replaced by what I hope is a more rational attitude toward drinking.

One of my uncles did his drinking—I ought to say debauching—sensibly. For most of the year, he drank not at all, because he couldn't drink a modest amount. If he drank at all, he had to get drunk, so he saved it up for the summer; then he would charter a small sailing schooner, gather together three or four merchant-companions from along Water Street, half-load the schooner with whiskey, and head for some small, uninhabited cove along the coast. There they would stay for several weeks, consuming the supply they had brought with them. Other uncles had their own individual ways of satisfying their craving for alcohol, and of ruining their careers.

My father was a solitary drinker, the worst kind. He would bring home his bottle or flask, or several bottles when he could afford them, and for days, or as long as the supply lasted, he would be drunk. I have known these alcoholic debauches to last a week, two weeks, and sometimes longer. Unlike many heavy drinkers, he ate heartily during these bouts, and that probably prevented the liquor from hurting him as much as it might have done. Then he would sober up, and my mother was always able to tell the right moment to help him to taper off. I have known her, dozens of times, to walk the mile and a half or two miles into town to the nearest public house, to buy him a flask of liquor for this purpose. Sometimes she managed to hide a little of his supply to serve when the tapering-off moment came. Once my father was sober, he would not take another drink for perhaps three months or even six months, then he would be sure to break out again. I remember scores of incidents that occurred in our home when my father was drunk, but they are not pleasant to remember or tell.

My father received the ordinary elementary education that was the most any boy could get in Newfoundland in the 1880s and 1890s—if you wanted more, you had to leave the country. From school, he entered his father's boot and shoe business, and after a while he began a career as a travelling salesman for the firm. He and some other salesman selling a different line from a non-competing company would jointly charter a small sailing vessel to take them and their samples to the principal harbours along the coast of the Island. The schooner was in fact a floating sample room, and the objective was to get signed orders for the firm from local merchants or larger shopkeepers. His co-charterer on one voyage was Simeon H. Parsons, a family friend and well-known commercial photographer, who took pictures of the magnificent scenery they passed on the trip.

My father had a number of adventures on these sales trips, and one I heard of in a curious way. The first time I was a candidate for election to the House of Assembly, in 1932, I travelled one day along the road from Happy Adventure to Salvage, eight or ten miles distant. I had hired a horse and buggy and its owner to drive me. We were within a couple of miles of Salvage when I saw a man coming toward us on foot. He had a canvas bag slung over his shoulder (which contained the relief or "dole" ration of food that he had just collected). Assuming that he was a voter, I stopped the horse when we came abreast to chat with him. I introduced myself as the new Liberal Party candidate for Bonavista South and asked him for his support. At the mention of my name, he showed an immediate lively interest, and he asked me my father's name. "Charlie," I told him, and he nodded vigorously and exclaimed, "He saved my life," and so I learned the story. This man, as a boy, lived at Salvage. My father's chartered schooner was lying at anchor in Salvage Harbour. It was Sunday afternoon, when no business could be done in a God-fearing Newfoundland outport, and my father was stretched out on the quarter-deck of the little schooner, reading. Suddenly he heard a splash in the water nearby, and he stood up to see what it was. It was this boy. He had been poling a small boat along toward the schooner, no doubt with a boy's curiosity to see who was on board, when the pole stuck in the muddy bottom and dragged him overboard. The boy couldn't swim a stroke, but he was lucky that day, for my father dived instantly over the stern of the schooner and quickly brought him to safety. I like to think that that voter voted for me on polling day!

My father might have continued working for the family firm, but for the fact that its ownership changed. I don't know how or where he learned the trade of lumber surveying; but I suspect that it was at the hands of his father, who had learned his own trade as a very skilled carpenter, for there's no great distance between the two trades.

My father was one of the most able-minded men I ever knew. He was a near-genius in mathematics, for example. I remember once meeting John Cowan, when he was an old man. Years before, he had been the Receiver General in a Liberal administration under Bond. (His grandson is now the Chief Justice of the Supreme Court of Nova Scotia.) John Cowan also was believed to be a mathematical genius or near-genius. He could run his eyes up a column of figures three digits wide and total it as accurately and quickly as a modern adding machine. My father could do the same thing. As a lumber surveyor, he could, with his racing iron, engrave the number of superficial board feet on each individual board or plank laid on the bench before him in rapid succession by the labourers, and keep mental count of large quantities before entering the subtotals on his tally board. He was reputed to be capable of surveying lumber, piece by piece, faster than any men had ever been able to place it before him. Every spring and summer, 600 or 700 sailing vessels came into the harbour of St. John's with loads of sawn lumber, below deck and above, for sale from the hundreds of small sawmills dotted all around the coast of the Island; every board of it had to be surveyed, and my father did the great bulk of it, though he was not the only surveyor in St. John's.

As I have said, liquor was his downfall. It might have been a different story had he been a social drinker. He had a good many chances to get ahead throughout his life, and he seized them and failed in every one of them through his bouts of drunkenness.

Once he had ten horses and carts, with a hired driver for each, which did the usual carting of the day. This was of two types. First, there might be a steady relationship with some firm that needed to have a lot of goods carted, such as lumber, cement, and other building materials, or groceries to be delivered to individual households. The least attractive part of that trade was hauling coal. The second kind of the carting trade was "hobbling". The driver would stand around with his horse in one of the various coves leading from Water Street, and wait for an individual order to cart something to some destination in the city. Each of the large merchant premises on Water Street had its own cove or side entrance to the waterside property where its wharves (finger piers) were, and each cove was named for the firm to which it belonged—there was Steer's Cove, Bowring's Cove, Ayre's Cove, Baird's Cove, and so on. These were public thoroughfares, and strolling down Water Street, one could see in every cove eight or ten horses and carts lined up with their drivers near them, waiting for a "hobble". It was a precarious form of living that was earned through hobbling. My father's ten horses and employed drivers engaged in both kinds of carting, and while it lasted, our family revelled in comparative plenty. But the trouble was that it didn't last. My father ended up with just one horse and cart, which he had to operate himself.

Then there was my father's involvement with the very successful construction partnership of Bowering and Miller, two outport carpenters who had formed their own small contracting firm in St. John's. My father, with his intimate knowledge of lumber and everything connected with it, was their valuable associate. His horses did all their trucking, and he helped them with their estimates of costs. They built the tuberculosis sanatorium on Topsail Road and added a wing to the General Post Office. That was another period of a couple or three years of prosperity in our family.

We paid for our brief times of prosperity with long periods of stringency, and sometimes hunger. More than once, my grandfather David, out of his none-too-adequate pension, had to help to provide food for us. Once our family went up on the Southside Hill and in a long day picked among us twenty gallons of partridge berries. Next day, my sister Marie and I peddled several gallons of them door to door on Freshwater and Merrymeeting roads in St. John's. We collected the best part of $2 cash from our sales, and this went for family groceries. A recollection of this flashed into my mind once as we were served berries at a dinner given for the provincial premiers at Rideau Hall in Ottawa by Field Marshal Viscount Alexander, the Governor General. But I didn't mention the incident to the relatively patrician Maurice Duplessis, Premier of Quebec, with whom at the time I was exchanging quips about the Labrador boundary.

Another time my father began to build up a small dairy herd, and he had actually acquired eight or ten milking cows when the venture collapsed. It was not his drinking that caused the failure this time, but a fire, with no fire insurance.

And that's the story of my father's lost career: he was the victim of his weakness for alcohol, the fact that he had no profitable profession to practise, the very large family he had, and just the poor times in which he lived in Newfoundland. Like thousands of other Newfoundlanders, he had gone off to Boston—"the Boston States"—looking for work; but after a succession of unprofitable jobs, he had, again like so many thousands of Newfoundlanders, returned home.

My father had a lively sense of humour and told a story well, and he used to enchant us youngsters with his tales. He was ugly when drunk, but very attractive indeed when sober. It is a tribute to his personality that, notwithstanding the bad times through which his drinking dragged us, all his children always thought of him with a lively, tolerant affection, if not with deep love. Our love was reserved for our mother.

The most brilliant of my father's brothers was David. He was, among other things, a born musician. It was said that he could play any instrument, and that he could sit down and play a tune by ear after hearing it only once. But it was as a lawyer that he really excelled. Uncle David was an articled student in the law firm of Sir Alfred B. Morine, himself one of the most brilliant lawyers and politicians in our history. Morine once declared that young David Smallwood was one of the cleverest lawyers he had ever known; and when David was called to the bar in St. John's, Morine offered him a place in the firm. David took it for a while, but in no time pulled up stakes in Newfoundland and headed off for Canada. Before I was born, he went west to Saskatchewan or Alberta, and began a law practice there. The family in Newfoundland soon lost track of him altogether, though his brother, my uncle Sandy, once ran into him in Alaska, where Sandy was prospecting in the gold rush. Indeed, I seem to remember that David joined with his brother in prospecting for a while.

That was the last ever heard of David until about 1915, when my grandfather one day received a picture postcard from his son. The picture was that of a great troopship, and on the reverse side, David told his father that he was en route to England in the Canadian Expeditionary Force. With such clues as the name of the ship and the postmark date on the back, I wrote to the Department of Militia at

Ottawa and was able to get my uncle's correct address in London. I promptly wrote him and had one letter back telling me how pleased he was to hear from a nephew he had never seen, and telling me that he was an official in the Canadian Forces Record Office in London. He was, of course, too old to be in the fighting branch of the army. That is the last time that any of us ever heard from or about him.

Another of my uncles, Jack, went off to Australia and that is the last that was ever heard of him. Uncle Duncan went off to California, and by all accounts he did very well. He was the inventor of a small adding machine which bore his name and sold in large numbers. I really don't know whether he invented the adding machine himself or bought the patents from the inventor. Aunt Fan, my grandfather David's only daughter, went to join her brother in California in the 1930s. She stayed there for a year or two, and then came back to Newfoundland. She spoke ill of her American sister-in-law; but as Aunt Fan was by then a rather embittered maiden lady in her early seventies, I never would accept her judgement of my uncle Duncan's wife. Duncan had some daughters, but to this day, I have never been able to trace them or any of my relatives in California, though I have tried hard enough.

Aunt Fan took her B.A. from Mount Allison University in New Brunswick. She studied nursing and practised it in Louisville, Kentucky, until her mother's death in the 1920s, when she returned to Newfoundland to care for her father. She was quite a remarkable lady—good-looking, highly intelligent, with a keen sense of humour. She came to live with me for the last few years of her life.

Uncle Sandy was the chief cutter in his father's boot and shoe factory, a most important job where salability of leather footwear is at stake. Like my father and Duncan, he too cleared out of the firm when the ownership changed, and went off to Alberta. From there, he went to Alaska in the gold rush; and with the money he made, he returned to Alberta and set up a partnership with an Englishman in owning and running a wheat farm. That must have been about 1908. One spring, he and his partner took a team of oxen hitched to a farm wagon to the nearest railroad station about thirty or forty miles away to pick up a load of seed grain. On the way back across the prairie, they lost their way; and for three days and nights, they endured first a very heavy rainfall and then a severe frost. The Englishman came out of it unscathed, but Sandy was badly paralyzed in both legs then and for the rest of his life. His brother Fred paid the cost of getting him back to St. John's, where he lived with his father. Uncle Sandy and I became great pals. In my grandfather's house on Springdale Street, there were four of us: my grandfather and grandmother, Uncle Sandy, and myself. I lived with my grandfather for several years after I went to work, so as to be near my job. Uncle Sandy persuaded his brother Fred to send him to England in the hope of a cure, and it was in England that he spent most of the time of the First World War. There was no cure, and he came back to live in his father's house in St. John's until he died, in his late seventies.

The one brother who had a successful career was the oldest son, Fred, and he was a very successful man. When he died, around 1916, he left an estate worth about $200,000. That wouldn't be insignificant even today, but at that time in Newfoundland, it was a great fortune indeed. It was Uncle Fred who became the sole owner of the boot and shoe business. My grandfather had intended that it belong to all the boys and his daughter as well, but that was not my grandmother's thinking. Probably with great insight, she recognized in her favourite son precisely the kind of business judgement that the enterprise needed, and so it turned out. He built the business into one of the largest in the country: the magnificent new factory building on Duckworth Street and two fine large retail shops on Water Street, one for men's and boys' footwear, and the other for women's and girls' footwear; and a thriving outport business, the largest of its kind in the country. Uncle Fred was also an important shareholder in several other business enterprises, including MacKeen's Tannery on Waterford Bridge Road. Little did I know as I walked past that tannery so many hundreds of times and peered curiously in the windows at the workings inside, enjoying the pungent leather and tanning smells, that I was gazing at my own uncle's property. Uncle Fred was the one businessman in the Smallwood family, the one certain money maker, though I really don't know how well Uncle Duncan did in California and I have no notion of Uncle Jack's life in Australia.

3

The Part That's Underground

A man who prides himself on his ancestry is like the potato plant, the best part of which is underground.

Spanish proverb

He that hath no fools, knaves or beggars in his family was begot by a flash of lightning.

English proverb

There are many kinds of conceit, but the chief one is to let people know what a very ancient and gifted family one descends from.

Benvenuto Cellini

Every generation revolts against its fathers and makes friends with its grandfathers.

Lewis Mumford

A mule always boasts that its ancestors were horses.

German proverb

(Some readers may well want to skip this chapter. To them, it will appear as one long exercise in conceit. But for the possibly 20,000 people, on both sides of the Atlantic, with Smallwood-Lawson-Jamieson-Brown-Gamberg-Devanna blood in their veins, it may just be the best part of the book!—J.R.S.)

I could have had fun with Sir Winston Churchill the first time I met him, on August 14, 1952, at 10 Downing Street, had I known that I was not the first Smallwood to meet a Churchill and that he was not the first Churchill to meet a Smallwood. The first meeting took place on July 15, 1705, at Ulierberg-Abby near Louvain, in Brabant, when the Duke of Marlborough listened to a sermon preached by the Rev. James Smallwood, Chaplain to Her Majesty's Foot Guards. I suppose that it would be the practice, following Divine Service, for the Duke to invite the Chaplain in for a sherry. The sermon must have been well received, for the General Officers wanted it put in print. This was done in London by T. Mead for Andrew Bell, at the Cross Keys in Cornhill. The British Museum, for a small fee, let me have a photocopy of it.

Six years earlier, another Smallwood, the Rev. James, also a Chaplain (to the Rt. Hon. the Earl of Romney and to "His Majestie's own Regiment of Foot Guards") preached a sermon on Wednesday, April 5, 1699, before the "Honourable House of Commons at St. Margaret's Westminster". The British Museum sold me a copy of that sermon, too.

The third favour of the Museum was a replica of a sermon preached at Carlisle on August 17, 1664, by the Rev. A. Smallwood, D. D., and the fourth a sermon preached on October 17, 1661, by the Rev. George Smalwood *(sic)* M. A., Rector of St. Margaret's, New Fish Street, in London. This last was preached "at the solemn funerals *(sic)* of the Right Worshipful Sir Abraham Raynardson, Knight, Late Alderman of London".

They were no illiterates, those Smallwoods, if the Rev. Matthew Smallwood, S.T.P., Dean of Lychfield, was a fair example. In May 1684, for a reason of which no hint is given, he put up some books from his library for sale at Gresham College in Bishopsgate Street, London. Copies of the catalogue "are given Gratis, at Mr. Chr. Wilkinson's at the Black Boy in Fleet Street, Mr. N. Ponder's of the Peacock in the Poultrey, Mr. Sam Smith at the Princes Armes in St. Paul's churchyard, Booksellers; at Widow Elford's Coffee-house in George-Yard in Lombard-street, at Widow Bourne's Coffee-house by St. Laurence Church, at Sam's Coffee-house at the West End of St. Paul's in Ludgate-street". A good advertiser, the Dean! There are 215 volumes in the catalogue, nearly all of them in Latin, and a few of them date back to 1484.

Even earlier than Dean Smallwood's book-sale in 1684, we have the will of Sir John Hurlestone, Archdeacon of Rychmonde, witnessed by the Rev. John Smalwoode *(sic)*, clerk, "Dean of the Middleswich Deanrie". That was in 1572.

And there are several references to Smallwoods who were scholars at Oxford and ordained ministers of the Established Church long before the sixteenth century—and long after. The Smallwoods came originally from the County of Cheshire, but in the course of time, they spread out into neighbouring Staffordshire and Wales and into Birmingham and London. Some of them went into business, some into the practice of law, and others into the army.

In studying my possible line of direct descent from the Smallwoods in England, I came across the case of Joseph Smallwood, who was born in 1695 and died on May 22, 1756. He had an extraordinarily distinguished career—although the most I can claim is collateral relationship. We are of the same tribe, but certainly I am not a direct descendant. That Joseph Smallwood was educated at St. Bonaventure's, Douay, France. He professed in 1717 and was ordained a priest in 1720. He was approved for preaching and hearing confessions in 1722 and for English Mission in 1728, in the Franciscan Order. From 1728 to 1732, he was Promoter of the Province; from 1732 to 1735, Guardian of Canterbury; and from 1737 to 1740, Guardian of London. From 1740 to 1743, he was Definator; and Guardian of London again from 1743 to 1746; and from 1746 to 1749, again Definator. He was Guardian of Canterbury for the final time from 1749 to 1752. Then he became Provincial of the whole of the Order of St. Francis for England and Wales, Douay in France, and Maryland in America.

I visited St. Bonaventure's School and St. Antony's Franciscan Friary on St. Antony's Road, Forest Gate, London, where the headmaster, the Rev. Howard Docherty, very generously showed me some early original minutes of the Order signed by Father Joseph Smallwood as Provincial of the Order around 1752 and a little later. Father Smallwood adopted the name Alexius in place of Joseph when he was ordained, though in fact I read, in the Westminster reference library in London, several entries of marriage ceremonies performed by him and signed Joseph. Father Docherty gave it as his opinion that Father Smallwood was probably a convert. There is no other reference to the name Smallwood in their records.

Though the Smallwoods originated in Cheshire, they did not all come from the village of Smallwood. This is a very old part of Cheshire; I don't know how old, but *The History of Sandbach* (1890) has this reference at page 273: "and Thomas de Leghes held land in Smallwood in the 24th Edward III (1350)", and it may well have been an ancient place then.

The first Smallwood known to have come to America was Randle or Randall Smallwood, in 1620. He settled in Virginia, which then was a very large part of America, embracing the territory today divided into West Virginia, Kentucky, Illinois, Indiana, Michigan, Minnesota, Ohio, and Wisconsin. Randle Smallwood almost certainly came to Virginia from Cheshire. I say almost certainly, because of his first name, Randle. One Smallwood after another in Cheshire had it, before and after this Smallwood. It was a popular first name among them and among other families in Cheshire.* Very little reference to him is made in the records, except for the fact that in 1627-1628 he was Provost Marshal of Virginia. He was the first Smallwood to hold public office in the New World—346 years ago.

It is important to me to know whether the first Smallwood in America was a Cheshire man. If he was, then Cheshire is the homeland of my tribe, for the Canadian-Newfoundland Smallwoods came from Virginia, and Randle Smallwood is our founder. We don't know much about him beyond the date of his arrival. The records do not even give the name of the ship he came on.

From Virginia, some of the Smallwoods moved the small distance to Maryland. James Smallwood may have been the first to do so, in 1664. He was a very prosperous and important planter, landowner, and merchant, and he also had a distinguished career as public man and soldier. From the day he moved to Maryland until he died in

*Sir Randle Baker Smallwood, of Cheshire, is a present-day example.

1714 or 1715, he was one of Maryland's most prominent citizens. For thirty years, he commanded the military forces of the colony. For twenty-two years, from 1692 until his death, he represented Charles County in the Maryland House of Assembly. In 1694, he became High Sheriff of his county and a member of the county's quorum. In 1692, he was appointed to treat and deal with the Indians, and in the same year he was authorized to raise his own company of soldiers, having received the rank of major in 1689. In 1700, he received the rank of colonel. Colonel Smallwood had eleven children by his wife, Hester, née Evans, an important family in Virginia.

This Maryland Smallwood had at least one notable eccentricity: he named three of his sons after three of his close business associates—Bayne, Pryor, and Leadstone. For several generations, these first names persisted in the Smallwood families of Maryland and of Virginia, to which some of them went back to live.* Colonel Smallwood's grandson Bayne, born in 1711, represented Charles County in the Maryland House of Assembly. His great-grandson, Bayne's son, was the famous General Smallwood.

General William Smallwood was, after Calvert, one of the greatest names in the colonial history of Maryland. Today in Baltimore, Smallwood Street is named after him, as is Fort Smallwood, a little distance away. His house and land, which he inherited from Colonel Smallwood, his great-grandfather, known as Smallwood's Retreat, is now a state park. There is a small village named Smallwood in Maryland.

General Smallwood was born on February 12, 1732, in Charles County, Maryland. He began his military career as a soldier in the French and Indian Wars. He took his seat as a delegate in the Maryland Assembly in 1761; was a delegate to the Maryland Convention of 1775; and joined the Association of the Freemen of Maryland, which advocated opposition by arms to the British troops employed to enforce obedience to the late Acts and statutes of the British Parliament for raising a revenue in America. In January 1766, commissions were issued to raise a Regiment of Maryland under Smallwood's command. His nine companies moved northward and won a reputation for valour in the battle of Long Island. He covered the

*One Bayne Smallwood turned up in Prince Edward Island in 1784 and was granted land. For a brief time, I thought that he might be the father of my great-great-grandfather Joseph, the first Smallwood to settle on that Island. I have not yet identified that Bayne.

retreat of General Washington. The Continental Congress elected him a Brigadier-General on October 23, 1776. His men fought at Fort Washington, Trenton, Princeton, and Germantown. He became a Major-General in September 1780, and he continued in service until November 15, 1783. He was elected delegate to the Continental Congress on December 4, 1784, but declined to serve. He was elected Governor of Maryland in 1785, and it was he who called the convention at which Maryland ratified the Constitution of the United States.

General Smallwood and General George Washington were close friends. Washington came frequently to Smallwood's home, and they both attended meetings of Alexandria Masonic Lodge held upstairs in Smallwood's house. General Smallwood was vestryman of Durham Episcopal Church, which stands near his home and is still in use. He cut a road through the trees from his house to the church. A sister kept house for him, for he never married. He died in 1792.

A great-great-grandson of Colonel James Smallwood, Samuel Nicholas (or Nicholls) Smallwood, born in 1772, became Mayor of Washington, D.C. He moved to Washington in 1794 and became the city's leading dealer in lumber and building supplies. In 1799, he was made superintendent of the labourers in the construction of the Capitol. He first entered public life in 1804, when he was elected to the Council of Aldermen, and was president of the Board from 1809 to 1811. In 1819, he was appointed fifth Mayor of Washington until 1822, when the constitution of Washington was changed and called for election of the Mayor by popular vote. He was elected Mayor in 1824 and served until his death. His son, William Augustine Smallwood, became a lawyer and then an Episcopal clergyman. He was elected Bishop of Indiana but declined the office.

The records of the State of New Jersey contain many references to Smallwoods who settled there from Virginia. The earliest that I have found is an entry of the marriage of William Smallwood to Jemima Down on March 15, 1736. In South Carolina on September 15, 1674, 100 acres of land were granted to Matthew Smallwood. In North Carolina on July 23, 1743, 365 acres were granted to Ignatius Smallwood. In 1788, John Smallwood was elected Vendue Master of the Town of New Bern, N. C. In 1789, Charles Smallwood was secretary of an early Masonic Lodge, No. 15, there.

In Georgia in 1805, five Smallwood men participated in the Georgia land lottery.

In Pennsylvania, the 1810 census showed four Smallwoods in the Philadelphia area.

The Ohio census of 1820 showed five Smallwoods living in four counties. In the spring of 1804, Walter Smallwood and his young wife came to Ohio from Virginia and purchased a building lot on the south side of Main Street, where he erected a house and blacksmith forge. Their oldest son, Louis, went to Lexington in 1832 and practised law. Their youngest son, Walter, became a judge of one of the Inferior Courts of Missouri.

Hezekiah Smallwood moved to Elizabethtown, Kentucky, and opened a brickyard in 1806. His grandson, William Hillary Smallwood, became a Captain in the U. S. Army in the civil war and was elected to the Kansas House of Representatives and to the Kansas Senate. He was elected Secretary of State in Kansas. Later he practised law in Duluth, Minnesota, and was elected a judge of the Municipal Court there. He died in 1919, the year of my first experience of an election.

A number of Smallwoods took part in the War of 1812, and in the Indian wars, and in the Mexican War. Smallwoods served in the American forces in the First and Second World Wars.

Benjamin Franklin Smallwood was an interesting member of my tribe—and the word *tribe* has very special significance in his case, for he was Chief of the Choctaw Nation in Oklahoma. His father, Elijah Smallwood, born in South Carolina late in the eighteenth century, journeyed as a young man to the Choctaw country in Mississippi, where he married a Choctaw woman. Elijah's son William by that marriage was half-Indian, and he attended school at the Choctaw Academy in Kentucky. William married a Choctaw-French girl, Mary LeFlore, and Benjamin Franklin Smallwood was their son. Born in 1829, he was well over half Choctaw Indian, and it was natural enough for him to be taken, as a child, to the old Indian Territory. He became a cattleman and shopkeeper. When he was barely of age, he was elected to the Choctaw Council, where he served as Speaker of the lower house on four different occasions. From 1847 to 1890, except when he served as a Captain in the 2nd Choctaw Regiment of the Confederate Army in the Civil War, he was active in the political life of the Choctaw Nation. In 1888, he was elected to the Chieftainship of the Nation. He died in what is now called Coal County, Oklahoma, December 15, 1891, nine years before I was born.

I mention these scattered and casual facts about the Smallwoods in the United States because they all descended from the Virginia family, and they are all of my tribe. I think that I have many more relatives in the United States today than I have in the whole of Canada, though there isn't a province of Canada where I have no relatives. They don't all bear the name Smallwood in either country.

The first Smallwood in what is now Canada was Joseph, my great-great-grandfather. He was a seaman, a master mariner, and the story of his life is succinctly set forth in his own statement to the Lords of the Treasury at Whitehall in London. It was dated December 14, 1778, at the seaport of Whitehaven in Cumberland County, England, and read as follows:

> To the Right Honourable the Lords Commissioners of the Treasury.—
>
> The petition of Joseph Smallwood, oldest son of Charles Smallwood, born in the County called Princess Ann County—near Norfolk in Virginia.—Humbly showeth.
>
> . . . [indecipherable] . . . said Colony of Virginia till the tenth day of October, one thousand seven hundred and seventy-five* when at the request of his father, who wished to prevent his being forced into the Rebel service and from his own disaffection to the cause of Rebellion Your Lordships said petitioner left Virginia having obtained the Command of a vessel called the Neptune† belonging to Messrs. Eilbeck-Chambre-Ross Merchants of Whitehaven, in the County of Cumberland and Kingdom of Great Britain—that the said vessel under the command of Your Lordships' said petitioner was afterwards employed for near twelve months in the service of the government as a Navy transport, at the expiration of which time she was with many other vessels ordered home from N. York‡—

*Four months after the Continental Congress made George Washington Commander-in-Chief of the revolutionary forces.

†Thanks to Daniel Hay, F.R.S.A., F.Ph.S., A.L.A., librarian and curator of the Public Library and Museum of Whitehaven, Cumberland County, England, I can report that she was 300 tons, launched in 1762, the twenty-third of seventy-two Whitehaven vessels captured or sunk during the American War of Independence. Whitehaven lost over 100 ships in that war.

‡New York continued to be in British possession for some years after the American Revolution commenced. So it was, too, with Philadelphia and some other seaports.

and was discharged out of the service at Deptford—that Your Lordships said petitioner being then in the merchant service—and bound with the said vessel to Halifax—with orders to touch at Philadelphia on Head quarter with necessaries for his Majesty's forces was unfortunately captured by a Rebel American frigate of 32 guns—called the Warren—J. B. Hopkins Commander and was carried to Boston at which place he remained a prisoner during the space of three months—that during Your Lordships' said petitioner's captivity at Boston—when it was discovered that he was a Native of America—every endeavour was used on the part of the Rebels to make him a Convert to their principles—for which purpose the first Lieutenant of the said frigate the Warren—or the Command of a Rebel privateer was offered him—both of which he rejected and continued unshaken in his loyalty till at the end of three months he was exchanged at Rhode Island as a prisoner of War from whence he proceeded to New York and took the first opportunity of returning to England.

Your Lordships petitioner, thus obliged to be a Refugee from his native country—being deprived of the assistance of his former employer thru the dissolution of the Commercial House of Eilbeck-Chambre-Ross & Co.—presumed from his knowledge of Your Lordships great goodness to many of his suffering countrymen under similar circumstances—with all humility to entreat Your Lordships to grant him such temporary relief as to Your Lordships shall seem meet—till a communication with America again opens—and . . . [indecipherable] . . . of his property . . . without danger to his person—or disloyalty to his Sovereign.

And Your Lordships petitioner, as in duty bound—will ever pray.

JOSEPH SMALLWOOD.

To this was attached a statement as follows: "We the underwritten do hereby Certify that Mr. Joseph Smallwood has fairly represented his situation—is a Man of Sobriety and good reputation; and well entitled to some aid as a Refugee. Whitehaven 14, December 1778."

Thirty-one persons signed, and to judge by their handwriting, they were all persons of some quality. Chambre, who had been a partner in the company that owned the *Neptune*, was one of the signers.

There appears to be no record of the response to Captain Smallwood's appeal for help; but if, as seems likely, he had by his loyalty to the Crown forfeited property in America, and was now landless and jobless, the Treasury probably would do something to help. It would not be more than he asked for, temporary assistance, in any case.* How did he occupy his time between 1778 and 1783, when he received his first lease of land in Prince Edward Island? There is no record of his activity in those five years, but surely an experienced master mariner would not be long without work in great maritime England; or perhaps he engaged himself, in one way or another, in the farming industry? He was to become a farmer in Lot 56† in Prince Edward Island, or the Island of St. John, as it was called until 1800. Had he had any farm experience in Virginia before going to sea? I wish I knew the answers to these questions about my great-great-grandfather. How negligent of me not to have asked them of his grandson, my own grandfather David! I cannot help wondering whether my great-great-grandfather Joseph ever put into St. John's on his Atlantic crossings. How could a sailing vessel fail to embrace the opportunity to break the long voyage across the Atlantic, if only to obtain supplies of fresh water?

Captain Joseph Smallwood's father, my great-great-great-grandfather Charles, whose sympathies were so strongly with the Crown that he had influenced his oldest son to move actively against what he called "the Rebellion", was evidently a prosperous citizen of Virginia. His will, made in 1781, indicates as much:

> In the name of God Amen. I Charles Smallwood of Norfolk County in the State of Virginia, Blacksmith, being of sound and disposing mind tho infirm of Body, do make and ordain this to be my last Will and Testament, in the manner and Form following Viz.
>
> First, I give and bequeath the Brick dwelling House I now live in, and Lot belonging thereto, as determined by the Division Stones now standing thereon, to my wife Ann

*I have since learned from the Public Record Office in London that the original of my great-great-grandfather's petition is noted "Nil", from which the P.R.O. tell me that they assume that his request was turned down.

†This had later to be changed to Lot 38.

for her natural life, and after her death to Thomas Ritson and Edmund Almond, of Norfolk County and my Son John Smallwood of Charles City, in Trust for the sole use and benefit of my eldest Son Joseph Smallwood, and the Heirs of his Body lawfully begotten, for ever, to be made over to my said Son Joseph, or his said Heirs, or sold, or otherwise disposed of for his or their use and agreeable to his or their direction, whenever required by the said Joseph Smallwood, his said Heirs, except my said Wife Ann survives my said Son Joseph, or his said Heirs, and in that case it is my Will that the said House shall be sold after my said Wife's death and the money divided equally betwixt my two Daughters Ann and Isabell Smallwood and their Heirs for ever, or in case my said Son Joseph or his said Heirs should be incapacitated by the Laws of this State from holding or enjoying the said House and Lot, or that it cannot be sold (by the above-mentioned Trustees Thomas Ritson, Edmund Almond, John Smallwood, or their Agents or Assigns) and the Proceeds remitted to him or his said Heirs, then and in that case it is my Will that the said House and Lot be sold, and the Money arising therefrom be equally divided, betwixt my said Daughters Ann and Isabell Smallwood, and their Heirs for ever.—

Secondly, I give and bequeath the House lately occupied by Mr. Edmund Almond, with the Smith's Shop, and Tools, and Lot they now stand upon, bounded by Division Stones now standing thereon, to my second Son John Smallwood and his Heirs for ever, also all my Lot, or Lots of Land at Newtown in the County of Princess Ann to my Son John and his Heirs for ever.

Thirdly, I give and bequeath my Negro Wench Jude to my said Daughter Ann Smallwood, and Wench Sarah in case she returns or can be brought home from the Enemy; if not, my boy Jim to my said Daughter Isabell Smallwood and their Heirs for ever, to be delivered to them my said Daughters on their marriage, in case that should happen before my Wife's decease, if they are to take possession of said Wench or Wenches, or boy, at her Death.—

Fourthly, It is my Will and desire that the remainder of my Negroes namely Armstead, Matt, Rose and Jim in case

Sarah returns home, Caesar and Bob be at the disposal of my said Wife Ann during her Life, also my Horse, Cows and Hogs, and all the House and Kitchen Furniture and Utensils, Beds and Bedding and likewise Armstead's hire due from Mr. Thos. Pleasants & Co., for the purpose of defraying Funeral charges laying in Winter's Provisions until the two Lots of Land at Ferry Point I lately purchased of Henry Herbert's Estate and Argyll Herbert.—

Fifthly, I. give and bequeath the two Lots of Land at Ferry Point aforesaid to be equally divided after my Wife's death betwixt my two said Daughters Ann & Isabell Smallwood and their Heirs for ever.

Sixthly, I give and bequeath the Negroes named Armstead, Matt, Rose & Jim in case Sarah returns home, Caesar & Bob, to be equally divided betwixt all my said children, Joseph, John, Ann & Isabell and their Heirs for ever after my Wife's death, and after payment of all my just Debts and the outstanding debts due me are collected the Proceeds are to be equally divided betwixt my Wife Ann, and said Children Joseph, John, Ann & Isabell and their Heirs for ever.—and the remainder of my Personal Estate I give to be equally divided betwixt my said Children, Joseph, John, Ann and Isabell & their Heirs for ever.

Lastly, I do hereby constitute and appoint Thomas Ritson of the Borough of Norfolk, and Edmund Almond of the County of Norfolk Executors of this my last Will and Testament. In Witness whereof, I have hereunto set my Hand and Seal this second day of November One Thousand Seven Hundred and Eighty-one.

Signed, Sealed, and delivered in
the presence of (the words & their
Heirs for ever being first interlined)

CHARLES SMALLWOOD.

Caleb Herbert
James Herbert
Edmund Almond

Charles Smallwood made a codicil to this will on July 5, 1784 or 1785, constituting his son Joseph executor of his will.

When he made his will in 1781, he was very cautious in his references to his oldest son, who of course had burned his bridges and was openly allied with the loyalist British. If the Americans won their revolution, would Joseph be able to return and claim the brick house? If not, and the house were sold, would the proceeds go in part to him? Charles took pretty well all contingencies into account in his will.

On May 6, 1791, Ann, the widow of my great-great-great-grandfather Charles Smallwood, sold for £65, which was well below cost, a lot of land at Ferry Point, "commonly called the Town of Washington, in the County of Norfolk", to form part of the site of a marine hospital that was to be built for "aged and disabled seamen".

In 1783, when the Revolution was over, Captain Joseph Smallwood prepared to move from Whitehaven to Prince Edward Island and sent his power of attorney "to my loving brother John" at Norfolk, Virginia, to transact all business in his behalf in connection with the property left to him in his father's will.

When, after a long life of liberal and humanitarian views and sympathies, you discover that you are descended from slave-owners, it is not a comfortable feeling. In 1794, Luke Smallwood, in Loudoun County, Virginia, was shown in his inventory to have "a Negro man named James valued at 54 Pounds"; this Negro was hired out for £10 and later for £12 in 1796 and £15 in 1797. In the estate of George Smallwood, of Jefferson County, West Virginia, 1825, three slaves are enumerated: "Barrett, man with value of $400; Maria, a girl of 16 or 17 years, worth $300; Gallon, a boy of 14 or 15 years, sickly, with defective eyes and a value of $200". Somehow, even a Smallwood's pride in the great General William Smallwood, fourth Governor of Virginia, wilts when he uncovers the fact that he had twenty-six slaves in Virginia—not many fewer than General George Washington had in that same state.*

My great-great-great-grandfather bequeathed land, houses, slaves, cows, a horse, and hogs to his wife and their four children, and there is no sign of any differentiation between the several kinds of property. Joseph, his oldest son, had at least one slave, a girl, after he settled in Prince Edward Island. Her name was Elizabeth, Elizabeth Smallwood, and I have a copy of the entry in the Church of England register of her marriage in Charlottetown on October 5,

*There were 697,624 Negro slaves in the American Colonies in 1790 and 59,557 free Negroes. Virginia had 292,627 slaves; Maryland, 103,036.

1808, to Sancho Robinson, Negro slave of Colonel Robinson. Colonel Robinson was an Empire loyalist who settled in Prince Edward Island after a distinguished career in the American colonies. Where did Joseph get his female slave Elizabeth? Did he have other slaves? Did Colonel Robinson bring Sancho, and perhaps other slaves, to Prince Edward Island from the revolting colonies? Were Elizabeth and Sancho still slaves in 1808, or were they free Negroes by then? Indeed, had they ever been slaves? Since slaves commonly took the surname of their owners, or were given them by their owners, it rather seems that these two had been slaves—though again it is possible that their parents were slaves and the children not. However it was, I'm glad that it never became known, while I was in politics, that I am descended from slave-owners!

Captain Joseph Smallwood, my great-great-grandfather, settled in Prince Edward Island in 1783 or 1784, with a lease on 200 acres of land. His wife, Margaret MacRobie, was undoubtedly Scottish. I have not discovered her precise origins or where they were married. It is possible that they were married before he left Virginia in 1775, but it is more likely that he met her during the five years of his sojourn in Whitehaven, Cumberland County, which is not far from the Scottish border. They had eight children, of whom James, my great-grandfather, was the fifth: John, 1785; Dorenda, 1788; Eleanor, 1790; Mary, 1792; James, 1794; William, 1796; Margaret, 1797; Catherine, 1802. They were all baptised in the Church of England at Charlottetown.

James Smallwood married Mary Brown, the granddaughter of a Scottish weaver, Laurence Brown. Laurence Brown sailed out of Greenock, Scotland, at five o'clock in the afternoon of April 8, 1770, as one of the sixty-family passenger list on board the *Falmouth* bound for Prince Edward Island. The Rev. William Drummond, a Church of Scotland minister, one of the passengers, kept a diary of the voyage that is now in the Public Archives in Ottawa, and it is from this diary that we learn so much of early events in the Island. The *Falmouth,* after sixty-one days at sea, made land at Stanhope on June 7, and came to anchor at seven in the evening.

Another of my great-great-great-great-grandfathers, Captain David Lawson, was one of the most important passengers on board the ship. Sir Hugh (later Lord) Montgomery and his brothers Robert and Archibald, who had obtained rights to a huge slice of Prince Edward Island, were sending him out as their agent for the issue of leases to the farmer settlers who came on the *Falmouth* and others who would come subsequently by many other ships.

On the evening of December 21, 1770, the Rev. Mr. Drummond officiated at the marriage of my great-great-great-grandmother, Jean Jamieson, who also had come out on the *Falmouth*, to Laurence Brown. John Jamieson, Jean's father, was a tailor, and he had come on the *Falmouth* too. He settled on Lot 33. Laurence Brown also settled on Lot 33.

Captain Lawson's family had accompanied him on the *Falmouth*. His son William, or it might have been another son, John, had a daughter named Isabella, who married Laurence Brown's son, John; and the daughter of that marriage, Mary Brown, married David Smallwood's father, James.

An interesting tradition has persisted in our family on Prince Edward Island, although no tangible proof—not even sufficiently persuasive evidence—have I been able to discover to establish the verity of this tradition. Laurence Brown, the Scottish weaver, after he settled in Prince Edward Island, corresponded with his uncle Samuel Brown back in Scotland.* At the same time, Robert Burns, Scotland's bard, was writing letters to his uncle Samuel Brown, his mother's brother. In fact, Burns lived with his uncle Samuel while he was going to school. Agnes, Robert Burns' mother, was the daughter of Gilbert Brown and the sister of Samuel Brown. The tradition is that Laurence Brown's uncle Samuel and Robert Burns' uncle Samuel were one and the same person. This would make Laurence Brown and Robert Burns first cousins, and Gilbert Brown, Laurence's grandfather. It is a pretty tradition.

Now I return briefly to the British colony of Virginia. The blacksmith, Charles Smallwood (Captain Joseph Smallwood's father), as I have already shown, was a man of some property, and I suspect that he inherited most of his initial wealth from his own father, my great-great-great-great-grandfather, master mariner Captain Charles Smallwood, who died in 1767. That Captain Smallwood was master of his own vessel, the *Experiment*, whose movements were recorded in contemporary newspapers: "1755. 28 Feb. Cleared Outwards in

*The Rev. William Drummond notes in his diary: "May 2, 1771. This day I packed my things in Sam Brown's chests. I exchanged with Belle Lawson for my trunk." One of these chests is presently in the possession of a descendant of Laurence Brown, my relative Wendell Kielly at Stanhope, P. E. I.

the Lower District of the James River, Dec. 18, Experiment, Charles Smallwood for Barbados with 1962 Bushels Corn and 98 Barrels of Pork. 1755. June 6. Experiment, Charles Smallwood, from Barbados, with 33 Hhds. Rum and 2 Barrels of Sugar. 1755. Sept. 1. Experiment, Charles Smallwood, from Boston, with 20 Barrels Mackerel, 2 Bags Hops and 2 Hhds. Loaf Sugar. 1755. Nov. 19. Experiment, Charles Smallwood for North Carolina with 3 Hhds. Rum and 150 Bushels Salt." He traded also to Bermuda, Antigua, and the Bahamas; and though I find no record of it, I wonder if he wasn't one of the American traders who were going in and out of St. John's and other Newfoundland ports?

Blacksmithing was in those days largely a matter of making the hardware for sailing vessels. No wonder Joseph, the blacksmith's son, followed in his own grandfather's trade as a mariner, so that in 1775 he was able to take command of the 300-ton *Neptune* for trans-Atlantic voyages. The maritime tradition was continued on Prince Edward Island by at least one of the descendants, William Smallwood, who owned ships that he built himself in his own yard at Mermaid on the Hillsborough River. James, my great-grandfather, and his brother John exported farm produce to Newfoundland in the 1850s and 1860s, but whether in their own vessels, I know not.

All of this brings me to the extraordinary, though quite natural, fact that nearly all of my great-, great-great-, great-great-great-, and great-great-great-great-grandfathers were contemporaries: Captain David Lawson, John Jamieson, Laurence Brown, Captain Joseph Smallwood, Charles Smallwood the blacksmith, and Captain Charles Smallwood the master mariner-trader (both of Virginia)—all of these lived and flourished between 1765 and 1795. Coming from both sides of the Atlantic, all except Captain Charles Smallwood and his son Charles met as contemporaries in Prince Edward Island from 1770 onward.

David Smallwood's wife, my grandmother Julia Cooper, was the great-granddaughter of the founder of Grates Cove, which lies at the point of the peninsula that separates Conception and Trinity bays. George Cooper reputedly came from London to St. John's around 1770, and tradition in our family has it that he was so well connected and recommended that the Governor of Newfoundland invited him to be his guest for a week or so at Government House, which then was in Fort Townshend. Family tradition further says that the Governor advised him, if he wanted a place exclusively for himself, to settle in uninhabited Grates Cove. I was reared on stories from my grandmother Julia, and her sister, Matilda Avery, of the gentility of their great-grandfather George: he insisted that everyone dress for dinner; he had special foods brought out to him from England; he brought a tutor from England to teach his children; and finally, the first school classes in Grates Cove were held in his large, rambling house. Long years after Julia and Matilda had died, my cousin Mrs. Wendell Farris, wife of Chief Justice Farris of British Columbia, told me that she had learned the same traditions from her own mother, my grandmother Smallwood's sister Kate. (Kate married the Rev. Joseph Howie of New Brunswick, and another sister, Jessie, married H. Paxton Baird, owner of a pharmaceutical firm in Toronto.) My own knowledge of Newfoundland history tells me, however, that the "English tutor" was not in fact brought out from England to teach my great-great-grandfather George Cooper's children.

John Hoskins, one of John Wesley's converts (he had known Mr. Wesley personally), set sail for the American mainland via Trinity town, on the north side of Trinity Bay. There, while he waited for a ship that would carry him westward to the mainland, he decided to improve the shining hour by holding a Methodist service in one of the fish stores. The Anglican fishermen would have none of it—no Wesleyan for them! They put him aboard a small boat and set him adrift, and the wind blew him across Trinity Bay to Old Perlican. There, too, with true Wesleyan zeal, he began to exhort the people to repent. The results were altogether different. Conversions rocked the settlement, and every living person in it became a fervent Methodist. Hoskins set up a day school, and it was as a teacher that George Cooper brought him to Grates Cove. He was a tutor, true enough, and an Englishman; but the only "bringing" that George Cooper did was the six or eight miles from Old Perlican to Grates Cove. Newfoundland has no J. Robert Mutch, so there is a lot that I do not know about the Cooper family of Grates Cove, apart from the fact that many of them later settled in other parts of Trinity Bay and other small bays, and that my great-grandfather Thomas Cooper took the Bay de Verde area census in 1847. George Cooper's wife was Margaret, but I don't know her surname. He himself lost his life when, as he stood on a flat rock on the landwash in Grates Cove, waiting for a small boat to take him out to the schooner by which he was going to sail to England, a heavy swell swept over the rock and carried him to his death.

My mother was Mary Ellen Devanna, although everyone called

her Minnie. She is still remembered by her large flock of grandchildren and great-grandchildren as Big Mom, although in fact she was of somewhat diminutive stature. I have tried hard, even making a visit to Dublin in 1972 and to the Channel Islands as well, to trace my grandfather Michael Devanna's ancestry in Ireland. The library of the Irish Club in London, and my study of the Irish genealogist and historian MacAuliffe in Dublin, have so far revealed only the fact that the family bearing the name Devanna, Devaney, or Devanney, with still other variants, was, like so many families of that remarkable nation of men, distinguished and "different". Grandfather Michael's father was Anthony Devanna, and he had been a soldier stationed in Halifax before coming to Newfoundland in the 1830s. His three sons, Michael, Richard, and John, were all born in St. John's.

My grandfather Michael Devanna married Mary Gamberg, the daughter of Charles Gamberg and Sarah Crampton. The first of the Gamberg family in Newfoundland was my great-great-grandfather John. He was born in 1786, possibly in Germany. He became a soldier of fortune and in 1815 fought in the Battle of Waterloo in the German army under General Blücher. Following the defeat of Napoleon, he joined the British army and was transferred to England. From there, he was sent with his regiment, or perhaps a smaller unit, to Halifax, Nova Scotia. It appears that he was demobilized there and that he set himself up as a house painter. I do not know the year of his arrival in Newfoundland, but I know that his wife's first name was Mary and that his son Charles, my great-grandfather, was born around 1820—whether in St. John's or in Halifax, I know not. John was a member of St. Thomas's Church of England parish in the east end of St. John's, though he was buried in Belvedere Cemetery. Charles was also a member of St. Thomas's for a time, but he became a convert to the Roman Catholic Church.

Charles Gamberg married Sarah Crampton, often called Cramp, of Freshwater Valley, just to the north of the city. The house in which my great-grandmother Sarah was born is still there on Freshwater Road; and I remember as a small boy, about 1908, being taken into the country to visit the Cramptons in that very house. Sarah died in 1890 at the age of seventy, and Charles in 1902, at age eighty-two.

The Gambergs followed John's trade of house-painting and became perhaps the most prominent painters in Newfoundland. The most notable work they did was the repainting of the famous ceiling of the House of Assembly and Legislative Council chambers in the

Colonial Building. These ceilings had originally been painted by the Polish artist Pindicowski, who, finding himself penniless in St. John's, had forged a cheque and was sentenced to serve a term in the penitentiary. He was given his pardon and permission to leave the country, in return for painting the ceilings in the Colonial Building and in Government House. When I first saw reproductions of the Polish art treasures that were stored in Canada during World War II, I was struck by the powerful similarity in the style of much Polish art and that of those ceilings. Little did I think, in all the years I sat in the Colonial Building and gazed at the ceiling, that one of my own relatives had done the repainting.

An appendix to this book demonstrates conclusively that our Smallwood-Lawson-Jamieson-Brown-Gamberg-Devanna family are a long-lived lot. We don't know how old they grew to be in Scotland, England, Ireland, and Germany; but we do know the champion. She was Laurence Brown's daughter, John Jamieson's granddaughter, my grandfather David's great-aunt, Catherine. Catherine, as my grandfather David often told me, danced the Highland fling on her one-hundredth birthday. I don't know what she did on the last day of her life, eleven days before she was 111 years old, but she was still able to read with her one eye almost to the hour of her death. From her childhood, she had only one eye, the other having been destroyed by a rooster that attacked her when she was eight years old. Many pieces have been published about her in the Prince Edward Island press, and her descendant, Mrs. Letitia Frizzel, has in her possession the only photograph of our centenarian-plus ancestor, taken a year before she died.

Stemming from those six root families—Smallwoods, Lawsons, Jamiesons, Browns, Gambergs, and Devannas—my tribe has overspread the face of North America, in every province of Canada, every state of the American Union. I haven't counted them; indeed, there must be several thousand of them whose surnames I have never heard. But it would surprise me greatly to discover that there were fewer than 10,000 of us on this continent today, not counting thousands more of us in Scotland, Wales, and England as well.

4

Apprentice Newfoundlander

Poverty with joy isn't poverty at all. The poor man is not one who has little, but one who hankers after more.

Seneca

Short of genius, a rich man cannot imagine poverty.

Charles Péguy

Twelve hours of hunger will reduce any saint, artist or philosopher to the level of a highwayman.

George Bernard Shaw

The St. John's to which my parents brought me when I was about a year old was proudly called by its inhabitants the oldest settlement of European peoples anywhere in the Western Hemisphere. That description was true enough, but it could also be called a dirty, shabby, down-at-heel seaport town of unpaved, muddy streets and one- and two-storey wooden frame houses of which perhaps 30 per cent were without water or sewage facilities—in 1930, there were still 2,000 families without either. Even some of the important Water Street merchants lived upstairs over their shops.* Shop clerks worked twelve to fourteen hours a day, and their last duty each day was to put up the heavy wooden shutters that protected the small windows of the shops. It was only a few months before I arrived in the city that the first streetcars began to operate, and they covered only a small portion of the city.

Square paving stones were laid on Water Street a few months before I arrived in the city, and they remained until Mayor Charles Howlett paved the street with asphalt in the 1920s. All other streets in St. John's were then just dirt passages: in wet weather, sometimes we went up to our ankles in mud; in dry summer weather, they were dusty and dirty.

Crossing-sweepers were common in the city. They were usually young urchins from the very poorest families. They stationed themselves at much-used street intersections, and as a pedestrian crossed the street, one of the boys would walk backward before him, brushing his birch-branch broom left and right to clear a faintly better path across. At the opposite side, the pedestrian usually gave him a cent, or a "big penny", actually an English penny, commonly seen in Newfoundland almost until Confederation in 1949. The last time that I remember seeing a crossing-sweeper was about 1926, when my

*But the trend to build stately wooden houses had started on King's Bridge Road, and on Circular, Monkstown, Rennie's Mill, and one or two other streets on the higher levels of the town. Later, they became known collectively to the irreverent as rogues' roost.

young wife and I walked across Duckworth Street to the top of Beck's Cove. Soft-hearted, she gave the lad ten cents, which neither she nor I could really afford that year. I never see a game of curling, with the players furiously sweeping the ice, without remembering the crossing-sweepers. No attempt was made, in the first quarter of the century, to remove snow from the streets. It piled high on them and stayed until the sun finally melted it in the spring.

In every street where the central water and sewer systems had not yet reached, and to a very great extent did not reach for another thirty years, there were water tanks. Some of these were made of wood, and the water ran from them continuously. Others were cast-iron with handles, and the water flowed from them only while the handle was held down. If the street was long, there would be more than one tank, for all the families would come here with buckets for their water. Every household had two buckets and a wooden hoop—used to keep the two buckets away from the carrier's legs so that he could carry the water home without slopping it. Some of these water tanks continued in use in St. John's well into the 1930s.

Sewage disposal was only a step ahead of the method used in medieval Europe, where the sewage was simply thrown out onto the street from second-floor windows—a stroll at night down a medieval European street must have been quite an adventure. In St. John's, along some streets sewage receptacles were placed at intervals of a few hundred yards; they were simply large earthenware pipes up-ended above gratings that led to the sewer pipe underground. People carried buckets of sewage to these hoppers last thing at night before going to bed or first thing in the morning before going to work. On streets where there were no hoppers or where hoppers had not yet been installed, there were the night-carts—horse-drawn carts followed by two men who would pick up the buckets of "night soil" placed in front of each house and empty them into the carts. The night-carts started to come along around midnight, and they carried oil-fed torches which gave off a flare of light and much smoke. I suppose that nearly a third of the present population of St. John's remember the night-carts and sewage hoppers—and remember the smell.

But if the old city was shabby and grubby, the land-locked harbour, snugly set inside the Narrows, was a romantic, thrilling magnet that drew the youth of the town every hour and minute they could steal away. At almost every finger wharf on the north side, the town side, of the harbour, there would be two, three, four, or five sailing vessels tied on, from every section of the Island's 6,000-mile coastline, with dried codfish, sawn lumber, sand, and vegetables from the outports; and the foreign-going windjammers just in from Greece, Malta, Italy, Spain, Portugal, the West Indies, or Brazil, with salt or rum or molasses or fruit—just in, or about to sail to those far-off seaports (so much farther off then than now) with salt-dried codfish. There were scores of those foreign-going vessels and hundreds of local outport schooners, and in the spring and fall the harbour would be full of them, so full that we could cross over the water from one side to the other by hopping and jumping from one vessel to the next. In March and April, the sealing fleet went out with 3,000 or 4,000 men to the Icefields in search of seals; when they came back in to discharge their load of fat-lined pelts, the wharves swarmed with unshaven seal-hunters whose canvas clothes were stiff with seal oil and grease after their four or five weeks at sea. And 3,000 longshoremen crowded the waterfront all year round.

What a paradise of excitement for the boys of St. John's! There were parrots and sugar-cane and conch shells that seamen brought from the West Indies, and great puncheons of molasses from Barbados and Jamaica laid out on the wharves, their bungs hanging out so that the gasses could escape—we would stick our fingers in the bung hole and lick the molasses off them, and on lucky days, we might get some sugar-molasses, the thick, sweet, congealed molasses that formed a deposit at the bottom of the puncheon. In the occasional winter, the water of the harbour covered over with a thin sheet of ice. Then the more outrageously venturesome, or just fool-hardy, boys went out on it and engaged in what must have been the most dangerous sport in the world for small boys: several of them together would press down on the thin, tough salt-water ice to make it buckle under their weight. By a miracle, the ice never broke and let the boys through into the cold harbour water. I was one of those boys more than once. I shouldn't have been, for my uncle Joe and his chum, the son of Dr. Simms, had met their death together, skating arm in arm, when they went through the ice on Quidi Vidi Lake.

One year, City Council caused some excitement by ordering that all goats be driven out of St. John's. The goats had always wandered around the streets, even on Water Street, overturning garbage cans, stealing into backyards, and generally making themselves a nuisance. Most people were glad to see the last of the goats, though the owners thought themselves ill-treated and nursed their sense of grievance long afterward.

The year of the Petty Harbour dogs was notable too. Petty Harbour, a picturesque fishing settlement eight or ten miles from St. John's, was the home of considerable numbers of large mongrel dogs, many of them crosses of Newfoundlands and Labradors, with perhaps a touch of wolf. They were strong, and the fishermen used them to haul firewood and fish-flake and stage material from the nearby forest. In "the year of the Petty Harbour dogs", the suburbs of St. John's and even the city itself were invaded by these animals, seeking food, night after night for weeks. They killed hens and sheep, and people began to be afraid that soon the hungry dogs would attack them. So the police were ordered out to search, find, and shoot them. Men living in the suburbs were loaned rifles by the police to join in the hunt, and my father was one of those so favoured. He already had his own double-barrelled shotgun, but this was not as good as a police rifle for hunting dangerous, hungry dogs.

It was about the same time, in 1910, that Halley's Comet had the whole town stirred up. Strange rumours ran wild through St. John's, and it is these rather than the comet itself that I remember.

I remember vividly the forest fire on the Southside Hill that lit up St. John's night after night and filled the town with smoke both night and day. It lasted a week, and everybody was up on the Hill fighting the fire. Hal King and I were among them, without our parents' knowledge. Luckily, the timber growing there was a dwarf species, but it was a fierce sight while it lasted.

In 1901, my father rented a couple of rooms over a small shop on LeMarchant Road at the corner of Lime Street. The widow who owned the shop lived in a room or two behind it and rented the second storey of the tiny house. The next year, we moved to the East End of town and rented one floor of a three-storey house on Bond Street—one of the few places in Newfoundland bearing Sir Robert Bond's name. We lived here for two or three years, and I can still remember several things that happened during this time. Once I took my sister Marie sliding on the snow-covered Garrison Hill, a short, steep incline, and crashed into the stone wall at the foot of the hill—I think it was the wall in front of the Parker residence. I carry to this day the marks of the stitches that had to be put in my forehead. Most houses in St. John's, if they were more than one storey high, had wooden ladders leaning against them at the back as fire escapes, and this three-storey house had its long ladder. I must have been between two and three years old when I almost brought my career to an early end. I climbed the ladder to the roof, then ran to the adjoining house, which was more than a foot lower, ran across that roof to the third house, which was even lower, and so on almost to the end of the block, where there was a sheer drop to the street, before someone caught up with me and stopped my fun. And I remember being in a large baby carriage that my father had got a carriage-maker to build, with my sister Marie, and being drawn through the streets by a huge Newfoundland dog that my father owned. This was perhaps the first time in Newfoundland history when I attracted considerable public attention! The dog had an unlucky end, though: Uncle Sandy, who was in Newfoundland on a short visit from Alaska, took it back with him when he went West again; and in Alaska, the Newfoundland was attacked by a pack of wild dogs and torn to pieces.

While we lived on Bond Street, I went to my first school, the first of five schools I was to attend between my third and fifteenth years. This was British Hall, a Church of England school that stood immediately across the street from the old tobacco factory, and no more than a thousand yards from Bishop Feild College, the last school I was to go to in Newfoundland.*

From Bond Street, we moved to Coronation Street—so named, I believe, from the coronation of King Edward VII a year or so before. This was a completely new section of St. John's immediately west of Springdale Street, and running parallel with it, where my grandfather David had his house. The new street was short, with two-storey houses on both sides. My father owned one of them, and it was then that I went to Centenary School run by the Methodist Church.

There were backyards behind the houses on Coronation Street and backyards behind those on Springdale Street. Between the two rows of backyards stood a field measuring about an acre, and my grandfather rented it and used it for years as a small "farm". He enjoyed this "farming" immensely, for he sprang from generations of

*Twenty years or more later, my friend, the lawyer George W. B. Ayre, at the moment a rich man, made a gift of British Hall to Bishop Spencer College for Girls; but almost immediately after he announced his intention, the stock market crashed. He was wiped out and subsequently spent a long term in jail. I visited him once in jail; and after he came out, I published in a newspaper that I was editing, the *Daily Globe*, his "Spatters From the Pen". Pen was an abbreviation of penitentiary, and the verses recounted his adventures and other events while he was in jail.

farmers. I joined him in the summer and got my first taste of growing crops. He grew immense cabbages, and potatoes and turnips. One year, he entered some of his choicest specimens at an agricultural fair in the Prince's Rink and aroused great wonder at the size of the potatoes in his exhibit; but to his chagrin, when one of the judges suggested that the largest potatoes be cut in two, they turned out to be hollow. In those days before the universal use of insecticides, cabbages were cut down by the cabbage grub, sometimes a whole field at a time. David had delivered to him from the shoe store on Water Street a large number of empty boot and shoe boxes, from which he fashioned paper guards that he inserted into the ground around each individual cabbage plant. His losses from the cabbage grub were trifling after that.

We lived on Coronation Street for three or four years, and the thing I remember most about it, apart from "working" with my grandfather on his "farm", was a fierce argument I had with Gordon Driscoll, a boy who lived across the street from me, on the meaning of the term *one fifty* in money. I argued that it meant fifty cents and Gordon that it meant three times fifty cents. (This is an incident that I would never have mentioned when I was in politics.) Another boy on the street, Ben Walker, grew up to have a successful custom tailoring business in Corner Brook. At the head of the street were the Hardings, and their son Dick was my friend for many years afterward.

About 1907, we moved to the Southside Road, almost at its western extremity, nearly two miles outside the city limits. We had a piece of land measuring about 150 feet along the road and going back about 2,000 feet up over the hill. From there I went daily on foot a couple of miles to St. Mary's School, owned by the Church of England, on the south side of the harbour. It was a long walk, so it was decided a year or two later to send me to the day school of Littledale Academy, which is now the large and beautiful St. Bride's College for girls. The day school was a small, one-room, single-storey wooden building that accepted boys and girls, who were taught by Roman Catholic nuns. (In later years, I always had great fun, when I spoke at public functions at Littledale, calling myself one of the earliest students of this famous girls' college, for I was not only a boy but a Protestant boy at that.) Catechism was taught every day, and I still remember the envy of the boys at Littledale when the nun would say, "Get out your catechisms. Joey, you can go outside if you want to"—as I always did.

We cleared the trees from two or three acres of our land on the Southside Road, and of course that meant fencing it, and I was the one who provided most of the fence. In those days, flour was the staple diet of most of the people in Newfoundland—bread and potatoes, bread and fish, bread and salt beef, but always bread. For its size, Newfoundland must have been one of Canada's best customers for flour. The flour used to come in wooden barrels weighing 198 pounds, and these wooden barrels were held together by flat inch-wide wooden hoops, and a number of wire hoops as well. Hundreds of thousands of the empty barrels were used by coopers to make into quintal* drums and half-drums, into which salt-dried codfish was packed for shipment to Brazil. The wire hoops were not used by the coopers, and my job was to "bum" as many of these hoops as I could from them—there were dozens of cooperages in St. John's—and to find them wherever I could, on dumps or just strewn about the untidy city. I hardly ever walked home without bringing some wire hoops. I would take several hoops, convert them from circles to long lengths, then hook them together, end to end, like reef knots. With enough hoops, I could make a strand of wire half a mile long or longer. Two strands, or better three, nailed to fence-posts gave us a fence that would keep the cattle out. And that's what fences were for in Newfoundland, and still are. It was almost unheard of to fence in cattle, sheep, or horses; instead, they were allowed to roam the public lands to pick up what wild grazing they could find. The area of cultivated land on the Island has always been trifling; and when men cultivated their little patches and pieces of land to grow enough vegetables for the house, it was vitally important to fence them to keep out the wandering animals. Many a tragedy there was when cattle or horses or sheep or goats broke in through a fence and ate or trampled the crop.

And so in the first ten years of my life, I had lived about a year in Gambo and nine years in St. John's, in a total of five houses, and had gone to four schools—two Church of England, one Methodist, and one Roman Catholic. To this day, there are no schools in Newfoundland that are not owned and operated by the churches, although there has been for the past three or four years a fast-moving trend to amalgamate the operation and physical facilities of some

*This old word for the British hundred-weight (112 pounds) has always been and largely still is the Newfoundland standard measure for salt-dried codfish.

schools owned by different denominations.

At my Southside home, I learned a lot of things: how to feed, clean out after, brush, and curry-comb horses; how to put the harness on them; and how to cure them when they had the colic. I learned how to ride them bareback and how to use them for gathering wood. I would put on the winkers, the collar and hames, and traces joined to a swingle-tree well clear of the hind legs, take an axe, and let the horse haul me up the hill by the swingle-tree. Then I would cut down trees, limb them out except for a small clump of boughs at the very top of each tree, drag the trees to the path and lay them top to top, butt to butt, eight or ten of them, put the chain from the swingle-tree around the lot at the slender end, fasten the hook, and then let the horse haul the sticks down the hill, the butts spreading out and making a wide, smooth path through the snow.

I would often go with my brothers and sisters up the hill to where it levelled out, almost to the shore of Beaver Pond. In those days, Beaver Pond was remote and unspoiled—the nearest neighbour was Tommy Linegar, who operated a tiny farm on Blackhead Road overlooking the city. The pond then was the home of great speckled trout, and no man knew it as Bob Lyons did.

Bob Lyons was one of a remarkable family in St. John's that owned and ran a watch-repair and jewellery shop on George Street, a couple of hundred yards from the Salvation Army soup kitchen. There were Harry, Gus, and Bob, and the one sister, Sis. They never married, and they lived and worked in their own brick house and shop. Was there ever such a shop since Dickens' curiosity shop! Bob was the youngest of the family—he would be in his fifties when I was a boy—and he lived for his one absorbing passion in life, trout fishing. He and my father were great friends and frequently went trouting together. Bob always used a bamboo pole, with a very long fishing line, a baited hook, and a brightly painted cork float. The float we always called a bobber, and we would watch it zealously for the slightest sign of down-movement that told us that a trout was nibbling at the bait. ("Watch your bobber" was a favourite saying to advise care and attention.) Bob, when he had nobody to go trouting with him, would go off by himself to Beaver Pond with an outrageously long bamboo pole, an even longer line, and a can of worms, get himself comfortably settled on a rock on the shore and cast the line almost half-way across the water. He would sit there for hour after hour, puffing away at his odorous clay pipe, never taking his eye off the bobber, and no doubt thinking all kinds of philosophical thoughts. And, miracle of miracles, always he'd come down the path over the hill to our house with two or three great trout for our pan.

There was another Lyons brother, but he was not part of the family jewellery business. He was a prominent commercial photographer, who photographed every important personage in Newfoundland for nearly half a century. He was the cause, in a way, of one of the tragic moments in my life. When I was organizing the *Book of Newfoundland* and seeking photographs in large numbers, I tried to locate the thousands of priceless glass negatives of the Lyons studio. Mr. Lyons had gone to his reward, and I found the heirs and discovered that someone had disposed of the negatives—he had sold them to a suburban farmer who wanted them for his greenhouse! I can't bear to think of it to this day.

We always kept a pig at Southside Road, and I was always very sure to be out of sight when the time came to slaughter it—I've never eaten fresh pork since. My mother kept ten or a dozen laying hens, and I can see her now "trying" the hens to find out whether they would lay that day.

We children had some glorious adventures pursuing the great Newfoundland pastime, trouting. (We never did call it trout fishing, except when we wanted foreigners to know what we meant, for how could you expect aliens and strangers to know that trouting meant trout fishing?) Many times my father would take me in the horse-drawn, square-body wagon six or eight miles to Bloody Pond, over the Old Petty Harbour Road, or to Third Pond or the fascinating Dixie Gullies. Bob Lyons always came with us when he knew that we were going. One morning, the three of us arrived at Bloody Pond before dawn. We unhitched the horse in a tiny meadow by the side of the road and decided to have some breakfast before starting to trout. But it was raining heavily, everything was wet, and we hadn't brought any dry kindling with which to make a fire. We just couldn't get anything to ignite, or if it did, the fire quickly went out. My father coaxed some of Bob's rum from him to help make the fire burn, until Bob began to complain bitterly as his supply shrank, and he insisted that my father's rum should be used in equal amount. We did get the fire going, a great roaring blaze that dried the grass around, and us; and with hot breakfast inside us, we felt just fine. Then Bob took up his great bamboo pole and said, "Come on, Joey, let's go trouting!" He led the way through the wet bushes to the edge of the pond. There was no path around the shore, and we had to use the rocks at the water's edge as stepping stones. Bob was clumsy, I as nimble as a mountain goat, but Bob kept calling loudly back to me to be careful not to fall in. I laugh still to remember the great splash ahead of me as Bob slipped on a greasy rock and measured his length in the pond. After a little bitter swearing to himself, he got up and resumed his cumbersome progress to our favourite spot where a small brook emptied into the pond, Bob still cautioning *me* to be careful. I remember that on that particular occasion, Bob caught an eel, which we all detested, and which meant to him that any further trout fishing would be useless at that spot for the rest of the day. (After the Second World War, when I visited West Germany for the Newfoundland Government, I marvelled to discover that the Germans regarded eel as a great delicacy. Then I learned that all Europeans think highly of eel, and I helped to bring about the export of live eels from Newfoundland to Europe.)

Often, we older children went off trouting without our father or Bob Lyons. We would tackle up the horse, take such food as we could find, and set off before midnight for Dixie Gullies. What adventure that was! And what the youth of today are missing, even in Newfoundland! We drove and drove in the dark until we came to the Ruby Line, and after an interminable time, we came at last to the Dixie Line, which ended at the Dixie Gullies. This was our great secret trouting paradise—secret because, of course, there were only two ways to get to it then: to walk, or to drive with horse and cart over the almost impassable Dixie Line. But what trouting! And the fun, to which I now confess publicly and contritely, of stealing Samuel Ruby's cabbages, potatoes, and turnips on the way in! We would climb over his fence and steal a head of cabbage and some small turnips, and even haul up some potato plants and finger around in the earth for potatoes. We would get to the Gullies just before dawn, in time to boil water for a cup of tea and eat a piece of hard-bread (Newfoundland's name for rock-hard ship's biscuit) before casting our fishing lines in the nearest Gully. After trouting nearly all day, we would have a great "scoff" of corned-beef or spareribs and the borrowed cabbage, turnips, and potatoes; then we would begin the return journey and reach home soon after dark.

The Ruby Line extended a distance of two or three miles. Samuel Ruby owned the land on both sides, and it was all fenced. He was one of the truly great figures in the early part of this century in Newfoundland, and even the last part of the former century. He was an Englishman by birth, and his greatness came from his pioneer farming effort. He had incomparably the largest land-holdings of any farmer. This doesn't really say very much, not nearly enough, for in Newfoundland until very recently no farmer had enough land to be worth mentioning. But even today, Samuel Ruby's holdings would be regarded with respect. Near his home he had cleared perhaps twenty-five or thirty acres for cultivation, and today there aren't fifty farmers in Newfoundland with that much cultivated land. The story we heard about Samuel Ruby was that sailors of all nationalities who came to St. John's and deserted ship could always find refuge on Ruby's farm. But Ruby charged a price. In return for a few weeks' board and lodging, the sailor had to spend long hours each day helping to clear the land, cutting fence-posts and rails, and fencing the vast extent of the Ruby property, running perhaps to several thousand acres. Samuel Ruby wrote the first book on practical farming ever published in Newfoundland. I used to have a copy of it long years ago, but I don't know if any copies are in existence today.

There was another kind of trouting that we liked very much. This was wintertime fishing, when we would fish through the ice on the ponds. Many a time, my older brothers and sisters and I would take the horse and catamaran—a two-runner slide—and drive off to the ponds and gullies five or ten miles from home. Each of us would cut several holes in the ice and lower a baited hook into the water. We would try to keep warm by walking briskly from hole to hole, trying the line at each hole and hauling up a trout when there was one. We would lay the trout on the ice near the hole, and soon it would be frozen as stiff as a board. It is interesting to us ice-hole trouters to realize that this is exactly how Clarence Birdseye discovered the vast and almost overwhelming principle of quick-freezing fish and other foods. He spent a few years in Cartwright, Labrador, for the Hudson's Bay Company, and although thousands of men before him had noticed that fish brought up through an ice-hole promptly froze board-hard on the ice, it was left to Birdseye to understand that this phenomenon could bring about the greatest revolution known for long generations in the food industry. In short, the quick-freeze refrigeration industry was born in Cartwright, but could just as easily have begun at Bloody Pond or the Dixie Gullies!

It was from my Southside Road home that I had my first thrilling travel adventure. A lumber-laden steamship went ashore near Renews, a fishing settlement about eighty miles south of St. John's, and Michael P. Cashin, the Member of the House of Assembly for that constituency, did the salvaging. For salvage insurance reasons, the lumber had to be surveyed, and my father was asked to go down the Shore to do it. He took me along with him. There was a rough, narrow gravel road along the shore, little better than a path through the trees, though nearly always in sight of the ocean. We went up with the mailman on his square-body mail wagon, I sitting or lying among the mail bags. I don't remember much of the actual drive, except waking up late at night while they changed horses about halfway along. But I do remember vividly the week or more we were at Renews, where we boarded at the home of Arthur O'Leary. I was taken about the settlement by the local boys, and in a small boat about the harbour, jigging sculpins and tom-cods, and I was shown how to make a whistle-pipe from a piece of alder. I remember my shame when my father began to drink heavily in the O'Leary house and lay helplessly about for days. I know now that I needn't have been ashamed; for Arthur O'Leary and his wife were not only generous hosts, but Irish as well, as the whole settlement was, and so they were quite familiar with and not unsympathetic to heavy drinking. Forty-five years afterward, I visited the O'Learys and made myself known, and they remembered me as a boy of six or seven. And when I had an audience of Pope Pius XII in Rome, Arthur was one of the few friends to whom I sent a cabled greeting. I had a lot of inward satisfaction as Premier in giving the Shore a better highway all the way to St. Shotts.

On Southside Road, I learned how to use a crosscut saw to saw sticks of wood into chunks that would fit into our Improved Success kitchen stove that was the only source of heat in the two-storey house. I learned how to cleave these chunks, if they were too large for the stove, into halves and quarters. I learned to work the land itself with mattock and prong and hoe, and to spread manure and plant potatoes and "hill" them up. I bought cabbage plants—or, better still, got them free—and planted them in our field, and I did constant weeding by hand. I learned to harvest the little crop of turnips in the fall, after the first frost or two had made them sweeter; I remember still how numb my hands were as I worked in that small field, helping to gather the eight or ten barrels of turnips for the house. We Newfoundlanders never measured anything by pounds or bushels or pecks—it was gallons or barrels always, whether of water, fish, vegetables, or crushed stone.

By the time I was ten, I was far more knowledgeable in some matters than most of the youth of St. John's, and far more ignorant in other matters. I had learned a lot about alcohol and its unpleasant effects—indeed, not until long afterward did I discover that the effects did not have to be unpleasant at all. I had learned a lot about living in a large family, and about poverty and hunger.

I had learned a lot about people, too, from our neighbours and my friends. There was the veteran of the road, John Baker, the cabman, and his beautiful horse, Barney. His family—Kate, Mamie, and Bride, and Bill, Jack, and Sam—all grew up into successful and respected citizens in the city. There were Danny Harvey and Alfie Rowe. Alfie was the hardest worker I have ever known; he turned himself into a slave in his determination to make a living. He managed to acquire a horse and box-cart, and he hauled quarter-tons and half-tons of coal to customers' homes, for so much per load. He worked his horse almost as hard as he worked himself. In the end, he had to give up that backbreaking trade and take something easy: blacksmith's helper.

And there were Mattie Churchill and Mike O'Rourk and the Sceviours and the St. John family* (then pronounced Sinjin, with the emphasis on the first syllable), who lived beside Nook's Brook and

*The head of the St. John family was a distinguished member of the seal-skinners' fraternity, for he was one of the most skilled among those craftsmen. Hundreds of thousands of seal pelts came into St. John's from the Icefields every spring, and each pelt had to have the thick layer of fat removed from it. This had to be done without damaging the skin, for the skin was worth much more than the fat. A skilled seal-skinner skinned many pelts in a day and rarely cut a skin. The pay was very high, and it needed to be, for there was work for only a few weeks every year. The fat would be rendered in great steam tanks at the sealing-ship owners' wharves along the south side of the harbour, and there were two products: the seal oil, and the blubber that was left after the oil had been rendered out. This blubber was prized by the larger farmers, and hundreds of horse-drawn box-cart loads of it were hauled away from the wharves every year and spread on the fields of Kilbride, Mount Pearl, and throughout the area. The smell, as you drove past those fields, was something that no one who ran into it would ever forget! But it was excellent humus for hungry fields, and they didn't mind the smell. The old, privileged position of the seal-skinners came to an end with the introduction of seal-skinning machines in the 1920s.

who after a while were succeeded by their relatives, the wonderful Horan family. Just over two years ago, I attended the funeral Mass for Mrs. Horan. She bore twenty-three children and reared nearly all of them. The children had to go to Mass on Sunday mornings in relays, because there weren't enough Sunday clothes and shoes to go around. When they grew up, they all became successful and much-admired nuns, magistrates, and businessmen. I was proud to have one of them, Jeremiah, as a candidate in the last General Election in which I led the Liberal Party.

A little farther westward, high up on the side of the hill, was the house of a young fellow that I didn't know—indeed, he wasn't born then—who afterward became an enormously popular radio and television personality and then a colleague in my Cabinet—John A. Nolan.

And there was John Syme. He was the first great capitalist in my life. He lived directly across the Waterford River from us, on Waterford Bridge Road; and native-born Scot that he was, he did a bit of farming as a sideline to his flourishing business in St. John's. He owned land on both banks of the river, his land on our side coming to the Southside Road itself and stretching narrowly along it for nearly half a mile. He had about the same area on the other side of the river, bordered by Waterford Bridge Road. He must have had ten or twelve acres, all of it cleared and cultivated, and most of it in grass to feed his small herd of dairy cows. His farmer and sole employee on the farm was Neddy Walsh, who lived in a little old-fashioned house midway between the river and Waterford Bridge Road. Neddy used to mow the grass with a hand-scythe, except for the headlands, and that was where I came in. The headlands were the stony edges of the fields near the fences, that the scythe couldn't get at. Only a hand-manipulated grasshook could be used here, and John Syme gave me the job of using it, in return for fifty cents a day. The job lasted two or three weeks, and although I used to think sometimes that his reason for standing over me as I worked was to make sure that I worked faithfully to earn my fifty cents, I know now that it was because he was genuinely interested in me and my boyish chatter. More than half a century later, when I was Master of the Masonic Lodge in Harbour Grace, I was delighted to discover in the records that John Syme had been present when the cornerstone of the lodge building was laid in 1867 or 1868. I must have been the world-champion grass-hook man, or boy. I really could use it! But I almost lost the little finger on my left hand—the marks are to be seen on it today—in spite of my skill and because of my speed.

And there was Nicholas Cousins, known to all around as Nick. He had what was for those days a palatial house a quarter of a mile to the east, built on a very narrow strip of land between the Southside Road and the railway track. He had a longish but very narrow garden beside his house, and he too employed me, to weed his flower beds, cut the grass, and generally tidy up the garden in which he took such delight. I remember him well because of an incident that has stuck in my mind ever since. As he stood watching me work one day, he enquired if I would like to have a piece of blueberry pie. There wasn't anything in the world at that moment that I wanted more, but some perverse instinct—perhaps a kind of foolish pride—prompted me to say no thanks and to persist in my refusal as he pressed the invitation. I was disgusted with myself and am disgusted to this day for refusing the slice of blueberry pie. Nicholas Cousins owned a cooperage plant in St. John's, probably the largest one in the country. His son Bertie succeeded him, and he built for himself a splendid new house on Waterford Bridge Road, opposite Charles E. Hunt's home and on the site of the magnificent home later built by Chesley A. Pippy.

My closest chums were Hal King and Alan Sceviour. Though they were slightly older than I, we became inseparable friends for several years. Alan Sceviour died not long after he came back from serving in the Royal Navy in the First World War, but Hal King lived to a ripe age and our acquaintance continued.

And then—and then the sky opened up, and a wondrous, beautiful new world was provided for me. It was provided by Uncle Fred, my father's oldest brother. Uncle Fred had volunteered to take his brother Charles' oldest boy, who was supposed to be bright and intelligent and promising, and pay all the expenses of putting him through college: school fees, pocket money, laundry, and other small expenses, as well as boots and shoes and clothing. And not only that! I was to go into boarding school, for Bishop Feild College had both day students and boarders. I suppose the idea was that the college would give me a good education, and the hostel would train me in behaviour. There were no real colleges in Newfoundland then, though five of the principal high schools of the country were so called: Bishop Feild College, Church of England; St. Bonaventure's

College, Roman Catholic; Methodist College; Salvation Army College; and Bishop Spencer College for Girls, Church of England. I have never known why the name *college* was used, for they were only the better-quality high schools of the respective religious denominations. In the case of four of these five colleges, the idea was mainly a bit of snobbery: the sons and daughters of merchants, lawyers, doctors, shopkeepers, and higher civil servants would attend them at a higher cost than that charged by other schools; they would learn and live in a more genteel atmosphere and enjoy, if that's the word, the air of the English public school.

Bishop Feild College had six grades: kindergarten, primary, preliminary, intermediate, junior associate, and senior associate. If you succeeded in senior associate, you were entitled to put the letters A. A. (Associate of Arts) after your name. On the day that I entered Bishop Feild College in 1910, I don't suppose that there were 200 A.A.'s in the whole country. As for university degrees, I doubt that there were a dozen persons among the 1,000 teachers in the country who had a B. A. or a higher degree.

But all that was unknown to me when the grand news came, and I was almost speechless with happiness. My brothers and sisters were excited, my mother joyful, and my father pleased too. I was fitted out with new clothes: two or maybe three suits of underwear, stockings, and Eton collars made of celluloid—celluloid, because they could be cleaned with a wet cloth and no laundry was needed. Indeed, at that time, many of the men who wore white collars had celluloid collars as well; but, then, not many men wore collars in Newfoundland in 1910.

5

Little Gentleman – For a While

At the feet of Gamaliel.

Acts 22:3

Education is the ability to listen to almost anything without losing your temper or your self-confidence.

Robert Frost

The five years at Bishop Feild turned me inside out, set my course in life, and were probably the most formative time of my life. It mightn't have intended to do so, but certainly the College by its teaching excited my passionate hatred of injustice and cruelty; it introduced me to the Church of England; it allowed me to become a recruit (and soon a bugler) in the Church Lads' Brigade; it provided the opportunity for the first strike that I ever led; it introduced me to boxing, gymnastics, and long-distance running (and the first Rugby football team in Newfoundland started by Thomas McNeill, the druggist); it saw me become a Socialist, increased my determination to be a journalist, and placed me cheek-by-jowl with the scions of many of the wealthy merchants in St. John's, thereby ending completely any danger there might have been (and perhaps there never was much) of my having anything less than a feeling of easy, effortless equality with the best or at any rate the richest of them. Bishop Feild strengthened enormously my already intense love of reading.

The college also built, or at least helped to build, something else that shaped my life: an unqualified, unwavering, unquestioned confidence in myself, my potential, and my destiny, at all times and seasons, whether I should be rich or poor, high or low, pragmatically successful or a failure. The one thing that my continued easy possession of this confidence did not depend on was money. Without two nickels or even two coppers to rub together, my confidence in myself was unassailable. I felt myself to be inferior to no one, except in physical strength, moral strength, and various skills and gifts in which, unless I was a fool, I couldn't help recognizing my own inferiority. But I didn't doubt that I could remove that inferiority if I really tried! I suppose that all this could be called enormous vanity, or was it really only the camouflage that an inferiority complex set up in self-defence? I doubt it, for I have noticed throughout my life that I have never even momentarily lost faith in myself, even during my poorest times and in the face of my greatest failures. And, of course, as I learned of the lives of so many, especially in North America, who came up from poverty to fame, I rather took pride in my poverty and failures, storing them all up carefully in the back of my mind as something that I'd be glad to look back upon when I became successful and famous. I even welcomed setbacks and bitter disappointments as things to be stored and remembered in later times—they would be a kind of personal treasury upon which I would draw at the right time. I have often wondered what a psychoanalyst would make of all this, but there has been a saving grace throughout it all: I can laugh at myself, I can see the fun of it, and I poke fun at myself in my own mind about it. At the same time, I have no doubt that this kind of faith in myself has enabled me to carry on through poverty and disaster countless times throughout my life. That's what four or five years at Bishop Feild did for me, so the college has a lot to answer for!

The very first day I was given my nickname, one that old Feildians still call me: "Splits". This is a Newfoundland word for stove kindling. Walter Leseman, who gave everyone his nickname at Bishop Feild, asked me, "What's your name?" and when I told him, he said, "Smallwood—in other words, splits." Walter himself was known as Crackie, from his uncanny talent in emitting the thin, shrill yelping of a crackie dog, an undersized mongrel.

I got into trouble on my first day too. A boy in the hostel pointed out a big red-haired fellow across the room and suggested that I call out, "Fox in the bread-box eating all the cheese!" I did so, not knowing what it meant, that it was somehow an allusion to red-headed people, or that the fellow was in fact the captain of the boarders, and that he didn't like being called "fox in the bread-box". His name was George Shaw,* and he sauntered over to me, seized me, bent me over his knee, and gave me a spanking that I can almost feel yet. Another big fellow among the boarders was "Slogger" Anderson, from Heart's Content. He was so called because in cricket he used to slog a mighty bat. After the spanking, perhaps to show that I was now forgiven, Shaw tossed me half-way across the room into Anderson's arms. Anderson tossed me back, and so I went half a dozen times across the room. Anderson was cut down in Flanders in the First World War, one of many of my Feild chums and acquaintances to be snuffed out. The boarders came from every part of the Island, the sons of outport merchants and doctors and magistrates mainly, and many of the day boys were sons of the financial elite of St. John's.

*He became an important shipping man as the principal owner of the Shaw Steamship Line plying between Newfoundland and Canada.

I was undoubtedly the poorest boy in the school, from the poorest family. Uncle Fred gave me ten cents a week pocket money, paid to me by the headmaster every Saturday morning. That was the official rate, but other boys received "unofficial" augmentations. Rarely did I get the full ten cents, for throughout the week for misbehaviour of one kind or another, I was sure to be fined a cent or two cents or even, for something serious, five cents; in the end, I actually received only two or three cents. My laundry was paid for in my school bill, as were my haircuts. Donnelly, the barber on Water Street, had the contract from the college, and we would bring him a note initialled by Mr. Wood, the headmaster, authorizing the haircut. Mr. Wood's neglect to read the actual note handed him for signing tempted us more than once to write, "Please cut the bearer's head off"; but Mr. Donnelly enjoyed the joke and accepted the note as proper authority for the haircut.

We had a scintillating array of teachers, about half of them Newfoundlanders and the others Englishmen. "Pompey" Hill, an Englishman who came to us from India, had an incredible moustache that curled on each side of his face into several loops and then jutted out into two sharp points several inches away from his cheeks. I think he must have used some kind of pomade to wax the moustache, and in class, one or other of his hands would forever be twirling it, reinforcing the curls and sharpening the points. He was proud of that moustache, and he gave a lot of his time and energy to its cultivation.

Pompey Hill was the finest example I have ever known of the absent-minded professor. He would be talking to us in history, for example, and stop dead in the middle of a sentence, look helplessly out the window, back at us, down at his desk, and then stand gazing absently at us while we waited, knowing exactly that he had "disappeared" again. Finally, he would ask a little ashamedly, "What was I talking about?" Of course, more than once somebody told him something altogether different from the real topic. While he was at Bishop Feild—and I think he lasted no more than a term or two—he ate with eight or ten of us in the Little dining room. He would get up from his place at the end of the table and walk down to the middle of it, seize the unsliced loaf of bread, and tear it in half and carry a big chunk of it back to his place. Sometimes he would take his plate of dinner out through the front door of the hostel onto the lawn and there, standing straight as an arrow and absently gazing directly ahead, fork the food into his mouth and chew stolidly. He was an endless source of fun and enjoyment for us, and we were sorry when he did not come back.

Another master, Sandy McBain, a Scot, had an artificial leg. I can see him now dragging his leg as he came into the classroom. Tasker Cook (afterward Sir Tasker, leader in the Upper House for Sir Richard Squires' Liberal administration) had an agency business on Water Street and represented several foreign companies. His son, named after him but known to us as Tack, was always bringing things into the classroom that he had pocketed in his father's office. One day, he had a sail needle, the kind used by sail-makers. He wrote on a note-sized piece of paper, "Please kick me in the behind", stuck the needle through the piece of paper, and dared the boys to stick the needle into Sandy's wooden leg. One of the boys took him up on it and jabbed the needle in from behind. We were startled by the howl that came from the master—the boy had attacked the wrong leg. Tasker Cook was agent for some cocoa company, and he used to have many miniature paper packages of cocoa for distribution as samples. Tack would bring pocketfuls of these samples into the classroom. One day, at least half a dozen of us had our mouths full of the dry sweet cocoa and couldn't answer the master when he addressed us, it was Tack Cook himself who opened his mouth to answer and sprayed the room with cocoa powder.

Another of our teachers was Obediah Bown. He used to alternate between exploding in laughter and getting very angry at some of my tricks. I had contrived to unlock a small room at the head of a stairway and found in it, from years before, a papier-mâché head of a monkey that had probably been used in some school play. All the boarders had prep in the evenings, from seven to nine, supervised by the house-master for the week. One night, when Bown was the house-master, I excused myself from the prep room and went and got the monkey head. I brought back a ladder and put it against the door, mounted it, put on the monkey head, and looked into the room through the transom. I had told one or two of the boys to look at the transom every now and then, and one of them looked and told the others, and soon all the boys in the class were stealing surreptitious looks at the monkey and trying to suppress their laughter. Finally, Obediah noticed that something was going on and followed the boys' looks. At that very moment, I was watching again through the transom. He started to laugh, and then collapsed utterly, spread his arms on the desk, put down his head, and laughed until he was weak. That was the only really funny thing about the prank.

It wasn't only the masters that we played tricks on. One of the students was a big lad named Azariah King, from Trinity Bay. In fact, he was a pupil-teacher, taking his final year before going teaching himself. Pupil-teachers enjoyed special status and sometimes substituted for masters in the prep room. The prep room was entered through a passageway; and one evening, as King came along to take prep, a dozen of us ambushed him. We seized his arms and legs, dragged him into the room, and—despite his struggles—managed to hold him face down over a desk while one of the boys paddled him energetically with a cricket bat. He yelled his threats at us, what he was going to do to every one of us, and we were afraid to let him go. When we finally did, we ran for our lives.

That short passageway had a rifle rack on each wall with wooden dummy rifles provided for the smaller boys in the College Company of the Church Lads' Brigade (CLB). One night, before a new English teacher walked into the prep room, twenty of us lined up in parallel rows, facing each other, with the dummy rifles held smartly at shoulder arms. The new teacher had to pass through the line, and as he did so, one of us barked the order, "Present arms!" We were all members of the CLB and knew our drill well. When the teacher had passed through, the order was barked, "Shoulder arms! Right and left turn, quick march!" We turned and marched briskly out of the room, restored the rifles to the racks, and then returned to class. The new teacher was visibly pleased, but I heard afterward that the other teachers in the college howled with laughter when they heard about it and made his life miserable for weeks.

My first strike at Bishop Feild College, or anywhere else, was about the food. The food wasn't all that bad, but as in all institutions, it was monotonous. When I read in one of the English school magazine weeklies about a slogan chanted by the boarders of that school condemning the small portion of molasses—*treacle* was the English term—for their pudding, I found our slogan: "More molasses, less pudding!" We didn't exactly win the strike, but I think that there was for a while a shade more molasses coady.

When there was cheese in the dining room, we would try to slip some of it into our pockets, together with a few slices of bread; later that night, we would go down into the furnace room to the big coal-fired furnace that heated the building, put the cheese on the bread, put both on the coal shovel, and hold the shovel inside the fire box so that the bread toasted and the cheese melted on it. Perhaps it was the fact that we had stolen the bread and cheese, and were breaking a rule by going into the furnace room, but certainly these were among the most delightful meals we ever had.

We had to be on time for our meals, and more than once, one or two of my chums and I returned from an expedition too late for dinner at six o'clock. I found the solution to that problem. There was an outside entrance to a small room next to the kitchen, and I would go there to coax the girls in the kitchen to bring us thick slabs of bread soaked in molasses for our supper.

My second strike was much more serious. At St. Thomas's Church, Church of England, a whole corner was set aside for Feild boarders, and if you didn't have a pass to be away on Sunday, you had to be in your place in St. Thomas's morning and night. Some obeyed the rule and some didn't, especially at night, when it was rare for a teacher to be present. Sometimes, instead of going to St. Thomas's for the evening service, a group of us went to the Salvation Army Citadel on New Gower Street, which we often felt to be more interesting than our own church. But one Sunday night, a master, Arthur Raley, was in church and noticed the very small number of boarders in the college corner. He wrote down their names and, when he returned to the college, checked the list of pass-holders for the day, thus discovering who had skipped church. We were gated for a week as punishment. This meant that for a week, we were not permitted to go outside the boundaries formed by four streets quite close to the college. The worst of it, apart from the indignity, was the fact that during this particular week, a special outing had been planned. Jimmy Alderdice had arranged through his father, Frederick C. Alderdice (manager of the Rope Walk and later to be Prime Minister of Newfoundland), to get a large Rope Walk stake-body truck to take some of us on a picnic in the country. Those of us who had girls were to bring them, and I had invited Kitty Parnell. Obviously, our being gated for the holiday was undemocratic, a foul infraction of the rules of common decency, an inexcusable breach of the principles of democracy, an early example of deviationism. I forget the exact form of the strike, but most of the boarders joined me, and one of our acts of protest was to refuse to go into the dining room for several meals. To compensate, we pooled our finances to buy some gingerbread and bottles of ginger-beer, the equivalent of today's pop and potato chips. Our strike came to the attention of the headmaster, and eventually he relented and reduced the period of gating, so that the expedition went off as planned. Forty years afterward, I was happy as Premier to return the favour to Jimmy Alderdice.

I have mentioned that I used to read English school magazines. There were the weekly magazines of the Gem Library and the Magnet Library. They told in series the adventures of Tom Merry and Company at one public school in England and of Harry Wharton and Company at another. I suppose there must have been millions of English school boys in the first ten or fifteen years of this century who grew up with these stories. Then there were *Chums* and *Boys' Own Paper*. (I have never in my life received a gift that gave me the thrill I had from getting one Christmas the bound annual of *Chums*, containing the fifty-two issues of the year.) Sammy Garland sold the magazines in his huge bookstore, and I bought every issue without fail. And not only those, but Claude Duval, Dick Turpin, Spring-Heeled Jack, and the Sexton Blake detective stories, all from England; and the Horatio Alger and Frank Merriwell stories, Buffalo Bill, Nick Carter, Old King Brady, and other detective stories from the United States. "Penny dreadfuls" our elders called them, but for me, as for millions of other boys, they had a magnetic appeal. Later, of course, would come R. M. Ballantyne, G. A. Henty, James Fenimore Cooper, Robert Louis Stevenson, and the whole distinguished band of adventure-story writers.

But with pocket money that couldn't be more than ten cents a week, and was nearly always much less, how was I to obtain all these papers and magazines from Sammy Garland? I did it by starting a circulating library among the boarders and some of the day boys. I charged them a cent for each periodical they borrowed. This gave me enough money to buy everything of that kind that was for sale in St. John's. I made no money profit for myself and didn't want to. But I did manage to do a lot of reading. It was one of the few times in my life when I played the part of a successful entrepreneur.

And I became a Socialist. At first, I only thought I was, for I hated injustice and cruelty and felt certain that wealth was most unfairly distributed. It was all very vague, but I had come across the word Socialist and decided that I was one. One day when my chum Andrew Lehr and I were visiting his father's dental office, as we sometimes did after school, I met a patient waiting his turn and we got talking. He was George F. Grimes, son of the Superintendent of Police for Newfoundland. George was then a grown man with a family, and he had just won a seat in the House of Assembly* as the most intellectual of the thirteen Fishermen's Protective Union MHA's led into the House by the great William F. Coaker. I blurted out that I was a Socialist, and he was gentle and patient and asked me what Socialism was. I told him that it meant that everybody would be equal, that people should all share and share alike, and that everybody should have the same amount. (I was only repeating what "everybody" knew.) He nodded sympathetically, but went on to explain that Socialism was not precisely what I had said and asked if I would like to read something about it. The upshot of it was that I received two or three pamphlets from him, the principal one being the American John M. Work's "What's So and What's Not So". Work had a cleverly simplistic style of writing, and his pamphlet was written for distribution at Socialist outdoor meetings and similar gatherings. Simplistic or not, it instantly clarified in my mind what Socialism was and wasn't, at least in broad outline. That was the first of scores and eventually hundreds of propaganda pamphlets, booklets, and newspapers that I read about Socialism, not to speak of hundreds of serious books and some very scholarly ones. Bertrand Russell, R. H. Tawney, H. G. Wells, George Bernard Shaw, Sir Sydney Olivier, H. N. Brailsford, Sidney Webb, Philip Snowden, Ramsay MacDonald, Leo Tolstoy, John Spargo, Prince Peter Kropotkin, Robert Blatchford, Norman Thomas, Upton Sinclair, William Morris, Edward Bellamy, to mention the barest minimum number, would scarcely be dismissed as mere pamphleteers. I spent unnumbered hours in the library of the Rand School of Social Science in New York dipping into what must have been one of the world's great collections of Socialist literature. I even wrote some of my thoughts on the subject in the Sunday magazine section of New York's Socialist daily when I worked on it. All of that came later; and in my Bishop Feild days, I was admittedly the most simplistic of simplistic Socialists. Certainly my Socialism, such as it was and is now, has coloured my thinking and conduct ever since.

While I was at Bishop Feild, I had my first contact with the highest of

*In the General Election of 1913.

high society in our country, His Excellency the Governor, Sir Ralph Williams. It was at the CLB summer camp near the beach at Topsail, twelve miles from St. John's. I had by psychological warfare persuaded Adolph E. Bernard, the captain of our school's "C" Company of the CLB,* to let me become a recruit while I was still below the strictly enforced age limit of fourteen. As the company drilled in the playground, no one could very well stop me from standing fifty feet away with my wooden dummy rifle and going through the drill in unison with the company. I became, of course, a very noticeable small figure every drill day, waging my cold war, and finally, in desperation, Captain Bernard had to let me join. Nothing would stop me from going to the summer camp at Topsail, and with my dummy rifle, I marched the whole twelve-mile distance from St. John's with the others. Vainly they urged me to climb onto one of the trucks hauling the Brigade's equipment to the campgrounds. On the day before camp broke a fortnight later, we had the usual visit from the Governor.† Because I was the youngest and possibly the smallest boy in the CLB anywhere in 1914 (my picture and a few words about me appeared in the CLB magazine in England), the officials thought it good fun to appoint me honorary aide-de-camp to His Excellency for the duration of the visit, so I walked about the camp all day, always keeping ten paces behind the Governor and standing stiffly at attention whenever he stopped.

Another event of that summer was my "trial" at the camp's annual "court-martial". All the officers of the camp sat behind a long table, and I stood at attention facing them, with guards on either side of me. I was found guilty of having overslept one morning in my tent and was sentenced to march at military pace from the camp field to the beach, stand at attention, stoop and pick up a beach stone, about turn smartly, and march back to the field and deposit the stone before the company commander's tent. Then I was to about turn and march again to the beach, ninety-nine times more, until I had 100 stones deposited. Eric Jerrett, one of Feild's best athletes, was the

*We called him Polly Bernard. He was born in France and was one of our best teachers. When the First World War broke out, he was one of the first to volunteer in Newfoundland, and eventually he became Colonel of the Royal Newfoundland Regiment in France. I had one or two letters from him while he was there.

†Someone spread the story, after he had retired from the Governorship of Newfoundland, that he had declared as he sailed out the Narrows, "Goodbye, Newfoundlanders—you're dirtier than the Boers!"

1. David and Julia Smallwood and their family—about 1885

2. David Smallwood – about 1910

3. A distant relative – Benjamin Franklin Smallwood, Chief of the Choctaw Nation, Oklahoma

4. The boarders at Bishop Feild College about 1913. J.R.S. is second from left in the front row

corporal who saw to it that the sentence was properly carried out. He must have been near-sighted, for at least fifty or sixty of the stones were actually carried up from the beach by other boys.

After breaking camp, we marched back to St. John's on a Saturday and passed the Catholic Cadet Corps encampment on the other side of the road. Colonel Charles O'Neill Conroy took the salute as we marched past; then our Commanding Officer ordered a halt, and I marched up to Colonel Conroy, as I had been instructed to do, and presented him with a big clay tobacco pipe dressed in CLB ribbons. When we got to Kitty Gaul's well at the side of Topsail Road, a couple of miles outside the city, we were halted again for a short rest, a drink of water, and a chance to comb our hair, straighten our uniforms, and brush the dust off our boots before completing the march to the CLB Armoury on Harvey Road. The CLB brass band came to meet us and led the way for the remainder of the march. I was instructed to march ahead of the band and was given an officer's swagger cane which I was to carry as though it were a rifle at shoulder arms. Saturday was a half-holiday in those days, and it seemed as though the whole population of St. John's lined LeMarchant Road as we marched smartly behind the band. It was the second time that I had attracted public attention.

In 1912 or 1913, I became a Boy Scout. There was then no patrol, or troop, or other form of Scout organization in Newfoundland; indeed, I was the only Scout in the country—a Lone Scout. To arrange this, I had to write directly to Baden-Powell in England. I wasn't able to buy my Scout clothing, but I did manage to get enough money to send to Gamage's in London for my hat. The brim tended to droop, but I learned how to stiffen it by ironing.

And I became an Esperanto enthusiast! I sent to England for the literature, and then the textbook, and worked away by myself at mastering the rules and some of the vocabulary. Even on my own, I made some headway on the artificial language, but eventually it died on the vine.

I was never a great athlete like my grandfather, but I was very good at trapeze and ring work in the gymnasium, at boxing, and above all at long-distance running. I always ran in the division above me and was therefore outclassed in age and experience, but I was always among the first to complete the course. A sensational thing happened in the ten-mile race one year. Just as we were lining up for the pistol shot that would start the race, one of the boarders, a lanky outport fellow from St. Anthony whose name I think was Strangemore, sauntered over and asked if he could get into the race. He hadn't practised, and he had no running shorts or shoes; but when they told him that there really was nothing to stop him, he hauled off his coat and vest, took off his collar and tie, tied his braces about his waist, and with his thick ankle-length underwear, ordinary pants, and ordinary boots, he crouched with the rest of us and started the run. He came in first, by a good margin, and I have always thought that he had the makings of another Tom Longboat.

The outstanding teachers at Bishop Feild College then were Ralph R. Wood, the headmaster; George H. House and Israel Samson, Newfoundlanders; and Adolph E. Bernard and Arthur Raley, a Frenchman and an Englishman. Ralph Wood was a son of the Rev. Canon Wood. He and his family lived in the hostel itself when I first went there; but soon afterward, he got a house on Cochrane Street, and we younger boarders welcomed the invitations we received, one at a time, to have Sunday morning breakfast with the Wood family.

Mr. Samson was known behind his back as Ikey, and with George House he was the manual training instructor. He was the only teacher in the school who administered corporal punishment—in all other cases, that was left to the headmaster: we would be sent to report to him and would tell him how many strokes he was to give us on each hand with his familiar wooden jam spoon. Ikey Samson would bend a boy over a desk, carefully adjust the seat of the boy's pants, and whack him (but not too hard) with a piece of thin board, saying, "First on one cheek, next on the other." The manual training department and the gymnasium were housed in a small wooden building beside the college. The caretaker, a kind man named Jacobs, used to clean up the manual training department after each use. There was always a pile of wood shavings, and Jacobs would stuff these into a large burlap sack and leave it in the entrance room that separated the two departments. I mention this detail because this sack played a small but memorable role on the last day I spent at the college.

Bishop Feild College was famous in Newfoundland for athletics, and I have often felt that Ralph Wood considered athletics to be more important than academic achievements. We had a great ice hockey team and perhaps some of the greatest hockey players ever known in any part of North America (except, of course, for modern times): Bert Tait, Jack Higgins, Reg Parnell, Tommy Winter, Duke Winter. Jack Higgins, when he was at Oxford University, was captain of the famous Oxford team that toured Europe to introduce the game. Later, he became an outstanding lawyer in St. John's, a prominent opponent of mine when I launched the Confederate movement,* leader of the Opposition in the House when I became Premier, and a beloved member of the Senate of Canada.

Sport was a branch of religion in Newfoundland. Each major religious denomination had its own teams in hockey, football, rowing, track events, and all other athletic activities. These teams opposed the corresponding teams of the other denominations, and the Church of England boys and girls would flock to the games to cheer for the Church of England players. The Roman Catholics and Methodists were just as ardent. To this day, it is very much the same. In a football game at St. George's Field, when Bishop Feild College played St. Bonaventure's, I happened to be standing near a group of young Christian Brothers, and they were even more excited by the play on the field than were the college boys. Most of St. Bon's team were big fellows, much bigger than most of the BFC players, and our boys had a tendency to turn away when a St. Bon's player charged toward them. One exasperated Brother yelled in disgust to his team, "There's only one thing to do if he turns his ass toward you – kick it!"

In the winter, we would go to the swimming pool in the Seamen's Institute. The Institute was a large brick building erected through the efforts of the great Dr. Wilfred Grenfell. A year or two before, with all of the students of the college, I witnessed the miracle of the laying of its cornerstone by King Edward VII by electricity from Buckingham Palace. The electricity came over the trans-Atlantic cable, and it was connected with a mechanism attached to the stone; when the King touched a button in London, the stone in St. John's slowly moved into place, while we cheered ourselves hoarse. The pool itself was a bit of a horror. The water was not filtered, and it was so murky that a boy would become invisible two feet below the surface.

In the summer, fifteen or twenty of us would get up an expedition and hike all the way to the brook that emptied out of Long Pond. Between high, sloping, tree-clad banks, the brook widened and

*A passionately patriotic Newfoundlander, he was desolated by the victory of Confederation. He draped his front door in crepe and wore black on his sleeve, in mourning for our "dead" freedom.

deepened to form two pools: Silver Pool and Sliding Rock. We had no bathing suits, but in the sheltered pools, that didn't matter. In the deliciously cool water we would be wonderfully refreshed after our long walk, but we would be just as hot and sticky again before we were half-way home.

In 1959, when we built Confederation Building to celebrate the tenth anniversary of Newfoundland's union with Canada (and to furnish ourselves with better offices), the Premier's suite occupied the eighth floor, one floor below the House of Assembly. My own office was at the front of the building and from it I had a marvellous view of St. John's. People from the mainland of Canada who came to see me were always thrilled when I led them to the windows. No Premier in Canada occupies offices with such a glorious view, and one of my most prized possessions is a painting of that very scene done by the Newfoundland artist Harold G. Goodridge.* But not the least interesting aspect of that wonderful view for me were Silver Pool and Sliding Rock, just a few hundred feet away, between the city and Confederation Building. Such has been the growth of St. John's. Indeed, our College Company of the CLB used to have skirmishes and sham battles, using blank cartridges in our rifles, over the very ground that now lies in front of Confederation Building!

Bishop Feild College is no longer where it was then, and the House of Assembly also has moved, but when I was at the college, the two buildings were not more than 2,000 feet apart, and I often sneaked into the visitors' gallery to listen to the speeches. It was then for the first time that I saw the leader of the Opposition, Sir Robert Bond; and William F. Coaker, W. F. Lloyd, and James Mary Kent, whom I was to meet afterward when I worked for the *Daily News*. These were on the Opposition side of the House, and across the way was the great Sir Edward Morris, the Prime Minister. Little did I think, as I listened to Morris in 1912, that I myself would be the fourth after him to be elected as the first minister of the Government of Newfoundland.

I have said nothing about my scholastic career at Bishop Feild, and

*At my request, he painted the mural in the large lobby of Confederation Building. It is a panorama of Newfoundland's development from the earliest times. He looked dubious when I suggested that he paint the faces of living men onto the figures of historic characters, but then he entered into the fun of it and today you see the faces of Mackenzie King, Louis St. Laurent, J. W. Pickersgill, RCMP Chief Commissioner Nicholson, Sir Leonard Outerbridge, and J. R. S.

that has been deliberate. It was not scholarship so much as other things that I got from my college: a love of reading,* access to a wide range of reading material, development of my self-confidence, a sense of belonging to something more than just St. John's, acquaintance with the disciplined and dignified orderliness of the Church of England, intensification of my hatred of cruelty and injustice, and in my general outlook on life, a feeling of easy equality with the best of them. In some subjects, I was exceptionally good; in others, exceptionally bad. I was extremely good in Latin and French, particularly French. But I did most of my arithmetic on my fingers. When Ikey Samson took us for an hour in algebra, he would say, "Get out your books at Lesson 10–Joey you can get out your novel and read it." He had simply abandoned any hope of teaching me algebra. Geometry was another story: here I excelled, and there was no one who could compare with me. George House took us for this class. He was the only teacher in Feild who brought the entire class up in a curved line in front of his desk, and invariably I was at the head of the line, the first to demonstrate the theorem. George House would demonstrate the theorem rapidly on the blackboard to refresh our memories. He had given it to us for homework, and I had never even as much as opened the book. All I needed was his rapid demonstration on the blackboard.

I was exceptionally good in English; I loved the feeling of words and was recognized generally in class for that quality. I would get into discussions with chums as we walked along the street, and to settle a point I would insist on our going to a telephone if we could find one, for there were not very many in St. John's then, and calling Mr. Wood to confirm my contention.

I nearly always came well down toward the bottom of my class, but more than once I had the highest marks for the week or the fortnight. When I didn't, Ray Clapp did. He was even smaller than I, and he had a sharp brain and tongue. It was quite normal for him to have top marks in our class, year after year. Sometimes, one of the masters would tell me to stay behind after class and would give me a talking to, asserting that I could get top marks whenever I wanted to. He would make me promise to come first for the next week, and I never failed to do so. This happened dozens of times–whenever I

*This was the main benefit of all my schooling in Newfoundland. By the time I was twenty, I had read about 1,500 books, over 12,000 when I was fifty, and probably close to 20,000 today. For years, I averaged a book a day.

really wanted to do it. I think that my failing was that I was satisfied once I knew that I could beat the others, but I wasn't interested enough to do it all the time.

Ray Clapp's father was a lawyer and Liberal Member of the House of Assembly for the district of St. Barbe, a huge area which now is divided into four constituencies. Ray went to live in England where he practised law, and there he changed his name to Mainwaring—pronounced, in good English style, Mannering. Ray came back once to Newfoundland when I was Premier, and we had fun reminding each other of escapades at Bishop Feild.

Andrew Lehr turned out to have a tragic life. After he left Bishop Feild, he went to Boston and got a job with Aetna Insurance Company. He and I boarded together for a while in Boston, and when I returned to St. John's, he insisted on coming with me. I didn't know it, but his father was furious with him for coming. Dr. Lehr used to pay him something every month to stay away from Newfoundland, and afterward I guessed the reason: he knew what was likely to happen to Andrew, and he didn't want it to happen in Newfoundland. Andrew boarded in a house on Brazil Street, and it was there that disaster overtook him. He went insane and was taken to the mental hospital. I was allowed to visit him once or twice. After some months, he became an outpatient of the hospital, and then he was allowed to leave the institution altogether. But a doctor who knew his case told me that there was no hope for Andrew, that he would spend the remainder of his life in a mental hospital. He did, but it was not a long life; he died in his mid-twenties.

One other chum, Mac Piccott, also came to a tragic end. Mac was the son of Archibald W. Piccott, then the Minister of Marine and Fisheries in the administration of Sir Edward Morris. The Minister was a giant of a man, but he had only one hand, having lost the other in an accident. Mac and I became close friends, and often after school he and I would go to his father's home on Howley Avenue, where we would steal his cigars and smoke them. One day we were both smoking as we strolled back to the college. When it got too close to the college to be safe, I threw away my half-smoked cigar and remarked, "That's the last time I'll ever smoke." And I kept my word for ten years. After that, I continued to smoke cigars for almost another ten years and then sank into the vice of cigarette smoking. Mac was determined to be a seaman and would think of nothing else. He went to sea before the mast, became an A.B., and I think might have risen to be a bosun. Then foul times fell upon sailoring. Mac couldn't get a ship; he became destitute in St. John's (his father had died leaving no money) and ended up living in a cheap boarding house on Lime Street. He was found dead one morning on the sidewalk near the house.

Billie Anderson, son of Dr. Arthur Anderson of Heart's Content, had a fine career. He was ordained a Minister of the Church of England, and he served the parish of Greenspond and later a parish in a small settlement on the southwest coast throughout the desperate period of the depression and the dole in Newfoundland. He was looked upon as a very saintly man indeed, and his name is remembered with gratitude in both parishes. Billie later went to Nova Scotia, and I think it might have been there that he died.

Ches Mercer went to live in New York and had a good job with Guaranty Trust Company. His brother, Roy C. B. Mercer, became a very prominent legal light in St. John's. Gebbie White was a son of the Church of England Bishop of Newfoundland, and he too went into the church and became a prominent and successful ecclesiastic, spending most of his time in the United States. Jack Chaplin, the son of the famous "King of Tailors", Mark Chaplin, was, I believe, the first casualty of the Royal Newfoundland Regiment in the First World War. If Jack Chaplin wasn't the first, another chum of mine, Billie Christian, certainly was. Billie wasn't old enough to enlist; but he was a big boy, and he succeeded in persuading the military authorities that he had reached the required age. He was dead long before he was eighteen. Jim Barr was one of our Feildian graduates to go through the war, and he finally got his commission. Con and Gerry Stein were the sons of a great railroad engineer, von Stein, who had been brought to Newfoundland by the Reids when they were building the railway. Jimmy Constable, from Grand Falls, was related to the great Scottish publishing family of Constable, and Jimmy received a letter from them once inviting him to come to Scotland and join the family. Another boy, Harry Burgess, came from Burin, and I believe his mother was a well-to-do widow. I still remember the twinge of envy I felt for the nice things she gave him. Clare Netten, a son of Canon Netten, was a very close chum. He died of pulmonary tuberculosis.

The friendship that I struck up with Albert Perlin has continued uninterrupted to this day. He succeeded me on the *Evening Telegram*, started his own excellent weekly, became chief editorial writer for the *Daily News*, and wrote and published fine short histories of Newfoundland—all as spare-time work stolen from his business. I consider him to be the finest regular writer for newspapers in Canada today. Dickie Field was a son of Canon Field. Ralph Tessier was on that first rugby football team with me, and as he was a big, powerfully built fellow, it was upon him that we practised tackling.

I was still at Bishop Feild when the war broke out, and it was a great thrill for us to go down by Quidi Vidi Lake and peer through the fence at the encampment of the Newfoundland Regiment in Pleasantville. When the First Five Hundred, as they were so proudly called,* marched from Pleasantville through the streets to the troopship at the water-front, I trotted along beside Polly Bernard carrying his officer's bag. I resented bitterly the fact that, going on fourteen, I was too young to go with my chums to war. How lucky I was.

Matthew Aupolok and I were chums. He was an Eskimo boy who was brought to the college by the Church of England missionary Mr. Stewart. The hope was that Matthew would one day be a missionary himself, but he died young, of tuberculosis. He had one of those short-handled, long-lash whips—the leather lash must have been fifteen or twenty feet long. He used it like an expert and tried to teach me to wield it. Matthew was gentle, calm, and intelligent, with a smile always in his eyes. His Eskimo greeting was a word that all of us took up—"auction-i", it sounded like, with a broad *i* as in idea (as *Time* would say).

I did not come out of my college a scholar or an academic success. I did come out with a determination to become a writer some day. Just before World War I, some organization in England sponsored an essay-writing contest for students throughout the Empire. Two of the three topics on which a student could choose to write were "Newfoundland's (or Canada's, or Australia's) Duty to the Empire" and "The Life of Lord Roberts". I chose the man from whom I got my middle name and read his autobiography *Forty-One Years in India*. I came second in my age class in the whole of the British Empire.

The cause of my leaving Bishop Feild in 1915 was a quarrel that I had with the house-master of the week. I don't remember what it was about, but I do remember that I fiercely resisted an injustice, real or

*Blue Puttees they were called, too, those "first" 500 and all the others, from the fact that, in the absence of khaki, they wore blue-coloured puttees. Soldiers without puttees were unthinkable in 1914.

fancied, done me. I ran out of the college and didn't go back. That night I slept in the vestibule separating the gym from the manual training room, and my bed was the sack of wood shavings that I mentioned earlier. Next morning, Mr. Wood suggested that I should go and see my uncle Fred; but when I went to his house on Gower Street, he was away somewhere, and I saw his wife, my aunt Bert. She was sitting up in bed, and she must have heard something from Mr. Wood, for she was very short and brisk in her pronouncement that the best thing for me would be to leave college and get a job. I have always felt that she disapproved of her husband's putting me through school, but perhaps I do her memory an injustice. After Uncle Fred's death, she lived mostly in Europe, a rich widow moving from Berlin to Paris to London and back again, for years. The last time I saw her was at the Cumberland Hotel in London, where she had a suite. She was pleasant enough to me then. I do not remember whether I left Bishop Feild that day or a little later. Perhaps my last bed at the hostel was not after all the sack of wood shavings.

While I was at Bishop Feild College, my mother became religious; and as so often happens, she went from one extreme to the other. Until she was nearly forty, she was quite indifferent to religion; but afterward it filled her life and, I am quite sure, brought her a kind of peace and happiness that she had never known. She was "converted" in the Bethesda mission of the Pentecostal faith on New Gower Street. Alice B. Garrigus, an American of quite remarkable personality, had opened the mission not long before. Crowds were attending her services, and my mother was one of many who, in the language of evangelicals, became "convicted of sin". She prayed urgently for forgiveness and was filled by an almost unassailable certainty of mercy and grace. She was in one of several groups who were baptised by immersion in Mundy Pond, near the City. The Pond was not then the polluted offence that it is today. Miss Garrigus, whom I got to know well, for I often visited the mission and her home upstairs, was an extraordinarily able and a saintly woman. She had an assistant, a Mrs. Boone, also an American. I still remember some of the more prominent members of the congregation: Herbert Eddy, C. L. March (who had a mattress factory at the foot of Springdale Street), the Leshanas, Miss Moulton, W. R. English, and Gordon Ryan. From that small acorn on New Gower Street, Pentecostalism in Newfoundland has grown into a sturdy oak.

In that profoundly formative time from ten to fifteen years of age,

I grew up in and was part of two different worlds that knew little of each other: the poor and the affluent—or if not absolutely affluent, at least comfortable. In one, I dressed well, had baths, ate regularly, went to church, engaged in sports, paraded in CLB uniform to church on special occasions, and took for granted all kinds of comforts and conveniences that the other world scarcely knew existed. In the other, I used an outdoor toilet; I had no bath-tub; my clothes were patched and passed down to the younger children; I was never certain of having a full meal; and I lived with the constant unease caused by my father's excessive drinking. By 1915, I knew both worlds well, because I was of both. I had known precious little of the first world until I went to Bishop Feild; and on many Sundays and in the school holidays, I continued my close participation in the other, then and after I left school.

6

Wage Slave and All That

That ephemeral sheet of paper, the newspaper, is the natural enemy of the book, as the whore is of the decent woman.
Edmond and Jules de Goncourt

Were it left to me to decide whether we should have a government without newspapers, or newspapers without a government, I should not hesitate to prefer the latter.
Thomas Jefferson

Don't laugh at a youth for his affectations; he is only trying on one face after another, to find a face of his own.
Logan Pearsall Smith

And so in my fifteenth year, I got my first regular paid job. It was with the weekly *Plaindealer* newspaper, owned by William J. O'Neill. The *Plaindealer* had been for years a well-known hard-hitting paper that was owned and published by Wiseman and Buckley. They were two printers who stumbled onto a big thing, but their streak of luck ran out and the paper fell on evil times. Just before it went broke, Bill O'Neill bought it and moved the few cases of type and the medieval press that constituted the "plant" to a rented building at the corner of Water Street and Springdale Street.*

When I joined the *Plaindealer* as a printer's apprentice, the staff of the paper swelled to four. The others were its owner and editor, Bill O'Neill; Tim Buckley, one of the former owners; and Johnny Gourley. Buckley and Gourley were excellent exponents of the old printing trade: well read, sensible, humorous, tolerant. Working with them was one of the real breaks of my life, for they adopted me and set out to teach me every secret of the printing trade as it was then. Every word and letter of the newspaper was set into type by hand, and the work of a printer's devil consisted mostly of sweeping the floor, washing the inky type with lye after it came off the press, running messages for the printers, and doing anything else that he was told to do. Tim Buckley and Johnny Gourley taught me more of the printing trade in the months I was there than an apprentice would

*The building was owned by the Newman firm of England's West Country, which had been doing business in Newfoundland for the best part of 300 years and is still doing so. After the *Plaindealer* days, it was rented by the Newfoundland Government as a liquor store, and now, with perhaps peculiar appropriateness, it is the home of the Press Club. Its basement, built of hand-hewn stone, extends westward along Water Street well beyond the building itself; and for perhaps over 200 years, in these cool stone vaults Newman's famous "Newfoundland" port wine has been stored for maturing. The practice through the eighteenth and nineteenth centuries was to bring the wine from Oporto in large oaken "pipes" in the holds of sailing vessels, store it for the appropriate number of years in these vaults, and then ship it back across the Atlantic in the same pipes to England for bottling for England's gentry. This process, which is followed to this day, is said to give the port a special "something" in its flavour or bouquet.

DIFFICULTY RATING: ★★★★★

12 9 B

Answer to previous puzzle

8	9	4	6	1	5	2	3	7
3	7	5	4	9	2	1	6	8
2	1	6	8	7	3	9	4	5
5	3	9	1	4	7	8	2	6
4	8	2	5	6	9	3	7	1
1	6	7	2	3	8	5	9	4
7	4	3	9	8	1	6	5	2
6	5	1	3	2	4	7	8	9
9	2	8	7	5	6	4	1	3

12/8

East
Pass
Pass

two
her four
hand
ny people
a forcing
shape
er route
nd let
e he

revious NYT crossword

ME ARTICLE
IN TOENAIL
AT AMASSED
TERNER SIE
ABIE MIDS
BANKVAULT
EADHORSE
ALL
EHANGOUTS
NER AWGEE
CATT ELSE
DDIN YTD
ETONCAP
CATERTU
ONEEYED

w
th
to
acc

TAU
Mak
you
in a c
comm
love. H
relatio
sary if y
forwar
★★★★

GEMINI
You'll be
mation th
a wild goo
facts, do y
refuse to l
lure you i
is not ben
your frien

CANCER (J
Work will
domestic
versa. Keep
and do not
Emotional
is apparent
stopped bef
into a corner

LEO (July 23-
let what othe
confusion or
an emotional
leaves you at
right for your
dren, your fr
romantic pa
against pers

o
d
ng
of
ds.

ring
015,"
ucer,
to be

at the
is be-
mains

stmas
er this
d three
5 tour-
distrib-
nyl Cafe

nd that's
d," Mil-
an's last
roved an
happen-

duced the
s stories
tradition
lled The
es Dave's

...es an honoured place in Christ... the Vinyl Cafe, the new story col...on published by Viking Penguin. And ...hares the volume with the classic Dave ...oks the Turkey, the first and most fa...ous of McLean's Christmas stories.

"I've been in publishing for more than a quarter of a century, and I have to say that it's almost impossible ever to distil what captures a reader's or listener's imagination," says Meg Masters, McLean's longtime editor. She's trying to explain the mythic place the hilarious turkey yarn holds among Vinyl Cafe listeners.

"Publishers are always trying to figure out what's going to be a hit — and you can't. But we can look at that story retroactively and point out the verbal and visual humour and madcap pacing. What is certain is that it became a hit the very first time Stuart read it. It snowballed into a favourite Christmas tradition."

The CBC quickly became aware of the impact on listeners of the turkey saga.

"It was a turning point," Milton says. "It turned Christmas into a big deal for us at the Vinyl Cafe. Once Dave cooked the turkey, we realized we would have to do something Christmasy every year."

A few months before McLean's death, he asked Masters and Milton about the possibility of a new book.

"We were both very excited by that," Masters says now. "We knew that Stuart loved to share his stories. He wanted the little world we had created, the world of Vinyl Cafe, to continue after it was off the air and after we were all gone. So we had that in mind after he passed. We had the last story he ever wrote and performed on stage — The Christmas Card — so we really wanted to get that out. There are also five other never-before-published stories in the new book. But the turkey is the essential."

deeply."

Finally she s... through.

"It made me feel ... It made me feel rea... all been so lucky with ... ing something we love... him perform that very... an incredible reminde... he loved standing on st... a story."

Meanwhile, as Christm... his still-grieving colleag... with affection the joy o... him.

"Stuart wasn't posses... writing," says Masters, w... McLean's book editor b... Cafe began on CBC.

"That was the interest... him. There was no way ... him into a direction he... go or put words into his... didn't like. But he was ve... and not just with me and... feedback from everybo...

Milton has lost count... times McLean would ap... after a show and quiz au... about how well he had...

"The first question h... was — what was your f... show and what part ... why. The audience b... editor because we le... it over the years."

Masters and Milt... McLean's presence... book.

"Working on t... says. "That's beca... There was this g... ing on it as well ... in his world."

normally learn in as many years. They advised me to read the monthly *Inland Printer*, the printers' bible, and suggested earnestly that I should try to take a correspondence course in lettering. As my pay was $1.50 a week, there wasn't much chance of my taking correspondence courses. I paid $1 to my mother toward my board, and the fifty cents I was able to keep for pocket money.

Then Bill O'Neill, who seemed to me while I worked for him to spend most of his time dodging bill collectors, surprised his three employees by ordering a linotype machine that would replace the hand-setting of type. A man called Shaw came down for the linotype company in Toronto to install the machine and to teach Tim Buckley how to operate it. Although the purchase of this machine undoubtedly was a great improvement for the *Plaindealer*, it meant that I had to get a new job somewhere else.

Wiseman, the other of the original publishers of the *Plaindealer*, had remained in the building where that paper had originally been published on Theatre Hill, and with a small printing plant he was now publishing a new weekly paper of his own called the *Spectator*. He had no staff at all—he set up the type himself and personally ran off a small number of copies on the tiny press. I got a job with him as printer's devil with an increase in pay to $2 a week, so clearly I was climbing in the world. But his publishing venture collapsed soon after, and I had to find my third job in less than twelve months. This one was to last for two years, and it was at the printing office of Robinson & Company, publishers of the *Daily News*, a morning newspaper.

It was not my first connection with the *Daily News*. A few years earlier, its new poured-concrete building on Duckworth Street had been erected by the building contractor William J. Ellis. Even the best contractors in St. John's still used primitive construction techniques, and Mr. Ellis obtained the crushed stone he needed for his concrete from people who crushed it by hand. He was paying twenty cents a barrel, or about $4 a ton, for the crushed stone delivered at the building site. My father obtained an order for a few tons, and I helped to provide the stone by breaking it up with a hammer. The building still stands on Duckworth Street, or at least part of it does, a monument to my very earliest efforts as a worker. It was a secret that I kept from the other staff while I was employed by the *Daily News*. Later, I was not ashamed to admit the fact.

At first, I had nothing to do with the newspaper, as my work was in the job-printing department. The foreman was Eliakim Hutchings, and he was more than kind to me. He constantly moved me from one part of the printing establishment to another, so that I could get a variety of experience in the trade. I nearly knocked myself out in one department. The company had the business of printing all letterheads for the Government, and the lettering had to be embossed or raised. This was done in the old way: a steel die was used to form a paper matrix; the steel die was inked, one sheet of paper was placed between it and the matrix, and then the two huge iron balls were turned on an arm at the top. One day, one of these balls hit me in the head and almost put an end to my career. I remember how we marvelled to see the first modern machine for embossing letterheads, in George Morgan's printing plant—it was a simple resin and heat process that made it possible to emboss letterheads almost as rapidly as they could be printed.

I spent the first year in the printing department, and then to my delight I got a job with the newspaper itself, in the mailing department. There was a small, brass, hand-operated mailer that cut off the printed name and address of the subscriber as a label from a long list and stuck it on each newspaper. My job was to operate the mailer, put the addressed newspapers in canvas mailbags lent by the General Post Office, pile the bags onto a hand-cart, and push the cart to the post office. There they would weigh the bags and give me a slip to carry back to the printing office. I think the company paid by weight at the end of each month. I worked at this and in the composing room for about six months, and then was moved to the front office as general helper to Ches Stevenson, the head bookkeeper. I don't know why he was called the *head* bookkeeper, for he was the only one. The rest of the office staff consisted of a stenographer, Mabel Porter, and me. My principal work was bill collecting.

St. John's was divided into eight or ten delivery routes, and as many boys carried the newspaper early each morning to the homes of the subscribers. There was considerable turnover among the carriers; a boy might be on a route for six months and then quit. After years of this sort of thing, the point had been reached where no one but the boys knew where the papers were delivered or the names of the persons who got them each morning. It was thus impossible to send bills to them, and my first job was to go over all the rounds, one each morning, and get the names and addresses where the papers were delivered. It was then, incidentally, that I became a newsboy, for the only time in my life. The paper carriers had quite a weight to carry, and I helped them with their load. As I went along with a few dozen papers under my arm one morning, I was hailed by a citizen who wanted to buy a copy. Startled a little, I hesitated only a moment before selling him a paper. From then on, for the next week or two, each morning I gladly welcomed any passerby who wanted to buy a paper, and even edged close to anyone going along the street, looking as expectant as I could. I can thus claim to have been a newsboy for the best part of a fortnight.

But the big thing was that I had got the first list of names and addresses of subscribers in St. John's that the paper had possessed in years. Then came the business of making out the bills, and after this, the more serious business of collecting the money. What adventures I had at that! For instance, there was the belted knight who hadn't lived with his wife for many years. He was a merchant prince, and having a bill for his wife running back for six or eight years, what more natural for me than to take it to him for collection? At the front office of his big firm, when I said I was from the *Daily News* and wished to see the president, I was directed immediately to his office. Tapping on the door, I heard an invitation from within to enter, so I did so and smartly presented the bill to His Lordship. Without a word, he looked at it; without a word, he turned stiffly to me in his swivel chair; and without a word, he handed the bill back to me. Thoroughly abashed, I took it and crept out. Back at the *Daily News* office, there were roars of laughter from the knowing Ches Stevenson when I told him what had happened.

When I had a long overdue bill for the paper delivered each day to a well-known judge of the Supreme Court, what could be more natural than to go to the Supreme Court building on Duckworth Street to collect? There were three Supreme Court judges in those times:* Chief Justice Sir William Horwood, Judge James Mary Kent, and Judge George M. Johnson. They occupied adjoining offices near the court rooms, and I picked one of them, that of Judge Johnson, and tapped on the door. Inside, I asked Judge Johnson where I might find Judge Emerson. I added that I had a bill to collect from him for the *Daily News*. "A bill?" he enquired mildly. "Yes, sir," I explained, "it's for delivering the paper to his house every morning for the past

*It was left to me many years afterward to get legislation passed to create a fourth judgeship for the same Court.

eight years." "Ah, yes," he nodded. He thought a moment and said, "Come with me." I followed him as he tapped on the door of Judge Kent and invited him (no doubt with a wink) to accompany us to the office of the Chief, Sir William Horwood. So the three of us entered the office of the Chief Justice. "This young man is from the *Daily News*," Judge Johnson explained, "and he has a bill to collect from Judge Emerson and he wants to know where he can find him." The three judges looked at each other soberly, and the Chief remarked with mock thoughtfulness, "It will be at one of two places—heaven or hell." "There is a third," remarked Judge Kent; and the Chief agreed, "Ah, yes, purgatory." By now, it had dawned on me that Judge Emerson must be dead and that the three learned judges were having their courtly fun with the young bill collector.

Two years I spent with the *Daily News*, and some of the friends I made during that time continued to be my friends throughout my life. Most of them, alas, are gone: the great John Alexander Robinson, editor of the paper, sometime Postmaster General and Conservative Cabinet Minister; John S. Currie, sometime Member of the House of Assembly, who during Robinson's career was the company's business manager and on Robinson's retirement became the paper's editor; and John Charles Puddester, who deserves a book unto himself. He came to the *Daily News* from the Reid Newfoundland (railway) Company about 1917. He was defeated several times in his attempt to get elected to the House of Assembly, finally made it, and made the Conservative Cabinet as well. He became one of the original members of the Commission of Government and its Deputy Chairman, and enjoyed the unique experience of being the first person in history to receive a knighthood from the monarch in person on New World soil. I witnessed the ceremony: it took place in the lovely garden of Government House in St. John's, and the knighthood was bestowed by King George VI. John Puddester's son Clayton was one of my early chums. And there was Andrew Wilson, who was learning his trade. His father was a foreign-going master mariner who took sailing vessels to "the Brazils", to the West Indies, and across the Atlantic to the Mediterranean countries with cargoes of salt-dried codfish. Andrew was always telling me that he didn't intend to continue at the printing trade—his ambition was to become a seaman like his father. And he did, briefly. He signed on with his father to go before the mast on the *Beverley*, of great local fame, and she went down with all hands on Andrew's first voyage. Another chum was Harvey Pike. And there was the pressman, Mose Pike, and his assistant, Tom Kearsey. They were two of the thirstiest pressmen I ever knew—or so I thought as I went countless times to bring back large containers of draught beer for them. George Holwell—kindly, humorous, understanding—also was my friend. And there was Johnny Fifield, a job-printing compositor. He was cadaverous, tall, and stooped, and one of the best of the old school of the printing trade. I worked for a while at the type-case next to his, and I remember vividly one day when he spent the whole morning and afternoon setting up by hand a large page of statistical tables in tiny 6-point type, the most odiously tormenting, nerve-wracking job in the whole trade. Toward the close of the work-day, his nerves snapped, and he took up his day's tedious work and hurled it to the floor, scattering the small type in all directions.

The *Daily News* was a Conservative newspaper, and though I worked on it, I was quite out of sympathy with its politics. It was at this time that I began writing pieces for the *Fishermen's Advocate*, the official daily newspaper of the great William F. Coaker's Fishermen's Protective Union. As a Socialist, I was an ardent supporter of Coaker, the FPU, and its official organ. I used to sign the pieces "Avalond", and I got a lot of secret satisfaction from seeing my pieces in print and sometimes from hearing people near me commenting on something that they didn't know I had written. But one day, there was a near disaster! I had one completed piece in my pocket in an unsealed envelope that I intended to carry down to the *Advocate* office. It fell out of my pocket, one of the printers in the *Daily News* office picked it up, and the secret was out. I don't know to this day whether the word reached the front office or whether the printers protected me. I suspect the latter, for I never heard a word of it afterward. Toward the end of my time with the *News*, I was getting $6 a week, having started at $3.

For most of the time I worked on the paper, I lived with my grandfather on Springdale Street, to be nearer the job, but I met my father every weekday so that we could have lunch together. Neither of us could afford to go to a high-class or even a middle-class restaurant; indeed, there really was only one good restaurant in St. John's, the Sterling. So we went to the Salvation Army soup kitchen on George Street, just a few blocks away from the newspaper building. It was called a soup kitchen, but in fact, besides the fine rich soup, you could get other plain, wholesome food and a cup of tea for only ten or fifteen or eighteen cents a meal. I have had a kindly feeling for the Salvation Army ever since, a respect and affection steadily strengthened by many subsequent contacts with them on somewhat higher levels.

One day, a thrilling piece appeared in the big Newfoundland newspaper, the *Evening Telegram*—a small want ad inviting applications for a job as a reporter on the paper. St. John's had many newspapers around that time. Besides the *Telegram*, there were the *Daily Star*, the *Evening Herald*, and the *Evening Advocate* in the evening; and the *Daily News*, the *Morning Post*, and the *Morning Advocate* as morning papers. The two large papers were the *Telegram* and the *Daily Star*. The *Telegram*, from its foundation in 1879 until the beginning of the 1920s, was not only Liberal, but *the* Liberal paper of Newfoundland, the "Thunderer", the unswerving champion of Sir Robert Bond, the Liberal chieftain. And now here they were, actually advertising for a reporter!

I wrote an application, making my handwriting as plain and readable as I knew how, and explained that I knew how to operate a typewriter. I became, in fact, the first reporter in Newfoundland to use a typewriter. I apologized for not knowing shorthand, but explained earnestly that I could write very rapidly and that I had a very dependable memory. I did not know it at the time, but the *Telegram*'s owner, William J. Herder, was a close friend of my uncle Fred, and that fact, together with my rather naive but somehow impressive letter, got me the job.

Never can I forget my joy at receiving a letter from Mr. Herder asking me to call on him, and never can I forget my joy at being told by him that I could have the job, and never can I forget my startled happiness and excitement when he told me that my pay was to be $12! I wondered if this meant $12 a week or $12 a fortnight or $12 a month. I would have been happy beyond words to get $12 a month, and would have considered myself lucky. I think I would even have been happy to pay the *Telegram* $12 a month to work on it—as a reporter. The pay turned out to be $12 a week. I walked out of that office on air, reported for work the next Monday morning as instructed, and began a career as exciting and as satisfying as any young fellow could ever hope to have.

One of my very first efforts for the paper was to cover the Victory Parade in late 1918 just after the First World War had ended. It was perhaps the biggest parade ever seen in Newfoundland up to that time, and I doubt whether any such event had ever before, or has since, been covered by any newspaper reporter in my way. I did it on horseback. I borrowed the horse from my father and perhaps the saddle too, if I had a saddle. I moved swiftly back and forth along the length of the entire procession, making my notes with some difficulty from my jolting vantage point.

The business and editorial staff then consisted of Mr. Herder himself, his bookkeeper Michael Martin, and one of the Herder boys, in the office; and the editor, Charles T. James, and two reporters, of whom I was one. The other was one of the most remarkable men I have ever known, Edward A. Smith. He was a son of the Rev. Canon Walter R. Smith, and a brother of my friend Warwick Smith, who had been Sir Edward Morris's private secretary for a time. Ned Smith, whose son Douglas now lives in British Columbia, was one of the most heroic men I ever met. No discouragement could hold him back, and no man ever strove harder under greater difficulties to make a living in a place and at a time when it was unbelievably difficult to do so. Ned Smith was succeeded by Pat O'Reilly, who quickly became my friend to the day of his death long years afterward. I myself was succeeded on the *Telegram* by my school chum Albert B. Perlin.

Charlie James, the editor, and I promptly became friends, though we disagreed and argued on almost everything. He was a Tory; I, a Socialist. He was an Imperialist; I, a radical who seized every chance to denounce Imperialism, in India, in Ireland, in Egypt, in Cuba, or wherever it was to be found. One subject of absolute disagreement between us was the wisdom or otherwise of the terms of the Versailles Peace Treaty. The full Treaty was brought in batches from the Anglo-American Telegraph office to our office, and James and I read them together, he with mounting exuberance, I with deepening disapproval. I told him again and again that the Treaty was madness, unenforceable, and contained the seeds of a second and even possibly a third world war. This was well before John Maynard Keynes wrote his *Economic Consequences of the Peace*, and long before it came generally to be recognized that the excessive reparations demanded would have to be reduced to little more than a token. I am still proud of my precocious prescience in the matter. I was only eighteen, and at that time Newfoundland was as remote from the outside world as it is from the moon now.

Charlie James had replaced Harry A. Winter, who subsequently became a Member of the House of Assembly and its Speaker, and a member of the Commission of Government later on, and finally a judge of the Supreme Court. Harry Winter had succeeded Dr. W. F. Lloyd, a Welsh-born Newfoundlander who "rose" (if that's the word) from the editorship of the *Telegram* to membership in the House of Assembly, to be Prime Minister of Newfoundland,* to be an Imperial Privy Counsellor, and finally, as the Rt. Hon. Sir William F. Lloyd, to retire as Registrar of the Supreme Court.

Lloyd, in his time, had replaced the original editor, Alexander A. Parsons. Parsons, after working briefly on the New York *Telegram*, returned to St. John's and was engaged by the printer, William J. Herder, to join him as editor of a new daily newspaper that Herder was about to launch. Herder had the business skill and money touch that guaranteed success. They made a great pair, and it was as a pair that they once went to jail for a principle: during a trial, they refused to divulge to the court the name of one of the paper's contributors, preferring a jail term to the violation of a journalistic tradition. In jail, they refused to put on the black and white striped prison garb and insisted on going around in their underclothing for the duration of their term. A long petition was got up by the people of St. John's, and Herder and Parsons were subsequently released and pardoned. After serving as editor of the *Telegram* for about a quarter of a century, Parsons received from a grateful Liberal Government an appointment to a very good job: governor of the very penitentiary in which he and Herder had once been prisoners! I knew Alex Parsons quite well; and I must now surely be one of the few persons in the world who can say that he has known, without exception, every editor that the *Evening Telegram* has ever had. Indeed, for some weeks in 1919, I acted as the paper's editor myself, and at nineteen I must surely have been the youngest one it ever had.

In those days, with two reporters on the staff, the work was simplicity itself. St. John's was divided into two, East and West. One re-

*He was a heavy drinker who went on periodic drinking bouts. When the Morris coalition administration fell, through Sir Edward's appointment to the House of Lords, it was decided by Coaker and Cashin to make Lloyd Prime Minister. But where was he? He had simply disappeared, but they had a shrewd suspicion that he was "on it" again. They searched for two days before they found him in a bootleg dive on a slum street just off Water Street. He was still drunk, but they got him to his home, cleaned and sobered him up, and took him over to Government House to be sworn in, hangover and all. Despite his drinking, Lloyd was an able, intelligent man.

porter took East and the other West. We came to the office at nine o'clock, and the first thing we did was to read the morning papers. If they had any news item that hadn't been in the *Telegram* the day before, we rewrote it in our own words for that day's paper. Amusing things happened on those rewrites. When the two *Daily News* reporters went to work at night, they too went through the evening papers and rewrote items for the next morning's paper, and sometimes forgetful reporters on morning and evening papers would be rewriting the same items for days on end! It took us until nearly eleven o'clock to finish rewriting the morning papers, and then off we went, the two of us, to our respective beats. We got back to the office around one o'clock in the afternoon and as fast as possible wrote up our stories from the notes we had gathered on our rounds. The paper came out around four o'clock in the afternoon, and it sold for one cent.

There was no city editor. There was no news editor. You might almost say that there was no editor, for the only thing the editor seemed to do was to write the day's editorial and spend the rest of the time proofreading or reading foreign newspapers for pieces that could be clipped for republication in the *Telegram* to fill out its pages. This left the reporters entirely on their own, to come and go as they liked within the general framework of the paper.*

But I was not content to come within the framework. And so, romantically fired as I was by the textbooks on journalism that I was reading, I went after a story wherever I saw it. In this way, without even first mentioning it in the office, I covered all of the early attempts at flying the Atlantic: Raynham and Morgan, Harry Hawker and Commander Mackenzie-Grieve, Alcock and Brown, Admiral Mark Kerr, the American "Nancies", and the di Pinedo four-continent flight. Mr. Herder must have been startled to see one of his reporters acting so independently. Once, I went over to Harbour Grace and stayed there a whole week covering Admiral Kerr's attempt to fly the mighty Handley Page aircraft across the Atlantic, sending stories by train each day to the paper. When I got the scoop on HMS *Cornwall*'s raid on Flat Islands in Bonavista Bay, I did at least dash

*In the whole of Newfoundland, there were ten reporters: *Telegram*, E. A. Smith and J.R.S.; *Star*, Reg Dowden and Edward D. Haliburton, who later became a member of the Cabinet of Nova Scotia; *Herald*, Richard Joy, who later became an assistant District Attorney in Washington, D.C., and James M. McGrath, who later as a distinguished medical doctor was the highly respected Minister of Health and then Minister of Finance in my Cabinet; *News*, Thomas J. Foran and Jack Coffee; *Morning Advocate*, John M. Browne and Will Crotty.

into the office at one o'clock, grab a handful of copy paper and my topcoat, and tell my employer as I dashed out again, "I can't stop to explain, Mr. Herder, but the *Cornwall*'s down in the harbour and she's going to Flat Islands and I am going on her!" All he had time to say was, "All right, son, but get a good story!"

It is worth telling that story. On my rounds one morning in 1919, I noticed the *Cornwall* anchored in the harbour and was instantly curious. I went to the captain of the Royal Navy training ship *Briton*, Commander MacDermott, and demanded to know what the *Cornwall* was doing in the harbour. My suspicions were strengthened by his transparent attempt to put me off with the bland explanation that she was just in on her normal routine. "Routine!" I scoffed. "At this time of year?" (It was months before naval ships would ordinarily be in St. John's.) I got no information from him, but a little after noon it suddenly struck me that I might get some information from the Minister of Justice, Alfred Morine. Morine had only weeks before come into office, with the defeat of the Lloyd administration, under the prime ministry of Sir Michael Cashin. Morine planned to be a Conservative candidate in Bonavista Bay in the election due a few months later, and I thought I had guessed the secret of the *Cornwall*'s presence in St. John's. So up I went to the Department of Justice and asked to see the Minister. When he was told that a reporter from the *Telegram* wanted to see him, he invited me in. I came to the point instantly. "Mr. Morine, the *Cornwall* is in the harbour—she's going down to Flat Islands, isn't she?" There had been some trouble down there with moonshiners. Magistrate Mifflin had gone to the islands with a policeman from Greenspond to arrest some suspected moonshiners, but they had been driven away by some of the people. It was Morine's idea that, with an election coming up, and he running in that very Bay, it was time to "show the flag", to prove to the people that they couldn't defy the law, and so on. It might have been good law, but certainly it was not good politics! Not knowing how much I knew, Morine looked keenly at me for a moment, tilted back in his swivel chair, joined his fingertips, and stared at the ceiling for a full minute. Then he sat forward again, pressed a button, and to the girl who came in said crisply, "Get the Inspector General on the phone." This was Inspector General Charles H. Hutchings, head of Newfoundland's police force. Into the phone Morine said, "Hutchings, there's a young man named Smallwood here. He's from the *Telegram*. He wants to go on the *Cornwall*, and I think it expedient for him to go. You will take him as your private secretary, and he will meet you at the King's Wharf." Then he turned to me and said briefly, "You'll be very discreet, won't you?" I would have promised him anything to go on the ship. I ran from there to the *Telegram* office, burst in upon Mr. Herder, and the encounter was as I have described. That was on Monday. We got back into St. John's on the following Saturday.

I was accepted on board as the Inspector General's private secretary and ate in the officers' mess, where, I confess, I relayed with appropriate modifications some of the detective stories I had read as they pressed me to tell them some of my adventures as the private secretary to the Inspector General of Police. We steamed around Bonavista Bay, gathered up about a dozen policemen, and discharged broadside after broadside at icebergs until the very bay reverberated with the *Cornwall*'s gunfire and the voters of the Bay were well cowed. (They were not, as Morine discovered on polling day—he was badly defeated.)

We got back into St. John's Harbour around 1:30 on Saturday afternoon and anchored out in the stream. I had my story already written, but the problem was to get ashore ahead of the Inspector General who was lunching on board. I wanted desperately to catch that day's issue of the paper. Finally, I saw a small boat and a boy rowing it. I beckoned to him, and when he came alongside, I slid down a rope to the boat and helped to row it to the nearest wharf. It was well past two o'clock when I ran into the *Telegram* office with my precious story, but Mr. Herder shook his head. It was simply too late for that day's paper, but they'd publish it on Monday. Meanwhile, he'd put a short piece in that day's paper saying that I had been on the *Cornwall* and that I had this story for Monday. I had to be content with this, but the short item that appeared that afternoon stirred up a hornet's nest at Government House, where the captain of the *Cornwall* dined with the Governor that evening. First thing Monday morning came a letter from the Governor pointing out that the *Telegram* reporter had gone on board the *Cornwall* under false pretences, that the captain was most annoyed, and that my story was to be brought to Government House for examination before being published. So off I went to Government House, where I found the captain with the Governor. The captain looked at me quizzically but said nothing as he reached out his hand for the story. I watched his face carefully as he read it. A trace of a smile came over it once or twice, so I figured that things were going well for me. In fact, he made one correction only: I had described the local pilot who had been on the *Cornwall* as the navigator of the trip, but the captain asked me to change that to the words *local pilot*.

I almost flew back to the *Telegram* office, and that day the story appeared in all its glory. More than 600 extra copies were bought by the crew and officers of the *Cornwall* as a souvenir of their Bonavista Bay adventure, and another 600 by the public of St. John's. The regular daily circulation of the *Telegram* in those days would be around 3,000 or 4,000 copies.

I think that I may say truthfully, if not modestly, that I created a new style of newspaper reporting in Newfoundland. It was for me a wonderfully romantic business, reporting for a newspaper, and I was thrilled to be at it. I sent away for all the books I could discover about newspaper work and read them, as they say, avidly.

For years, I had been a compulsive reader. Reading was almost like a drug for me, and it has remained thus all my life. There was no public library in Newfoundland then (I tried a few years later to get one started), so mainly I had to buy my books. I did this chiefly in Sammy Garland's remarkable bookstore, where I had bought my penny dreadfuls as a boy. The three storeys and the basement of Garland's building on Water Street were filled with thousands of books—good, bad, and indifferent. It must have been one of the biggest, most adventurous bookstores in North America, and I think that I got to know it better than Mr. Garland did. Since I was eleven or twelve years old, I must have spent as much as $100,000 on new and second-hand books—I have nearly 15,000 books in my library now, and some of them I bought second-hand over half a century ago. I read day and night, walking along the street, in streetcars, on trains and on airplanes, and on board ships. I read anything and everything, with prodigal, untrained, unguided enthusiasm, blundering my own way, forming my own judgements, following my own personal taste; classics, penny dreadfuls, detective stories, adventure, travel, biography and autobiography, poetry, history, religion, economics, mythology; the best and the worst, the noblest and the most mediocre, even trash; books on everything under the sun, and mail-order catalogues when nothing better was at hand. I plunged joyously into every book that I could lay my hands on, and every book was a journey into gladsome territory. Sometimes I would write to the author of a book that puzzled or thrilled me. J. Patterson

Smyth must have been a bit puzzled himself when I wrote to him about his *Gospel of the Hereafter* and asked him to elucidate some of the points he had made in his book. He did, however, answer my letter. I wrote to John A. Hobson, the British economist, and he wrote back with an answer to the question that I had put to him on the problem of generating new capital in Newfoundland.

I ran into a young Jewish businessman about this time, Sam Miller, and he lent me a pamphlet that he had picked up in New York shortly before. It was written by the American Arthur Rhys Williams, and it explained the Bolshevik Revolution of 1917 in Russia, speaking of the Bolsheviks, Mensheviks, Cadets, Octobrists, and the rest of the political parties and groups whose names I had seen in the rather sparse references that the meagre cable news services supplied to our local newspapers—the local papers used to get a paltry 1,000 words a day to cover the whole world. This was the first extended account that I had read of the Russian Revolution. It didn't make me a Communist, but it certainly made me hope that at least some of the purposes of the revolution would be realized. I felt then, as I know now, that the world would never be the same again after that. I wrote a piece under my own name in the *Telegram*, explaining what Bolshevism was and informing my readers carefully how to pronounce the word Bolshevik—it was not *vik* but *week*. I'm afraid that I was misleading my readers, but I was only accepting Sam Miller's pronunciation of the word, and he used to have difficulty with his *V*'s.

About this time, I joined the Methodist College Literary Institute, widely known as the MCLI. One had to have attended Methodist College or to be a Methodist to join the Institute, and as a member, one became part of the intellectual elite of Newfoundland. Founded in the 1860s, it had attracted many of the most interesting personalities, and it was admittedly the finest training ground for debating and speaking in the country. Even the great Sir Richard Squires had been an active member, and I believe that Sir Robert Bond was too, in his day. When I joined, the leading members were Dr. Solomon P. Whiteway, white-haired, low-voiced, gentle, tentative, and always literary and liberal in his remarks; Captain Abram Kean, the greatest sealing captain that Newfoundland has produced and always an interesting speaker; William White, a successful businessman who had acquired part of the Smallwood Building on Duckworth Street after Uncle Fred died; the scholarly, thoughtful William Drover, who, though a Tory in politics, was actually one of the most liberal-minded of men; Calvert C. Pratt, then a keen St. John's businessman with Albert E. Hickman, but destined to become a millionaire in his own business and a Canadian Senator; the two brothers, Fred and Joe Moore, who spoke as one and who could be counted on always to take the most conservative position that it was humanly possible to take on any topic debated—one of them was later elected as the Member of the House of Assembly for White Bay; Reggie Hearder, a gentle young Englishman, and Albert E. Parkins, also an Englishman, who had a daughter, Eleanor, the object of my first "crush", if so feeble a word can justly be used for the wracking experience; and the towering Herbert J. Russell, destined to become the head of Newfoundland's railway system. Later, the leading personalities were Ray Gushue, who, at my prompting, became the first president of our university when it was created under my premiership; Hal Puddester, Sir John's son, destined to become a judge of the Supreme Court; Bert Butt, a thoughtful debater in whom, alas, action was nearly always lost "in the pale cast of thought"; and, superlatively, Nimshi Cole Crewe, a colourful genius of a man if ever there was one, and my closest friend and confidant for nearly twenty years—a man who had great influence in the shaping of my mind.

The most experienced journalist in Newfoundland was Sir Patrick T. McGrath. For years, he wrote freelance articles for newspapers and magazines in the United States and Canada and even England, as a sideline to his two great preoccupations as editor of the *Evening Herald* and private political advisor to the Prime Minister, Sir Edward Morris. But his experience as a journalist was confined solely to Newfoundland. In contrast, Dr. Harris M. Mosdell, the editor of the *Daily Star*, had worked on a newspaper in Toronto, I think the old *Mail and Empire*, and had good experience in daily journalism as it was practised in a large city. The *Star* reflected this: it was a sprightly newspaper in many ways, and certainly a brighter and livelier paper than the old *Telegram*. The young politician, Richard Anderson Squires, was its owner. He had launched the *Star* to promote his fierce ambition to become Prime Minister of Newfoundland. Mosdell, seeing my work on the *Telegram*, determined to get me away from that paper and onto his own staff. He must have talked it over with Squires, for the approach to me came, not from Mosdell himself, as would have been natural, but from Squires. I was asked to drop in on Mr. Squires at his law office in the Bank of Nova Scotia Building. I thus had my first meeting with the man with whom later I was to become very closely associated. When he invited me to join the *Star*, I gave no indication of my feeling in the matter, and the interview ended with his request that I should drop in and see Dr. Mosdell. When I did, Mosdell complimented me on my work and suggested that he could teach me a lot about working journalism if I came with him on the *Star*. I told him frankly that I was getting along all right on the *Telegram* and felt quite at home there. He offered me $18 a week, but I told him loftily that the money side meant little to me.

A day or two later, Mr. Herder came into the reporters' small room and said without preamble, "Son, I hear you're going to leave us and go on the *Star*." "You've heard wrong, Mr. Herder," I told him earnestly. "They're asking me to, but I haven't said yes or no." "We like you here," he said, "you're doing good work, and you'll find that we'll treat you as well as the *Star* or anyone else."

We talked a little more, and Mr. Herder suggested that I drop in and see Harry D. Reid. This suggestion didn't altogether surprise me, for I had formed an impression that there was some kind of close association, or even connection, between the *Telegram* and the Reid Newfoundland Company, operators of Newfoundland's trans-insular railway, of which Harry Reid was then the head

I had been dropping into Mr. Reid's office one or two mornings every week for nearly two years, to pick up any items of news that he might have to give. Those were the days of free railway passes, so one day in his office, as we chatted and joked, I said to him, "What about a pass on the railway, Mr. Reid?" He didn't hesitate but took a book of passes from the drawer in his desk and started to fill it out with his fountain pen. When he filled in my name, I said to him, "Add the words 'and friend'," but he put it more precisely, "and one friend". He signed the pass and handed it to me. I now had the right to travel free with one friend from any station to any station in Newfoundland for the period of a year. It must have been one of the last such passes ever issued, for within a year the Government had taken over the management of the railway.

Mr. Herder must have spoken to Mr. Reid before I got to see him, for Reid knew why I came. All he said to me was that the *Daily Star* had no future,* that the *Telegram* did, and that I would be well ad-

*He was right, as it turned out. Dr. Mosdell's skill couldn't save the paper, even when it was joined by the anonymous writing of Alex A. Parsons, the old *Telegram* editor, of Arthur English, and of John J. St. John, and by the business acumen of David R. Thistle.

vised to stay with the *Telegram*. When I got back to the office, Mr. Herder asked me what pay the *Star* had offered me, and I told him. "We'll pay you that right away," he announced.

It wasn't long afterward that the *Telegram* installed a beautiful, big, new newspaper press, and there were rumours about the town that the money for the press had come as a loan or investment or gift from the Reids. I know nothing about that, but I do know that the *Telegram* and the Reids were thick at that time and that the Reids were at daggers-drawn with Squires and his newspaper.

I continued to work happily on the *Telegram*; and before I left about two years after I had joined the paper, Mr. Herder raised my pay to the unheard-of pinnacle of $25 a week. That was far more than any other reporter in Newfoundland was paid. In fact, it was about the same salary that the editor himself received.

It was while I was on the *Telegram* that I became a politician; but before becoming a politician, I joined my first trade union, in 1918. This was the Newfoundland Industrial Workers' Association. The NIWA was the largest union of industrial and commercial workers that Newfoundland had ever seen: it had nearly 2,000 members, almost all of them in St. John's. It was rather a hodgepodge union, taking all kinds of employed people into its ranks, including even a newspaper reporter, myself. W. J. Naufts was the principal officer. William J. Willar, one of the most impressive orators that I ever heard, commanded enormous respect in the union, as did John Cadwell, a big, handsome man who worked at the foundry. A popular member and officer was E. J. Whitty. The general secretary was a remarkable Newfoundlander, Warwick Smith. He had begun to study law but had to give it up for health reasons. He had then gone to work with Sir Edward Morris, when he became Prime Minister of Newfoundland in 1908, and he told me many amusing stories of his close contact with Morris. Most of them centred around Morris's habit of calling him into his office and, in the presence of some constituent of St. John's West who had failed many times to get in to see the Prime Minister, sternly reprimanding him and pronouncing his dismissal as the culprit who had kept the constituent from seeing his Member. Always the constituent protested, in alarm, that he didn't really want Mr. Smith to lose his job on his account, and always Morris unwillingly acceded to the constituent's request. Warwick Smith had great influence in the NIWA.

The NIWA had its own weekly newspaper called the *Industrial Worker*, and I was its editor. This was only a part-time job, of course, for I continued working for the *Telegram*. My successor as editor was my old school friend Samuel J. Hefferton, who soon after also succeeded me as a reporter on the *Telegram* and many years later became a valued colleague in my first Cabinet. Today I do not possess even one copy of the *Industrial Worker*, and I doubt that anyone else does.

The union decided to establish a consumers' cooperative society that would operate a retail grocery shop in the city. Neddy Whitty became its manager for the limited number of years that the co-op operated; it was located at the foot of Flower Hill in the heart of the working-class section of the city.

The union also decided to establish a sort of branch cooperative society in the papermill town of Grand Falls in the centre of the Island. That society was lucky enough to have in its membership a few British paper-makers, who persuaded the committee to ask the great Cooperative Wholesale Society of England to find them an experienced cooperative manager. It was, I think, only because of the superlatively capable managerial skill and personality of Harry Fletcher that the Grand Falls Co-op was able to survive even the annihilation threatened by the disastrous general strike of 1921 in the big papermill. The society has gone on from strength to strength, until today it is one of the strongest cooperative societies in Canada. I don't imagine that very many of its present membership have ever even heard of the NIWA or of the parent society, if it can be called that, at the foot of Flower Hill.

It was possibly as a natural outcome of the NIWA that Newfoundland's first Labour Party was launched—it was called the Workingmen's Party. As a Socialist of nineteen, two years too young to vote, I threw myself heart and soul into the election that took place in early November 1919. The Party decided to contest only one seat, that of St. John's West. The great Morris had gone to the House of Lords, and his People's Party was now led by Sir Michael Cashin; the reorganized Liberal Party, with the word Reform added to it, was led by Richard Squires, a brilliant student of Sir Edward Morris. Both these heavyweights were running in St. John's West, but we entered the fray with boundless enthusiasm, if precious little political skill. Like St. John's East and several other constituencies, it was a seat that was entitled to elect three members to the House, and our three candidates were William J. Linegar, John Cadwell, and Michael A. Foley. My paper, which was energetically supporting Sir Michael Cashin (and I apologize for the inadequacy of the word, which falls lamentably short of indicating the kind and degree of energy that newspapers put into their election campaigns in those times), didn't like my attitude one bit. Mr. Herder remarked that he didn't think I was in sympathy with the paper's politics and I said firmly that indeed I was not. He grumbled a little, but I heard no more of it from him. Our candidates lost, but Richard Squires and Sir Michael Cashin were both elected. This was the first and last election in Newfoundland in which I supported Labour Party candidates, though I did so in the United States and in England. In Newfoundland, I became strongly convinced that the Liberal Party, so long as it lived up to its own tradition, was soundly and constructively a Labour Party in almost everything but name.

I finally left the *Telegram*, not to work on any other Newfoundland newspaper, but to go to Canada. It was not that I had any particular interest in going to Canada, for my real destination was the United States. It was my ambition to be an efficient newspaperman, and I knew the paper that I wanted to work on—the New York daily *Call*, the organ of the New York Socialists. But I had sense enough to know that my experience in journalism in St. John's scarcely fitted me for a job in New York. I thought that I would bridge the gap by working first in, say, Halifax in Canada and then perhaps in Boston in the United States. And this is precisely what I did. Mr. Herder gave me a very good letter of recommendation to W. H. Dennis of the *Halifax Herald*, as did Sir Patrick McGrath. At the St. John's railway station the day I left for Halifax, quite a crowd of friends turned up to see me off. I remember that most of the Jewish community in St. John's were there, and that they presented me with a bouquet of flowers and wished me good luck in my new endeavours. (I had done the community some small journalistic service.) The leader of the Jewish group was the brilliant young violinist, Dave Swedlin.

And so I began my travels around the world. The Chinese say that a tour of a thousand miles begins with one step. My "tour" has gone over half a million miles, and its first "step" was the 700 miles from St. John's to Halifax. It was my first time across the Island. I was entranced, and I wrote back an account of my impressions to the *Telegram*.

I arrived at Halifax on the last day of June 1920, and on that same day presented my letters of introduction and was hired as a reporter. W. H. Dennis was the son of Senator William Dennis and later became a Senator himself. When I reported for work the next day, I came under the immediate command of one of the finest newspapermen that ever lived, Edgar Kelly, the *Herald's* city editor. He had an acid tongue, mordant wit, endless cynicism, and underneath it all a kindly heart—and he was a thoroughly competent editor. He gave me more training in practical newspaper writing than anyone else ever did. It was on the *Halifax Herald* that I discovered that I was extremely good at interviewing people. Perhaps it was my youth (and I was much younger than my nineteen and a half years) and naïveté and obvious boyish idealism; but whatever it was, I discovered that I got on well with the people whom I was sent to interview.

Once I did an interview with Grant Hall, the president of Dominion Atlantic Railway, which operated throughout Nova Scotia. He came only occasionally to Nova Scotia, and I interviewed him on board his private car at the railway station, where he invited me to join him and Mrs. Hall for breakfast while the interview proceeded. I got a good story from him, and so I told Kelly. "All right, go ahead and write it." It was only when I turned in the typewritten piece to him that he told me that Grant Hall for years had been regarded as a most difficult person for a newspaper interview. He usually refused to see reporters, and when he did, he told them nothing. I was surprised to hear this, for I had got on extremely well with him. That was the first of countless press interviews that I conducted in Canada, the United States, and England.

My Bishop Feild College chum, Ed Haliburton, who, after his return from the war had worked for a while as a reporter on the *Daily Star* in St. John's, was now a student at Dalhousie University and was working on the *Halifax Chronicle*. He rose to be one of the most widely respected public men in the whole province of Nova Scotia.

Among my activities on the *Herald* was that of helping to start the famous Nova Scotia schooner races, and I did some work for a new weekly that Dennis started, called the *Atlantic Leader*. He tried to persuade me to go back to St. John's to represent the new weekly there, but my mind was set in the opposite direction.

A small group of Haligonians used to drop into the editorial offices of the *Herald* every night of the work-week to talk about politics, and the day's news, and Nova Scotia's woes as a Canadian province, and the greatness of Nova Scotia before Confederation. I listened with interest to their talk; but if my grandfather David had not converted me to be a Confederate, what I heard from those Nova Scotians certainly didn't either. I got quite an education from them, all of it bad for a future Confederate in Newfoundland.

I barely resisted the temptation while I was in Halifax to join two or three fellows I knew who went west on the harvester special. Thousands of men used to go out to the Prairie Provinces every fall to help in the harvest season on the farms and ranches, and they could travel on the train at absurdly low rates.

The closest friend I had in Halifax was George MacLeod. He had come from British Columbia to study law at Dalhousie University, and he had a part-time job on the *Herald*. It was he who became my savings bank. Somehow or other, I had to save enough money out of my wages, then around $30 a week, to get me safely to Boston and keep me going until I found a job there. So every pay-day George demanded $5 or $10 for the "fund", and with no great alacrity I gave it to him. It was lucky for me that I did; for when I finally decided that I had perhaps learned as much as I was going to learn on the *Herald* and started off for Boston, George was able to give me back between $50 and $100, a relative fortune. I worked on the *Herald* for several months, and then took the train to Yarmouth and the overnight ferry to Boston.

(left) 5. J. R. S. the young reporter about 1919

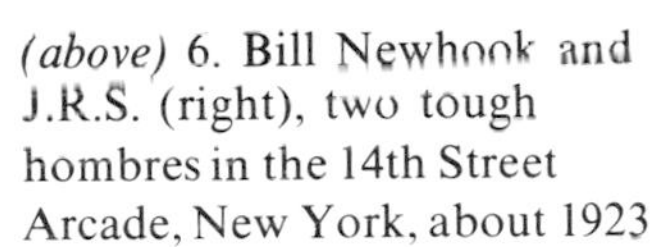

(above) 6. Bill Newhook and J.R.S. (right), two tough hombres in the 14th Street Arcade, New York, about 1923

(left) 7. Joseph and Clara Smallwood with their first child, Ramsay, in 1926

8. The Barrelman, about 1937

9. Charles and Minnie Smallwood with their thirteen children, 1940

7

Some Training for the Premiership

Travel, in the younger sort, is a part of education; in the elder a part of experience.

Francis Bacon

Many shall run to and fro, and knowledge shall be increased.

Daniel 12:4

If an ass goes traveling he'll not come home a horse.

Thomas Fuller

My first experience of America was a little disconcerting to one who had built in his own mind a strong concept of the greatness of democratic America. I had with me a postcard from my school chum Andrew Lehr, giving the address of his boarding house in Boston. It was 8 Allston Street, and Allston Street was just behind Scollay Square, only a few hundred yards away. I got a taxi at the ferry pier when we landed in the morning, piled my trunk aboard (and my huge George Turner map of Newfoundland), hauled out the postcard, and directed the driver, "8 Allston." He nodded and said, "Allston? O. K.," then started off, I watching the meter narrowly. When it got up to $2 or $3, I began to wonder how far Allston Street must be. When it got nearly to $6, I concluded that I was being taken for a ride in more than one sense. I watched for a policeman and when we came nearly up to him, I said to the driver, "Stop, stop here." I explained the situation to the policeman, and there was a wrangle between him and the driver in which the driver pretended that I had intended him to take me to the suburban town of Allston. I exclaimed that I hadn't even known of the existence of the suburb and asked triumphantly, "Didn't I tell you that I wanted to go to number 8 Allston? What did you think number 8 meant?" That clinched it, and the policeman, taking the cab's licence number, ordered him to turn around and take me back to Allston Street without any further charge. When we got to number 8 and I offered him Canadian money, which was all I had, he said contemptuously, "That money is no good. I want American money." I argued with him, and he made a concession: he would take it at fifty cents to the dollar! The Canadian dollar was down that year to about eighty cents, so I said, "Let's go to the nearest bank—and leave that meter off." I changed the money and paid him off.

Having got my trunk (and map) stowed away in a room, I set off for the office of the Boston *Herald-Traveler.* The city editor was a man named O'Brien, and he guessed immediately that I was from "down East", by which he meant Nova Scotia or somewhere around there. I explained patiently that I was from Newfoundland. (In those days, and right up to Confederation, nothing annoyed Newfoundlanders more than to get letters addressed "St. John's, Newfoundland, Canada".) Anyway, O'Brien gave me the job and immediately my first assignment. "Have you ever heard of Boston Common?" he asked, and I said that of course I had heard of it but that was about all. He explained that it was in a way America's Hyde Park and that my assignment was just to wander around in the park, listen to the stump orators, and write my impressions. I added to my education that day! The single tax speaker educated me as to the meaning of the term *real estate*. I shamed myself before the audience by arguing that real estate meant only buildings, and he had great fun showing up my ignorance. Then I came to another speaker, who was holding forth for a party I had never heard of, the Socialist Labor Party. I found out afterward that this was a party founded by the great Daniel De Leon. (I call him great because it was from him that Lenin derived some of his basic ideas, and surely that should be enough to justify the word.) This particular speaker finished his meeting while I was there, and I went up to him and began to ask him about his party. After a while, he asked me where I was from and I told him Newfoundland. "What part?" he persisted and I told him St. John's. "What part of St. John's?" and I told him the West End. Then I learned who he was. His name was Maher, and he was from the East End, and I knew his father fairly well—he owned a tinsmith shop on Duckworth Street, opposite the Customs House. I told Maher that his father, a devout Irish Roman Catholic, would be horrified if he knew that he had a son preaching Socialism. Maher said grimly, "He knows, and you're absolutely right."

I got on very well at the Boston *Herald-Traveler,* but I felt after two months that I was ready to face New York. Andrew Lehr insisted on coming with me to New York, but as he didn't find a job there and had saved practically nothing, I had to foot the bill for both of us. I was lucky enough to get a job the very first day, on the New York *Call* as I had hoped. Louis Baury, the city editor, had been an editorial reader for the great Macmillan publishing firm on Fifth Avenue, and he had walked out indignantly when the firm disagreed firmly with his verdict on a manuscript that had been offered for publication. He had got this position on the *Call*, and a brilliant job he made of it. One of the first men I met in the *Call* city room was a Newfoundlander named Gerald M. P. Fitzgibbon, from St. John's. Gerry was one of the most remarkable men I ever knew. Afterward, in St. John's, I met men who had been school chums of his, and they told me story after story of his remarkable ability to hypnotize people. He was a great athlete too, and he became champion cross-country runner of New York State under the colours of the Hibernian League.

Fitzgibbon was one of the really great stump speakers of the Socialist Party in New York—he and August Claessens, "the little giant of the soap box", were perhaps the two greatest in all of New York. Fitzgibbon told me that his favourite style was to use wit and humour in his speaking. "You get them smiling, and when they smile their mouths open, and when their mouths are open is just the moment to give them what you have." "And," added one of the group standing nearby, "Gerry is a mind-reader." I smiled at this, and Gerry said seriously that yes, he was a mind-reader, and offered to give me a demonstration. "Think of a word," he said, "the name of a place in the news or a person or any word you like; and then write it on a slip of paper and crunch it up in a pellet and give it to me and I'll tell you what's on it." I walked to the other end of the room and wrote the word *Minsk*. This was the name of a town in Russia that was the current centre of fighting between the Bolshevik forces and those of General Wrangel or Admiral Denikin or some other opponent of the Bolsheviks. I made sure that no one saw me write it and that the movement of my hand could not be seen, crunched the paper tightly into a pellet, and walked back and handed it to him. He held it loosely in one hand and said to me, "Look straight into my eyes and think hard on the word that you've written." I did so, and in a few moments he announced the word! "But you've spelled it wrong," he said. "I spelled it right, I think," I insisted. And he said, "No, the proper spelling is Ominsk," and he was right.

After a while, Gerry disappeared—he didn't come around the *Call* office any more. I had left New York, gone back to Newfoundland, and returned to New York before I saw him again, and then he told me of his latest activity. He was inviting reporters from all the newspapers of New York to come to East River to witness his performance. He outlined the plan. "They'll handcuff me with my hands behind my back, and my ankles shackled, and the shackle and handcuffs linked with a chain behind me; and then they'll seal me up in a canvas bag, and throw me over into the water. I'll come up in less than half a minute." "My God, Gerry," I exclaimed, "suppose you don't come up!" "Oh, I'll come up all right," he declared confidently, and up indeed he came, and great was the publicity thereof. Yes, he was a remarkable fellow. When I returned to Newfoundland that first time, I went to see Gerry's father, Thomas Fitzgibbon, a bearded Irishman who kept a small dry-goods store above which he and his wife had their home. She wept when I told them about Gerry, but the father seemed to be a bit hard toward him. Thomas's nephew, Joe, worked in the store with him and had been elected the year before as a Liberal Member of the House of Assembly under the leadership of Squires. Subsequently, Joe Fitzgibbon became Deputy Mayor of St. John's and one of the most generally admired, even loved, public men of the town.

What an exciting crew the men who ran the *Call* were, especially to a young Newfoundlander a bare few months away from his Island! Charles W. Ervin, the managing editor, whose autobiography is well worth reading, was an outstanding American liberal. James Oneal was the editor, and a great historian of the American labour movement. Ryan Walker was the cartoonist, and it was he who invented Henry Dubb, to represent the thick-headed worker who wouldn't become a trade unionist and a Socialist. David Karsner was the editor of the paper's Sunday magazine, and he and I became good friends. Eddie Levinson worked afterward as deputy editor of the *New Leader* and later as labour editor of the liberal New York *Post*. He had a distinguished career in charge of public relations for the United Automobile Workers and was the author of a successful book, *Labor Spy*. Richard R. Rohman had been to Paris, working on the Paris edition of the *Herald-Tribune*, so he was quite a romantic in our eyes. Pincus (Philip) Hockstein and I hit it off together until he went off into what the other fellows called "the sticks" as a reporter on the *Staten Island Advance*. He rose to be the paper's editor; and from that moment, his career with the Newhouse newspaper chain moved steadily upward until he was managing editor for all the papers of the chain. There was E. Haldeman-Julius, who was to become famous in America as the originator and publisher of the world's first great mass production and mass sale of books. These were the Little Blue Books, and later the Big Blue Books, running to close to 2,000 titles and selling in the hundreds of millions. The little books sold for five cents and the bigger ones for more than that. He had some financial backing—from his wife's people, I believe—and was able to buy out what was left of the printing plant that printed the famous, or infamous, *Appeal to Reason*, in Girard, Kansas. He modernized the plant, put in fast new presses, and generally became the Henry Ford of his day in the book printing and publishing world. All these men at the *Call* were ardent Socialists, the younger ones having served their apprenticeship in the "Yipsels"—the Young People's Socialist League.

The *Call* was in continuous, not just continual, financial difficulties, and constant appeals went out to the Socialist-leaning unions in New York and to wealthy individual Socialists. The most prominent of these was the clothing manufacturer Morris Berman, who had come up from the ranks to considerable success and wealth. Whenever he was asked for a contribution for the Socialist Party or the *Call*, his answer always was, "Yes, I'll give you a thousand dollars [or five or some generous figure] the minute you match it." This enabled the Party to go out and say to the unions and others, "If you will contribute a thousand dollars, Morris Berman will match it." It always helped. The paper, for its unenthusiastic attitude toward the war, had lost its cheap mailing privileges under Postmaster General A. S. Burleson, whose name and everything about him were heartily detested by Socialists; and for years, it had been in a chronic state of crisis. When I went back to Newfoundland a little before Christmas 1921, the paper was still staggering along; but soon after I returned to New York the following year, it finally collapsed and was replaced by the new weekly, the *New Leader*. James Oneal, Eddie Levinson, and a few others of the old *Call* crowd joined the staff, and I promptly attached myself to it as well.

One of my first assignments with the *Call* was an interview with Frank A. Vanderlip. In 1920, Vanderlip was the most prestigious banker in America, not only as head of the National City Bank, but as a sort of senior statesman for all bankers in America. He had once described American businessmen as a race of economic illiterates.

The interview arose out of my reading in one of the papers a tiny item saying that the villagers in Sparta were angry over an eviction order issued for Mr. Vanderlip, who had bought them out without their knowing it and wanted the land to add to his country estate. I had taken the item to Louis Baury and expressed my indignation that this sort of thing could happen in a great democracy like the United States. He had looked shrewdly at me and suggested that I go and see Vanderlip about it.

I took the train to Scarborough on the Hudson, where Vanderlip had his mansion; it was quite close to Sing Sing Prison. At the railway station, I hired a taxi to take me to the mansion, and when we got there, we drove through a great gate and up a long tree-lined private road to the front entrance. To my astonishment, the door was answered by a man dressed in silk breeches to the knees and wearing the rest of the garb of the sort of domestic functionary that I believed then was quite common in the stately homes of England but surely unknown in democratic America. I gave this footman, or whatever he was, my name and stated my mission with Mr. Vanderlip, and he told me to wait a moment and disappeared. He didn't come back, but a grey-haired, elderly gentleman came smiling toward me and invited me in. I followed him through the broad hallway into a large, high-ceilinged room that had mahogany walls, a deep carpet, and a great open fireplace with logs burning in it. Mr. Vanderlip showed me to a large chair at one side of the fireplace, opened a silver box containing cigars and held it out to me, and took his place in the chair opposite. He dismissed the matter of the village, saying simply that he had paid good prices for the properties and that the tenants would be all right. I couldn't pry much more out of him on that topic, for he did the prying. He asked me about myself, about my paper, and about Socialism. Among other things, he asked, "What will happen to my home when the Socialists come in power? Will the leaders of the Party live in it?" He looked a little shamefaced at my reply. "No, sir, certainly not. I think that your home and grounds and a lot of other homes and grounds in the area would be used as summer camps for the children of New York's slums." Louis Baury laughed when I got back to the office and told him of the conversation. "Vanderlip knows more about Socialism, and what it means, than most Socialists," he said.

About the same time, I interviewed James Weldon Johnson, the American poet.* It wasn't for his poetry that I saw him, but as the secretary of an organization of which I had never heard up to then: the National Association for the Advancement of Colored People. The American Marines had a day or so before entered Port-au-Prince to take possession of the black Republic of Haiti, in particular to occupy the Customs Houses of that land to make sure that enough money was gathered to pay the interest on loans borrowed in the United States by the Haitian Government. What was more natural than that a reporter from a Socialist paper should go to a black man

*He was the author of *Autobiography of an Ex-Colored Man.*

who was secretary of the great organization of black men, for his comment? It was my first close contact with a black man.

Nineteen twenty was a presidential election year—the candidates were Warren G. Harding for the Republicans, James M. Cox for the Democrats, and Eugene V. Debs for the Socialists. It was my first experience of an election in America, and only my second experience of any election. In New York State, the three parties contested the governorship, of course, and the seats in the State Assembly, not to speak of the city government. The Socialist candidate for Mayor of New York was the able New York lawyer, Morris Hillquit, and he would have been elected—the first Socialist ever to win that office—except that many, and perhaps most, of the votes cast for him were never counted. This is what happened.

The night of the election, a frantic telephone message came to Louis Baury from somewhere in the Bronx: "They're getting away with murder here!" Baury jotted down the address and told me to get there fast to see what was going on. I ran downstairs and jumped into a car that the Party was rushing to the scene. I was one of four or five in the car. When we reached the address or were only a few feet from it, the car came to a stop, and it was instantly surrounded in the darkness by half a dozen men who seemed to materialize from nowhere. Their leader looked in the window of the front seat and said, "Get out, all of youse!" He shone a flashlight into the face of the occupant next to the driver, then exclaimed, "Oh, it's you, Mr. Hillquit. I'm sorry, Mr. Hillquit, but I didn't know it was you. It's all right, Mr. Hillquit, everything's O. K." He muttered a word to the others, and they all disappeared as quickly as they had come. The man in the front seat was not the candidate, but his brother Edward. I have no doubt at all that it was his presence that saved us from being beaten up that night, and the others thought so too. We got out of the car and went into the polling station where the ballots were being "counted" by the Deputy Returning Officer (if that is the correct title in New York for the Newfoundland counterpart).

As soon as we got inside the door, our Socialist Party agent slipped over to us and said in a low voice, "It's murder, just murder." He explained what he meant, and then we saw for ourselves. The returning officer would reach down into a large box for a ballot, open the ballot, and lay it to one side; then he would quickly reach for another and do the same thing. But fast as he was opening the ballots, he was much faster in announcing the party for each one. There was no connection whatsoever between his opening the ballots and his announcement; in fact, he must have announced many more votes that there were ballots! The practice was to announce the party rather than the candidate's name. There were three parties, of course—Republican, Democrat, and Socialist. He would call rapidly, "Dem, Dem, Dem, Rep," and then, "Dem, Dem, Dem, Dem, Rep, Rep, Soc." When an objection was raised to what was going on in the counting, the Deputy Returning Officer ordered the police to remove the objector; and outside on the street, the goon squad beat him up and threw him into the gutter.

The Democrats "won" the election in that polling station, and so it was, I learned, in station after station. It was surely the most brazen theft of an election ever witnessed. Neither the dozen Socialists who were elected to the State Assembly of New York nor those elected to the city government were allowed to take their seats. A court case was entered in behalf of Morris Hillquit; but the next mayoralty election had taken place before the case was disposed of, and Hillquit never did "win" the election.

One of the interesting things that happened to me during that first year in New York was the opportunity to cover the story of the "rebirth" of free speech in Mt. Vernon. Mt. Vernon is, of course, a famous name in American history, but the Mt. Vernon in this incident is in New York State, not far from New York City. The Mayor, Elmer J. Kincaid, had announced that no Socialist Party or any other open-air meetings would be permitted in his city in the future without a permit from him. He had in fact got his council to enact a municipal ordinance requiring such a permit for each individual meeting. The tiny Socialist Party branch in Mt. Vernon reported this to Party headquarters in New York, and the Party in turn reported it to the American Civil Liberties Union, whose leader, Arthur Garfield Hays, was eager to take up the challenge. Hays organized a protest meeting to be held at a central street corner in Mt. Vernon, a corner relatively free of traffic, so that there should be no excuse based on interference with traffic. The speakers were the Rev. John Haynes Holmes, the Rev. Norman Thomas, and the reputable trade unionist Rose Schneiderman. I drove with the three of them to Mt. Vernon and was no more than a foot away as they began their widely advertised meeting. Mt. Vernon's chief of police, with a couple of policemen, stood nearby, and a large crowd gathered to witness the events.

Holmes was the first speaker, and he had no sooner opened his mouth than the chief of police asked him if he had a permit for this meeting. Holmes said that he had, and the chief quite politely asked to see it. Holmes passed him a printed copy of the Constitution of the United States, and the chief protested that he meant a permit from the Mayor. When Holmes admitted that he had no such permit and said that he didn't feel that he needed to have one, the chief told him that he was sorry but that he would have to stop Mr. Holmes from speaking. Holmes thereupon quietly stepped to one side, and Norman Thomas took his place. Thomas, of course, became the Socialist Party's almost permanent candidate for President of the United States. What he did that night was to say, "Ladies and gentlemen, I'll now read to you the Constitution of the United States," and the magnificently ironical position developed at once when the chief of police interrupted to ask him if he had the Mayor's permit. Thomas managed to look surprised and asked mildly if it was necessary in Mt. Vernon to have a permit to read the Constitution. The chief of police was embarrassed, but he insisted that if Mr. Thomas persisted in holding this meeting he would have to order his men to arrest him. Thomas said that he couldn't help that, but that he must insist on enjoying the right to read the Constitution of his country, and resumed the reading. The chief of police, now looking miserable, nodded to the two policemen and said, "You are all under arrest." So we drove down to the police station where the three speakers were booked and of course given bail. I telephoned my story in to the city room with delight, remembering the fame of Mt. Vernon in American history, but knowing really so little in detail of that history that I probably thought that this Mt. Vernon was the famous Mt. Vernon; so I began my story, "The battle for free speech began again in Mt. Vernon tonight."

Afterward, the local court convicted the three speakers, but the case was appealed to the Appellate Court of the State, which threw it out with the ringing declaration that the municipal ordinance was quite unconstitutional. So I was in at the birth of another famous fight for freedom! Actually, while Holmes and Thomas were speaking, I, standing behind them, had used their backs to steady my writing pad so that I could scribble a few notes of what was said. Back at the paper, they were delighted with my story, which was in a style and with an approach that perhaps only a non-American would have had just then.

I wonder if any young fellow from Newfoundland ever had as

many and such a diversity of exciting experiences, acquaintances, and friendships, and participated in as many exhilarating, even historic, events as I did in New York between 1921 and 1925. If anyone did, he is to be envied. I came to know Marcus Garvey very well, the one man who could claim to have started the black nationalism movement in Africa, America, England, and the West Indies. When I met him first, he was at the crest of the wave. He had launched a substantial movement of black people in the United States under the name Universal Negro Improvement Association. Up in Harlem in Liberty Hall, he was holding a great national convention of the association, and I covered every hour of it. Garvey himself was of medium height, stout, with broad shoulders and a deep chest and a beard like Lenin's. He wore a brightly coloured, bedecked uniform that must have been his own creation, for it was like no other uniform on earth. He had a dramatic group known as the Black Cross, consisting of attractive black girls in nurse's uniforms with black rather than red crosses. Several hundred stalwart black men were dressed in gay uniforms—they were a sort of elite guard of the movement. Garvey demanded to know what evidence there was for the belief that God was white. Why should He not be black? He was one of the most mesmerizing speakers I ever heard, a most powerful orator who stirred the emotions not of the black people alone, but of at least one white man who attended the convention.

Garvey wanted to have the black people in America move back to Africa. That very year, he announced the formation of the Black Cross Steamship Line that was intended to carry them there. The newly formed company had brought its first ship into port; she was moored in East River, and for a dollar you could go aboard and inspect her, which tens of thousands of black people did. Garvey soon found himself in deep trouble, for he had mailed to many states thousands of his pamphlets and circulars offering shares in the steamship company for sale. After I had left New York, he was arrested, tried, and convicted (unjustly, I am sure) of using the mails to defraud, and was sentenced to jail.

The last time I saw Garvey was in Hyde Park in London several years later. I had listened to most of the soap-boxers, as I always do when I go to London, and then spied a speaker back from the Corner deep into the meadow behind, so I wandered over to see who it was. I felt ashamed for Garvey as he uttered futile complaints about the treatment of black men in London, surely one of the most tolerant cities in the world. I asked him a question. "Mr. Garvey, I met you when you were the leader of a great movement of Negroes in the United States, when you had your new steamship line, and all that sort of thing. But I left America about that time and I've never heard the outcome of it all. What happened?" Garvey was on guard in his reply; he didn't know whether I was friendly or hostile; whether I knew the sequel to the American project; and if so, whether I was going to tell it to the audience. He needn't have worried, but he mumbled something about the interests of the white man in America being too powerful up to then to allow the black man to get on his feet.

After leaving New York, I had asked Sir William Coaker if he had heard of Garvey, because Coaker used to go to Jamaica for a few weeks every winter and Garvey was a Jamaican. Coaker had heard or read a lot about Garvey's activities in Jamaica. When he got out of jail, he went back to the island and tried to launch a new political party based on his own theme of black nationalism, but the party succeeded only in getting Garvey himself elected to the Jamaica Legislature. He really was a failure there. The blacks of the island were not ready for black nationalism; perhaps, indeed, nowhere in the world were they ready for it in the early 1920s.

Years later, when I was Premier, I dined with the editor of the *Gleaner* in Kingston, Jamaica, and asked him if he had ever known Marcus Garvey. He hadn't, but he knew all about him. He asked me if I'd seen the street in Kingston that was named after Garvey and the statue of Garvey that had been erected to his memory. I had, but one thing I lacked: copies of Garvey's books. To my delight, the editor promised to get them for me, and they are among my prized possessions today. Marcus Garvey was one of the most dynamic personalities I have ever known. His trouble was that he was too far ahead of his times.

I hadn't been in New York long when I began to realize that something had happened to me, something that changed the course of my life. I hadn't thought it out particularly before leaving Newfoundland; but in a very general kind of way, I came to America not only to follow my romantic ambition to be a writer on the Socialist daily, but probably to settle down there and even become an American citizen. Many Newfoundlanders did this, though perhaps most of them eventually went back to Newfoundland. Probably I would have remained in America had I left Newfoundland a year or so before I did, before I had got into the middle of a General Election in Newfoundland and had become involved with the Labour movement. In short, I had become a Newfoundlander before leaving for America—almost, you might say, a professional Newfoundlander. That, I suppose, was why I carried a huge map of Newfoundland with me to hang in my rooms in Halifax, Boston, and Manhattan. And perhaps that was why I went every week to Greenpoint in Brooklyn to meet the Red Cross boat from St. John's, in the hope of meeting some Newfoundlanders whom I might know and get the latest news from home. And what came over me just before Christmas 1921 was a yearning to go back to Newfoundland; not the ordinary homesickness that people feel, but something much more compelling. This instinct and my interest in the work I did in New York were in conflict for the next four or five years, and so I found myself going back to Newfoundland several times and just as often returning to New York. In 1921, I went back by train, stopped over at Halifax for a day, and wrote a piece for the *Halifax Herald* telling of my adventures and experiences in New York. I still had the railway pass that Harry Reid had given me, so I had to have enough money only for two passages to Port-aux-Basques, for Andrew Lehr insisted on going back with me. I telegraphed my father asking him to telegraph $50, and he did.

What a narrow escape we had in Port-aux-Basques! When the train started off for St. John's, the conductor came up to collect our tickets, and I nonchalantly showed him my pass for Joseph R. Smallwood and one friend. He passed it back, and I was dumbfounded when he told me that this pass was no longer any good, that the Newfoundland Government had taken over the railway and passes were no longer being issued. I recovered quickly enough to remind him that this pass had been issued to me by the president of the railway himself and that in common fair play, they should honour it on this one occasion at least. The conductor telegraphed ahead to St. John's, reported the facts, and got back instruction to accept the pass. I arrived in St. John's broke as usual.

When the House of Assembly opened that winter, Dr. Mosdell sent for me and asked if I would cover the session for the *Daily Star*. I think that I may claim to have written that winter and spring the best newspaper coverage there had been of House of Assembly sessions. Mosdell asked me also to cover the Thursday night debates of the

MCLI, and I did so, much to the gratification of the members; for they took the Institute and themselves very seriously in those days, as doubtless they were right to do.

After a short time as a reporter on the *Evening Advocate*, I wanted to get back to New York, so I went to Albert E. Hickman and asked him for a passage on his tramp ship *Yankton*. He agreed, and it was the roughest passage I ever had. I remember it above everything else for one special reason: it was during this trip that by the sheerest coincidence, the most startling coincidence, I read in succession Theodore Dreiser's *Sister Carrie*, Gustave Flaubert's *Madame Bovary*, and Hermann Sudermann's *Song of Songs*. I suppose that it might be beyond the capacity of even a computer to figure the degree of probability that ever again any person by mere chance will read these three particular books in succession, not knowing the nature of any of them until he had read them and then discovering that all three of them deal at the hands of a master with precisely the same theme.

I got back to New York safely, in spite of the *Yankton*, and went to see Carr van Anda, managing editor of the *New York Times*, about a job. Not long before, Charles R. Miller, editor-in-chief of the *Times*, on the suggestion of his executive assistant and biographer, F. Fraser Bond (Sir Robert Bond's nephew), had visited St. John's on vacation, and I had interviewed him. The interview with Miller filled an entire page of the obscure daily in St. John's on which I was working at the time. Miller wrote later from his New York office asking for a dozen copies of that issue; in his long career, it was the first time that he had been interviewed for publication by a reporter. I asked him for a letter of introduction to his editorial staff in New York. He wrote it in his own handwriting, and it contained the sentence, "I can personally vouch for his fidelity as a reporter." When I presented the letter to Mr. van Anda, he exclaimed, "Young man, do you realize how fortunate you are to have a letter like this from Mr. Miller?"

Mr. van Anda gave me a job as a reporter to take effect a few weeks from then. He told me that the *Times* always had a waiting list of about 1,000 people who were eager to get jobs, and that a reporter's job on the *Times* was one of the most eagerly sought openings for young newspapermen. I was delighted to have the job, but with no money in my pocket I wondered how I was going to survive.

I hung on to my boarding-house room briefly, but the $6 or $7 a week that it was costing me made too deep a hole in my savings. I told another roomer on the same floor that I was going out of town for a short time—though of course I wasn't—and asked him to take my few belongings (no longer including the map) and hold them for me. I decided that I could survive each day on forty cents, with a ten-cent breakfast and a thirty-cent dinner at night consisting of a plate of pork and beans, bread, coffee, and a piece of apple pie; but where was I going to sleep? I found a place near the Forty-second Street Public Library, on Sixth Avenue, now known as the Avenue of the Americas. The elevated railway ran on it then, and this was the chief drawback to the room I got for the first night: it cost only fifty cents, but at very short intervals, a train would roar past. I had to pay the fifty cents in advance to the clerk downstairs, who gave me a key and expected me to find the room myself. I soon realized that I was in one of New York's flop-houses. I didn't mind—my spirits never were much, if at all, affected by my pecuniary state from day to day, time to time, or place to place. Next morning, I went out to the library and spent the day reading. I stayed in the same flop-house for several nights and then decided to look for a cheaper hostel. I found one much farther downtown, not far from the Bowery though not on it, for twenty-five cents a night. It was a six-storey building, and each floor was identical. All the partitions had been taken out, and the whole floor had been given new partitions of chicken wire. You could see from one end of the floor to the other and from side to side, for the "rooms" were mere cubicles divided from each other by the chicken wire, each cubicle having a door that locked from inside. There was a cot, but I didn't feel like undressing and getting under the covers; so I spread out a newspaper that I had and lay on the paper. A bell rang at seven o'clock in the morning, long and loud enough to wake the dead, and everybody had to get up and out. We had received our twenty-five cents' worth; so it was out again to go to the public washrooms for a wash and a shave (the only baggage I carried around with me was my safety razor), get my ten-cent breakfast, and then wait around for the library to open.

One day, I suddenly remembered a resolve I had made back in St. John's that I would look up the motion-picture producer Ernest Shipman. Ron Young had told me about him in St. John's. Ron, who beyond comparison was the most knowledgeable man in Newfoundland where movies were concerned, was running the Nickel Theatre, a movie house. He told me that Shipman was a Canadian who had produced movies based on the novels of Ralph Connor—

"The Man from Glengarry", "Cameron of the Royal Mounted", "King Spruce", and "The Rapids", and others. His ex-wife, Helen Shipman, was a popular actress. "Why don't you get Shipman to come down and make a picture in Newfoundland?" Ron asked me. And I said yes, I'd try. So now I looked him up in the telephone directory and headed off for his office. He was pleasant enough, and certainly interested in what I had to suggest. There was something vaguely familiar about his face, and I tried to remember where I might have seen him before. Before our meeting was over, I realized what had puzzled me: he was almost a double for Mackenzie King, the man who had recently become Prime Minister of Canada.

Shipman explained the procedure he had followed in making his movies, one which he intended to continue to use. He would go into a town in a Canadian province, gather a number of businessmen and others with capital, and propose the formation of a local company that would finance the production of a movie film. The local people would put up 60 per cent of the $100,000 needed, and Shipman would put up the remaining 40 per cent; but they would agree to share the profits of the picture fifty-fifty. Then he would move in and produce the picture. His pictures had made good money, and the various companies were pleased. "Do you think that the business people of St. John's would go for a scheme like that?" he asked. I didn't hesitate, for I didn't know St. John's businessmen as well then as I did later. Yes, I thought they would. "Would you go down and organize them for me?" Shipman pressed. I had to make a decision, and I made it there and then. I was delighted to have a job on the *New York Times*, or at any rate to have one coming up in another week or two, but I was more delighted over the prospect of getting a film made in Newfoundland. By now, I was committed beyond cure to Newfoundland; I was carrying a torch, and I am afraid that the *New York Times* lost out in the fierce battle for my services. Shipman wanted a day or two to think it over and asked me to come in to see him on the following Monday. If he had decided favourably, he would underwrite my expenses and salary to go to St. John's as an advance agent for him, to get a group interested enough to meet with him when he came himself. This was agreed, and I went back to the library well fed and with two jobs in prospect.

By then, my funds were so low that I really couldn't afford the luxury of twenty-five-cent "bedrooms". It was a choice of eating or flophousing. I chose food, and that night I joined the down-and-outs who slept on the marble benches in Bryant Park immediately behind the library. I had often walked through it, once or twice quite late at night, and seen the occupants stretched out asleep on the hard benches, with a rolled-up newspaper, probably gathered from a trash can, as a pillow. If they could do it, so could I; so with a newspaper, I curled up and fell asleep. I was awakened by means of the customary courtesy paid to all sleepers in Bryant Park by New York's "finest", the police force. The whole force didn't come to Bryant Park—only one cop—but he was a model of efficiency. He made his procession past all the marble benches, tapping each sleeper smartly on the soles of his feet with his night-stick. I have personal knowledge that this method of awakening is quicker and surer than the best alarm clock. All over the park, men sat up yawning and rubbing their eyes. I wondered where I was going to get a wash and shave before the library opened at ten o'clock and solved the problem by asking the fellow on the next bench. I slept two or perhaps three nights in Bryant Park. Dozens of times since then, I have made my pilgrimage to the park, and I think I have identified the marble bench on which I slept; but no memorial plaque has been attached to it, and the secret of its identity is locked in my breast.

Shipman decided that he wanted to try Newfoundland, so off I went at his expense on the very first boat. In St. John's, I saw C. A. C. Bruce, T. A. McNabb, one of the Reids, Jack Kielley, R. B. Stafford, and several others, and explained the proposal to them. They were cautiously interested and said that they would like to meet with Ernest Shipman himself. I understood quite well that they weren't going to be impressed by me, but might or might not take Shipman seriously when they met him. Shipman and his current wife arrived after a fortnight; I brought him together with the businessmen, and he started a series of meetings.

On Saturday night, I took the Shipmans out to the Williams Inn at Forest Pond; and after we had eaten, the three of us got one of the Williams' rowboats and went out on the pond trouting, although it was raining cats and dogs that night. Alan Williams' face was a study when we came back, for Ernest Shipman had a dozen huge trout. Alan just didn't want his customers to be catching so many of his biggest fish! (That night, by the way, was the night the respected Charles R. Duder died, in Bay Bulls Big Pond, when the boat from which he was fishing capsized.)

Shipman was growing quite enthusiastic about the prospect of making movies, not only in Newfoundland, but in Nova Scotia, New Brunswick, and Prince Edward Island as well. Nothing would satisfy him but that I should go to Halifax, Saint John, and Charlottetown, and do the preliminary sales and promotion work as I had done in St. John's. I demurred, but he pressed me hard. Warning him that my heart wasn't going to be in my work in those Canadian provinces as it was in Newfoundland, I nevertheless set out on the job. In all three cities, I got groups of prominent businessmen together, and in each city a local company was formed according to the Shipman formula, to make movies. Shipman followed after me and personally attended to the business of forming the local companies. The nearest we got to the actual making of a film was at Charlottetown.

Before Shipman came to Prince Edward Island, I had seen the Lieutenant-Governor, the Premier, the Mayor, and several prominent businessmen. The most prominent of the businessmen was John O. Hyndman. The Premier, John H. Bell, was very kind to me and appeared to be as anxious to get a Prince Edward Island film made as I was to get one made in Newfoundland. Other men with whom I discussed the project included Mayor Jenkins, who owned a high-class grocery business and turned out to be a relative of mine; and Frank Heartz, a wealthy Prince Edward Islander who had made a lot of money in Western Canada. I found in him a most likable personality, and I was pleased some years later to learn that he had become Lieutenant-Governor of his province.

I made great friends with Frederick J. Nash, editor of the *Patriot*. He was a very distinguished man, and with his long hair he would be in perfect style today. As I sat across the desk from him, I kept glancing at two portraits of himself that hung on the wall behind him. As I made no comment on his having two identical photographs of himself, framed, side by side, on the wall, at last he himself raised the matter. "You're wondering why I have two pictures of myself on the wall, aren't you?" he enquired. I nodded and he explained, "Only one of these is a picture of me. Of course, you know who the other one is." I was a bit ashamed to admit it, but I didn't. It was Sir Wilfrid Laurier, the great Liberal Prime Minister of Canada for the first ten or twelve years of this century. The *Patriot* was the Liberal paper, and Fred Nash was an ardent Liberal. He cultivated his already remarkable resemblance to Laurier, wearing his hair long, the statesman's collar, and the Prince Albert coat, so that in actual fact many people mistook him for Laurier. He told me that once in a restaurant in Montreal, he was given a table near the window, and after a while he happened to glance out on the street and there was a big crowd standing staring, as they thought, at Laurier. On another occasion, he had gone to meet the ferry that was bringing Laurier for an election meeting. Laurier boarded the train, and they started for Charlottetown. At every railway station, crowds came out to greet Laurier; but he was very tired and wanted to lie down to take a rest before the big meeting. He asked Nash to go out on the rear platform and wave back to the crowd, and Nash told me that no one ever suspected that it wasn't Laurier.

Shipman spent a few days in Charlottetown, meeting with the group that I had got together. Then he told me that he simply had to get back to New York, but that I should stay on in Charlottetown to represent him. The work had begun to appeal to me, so I agreed. I had thought about the matter, as a result of conversations with Prince Edward Islanders, before Shipman came and had reached the conclusion that the movie to be made in Prince Edward Island ought to be based on their famous fox-ranching activity, which as late as 1921 was still a flourishing business there. Shipman concurred and said that he would send his favourite scenario writer to join me in Charlottetown. Faith Green had done several quite successful scenarios, and I waited expectantly for her arrival. I was disappointed to discover that she did not have an idea in her head for a scenario; but when I told her my idea, she agreed immediately and we set to work.

Faith Green was in her late fifties or early sixties, I was twenty and a half, and I suppose we must have been the strangest team of movie-writers that the industry has ever had. The sequel to all this is disappointing: not one movie was made by Shipman or the companies that he had organized. As far as I can see, the only good that was accomplished by all my work in the four capitals was the opportunity it gave me of getting to know more of the places which were destined, little as I thought then, to become what I myself was to name them: the Atlantic Provinces. The term *Maritime Provinces* is still commonly used, but it refers exclusively to the three older provinces.

I decided to go back to New York. I continued to do some work for the *Call*, which was soon to fail. I also worked and spoke for the Socialist Party, and continued to meet fascinating people. I had to earn at least enough to eat and sleep, though I had no ambition at all to earn more than that. You might say that it was five years of intensive study and a minimum of earning money. I got the customary remuneration for my open-air meetings for the Party—around $10 a meeting for two or three meetings a week—and I was expected to have a collection taken from the audience to contribute toward my fees. I was ashamed to seek a job again at the *New York Times*, and it was useless to try for a job on the remaining newspapers, for it was the time of fast-disappearing dailies in New York. One by one, they went under, one paper buying out another and merging what they called the best features of each. Frank A. Munsey was the active leader in that trend, which put hundreds of reporters out on the street. They got jobs mostly in public relations with various types of enterprises or sought employment with the trade magazines.

I worked enjoyably for a half-year with the Allen Business Papers at 1225 Broadway. One of their magazines was *American Hatter*, whose editor, Ernest Hubbard, was as fine a character as I ever met. I went to a hat factory in New Jersey and spent long enough in it to enable me to write a series of articles on hat-making. I responded to an ad from the McGraw-Hill publishing house for an editor and got the job. They published a large number of trade and industrial magazines, as well as technical textbooks. I was hired as editor of the *Electrical Merchandiser*, and I didn't like it. Their building then was ridiculously narrow but toweringly tall, away over on the west side of New York, and the editorial offices were on the top floor. The only time I have ever had a headache in my life was the first day on that top floor. When I mentioned it to the fellow at the next desk, he said, "Lift your feet off the floor." I did, and the swivel chair swayed from side to side with me in it. "This building sways almost a foot each way," my informant told me, and that's what caused the headache.

I quit that job after a month or two and got one much more to my liking. As a matter of fact, it was one of the most interesting of my life. The Gilliams Editorial Syndicate wasn't the literary mammoth the name hinted, but was just Mr. Gilliams and his daughter in the office. He was a former newspaperman who was now almost elderly, but he had for clients a large number of newspapers across America that took his feature articles for their Sunday editions. Gilliams wrote very little himself, and that's where I came in. I was supposed to write three feature articles each week, and these were duplicated and sent to the subscribers with illustrating photographs or draw-ings. It was common then for Sunday newspapers to publish the full-page article made up with less than one-quarter of the page for reading matter and more than three-quarters for illustration. I had a free hand in the pursuit of any idea that I had for the article. I would watch the daily papers closely for leads, and it was a fruitful source, but it took me to some of the strangest and often bizarre people and places. I turned out these journalistic masterpieces each week for the best part of a year, but today I haven't a copy of even one of them.

Twice I decided (or the gravely attenuated condition of my exchequer decided) that I should try my hand, for the first time in many years, at physical work. I heard that in the big shipyard on Staten Island a fellow could get a job, so over I went to see the boss, and surely enough I got the job. "Do you know tools?" the boss asked me, and of course I lied cheerfully and said that I did – after all, I knew an axe and a hammer and a saw and a chisel and a screwdriver. They had a big tool house, with every tool hanging from a hook or nail; and every time a worker took a tool, he hung a brass check on the nail with his number on it. I learned the name of each tool I took by simply writing it down. What annoyed me about the job was being down in the engine room of a large steamship and, with a slender, bent steel rod, hooking the congealed oil and grease out of the long vanes of the engine's rotors. There were, I felt, thousands of miles of those rotors! It was the most uninspiring thing I ever did in my life, and I quit the job after less than a month at it, out of unendurable boredom.

Another time I got a job that wasn't a bit boring, but the muscles of my arms are aching from it still. It was in a small machine shop on East Twenty-third Street. The boss was a German, a squat, stout man who spoke very quietly and didn't believe for a moment that I had ever worked in a machine shop before, or that I would last out the day. He had good reason for thinking the latter, for it was a terrible job. There was a big coarse emery stone revolving at considerable speed, and there were hundreds of three- and four-foot lengths of rusty iron, each the exact shape of a piece of railway track. He showed me what to do, and it looked foolishly easy. He took two pieces of thick wadding as hand pads and a piece of the rusty iron. He pressed the iron against the emery stone, and thousands of bright sparks flew toward him and onto his feet. If he let the piece of iron stop against the emery stone, it instantly gouged a hole in it; so he applied a steady, even pressure and kept pushing the rod until it was half-way down. Then he reversed it and did the other half. As soon as one rod was finished, I was supposed to go on to the next. By lunch-time, my arms were numb, and I could scarcely hold the light lunch I had brought with me. I felt like quitting the job there and then, but I was ashamed to do so. How I welcomed four o'clock when the day ended! Nothing but sheer shame took me back next morning, and I'm sure that the German boss was surprised to see me. (I learned that he had had scores who stayed a day or part of a day, and very few indeed who lasted beyond the first day.)

Eventually, early in 1924, I went to work for the *New Leader*, the weekly successor to the *Call*, and stayed there until I went back to Newfoundland permanently.

What a glorious opportunity there was in New York for a young man to resume and vastly improve his interrupted education! For years, I went night after night to classes and lectures in the Rand School of Social Science on Fifteenth Street, just off Union Square, where Algernon Lee was the director, and where Alexander A. Goldenweiser, E. A. Ross, Will Durant, Thorstein Veblen, Scott Nearing, Joseph Shipley, and a dozen others lectured on literature, history, economics, sociology, art appreciation, current events, and a whole catalogue of other topics. Down in the basement cafeteria, every kind of "-ism" was debated loudly by every kind of radical in New York, so loudly sometimes that one couldn't hear the man across the table: Socialism, Communism, Anarchism, Syndicalism, and the nuances and subdivisions of each and of others. It was surely one of the most exhilarating places in North America in those early years of the 1920s—a very far cry indeed from the St. John's that I had left.

If I had been tempted to be a Communist, and I never was, the conduct of the local Communists on dozens of occasions when I was a Socialist street-corner speaker would have cured me. I must have spoken at hundreds of open-air meetings all over Manhattan and in the Bronx and in Harlem, across the river in Jersey City, and in at least half a dozen neighbouring Jersey towns. We were in constant demand to go and speak at strikers' rallies. There were always strikes going on throughout New York, and the unions didn't always have acceptable speakers in their own ranks. Even unions that were not Socialist-leaning were glad to have us. I spoke at many such meetings. No sooner would we have our Socialist Party meeting going, and be getting along well with a sizable audience, than a Communist group would set up a rival meeting directly across the street from us. The Communist speaker always seemed to have a more powerful voice, and our crowd would begin to melt and his to swell. No orator of any persuasion could be expected to be tolerant of an "-ism" that would sink so low as to take his audience away from him!

I was on the panel of speakers of the Socialist Party in New York, and I soon discovered, as Party headquarters did too, that I got on wonderfully well when I spoke to groups of Jews and immigrants in the ghettoes and to black people in Harlem. Just as some people are born tone-deaf and are not able to distinguish one note of music from another, so I was born without even vestigial remains of racial prejudice, and I think that the audiences understood this instinctively. At any rate, I was one of the very few Gentiles who would be sent by the Party to Jewish areas and one of the very few whites to go to Harlem.

I suppose that the most celebrated journalist in America in the early 1920s was Charles W. Wood. He attracted the attention of Ralph Pulitzer, publisher of the New York *World*, by his writing in a small Socialist weekly that he was editing in Albany. Pulitzer telegraphed Wood, "Interested your writing Stop Drop in and see me." Wood telegraphed back, "Too busy Stop Suggest you drop in and see me." Pulitzer telegraphed to say that he really couldn't leave New York just then, so Wood wired back and suggested Schenectady as a compromise! Wood ended by going to New York, and Pulitzer invited him to join the *World*. On that paper and in *Collier's* magazine, Wood's interviews with American industrial tycoons attracted nation-wide attention. It was Wood's interview with Henry Ford that announced Ford's firm, final decision not to allow himself to be nominated for the Presidency of the United States—hundreds of Ford-for-President clubs had sprung up all across the country, and there had been enormous excitement over the Ford-for-President theme. The first time I met Wood, he told me that his mother was a Newfoundlander, one of the Bartlett family of Brigus, the family that produced the famous Captain Bob Bartlett who took Peary to the North Pole. His father, a Methodist minister, had been stationed for a time at Brigus and there met the girl he married. Wood was a Socialist of an artistic, esoteric kind, and he used his interviews with American industrial leaders as pegs upon which to hang propaganda for his own theories. His principal theory was that politics, political parties, and regulation-type government were all a waste of time; that what counted was production of goods, ever more plentifully, ever more efficiently, and that thus the welfare of all would best be served. As far as I could gather, he was essentially a syndicalist and thus, perhaps even without his knowing it, a follower of Daniel De Leon.* His favourite fun, when he met left-leaning intellectuals, was to ask if they cared to join him in his forthcoming expedition. They would ask what expedition, and he would explain that he was gathering a thousand persons together to lead them to the Inner Gobi Desert in central Asia to start a new colony that would enable the human race to make a new beginning. Each person joining the group would have to contribute a substantial sum of money to swell the joint capital.

Wood had a well-developed sense of humour. One day in his office in the *World* building near City Hall, he said to me, "I'm going out for a haircut. Do you want to come along with me?" And when we got to the barber shop, he said, "Come in and have a haircut on me"—the only time I've ever been offered the treat of a haircut. We were strolling along the street another day when, coming to a corner store, he pushed the swinging half-doors open and went inside. I followed him and found myself in what was either an absolutely perfect reproduction of an old-fashioned pre-Prohibition saloon, or no reproduction at all but an authentic original. I'm inclined to think that it was an original, and that it was a corner pub that simply never had heard about Prohibition but continued to operate as usual at the same old stand! We went up to the bar, I placed a foot on the brass rail as I saw him do (it was the only full-fledged saloon that I had ever been in), we leaned our elbows on the bar, and Wood called for whiskey, at the same time asking me what I would have. I had a soft drink; and as we stood there, we were joined by another man who turned out to be Courtenay Savage, principal reader for the famous Theatre Guild. "Hello, Charley." "How're you doing, Courtenay?" "What are you doing these days?" "Oh, the usual stuff—that is, except for my expedition. Have you decided to join us?" "Yes, I think I will." "Any interesting plays lately, Courtenay?" "Nothing exciting. By the way, Charley, did you ever think of writing a play yourself?" "As a matter of fact I'm writing one right now." "That's great, Charley. How about letting me be the first to read it?" "Sure, Courtenay, I

*I knew De Leon's son, Solon De Leon, quite well. He was the librarian at the Rand School, and I was one of the library's best "customers".

certainly will. Would you like to hear what my play is about?" "You bet, Charley. What's it about?" "Well, it is largely dialogue. There are only two characters in the play, both of them unborn, and the dialogue is around the question: 'Is there a life?' " And so for an hour I stood between two brilliant men who chaffed each other with their sallies.

John Murray Anderson was one of the most original creative artists in the whole theatre world of America, and he was a native-born Newfoundlander. Antique collector and dealer, rival to Vernon Castle, playwright, producer of the Greenwich Village Follies, rival and the successor to Florenz Ziegfeld, producer of a large number of movies—an authentic giant in his field. His father, the Hon. John Anderson, owned a large haberdashery business in St. John's. He earned his nickname, Daylight Anderson, by inducing the Legislature, through his indefatigable propaganda efforts, to make Newfoundland the first country in the world to adopt daylight saving. The senior John Anderson and I were great friends, despite the age disparity; and when his son, John Murray, paid his first visit in many years to St. John's, I interviewed him at great length, giving him almost a whole page of my newspaper.

Anderson welcomed me warmly when I telephoned him from my rooming house in New York, and invited me to come along and join him at his apartment. His brother Hugh was with him, and the three of us went to a large empty theatre and took our places in seats a few rows back from the stage. Then there passed across the stage in slow succession, one at a time, forty or fifty of what I thought were some of the most beautiful girls in the world. For days, Murray Anderson had been watching these parades of "lovelies", and thus far he had chosen only four or five for the two chorus lines that he intended to have in the forthcoming edition of Greenwich Village Follies. I was impatient with his willingness to let all of those beautiful girls slip out of his clutches, for he selected not one of the group that afternoon. Later, when I saw the two chorus lines in the Follies, I understood. One line of thirty or forty girls were tall, willowy, and beautiful; while the second line were shorter, equally beautiful, and all of them brunettes.

At about seven o'clock in the evening, Anderson called off the work for the day and turning to me said, "Let's go and eat." It was my first experience with a bootleg restaurant; it was in the basement of one of New York's old brownstone houses. We dawdled there until close to midnight, and then I followed Anderson and his brother back to Murray's big apartment. Murray said languidly to Hugh, "Get some people in," and Hugh went to the phone. Soon after, in stormed Bert Savoy, then America's most famous female impersonator and chief performer in the team of Savoy and Brennan. A little later, Polly Moran arrived, of "Sheriff Nell" movie fame; and then, as though that were not enough, Marie Dressler, the immortal Tugboat Annie of the movies; and finally, a tall blonde English girl who had just won a beauty contest in England and was on her way to Hollywood. Murray Anderson introduced me to his friends as they came, and Bert Savoy, who had visibly dined and wined well, held my hand, and said earnestly to me, "Brisbane, I agree with some of your stuff, but I hate you for what you wrote this morning!" Arthur Brisbane was America's supremely great daily columnist. His piece headed "Today" appeared on the front page of every Hearst newspaper in the country. I was flattered.

An hour or two after they arrived, close to two o'clock in the morning, Bert Savoy, who had continued drinking, got into a towering passion of attack on Murray Anderson. It ended when he suddenly screamed, "I hate you, Murray Anderson, I hate you!" and with that spat in Anderson's face—Anderson was paying him $2,500 a week, a princely sum then. Hugh Anderson quietly gathered them all up and got them out of the apartment. He went with them too, so that Murray and I were left alone. We talked about Newfoundland and its tragic history, and the condition of the people; and I found him, with his sympathetic artist's temperament, to be remarkably of one mind with me in his attitude. He rather startled me, though, by one remark he made. He argued that the Newfoundland people, by their very means of making a living, had developed a deep instinct of destructiveness. "They kill codfish and other fish; they shoot seals and other game; they cut down trees—it's kill, kill, kill—destroy, destroy, destroy." There was too much truth in his description of the way a majority of Newfoundlanders down through our history had earned their living for me to be able to argue credibly against him, though his suggestion shocked me. We talked until seven o'clock in the morning, and I walked back to my room on West Fifteenth Street.

In New York, except for the first two visits, I boarded at 123 West Fifteenth Street, with Mrs. Taylor. She was a mother to me, and her son Arthur and I became friends. He had been an actor, but now his health wouldn't allow him to work, so he hung around the house a lot. His mother bought him an abandoned farm of 180 acres on the bank of the Delaware River in New Jersey near a place called Frenchtown, not far from Philadelphia. Arthur knew absolutely nothing about farming; in fact, I'm doubtful that he ever saw a farm in his life until he owned this one. It had a fine old stone dwelling, a large barn, and a very good cherry orchard. Otherwise, it was a run-down disaster. I went out frequently for a week or more at a time to the farm, and in the kitchen garden that summer, I grew enough tomatoes to supply a small town! I got the plants from an old farmer named Bloom on the adjoining place. I kept telling Arthur that he should have a cow on his farm and couldn't understand his disinclination. We heard of a cow for sale eight or ten miles away and went off to fetch it in his Ford pick-up. When we got the cow home, I discovered why he had been unenthusiastic—he didn't know how to milk it, and try as I might I couldn't teach him. So, for my pains, I had to milk the cow. We used to drive from Manhattan to Frenchtown in the pick-up, and I can't count the hours we spent on the way to the farm, parked on the side of the road, rebabbitting the crankshaft. This crankshaft used to splash into a pan of oil underneath the truck; but the trouble was that when the truck went uphill for any distance, the oil ran to the back end of the pan, the crankshaft got no lubrication, and the babbitt lining burned out. The loud noise it made always warned us; then we had to take off the pan, carefully saving the oil, take off the crankshaft, and melt new babbitt and put it in. I became quite an expert at it, and except for the printing trade and one or two aspects of farming, this was the only manual trade that I ever mastered.

Next door to the Taylor boarding house lived the Solomon family. The father owned a saddlery and leather shop downtown, and the mother was one of the sweetest women I ever knew. There were two daughters, Ann and Belle, and two sons, one of whom became a successful medical doctor afterward. I had the distinction of writing the bar mitzvah speech that Sammy delivered in the synagogue, for I became virtually a member of the family, spending almost as much time in the Solomon home as I did in my own boarding house.

I got to know Lincoln Steffens very well, at the Civic Club, where Socialists and Liberals met frequently for fun and an intellectual kind of entertainment. Steffens had the personality to match his great skill as muckraker and writer. It was he, of course, who uttered the famous words after he visited the Soviet Union soon after the

1917 Revolution broke out, "I've seen the future—and it works!" (I wonder if he would say that today?) Steffens was one of two of the best-known American muckrakers that I met, the other being Upton Sinclair.

It was also at the Civic Club that I met Art Young, the cartoonist. Because he was a radical and, in a literary or artistic way, an admitted Socialist, Young was unwanted as a cartoonist, great as he was. He was then publishing a little paper of his own called *Good Morning*, with the sub line: To Laugh That We May Not Weep. He was a big man, with long curls, and in that respect he would be in perfect style today. I consider two of his cartoons among the greatest ever drawn. One showed a couple of raggedy hobos sitting on a bank on the side of a railroad track. One of them was stewing some coffee in a tin can held over a tiny fire; the other was reading part of a page of a newspaper that had probably been thrown out the window of a passing train, and he was saying, "I see England owes us eleven billion dollars." The other showed a slum kitchen in a slum tenement building. A big hairy fellow stripped to his undershirt was sitting sprawled over the rickety kitchen table. His slatternly wife was standing by the kitchen stove cooking something for their meal. He said, "I golly, but 'tis hot," to which she rejoined, "You complaining about hot, and you down in a nice cool sewer all day!"

Of course, we young Socialists thought the world of Upton Sinclair, and when he came to New York and made an appearance at the Rand School, we all flocked to hear him. I think that the first time I met him was on the occasion of the unveiling of Willy Pogany's murals on the walls of the principal hall in the school. How quickly fame perishes! It's strange to realize that in spite of Sinclair's fifty or sixty books and his waging of the celebrated EPIC (End Poverty in California) campaign for the governorship of California, his name is rapidly going into the limbo of forgotten things.

It was through Frieda Kirchwey, editor of the *Nation*, that I first met Heber Blankenhorn, and it was through Blankenhorn that I almost changed the whole course of my life. Around that time, several labour banks were starting in America, and Blankenhorn was an advisor to the bank operated by a number of standard railway brotherhoods. The brotherhoods were planning to launch a weekly newspaper to which more than a million railroaders would be subscribers through their union dues. The paper was to be called *Labor*, and they were looking for an editor. Blankenhorn urged me to let him recommend me for the job, but it meant living in Washington, D. C., which I wasn't at all anxious to do. I had met Blankenhorn in the first place because of an article that I had written for Sir William Coaker's paper in St. John's, a fanciful piece in which I supposed that Henry Ford became interested in Coaker because Coaker's middle name was Ford. The article went on to say that Ford had volunteered to help Coaker finance some large projects that he wanted to launch for the betterment of the fishermen. On reading the piece, Coaker had wired me, "See Ford Ask him invest one million in Fishermen's Union Trading Company." I showed the telegram to Blankenhorn. I told him all about Coaker, the Fishermen's Protective Union and its associated companies (trading, publishing, shipbuilding, electric), and the union's own town and seaport of Port Union; and I sought his advice as to how I might proceed to obtain Coaker's million dollars for him. (I dismissed the thought of Henry Ford as a likely source.) Blankenhorn was interested but pointed out that Newfoundland itself was almost completely unknown, and that as far as Coaker and his movement were concerned, they might just as well be on another planet. What was needed was publicity, and he suggested that I start by writing an article for the *Nation*. I did, and the *Nation* published it, but nothing came of the million-dollar idea.

Coaker figured in another incident in which I was involved in New York. Plutarco Elias Calles had just been elected President of Mexico and was to be installed as President by his predecessor a couple of months hence. This was possibly the first time in Mexico's history that one president succeeded another without bloodshed. Calles went to Europe before his inauguration and stopped in New York on the way. He spoke at several Socialist rallies while he was in New York—in Spanish, of course—and I covered his meetings. He had asked for a dependable young Socialist to act as interpreter for him, and a New York *Call* friend was given the job. His name was Robert Haberman, and he was a young Jewish fellow from Eastern Europe who had learned to speak Spanish fluently. I had a special interview with Calles, with Bob Haberman acting as interpreter. Bob was offered a permanent job by Calles and, changing his first name to Roberto, he went off to Mexico with the president-elect. Haberman came back to New York on a visit a year or so later. In the interval, he had risen rapidly to become the man behind the throne in Mexico. He and I talked about Mexico, and it came out in the conversation that Mexicans ate a considerable amount of salt-dried codfish. "Where do they get it?" I asked. "It comes from Spain," he told me, and I was astonished. "But Newfoundland supplies Spain with her codfish," I explained. "It must be Newfoundland codfish that you're getting; Spain must be re-exporting some of it to you." He shrugged and said, "Why don't you run down and see?" That was all very fine, but it took money, and as usual I was either broke or close to it. I wrote Coaker in Newfoundland and told him the story, suggesting that either he should go to Mexico himself or send money to me to go. He did neither.

Meyer London was one of our Socialist Congressmen in Washington, and Victor Berger was another. London lived in New York, and I got to know him very well; I saw less of Victor Berger, because he didn't often come to New York. At that time, the one city in America that had a Socialist mayor was Milwaukee, and his name was Dan Hoan. I knew him well too.

Judge Jacob Panken was a popular Municipal Court judge elected on the Socialist ticket, and I first got to know him when I interviewed him in his apartment on Second Avenue, at the edge of the great Jewish ghetto, a few hours after he returned from a visit to Europe. He didn't want to talk about anything but a man named Hitler, who, he said, was probably the greatest threat to Europe's peace and democracy that existed. He had heard Hitler harangue a crowd, and he confessed frankly that he was frightened. That was in the very early 1920s, and it was the first that I had ever heard of this fellow called Hitler.

Just before the *New Leader* started up, Eddie Levinson, Pincus Hockstein, and I decided to start a paper of our own, and that was the nearest I ever came to becoming a newspaper publisher in the United States. It was an ingenious idea, and a pity that it did not take. It was to be a labour and trade union weekly, with each one of perhaps a dozen or more large trade unions taking a page each week for their own notices, union information and gossip, and union propaganda generally. A certain number of copies of the paper would be printed with each union's page in it, and these would be delivered to the union; so with the other unions as well. We got out one issue of the paper, without any advertising revenue, in the hope of using it as a sample to persuade the unions to back it. I remember that of the three of us, mine was the only picture to appear in it—it was to illustrate a story to the effect that I was going to Canada to attend an important conference being held to form a Labour Party for that country. In the event, I don't think the conference was actually held.

During the presidential election campaign of 1924, I worked hard for the Socialist Party. I was one of a number that made a swing around the state, and it was a fascinating experience. A relay of speakers was sent to fifteen or twenty cities, in each of which the speaker would report to local Party headquarters and be told where he was to speak. I was routed to eighteen cities, but I remember only fifteen of them: Ithaca, Elmira, Jamestown, Buffalo, Niagara, Rochester, Oswego, Watertown, Ogdensburg, Syracuse, Utica, Schenectady, Albany, Troy, and Poughkeepsie. In Albany, on the night of my speech I had as a rival Charles Evans Hughes, the United States Secretary of State. Hughes delivered a notable address at the University in Albany that night, in which he advocated for the Senate a modification of the British practice of having Ministers in Parliament orally answer questions of parliamentarians. My meeting was held at the foot of the hill where Hughes was speaking, and my audience was much smaller and far less distinguished. This was noticed by the editor of the *Knickerbocker Press*, whose editorial next morning pointed out the contrast between the two speakers, somewhat to my disadvantage.

In Buffalo, I shared a platform with Frank R. Crosswaithe, "the Negro Debs". He was one of the most inspiring orators that I have ever listened to. Crosswaithe was an organizer then for A. Philip Randolph's Union of Pullman Porters. He was a convinced Socialist and was in great demand as a speaker at Socialist rallies. I ran into Crosswaithe at Party headquarters in Buffalo. He too was making the swing round the state, going in the opposite direction. He suggested that we team up for the Buffalo meeting, and I was very pleased by the invitation.

Buffalo was then a stronghold of the Ku Klux Klan, but at the time, I was not aware of this. The meeting was held at night in a large open square, and there must have been 10,000 people in the audience. I was the first of the two speakers. I mounted a little stepladder to the platform, which was draped with an American flag, and launched into my speech. It was an attack, a particularly vehement one, on the Ku Klux Klan. I told the story of John Brown in his death cell kissing a black baby in preference to the crucifix, in response to a coarsely worded challenge of one of the prison warders, put to test Brown's sincerity in his efforts against slavery; and of Brown's being menaced by black men in the line through which he had to pass to reach the gallows. It was admittedly an inflammatory speech, and although I was blithely unaware of it, the black men in the audience, including Frank Crosswaithe, were deeply concerned for my safety. The platform itself was encircled by a couple of thousand negroes, but they in turn were surrounded by thousands of white men. I realize now that anyone on the outer fringe of the crowd could have taken a shot at me and easily escaped.

At the foot of the platform, Frank and the local leaders of the party conferred hurriedly as my speech proceeded. They decided that Frank wouldn't speak, and I was surprised, when the chairman got up pretending to introduce Crosswaithe, to find Frank and myself being hustled into a car that was backed up to the platform and closely surrounded by a large number of black men. Once we got beyond the outer ring of the crowd, our car put on a fierce burst of speed down the street, around the corner, down another street, and around another corner. Frank explained that we were doing this to throw off any possible pursuers. We drove thus for over half an hour, and then Frank asked me what I proposed to do. When I said that I thought I would go back to my hotel, he suggested that there might be a mob waiting there for me or that one might get there after I arrived. I said that I supposed this was possible and asked if he had anything to suggest. "You could get out of town," he said earnestly, "or if you like you can come to my hotel." His hotel was an exclusively black one in an exclusively black neighbourhood, and I said that I thought I would like to go to his hotel. I slept the night in the spare bed of his room; and after we turned out the light, we talked, or mostly he talked, for a couple of hours about his life and career. He had been born in the Virgin Islands and was thus an American citizen. He was university educated, and I felt ashamed even there in the dark to hear him tell, in quite matter-of-fact tones, of the countless insults he had received all his life, and was still receiving from white men not fit to lace his shoes. I learned a lot that night of what it felt like to be an educated, talented black man in the 1920s.

Long years after our adventure together in Buffalo, when I was Premier, I had an appointment at Nelson Rockefeller's offices in Rockefeller Plaza in New York. I was hoping to interest Rockefeller's International Basic Economy Corporation in the development of some of Newfoundland's natural resources, particularly in Labrador. It was Frank Crosswaithe who drove me in his big Cadillac to

Rockefeller's office. I had asked some old Socialist friends if Frank Crosswaithe was still around, and so learned of his appointment as a member of the powerful Housing Commission of New York. I called him up, and we arranged to get together. He was still a Socialist, still a trade union organizer, still devoted to the Labour and Socialist movements. As a member of the Housing Commission, he had the use of a chauffeur-driven Cadillac. I wondered with a chuckle what Nelson Rockefeller would think if he knew that Frank Crosswaithe, the Socialist and trade union orator, had driven me to the IBEC office.

In Poughkeepsie, Mrs. Eleanor Roosevelt, wife of New York's Governor, had me as her rival. My encounter with Mrs. Roosevelt, if not the highlight of her speaking tour, was assuredly a highlight of mine. It started at the railway station at Poughkeepsie. As I got off the train with my suitcase, I saw a man in a dark uniform and chauffeur's hat look expectantly at the passengers streaming past him and evidently decide that I was the passenger he wanted. "You are Mr. Smallwood?" He took my suitcase and asked me to follow him. He took me to a big Rolls Royce limousine, and I sat back like a lord as he drove me to the King Court Hotel. He carried my suitcase in and then left. I signed the register and decided to satisfy my curiosity. "Does the car belong to the hotel?" I asked the clerk, and then I learned the story. The car belonged to a man named King; so did the hotel and a lot of real estate in Poughkeepsie. King was one of the wealthiest men in the city. He had been raised in New York's ghetto, where he started his business career with a pushcart. He was not one of those who spurned his origins but was, on the contrary, a sincere Socialist. In this election, in which the Socialist Party was backing the Third Party candidacies of Senator Robert M. ("Battling Bob") LaFollette and Senator Burton K. Wheeler, he like all of us supported the Party's stand. I was his guest, as all visiting Socialist speakers were, the clerk told me.

After I got stowed away in my room, I bought the evening newspaper and there, on the front page, I got the news. The top left column spoke of the Teapot Dome meeting to be held by Mrs. Eleanor Roosevelt in the big public square that night. The Teapot Dome scandal was a major embarrassment for the Harding administration, so the Democrats had made a papier-mâché replica of a teapot, painted it the right colour, and set it squarely down upon a large touring car. Steam emerged from the spout, which stuck out in front of the car's hood, and the opening of the teapot, where the lid would be, came over the seats, and the handle stuck out over the rear of the car. Mrs. Roosevelt and Nancy Smith, Governor Al Smith's daughter, and a third woman constituted the group. They too were making the swing around the state, and Poughkeepsie was their first stop. At the top of the page in the third column was a bit of publicity about me and my meeting that same night in the public square. In the second column, wedged in between the other two, and having a border around it, was the exciting story that there was likely to be a clash between the two parties: each party claimed to have the necessary municipal permit; obviously, neither party was going to be willing to yield to the other; and equally obviously, two meetings couldn't go on simultaneously. I read these stories as I strolled down the street to report in at Party headquarters. "What's all this about?" I asked, tapping the newspaper. "Pay no attention to it," I was reassured. "We have the permit—look, here it is, see?—so the other crowd will have to take a back seat." I didn't like that one bit. I knew that Mrs. Roosevelt and Nancy Smith would draw a big crowd, especially from Vassar College, and that it could well be a fatal mistake for the Socialists to be less than gallant in the situation. "Let them speak," I advised. "They won't take long, and the crowd will be eager to hear our answer to them, and we can make it a tremendous propaganda victory for the cause." My strategy was approved, and that night at least 12,000 people jammed the square. Mrs. Roosevelt's teapot and our portable platform were not more than twenty feet apart. Nancy Smith spoke, almost inaudibly, for two minutes. Mrs. Roosevelt spoke for perhaps ten minutes, and she began and ended her speech with a kindly reference to our courtesy in yielding our time to them. I didn't know, as I held forth in what I now admit was a good speech, that in my audience there sat listening to me a lady who was destined to become probably the most distinguished First Lady of the land. I had great fun reciting the names of the seventy-two industrial and financial companies of which the Democratic candidate, John W. Davis, was a director. "Mrs. Roosevelt tells us that Al Smith is for John W. Davis," I cried, "and she asks us to believe that if Al Smith is for John W. Davis then John W. Davis must be all right. I suggest to you, on the contrary, that it may only show that there's something wrong with Al Smith!" Cheers from the large contingent of Vassar girls! Oh, but it was a glorious meeting, the best one of my life to that moment. Years afterward, when I was Premier, I called on Mrs.

Roosevelt in her flat in Manhattan to invite her to come to St. John's to open the magnificent new campus of our university; and as we talked and sipped our tea, I asked her if she remembered the meeting. She said she did indeed and was kind enough to say that she remembered the "nice young man" who spoke for the other side. Of course, I told her that I was that speaker, and we had great fun recalling the night in Poughkeepsie.

Fiorello La Guardia ran for Congress that year, and although he was not a full-fledged Socialist or a member of the Socialist Party, he ran on the Socialist ticket. I got to know La Guardia fairly well—not intimately, but well enough for him to recognize me when we met at frequent intervals in the campaign that year. I never did meet him after he became Mayor of New York, not even when he visited St. John's. On that occasion, spectators witnessed the unbelievable scene of America's most colourful Mayor and St. John's equally colourful Mayor, Andrew G. Carnell, throwing their arms about each other and engaging in a fierce and funny struggle, each to be more colourful than the other.

Clarence Darrow often came to New York—Darrow, the towering giant of the American courtroom; the satanically brilliant orator who could reduce even stern judges to tears; the genius who rejected the opportunity which any other lawyer would have fought to get, that of a jury trial, and elected to place the lives of his young clients, Loeb and Leopold, in the judge's hands and won their lives for them. Frequently I hurried to the halls where he engaged in debate with some of America's ablest and most eloquent speakers. "Is the Human Race Worth Working For?" For the affirmative, John Haynes Holmes, the humanitarian; for the negative, Clarence Darrow, the humanitarian—Darrow, who had throughout his life fought for the underdog and for every great cause, arguing with supreme skill against every principle that he had ever held and still held dear! Can there be more powerful, unalloyed, intense intellectual pleasure than hearing a debate like that? He debated with Scott Nearing, then a far-to-the-left Socialist, destined to go so far leftward as perhaps to lose the title Socialist and acquire that of Communist. And he debated with Norman Thomas—oh, if only one could bring back moments like those!

I was one of the millions who signed the petition to President Harding for the release of Eugene V. Debs from Leavenworth. In that institution, the thousands of prisoners would stand as Debs came into the dining hall and sit only after he had done so. David Karsner, editor of the *Call's* Sunday magazine, who wrote the book *Talks With Debs at Terre Haute*, used to tell me much about those talks. Harding, who will never be accused of being one of America's greatest presidents, was nevertheless magnanimous enough to send for Debs. Debs travelled to Washington, unaccompanied by prison officials, where Harding chatted briefly with him in the White House. It is difficult to describe the excitement among the Socialists of New York when Debs made his first speech after his release from prison. Twenty thousand jammed Madison Square Garden that night and paid tens of thousands of dollars to hear him, and thousands of others tried vainly to get in. The tall, gaunt, bald, saintly looking, humorous Debs, America's greatest orator since Wendell Phillips, with a voice that could charm laughter, tears, and anger out of any audience; Debs, the idealist, philanthropist (his guardian-companion had to watch him narrowly to see that he didn't give away his topcoat or the last dollar in his pocket), this genius at making friends for his cause and, whether he wished it or not, for himself—the pandemonium broke out as those in the higher galleries glimpsed his entry into the Garden, surrounded by forty or fifty uniformed policemen, who had their work cut out to shield him from those who wanted to shake his hand or clap him on the back, or just touch him. Thunderous applause and wild cheering broke out from those higher galleries, the greater crowds below realized that he was among them, and men went into a mad delirium of joy. The cheering and cries were like the roaring of the sea, and they lasted for twenty-three minutes. I timed it by my watch, for I had expected something like this to happen. It is one of the regrets of my life that I never met Debs personally, but I attended each of his four or five great meetings and walked out on air from each of them, a better man than when I went in.

Big Bill Heywood, the tremendously able leader of the IWW (Industrial Workers of the World, known as the Wobblies) was out on bail when I interviewed him. The very next day, he skipped his bail and smuggled himself away to Moscow. It was in Moscow that he died, and it was in Moscow, at the Kremlin Wall, that I pointed out to Richard Nixon the plaque that the Soviet Union had erected to Heywood's memory, close to the plaque commemorating that other remarkable American, John Reed, who wrote the first great book on the Russian Revolution of 1917, *Ten Days that Shook the World.*

I spent a very large part indeed of the five years in New York going to political meetings of all kinds, particularly Socialist meetings, and attending countless lectures at the Rand School and at the Labor Temple at the corner of Fourteenth Street and Second Avenue, where I took the lectures on philosophy given by Will Durant.* I often heard Durant debate with Harry Wadsworth Longfellow Dana at the famous Cooper Union Institute in Cooper Square. There Everett Dean Martin delivered his famous lectures on Social Psychology; I took lectures from him for two or three winters.

Wherever there was an outstanding speaker, if I knew about it, I was there to hear him, often gate-crashing to do so. I heard Bertrand Russell speak or debate several times, and I had to gate-crash to hear him in the Horace Mann auditorium of Columbia University. The hall was jammed, and John Dewey himself was Russell's chairman. Russell spoke for possibly three-quarters of an hour, and if he had spoken in Aramaic, I would have understood him as readily; for in fact I didn't understand a single, solitary sentence of his speech. Suddenly, about half-way through, something happened that made me think that I was not alone, that perhaps most of the audience were suffering from the same failure. It was when Russell, to give what I'm sure he felt was a primitively simple explanation of a point that he was making, pointed to a large brass urn containing a flower that stood on the stage and said, "We are all now looking at this object over there. [He pointed.] I see what I call a brass urn with a flower. No doubt you see what you call a brass urn and a flower. But how can we ever know that what I call a brass urn and flower are what you call a brass urn and flower?" And then he added, as though to clinch the matter, "That's clear to you, of course," at which there was a quick burst of almost hysterical laughter from the audience, in which I joined. It was after that night that I christened Russell "a brain on two spindly legs".

While I was in New York, I had the exciting experience of interviewing Russell. It was in his bedroom in the home of Dr. Horace M. Kallen, the head of the New School of Social Science, with whom Russell was staying. The philosopher was leaving that morning by steamship for England, but Dr. Kallen told me to go on up to Russell's room. When I tapped on the door, Russell called for me to come in, and I found him in bed. I introduced myself as from the

*These lectures he eventually published as the highly successful *Story of Philosophy*.

New Leader, which he knew, and he said he was at my disposal. I conducted my interview while he got out of bed and dressed, and I noted and reported in my story that he wore no undershirt, and that his top shirt had a collar still attached to it at the back by a collar button, with the tie still in the collar. He had had the proverbial Englishman's cup of tea brought to him in his room, and with no more breakfast than that, he went downstairs and had a taxi brought to the door. I helped him to put his suitcases aboard the taxi and accompanied him to the ship's side as we continued the interview. Bertrand Russell is assuredly one of the half-dozen men in the world that I am proudest to have met.

It was in the 1920s that I undertook the research on what I hoped would be my magnum opus—a collection of popular biographies of some of the great liberators, as I liked to call them. I spent several years, in my spare time, in the great public library at the corner of Fifth Avenue and Forty-second Street, reading and making notes from everything I could find there on the lives of Simón Bolívar, Toussaint L'Ouverture, Louis Kossuth, Joseph Mazzini, Giuseppe Garibaldi, Thaddeus Kosciusko, and one or two others as well. I filled dozens of notebooks, at least one of which I still have. Maybe someday I'll get around to writing that book.

The years in New York were glorious and exciting and wonderful. But I was a Newfoundlander, and when the opportunity came to go home again, I seized it.

8

Agitator, Editor, Author – and Preacher

Oh, London is a fine town,
  A very famous city,
Where all the streets are paved with gold,
  And all the maidens pretty.

George Colman, Jr.

By labour and intense study . . . I might perhaps leave something so written after times as they should not willingly let it die.

John Milton

John P. Burke would have become President of the American Federation of Labour if he had been leader of a larger international union, and even the fact that he was a Socialist would not have deprived him of the honour. He was one of the most universally respected of America's trade union leaders; but his International Brotherhood of Pulp, Sulphite and Paper Mill Workers was just too small to be a springboard to the leadership of the Federation. Burke used to come down to New York from Fort Edward, a small upstate town where his International had its headquarters. Often when he came down, he and I would go for walks together and talk our heads off. One hot day, as we were walking up Fifth Avenue, we came to St. Patrick's Cathedral, and I suggested that we go in to cool off. I had a private reason that I did not mention: the fact that cathedrals have always had an irresistible attraction for me. I had another reason, though, that I was able to tell Burke, and that was the fact that the inspiration for the building of the noble New York edifice was received by Archbishop Hughes of New York while he was on a visit to St. John's for the official consecration of St. Patrick's Church in the West End of St. John's. As we sat in one of the pews and silently revelled in the quiet coolness of the interior, I whispered to Burke, "I imagine you're a Roman Catholic, John?" "I was raised one," he whispered back, "but I don't count myself one any more." He had lost his faith, and I think that perhaps he was substituting Socialism for it. He told me when we came out of the cathedral that his mother, who was still living, would be heartbroken to know his present views.

It was John Burke who set my new course in life. Repeatedly he asked me to go back to Newfoundland and reorganize a branch of his International there. This was Local 63 at Grand Falls. I finally agreed and set off for home in February 1925. What a year that turned out to be for me!

At one time, Local 63 had 1,700 members, but by 1925 the membership, Burke admitted ruefully, was down to 1,400 or possibly fewer. In fact, when I got to Grand Falls, I discovered from Andy Lynch, the secretary of the local, that the membership was not much above 100. Jim Bragg, the local president, confirmed the figure. I realized that it would be a much tougher job to rebuild the organization than it had been to form it originally. It was a far cry indeed from the days of the redoubtable K. M. Brown and the three-month strike in the mill of 1921. It was my first experience in union organizing; but by frequent advertising (mainly through posters on public billboards), endless meetings, and surreptitious gatherings that I held inside the mill itself, I slowly built up the membership over the next few months to about 900. By late spring, the local was in fair shape, and there was no doubt in my mind that I had well earned the $46 a week that the International was paying me. I made friendships at Grand Falls that have lasted to the present.

John Burke was very keen on my going to Corner Brook, where a big new pulp and newsprint papermill was getting into production, to organize Local 64 for him. I was keen too, but there was something else that I wanted to do in Newfoundland: to form some kind of federal organization that would bring together Newfoundland's handful of unions. The unions were pitifully few in number, nearly powerless, generally unknown to each other, and lacking any kind of central body that could inspire them with a sense of cohesion or power. John Burke wrote back a trifle coolly when I told him of my intention to try to form a Newfoundland Federation of Labour. He said that he realized the importance of Newfoundland's having a Federation of Labour but reminded me that the International was paying me to work for Local 63 and to organize Local 64. If my Federation effort didn't take too much of my time away from the International's business, however, he wouldn't object too strongly.

My plan was thus damned with faint praise from my paymaster. Where I would have loved to be free to throw myself body and soul into the task, I was forced to limit myself to writing letters to the few unions in St. John's. In Grand Falls itself, there were locals of the International Brotherhood of Paper Makers, the International Brotherhood of Electrical Workers, and the International Association of Machinists. A majority of the unions in St. John's and all three locals in Grand Falls, as well as my own Local 63, agreed to the formation of the Federation. I was urged to become the Federation's president and was accordingly elected to that office. There were no funds, my freedom of action had been limited (properly, I realize) by John Burke, and there was no one else in a position to exercise the necessary leadership. The Federation died on the vine.

With Local 63 showing every promise of sound development, I

headed off in the early summer of 1925 for Corner Brook. The town was still the crudest of mushroom frontier construction camps, and the mill was really only at the stage of being run in. The paper-makers, electricians, and machinists had already got their locals started, but more than half of the workers who were eligible for membership in Local 64, when it came, were still quite unorganized. By then, I knew at least the linguistic patter of pulp and papermills, and I had some practical experience at organizing or, even more educative, reorganizing a union. So I tackled the job (despite the bungling, ineffectual efforts of a Canadian named Roberts who had been sent in to help) of building the local. I held secret meetings during work hours inside the mill and other meetings in the union hall. The whole population of Corner Brook turned out each Sunday afternoon to watch the arrival and departure of the railway passenger trains between St. John's and Port-aux-Basques, and this provided a ready-made meeting every week! I would mount an empty oil drum and hold forth, practising my oratory, telling of the need for 100 per cent trade union organization in the mill and in the town as well. Absurd stories were told, years afterward, of my organizing and speaking efforts in Corner Brook. One story had me standing on an empty oil drum afloat in the harbour just off from the mill, and from it addressing the workers on shore!

By late summer, Local 64 was well and truly laid and fairly set on its course. Then two things happened in quick succession, one of which again changed the course of my life: I got married, and I walked across Newfoundland.

Throughout my union organizing months in Corner Brook, I boarded with Mrs. Serena Baggs in Curling, three miles westward along the railway from Corner Brook. She was the widow of a sea captain, and she kept three or four "genteel" boarders. She had two lovely daughters, one of whom became the wife of Canada's distinguished radio and television personality Joel Aldred. Visiting with Mrs. Baggs that summer was her cousin from Carbonear, Clara Oates. In a very few weeks, we were engaged and planned to be married in the fall.

I had no car, and the highway between Curling and Corner Brook was almost impassable for a car in any case; so I walked back and forth the six miles along the railway track each day. One day, I was stopped by the four section-men who were responsible for maintaining the track between the two towns. The foreman of the crew said in his Jack-o'-Tar* accent, "You are Mr. Smallwood?" "Yes." "You are the man who have made union in Corner Brook?" "Yes, that's right." "Why you not make union for us fellers?" "What fellows?" "Us fellers, section-men." "Haven't you got a union now?" "No, no union." "What do you want a union for?"

And then I heard the story. Until the spring of that year, the section-men had for many years been getting twenty-two and one-half cents an hour for the crew and twenty-five cents for the foreman. In the spring, the rates had been raised to twenty-five cents and thirty cents; but now the order had come along the line from the general manager in St. John's that on November 1 the pay would be cut back to the former rates. The story made me angry, and I determined to do something about it. A section-foreman and three men would have a stretch of seven to ten miles of railway track to maintain: plucking out rotten sleepers or ties and replacing them with new ones, loosening the gravel and packing it again tightly under each sleeper, straightening rails, driving home the spikes that had loosened, repairing the culverts or building new ones, and a host of other things which made the difference between rails and roadbeds that were safe or unsafe for trains.

Our railway had received a terrible battering in the First World War through being forced to carry more freight than had ever been dreamed of for it, and the whole system was in a run-down condition. "Two streaks of rust" was how one public man described the railway. The rails were too slight, only 50 pounds;† they were old and pieces had spalled off them. In hard fact, the railway was heavily dependent for its continued operation on the very men it was mistreating.

I briefed myself thoroughly on the situation, thought it over, and a few days later sought out that same section crew to tell them that I accepted their invitation. I outlined how I intended to proceed, and they were charmed. Counting the branch lines to Lewisporte, Bonavista, Placentia, Heart's Content, and Carbonear, there were about 600 section-men in the country, four of them every seven or eight miles, spread over a total distance of about 783 miles. Obviously, I couldn't call a meeting. I could only go personally to visit them, and this is what I had decided to do.

**Jack-o'-Tar* is Newfoundland's term for one who is part French and part English.
†Soon after, the rails were replaced with 70-pound stock, and after Confederation these in turn were replaced with 85-pound rails.

I took a train to the western terminus at Port-aux-Basques, and there I held a meeting of the four section-men and eight or ten other railway employees who were not eligible to join any of the existing unions there. I found them to be angry about the forthcoming cut in their pay and quite willing, though not overwhelmingly anxious, to form the new union and pay the fifty-cent fee that I had set as the price of membership. This fifty cents was the joining fee and the first year's dues combined. They all joined, and I wrote their names down in my book and accepted the $6 or $7. Lou George, the railway agent in Port-aux-Basques, was then the president of the Order of Railroad Telegraphers. As that union was not a strong one, Lou asked if I would act for him in soliciting new members as I travelled across the country. I agreed, and I did in fact enlist a fair number.

Next morning, I set out on the walk to St. John's. Eight or nine miles from Port-aux-Basques, I came to the second section crew. I explained the plan to them, entered their names in my book, and collected fifty cents from each of them. That done, I resumed my walk until I came to the third section crew, enrolled them, and collected their fees. I walked that first day about sixteen or seventeen miles and got a bed for the night in some section-man's house beside the track. Next day, I resumed the walk and did eighteen or nineteen miles; and the next day, and the next, day after day. I didn't miss a section crew or fail to get even one man to join. Sometimes a man wouldn't have the half-dollar, but always one of the others volunteered to lend him the money. My longest walk in any day was thirty miles, but much more frequently it was eighteen to twenty. I slept in shacks, on couches in kitchens, on floors. It was good to arrive back in Curling, where my fiancée still was with her cousin Serena, and to have nearly a week's rest. I was able to enroll the labourers, coal shovellers, and others at Humbermouth, a divisional headquarters of the railway, not having even one failure among them. Then I started off again, heading for Bishops Falls, the next divisional headquarters of the railway, roughly half-way across the Island. This meant walking over the Topsails, the highest point of the railway, where epics of suffering and courage among railway crews had occurred for the quarter of a century or so that the railway had been running across the Island. Trains would often be buried in the snow there for ten or even twenty days at a time. I remember one train that was stopped for twenty-three days on the Topsails, the passengers still on board, food down to the minimum scraps, and plucky trainmen hiking to the nearest settlement, forty-one miles away, for more provisions. The only representatives of the railway at this point were one section crew of four and the railway agent, a young fellow named Cluney Adams, who had a one-room shack containing the telegraph key, his bed, a kitchen table, and a few dishes. I slept on the floor of the shack that night.

In Bishops Falls, I was able to have a few days' rest and to enroll two section crews and a number of men who worked around the divisional headquarters. The next rest I got was at the nearest divisional headquarters to St. John's, Clarenville, except for a day and night I spent with Sir William Coaker at his home in Port Union, when I did the Bonavista branch. On that branch at Lethbridge, I met the only railroader in Newfoundland who refused point-blank to join the new union.

At Whitbourne, I had the honour and, of course, the pleasure of my second meeting with the great Sir Robert Bond, who had been Prime Minister in the year that I was born and for the eight years after. Bond had a "gentleman's" farm at Whitbourne that he called The Grange. He had a large rambling house on it, and across the way a fairly large barn with dairy cows. He employed one or two men and shipped the milk three times a week by train to St. John's. He had got a grant of a stretch of Crown land that must have amounted to nearly twenty square miles. Eight square miles of it he had earlier sold to his leader, Sir William Whiteway—a piece eight miles long by one mile wide. After I became Premier, I bought from Sir William Whiteway's heirs half of that eight-mile stretch of land, a piece measuring four miles by one mile; later, I passed ownership of it over to my two sons. I didn't need that piece of land, but bought it solely so that the succession of ownership of it would be Bond, Whiteway, Smallwood.

The first time I had met Bond was in 1919. In that year, as a reporter for the *Evening Telegram*, I had attached myself to a delegation of old-time Liberals who were calling on Bond at Whitbourne to try to persuade him to re-enter politics and lead the Liberal Party again. Bond gave a resolute no for his answer.

I had been walking along the railway track for nearly two months, I had worn out several pairs of shoes, and I was down to one quintal (112 pounds) in weight. I had had one adventure after another; I had met my first snowstorm of the season as I trudged along the Bonavista branch line; and I had made acquaintances who are my friends today. From Port-aux-Basques half-way across the Island to Windsor, I had carried my clothes and a few other necessary belongings in a small suitcase slung on a stick over my shoulder. It was anything but comfortable as it swung back and forth in unison with my stride. At Windsor, however, young Gordon Maidment gave me a knapsack, which somewhat resembled the knapsacks you see today on youngsters hiking all about the world, but smaller and much less fanciful. It was an immense improvement over the suitcase.

Having gone down the Heart's Content branch line, I got a lift by horse and wagon across the peninsula from Heart's Content in Trinity Bay to Carbonear in Conception Bay. Here my fiancée lived in the great rambling home of her father and his ancestors, the home where one of the first schools ever held in Carbonear was conducted, and one that contained some very attractive antiques, mahogany furniture, and sterling silver. My fiancée had returned here by the time I reached Carbonear, so we made the necessary arrangements for our wedding before I resumed my walk to St. John's. I simply had to be in the capital before November 1, when the pay-cut was scheduled to come into force.

I was lucky, for having got again onto the main line, as I was walking to the railway station at Avondale, thirty-six miles from St. John's, what should there be also coming toward that station from the direction of St. John's but a freight train, at the end of which was a private car used by the general manager when he travelled. The train stopped, three men got off the private car and walked toward the station, and the four of us actually met in front of the door of the station! It was Herbert J. Russell, the general manager of the railway, an old MCLI friend of mine; Colonel Michael S. Sullivan, then the chairman of the Government's Railway Commission; and the railway's chief engineer, W. F. Joyce.

"Hello," Herb Russell greeted me, "what brings you here? Where are you coming from?" Sullivan and Joyce smiled broadly as I replied, "I guess you know where I'm coming from, Mr. Russell," and he admitted that he did but that he wasn't sure of what I was up to. The papers had learned of my walk across the Island, and bits and pieces had appeared about me from time to time during recent weeks.

I told the group that I had met and talked with every section-man in the country, as well as the divisional headquarters' labourers; that all but one had joined the union; and that we were absolutely determined not to lose the pay increase.

"We can close down the railway, gentlemen," I told them, "because you know the condition of the rails, and the section-men know it; and, what's more important, the locomotive engineers and firemen know it. And we all know that there's not a locomotive engineer on the railway who would be willing to take his train over any length of track that he knew the section-men had not attended to for so much as a week."

"I wasn't expecting this from you," Russell said. "You believe in nationalization, and here we have the biggest example of nationalization in the country."

I admitted that this was true, and that I wanted the railway to succeed now that it was owned and run by the Government. But nobody had the right to expect the railway's success to depend on cutting the pay of the few hundred men who were already the lowest-paid group in the system.

They knew that I carried all the trump cards, and as they travelled across the Island that day and the next, they kept their pledge to me: they instructed the four roadmasters to inform all section-foremen that the pay-cut was off.

Their train went off westward; and as an eastbound express train to St. John's was due to arrive shortly, I decided to call it a day, board the train, and go home. I hadn't actually walked all the way across the Island by the main line, but with the five branch lines thrown in, I had walked a total of 747 miles between Port-aux-Basques and St. John's—197 miles more than the length of the main line.

I reached St. John's by noon that Saturday, and by noon on the following Saturday, I had published the first issue of a weekly paper that I had decided to start, the *New Outlook*. A large religious denomination complained that the name too closely resembled that of their official organ, so I changed my title to the *Labour Outlook*. I mailed a copy free to each of the 600 men who had joined the union. That first issue contained the full story of my meeting with Russell, Sullivan, and Joyce, and told them what they had already heard from their roadmasters. I continued to send them the paper without any charge over and above the fifty cents that they had already paid me.

Then something happened to change things again. Dick Hibbs, an old friend of mine from FPU days, was publishing the *Daily Globe* in the same building and printing plant that had been the home of Coaker's *Fishermen's Advocate*. Coaker had closed down the two daily editions and was now publishing the weekly in a plant that he had set up in Port Union (where it is published to this day). Hibbs was barely making ends meet with the *Globe*, but he wasn't happy with the editor, Dr. Mosdell, the former editor of the *Daily Star*, now defunct. It was in Hibbs' *Globe* plant that I was getting my new weekly paper printed, and a fortnight or so after my paper started, he called me into his office and offered me the editorship of his daily. I had two immediate objections: I wouldn't take another man's job from him, and I was already publishing my own paper. He had prompt answers to both objections. Dr. Mosdell was going in any case, so that I would not be taking his job from him; and he would send the *Globe* every day for three months to my subscribers. I didn't bother to tell Dick that my "subscribers" were really getting a free paper from me. I took the job and thus found myself for the first time editor of a daily newspaper, except for the short period in 1919 when I had been acting editor of the *Telegram*.

The *Globe* was in fact, if not in name, the official organ of the Liberal Party, which was then in opposition to the Tory administration of Walter S. Monroe. The leader of the Opposition was Albert E. Hickman, one of the most aggressive businessmen in Newfoundland and, at the same time, one of the most unsuccessful politicians we have ever had at the head of a political party. Sir Michael Cashin was the real heart, indeed the only driving force, of the Opposition. He was not himself a Member of the House, having retired after about forty years of service. He was very angry with Prime Minister Monroe, but his feelings were relieved to some degree by the actions of his son, the irrepressible Peter J. Cashin, who was a Member of the House. Peter had been elected as a Tory and had sat in the House as part of the Monroe administration. But having quarrelled violently with Monroe, he crossed the floor and sat, if not formally with the Liberal Opposition, most assuredly with them in fact. Indeed, he virtually took over the Opposition, and Newfoundland was to witness some of the most extraordinary events in the House as a result. Peter was inclined to deliver slashing and altogether unparliamentary speeches, for which the Speaker ought to have dealt with him; and one day he was going aboard his former colleagues when one of those colleagues made the mistake of interrupting him with some harmless remark. Peter glared at him and snapped, "The Minister of—interrupts me. Well, now, I'm going to tell the House about him. He's the very man who went around in the Party getting signatures for a round robin to the Premier demanding the dismissal of

Morine."* "That's not true!" exclaimed the Minister. "Oh, yes, it's true enough, and that's not all, for you're the very man who came to my father's house one night and damned the Premier and all your colleagues, and Morine, and told my father that you'd never be satisfied 'til you got Morine out of the Government." "That's a lie!" exclaimed the Minister. "It is no lie," retorted Cashin. "I was there, and I know!" "I didn't see you there," the Minister was unwise enough to say, and Cashin pounced on him in brutal defiance of all parliamentary practice, procedure, and principle. "No, you were too blind drunk to see me!"

Until then, the Chairman (the House was in Committee of the Whole), John C. Puddester, had not interfered, but he decided that this had to stop. "The honourable Member is out of order," he declared. "How am I out of order?" Cashin demanded to know. "The honourable Member mustn't address another honourable Member by name, or address him as 'you', but should address the Chair." A grin of delight overspread Cashin's face. "I'm addressing the Chair," he said triumphantly. "No, you're not addressing the Chair," the Chairman insisted. "Well, I'm addressing what's in the Chair," Cashin grinned back. "That shows that you don't know the difference between me and the Chair," Puddester was unwise enough to say. Cashin replied, half choking with laughter at the wit of his own remark, "To tell you the truth, I don't see much difference between you and the Chair!" What Puddester ought to have done, of course, then and much earlier, was to raise the Committee, leave the Chair, and report these serious infractions to the Speaker.

I witnessed those days and made the implacable decision that if the time ever came when I should have any authority in the House, things would be a lot different. And when I had the authority, and in the first dozen years or more of my premiership, I insisted on decorum and dignity in the House (always allowing for the occasional breaches caused by brief outbursts of temper). I was often criticized for my attitude, but only by those who had not witnessed the terrible disorder of those earlier years in the chamber and had not known the terrible effect upon the minds of most responsible people of the country.

Peter Cashin was admittedly one of the most colourful men ever to

*Sir Alfred B. Morine had been leader of the Government in the Upper House and was one of the stormiest of all figures ever known in Newfoundland politics.

sit in that chamber. He was fluent, rough, and direct, and sometimes not unwilling to do a little plagiarizing. Quite clearly, he had read William Jennings Bryan's "Cross of Gold" speech of 1896: "Having beside us the producing masses of this nation, and the world, supported by the commercial interests, the labor interests, and the toilers everywhere, we will answer their demand for a gold standard by saying to them: You shall not press down upon the brow of labour this crown of thorns, you shall not crucify mankind upon a cross of gold." This is how it came out of Cashin. Having told the House of the misdeeds of the Government and described the consequent sufferings of the fishermen, he cried in ringing tones, "You've crucified the fishermen. You've stabbed him. You've taken a stiletto—a golden stiletto—and stuck it into his belly—and the point has come out through his back—and you've hung your hat on it!"

Sir Michael clearly was getting a vicarious satisfaction from Peter's speeches. He liked me to drop into his office on Water Street to discuss the unfolding political situation. He threw a few dollars into the *Globe* pot every now and then to help keep it going. And he'd demand to know, "What's that fellow Hickman doing to help?" The answer was pretty well always the same. "Nothing."

I used to drop in most days to see Mr. Hickman, who after all was leader of the Party. He was never willing to yield more than the very minimum of his time or thoughts away from the conduct of his large and fast-growing commercial interests. Politics for him was only a pastime, and Liberals in Newfoundland were growing daily more discontented with his leadership, or lack of it.

Near disaster struck the *Globe*. Dr. Mosdell entered an action in the Supreme Court for wrongful dismissal—or more accurately, breach of contract—against the paper. He claimed the sum, large in those days, of $700 for unpaid salary. Dick Hibbs defended himself in court, but Mosdell got the verdict.

Two days later, Mr. Cross, the bailiff, walked into my office and handed me a document from the court which in effect put the broad arrow on the *Globe* building and plant, on the newspaper itself, and on everything connected with it. It was about mid-day, and the paper was due to come off the press at 2:30. But no newspaper would come off the press, Cross told me, until the award of $700 was paid to him for Dr. Mosdell. I assured him that I would get the money, though it might take me a short time. Meanwhile, couldn't I let the printers go ahead and get the paper ready for the press? He pondered that for a moment and then agreed, provided that no papers were actually printed on the press until the money was paid. So, leaving him in possession, I went to Mr. Hickman and explained the situation to him. He didn't want to be bothered and asked if I'd gone to anyone else for help. I said no, and he shrugged his shoulders and said that he was tired of paying bills for the *Globe*. Precious little did he ever pay, as I well knew. So then I went to see Sir Michael Cashin, but he was out. I left word that it was of the greatest urgency that he should contact me the moment he came in. I hurried back to the office and awaited his telephone call, knowing that he virtually had no choice but to pay off Dr. Mosdell's account and allow the paper to publish that very day; for that issue contained a slashing speech that Peter had made in the House a day or so before, and Sir Michael was most anxious to obtain a supply of copies for his own distribution. It was nearly two o'clock before he called me. I explained the situation carefully over the phone, telling him that the bailiff was there in the office sitting beside me. "How much?" Cashin asked succinctly, and I told him. "I'll be right along."

The practice was for the first copy off the press to be brought to me for a quick glance over each page to see that everything was in good order, with no wrong headlines and the like. Sir Michael came into my office, sat in my chair, and as he was handing the cheque to me, a boy hurried up from the pressroom with the customary first copy. I was thus able, as Cashin handed me his cheque, to hand him that day's paper with the remark, "I guess this is the first time you ever paid $700 for one copy of a newspaper, Sir Michael."

I have got a little ahead of my story here, for most of these things happened in the following winter and spring, 1926.

I had been editing the *Globe* for a little less than a month when I was married. The wedding took place in my fiancée's home in Carbonear, and a houseful of relatives and friends attended as the Rev. Walter Bugden of the United Church of Carbonear performed the ceremony. My marriage to Clara Isobel Oates was one of the most fortunate events of my life, though perhaps not always of hers. She has been the soul of loyalty from that moment, a helpmeet in the sincerest meaning of the word, a loyal and loving wife, and a wonderful mother to our three children, and through them to our eleven grandchildren and our two great-grandchildren. I don't know what I would have done without her, for I was then, and have continued for most of my life since to be, the most undomesticated of husbands, devoting by far the greater part of my time and thought to public rather than private family affairs. I have been extremely fortunate in the particular family into which I entered by my marriage.

In 1925, I had reorganized Local 63 at Grand Falls, organized the first prototype of the Newfoundland Federation of Labour, organized Local 64 at Corner Brook, walked over 700 miles along the railway track, successfully prevented a cut in pay for the section-men, started a weekly newspaper, become editor of a daily newspaper, and got married. An eventful year.

My period of editing the *Daily Globe* was one of personal happiness and strong political discontent. In my basic philosophy, if so grand a word may be used to describe it, I was a Socialist. In my politics, I was a Liberal, because I felt that Liberalism in Newfoundland, with its roots set deeply down in the fishing and working classes generally, and its honourable record of taking always the side of the people, was as close as it was reasonable or practical to think the Island could get to Socialism. It was Liberalism that had, through the great Dr. William Carson, waged that original battle for the right merely to live in Newfoundland, to enclose a piece of land, to put a chimney in your house; the historic fight to make the English-appointed governors of Newfoundland live on the Island all year long; the fight to force the Governor to have a small advisory council of local people; the fight for sweeping reform of the Supreme Court; the fight for representative government. It was Liberalism that had brought in manhood suffrage and the secret ballot. It was Liberalism that had built the railway across Newfoundland; Liberalism that had built the great pulp and paper industry at Grand Falls, and again at Corner Brook. All down through the years, it seemed to me, Liberalism had done those things that Socialism would have done, except for the impossible socialization of industry. I found no difficulty whatsoever, as a Socialist, in being a Newfoundland Liberal, and indeed a Canadian Liberal when I became a Canadian. But I was discontented with the state of the Liberal Party in Newfoundland—acutely discontented. I considered it intellectually bankrupt. Politics in the last half-dozen years or more had degenerated into name-calling, vituperation, slander, a barefaced tug of war between the Ins and the Outs.

I wrote for the *Globe* a series of articles under the heading, "What is Liberalism?" They attracted much attention. Sir Robert Bond wrote me a brief letter of congratulation, as did the Chief Justice, Sir

William Horwood. The articles pointed out that people were fast losing faith in parties and politicians; that the differences between the parties were blurred; and that people soon would be saying, "A plague on both your houses." The articles, copies of which I still have, were the only statement of the principles and basic policies of Liberalism in Newfoundland ever written, that I know of. I felt quite strongly Newfoundland's need to be rid of the Monroe administration, which was almost unashamedly pro-merchant and anti-fisherman in its legislation: it had abolished the income tax and the business profits tax; cut the bank tax in half; and greatly increased the ad valorem customs duties and taxes on fishing gear, on tobacco and cigarettes, and on ready-made clothing, leather footwear, and other basic necessities of fishermen and labourers generally throughout the country.

In my view, it was imperative that the Liberal Party, if it was to win, be led again by the Rt. Hon. Sir Richard A. Squires. This meant not only that Mr. Hickman would have to go, but also that Sir William Coaker would have to back Squires. I saw Coaker whenever he came into St. John's from Port Union and pleaded the case. He soon saw for himself that Hickman must not continue as leader of the Party, but realized that it was not going to be easy to get him out. At Coaker's suggestion, I made Mr. Hickman what I thought was a practical proposal. I saw him at his house on Circular Road and suggested that when the Liberals came in power, he should take an appointment to the Upper House and become leader of the Government there; and that he should accept a knighthood. I will never forget the look on Hickman's face or the tone of his voice as he exclaimed that he didn't want a seat in the Upper House, and if he was to be Leader of the Liberal Government he wanted it to be in the Lower House, the House of Assembly; and that he wasn't interested in having a knighthood. This rejection was unexpected, and after a little more discussion, I asked him to tell me frankly what he wanted. I was knocked over by his answer. "I want my money back," he said firmly. "I put $23,000 into the Party's campaign fund last election, and I'm not going out until I get it back." Coaker chuckled when I reported back to him, and we agreed that it wouldn't be all that hard to get Hickman out of the leadership when the time came.

But who should replace Hickman? I was for Squires, but Coaker wasn't so sure. He wasn't convinced that the people, especially the fishermen, would go for it. I argued strongly that not only would the people go for it, but that they'd go for no one else. And so it became my job to reconcile Coaker and Squires, and that was far from easy.

Squires mistrusted Coaker even more than Coaker did Squires, and I seemed to be up against a stone wall. It was during those talks with Squires, at lunch with him at his home at Midstream one day, that I attempted a description of Mr. Hickman: "You're familiar with Joyce Kilmer's poem 'Trees'," I said. "Well, if Albert Hickman saw what must have been some noble trees that inspired Kilmer's poem, he'd whip out a pencil and an old envelope and begin to figure how many board measure feet of lumber he could saw out of them!" Squires laughed appreciatively; but it came my turn to laugh inwardly some weeks after when Squires, forgetting the source of the story, said seriously to me one day, "You know, Smallwood, Albert Hickman is no politician. He just hasn't got the qualities to make a politician. For one thing, he's totally lacking in any kind of imagination except for business. In here at Midstream, I have some beautiful trees growing, and it's a joy for me to stroll around among them. But if Albert Hickman saw them, he'd be wondering how much lumber he could saw out of them."

I couldn't get Coaker and Squires together. Each demanded that the other should express a wish for the meeting, and neither would do so. I attempted a compromise meeting by my invitation at my own four-room flat on Balsam Street, but that didn't work. In fact, it was not until I went to London in early 1927 that I was able to make any headway at all; and then the best I could do was to bring about a meeting between Coaker and Lady Squires. She was spending the winter there and used to have me come to her apartment every Sunday for dinner, and to wander about London and go with her to Spiritualist meetings in Aeolion Hall in the West End. Coaker was on one of his visits to the fish markets along the Mediterranean, and he looked me up when he reached London on his way home. It took a little persuasion, and doubtless Lady Squires was in touch with Sir Richard back in St. John's, but at last she agreed to meet with Coaker (after many vehement denunciations of him) when he came. I left them together, but each of them reported to me afterward, and I was satisfied that progress was being made. I was back in St. John's again before I finally managed to bring the two men together. I had the great satisfaction then of knowing that they had agreed to go together to the country in the election that was due in 1928. Squires won the election 28 to 8 against Frederick C. Alderdice, who had replaced his cousin Monroe as the new leader of the Tory Party and as Prime Minister of the country.

It was during my time on the *Globe* that I decided to publish a Newfoundland *Who's Who.* There never had been one except on a small scale, and I was ambitious to have a full-length volume. I suggested to Dick Hibbs, who controlled the printing plant, that we form a partnership and share the profits fifty-fifty, and he agreed, provided that I did the work. I had the book more than half completed when Hibbs had to stop publishing the *Globe* for lack of funds. This left me without a job, but I determined to finish compiling the *Who's Who* so that it could be published and we could get our profits. But this turned out to be a task requiring much more time than I had expected, especially as Hibbs wasn't in any hurry to publish it. After a few months of intensive work and no income, I reached the end of my tether and accepted Hibbs' offer to buy me out. I got enough money from the sale to pay my steerage fare to England and leave a little with my wife, who went back to Carbonear to live with her parents.

I had long wanted to go to England, and now seemed to be the time. It was late in 1926, and I travelled by the "home" boat to Liverpool. I went up to London by train and had my first adventure on my very first night in England. At the railway station in Liverpool, I bought some English newspapers, including the *Daily Herald*, the Labour Party paper, and on the train to London I looked over the list of meetings that were being held there that night. I chose a meeting of the local Labour Party in the London constituency represented in the House of Commons by Dr. Hugh Dalton. Two or three of those present were Communists, and when one of them pitched into Dalton, I was on my feet in quick reply! My trans-Atlantic accent, horn-rimmed glasses, and general manner of speaking certainly aroused the curious attention of the crowd, but the Communist was back at me in a flash, and then Dalton put his spoke in. That first night in Britain was one I would remember.

What a time I had on that visit to England! I looked up Dr. L. Haden-Guest, the Labour MP for the London constituency of North Southwark. I had met him in Corner Brook in 1925, when he was one of a party of half a dozen British parliamentarians who came to see the new papermill. He and I had gone for one or two walks along the road between Corner Brook and Curling, and had talked much about Newfoundland and the condition of the people. He was glad to see me in London and told me that he would like me to write something for a new magazine that he was about to launch. This was a review specializing in a Socialist policy for the Empire. He was one of a group within the Parliamentary Labour Party who had a special interest in the Empire. George Lansbury was chairman of the group, and Lord Olivier* an interested member—as Sir Sydney Olivier he had written some of the famous Fabian essays. I had one interesting chat with Lord Olivier. It was in a bus, and I happened to sit next to him as we both got on board after coming out of a meeting of the group where the speaker was Stanley Bruce, the Prime Minister of Australia. I did write for Haden-Guest's magazine, and I believe that it was for him that I interviewed the first Canadian Premier that I ever met. This was the Premier of Alberta, and his name, I thought, was very appropriate for a western province of Canada: Greenfield.

Shortly afterward, Haden-Guest fell out with the Labour Party, primarily because of incompatibility between him and the Party's leader, J. Ramsay MacDonald. Haden-Guest went all the way: he resigned his seat in the House of Commons; and in the ensuing by-election in North Southwark, to everyone's surprise, he offered himself as an independent constitutionalist candidate. It was the first election that I had a chance to get into in England, and certainly I wasn't going to miss the opportunity. Not for a moment did I hesitate in my choice of parties. I helped to elect George Isaacs, and so did the whole of the local Labour Party organization to a man and to a woman. Leonard Styles organized the campaign against Dr. Haden-Guest as ardently now as he had done for him before. It was in this by-election that I made my only election speech in England. The great Ramsay MacDonald himself was due to speak at a big outdoor rally in North Southwark, and to make sure that a large crowd would be there to greet him, a relay of speakers was put on to build up the audience and hold their attention. I was one of the relay. Thus, I have always been able, with perfect technical truth, to say that Ramsay MacDonald and I spoke at the same public meeting! I felt that I had every right to do so: I was an admirer of MacDonald, and my wife and I had named our first child after the two men that I admired most at the time, Ramsay Coaker. The mountainous David Lloyd George came down to speak for the Liberal candidate, and of course

*As Sir Sydney Olivier, he had been Colonial Secretary of Jamaica, and he had befriended a brilliant young Jamaican who grew to be a very successful lawyer and Premier of Jamaica, Norman Manley.

I went to hear him. He was a disappointment that night, but at least I can say that I heard him.

I had tea on the Embankment Terrace of the Parliament Buildings with Jimmy Maxton, the wild, brilliant, sweet-faced, sane Clydesider who was possibly the most universally respected revolutionary in the Commons. I had long talks with Fenner Brockway, who, for his sins, ended in the House of Lords. And I met Arthur Henderson, the man who, perhaps more than any other, built the superb organization of the Labour Party. He had represented the Labour Party in Lloyd George's war-time coalition and became Foreign Secretary in the first Labour Government. Henderson paid me a very great compliment indeed. Herbert Tracey, head of the joint publicity department of the Labour Party and the Trades Union Congress, whom I got to know very well, asked me to write a piece for the official organ, the *Labour Magazine*, explaining why it was that organized labour in the United States had not formed a great Labour Party as the British had done. My article attracted a lot of attention and was reprinted in a number of other periodicals. Arthur Henderson told me that, although he had been frequently to the United States, as fraternal visitor to American Federation of Labor conventions and other great labour conferences, it was not until he read my article that he really understood why American labour had not followed the British example.

Herbert Tracey asked me if I knew a man named Harry J. Crowe, and I was astonished by the question. "Why, do you know him?" I queried, and it turned out that he'd collaborated with Crowe in the writing of a book in which Crowe advocated the confederation of Canada, Newfoundland, and—the West Indies! Crowe, of course, was famous in Newfoundland for his successful promotion of large timber developments. He was a lifetime advocate of the union of Newfoundland and Canada. I met him once or twice. At lunch with Tracey one day, I met a man whose name, in some circles in Canada, is well known: John Grierson. He was the first commissioner of the National Film Board of Canada. When I met him, he either had just come back from a tour of Canada or was about to begin it. There was nothing talked about at lunch that day except movie-making.

Father Tom Nangle and I became warm friends in London. He was the enormously popular and respected Roman Catholic padre of the Royal Newfoundland Regiment in the First World War. He had come back to St. John's after the war and led a movement for the building of a great ornamental monument as Newfoundland's war memorial, and thousands followed him. Others, however, had favoured the building of another kind of memorial to Newfoundland's war dead – a small university college. The college idea was led by Dr. Levi Curtis, Dr. W. W. Blackall, and Dr. Vincent P. Burke. Newfoundland was badly split on the issue; but in the end, both factions won, for both memorials were built – the monument on the Queen's Beach, and Memorial University College, which became the foundation of our magnificent Memorial University of today. In 1927, Nangle was in London, representing the Newfoundland Government in the building of the great war cemetery at Beaumont Hamel in France. Sometimes he wore his military uniform as a colonel, but just as often he wore civilian clothes. He was a very attractive personality indeed, and he didn't have an enemy in the world.

Years afterward, when I was Premier, I had a letter from him. He had by then been living for many years in Southern Rhodesia. He had been editor of a newspaper and a member of the Southern Rhodesia parliament, and at the time he wrote to me, he was a tobacco farmer. Having read a small item in a British newspaper that I had succeeded in getting a copper mine going at Tilt Cove, he wrote to tell me that he owned some shares in a mining company that had owned the Tilt Cove deposit, and he wondered if the shares were worth anything. I wrote back and told him that they were worth $1,000 or $2,000, or some such figure, and suggested that he send the shares to a bank in St. John's if he wanted to cash them. He sent them to me instead, and I got the Royal Bank of Canada to handle the transaction. Colonel Nangle was grateful to me, so he wrote back and went on to tell me the story of his life since the days when I had known him in London. He had lost his faith completely, had ceased to be a priest or a professing Roman Catholic, and after a time had married and now had a grown family of whom he was very proud. He told me that his neighbours knew who and what he had been, but did not hold it against him. This explained why he had not accepted my invitation to come, with a couple of dozen other distinguished Newfoundlanders from all around the world, as the Newfoundland Government's guests at the opening of the new campus for the university. Before he died, Colonel Nangle sent me the unique collection of documents he had carefully collected and preserved throughout the wartime career of the Newfoundland Regiment. These will eventually be presented to the most appropriate people to have them in our province.

I got to the meeting, uninvited and unknown, at which the English branch of Leon Trotsky's Fourth International was founded. I went to every Socialist, Communist, Liberal, Tory, philosophical, and religious meeting that it was practically possible for me to attend. I spent much of my time in the House of Commons, and of course in the Public Record Office and the British Museum. If there was an "-ism" to be explained or debated anywhere in London, I tried to get to it—it was like living New York all over again in the English atmosphere.

After the first few nights in the Ivanhoe Hotel in Bloomsbury, near the British Museum, I got a room in a Bloomsbury rooming house, 89 Guildford Street, also quite near the Museum. It turned out to be a well-known address, for directly across the street was the rooming house in which Jacob Epstein had his studio on the top floor. Epstein was not famous then, and not perhaps as careful of his reputation as he might have become in later life; for more than once I saw and heard him in loud voice debate with his very beautiful model standing in their doorway. I have always felt a quarter-inch taller for having lived across the street from one of the great sculptors of this century.

I made the acquaintance of a man whom I had never actually met when he was in Newfoundland, Edward Patrick Morris. He had left Newfoundland in 1918 as Prime Minister Sir Edward Morris, and very soon after arriving in England, he became Lord Morris. We had a splendid talk for two or three hours when I called on him at his office. Morris told me tale after tale of his political life in Newfoundland, and I'm sorry now that I remember only one of them. It was his last General Election, in 1913, and some of his advisors had succeeded in persuading him that the great Coaker was not very strong along the northeast coast; that all that was needed was for Morris himself to make a tour of that coast to hold it, or a substantial part of it, for the People's Party which he led. So the Prime Minister chartered a small steam-driven ship, not much bigger than a tug, and set out on his tour. He met with a pretty rough reception everywhere, but kept on doggedly, always in the hope that the next harbour would be different. And then in one of those "next" harbours, he held a meeting in the local Orange Hall, which was crowded from stem to stern with irrepressible supporters of Coaker and the FPU. He attempted to speak but was met with a ceaseless barrage of catcalls, cheering for Coaker, and shouts of "Down with the Tories". When a crowd of young fellows outside the hall began rolling stones down the steeply sloping roof of the hall, creating inside an absolute pandemonium of noise, Morris finally gave up the meeting and the tour.

He told me that before starting back for St. John's next morning, he went to the home of one man who had been in the audience, in the very front row, who had not joined in the rowdy interruption of his speech but had never taken his eyes off Morris throughout the speech. A woman came to the door in response to his knock, and he asked if he might see the man of the house. She looked uncertain and embarrassed and said that she didn't think it would be any good for Sir Edward to see her husband. Morris pressed the matter, saying that he was not going to embarrass her husband—he wished merely to thank him for the courteous attention he had given him at the meeting last night. The wife stuck to her story that it wouldn't do Morris any good to see him. Morris said again that all he wanted was to thank her husband for his politeness at the meeting. And then she told him that her husband was a very ardent Coakerite, but he had the misfortune to be stone-deaf. It seems too good a story to be true.

I asked Lord Morris, "These stories that you've been telling me of your life in Newfoundland make me curious—do you mind if I ask whether you're happy over here in England?" Morris considered before replying, and then said, "I knew everyone back home, and everyone knew me. I would leave my house in the morning to go to my office, and as I walked along the street to Rawlins Cross and down Prescott Street and along Duckworth Street to my office, everyone I met knew me, and it was 'Good morning, Sir Edward' and 'Good morning, Bill,' 'Good morning, Pat,' 'Good morning, Tom.' Everyone knew me, and I knew everyone. Oh, yes, I had my friends. Over here, well, of course, I have friends too. I like my work, I have a nice home, and of course a seat in the House of Lords." Then he was silent for a moment and resumed, "You're a younger man than I am, and you'll survive me, and being a journalist no doubt you'll write my obituary. Put this sentence in it: 'He was an old tree transplanted'."

During my stay in London, I wrote my first book, a slender volume that I completed in three days and nights on one of my Newfoundland heroes: *Coaker of Newfoundland.* I was proud to have the one illustration in it, a line drawing of Coaker's head, done by an artist who had just before achieved fame as the illustrator of the book *Mathematics for the Millions*, J. F. Horrabin. My book was published by the Labour Publishing Company and sold a few thousand copies in the next year or so.

In the summer of 1927 I returned to Newfoundland and almost immediately set out for Corner Brook, where I had so many friends. Then things happened to me in quick, dizzying succession. I got a job with the new owners of the pulp and paper mill, International Power and Paper Company, whose president, E. A. Charlton, and I became warm friends. The great question of the day in Newfoundland then was whether or not a third pulp and paper mill would be built. If so, then the Gander Lake and Gander River watershed would be its foundation, and the mill itself would be built in Gander Bay at the mouth of the river. In 1927, the International Company had options on the Gander areas and the question in everybody's mind was, would they build?

Charlton sent a small group of men to Gander Bay, under the leadership of a distinguished civil engineer from Toronto, to supervise some physical and topographical surveys in the area. He gave me a job with the group, and I was responsible in particular for the local Gander Bay men who were employed to drill out the area that was to be the site of the mill itself. Parallel lines were cut through the trees as pathways for the drill. It was my job not only to supervise the work itself, but to measure the core brought up in each hole drilled. Each night I would write up my notes, with a diagram of the hole showing how many feet or inches of topsoil, subsoil, sand, pug, or anything else lay between the surface and bedrock. Another group installed water gauges near the mouth of the Gander River and made daily readings of them. Grant Patterson led a group that did topographical surveys.

Most of us boarded in the fine old house of Charlie Rowland. He had lingered on for years in Gander Bay as a sort of watchdog over the timber and other interests of a large company that had once operated there, and he was vastly interested in the possibility of the new papermill. He was full of fun, and night after night engaged all of us in hot debate on all kinds of topics—there was nothing else to do at night in Gander Bay, and we enjoyed it greatly.

I was the victim of one of his practical jokes. Late one Sunday afternoon, there came a knock on the back door of the house. Charlie Rowland, who answered the knock, came into the front room where we were all sitting and told me that I was wanted at the door. I went out and was greeted by two men who enquired, "Are you Mr. Smallwood?" When I admitted it, they asked earnestly, "Will you take the service tonight, sir?" "The service?" I asked puzzled. "Yes, sir, in the United Church here." "You mean you want me to take the service in church tonight?" I asked in great surprise; and they said yes, it was only once every few months that they got a minister to hold service for them, and as I was a minister, they thought that I might be willing to take the service in their church tonight. At once, I knew that this was Charlie Rowland's doing, but I merely told them frankly that I was no minister, that they were quite mistaken. They were disappointed and said that they had truly hoped that I would take the service. "What do you mean by 'taking the service'?" I enquired. "I have never taken a service in my life, and I just wouldn't know how to do it. If it came to preaching the sermon, I might make a hand at that, but not taking the service." They brightened at this and explained that it was the sermon that they wanted. They would take the service themselves, if I would only come and preach the sermon. I made a quick decision and told them that I'd to it. "What time does the service start?" I asked them, and they told me 6:30. "I'll be there," I promised, and they went off happily.

When I came back into the front room, Charlie obviously was dying to know what happened, but I made no reference whatever to the call. At last, he could stand it no longer and asked me point-blank, "What did the two men want?" "Oh, nothing in particular," I answered nonchalantly. "They thought I was a minister and wanted me to take the service in their church tonight." There was a laugh around the room, and Charlie Rowland pursued the matter. "And are you going to take it?" "No," I replied, "but I am going to preach the sermon." They didn't know whether to believe me or not, but I went and got the New Testament and hunted for the verse that I intended to use as the text of my sermon. I knew exactly what I intended to say.

At 6:30, I walked up the road to the church and went into it in my long rubber boots and rough clothes—I had no others with me—to find the little church packed. They had waited there for precisely one hour before I arrived, as a result of the difference in time—"God's time" versus daylight—observed by the people of Gander Bay and by us in Charlie Rowland's house. I was led to the front row pew, and my two visitors of the afternoon proceeded to conduct the service. When it came time, one of them introduced me; and I took my place, gave out the text, and launched into my sermon. It was my first, and I had no idea how long it would take me, but I was told next day that everybody in the church had been very pleased with it and had declared their willingness to stay all night and listen as long as I wanted to speak. My sermon lasted just over an hour! Either because of the sermon or for some other reason, the mill never was built in Gander Bay.

Back in Corner Brook, I decided to publish a new paper. The *Humber Herald*, I called it. There was a weekly newspaper at Curling, three miles away, owned by the International Company. It was a fine staid old paper, but I felt that Corner Brook needed more of a crusading type of publication. Jonathan M. Noel was a fine, old-fashioned Newfoundland outport shopkeeper from Freshwater near Carbonear, and he had built himself a large building on the main street of Corner Brook's west side. He sold dry goods and bits and pieces of hardware, did picture framing, and took orders for photographic enlargements; and in between these and a hundred other such activities, he continued the small commercial printing enterprise that he had started back home in Freshwater. He had a one-storey addition on his large wooden building where he did his printing. I was astonished to discover that he held the compositor's "stick" upside down in his hand, set the type in it upside down, and did almost everything in reverse. He had never seen it done by anyone else, was entirely self-taught, and was much surprised when I told him the truth; but he didn't change. He was enormously thrilled when I suggested that he let me print my new paper in his little print shop. I set up the type myself by hand, letter by letter, word by word, out of my head, without bothering to write anything beforehand. I found that there was barely enough type in the plant to make one tabloid-sized page. When that one page was set, Mr. Noel locked it up in the proper forme, put it on his small foot-pedal press, and printed the 1,000 copies. It was my job then to wash the type and distribute it, letter by letter, back into the type-case. Then I set up the next page, following the same method, and this page too was put on the press by Mr. Noel and the 1,000 copies printed, and so with the other two pages.

The first issue of the *Humber Herald* consisted of four tabloid pages and sold for one cent. It sold out completely, and Mr. Noel was beside himself with pleasure and excitement, to think that he had lived to see the day when a newspaper was actually printed in his little plant. I worked harder than ever the second week, made up the paper to six pages, and got Mr. Noel to print 1,500 copies, which also sold out to the last copy. In the third week, I worked even harder, and got out 2,000 copies of an eight-page tabloid. The fourth issue was the same size as the third, but sold more copies.

By now, everyone was interested in the *Humber Herald*, and I decided to form a company that would raise the capital to buy a big press, a linotype machine to set the type mechanically, and some new display type for the advertisements that I was having no difficulty in obtaining from the Corner Brook businessmen. Jonathan Noel agreed to put his little plant into the company for shares; Merve Pickering, a boss-machine tender in the mill, put some money into it. I got in touch with the Sears Company in Toronto, and they sent a man down, and I arranged to get the press and linotype on easy terms, with a comparatively small downpayment. This settled, I suspended publication so that we could get ready for the larger venture. I helped to dig out the big hole in the floor of the annex, for we had to install heavy concrete foundation walls to hold up the heavy press and leave a pit underneath it. Then I borrowed a wheelbarrow and went up and down the unpaved street (which in my first issue of the *Humber Herald* I had named Broadway), picking up rocks and stones and going back to the building with load after load of stones to be used for the concrete that we needed. It was the second time in my life that I had worked with stones going into the concrete of a newspaper building.

The new *Humber Herald* flourished, and I was able to devote more time to furthering my ambition to be the Liberal candidate for the Humber constituency in the General Election that was due to take place in the fall of that year, 1928. I went into every nook and cranny of Humber District from Kitty's Brook, near the Topsails, all the way out to the entrance to Bay of Islands, including Humber Arm, Penguin Arm, and Goose Arm, until I was known to just about every living soul in the great District and knew most of the voters in it. I held meetings in many places and addressed meetings of lodges, church groups, and unions. I walked out and back over the rafted ice along the shore of Humber Arm to Lark Harbour.

Of course, I wrote to the leader of the Party, Sir Richard Squires, keeping him intimately informed of my every move, with the obvious purpose of persuading him that I could win the constituency for him. John A. Barrett also wanted the Liberal nomination, and he too was writing to Sir Richard. When he didn't get it, he ran as the Tory candidate.

And then—disaster! A letter arrived from Sir Richard telling me that he had decided to run in Humber District himself. Furthermore, he wanted me to be his campaign manager, as he would not be able to visit the constituency for more than a day or two at the most. This was because he intended to travel throughout the whole country by train, steamship, motorboat, and sailing vessel. It was a devastating blow to my hopes when I picked up the letter at the post office and read it. I rebelled instantly, but put the letter in my pocket and started off on a long walk to Mount Moriah and back to the post office. The ten-mile walk cooled my mind and allowed me to think clearly. I went up to the telegram window and sent this telegram to Squires. "Not for any other man would I do this but I will step aside and manage your campaign as well."

The word quickly got around that I was not to be the candidate, and very soon Tommy Coombs, the most prominent Tory in Corner Brook, asked me to drop in to see him. He commiserated with me and told me that he thought that I had got a rotten deal. "I wouldn't put up with it if I were you," he declared, and I asked him what he would do. "Do! I'd run anyway, if I were in your shoes, as an Independent, an Independent Liberal." "And where would I get the money to finance my campaign?" I asked, knowing precisely what his answer was going to be. "I'm authorized to finance your campaign generously, from start to finish," he assured me. I smiled back at him. "And split the Liberal ticket and let Mr. Barrett in! Nothing doing, Tommy. I'll keep my powder dry for another day."

I organized a great election campaign for Squires, aided enthusiastically by Michael A. Foley, Bob Simmonds, Jim Penney, Sammy Hilliard, Pierce Fudge, and other staunch Liberals. Squires came to Corner Brook by a three-car train that he had hired in St. John's. I had a boat waiting for him, and the two of us went off on a whirlwind two-day tour of the Bay. I acted as chairman for his every meeting, and as his voice was failing, I did most of the talking, to give the customers their money's worth, so to speak. We had an arrangement whereby I could let Squires know when, in my judgement, he had spoken long enough to make the right impression on his audience. I would scrape my shoe back and forth on the floor of the platform until he showed by a nod that he had heard and understood. We wound up the campaign the night before polling day with a great rally in Curling, followed by the meeting to end all meetings, in the Regent Theatre in Corner Brook. To start with, we couldn't even get into the Regent! Every law of safety was broken. The hall was a solid mass of flesh from wall to wall, from the entrance door and outside on the street up to the edge of the platform and on the very platform itself! We got in by climbing up a ladder at the back of the building and squeezing in through a window backstage. We had to push our way through the crowd on the platform to get to the front of it, and when we did, a pandemonium of cheering broke loose. I spoke first, and in that day of no voice amplification, no microphones, and no loud speakers, my countless street-corner speeches in America stood me in good stead. Even so, in my last speech of that campaign, my tenth for that day, I had to cup my hands about my mouth to try to make my voice carry. When I introduced Squires, I had to squirm around behind him, and he squirmed to get in front of me—such was the jam of people. Though his voice was very good, Squires was dog-tired, bone-weary, and his mind befuddled from sheer exhaustion. It didn't really matter, for it was not his speech but the sheer magic of his person that won the day.

He asked me during that last day what, in my opinion, his majority would be. I said frankly that I hadn't thought of it that way, but that if he wanted to know I'd figure it out. I then took every polling station in the constituency, estimated the proportion and the number of voters who would vote, and wrote two columns of figures: one for Squires, the other for Barrett. Then I added up the two columns: Squires 3,050; Barrett, 615. Squires laughed at my forecast. "After you've been through as many elections as I have," he reminded me, "you'll learn to make a realistic forecast." "No doubt," I admitted. "But this is how the vote is going to turn out tomorrow."

And it did. John Barrett got 632 votes—I was 17 votes short. Squires got 3,011—I was 39 votes out. I acted as scrutineer for Squires at the counting of the ballots—it went on from midnight to seven the next morning—and was the first to congratulate him on his election. As we shook hands, he said, "Smallwood, that is the most astonishing election forecast that I ever heard of."

9

More Training – for Something or Other

All Government without the consent of the governed is the very definition of slavery.

Jonathan Swift

In the long run every Government is the exact symbol of its people, with their wisdom and unwisdom.

Thomas Carlyle

Democracy is the recurrent suspicion that more than half of the people are right more than half of the time.

E. B. White

Squires had been swept back into office, but the times were not good. People who complained about unemployment and hard times in 1929 didn't dream of what was ahead of them: the Wall Street-crash to come in the fall of that year, the start of the world depression, the rapid intensification of the universal revolution, all to be reflected in Newfoundland by such poverty and misery as we had never known—and we had not known much of anything else. Squires was soon in trouble; but little did he think that, by comparison with what was coming, he really was in clover in the summer of 1929.

I was still editing the *Humber Herald* but was rapidly losing my taste for it. Merve Pickering, its major shareholder, had lost his job in the mill and was forced to leave the country. Jonathan Noel acquired his shares and was now virtually the owner of the company, for I had not been the kind of shrewd financier who would provide, or connive, for his own future. Moreover, Noel repeatedly interfered with my editing. I therefore welcomed all the more a letter that I got from the Prime Minister early in 1930, asking me to come to see him in St. John's. I went with alacrity, leaving the *Humber Herald* to Mr. Noel, who lost no time in selling it to the papermill company, which already owned Corner Brook's *Western Star*. The *Herald* was merged with the *Star*, and that was the end of it.

In St. John's, I reported to Squires, but he gave me no hint at all of his reason for sending for me. He merely asked me to stand by, and so I continued to board at the Brownsdale Hotel on New Gower Street. I hung around for two or three weeks, growing more curious and impatient every day. And then at last Squires telephoned for me, and I hurried to his office.

"The plant that prints the *Watchman* is going up for sale," he told me briskly. "I want you to go to the sheriff's office and buy it for me. Here's the money,"—he handed me a wad of bank notes—"it's $3,000, but maybe you'll get it for less." The *Watchman* was the Opposition Party's propaganda weekly newspaper. It was edited and managed by my friend Charlie Jamieson.* The printing plant was owned by George H. Andrews, and in it he had for a while been printing a newspaper edited by Alexander Parsons. The paper had folded; Parsons had sued it for unpaid salary and had got a judgement in his favour and a court order for the sale of the plant by public auction to satisfy the debt.

When I got to the sheriff's office, I found only one other potential buyer present: George Andrews himself. He kept bidding me up and wouldn't stop until the price was several hundred above the $3,000 that I had in my pocket. It was finally knocked down to me. I quickly obtained the key from the sheriff, hurried to the building on George Street (almost opposite the former site of the Salvation Army soup kitchen!) and went straight to Charlie Jamieson's office. Quickly I found what I was looking for: the printed mailing list of the *Watchman*! All of the Opposition Members of the House of Assembly had provided mailing lists for their own constituencies and paid so much a year to have the paper sent each week to a select number of voters. I dearly wanted that list, and to make sure that it stayed hidden, I took it back to the hotel. That afternoon, Charlie Jamieson came hurrying into the building and to his office, which was now mine, and said that he had come to get his mailing list. I told him to go ahead and get it, but when he looked in the drawer where it had been kept it wasn't there! He complained, but I waved him aside. "Don't bother me about your mailing list, Charlie. I have my work to do."

And I did. I had offered George Andrews a job and got hold of a couple of other printers, and they were hard at it early that Wednesday afternoon, setting up in type the pieces that I was pouring out from my typewriter for a new weekly newspaper that I had guaranteed Squires I would have out on Saturday—the *Watchdog*. The newsboys turned up Saturday morning as usual, and soon the streets of St. John's echoed with the sound of the boys calling, "*Watchdog! Watchdog!*" Although, truth to tell, most of the boys thought they were still selling the *Watchman*, and so called in their cries. Certainly every Tory bought the paper. But no longer was it their paper. Over the editorial column, where there had appeared each week a large picture of the Opposition leader, Frederick Alderdice, there now appeared a handsome picture of the Prime Minister, Sir Richard

*His son, Donald, was elected Liberal Member of Parliament and became a member of Prime Minister Trudeau's Cabinet.

Squires. And the reading matter!—that was an offence to heaven itself in the mind of any dedicated Tory. I mailed a copy every week to each name on the Opposition's mailing list.

Rarely have I had so much fun, and the fun was all the greater because for a while the Opposition couldn't find another printing office able and willing to print their paper; and, above all, because they sued us for what I might call plagiarism! They claimed that we had deliberately published a paper intended to deceive people into believing that they were buying the *Watchman.* The shrewd and competent Leslie R. Curtis was my lawyer (he was Sir Richard's law partner), and the brilliant Harry A. Winter was the Opposition's lawyer. Supreme Court Judge James Kent heard the case, and he had all he could do to keep a straight face as I explained that we were printing the *Watchdog* in the same printing plant that had printed the *Watchman*, using the same linotype, the same type generally, the same press, so that there couldn't help being some similarity of appearance. But we had been very careful to change the name (even I found it hard to keep a straight face here), for after all who could mistake a watchman for a watchdog? Judge Kent threw the case out.

Unemployment and destitution had sucked Newfoundland into their maw. The people were desperate. They didn't know that the depression was universal, so they blamed Squires for the hard times. One day, I was in Victoria Village, as it was called then, a famous Liberal stronghold; and one of a group of men with whom I was chatting asked, as one Liberal to another, "Why is Squires letting this state of affairs go on?" The group listened expectantly for my explanation. Virtually every man in Victoria was unemployed. I answered, "He's letting it go on here in Newfoundland for exactly the same reason that he's letting it go on in Canada and the United States." I might as well have used Sanskrit.

And then there was the riot. In April 1932, a big meeting was called at the Majestic Theatre, and Eric Bowring was to be its chairman. So I went to the Finance Department and searched back through the public accounts for a quarter of a century, and in a special edition of the paper described in detail the large sums of public money that had gone to Bowring's firm. As the crowds poured into the Majestic that night, free copies of the *Watchdog* were handed out at the door. I went to the meeting myself, and before it was over, I rose to my feet to ask the chairman if I might be permitted to speak.

Gentleman that he was, he said Yes, of course, and invited me to the stage. I met an uproar of cries from the audience: "Put him out!", "Throw him out!", "Give him a hearing!", "Let's hear what he has to say!". I strolled up the aisle, and Eric Bowring himself reached down to help me onto the platform. "Beware of the Greeks when they come bearing gifts" was my opening sentence. "Beware of Water Street when they come with political advice!" And from there I launched into a bitter attack on Water Street's merchants. I will never know how the meeting would have ended. I was near the wing of the stage, and before I could do anything, I was seized by two men who lurked behind it. They took turns holding and punching me, and finally threw me bodily into the street.

Next day, the merchants declared a holiday. All the department stores were closed, and the employees understood well that their employers expected them to march in the parade that had been announced. The parade marched to the House of Assembly, a mob quickly formed, every window in the building was smashed, and furniture, including a piano, was dragged out of the building and set on fire.

Five of us had barricaded ourselves in the Speaker's room adjoining the main Chamber: Sir Richard and Lady Squires (she had been elected to the House), Inspector General Charles H. Hutchings of the police, the Hon. James Bindon, and myself. It was dark by now, and perhaps as many as 10,000 men jammed the grounds of the building. A continual roar of voices filled the air, and rocks and bricks kept hurtling into the room where we were. Then in the darkness came a knocking on the heavy mahogany door that we had bolted and barred, and a voice called, "Are you there, Sir Richard? Are you there? We have come to escort you out." It was L. Edward Emerson, one of the Opposition Members of the House, later to become Commissioner for Justice and subsequently Sir Edward Emerson, Chief Justice of the Supreme Court. When no one answered, Emerson repeated his question and said urgently, "We're afraid they may set fire to the building—you'd better let us take you out." It was Lady Squires who answered. "You should have thought of that," she said bitterly, "when you people got up this parade." "My God," exclaimed Emerson, "are you there too, Lady Squires? You'll simply have to come out with us." She declared that she would never leave. I whispered urgently to Squires that he should make her go. He did, and the group got her safely out through the least conspicuous part of the building. Then they came back for Sir Richard, and again I advised him to go. With his glasses off and a cap pulled down over his eyes, he left, guided by an escort of half a dozen men. He had got through the thinnest part of the crowd and was almost on Bannerman Road, on the eastern side of the building, when he tripped over an iron gate that had been smashed down. This attracted the attention of some of the crowd, and the shout went up, "Here he is—Squires is here!" In a trice, Squires was surrounded, and the mob began to move with him through the front gate across Military Road and into Colonial Street, shouting, "Drown the bastard!" "Down to the harbour with him!" Fortunately, the street was too narrow to allow the whole mob to pass through together. As Squires was hustled along, a man standing in his own doorway said urgently, "Come in here, Sir Richard," and Squires slipped inside, hurried through the hallway, and went out through the back door of the house into the garden. Someone broke an opening into the fence to allow him to go through into the garden behind, and from here he gained entry through the back door into a house on Bannerman Street, which runs parallel to Colonial. There, he put his glasses back on and telephoned for a car. Meanwhile, crowds of people continued to push down Colonial Street, not realizing that Squires had been rescued. That night, Sir Richard was driven to three different homes to elude the mob.

But the mob was no longer after him—it was after rum or any other alcohol that could be found. Using a large wharf stick as a battering ram, some men smashed their way into the Liquor Control building at the corner of Springdale Street and Water Street (the old *Plaindealer* building, where I got my first job) and began a systematic looting of the liquor. Like a bucket brigade, they kept passing the bottles through to the crowd outside. Smashing and looting went on about the town, and the police were quite incapable of controlling the crowds. The Great War Veterans' Association (now the Canadian Legion) mobilized its membership, and for the rest of the night until well past daylight next day, squads of war veterans marched through the streets.

Jimmie Bindon and I left the building a little after Sir Richard by going in through the Chamber, down the winding stairway to the ground-level basement, and out through a smashed window. We walked diagonally across Bannerman Park to the gate at the corner of Circular and Rennie's Mill roads, and then separated. I went home and, after a quick meal, insisted on going out again to walk about the city and see what was happening. My two brothers-in-law, Fred Cook and Bill Green, decided to come with me for protection. I wore a cap and walked between Fred and Bill, and the whole time I kept one hand in my pocket, holding my weapon—a carpenter's hammer! I had no need to use it, for no one recognized me.

Next morning, the town was full of rumours. Squires had resigned. The Government was out. The Governor had sent for Alderdice to form a new administration. British naval ships were on the way in to the harbour. I went to Squires' law office on the top floor of the Bank of Nova Scotia building, and while I was chatting with Leslie Curtis, who should come in but Sir Richard himself. He stayed only a few minutes, for his well-known car and his chauffeur, Tom Crossman, were parked at the curb and there was a chance that another mob would gather. "Is it true," I asked him, "that you've resigned?" "My body may resign," he smiled back at me, "but I never." What Squires was attempting to establish that morning was the fact that he was carrying on as usual, visiting his law office as he did briefly every day. He left us after a few moments and went straight to the Prime Minister's office. Again his car was parked at the curb, and when Squires came back down the steps from his office, there was a group of a couple of hundred or more clustered between him and the car. Smiling right and left, he stalked through the crowd to the car, and not a hand was laid on him. Rather, there was a sort of grudging admiration. But if no hand was laid on him, one was laid on his pipe. It was clenched between his teeth, when one fellow reached out his hand, grabbed the pipe out of Squires' mouth, and stuck it in his own.

All of this, of course, was the poorest of poor preparation for a General Election! Squires decided to go to the people, and the election was held in early June 1932. The result was inevitable—Squires was wiped out. He was even defeated personally in Trinity South, where his successful opponent was Harold Mitchell. I had no difficulty getting a candidacy this time; but before I even mentioned it to Squires, I worked with him day and night helping him to get candidates to run in the various constituencies, drilling the candidates individually, making preparations for their departure to their respective constituencies, writing Squires' manifesto, and attending to the thousand details that go with the waging of an election campaign. I revelled in it!

The candidates had left for their districts and Squires himself was about to head off for Trinity South before I actually mentioned a candidacy to him. There were two districts not filled, and Squires said promptly, "Yes, and I want you to go up to Fortune Bay and lick this fellow Mosdell." Dr. Mosdell, who had edited Squires' paper, the *Daily Star*, had run as a Liberal candidate in Fortune Bay in the 1928 election, but after a couple of years in the House, he had crossed the floor and declared himself to be an independent Liberal. It was as an independent Liberal that he was running in this election. "I'll go to Fortune Bay if you insist," I assured the Prime Minister, "but it's not where I would like to go." "Where would you like to go?" Squires asked, and I told him Bonavista South, which still had not been filled. Why did I want to go there? I explained that Fortune Bay was overwhelmingly a Church of England area, and I was a non-conformist. Bonavista South was a district that I could cultivate. Those were all-important considerations in Newfoundland politics then and for many years afterward. I knew, I told him, that I wouldn't be elected even in Bonavista South this time, but at least I would be able to make myself known and thus lay a foundation for the future. Squires agreed and gave me $250 as my campaign fund. I spent some of that to get a tiny leaflet printed with my picture for distribution and set off for the District. At Port Union, I went to The Bungalow and had breakfast with Sir William Coaker. "You're going to get yourself killed in Bonavista," Coaker told me cheerfully. "The District is in a bad mood—the whole country is in a bad mood. I'm afraid there's going to be trouble, unemployment—the fishermen aren't able to get supplies to go fishing. It's no time for an election, and if I were you I would just go quietly around the District and hold no meetings and just put in an appearance." Encouraging advice for a young man contesting his first election! "What parts of the District have you been in?" Coaker asked me. "None, no part," I answered. "You've never been in the District at all?" Coaker asked in great surprise. "No, never. I've never set foot anywhere in it." "What people do you know there?" Coaker wanted to know. "Not a soul," I had to admit, and Coaker shook his head. "Take it very easy when you get there," he cautioned again.

I didn't take his advice. I fancied myself as a speaker, and I was reluctant to give up the one advantage I had. But partly because of Coaker's advice and more because of my strong feelings of disillusionment with the state of both Newfoundland's economy and its politics, I waged a campaign that must surely have been unique in the country's history up to that time. I did two things: I went down among the flakes and stages of the fishermen, mixed with the men, stood on the occasional upturned boat on shore and gave them a little talk, visited many of them at their homes, and generally tried to make friends with them; and I held as big a meeting as I could organize in each settlement. I canvassed among the men during the day, then addressed them all together at night. That in itself was not what made my campaign so unusual, but rather the nature of my speeches. I told the people bluntly that I could see no hope whatever for Newfoundland unless very drastic changes were made.

"Close down the House of Assembly," I cried. "Bolt and bar the doors and windows of Colonial Building. Do away with the Government—not just the Government we have now, but any government. Send a petition to the King asking him to appoint a Commission to run the country for the next ten or fifteen years."

Then I developed the theme. "It's time to have a long political holiday. Party politics has become meaningless except to ruin us—just a continual squabble between the Ins and the Outs. Both parties have gone intellectually bankrupt."

And then I tried to drive home my meaning. "Are there any men here, or women, in this hall who really believe that it'll make any real difference to them which side wins in the coming election? If you do, you probably believe in Santa Claus, too. Don't waste shoe leather. If you live next door to a polling booth, at least you won't wear out any shoe leather going in to vote. If you live a hundred feet or more, don't waste that much precious shoe leather!"

And then I went out on a limb. "Mark my words, whoever wins in this election, they won't be there long. It might be six months, or a year, or a year and a half—but I guarantee you here and now that inside of two years the House of Assembly will be closed down, the Government will be turned out, and Newfoundland will be under a Royal Commission appointed by the King. I guarantee you this."

In St. John's a couple of weeks after I had had breakfast with him, Coaker told friends of his that he wouldn't be too surprised if I were to get elected. "He's another Morine," he said, and that was intended to be a great compliment. But I wasn't elected—I was badly defeated by my friend Herman Quinton, who had been elected four years before and was running now for re-election.*

*When I launched my campaign for Confederation, Herman became one of my staunch supporters. When we won Confederation, I invited him to be our Liberal candidate in the District of Burgeo-LaPoile and subsequently brought him into my Cabinet as Minister of Finance. He was with me on my first industry-seeking tour of West Germany. He later went to the Senate, and his death not long after was a sad event in my own life.

Squires' party was virtually wiped out in that election of 1932, with only two of its thirty-six candidates elected: Frederick Gordon Bradley in Humber District and Roland G. Starkes in Green Bay.

But no more than six months after that election, my name shone as brightly in Bonavista South as that of an authentic prophet! Everybody remembered my words, and very few now doubted that my prophecies would be fulfilled completely. And, indeed, they were! Newfoundland had truly come to the end of its financial tether, couldn't raise a dollar in the money markets of the world, and was devastated by unemployment and the most acute misery among a semi-starving population. A Royal Commission of Enquiry into Newfoundland's condition was appointed by the British Government, consisting of Lord Amulree as chairman and the Canadians Sir William Stavert and Dr. C. A. McGrath as the members. The secretary of the Commission was the very clever Peter Clutterbuck, who later, as Sir Peter, became Britain's High Commissioner to Canada.* The Royal Commission sat for months, travelled about the country and to Ottawa, examined many witnesses and documents, and in the end recommended precisely what I had prophesied in my speeches in Bonavista South. But I am getting a little ahead of my story.

The shape of my thinking about Newfoundland at that time is best seen in my action on the occasion that every political candidate had long believed to be precious: the night before polling day. That was always the night when candidates would plan to hold their last great shove-off, in the largest settlement in the District, to help create or intensify the drive for votes the next day. I chose instead to address a meeting that I had asked the Bonavista branch of the Fishermen's Protective Union to hold. I was not altogether surprised when only a handful of members turned up. In Newfoundland's largest fishing settlement, with over 800 fishermen, there weren't more than two or three dozen fishermen who were still members of the FPU, and even at that they formed the largest of the few remaining councils of the once mighty Union. I spoke for a couple of hours and told them that it was more important to Newfoundland to establish a powerful fishermen's union than to elect a government. They knew me for a

*At a cocktail party given in Ottawa in Clutterbuck's honour, Jack Pickersgill remarked to United States Ambassador Wigglesworth, "How does he live with a name like that?" One who overheard the remark told another group, "I just heard Pickersgill laughing with Wigglesworth over the name Clutterbuck."

strong supporter of Sir William Coaker, the great founder of the FPU; they were very unhappy about the catastrophic decline of the Union; and they pricked up their ears when I hinted broadly that when this election was over and the dust had settled, I might be back in Bonavista on more important business than a mere election campaign.

And I was. At first Jim Parsons and his wife, and then for a longer time my dear friends Gus Ayles and his wife, put me up at their home until I was able to find a house on The Scrapes to rent, at $8 a month, so that I could bring my family from Carbonear. I held my first meeting in the small workshed in the Ayleses' backyard. There were only eighteen or twenty men present, but they were some of the most reputable, responsible skippers among Bonavista's fishermen: Gus Ayles, Lar and Jack Keel, Rufus Marsh, Leopold and Simeon Way, Hezekiah Keel, George Sharpe, Will Hayward, Ed Skiffington, Louis Butler, Jabez Ryder, Absalom Powell, Stewart Butler, Stephen White, Bernard Russell, Hubert Whiffen, Mark Mouland, Doug Rolls—all were fine men. They agreed unanimously to my proposal to form the Fishermen's Cooperative Union, and we did it there and then that night. I wrote a constitution for it and, borrowing an idea from the Loyal Orange Association, decided that each meeting would begin and end with the recitation of a "lecture". The officers and members would stand and the Master Fisherman, by which name the chief elected officer of each local branch was known, would ask the question, "Who are we?" to which the whole body of members would reply, "We are fishermen." "How do we make our living?" Holding up their hands, "By fishing." "Who gets the fruit of our toil?" "Not the fishermen," and so forth to the end of the "lecture". This was quite frankly intended to be propaganda, and it came to be memorized by every one of the 8,000 fishermen that I succeeded in enlisting in the Union between 1932 and 1935.

Leslie Curtis, who was my personal friend and benefactor, "lent" me a few hundred dollars to buy the *Margaret P.*, a ketch rigged sailboat with an eight-horsepower gasoline motor to help her along. She was thirty-eight feet long on top, and she had a cabin that could sleep three or four men. I got a retired seaman, "Captain" George Miles, nearing eighty, to be skipper of my boat and young Harold Mouland to be her engineer. We poked our way up and down the northeast coast of Newfoundland so that I could organize branches of the Union and then go back occasionally to visit them. I got to know thousands of fishermen, and it would take another book to describe my experiences and adventures, including five years of poverty for my family and me.

Our poverty was only a pale reflection of the fishermen's grim poverty, for Newfoundland in those years suffered agonies of malnutrition, beriberi, an alarming increase in the scourge of pulmonary tuberculosis, and all the other terrible effects of poor and inadequate food. Since those days, whenever I have read or heard of similar conditions in India, the West Indies, or other parts of the world, I have known exactly what they meant. I got a new education during those years, a new knowledge and understanding of Newfoundland, and especially of Newfoundland's fishermen and of life in the outports. The fishermen paid dues of fifty cents a year to the Union. Half of this was retained by the local branches, and half went to the national headquarters at Bonavista. Members didn't always pay their dues; but even if they had done so, and every dollar paid had gone to the national treasury without any hold-back, the FCU would have been the most poverty-stricken organization in the country. Such were the times.

The hard times were about to force a radical change in the government of Newfoundland. While I worked for the Fishermen's Cooperative Union, there was no respite in my interest in politics or in the Liberal Party, and I visited St. John's whenever I could.

Gordon Bradley was the Leader of the Opposition in the House of Assembly. His following there consisted of Roland Starkes. They were what I used to call orphans of the storm, the storm that had swept across Newfoundland in 1932 and carried the Tory Party into power under Frederick Alderdice. In the one session of the Legislature so far held in this General Assembly, I had worked hard to put vitality into our two-man Opposition. On the opening day of that session, Bradley had given the Government notice of 200 questions to which he wanted answers, and Starkes had given his notice of 100 additional questions. On each day of that session, the two men had given notice of large numbers of other questions, for a total of nearly 1,000 for the session. I had written nearly all of them. The very first question on the opening day of the next session would call for the tabling in the House of the public accounts for the previous year, or even for several years. Believe it or not, the public accounts then and for some little time to come consisted of a set of huge ledgers, one for each year, into which entries were made with pen and ink. Every dollar of expenditure for the year was entered; and if the Opposition, whoever they were, got their hands on the public accounts, they would have enormous scope for the asking of questions. This was where the bodies were buried, and the work of a smart Opposition was to find the concealed bodies, or the camouflaged bodies—or, even more interesting, the bodies that weren't there at all but somewhere else. I had haunted the House every sitting, and more than once I had sat in the gallery to listen to my own speeches, which I had taken sheer delight in writing, delivered by Roland Starkes. He was able to deliver his own speeches, but unless I could persuade him to do it for me, I had no way of delivering my speeches in the House. I was passionately convinced that the House should be done away with altogether for a period of years; but as long as it was there, and as long as party politics continued to be played, I had to take my part in the game.

So it happened that one afternoon late in 1933, Bradley and I were waiting impatiently in his law office in the Renouf Building at the corner of Church Hill and Duckworth Street. Gordon, both feet on the desk as he tilted back in his swivel chair, was phlegmatic. I paced the floor. We'd talked ourselves out in our efforts to guess what was going to be in the document that would be delivered to him at any moment now. This was no less than an advance copy—a couple of hours ahead of the public release of it—of the report of the Amulree Commission that had been examining Newfoundland's affairs for months and was now going to tell the world what was the best course for Newfoundland to take to get the country out of its misery. I shall never forget those last few minutes before the messenger arrived from Prime Minister Alderdice's office. Bradley ripped off the wrapping—his feet were off the desk now—and I hung over his shoulder as he went through the report. He scanned the pages hurriedly until he came to the main section, the one that set forth the Commission's proposals. Bradley's spirits sank fast as he read them, but mine soared. I was elated. This was very bad news for him, but the best of news for me. When he had read through to the end of the proposals, he slammed the book down and swore.

Though my spirits soared over the recommendations of the report, I was enough of a party politician to be able to see how this thing should be handled in the House.

What the Report recommended is very simply told:

1. The House of Assembly was to be done away with.
2. The elected Government was to be done away with.

3. There were to be no more elections.
4. A "Commission of Government" was to be set up to rule over Newfoundland.
5. All of the Members of the Commission were to be appointed by the Government of the United Kingdom; three of those so appointed were to be persons from the United Kingdom and the other three from within Newfoundland. The six-man Commission was to be presided over by His Excellency the Governor.
6. The Commission of Government was to be a combined Government and Legislature for Newfoundland. (In practice, the utterly absurd procedure was followed in the private, secret meetings of the Commission of giving first, second, and third "readings" to the various "bills" that the six-man Government "introduced", which subsequently, as a "Legislature", they solemnly proceeded to "enact" into law. No Hansard was issued, and the nearest the public ever got to knowing what decisions were made was when a communiqué was issued after each meeting. These communiqués were numbered seriatim throughout the years of the Commission's life.)
7. In return for this sacrifice on Newfoundland's part, Britain would convert Newfoundland's public debt to a substantially lower rate of interest and would put Britain's credit behind Newfoundland's bonds.* Furthermore, the British Treasury would make good any deficit that Britain's own Commission of Government incurred in its annual budget. No expenditure could be made above a certain modest figure without first being submitted to the British Government and receiving their approval.

These, with a number of other less important details, were the main recommendations of the Amulree Commission. Forty years later, it may seem surprising that I, a Socialist and a Liberal, or indeed that many Newfoundlanders more conservative in their views, could have swallowed such a dose of bitter medicine. Forty years ago

*The bonds were down to $60 for a $100 bond and unsalable at that price, except in a strictly limited small circle of persons who were strongly suspected afterward of having had secret prior knowledge of the imminent British intention to guarantee the bonds. The bonds bounded back to par and substantial profits, so it was believed, were made by the few.

it was easy to swallow, for Newfoundland was in dire straits. A hundred thousand of the country's population of fractionally more than a quarter of a million were on the dole—more than a third of the population. The dole was six cents a day—$1.80 a month—for each person: no more, no less. It was not given in cash (that reform, at the prompting of my colleague Stephen A. Neary, I was to institute many years later). It was then a written order, signed by one of the Government's relieving officers, to some grocery shop, and the written order spelled out precisely what the holder could get: so many pounds of beans or peas, so many pounds of margarine, so many pounds of flour, and so forth. The flour, all of it imported from Canada, was by special arrangement heavily fortified; it was dark brown in colour, and the bread made from it, though more nutritious, dried very quickly and was anything but tasty or appetizing. Our people for long generations had prized and praised the housewives who could bake snow-white bread for their families; and with bread being so large a part of the Newfoundland diet, its appearance and flavour were of prime popular importance. It was a sad moment indeed for each family as it was forced, to avoid starvation, to have its first baking of the dole flour.

Oh, yes, Newfoundland was in a bad way.

The codfishery was worth $11¼ million in 1929, $8½ million in 1930, and $4¾ million in 1931.

The seal hunt had produced 201,000 seals in 1929, 241,000 in 1930, 88,000 in 1931, and 48,000 in 1932.

The country's iron ore was worth $4 million in 1929, $3¼ million in 1930, $2 million in 1931, and half a million in 1932.

Passengers carried on the railroad and coastal steamships were 220,000 in 1930, 191,000 in 1931, 115,000 in 1932, and 113,000 in 1933.

Newfoundland had to import practically everything it consumed, and these imports were paid for with the proceeds of its exports. Exports were $40 million in 1930, $33½ million in 1931, $26½ million in 1932, and $24½ million in 1933.

The result? In the same four years, the country's imports were $31¾ million, $25½ million, $18 million, and $15 million.

No wonder that more than a third of the people were starving on a dole of six cents a day! No wonder the Government's revenue, which depended overwhelmingly on ad valorem customs duties on imports, fell disastrously to $7½ million, of which $5 million had to be sent out of the country in annual interest to the holders of Newfoundland bonds, leaving $2½ million to pay for civil servants' salaries and pensions, military pensions, police and courts, roads and bridges, teachers and schools, public buildings, lighthouses and fisheries, and all other services for a whole year of the one and only Government there was in Newfoundland, except for the municipal council of St. John's. No wonder the total vote for education had to be reduced from a million dollars to three-quarters, and then to half a million *for the year*! No wonder teachers' salaries had to be cut down to $60, then $50, then $40 a month. And no wonder tuberculosis and beriberi cut like a knife into the homes of thousands and threatened to wipe us out. (For some years before the coming of Confederation, every Newfoundlander entering Canada had to produce his X-ray plate for the immigration officials' examination.)

In the United States, across Canada, and in Newfoundland, the same word was employed to describe the amount of unemployment, poverty, disease, and hunger there was in each country: depression. But it was totally incongruous to use the same word to describe the wildly different conditions in the three countries. In Newfoundland, depression meant hunger, real hunger; hunger for over half the population; hunger that left people hungry day after day, for months, for years; hunger that so weakened families that their resistance to disease was reduced close to the minimum. Many of the men who were fortunate enough to get jobs in the pulp and paper companies' logging camps came in ravenously hungry and had to eat for two and three weeks before they put enough flesh back on their bones to be able to swing a bucksaw again. The report of the Canadian medical team that investigated the state of people's health in superbly beautiful Bonne Bay shocked us all. We were all of us frightened of tuberculosis, suspicious of neighbours and friends—and relatives—afraid to get X-ray photographs taken of our lungs, and afraid not to. We had the highest incidence of tuberculosis to be found anywhere north of the Mexican border. We also had the highest rates of infant mortality, maternal mortality (deaths of mothers in childbirth), and contagious, infectious, and otherwise communicable diseases in North America. The one-third of our people who were on the six cents a day, $1.80 a month, dole deteriorated visibly in health, for the dole was simply not enough to sustain life. It was I, in the *Optimist* weekly (what a name for a newspaper then!), who wrote up the story of the family that perished of starvation in Shoe Cove,

Green Bay; and it was this story that led the government of the day foolishly to invoke an ancient British statute for the prosecution of the small group of unemployed printers who published the paper in the hope of earning a few coppers for themselves.

You could smell the poverty. People's houses went unpainted, though they had always been so proud (and now they are proud again) to keep them painted brightly. The curtains and blinds on the windows were in tatters. The furniture was dilapidated and rickety, a lot of it past its use. Bedding was threadbare. Pots and pans were worn out. Dishes were cracked, the edges of cups chipped and the handles gone. Spouts of teapots had disappeared. People's clothes were patched—Sir John Hope-Simpson marvelled at the numbers of people who had no underwear other than old flour-sacks; sometimes people had no underwear of any kind. I got a berth on a ship going seal-hunting to the Icefields one spring for a man from Bonavista, and when he came to St. John's to join the ship, I discovered that he had nothing to wear but a cheap threadbare suit. I told Ches Crosbie, who had given me the berth in the first place, and he staked my friend to a suit of fleece-lined underwear for protection against the frozen floes off our northern coast. The man spent six weeks at the Icefields hunting seals and earned over $60—he had struck Klondike and was the envy of hundreds of fishermen in Bonavista.

For the women, one of the most keenly felt hardships was the lack of kerosene oil for the lamps. The men suffered from the scarcity of tobacco. There was a descending order of aristocracy: machine-made cigarettes for the affluent; Target for rolling your own; Bugler, cheaper, for the same process; hard plug tobacco from which you cut off bits and pieces that you rolled and rubbed between your palms until it was fine and pliable enough to roll into Zig-Zag cigarette papers; dried tea-leaves, the dust in your pockets, and a token of tobacco all rolled together. I myself, as my fortunes veered, went up from Bugler to Target, though more than once I was down to plug tobacco.

Once I walked over the hills the five miles to Tickle Cove from Keels, in Bonavista Bay; and as I entered Tickle Cove, a resident, full of curiosity, greeted me. After learning who I was and what I was up to (forming local branches of the Fishermen's Cooperative Union), he suggested that I must be hungry and in need of a meal. He took me to his house and got a meal going for me. He burned "blasty boughs" in the dilapidated kitchen stove to boil some water in an empty biscuit tin, and this he poured into another tin to make tea. Meanwhile, he had put the square, flat lid of the biscuit tin on the other damper of the stove, and on it a thin slab of fatback pork to be rendered. Then he laid a thick slab of dole bread in the rendered pork fat (this was in lieu of the margarine that he didn't have), and my meal was complete: the black, sugarless, milkless tea in a handleless cup with badly chipped drinking edge; the slab of grease-soaked brown dole bread on a cracked plate; the whole eaten at a rickety table at which I sat on a flimsy empty wooden box that took the place of a chair. It was his best, and he gave it generously. (Incidentally, Tickle Cove voted heavily against Confederation.)

Newfoundland clearly was flat on its back, on the rocks, run ashore, bankrupt. With even my amateur dabbling in economics, I could see this, and I could see that the political parties were not dealing with the problem but were arguing about trifles.

And I could see something that Lord Amulree and his colleagues failed to see: that their talk of corruption in the Newfoundland Government was farcically unreal. There wasn't as much corruption in a decade in Newfoundland as there would be in any six months in many Canadian provinces, or in a week in any American state. The difference lay in the fact of the Newfoundland parties' intellectual bankruptcy. Lacking deep-seated and strongly held views on vital matters, the two parties slandered each other, each trying to convince the people that its opponent was a dirty embezzler or pickpocket—that was the sum of their propaganda. That kind of propaganda convinced a lot of Newfoundlanders, and a lot of others, that Newfoundland politics was corrupt and rotten. For a few years before the Royal Commission report, I had grown to be unalterably convinced that what Newfoundland needed, above all else, at least to start with, was a complete political holiday; a complete cessation of party politics, and the substitution of an appointed government in place of one that was answerable to a House of Assembly and thus to the people. It was savage surgery on the ancient British Colony, made up as it was of people of solid English, Irish, Scottish, and Welsh stock, with a little savour of French, Jewish, and other strains from Europe—savage, but life-saving.

I have taken a lot of space to describe the situation in Gordon Bradley's office as I saw in that afternoon in 1933, but it needs to be put on the record.

It is necessary, too, that notice be taken at this stage of a few words in the recommendations that came politically to be neglected, or forgotten, or deliberately or even ignorantly suppressed. How long was this blatant denial of democratic self-government to last? When would responsible government (which means simply government dependent on the continuing support of the Legislature) be restored to Newfoundlanders? This was answered in all of the relevant documents, starting with the recommendations of the Royal Commission, the report itself, the White Paper issued a few hours later by the British Government, the Newfoundland Act of the British Parliament, and the new Letters Patent issued as Newfoundland's Constitution. The same words are repeated throughout those documents: "It would be understood that, as soon as the Island's difficulties are overcome and the country is again self-supporting, responsible government, on request from the people of Newfoundland, would be restored." Could anything be plainer? Would it be dishonest, or just stupid, in quoting that important condition, to leave out the words "on request from the people"? Before the issue became timely, Harry A. Winter had pointed out that the scheme had made no particular provision for enabling the people to make their request. Would they do it by petition? Or by the holding of numerous public meetings? Or by sending a delegation to Westminster? And no suggestion was made in the scheme for determining whether or when Newfoundland had become self-supporting again. These things ought to have been made clear in 1934, as in fact they were in 1945; but the essential fact is that the two basic conditions themselves that had to be met before responsible government would be restored *were* clearly stated: when Newfoundland "is again self-supporting" and "on request from the people".

All this I saw or felt that afternoon in Bradley's office, and I was pleased. Bradley was deeply depressed. "Where does this leave me?" he demanded. "My life is finished. There'll be no more public life for me, and I've let my law practice almost disappear since I came into politics. Now everything's gone." I tried to cheer him up and declared that I'd give an arm to be in his position, to be Leader of the Opposition, or just to have a seat in the House. "You would, would you?" he boomed. "And with your views on this report, what would you do in the House? Would you support the Government? Would you support these recommendations?"

I wouldn't do either, I told him. If I were in his shoes, I would prepare two speeches. One speech would be a plea for time. Prime Minister Alderdice had announced that the House was to be called together immediately to deal with the report, and I argued to Bradley that a strenuous effort should be made by the Opposition to stop the thing from being railroaded through. The Government would be introducing a resolution calling for a petition from the Legislature to the King, praying him to cause the Parliament of the United Kingdom to put the Amulree scheme into effect. Once that petition passed the House, the thing was over. That would be the last action of the House for probably many years to come. All the more reason, therefore, for not rushing into it, for giving the House and all the people a chance to study and consider the proposals. Bradley agreed that the speech should be made, took out his writing pad, and challenged me to go ahead. I paced the floor and dictated the speech to him, and I can vouch for the fact that few men in the whole of Newfoundland were capable of delivering it with the voice, stance, and eloquence that he displayed a few days later. "But suppose they won't listen?" Bradley said, and I agreed that in all probability they wouldn't. "You should have your main speech prepared for when that happens," I told him, "a speech in which you could put your main arguments against the scheme." Bradley got his pad out again, and I dictated the second speech. As I recall that speech today, I am surprised by my own quite unconscious prescience that afternoon. After all, I wasn't stating my own thoughts about the scheme, but only what I believed Gordon Bradley's should be, once he got around to formulating them. The speech that I dictated to him was merely anticipation of what I believed his speech would be, provided he could get his mind on the topic and away from his own personal predicament. I pointed out in the speech that even if the new system of government brought about what some people believed to be necessary, a political holiday, it was inevitable that in the absence of elections, of a House of Assembly, and of popular representation, the deep-seated democratic instincts of a British people would eventually reassert themselves. I made the point that this was going to be in essence mere absentee government. I went on to say—and this, I think, was real insight at the time—that the British Government, which would control the Commission of Government's budget, would scarcely be willing to give the Commission much of a financial free hand in Newfoundland. We talked until nearly eight o'clock that evening, and then we walked together back to Bradley's house on Circular Road for a bite to eat. He was still deeply depressed when I left him.

The House met and, notwithstanding Bradley's and Starkes' speeches, passed the petition to the King and then closed up shop. Bradley had just about the last word in that House; and there was not another House until, sixteen years later, it opened under Confederation, at which time I might be said to have spoken the next word. The Amulree report was still being published serially in the newspapers for a considerable time after the die was cast and the petition had gone to the King, the House had closed, and the whole new system was in train! There was no television then, radio broadcasting was weak and inconsequential, and even the newspapers that did publish installments of the report reached only a small fraction of the population. It is fair to say that the great change in our Constitution—so basic as to be a constitutional revolution—had been put into effect while as yet our people had scarcely the foggiest notion of what it was all about. Was there indignation among the people when they did know what it was about? There was none, or virtually none; instead, there was a deep sigh of relief from the people as they believed that now things were going to be better—better for them. Harold Mitchell, who had won Trinity South over the great Squires, proposed publicly—and his proposal was not publicly scorned—that a gigantic bannered arch of welcome be built across the Narrows, the high-walled entrance to St. John's Harbour, underneath which the ship bringing the Commissioners from England would pass. I rejoice a little that I do not have to record that the arch was erected—for it was not. The proposal fell of its own weight.

The rest is soon told. The three British Commissioners arrived in February: Sir John Hope-Simpson, Thomas Lodge, and John H. Penson, who had been Newfoundland's English Auditor General. The Newfoundland Commissioners were Frederick Alderdice, John Puddester, and William R. Howley.* The Governor was Admiral Sir David Anderson. My friend William J. Carew, who had been special private secretary to every Prime Minister beginning with Sir Edward Morris, became secretary of the Commission. The Commission wrought many reforms and improvements in the structure of government. The civil service was reorganized, institutionalized, given a scale of grades and a scale of salaries, and gradually by recruitment made into an incomparably better service than we had ever known. The Commission worked splendidly, even magnificently, if their objective was "good" government, careful government, fastidious gov-

*The usual Anglican, nonconformist, and Roman Catholic representation!

ernment, dignified government; government that functions smoothly as a machine, but a machine that produces nothing more than smooth-running government. They built a few, a pathetically small number, of small outport cottage hospitals, and they pioneered in the building of a few bait depots for the fishermen. They were long on efficient, smooth-running administration; but lamentably, maddeningly short on economic development, economic building, the development of the natural resources of the country. *Development* of the resources? They didn't even search for them; they didn't send out drills or use any of the modern means of detecting and measuring natural wealth; they gave no sign that they believed that Newfoundland had natural resources. They were themselves, as a government, near-perfect civil servants organizing a near-perfect civil service. They had no leader, no man who could weld the Commission into a strong unified body determined to carry out any program higher or more urgent than that at which they were so good: departmental smoothness, civil service excellence.

Bradley went back to live in Bonavista but soon afterward accepted appointment as a chief magistrate in Grand Falls. He stood that as long as he could; but hating the Commission of Government with every fibre of his being, he finally threw it up and went back to live in Bonavista again, where he was freer to voice his lurid opinions of the Commission in articles that he wrote or inspired for the *Fishermen's Advocate* under the editorship of his friend and mine, Charlie Granger. I continued my work for the fishermen through the Fishermen's Cooperative Union until even I had to admit that I could carry on no longer.

10

Broadcaster —Historian

History would be an excellent thing if only it were true.
Leo Tolstoy

S. T. Coleridge: "Pray, Mr. Lamb, did you ever hear me preach?"
Charles Lamb: "Damme, I never heard you do anything else."

Anybody can make history; only a great man can write it.
Oscar Wilde

My children were growing up—there were three of them, Ramsay, Bill, and Clara—and I was without any income whatsoever. I couldn't even keep up the $8 monthly rent for my house in Bonavista. We lived mostly on group collections of what the fishermen called garden fruit—the potatoes, turnips, carrots, parsnips, and cabbage that they gathered and brought to my house in the fall—and we depended on collections of firewood that they brought us too. After four years, I was battered reluctantly into recognizing the brutal fact that I would have to give up the work of organizing the fishermen. In any case, I had begun to wonder strongly whether this kind of primitive, simplistic fishermen's union activity was going to do much if anything more than to put an occasional extra quarter or half-dollar in the fishermen's pockets. In spite of my doubts, it was with deep regret that I decided to resign my position as national chairman of the FCU and go back to St. John's.

I had formed a branch of the Union at Pouch Cove, eighteen miles from St. John's, one of a group of branches that I organized along the St. John's shore: (the others were at Flat Rock, Torbay, and Bauline). In Pouch Cove, I had formed a fishermen's producers'-consumers' cooperative society. The society members, mostly with free labour, had built a magnificent new building; John S. Noseworthy and Stan Sullivan of Pouch Cove, and a young man named King from Bauline managed it; and I had gone to Ches Crosbie asking him to give the new co-op some commercial support. Crosbie had done so willingly;* so now that I was back in St. John's, it was natural enough for me to ask him to back me in a venture that I had long had in mind and had now decided to put into effect. This was nothing less than the preparation and publication of a handsome, exhaustive encyclopedia of our country: what would be *The Book of Newfoundland.*

Crosbie invited me to have breakfast with him at his home, and it

*I had, and have to this day, boundless respect and liking for him and for his memory.

was there that I put the proposal to him, spelling it out in the greatest possible detail. I literally hadn't a dollar to my name, and he would have to foot every bill. He agreed cheerfully to do it, though we thought then that it would run to nearly $20,000 (in fact, it ran to much more), and he gave me the use of the second floor of his building on Water Street, across from the General Post Office, upstairs over his own offices. I was lucky to get Leo P. Mokeler as my secretary and assistant. I commissioned a clever young writer not long out of school, Michael Harrington, to write a number of articles that I wanted done for the book, and I paid two or three others to write for me as well. At the beginning, I had made out a long list of the topics and themes that I wanted to be written up for the book, and these, taken together, would comprise a very complete and thorough description of Newfoundland. Next I had to match the themes with the names of those best able to write them. Then I had to persuade these people to do the writing. Then, even more difficult, I had to hound them to get the articles into my hands. A few articles I could publish with very little editing, but most of them I had to rewrite entirely.

As the months passed, the work became ever more burdensome, until I found myself in command of a small army of salesmen out in the field booking advance orders for the book, supervising the sale of advertising space at the back of each volume, and laying out the work of some ten or twelve girls whom I employed to do typing and retyping of the many articles. I had tremendous help in the advertising part of the book from Oliver L. (Al) Vardy, a very able salesman who had just come back to his native Newfoundland. He had heard me speaking over the radio about the *Book of Newfoundland* venture the first night he was in St. John's, and came to see me next morning to ask if he could fit into it. I took him out to one or two prospective advertisers, and he listened carefully as I went into my sales pitch and clinched two contracts. Walking back to the office with me, Vardy told me that he thought he would need no further tuition but would be able to handle it on his own from there on. He did, on commission, and earned more thousands of dollars in the next two or three months than I had ever earned in a full year in my life, more than I was destined to earn in any one year for years to come.

I had arranged for the books to be printed in England. During the last three days before I boarded the Furness-Withy passenger boat with all the manuscripts and illustrations for the book, I didn't leave the office at all, or take off my clothes. For seventy-two hours, up to the moment of going aboard the boat, I put on that last great spurt.

I got a room in London and operated mainly from there; and about once a month, I went down to the little town of Bungay, in North Suffolk, to the printing plant of Richard Clay and Sons. A batch of galley proofs came to me by mail each morning in London, and I corrected them and mailed them back to Bungay. Then page proofs began to arrive. For a while, galley proofs and page proofs overlapped, and I had my work cut out to cope with them. Three months after I reached London, the book was ready for the press and I took the ship home to St. John's.

The Book of Newfoundland came out early in 1937, two large, beautifully printed and bound volumes, with dozens of interesting articles and about a thousand photographic illustrations. One volume had an article on the wild birds of Newfoundland, with splendid illustrations in full colour. The other had an article, similarly illustrated, on the wild flowers of Newfoundland. It was a set of books the like or equal of which has never to this day been published about any other province of Canada. Ten thousand sets were printed, and they sold for $5 a set—the book bargain of the century. The trouble was that they didn't sell, a sad commentary indeed on the financial condition of our country in those years just before the Second World War. I had drawn no salary whatsoever out of the venture, from beginning to end. My hope had been that I would get something by way of dividend, but there was none. At last, when the war broke out and thousands of United States and Canadian troops, sailors, and airmen poured into Newfoundland, the books went like hot cakes and were sold to the last set. Ches Crosbie, I am glad to say, got his money back, and *The Book of Newfoundland* remains as a memorial to his big heart and generous pocketbook.*

But here I was, broke again. I had no money, no job, and a wife and three children to support. Al Vardy's success was my clue. While in London, I had heard from Leo Mokeler that Vardy had blossomed

*In 1966, I decided to publish volumes three and four of *The Book of Newfoundland*, to be the same in size and appearance as one and two, but of course with entirely new writing and illustrations. I decided also to reprint volumes one and two, which were so scarce by then that they commanded a price of $200 a set. I had 10,000 sets of three and four printed and 5,000 reprints of one and two, and I made a profit of about $60,000 from both publications.

forth as an enormously popular radio news broadcaster. His was the first real newscast in Newfoundland, and he did it with style and with very real competence. The Newfoundland Butter Company (manufacturers of margarine) sponsored the program, and at that time Vardy was the highest-paid person connected with broadcasting in the country. The night I went aboard the boat to England, he and I had had a brief chat, and he had wondered what he would turn to next. I suggested that he work up a news program on the air, and this is precisely what he did. Now I needed a job myself, and as a start I decided that I would write a column for the *Daily News*.

John S. Currie, its editor and principal owner, agreed to pay me for the column at $20 a week. Ches Crosbie let me continue to use the office upstairs, and Leo Mokeler, having nothing better to do for the moment, hung around the office and helped me in one way or another—mostly by being a patient listener to the many speeches I made to him about Newfoundland and its future. The column was called "From the Masthead" and it was by "The Barrelman". The barrelman is the member of a ship's crew who climbs to the masthead and, from the protection of a barrel-shaped enclosure, peers about to sight whales or seals or ice packs, and calls the information down to the bridge below. My column consisted of anecdotes about Newfoundland, bits and pieces and scraps of information about the country and its people, and in general was devoted to a sort of glorification of Newfoundland and everything good within it. Thomas H. O'Neill, father of Judge Hugh O'Neill, was the source of many excellent anecdotes, and Mrs. Genevieve Dolan sent me some lovely stories from the West Coast.*

The column attracted considerable attention, and when I concluded that the time was ripe, I went to see William F. Galgay, the general manager of radio station VONF and my friend. Since the installation of the Commission of Government, the station had become a public corporation. I proposed that he allow me to go on for a week or two with an unsponsored program much along the lines of my daily column. For fifteen minutes each night, from a quarter to seven until seven o'clock, using a ship's bell to signal the start of the program and to separate its various items, I continued for about a

*It was around this time that I made an avowal to Leo Mokeler that he may remember. I had my wife and three growing children to support, and my income was $20 a week. "I'd be willing to indenture myself for life to anyone who'd guarantee me $100 a month to my death," I told Leo, and I meant it.

week. Then I went to see Frank M. O'Leary, who had a successful commission agent's business on Water Street, and suggested that he listen for a night or two to my program and decide whether he would like to sponsor it. He told me that he had already listened to it and liked it very much. He agreed to pay me $30 a week, and he of course would pay the station for the time. It was not a big salary, but more than I had been getting, and it was bound to lead to something better. (The something better was Confederation with Canada.) That was the start of my Barrelman program: "F. M. O'Leary Ltd. presenting The Barrelman in a program of making Newfoundland better known to Newfoundlanders." For more than six years, I wrote The Barrelman and spoke it over the air six nights a week for fifteen minutes each night. I wrote many hundreds of thousands of words—indeed, more than 2,500,000 of them.

The Barrelman program was sensationally popular among the outport people, the most popular one on the air. It was a peculiar blend of Newfoundland history, geography, and economic information, with stories of courage, endurance, hardship, inventiveness, resourcefulness, physical strength and prowess, skill and courage in seamanship, and a hundred other aspects and distinctions of our Newfoundland story—all of them "making Newfoundland better known to Newfoundlanders" and intended to inspire them with faith in their country and in themselves, and to destroy what I continually denounced as our inferiority complex. I went around the world, figuratively, to find Newfoundlanders who had become successful in many fields of human endeavour: Newfoundlanders who had become admirals, generals, bishops and archbishops, Members of Parliament, mayors of cities, presidents of universities, industrial leaders, financiers, artists, actors, singers. Newfoundland was proud that it had produced, in the First War, a winner of the greatest of all British decorations, the Victoria Cross; but I found a second Newfoundland winner of the V.C.—Sergeant Croke, of the Canadian Army. We were proud that we had a Newfoundlander in the House of Lords, Lord Morris, but I found that he was the third Newfoundlander to have a seat in that House. And so it went night after night, always with fresh evidence that Newfoundland was a fascinating place, populated by brave and resourceful men and women, who rarely failed to accomplish big things once they had the opportunity. That was the rub: having the opportunity. "Proving once again, ladies and gentlemen, that Newfoundlanders have what it takes, every time they get the chance!" I took no offence when someone publicly called me a blind patriot.

Of course, in a fifteen-minute talk program that went on six nights a week throughout the year, except for the month of July, I had to lighten the program with some humour; and here, almost by accident, I hit on what was then, though it is no longer so much so, the common vein of Newfoundland's humour: the tall tale. This depends upon vast exaggeration, and once it had been the kind of humour that Americans liked, back in the last quarter of the previous century and the early part of the present. The great masters of the art were Mark Twain, M. Quad, Josh Billings, and Finley Peter Dunne. The first tall tales I told in my program were three or four that I had heard from my grandfather David, and he had brought them with him from Prince Edward Island. Then an avalanche descended upon me! Newfoundlanders, especially outport people, loved my tall tales, and they wrote me hundreds of tales to tell; some of the best of them probably were made up locally. I remember one about a man who was out in his small rowboat with his double-barrelled shotgun, hoping to shoot a wild sea-bird for his dinner table. Not a bird did he see. Then he heard distant thunder. At any rate, it sounded like thunder, but it wasn't: it was the sound of the wings of tens of thousands of wild ducks approaching from the north. They blackened the sky as they flew high over the small boat. The fisherman aimed his shotgun at them and fired both barrels. He had time to load again and fired – but not a single bird came down. Not one. The vast flock finally passed beyond him, but he didn't take his eyes off them. And then, lo and behold, fifty ducks fell out of the cloud into the water. He hastened to pick them up and went ashore with a boat-load. The birds had been too tightly crowded together to allow the dead ducks to fall when they were shot. It was only when the flock loosened out a little, after passing the fisherman, that there was room for them to tumble into the sea. The fishermen loved that story, and hundreds more that I was able to tell.

When war broke out in 1939, Frank O'Leary wanted to use the program to do something to help the cause.* Between us, we worked out the idea of The Fish Appeal. This was a plan by which each fish-

*If ever a man deserved to be made an officer of the Order of the British Empire, that man was Frank O'Leary, and Newfoundland was pleased when he got it. Subsequently, before his death, he was appointed by the Pope to be a Knight Commander in the Order of St. Gregory.

erman would donate a salt-dried codfish, and all the fish would be sold to the highest bidder; the proceeds would be used to buy cigarettes and comforts to be sent to our boys in the army, navy, and air force in Britain or wherever they were. I pushed this appeal vigorously every night for two or three years, and we raised thousands and thousands of dollars. It was a rare fisherman indeed who contributed merely one codfish. Retired fishermen and others who were not engaged in the fishery sent money in place of fish.

I received a staggering amount of fan mail. People wrote me from all parts of the country. In the outports that had no electricity, and that was the overwhelming majority of them, there were only battery-operated radios. Batteries were expensive to keep up, and so not too many families could afford to have a radio. Those who did not would crowd the homes of those who did, but the owners were careful always to turn on their radios only, or mainly, for three programs: mine at a quarter to seven; Al Vardy's at seven o'clock; and the famous Gerald S. Doyle local news bulletin at a quarter to eight each night. In short, my program gave them entertainment and enlightenment about Newfoundland, Vardy's gave them the world news, and Doyle's gave them Newfoundland news.

I took the month of July off each year, and as I had acquired a second-hand car, I was able to spend that month poking about the country, wherever I could find a road to take me. In this way, I visited hundreds of Newfoundland fishing settlements and other places. (By car, by coastal steamship, and on foot, I have visited 1,000 of the 1,300 settlements there were in Newfoundland at that time.) In each settlement, I would talk with the oldest men and women and try, by probing, to reconstruct the history of the settlement: who was the first settler, where did he come from, how old was he, who was his wife, where did he meet her, how many children did they have, where exactly did he settle? And a hundred other questions. From this probing and my own intensive research, carried on six days a week through six years, I knew more, probably many times more, than any other person in Newfoundland about the history of the settlements. I later put much of this information in my *Gazetteer of Newfoundland*, the first complete gazetteer ever written of our country. This gazetteer formed part of a *Handbook, Almanac and Gazetteer of Newfoundland* that I published in 1940 and again in 1941.

I was accompanied on many of those automobile tours on the eastern side of the Island by my close friend Nimshi Crewe, then Deputy Auditor General, who usually contrived to get his vacation for the same month. He, too, was a walking encyclopedia of Newfoundland outport life and history, and he often joined me as I chatted with groups of fishermen and was able to throw in an occasional shrewd question or observation. But he had his own mission on those trips with me: he was a dedicated collector of antique English mahogany furniture, grandfather clocks, sterling silver, and indeed anything bearing on the history of Newfoundland. After John Murray Anderson and John G. Higgins, I think that Nimshi Crewe had the most distinguished collection of antiques in Newfoundland. His house was furnished mainly with antique mahogany furniture, and it was a pleasure to have a meal with him and his fine family, and dine with his beautiful sterling flatware taken from the superb old English sideboard in his dining room.

I reached the dangerous point, as he and I travelled together, of becoming interested myself in antique mahogany furniture, but I sternly repressed the temptation. I would never become as expert as he in understanding and recognizing genuine antiquity in furniture, and in any case I doubt that our friendship would have survived rivalry from me. I settled on a simple hobby of my own: collecting lustre-ware dishes. As we went into each individual outport, I would concentrate on gathering history and local lore, grist for my Barrelman mill and my own general knowledge of Newfoundland; Crewe would go from door to door seeking antiques, and I would keep a sharp eye peeled for lustre-ware. Often, after I had garnered all I could of history, Crewe and I would agree to divide the harbour in two: I would take, say, the north side and he the south. And so we would canvass every house, knock on the door. The woman of the house would come. "Good morning, ma'am, I'm looking around to see if there are any antiques in this harbour—you know, before now things. Old chairs, tables, or anything really old. I would like to buy it if you have any." Ninety-nine times out of a hundred the answer would be either no or else yes, but we're not selling it. I would get the occasional piece of lustre-ware and ended by having what must surely have been the largest collection ever put together in Newfoundland and one of the largest anywhere. It ran to more than 200 pieces—copper lustre-ware, silver lustre-ware, and some beautiful ornamental pieces. In the end, I decided to narrow my collecting activities drastically, to look only for cups and saucers, side plates and dinner plates, salt and pepper shakers, sugar bowls, milk jugs, and butter dishes. My ambition was to be able to set a table for six completely with lustre-ware and sterling silver. I had no great difficulty with the silverware, for my wife's people's collection was large and she had obtained some of them, and I had a few pieces of my own grandmother Smallwood's collection. The tableware in lustre was another story, and I never did succeed in getting more than three cups, two saucers, and some plates, and a few other odds and ends.

What fun it was! What happiness, to be close to the heart of our people and our outports! I used to carry a canvas tent in the back of the car, with tins of food, a tin kettle, and a few other tools for camp life. Crewe wouldn't sleep in the tent but insisted always on wandering around until he found some house that would give him a comfortable room and bed for the night. Half the fun for me was the camping; but the whole community of Green's Harbour enjoyed the fun when I, not knowing the difference, went a quarter of a mile along the road from the settlement and in the dark pitched my tent in the centre of an old, unfenced cemetery at the side of the road. I wondered, as I turned in to sleep, why the ground on which I slept was so uneven, but it wasn't until next morning in the daylight that I discovered that I was sleeping snugly between two graves. Years afterward, as I campaigned for Confederation or for a General Election and drove around Trinity and other bays, I looked for the various spots where I had pitched my tent. I always notice particularly the spot just outside New Melbourne where, without bothering to pitch the tent, I slept in a sleeping bag in the dry ditch at the side of the road. I remember the youngsters who woke me up next morning and joined me as I boiled the kettle for tea and opened a can of beans for breakfast.

At the end of a month of that kind of travel, I would go back to St. John's and resume my broadcast with as much zest as ever. I loved the outports, and still do, and never made any bones about it. Once, indeed, having spent the month in the outports, I began my resumed program with the words, "Ladies and gentlemen, good evening. I have just returned to St. John's from a month's visit to Newfoundland, and . . ." That's how I felt, too. Although, to be fair, I ought to point out that even St. John's, to a very large extent indeed, is a Newfoundland outport. Thousands of its people are outport people who have come to live in the city. Large sections of the city are populated overwhelmingly by outport people. In the northwest corner of St. John's, there lies the great Newfoundland "outport" of Little Bonavista. These outport sections of St. John's invariably supported me when I was in public life. They voted for Confederation in both referendum elections, and it was mainly because of the outport people in St. John's that the capital city in the second referendum actually gave Confederation one-third of the total vote of the city. I never did succeed in winning more than one-half of the St. John's seats in the House of Assembly elections, and in my last election of all, my seventh, I didn't win a single seat in St. John's.

Throughout my years as Barrelman, I virtually lived at Gosling Memorial Library doing daily research for my radio program. And I read every word of the typewritten copies of the Colonial Records for the period 1749 onward. I read, too, every page of every newspaper back-file. In the vault of the Home Affairs Department, I came across a small hoard of historic documents. I found still more in the attic of the Supreme Court building. All of this intensive reading, carried on for five or six days a week throughout the year for five or six years, meant that I was the only Newfoundlander who had ever made his living, or at any rate a large part of it, out of Newfoundland history.

My reputation as a Newfoundland historian got me two jobs that I prized greatly. One was commissioned by the Hon. Robert B. Job. He was a direct descendant of Dr. William Carson, a man whom I always describe as the greatest reformer in Newfoundland's five-century history. He was the father of agriculture, and he built the first road. He established our present great General Hospital. He reformed the Supreme Court. He succeeded in forcing the British Government to order Newfoundland's governors to reside full time in the Island from the time of their appointment. He forced the appointment of a small council of local advisors to the Governor. He launched and led the movement for representative government, and became the Speaker of the House of Assembly. He was a Scot and brought with him to Newfoundland the sharply defined ideas of political freedom of the Edinburgh school. I was delighted, then, when Mr. Job asked me to write the story of Carson's life. I wrote "The Life and Letters of Dr. William Carson" and delivered it to him. He paid me $250, but I would have been willing to pay him as much for the privilege of writing it. It has never been published, though Mr. Job incorporated a few of its facts in a small book that he wrote himself,

John Job and His Descendants. I have the ambition to see my book published.

The other job was given to me by Cyril B. Carter, a director of the great mercantile firm of James Baird Ltd. He was a descendant of Surrogate Robert Carter of Ferryland.* Mr. Carter had the idea, which was possibly justified, that Robert Carter and his descendants had been given the right to fly the white ensign. I knew a lot about Robert Carter, and I was delighted to accept the commission. Robert Carter was appointed a surrogate in 1749 at Ferryland, and he played a noble part indeed in the defence of that settlement and the Isle au Bois against the French invader in 1762. He played a large part, too, in the defence of St. John's on that same occasion. I would scarcely think that there are many families in North America today with so long a record in the practice of law. Robert Carter served as a part-time magistrate for almost half a century. His son William was a judge in the Court of Admiralty at St. John's for long years. William's son, Peter Weston Carter, was a judge of the Central District Court at St. John's for nearly fifty years. Peter Weston Carter's son, Sir Frederick B. T. Carter, was not only a practising lawyer but Prime Minister of Newfoundland and, with Sir Ambrose Shea, represented Newfoundland at the great Confederation Conference at Quebec, thus ranking as one of the Fathers of Confederation. Sir Frederick's grandson, Harry P. Carter, a school chum of mine at Bishop Feild College, was a high-ranking official of the Department of Justice for many years. I wrote the story of Surrogate Robert Carter, delivered it to Cyril Carter, who paid me for it, and I have not seen it since.

I was connected with one other small book during my Barrelman days. The Department of Education commissioned me to write a book of Newfoundland stories having historical and factual basis, for distribution in the schools of the country. Mr. Leo F. English collaborated with me on that book, contributing several of the stories in it.

My Barrelman broadcasting had two major results: Frank O'Leary's name became a household word, his business expanded phenomenally, and I suspect that he became a millionaire; and my voice and personality became part of Newfoundland's very culture.

*A surrogate was a deputy to a naval commander plying the local waters, and he could try minor cases; the naval man was the real judge. Sometimes his quarter-deck justice happened to be just.

11

Pigs Is Pigs — and Confederation, Maybe?

To plow and to sow, and to reap and to mow, and to be a farmer's boy.

Anon

To market, to market, to buy a fat pig, Home again, home again, jiggety-jig.

Anon

A farmer is always going to be rich next year

Philemon

May the countryside and the gliding valley stream content me. Lost to fame, let me love river and woodland.

Virgil

I had always felt an attraction to farming, and in 1939 I gave way to that attraction by buying forty acres of land on Kenmont Road, in the northwestern suburb of St. John's. It had an old dwelling on it and a large new barn. About four of the forty acres were cleared and capable of cultivation. The Second World War was on in full force, and food prices were rising every day. I bought 1,000 laying hens, which I soon increased to 1,500, considered then in Newfoundland to be a huge flock! I had customers for every egg at $1 a dozen. They were glad to get fresh eggs at that price, for the retail price in St. John's was twenty and thirty cents a dozen more than that. I used to carry eggs with me to the Newfoundland Hotel, my best customer, when I went to the broadcasting studio on the top floor of the same building.

Then I ran into the difficulty that plagued and in some cases utterly ruined the other poultry-men around St. John's. This was the poultry feed shortage. We were at the mercy of Canada for our animal and poultry feeds, and the local importers in St. John's were complaining bitterly about the irregularity and undependability of the Canadian exporters. When a laying flock is in production, it is highly hazardous to vary the feed. The birds can be thrown into a moult very easily if the feed is changed, and egg production falls catastrophically. I, like all the poultry-men, scoured St. John's from one importer to the other and was glad enough to be able to buy a few rationed bags of feed of any brand whatsoever. The result was inevitable. My 1,500 birds laid what you'd normally get from a flock of a hundred. They didn't earn even the cost of their feed. And there was no prospect of any improvement in the feed situation. I sold the whole flock live to a man who supplied foodstuffs and other goods to the Spanish and Portuguese fishing vessels coming into St. John's. The fishermen kept the birds on board to produce eggs and for fresh meat on their long voyage at sea. Thus ended my first poultry venture.

Then I went into the business of raising hogs from weanling age to market weight. All of us who raised market hogs around St. John's at that time, and for a long time after, fed them with the edible swill that accumulated in huge quantities at the big United States Air Force Base at Fort Pepperrell. Dave Squires and his brother Will were the biggest of the hog-raisers in Newfoundland. They had the contract to take all the edible swill from Fort Pepperrell, amounting to thirty and forty steel barrelfuls each day, and they supplied me. This was highly nutritious food for hogs, but of course it ought to have been thoroughly boiled before being fed to the animals. Later, when I went to Gander, I was perhaps the first hog-raiser in Newfoundland to put in a system for boiling all swill. Up to then, we fed it just as we received it, without realizing that we were running the daily risk of losing our whole herd. I began with fifty hogs, importing them as weanlings from Knud Jorgensen and later from Wellington McNeil on Prince Edward Island. Gradually I increased the number to 150, which was then perhaps the second or third largest such establishment in the country. Suddenly disaster came upon us, all of us, in the form of what I believe was necrotic enteritis. Even the leading veterinarian of Newfoundland, Dr. Alex Bishop, manager of the Newfoundland Government's hog farm, had serious losses. There was no truth, I am convinced, in the belief of some hog-raisers that our losses were caused by an epidemic of hog cholera. There just wasn't anybody in the whole of Newfoundland who could tell definitively what the trouble was. I saw the Commissioner for Natural Resources, Robert Ewbank, about it, and he promised to telegraph to the federal Department of Agriculture at Ottawa to ask them to send to St. John's a veterinarian experienced in hog diseases. He got a reply that Ottawa didn't have one to spare just then. I telegraphed to the Ontario Agricultural College at Guelph a minute description of the symptoms and got back a reply saying that they were morally certain that it was necrotic enteritis.

I lost some stock but didn't go under. In fact, I was getting along very well with my farm and my Barrelman broadcast. I was producing the large monthly tabloid newspaper *Barrelman* for Frank O'Leary, publishing the occasional literary production, doing some writing for two or three retail stores on Water Street, and in general was better off financially than I had ever been before. It was at this peak in 1943 that destiny struck again, in the person of Group Captain David Anderson.

Anderson was the Commanding Officer of the Royal Air Force

Transport Command station at Gander Airport. Without a doubt, he was one of the most colourful personalities of the RAF. In England, he had test-flown the prototypes of the Mosquito and Spitfire fighters, but had seriously damaged his prospects in the RAF when, at the very time when the Air Force was trying to persuade the Chancellor of the Exchequer to give them more money, Anderson took the Chancellor on a flight and crashed his plane! He survived the black looks of the Royal Air Force and in the first part of the Second World War found himself in Washington, D. C., as Air Attaché to the British Embassy. He was married to a wealthy American woman, and I remember seeing a piece in *Collier's* magazine that said Anderson alone was worth as much as all the rest of the ambassadors when it came to making friends for the British among Americans. Now he was in Gander, and he had decided that it was a shameful waste of the King's money to be throwing away all the good waste food from the mess halls in Gander—British, Canadian, and American—instead of producing pork with it. So he had taken a Catalina Canso bomber to Charlottetown, loaded it up with weanling pigs, and flown them back to Gander.

He had hired a local man to look after the twenty-five or thirty pigs, but I doubt if the man had ever seen more than perhaps one or two pigs together in his life before. Andy heard of me and my hog venture on Kenmont Road, so he flew in to Torbay and drove out to see me. He wanted me to go back with him that very day to see his pigs in Gander. I had to record a couple of programs before leaving town, so he undertook to send the big flying boat back for me some days later. In Gander, I saw his small piggery and offered some useful advice. Over a meal at his home in The Barn, as he called it, we discussed the idea of using all of the large quantities of edible swill—surplus and waste food—generated every day at the great airport. I told him that there should be enough swill to feed a thousand pigs or more, and the talk led around to the idea of our organizing a big new hog-raising venture. The company would be owned by me or my financial backer or both of us, on the one hand, and the RAF Welfare Fund on the other. The more we discussed the idea, the more I was attracted to it, and I promised to let him know.

Again I went to see Ches Crosbie, and he agreed to finance me, so we went ahead with the scheme. A few hundred feet away from the main hangar on the RAF side of Gander, we built a huge piggery building 300 feet long by 40 feet wide, and with a handsome double monitor roof—surely one of the finest piggery buildings ever built anywhere in Newfoundland or the rest of Canada. We put in two huge steam-jacketed boilers, each with a jet of live steam as well. Truck loads of edible swill were brought each day and furiously boiled in the two large tanks. Andy's ingenious mind devised a magnificently efficient system of feeding the pigs, although the system meant that the pigs could be fed only on one side of the building at a time. The noise from the other side as the hungry pigs squealed an impatient protest could be heard, when the wind was in the right direction, all the way across the airport! I can still see the delighted grin on Anderson's face when this incredible squealing started every mealtime.

Every VIP who came through Gander was welcomed by Anderson and taken to The Barn for a drink or meal; and rarely, if they had the time at all, did he fail to bring them down to show off the piggery. I remember, among hundreds, Bert Balchen, the American flier who did such valuable work during the war, visiting our piggery and telling of his experiences in the lumberwoods of the northwestern United States, when as a young fellow his principal work was to swill-feed the pigs. And I remember vividly the four or five dignified, distinguished Chinese statesmen on their way to the founding meeting of the United Nations at San Francisco. They marched solemnly behind Anderson down the long centre aisle of the piggery, each of them holding a small phial of perfume (I assume) under his nose. I was so proud of the hospital cleanliness of that piggery, of its wholesome smell, and here were these Chinese statesmen insulting me to my very face! I am glad, at all events, that they were not Maoists! Perhaps the perfume was mainly used to smother the smell of corruption in Chiang Kai-shek circles of that day. Anthony Eden, true English gentleman that he was, and because he was an English gentleman, showed great and intelligent interest in the pigs, as did the great Field Marshal Jan Smuts.

One day, Andy had me with him to greet a small group of English VIPs on their way to London from Washington, all but one wearing the uniform of Air Vice-Marshal. After a drink and a meal, we went down to the piggery; and upon our return to The Barn, the civilian VIP and I got into deep conversation. The topic was an important one: what is the best manure for the various crops? Horse manure, cow dung, sheep manure, poultry manure, pig manure? He was impressed, I think, to learn that I had read Lord Russell's books on agriculture, the same Russell who had done famous pioneer work in India. This civilian was pretty knowledgeable, too, and I began to wonder who he was. I hadn't caught his name, so I asked him frankly what it was. "Somervell," he said. "Somervell," I mused. "You're an author." "No, you may be thinking of my brother." "Didn't he write one or two books on economics or economic subjects?" I asked, and he agreed that it was so. "But you haven't written any yourself?" I asked him, and he said, "No, but my father wrote a book." "What was it about?" "It described his own system of teaching English," Somervell explained. "He devised a special system of his own, and one of his students was Winston Churchill." "By gad, he must have been a good teacher!" "That's what the President said to me yesterday," Somervell said. "The President?" I asked. "Yes, President Roosevelt." "You were talking with President Roosevelt yesterday?" "Yes, we had a long talk."

After we had seen the group off on their unheated Lancaster bomber, I remarked to Anderson, "An interesting fellow, that Somervell. Is he a gentleman farmer, or what?" "Don't you know who he is?" Anderson demanded. "He's the Attorney General of England!"

So among my souvenirs is remembrance of the time I discussed the relative values of horse, cow, sheep, pig, and poultry manures with the son of the man who taught Winston Churchill his English.

The piggery was going along swimmingly when an obstacle arose. Across Canada, the Government insisted on careful, skilled inspection of every hog after slaughter, to make sure that the pork was thoroughly wholesome for public consumption. The Royal Canadian Air Force establishment at Gander, with several thousand men in it, consumed large quantities of pork; it was an obvious market for our piggery. But there was no inspection of the carcasses. As soon as we discovered why the RCAF was not buying our pork, Anderson got busy and the next thing we knew was that the famous surgeon, Wing Commander John A. Sifton, was enlisted on our side. Sifton was the superintendent of the large Banting Memorial Hospital at Gander, named after the great co-discoverer of insulin, who had lost his life in a plane crash not far from Gander. Sifton is one of the most distinguished names in the whole of Canada, of course. I took secret delight in seeing this accomplished medical man come to our piggery at the end of each slaughter and personally examine the necessary glands in each carcass that indicated the state of the animal's health. There he was with his long white coat and rubber gloves, delicately slitting open one gland after the other and giving tuition to an officer of the RAF security police who'd been chosen for the training. All our hogs were so inspected thereafter, and we had no trouble selling pork to the RCAF or anyone else.

I was still not satisfied. We were raising perhaps as many as 2,500 hogs a year and merely selling the carcasses as shop hogs. Why couldn't we process the pork into hams and bacon, loins and chops, and fatback and pork sausages? Thus we could increase the value of our production far above the mere shop hog level. I persuaded Anderson that we should take a shot at it, and he told me to go ahead. I made enquiries by letter of where I might get a good man to come to Gander and show us how to do it. The man most highly recommended was Tom Olsen, a Canadian of Danish birth, who was said to be the greatest authority on pork in the whole of Canada. He had been pork superintendent for Canada Packers in Toronto and had left to form his own independent company. He was evidently a greater technical expert in pork processing than he was a businessman, for his business had failed. When I heard of him, he was superintendent of Wellington Packers, a small firm in Guelph, Ontario. I wrote to Tom Olsen and asked if he would come to Gander and undertake the job of training a small team. He wrote back and said that it would not be practical; that someone should come to Guelph and be taught the trade under his personal tuition in a plant that was already equipped and operating. So I went to Guelph and spent each day for a week in the plant and each night at Olsen's home. I made countless notes, so many and so thorough that I finally asked Olsen what book there was that described this process. He knew of no book, and so was born the idea that he and I would collaborate in the writing of what would be the great book of books on the subject of pork processing. I never did get around to it, and now it may be too late.

Back in Gander, we built a beautiful smokehouse, and from Pemberton in Toronto I obtained most of the equipment needed for our processing. I personally trained each man in the different phases of processing; what I didn't remember, I had only to consult my notes to revive. We put out magnificent hams and bacons, and boiled hams, and spareribs, and fatback pork which we put up in barrels, and sausages as good as were ever made outside Europe. Government House took two or three dozen sausages every week from me, and I had many distinguished customers throughout the country, including a substantial number of meat shops that bought them for re-sale. I was on the way to becoming a great rival of Canada Packers, Swift Canadian, and the other meat moguls.

If in my own mind my pig establishment was making me important, I was quickly cut down to size by a visiting United Church minister. The RCAF maintained a non-denominational chapel, and this was used by all the principal religious bodies in Gander. There was an altar at each end of the chapel, one used by Roman Catholics and the other by all the others. The pews had reversible backs, so that the congregation could face either way. One Sunday morning, my brother Reg, who was the general foreman of the piggery, with his wife and children and my wife, my two sons, and my daughter, joined me in going to church. We occupied one whole section of the front pew. What topic would you suppose the visiting minister preached that morning? The prodigal son! He waxed eloquent as he described the plight of the prodigal son, who sank to the very depths of degradation: feeding the pigs. How could men sink lower? Could there be a humbler or more degrading occupation? As his eloquence flourished, the broad smiles on the faces of the whole congregation changed into titters from a few, and that in turn caused a few others to burst into quite audible laughter. The poor minister stopped in bewilderment, and this quickly sobered up the congregation. We Smallwoods in the front row, every one of us, enjoyed the affair as much as anyone. He was contrite after the service was over and we told him the joke.

I have said that destiny, in the person of Group Captain David Anderson, had put the finger on me and brought me to Gander. Anderson did more than that: he made me stay in Gander. I was astonished to learn, and he appeared to be sincerely surprised at my astonishment, that I was to stay full time in Gander to run the piggery venture. This would mean my giving up my Barrelman program and living in Gander without income. Andy was determined about it, so I had to give in.

Running the piggery couldn't possibly absorb my energy or time, so I turned to other activities. I promoted some debates on the RAF side of the airport, and all Gander chuckled next day at the remark of one man, an employee of the Works and Building Section, as he joined those who spoke from the floor. The subject was "The Most Important Section of R.A.F. at Gander is . . ." and then followed the various departments: aircraft maintenance, signals, catering, mechanical department, works and buildings, and so forth. Speakers stoutly upheld the different activities of the airport, always contending that the movement of aircraft couldn't possibly continue without this or that department. *Movement* became the key word, and a worker from the plumbing section of Works and Buildings clinched the matter for all time. "You all talk about 'movement'. There will be no 'movement' unless Signals does its work, no 'movement' unless Aircraft Maintenance does its work, and so on. But let me tell you gentlemen tonight that not only the aircraft, but all 'movement' will stop in Gander a day or less than a day after the plumbers fall down on their job!"

I organized three separate unions in Gander and laid the groundwork for the organizing of a new consumers' cooperative society. When the RCAF pulled out after the war, I succeeded in capturing their fine library that had served the whole of the Canadian personnel in Gander. I turned it into a public library for Gander. I managed, too, to get the huge drill hall, with its swimming pool, from the RCAF for the use of Gander's civilian people. And when the RAF Transport Command withdrew from Gander, I bought, for the reasonable figure of $300 or $400, the library on that side of the airport. These books, numbering between 1,000 and 2,000, I decided to donate to Gambo, my birthplace. I delivered them to Father Walsh and asked him to provide the space that would make the books available to readers there.

Over on the American side of the airport, there was a Jesuit priest, Captain Lynch of the United States Air Force, and I heard that he was going to have Monday night meetings of young Roman Catholic men. It was to be a kind of debating club and generally a place for serious discussion. It was a veritable life-saver for me, for I missed sorely the intellectual clash and contest to which I had long been accustomed. I rounded up twenty-five or thirty young Roman Catholic friends of mine on the RAF side, including John Murphy, Gerry Wakeham, Clarence Macdonald, Dick Gaul, and Tom Kelly, and they agreed to go with me each Monday night to Captain Lynch's meetings. Most of the young fellows, I found, were shy about asking questions or getting on their feet to discuss the topics introduced, so it fell to me to be the devil's advocate and to stir things up by asking questions, some of them awkward, some embarrassing, but all of them to the point. Lynch was a brilliant man with a lively wit. He had made frequent use of the word *inspiration*, as applied to the original writing of the Scriptures and the Apostles, and I took him up on it. "Do you tell us that inspiration was confined to the authoring of the Scriptures and the Apostles?" I demanded. "Surely inspiration has continued to this day! Surely men have been inspired all down through the ages!" Captain Lynch held his ground, and I persisted. "Do you mean to tell me that a man like Abraham Lincoln was not inspired?" I demanded of him, and he neatly turned the tables on me by shaking his head and saying with a smile, "No, I don't admit that Lincoln was inspired—as a good Democrat, I can't admit that!" My example did encourage a few of the others to join in the questioning and discussion; but for the most part, they would call me aside afterward and suggest questions for me to ask at the next meeting.

I did a lot of flying around the Island with Anderson, who loved to fly and who seemed never to be at a loss to find some way of flouting King's Regulations by being in the dead centre of some part of them that appeared to justify his violation. He found on the base an old fellow from Fortune Bay who was a very handy man as a carpenter, and put him to work building some snipes for sailing on Gander Lake. Daily he went into the workshop, with his four dogs, to see how the snipes were coming along. One day he complained mildly that the progress was slow. The old fellow admitted as much but said the work would go faster "if I had me own axe". "Well, why don't you use your own axe?" Andy demanded, and the old fellow explained that it was in his home in Fortune Bay. "We'll go and get it," declared Andy. "Get your coat on and come along." Andy set off in the big Catalina Canso flying boat to fetch the axe; and as he brought back a large number of live lobsters as well, he was able to satisfy King's Regulations by reporting his admirable addition to the food supply of the base.

Once he took me to Buchans, the mining town in the centre of the Island, where my wife was holidaying with her sister, Mrs. Milley. A new "dirt" runway had been gouged out by bulldozers; and our plane, a tiny single-engined Tiger Moth, was the first ever to land on it. It had rained, and the runway was four or five inches deep in thin watery mud that sprayed every inch of the plane as we landed. It was so bad that Andy decided, when we left to come back, to take off from the road beside the runway. What a trip back that was! I sat in the seat behind him and was entranced by the route he followed: down the shore of Red Indian Lake to the beginning of the Exploits

River, down the river itself for fifteen or twenty miles, and then bearing off across country toward Gander. I peered down over the side, absorbing every inch of the country that I loved, and then straightened up to have a look forward, over Andy's shoulder, when my blood froze at the sight that met my eyes. We were headed straight into the side of a mountain! It was Mt. Peyton, and this was the end of everything. Nothing could stop us now from crashing into the mountain and being beaten into tiny fragments of plane and flesh. But we didn't crash. Andy must have approached within a bare few hundred feet of the mountain, when he tilted the nose upward, and we skimmed up the side and over the top and down the other side for 300 or 400 feet before levelling off again. When we reached the western end of Gander Lake, nothing would do for Andy but to follow the actual contour of the lakeshore, twisting and turning, banking sharply, as we followed the outline of every indentation, every cove and inlet. I was a little frightened at first, and then remembering Andy's skill, I settled back and enjoyed the breathless excitement of it. "How'd you like it?" Andy asked me with a grin as we climbed out of the plane at Gander, and I grinned back, "Any time."

Joe Gilmore and I became good friends. He was the famous chief of all aircraft maintenance at Gander, and the trans-Atlantic pilots who ferried bombers across to Britain swore by him, for he was famous for his skill, knowledge, sound judgement, and dependability. He was not himself a flier, but he had learned to fly small planes, up to the size of a Norseman; and his dearest love was to get into the air with one of them. I too enjoyed this, and we often schemed together to justify his taking the Norseman or one of the Moths on a flight somewhere or other. Once we decided that he should take me around the settlements on Bonavista and Trinity bays on a selling tour for the piggery. We lost the plane at Clarenville. Joe had moored her just offshore, but a sudden summer storm came up and one of the pontoons sprang a leak and filled with water, bringing her well down on one side into the water. The wind caught the up-tilted wing and whipped the plane over on her back, and she went down by the nose. When Joe and I were awakened at two o'clock in the morning and hurried down to the scene, nothing was to be seen but a bit of her tail above water. That ended that flight. With help, we got her ashore and mounted her on a railway flat car for the return journey to Gander.

Group Captain Brown, Andy's successor, was flying the Norseman when I suppose I had the narrowest escape from death in my life so far. We were flying to Buchans to deliver two dachshunds that Andy had left behind in my care to sell for him. I had arranged with Cyril Courage, Royal Stores manager at Buchans, to buy the dachshunds, and now Brown was flying them to Buchans for me. Joe Gilmore sat in the co-pilot's seat, and I and my son Ramsay and the dogs sat behind. As we approached the foot of Red Indian Lake, Brown was peering about the country, which he hadn't seen before, when suddenly, a few miles up the opposite shore of the lake, he spied a small settlement. It was Millertown, a pulpwood logging headquarters for the Grand Falls papermill. Brown headed in that direction and tilted the nose of the Norseman almost straight down to get a close look at it. We gathered speed. It made me a little uneasy, but I was inclined to depend on Brown until I glanced at Gilmore. He was clearly alarmed. He looked at Brown, and then down again, and back, and suddenly he seized the wheel with a shout at Brown and pulled back, at first gently and then quickly with all his strength. We were not very high off the ground when she levelled out and Brown resumed control. When we landed at Buchans, he gave Gilmore a mild perfunctory reprimand, for of course Gilmore had committed a frightful breach of discipline. But I was inclined to agree with Joe when, at the first moment he could, he said fiercely to me, "The madman! The madman!" Gilmore explained to me that the Norseman was in a power dive when he seized the controls, and that even then we were in danger of tearing the wings off.

Poor Joe Gilmore! One day, a pilot had landed the Norseman on the harbour ice in Gander Bay, and she had sunk partly through the ice, nose down, with her engine in the salt water. It was agreed that she needed a thorough overhaul. Joe was to fly her by stages to the Norduyn plant in Montreal, stopping overnight at Harmon Air Force Base at Stephenville and again on Prince Edward Island. Regulations required that she be accompanied over salt water by another plane, and the Catalina Canso went along with her. It was a thrilling prospect, to fly to Montreal in a single-engine plane, and I was looking forward to it with enormous zest. But Group Captain Brown grounded me, saying that he wanted me for some business or other in Gander. I didn't have the heart to go out onto the tarmac with Joe as he went to the Norseman, so I shook hands with him in the hangar and, sick with disappointment, turned back to my house. Joe got as far as Prince Edward Island, where the Norseman came hurtling to the ground in flames, the engine itself being found later many feet underground. Joe's body was brought back to Gander for burial. His wife and family were utterly desolated, and all Gander was in deep mourning. I started a drive to raise a fund for the family and struck up every air crew that passed through Gander for weeks afterward. I don't remember the amount that I raised, but it was a good many thousands.

Several times while I was at Gander, I got a chance of a free airplane ride to Montreal on board an RAF Transport Command aircraft. Since they were unheated, I'd wrap myself up in a blanket and with the help of lots of hot coffee keep myself reasonably comfortable throughout the flight. I'd take my chances on getting a return flight from Montreal, but it could be done. On one of those flights late in 1945, I went on from Montreal by rail to Toronto, where I wanted to talk with some grain merchants and at the same time visit one or two animal and poultry feed mills; for I was thinking actively just then, as I did even more actively some years later, about the fact that Newfoundland didn't have even one such mill. I felt that the raising of any kind of livestock—hogs, poultry, beef, or milk cattle—would continue to operate under a very serious disadvantage as long as we lacked a feed mill. (I counted it one of my best accomplishments as Premier that I brought the first feed mill to Newfoundland.)

When my work was done in Toronto, I returned to Montreal by overnight train and went straight to the Ford Hotel on Dorchester Street. After I had registered, I gave my bag to a bellhop to take up to my room and, buying the *Gazette*, the morning paper, at the newsstand, went into the dining room. I remember that I laid the *Gazette* folded on the table and picked up the menu and placed my order with the waitress before I took up the paper to read it. My heart pounded when I saw the headlines on the front page: Prime Minister Clement Attlee, in the House of Commons, and Lord Addison, the Secretary of State for the Dominions in the House of Lords, had made the statement that Newfoundland was to be provided with an opportunity to decide for itself what form of government it would have for the future. First, they explained, in a secret ballot, almost exactly as though it were a General Election, the people would elect forty-five persons to a National Convention. The country would be divided into separate constituencies for this purpose. The National Convention would have one supreme purpose: after enquiring carefully into the financial and economic state of the country, and determining the extent to which the degree of prosperity it enjoyed was the temporary product of the war, it would recommend to the United Kingdom the form or forms of government that would be the basis of the second great event, to follow afterward. This was a national referendum that would be held among the people. On the ballot paper in that vote, there would not be the names of any candidates, for there would be no candidates; rather, there would be a choice among alternative forms of government. Again, the ballot would be secret; and as provided in the subsequent legislation, if there were more than two forms of government on the ballot and none won a clear majority, then the form receiving the smallest number of votes would be dropped and a second referendum would be held.

I raced through the newspaper story and then read it more carefully, and then once again. I ate very little of that meal but soon went out into the streets of Montreal and walked for miles as I thought the matter over. Here, at long last, approached the moment and the opportunity for Newfoundlanders to settle their own fate. Now it would be in our own hands, and now Britain had provided the answer to the puzzle that Harry A. Winter had propounded in my paper only a few years before: how were the Newfoundland people to make their decision? Once Newfoundland became self-supporting again, responsible government, on request of the people, would be restored. That was the promise made by the British Government in 1933-1934. But how were the Newfoundland people to make their request? And who was to determine whether Newfoundland had again become self-supporting? No suggestion of answers had been provided in the original scheme, as Harry Winter had pointed out, but now here they both were.

I was going to be in it. All the King's horses and all the King's men wouldn't stop me. All of my work and training up to that moment made my entry inevitable. But on what side? What form of government would I want? I wasn't sure of what I wanted; I knew only what I didn't want. I didn't want the present system of non-elective, non-representative government, appointed for Newfoundland by the British Government. I had wanted it, back in 1932, two years before it came. I had welcomed it warmly when it came. I had supported it for most of its existence. I felt certain that I would prefer it to a simple, unconditional return to responsible government. Was there a good condition that could be instituted? Was there a scheme that would give us responsible government that would work? That was the problem that tormented me, and which I knew, from my intimate association with the thousands of Newfoundlanders living in Gander, concerned our people insofar as they noticed the matter at all. These Newfoundlanders at Gander hailed from every coast, every bay, and hundreds of individual settlements throughout the Island. They were incomparably the most representative group of Newfoundlanders in the country. I knew their feeling; and knowing their feeling, I knew the feeling of Newfoundland in general. The feeling was one of considerable respect for the integrity, efficiency, and goodwill of the Commission of Government. Most people thought it was the best government we had ever had. Only the most thoughtful people were very much disturbed by the non-representative nature of the Commission. Only a small proportion of Newfoundlanders was much concerned about the fact that the Commission was responsible, not to the people or to an elected House of the people, but to the British Government in London. In short, the great majority of Newfoundlanders were entirely pragmatic about the matter: "No matter how we reached the shore, so we both reached it." Never mind how the Commission of Government got born; never mind the fact that they were not constitutionally answerable to us; never mind the fact that we had no constitutional rights whatsoever. It was a pretty good government—what's all the excitement about? I knew this feeling, and I was one of the small number—perhaps the only one—of political observers in Newfoundland who knew it. And I knew it that day, December 11, 1945, as I walked back and forth through the downtown section of Montreal.

I remembered the long walks and talks that Gordon Bradley and I had had, back in 1930, around Quidi Vidi Lake, and Bradley's determined voice declaiming to me, "Joe, you mark my words! Confederation with Canada is our only hope, our only salvation!" I remembered my asking him why he thought so, and not being much impressed by his answer. But I remembered also the resolve I had made then, and not kept up to now, that I would make my own study of the matter. I would find out for myself what this Confederation thing was all about; what it was, how it worked, what effect it would have on Newfoundland were we to become part of the Canadian Confederation.

Before the day was over, my mind had cleared. I would make that intensive study of Confederation now, and I would discover whether or not Confederation was the missing condition to successful responsible government in Newfoundland. My mind, at that point, was wide open on the subject of Confederation. I really didn't know Canada. I had been in Halifax, Saint John, and Charlottetown, and I had concluded that they weren't all that far ahead of my own St. John's. Once only had I been to Montreal. I knew practically nothing of Canada's history. I knew not one Canadian public man, except Premier Greenfield whom I had interviewed in London, and he was now no longer in public life. It would require a thorough examination of the question, from the very beginning, and that was precisely the kind of task I had always revelled in.

That night I went to Ewart Young's apartment, and we were both excited, and we talked loudly and debated the issue. Ewart was an able Newfoundland journalist who was living then in Montreal. He was an ardent Confederate already, as Bradley had been. I admitted guardedly that I was interested.

I caught an RAF bomber back to Gander next day, and that night sat down and wrote ten letters: one to the Prime Minister of Canada, and one to the Premier of each province. I confess that I had to telephone a friend to make sure that I had all of the names of the nine provinces and to learn from him the names of most of the provincial capitals. I daresay these letters are still in the files in some of the provincial capitals—unless the premiers took them with them on their retirement. The letter itself, as I recall, was quite simple, something like this:

> The Honourable
> The Prime Minister of Nova Scotia,
> Halifax, Nova Scotia.
>
> Sir:
>
> As you may have read, Newfoundland is soon to have a National Convention to recommend the form of government that Newfoundland shall have in the future. This National Convention is to recommend to the British Government what forms of government should be placed on the ballot paper in a national referendum of all the people to be held subsequently.
>
> I have decided to offer myself as a candidate for election to the National Convention, and I wish to make a careful

> study of what effect would be had upon Newfoundland and her people if Newfoundland were to become a Province of Canada.
>
> Would you be kind enough to assist me in this study? I would like to have copies of some of your more recent budget speeches, estimates of revenue and expenditures, annual reports, your Provincial Constitution, any books or magazine articles that would throw light on the subject, and anything else that you think would help me in my study.

Quite soon the material began to pour into Gander, from the nine provinces and from Ottawa. I buried myself in a small mountain of printed material, working at it day and night. Often I had to pull down the blinds to shut out the dawn before I turned in for a few hours of sleep. For several weeks, I continued this intensive study and made innumerable notes. I remember that I had been sleeping a mere two hours one morning when there was a knock on my bedroom door, and I opened it to find the Rt. Rev. Monsignor Finn, of Grand Falls. He was in Gander and had dropped in to see me, and I invited him to sit on the side of the bed. We talked Confederation, and he told me this incident. As a young priest, he had gone to visit Bishop Power at St. George's, for they were friends. That was around 1919, and Bishop Power showed him a document that he had received from the Hon. Charles Doherty, the Minister of Justice and Attorney General of Canada, who was the bishop's friend. Father Finn was able to repeat for me the principal contents of that statement. It was a description of the terms and conditions that Canada had offered to Newfoundland if the Island were to join the Canadian Confederation. The public debt was to be taken over, a bounty was to be paid to the fishermen on their fish, and there were other attractive proposals. Behind that offer lay Canada's conviction that Germany was probably going to win the war. The submarine warfare of 1917 was terrifyingly successful, and was sinking British shipping much faster than it could be replaced, and it looked very much as though Britain might be starved into surrender. "Where would that leave Canada?" the Canadian Government asked itself. They decided that they would invite the Royal Family to come to Canada and would then settle down to the stern task of defending Canada from probable German invasion. But what of Newfoundland? Newfoundland was the sentinel of the St. Lawrence. The direst conceivable peril would face Canada if the Germans took possession of Newfoundland. So, obviously, in that thinking, Canada would have to take over Newfoundland. But that would require Newfoundland's ready consent, and so the offer was made. It was made to Sir Edward Morris, Newfoundland's Prime Minister. The bishop told Father Finn that he had learned that Morris had not shown it, or even mentioned it, to his Cabinet. Instead, he had gone to England and shown the document to the British Government. Lloyd George pooh-poohed the Canadian fears. Morris did not return to Newfoundland, but cabled his resignation as Prime Minister to the Governor and entered the House of Lords as Lord Morris of Kilbride. (Years later, I asked Jack Pickersgill to have a search made for that document, but he told me that he had no success.)

I ended my weeks of reading a staunch and confirmed Confederate, with one proviso only: that we should get satisfactory terms and conditions from Canada. My course was set. I was going to get myself elected to the National Convention and then get the Convention to ask Canada for her best terms.

One of my first converts to Confederation was Anthony Mullowney, the Superintendent of Works and Buildings at the Gander Airport. With the war over, the RCAF, the RAF, and the Americans began to pull out. The Canadian Government set up the War Assets Disposal Corporation (WADC) and the very first sale they made anywhere in Newfoundland was that of 3,000 grey woollen blankets. Tony Mullowney and I heard of them and resolved promptly to buy them, if we could get them cheaply enough. Our plan was to sell them quickly and use the profits to finance our individual campaigns to be elected to the National Convention. Tony, a native of Summerville, on the south side of Bonavista Bay, was going to run for Bonavista South as a Confederate. We decided to offer $1 each for the blankets, but where were we going to get the $3,000? I solved the problem in the usual way: I telephoned to Ches Crosbie in St. John's. He was amused by the thought of my engaging in a trading venture but said that he would telephone to the bank manager in Gander. He did, and we got the $3,000 and closed the deal. Now we faced the big problem of where to sell them. We began to compile a list of businessmen around the outports, planning to send each of them a circular letter offering the blankets for sale in small lots of two or three dozen each. We were up to our necks getting this sales campaign ready when who should arrive at Gander but Darius Powell for Bowater's woods department. He came expressly for the purpose of buying the whole lot of blankets from the WADC for the Bowater logging camps in western Newfoundland. He was chagrined to discover that they were already sold. Powell quickly came to me, wanting to know if we'd sell him all 3,000 blankets. Tony and I talked it over and agreed to sell—for $3 a blanket. That would make a "modest" profit of $2 for each blanket, or $6,000.

It was the bargain of the century for Bowater, but Tony and I wouldn't do so badly either. I telephoned Ches Crosbie and proudly told him that we'd sold the blankets for $6,000 profit. He chuckled appreciatively, and I told him airily, in fun, "Any time, Ches, any time at all that you want a bit of profitable trading done, call on me." With his usual generosity, Ches told me that I could keep half the profit. I divided it with Tony Mullowney, $1,500 each, and with it I promptly paid off some accumulated debts. It ate up my share completely. Tony later changed his mind about running for the National Convention and insisted on my taking back his share of the spoils, to help finance my campaign for Confederation. Surely Tony Mullowney deserves to rank as a Newfoundland Father of Confederation.

Bishop John O'Neill of Harbour Grace, into whose diocese Gander fell, decided to establish a parish there, and he sent Father Philip McCarthy from Grand Falls to do it. Father Phil and I became warm friends, for night after night we were the guests of our mutual friend Tony and his wife Letty. Tony and I set out to convert Father Phil. And when Bishop O'Neill arrived to hold the first meeting of the potential parishioners, he had dinner at Tony's, where Father Phil and I were the other guests. I washed up the dishes after the meal, so that the Bishop and the other three could go on to the meeting. Then I waited not too patiently for their return, for I wanted to go after the Bishop with a view to converting him to Confederation, too. He fought back but faintly, and I entertained some inward hope that I would capture him for my cause. I did, indeed; but not for years to come. And then, what a man he proved to be! What a man! A great service was held in the Pro-Cathedral at Grand Falls to mark a milestone in his life as priest and bishop. I was there and, as Premier, was given a seat of honour in the front row. Bishop O'Neill, in his moving speech in reply to all the addresses of greeting and congratulation, said frankly that he had opposed Confederation when I espoused it, but now he was happy to say frankly that he had been wrong, that

Confederation was good for Newfoundland, and that I had been right in the stand I took. Handsomer words were never spoken.

Where I was to run for the National Convention was more or less settled for me. David Anderson's insistence in 1943 that I live in Gander had historic results—historic, that is, if I can be credited with part of the responsibility for changing Canada's and Newfoundland's history by turning Canada into a federal family of ten and Newfoundland into a province of Canada. For see what happened: when the Commission of Government announced that there was to be elected a National Convention of forty-five members, each of them representing a geographical slice of the country, they made the stern condition that no person could run for election except in the "slice" where he was residing. I think that "ordinarily resident" was the term. This meant that as I was now, thanks to Andy, ordinarily resident at Gander, I would have to run as a candidate for election to the National Convention in the constituency that contained Gander. The airport itself was divided: the eastern portion of it, where I resided, was put into the constituency of Bonavista Centre, which also contained my birthplace, Gambo. Whatever chance I might have of being elected to the National Convention for Bonavista Centre, I would have no chance whatsoever if I were reduced to running in the constituency that contained my home on Kenmont Road, St. John's West Extern—that is, if I ran as a Confederate. In the General Election of 1869, the people of Bonavista Bay had voted triumphantly against Confederation with Canada, and no constituency in that bay would normally be classed as one that a Confederate would be anxious to contest—indeed, we knew of no constituency that would. A Confederate's chances in Bonavista Centre would, nevertheless, be far greater than in the farming constituency of St. John's West Extern. We might or might not be a province of Canada today had not Anderson insisted on my living in Gander, or had the Commission of Government not inserted the residence qualification to election to the National Convention. Gander itself was to be the birthplace of the drive to unite Newfoundland and Canada as one country.

My farming venture on Kenmont Road turned out to be one of the most profitable "farm" ventures in Newfoundland's history, surely! It cost me $3,000 to acquire it, about $1,000 to improve its dwelling, and another $2,000 to build a new bungalow on it—$6,000 in all. That whole section of Kenmont Road came into intense demand for industrial and commercial sites. Had I waited a year or two longer than I did, I could have got a much higher price for it. This was shown by the sales of land all around me. But I did well—I got $125,000 for it. This was free of all taxes, for the sale meant recovery of capital and capital gains, both then exempt from taxation. I paid off some debts and made some useful investments with the proceeds.

Hard to concentrate

The Confederate

12

A Crusade Is Born

Who asks whether the enemy were defeated by strategy or valor?

Virgil

All victories breed hate.

Baltazar Gracian

When the heart is afire some sparks will fly out of the mouth.

Thomas Fuller

I was now a Confederate, but what was I going to do about it?

I was going to bring Newfoundland and Canada together as one country. I was going to get the National Convention to ask Canada to state the terms and conditions of Newfoundland's entry into the Confederation. If the terms and conditions were acceptable, I was going to try to persuade the Newfoundland people to vote for Confederation. But first I had to get myself elected to membership in the National Convention. And the whole thing was really one: persuading the Newfoundland people to vote Confederate, persuading the National Convention to ask Canada for the terms and conditions, getting myself elected to the National Convention. Propaganda was the great need, but propaganda in the best sense of the word: factual, informative, truthful, sincere. Clearly, I would have to employ whatever experience and skill I had as a propagandist, and probably much more than I had.

Our people had no notion at all of what Confederation was or what it meant. They had no conception of a federal system of government. Their only experience of government was what they had had before the coming of the Commission system. In Newfoundland up to this time, one Government alone (assisted in a minor way by the municipal council of St. John's) had performed all the functions of government that in most other countries were performed by federal, provincial or state, municipal, county or other forms of local administration. Schools, local roads and local streets, relief of the poor, street lighting (where there was any), traffic rules in even the smallest hamlet in the country, hospitals and health—all, without exception, came under that one Government that was responsible to the House of Assembly. The only connections that the people had with it were the election of their Members to that House of Assembly and their relations with the elected Member. The Member was expected to get a sick member of a constituent's family into a hospital; to get the Government's Relieving Officer to issue relief to a needy family; to get a grant of money from the Government to repair a local road or fix a local bridge or do anything else that needed to be done. The extraordinary practice prevailed of having the elected Member for the District receive in his own hands every dollar of cash that was granted by the Government for a local road or bridge or other works, and for that Member to spend it! He would select some person in the settlement concerned to employ the men to do the work. Rare indeed was the Member who had any knowledge of accounting, and financial controls were words from an unknown tongue. (Yet it is just as extraordinary a fact that the overwhelming bulk of this money was honestly, if not always efficiently, spent to accomplish the purposes intended. They were pathetically small amounts in any case.)

It was to people whose knowledge and experience of government was so simply defined that I undertook to explain the complexities of Confederation; and not merely to explain, but to convince them of its rightness for them—a mammoth task! When I launched my speaking campaign in Bonavista Bay, I took three to four hours for every speech, often using a blackboard, to make sure that even the slowest intellect in the audience would understand as vividly as I did myself what Confederation was, and what we might expect it to do for Newfoundland in general and the common people in particular. Later, as my campaign went into its final phases, I employed a simile that many Newfoundlanders readily understood. Scores of Lodges of the Loyal Orange Association, of the Knights of Columbus, of the Odd Fellows and other fraternal societies existed throughout the country, with tens of thousands of members. I pointed to them as examples of the federal system: each individual Lodge or Council or Branch was autonomous in purely local affairs, but was part of a much larger country-wide body, which in turn might be part of an international organization. The country-wide body ruled in certain things, and the international organization ruled in still higher matters. I think that this explanation was the first to give many of our people at least some grasp of what Canada's federal system was like. It enabled them to understand how it could be that, under Confederation, a province would have its own elected Provincial Government, to handle purely local matters, while at the same time there would be a great Central Government at Ottawa that would coordinate national affairs for all the provinces. This Central or Federal Government would be answerable to the Parliament of Canada, just as the local Provincial Government would be answerable to the Provincial House of Assembly. Each Legislature and each Government would have its duties and rights clearly spelled out. And, I used to say triumphantly, Newfoundlanders, like the people in the other nine provinces, would have the right to elect that Parliament of all Canada and would be represented in it by their own Members of Parliament and their own Senators. In addition—a fact that appealed to so many people then (and all people today!)—Newfoundlanders, besides paying Canadian federal taxes to the Federal Government of Canada, would share in the huge amounts that this Government paid out to individual provinces! I drove home, repetitively and endlessly, the fact that there were "have" and "have-not" provinces, that Newfoundland would be one of the have-nots, and that therefore we would receive from Ottawa far, far more than we contributed.

On March 1, 1946, I launched my campaign for Confederation. I did it by writing a series of eleven articles that I took in to St. John's to the Hon. John S. Currie, editor of the *Daily News*, asking him to publish them. He was strictly anti-Confederate, but a personal friend of mine and a man of fine spirit. "Yes, Joe," he said, "I'll publish them, but I would prefer to have them appear as letters to the editor from you. If I publish them as articles, it will look as though I had commissioned you to write them, and that would suggest that I favoured or our paper favoured Confederation with Canada." "That's all right with me, but will you publish them daily without interruption, so that they will appear as an unbroken series constituting one whole?" He said yes, and so they appeared. Except for one or two gaucheries, the eleven letters, and two or three others that I added in reply to real or fancied objections raised to them, were truthful, accurate, and for many readers a great revelation of what Confederation would mean, or do, for Newfoundland.*

Having nailed my colours to the mast as a staunch Confederate (always provided that Canada would offer us acceptable terms and conditions of entry), I now took my second step. This was to embark upon a speaking tour in Bonavista Bay. I had received an invitation from several men in or near Gambo, men who worked at Gander, to

*Afterward, in Ottawa, when our first delegation from the National Convention negotiated the terms of Confederation, some Canadian negotiators professed surprise at how much I seemed to know about their own system. When I spoke of federal spending on roads in the provinces, and one of the Canadian Ministers said that no federal money was ever spent on provincial roads, I was able to point to several instances where precisely this had been done, naming the places and occasions, and he hurriedly acknowledged that I was right.

come to address a meeting. I went one Saturday night, April 6, 1946, and for nearly four hours spoke in an unbelievably crowded LOA hall at Middle Brook, one of the three settlements of the Gambo community. Not often in my life have I seen so much of the space of a hall occupied by human bodies as in that hall that night. It was hot, and as I warmed to my speech, it became hotter. After a while, without interrupting my speech, I took off my coat and vest and hung them on the back of a chair; half an hour later, I took off my collar and tie, and now I was properly stripped down to it. It was my first speech about Confederation, and that crowd of fine men and women was not hesitant to express its approval and support. "He's another Winston Churchill!" one of the citizens proclaimed delightedly to the crowd. They stood to a man and a woman to uphold a motion from the floor expressing support for my ideas.

Word of that remarkable meeting spread along the centre and north side of the Bay, and it wasn't long before I received a letter of invitation from the island of Greenspond. It was sent to me by the well-known and beloved Captain Peter Carter, the equally beloved Captain Charlie Downer, and the respected H. William Barrow. They had seen one or two of my *Daily News* letters and heard of the Middle Brook meeting, and they wanted to know about this Confederation. On May 7, Ron Sturge took me to the island from Gambo in his small motorboat. The Greenspond meeting was a duplicate of the Middle Brook gathering: it was jammed with people to the last square inch, and again I delivered a four-hour speech, for the first time using a blackboard. An Anglican clergyman put some very sympathetic questions to me after my speech, and clearly, I made a profound impression on that great audience.* (Out of 500 votes cast there, I received 495 in the first general election.)

My next meeting was at Fair Island, in the SUF hall, May 9, with Captain Malcolm Rogers as my chairman. On the same day, in the afternoon, I had a meeting in the school hall at Silver Hare Island, with Captain Sam Matthews taking the chair. Then came Bragg's Island on May 10. It was here that I began a practice that I often followed afterward. This was to go to the last house out at the extremity of the settlement, on one side of the cove or harbour, and work my way clear around the settlement to the last house on the opposite

*I carefully refrained from making any mention of the fact that my grandfather David and his family had lived there in the 1860s, or that he had flown his Confederate flag in the 1869 election.

shore, calling at each house, making the acquaintance of its occupants, and inviting them to come along to my meeting in the hall—almost always an Orange hall or an SUF building—that night. It was good technique, for many of my audience were by now personal friends, and invariably I got an enthusiastic welcome and the closest possible attention. I don't remember speaking for less than three hours at any such meeting, and often it went to the full four. These meetings were not only to convert the people to Confederation, but to persuade them to elect me as their representative to the forthcoming National Convention. "Don't vote for me," I pleaded at every meeting, "unless you want to be represented by a man who will fight to get Canada's terms and conditions of Confederation. Somebody else will be asking you to elect him [I would change the tense whenever that opponent appeared at the same meeting] and if he is against Confederation, I plead with you to vote for him, not for me, if you don't want to be represented by a man who'll fight to get Canada's terms of Confederation."

There was only one place in the whole of central and northern Bonavista Bay where I met with any opposition at all. This was a large place, relatively speaking, where 500 votes were cast in the election. A lady in the audience stood up and interrupted my speech with a question. I answered the question politely. After a while, she was up again, and again I answered her politely. I noticed the restiveness of the audience when she stood up a third time, and at her fourth interruption, there were shouts of impatience. I answered her rather tartly, and the whole audience applauded their approval. It turned out that the lady was not the most popular woman in the area, and the audience was itching to have me go aboard her in my replies and was impatient with my politeness. (One vote was cast against me in that place, and for weeks the people tried to figure out who it could have been. They decided in the end that it must have been a visitor who was in the settlement that day.)

That was the only interruption I had in my whole National Convention election campaign, but it reminds me of another incident that had occurred some years earlier, during the campaign for Sir Richard Squires in the election of 1928. I led a group of four of us to hold a meeting for Squires in the local school at Summerside in Humber Arm across from Corner Brook. The meeting was crowded, and down at the back, near the big bogey stove that heated the room, was a man who had evidently come to the settlement from somewhere else after bending his elbow a bit and who wanted to have some fun. I put on Jim Penney first, and he hadn't spoken more than a few minutes when the first interruption came. He tried to ignore it, but that didn't cure the problem. Then I put on Michael Foley, a fluent Irish tongue if ever there was one, and he got away without interruption for twelve or fifteen minutes; and when it came, he tried to quieten the drunk by jollying him along. That didn't work, and the drunk got a little noisier. I saw that stern measures would have to be taken, so I told the chairman to introduce me as the last speaker. Because I had then a bit of a reputation as a speaker, I spoke for quite some time before I was interrupted. Then I was ready. "Oh, my friend, I was wondering when we were going to hear from you again. In fact, I was beginning to be afraid that you were going to ignore me. Now, friend, I want you to listen to something very special that I have for you—this is not for the rest of the audience, but just for you alone: something very special, and I want you to take in every word of it."

The audience, and the drunk, were interested at once, and I went on, " 'Twas a cool raw morning, just as dawn was breaking. There was this field, and this big tree growing in the middle of it, and down on the bottom branch of it, this little bird." At this, my drunk recovered enough to sneer, "A little bird!" "Yes, a little bird, a small little bird, cold and miserable, and hungry, and discouraged, and wondering miserably where she was going to get her breakfast. And just in the depths of her despair, a horse came along and stopped right underneath the tree, and did what many a horse has been known to do before, and then walked on. The bird hopped down onto the ground and had a right royal hot breakfast. Now the world looked different, and the bird, warm and well fed, flew up to the tip-top of the tree and let out with shrill singing of happiness and goodwill. A hen hawk flying overhead heard the singing, spied the bird on the top of the tree, curved down, and with one swoop seized the bird in its beak and made off with it. And that was the end of the little bird."

The drunk was ill-advised enough to attempt a comeback, "The end of the little bird!" he sneered. "Yes," I said, "that was the end of the little bird. But it is not the end of the story. The end of the story is a moral, and the moral is this: 'When you're full of shit, keep your mouth shut!' " The audience exploded into a riot of laughter, and the drunk slipped out of the hall.

One day during my 1946 campaign, I got off the freight train at Alexander Bay station to take the three-mile road to the coastal settlement of Glovertown. I noticed that some sparks from the engine

10. J. R. S. spcaks to the National Convention—and to the people of Newfoundland

11. Writing speeches for the Confederates

12. The first plenary meeting in Ottawa, with Prime Minister Mackenzie King and Louis St. Laurent, 1947

13. J. R. S. – propagandist

14. Counting the telegrams that demanded that Confederation be placed on the ballot

15. J. R. S. with Mackenzie King at the Liberal leadership convention, August 1948

(above) 16. Albert Walsh and Prime Minister St. Laurent signing the Terms of Union in the Senate Chamber, December 11, 1948

(left) 17. J. R. S. holding his first press conference as Premier, immediately after being sworn in, April 1, 1949

(right) 18. Victory!

20. J. R. S. with Alfred Valdmanis

(left) 19. Newfoundland's first appearance at a Federal-Provincial Conference, Ottawa, 1949

(right) 21. J. R. S. and J. W. Pickersgill – an unshatterable partnership

22. Pickersgill and Smallwood on the campaign trail

23. J. R. S.'s favourite way to campaign

had started a small grass fire on the side of the track a few hundred feet back from the station. It wasn't very big, but I thought that the train hands or station men should take no chances, but go and put it out. Quite evidently they didn't, for I wasn't in Glovertown more than an hour when the word spread in some, though not great, alarm through the settlement that a forest fire was burning near the railway station and, the wind being the way it was, that it would probably sweep down upon the town. There was no one in Glovertown with authority to organize the people into corrective action, and of course the Newfoundland Fire Patrol people were far away. I hurried back over the road a half-mile from the settlement to suggest to the few families living along the road that they might be wise to get their household effects out and down to the waterside. Some of them did, and some did not. As the flames roared inexorably toward the town, other families began to move their furniture to the edge of the harbour. In the next three or four hours, that forest fire destroyed seventy houses, shops, and other buildings, and was the greatest disaster that ever struck Glovertown. I had chartered my friend George Turner's boat to come from Happy Adventure and pick me up at Glovertown to take me to some of the Bonavista Bay islands for public meetings, but the fire interrupted that program. I offered to take in the boat with me some homeless people who wanted to go to Port Blandford, on the railway line, at the head of Clode Sound. There was a full boat-load of us, and I'll never forget that rough and, to me at least, rather frightening passage in the black, stormy night as we punched and battered our way in a rough sea the 30 miles to Port Blandford. There I caught a train to St. John's, and as I was the first to reach the city from stricken Glovertown, I was invited to go on the air and tell Newfoundland about it. I gave my account and in my statement launched an appeal for donations to a fund that I had decided to raise for the succour of some of the poorer families of the settlement.

The election took place on June 21, and I was elected to the National Convention with a comfortable majority: 2,129 votes for me; 277 votes for my opponent, Kitchener Pritchett.* Everybody in Newfoundland knew by now that I had run as a Confederate, and with 89 per cent of the votes cast, I would enter the National Con-

*I had a moment of panic on nomination day when, for most of the period during which candidates could be nominated, no one else appeared. Wasn't Mr. Pritchett going to be nominated? I was desperate, for if I got elected by acclamation it would be no victory at all for Confederation. I and some of my friends exerted strenuous efforts to get Mr. Pritchett nominated in time.

vention with the largest percentage majority of any of the forty-five members. It was at least a promising start for Confederation! If one constituency could be won to Confederation, others could; and if you let your hopes run away with you, the majority could. I was the only declared Confederate to be elected as a Confederate to any public body in Newfoundland in nearly eighty years. Whiteway, Bond, Morris, Squires, and Morine were Confederates, but with the exception of Morine, they had remained prudently silent on their Confederate views. Morine, a Canadian by birth, was known to be a Confederate, but even he was careful not to make an issue of it in any election. Gregory Power, a declared Confederate, was a candidate for election to the National Convention from Placentia East, but he fell short of a majority.

No man had read my letters to the *Daily News* with more interest than J. Scott Macdonald, Canada's High Commissioner to Newfoundland. I had gone to his offices on Circular Road in St. John's to obtain some statistics that I needed, but had not met him personally. Now that I had been elected a Member of the National Convention, I wanted a meeting with him, for I had decided that my next move must be to Ottawa. What if Canada were not interested in my theme of union? I really had no evidence at all that Canada would welcome an approach from the National Convention. This might prove to be a fatal flaw in my proposed course of action. If I should succeed in getting the National Convention to ask Ottawa to receive a delegation from the Convention to discuss terms, and Canada said no to the request, what an utter fool I'd look and feel! I'd better plug that loop-hole if I could. And then there were still some things I wanted to know about the Canadian federal system. It was one thing to know that the Parliament and Government of Canada had constitutional responsibility for this or that problem or work in Canada. The question was, how would the federal authorities carry out that work in practice? After all, it was not enough to know what the federal authority had the responsibility to do; it was just as important to know how and to what extent they did it. I still had enough money to get me to Ottawa and pay my hotel bill there, thanks largely to Tony Mullowney, but I knew nobody in Ottawa, and that was why I saw Scott Macdonald. Would he notify his Government that I was going to Ottawa, and would his Government be willing to fill in the gaps in my knowledge? Macdonald promised to get in touch with Ottawa; and in the meantime, I was encouraged by his personal opinion that I would be well received.

I discovered when I got to Ottawa in August 1946 that the Hon. Frank Bridges had been appointed to be my guide. He was Canada's Minister of Fisheries and MP for York-Sunbury, New Brunswick. He asked me what I wanted to know, and it was he who made the necessary arrangements and introductions for me in each of the departments of the Canadian Government: Agriculture, Transport, Public Works, Fisheries, Health and Welfare, and a dozen others. I spent half a day in some departments, less than that in some, and more than that in others. I wouldn't say that there were many men in Ottawa who knew more than I did of the nature and variety of the operations and work of those departments! I worked twelve and fourteen hours a day at it, for some Ministers and Deputy Ministers were willing to meet me at night. The Department of Finance and the Bank of Canada, and C. D. Howe's great department were exceptionally helpful to me.

The one man who assisted me above all others was Dr. R. A. MacKay. He had been a professor at Dalhousie University, a member of the Rowell-Sirois Commission, and later became Canada's ambassador to Norway and Iceland. When I was in Ottawa, he was in the Department of External Affairs. We became close, and I freely confided to him my own purposes and ambitions in this whole drive of mine.

I didn't know it then, but the best friend I had in Ottawa on that visit, and ever afterward, was John W. Pickersgill. He remembers well the occasion of our first meeting, though I do not. I had never heard of him, didn't know of his long-held personal interest in Newfoundland, and had no conscious reason to notice him closely. He was Prime Minister King's special executive assistant. Because Mr. King was in England at the time of my visit, I couldn't meet him, but Mr. Pickersgill arranged for me to meet the acting Prime Minister, the Rt. Hon. Louis S. St. Laurent, in a small office just off the Chamber of the House of Commons. I met Mr. St. Laurent for merely a few minutes, but even then he impressed me deeply as a courtly and gracious man. In guarded, very general terms, he expressed the hope that it might turn out to be feasible for Newfoundland and Canada to join together in Confederation.

I have often wondered what he and the other Ministers of Canada must have thought of me at that time? From Scott Macdonald in St. John's, they knew at least this much: that I had run for the National Convention as a professed Confederate, had been elected with a very large majority as a Confederate, was the author of those letters in the *Daily News*, and clearly intended to induce the National Convention to ask Ottawa for the terms of Confederation. Macdonald would doubtless have given them at least a sketchy outline of my career—pigs, trade unions, Socialist propaganda, some books, impecunious, energetic. It was not, in the eyes of cautious Ministers, a prepossessing picture. I suppose that they may have felt that they were perhaps damned if they did and damned if they didn't pay me at least some perfunctory attention. I know now, long years afterward, that the Canadian Cabinet was by no means falling over itself to have Newfoundland join Canada. I think that Mackenzie King himself did generally, if rather lukewarmly, welcome it. Brooke Claxton, C. D. Howe, and one or two others were a little warmer than Mr. King in their willingness to have Newfoundland in. Mr. St. Laurent, more than any of them, was willing to stretch a point in Newfoundland's favour. But behind them all was the grey eminence, Jack Pickersgill, without whom Newfoundland might not even yet have become a province of Canada. Scott Macdonald, too, was as ardent as anyone in support.

So I did have two staunch supporters, Pickersgill and Macdonald, and probably R. A. MacKay, with a few of the Ministers likely to support the idea. But the whole Cabinet, following Mackenzie King's lead, was fearful lest Newfoundland get the idea that Canada was eager to have Newfoundland, so eager perhaps as to be willing to scheme and connive at it. Even the Ministers who most favoured the idea were at one with their colleagues who insisted that there must be no Canadian interference whatever, but that the decision must be left strictly to the Newfoundland people themselves. It is laughable to hear, though we hear it often enough nowadays, of the Canadian "plot" to entrap Newfoundland into the Confederation. There were moments, I do confess, when I wished that there might be at least an element of truth in the suspicion. At any rate, everyone was polite and friendly to me in Ottawa, and I came back to Gander hopeful, even confident, that the Canadians would say yes to a request for the terms from the National Convention.

My old friend, Gordon Bradley, one of the two survivors of the Liberal debacle in 1932, had been elected to the National Convention in Bonavista East, and I knew he was a Confederate.* A few

*One night after the National Convention election, I took Bradley to Canada House on Circular Road to meet Scott Macdonald. On the way, we walked the full length of Circular Road, east to west, strolling along casually, talking loudly and fearlessly—for the benefit of anyone who might have seen us—of the United Nations, the Second World War, and the fiscal system of the Peruvians. And so, still casually, we ap-

days before the Convention opened, we met at his home in Bonavista. After we had discussed matters for many hours, I said to him, "Gordon, Newfoundland will have a Minister in the Canadian Government, and of course a Premier of her own. You're the senior man, and you have first choice. I'll take what you don't want." He said that he wouldn't be found dead occupying the office of Premier. He had had enough of Newfoundland politics to last him all his life. "I take it, then, that what you want is to be Newfoundland's Minister in the Canadian Government?" He replied that he doubted that Newfoundland would ever have a Minister in the Canadian Cabinet, or that Newfoundland would ever be a province; but should Newfoundland actually become a province, and the opportunity come to him, then he certainly would want to be Newfoundland's Minister. I thrust out my hand to him and said, "Good for you, Mr. Minister, and I trust I may have your support for me for Premier of the new province?" He laughed and said, "You're welcome to it, Joe!" I insisted that we shake hands on the bargain, and we did. I was very happy, for I wouldn't have wanted to be "found dead" occupying the office of a Federal Minister. A couple of years or so afterward, Bradley, Senator Ray Petten, and I were together at the Liberal Convention at which Mackenzie King passed back the reins of leadership and Mr. St. Laurent was elected in his place. When I was asked to address the Convention, I told them of this conversation and this pact, and those 3,000 delegates roared with appreciative laughter. As is now so well known, the offices we shared between us in Bonavista that night were in fact occupied according to schedule.

On my return from Ottawa, I spent a few days in Gander, then set off by train on the Great Adventure in St. John's. Pierce Fudge, one of the two men elected for the Humber District, was on the train, coming in from Corner Brook. I was delighted to have this undisturbed chance to feel him out and, if he needed it, to convert him to Confederation; or if not all the way to Confederation, at least to the idea that we must ask Canada for her terms of union. Pierce Fudge and I were old friends from the days when I lived in Corner Brook, and he and I had campaigned for the election of Sir Richard Squires.

---

proached the gateway to Canada House and slipped in through the front door, where Macdonald was already standing so that he could open it almost before we could touch the doorbell. He, too, was anxious for anonymity just then! I showed off Bradley proudly, for he was an impressively large man and possessed a magnificent voice; and once over his initial shyness at meeting new people, he emerged quickly as a fine conversationalist. I had told Macdonald that Bradley was quietly with me in my striving after Confederation, and here was the evidence.

He was the first of the elected Members of the National Convention (apart from Bradley) whom I tried to win to my cause. To my surprise, he rejected my ideas, and I think that perhaps of all who took their seats on the opening day of the Convention, he was among the half-dozen most strenuously opposed to Confederation. He was a great admirer of Peter Cashin and of Ches Crosbie, both opponents of the idea.

I put up for a while at the Newfoundland Hotel, where a good many of the newly elected Members stayed, and my next approach was to Michael Harrington, one of the three Members from St. John's West. Harrington was the youngest Member of the Convention, I think. This was the man who had done some very good writing for *The Book of Newfoundland* for me, and when I retired from my Barrelman broadcast, Frank O'Leary had given Michael the job. I had gone on the air myself to introduce him and give him the best possible send-off in his new career. Besides quite a lot of material that he originated for the Barrelman program himself, he made use of a good deal of the material that I had written and broadcast before. Harrington came to talk in my room in the hotel and have dinner with me one night. I told him frankly that I was going to try to persuade the Convention to seek the terms of Confederation and just as frankly asked him for his support in that purpose. He was friendly enough but quite non-committal. Later, when the great debate went on in the Convention, he astonished me by informing the Convention that I had tried to bribe him with a seat in the Senate of Canada. I hadn't. I had, of course, pointed out that under Confederation we would have our own House of Assembly, be entitled to elect so many Members to the Canadian House of Commons, and be entitled to so many Senators, judges, and other appointments in the Canadian system: all of which would bring Newfoundland back with a bang into the system of democratic representation. We would have, not just one, but three Houses, one in St. John's and two in Ottawa. I was deeply disappointed in Harrington, though I understood well enough that he was a Newfoundland idealist-nationalist, more poet than politician, and that in his eyes, despite his outward friendliness to me, I was doubtless what Peter Cashin a few days later called me: a Judas Iscariot, a Newfoundland Quisling. I shouldn't be surprised if Harrington looked upon me in even worse light than Cashin did, for Harrington would be thoroughly sincere, if thoroughly naive. But I admit that his attack on me in the Convention hurt my feelings.

I enlisted Gordon Bradley's help on my next approach. This was to my old MCLI friend, A. B. Butt. Bert Butt, too, was an idealist. He walked with Bradley and me to Cuckold Cove, near the foot of Quidi Vidi, and as we sat on a patch of grass and looked out over the Atlantic Ocean, I tried to win him, if not to Confederation, then at least to the idea that the Convention should ask Ottawa for the terms. I was again disappointed when he argued against it.

So far, my score was zero: three attempts, and three failures. The Rev. Lester L. Burry, an old friend from Corner Brook times (we had been on a debating team there), now a much beloved United Church missionary in Labrador, would have been my first convert to Confederation, but for the fact that he was already in favour of it. No man, not even Sir Wilfred Grenfell, ever had the welfare of Labrador's people more at heart than did Lester Burry, so he couldn't help being a Confederate. I was delighted, too, to make the acquaintance of Ike Newell, the big, smiling, exceedingly bright, cooperative field worker for the International Grenfell Association movement in and for miles around St. Anthony. He kept insisting (whether to jolly me or not, I still don't know) that he wished to keep an open mind on the best form of government for the future, but of one thing he was sure: we simply had to have the terms of Confederation.

My old House of Assembly friend, Roland Starkes, didn't even need to be asked. "I'm with you, and proudly," he said succinctly, and that was it indeed. I was encouraged by the attitude of Edgar L. Roberts, from the St. Barbe coast, and by that of Charles H. Ballam (who was destined to be Minister of Labour in my Cabinet for a good many years). I was more than impressed by William J. Keough, the cooperative field man in the Port-au-Port area and now the National Convention Member for St. George's. Not many men have I known in this life with his sincerity, integrity, and high sense of honour. He was perhaps the greatest phrase-maker in Newfoundland's long story. He, too, was destined, after sore tribulation, to be a dear colleague for many years in my Cabinet, to the very hour of his death. The other cooperative field worker elected by Port-au-Port, Michael McCarthy, was friendly. "Of course we have to have the terms of Confederation," he agreed. "We can't do less."

The southwest coast of our Island had had more and longer business and social relations with Canada (Nova Scotia, mainly) than any other part of our country. I was confident about the attitude of Percy Figary, the popular railway union leader at Channel–Port-aux-Basques and Member for the Burgeo-LaPoile coast. The other two Districts of that coast were represented by John T. Spencer, Hermitage, and William J. Banfield, Fortune Bay. Spencer was quiet and unassuming, but I felt that I could depend on him absolutely. Bill Banfield was not only one of my strongest supporters, but gave me the encouraging news that he was working on his father-in-law, the highly intelligent Kenneth McDonald, and that he was confident that McDonald would support me. This was important, for McDonald was one of the two Members elected by the great Grand Falls District.

Daniel Hillier, Burin West, a quiet, unpretentious man, assured me earnestly of his support, and kept his word to the end. S. F. (Ted) Vincent, who had been elected by Bonavista North, the adjoining District to mine, couldn't help being a Confederate. The people of his District were pretty definitely Confederate, and Ted himself became one of my most ardent and helpful campaigners along the big stretch of the northeast coast.

And there it was. In a Convention of forty-five Members, I didn't have a chance: I would be voted down, and Confederation would die there on the floor. It would die, that is, if it were left entirely to a vote of the forty-five. But perhaps not; not if I could get it out of the hands of the forty-five and into the hands of the Newfoundland people.

When the Convention was sworn in and opened by the Governor, Sir Gordon Macdonald, on September 11, 1946, I sized up the Members much along these lines:

For getting the terms—16

Rev. Lester L. Burry (Labrador)
William J. Keough (St. George's)
Michael J. McCarthy (Port-au-Port)
John T. Spencer (Hermitage)
Kenneth McDonald (Grand Falls)
Daniel Hillier (Burin West)
Samuel F. Vincent (Bonavista North)
Isaac Newell (White Bay)
Thomas G. W. Ashbourne (Twillingate)
Edgar L. Roberts (St. Barbe)
Charles H. Ballam (Humber)
Roland G. Starkes (Green Bay)
William J. Banfield (Fortune Bay)
Percy Figary (Burgeo-LaPoile)
F. Gordon Bradley (Bonavista East)
Joseph R. Smallwood (Bonavista Centre)

Possibility of support—7

Reuben Vardy (Trinity North)
Edward P. Reddy (Burin East)
Alfred Watton (Fogo)
Leonard J. Miller (Placentia East)
Dennis L. Ryan (Placentia West)
Frank A. Fogwill (St. John's East Extern)
Hon. R. B. Job (St. John's East)

A fighting chance of support—2

Major Peter J. Cashin (St. John's West)
Chesley A. Crosbie (St. John's West)

Definitely opposed—11

John Hannon (Harbour Main)
Wilfred Dawe (Port de Grave)
Michael F. Harrington (St. John's West)
Edgar L. Hickman (St. John's East)
Malcolm Hollett (Grand Falls)
David I. Jackman (Bell Island)
Thomas Kennedy (Harbour Main)
Albert E. Penney (Carbonear)
Albert B. Butt (St. John's West Extern)
Pierce Fudge (Humber)
Albert J. Goodridge (Ferryland)

Uncommitted—9

P. Wellington Crummey (Bay de Verde)
Colin G. Jones (Harbour Grace)
Kenneth M. Brown (Bonavista South)
Gordon F. Higgins (St. John's East)
Edmund C. Craniford (Trinity South)
Archibald Northcott (Lewisporte)
John J. McCormack (St. Mary's)
Joseph Fowler (Port de Grave)
Captain Charles L. Bailey (Trinity South)

I planned to introduce a resolution asking that the Convention send a delegation to Ottawa to find out the terms that Canada would offer us to enter Confederation. With forty-five Members in the Convention, my resolution would need to have at least twenty-three votes; and I felt, as I looked about the Chamber on opening day, that I could not definitely count on more than sixteen, including myself, to support the resolution. But there were the seven that I thought that I might have a chance of getting, which would make the magic total of twenty-three. Could I win over three or more of the uncommitted group?

It was not at all, in my own mind, as hopeless as it looked on the surface. First, there was Ches Crosbie. We had been fairly close for several years, and it was I who had persuaded him to run for the National Convention in the first place. I had come in from Gander specially for that purpose, and I attended the first meetings that he called of his friends at his home on Rennie's Mill Road. I had taken him down to the studio of the radio broadcasting company, after they had closed down their broadcasting for the night, to have him record short speeches that I had written for him, so that they could be played back and I could point out for correction his mistakes of enunciation and the like. I was convinced that Crosbie wanted to be Premier, and throughout a large part of the life of the Convention, I did everything in my power to persuade him to support my motion for terms. "You don't have to be a Confederate, Ches, to be willing to get the terms. And even after we get the terms, you don't have to support them if you don't like them." I told him, not once, but half a dozen times at least, that if he wanted to become Premier, I would help him to the utmost of my knowledge and ability, and be a man-Friday to him after he took office, if only he would now support my motion. He often slipped into my apartment on Duckworth Street East late at night (his cousin, Dick Chalker, the building's owner, lived upstairs in the same house),* and we would chat about the situation. For a long time, he didn't say yes or no; and for a long time, I had a secret hope that he would be with me. In the end, he voted against my resolution, and later he even refused to sign the terms of union between Canada and Newfoundland. When I ran for Premier, he supported me strongly and continued his support to the day of his death.

*Chalker asked Steers Ltd. to insure his house at Lloyd's of London against damage from riot or civil commotion, so he took it good-naturedly when his friends twitted him about having Smallwood as a tenant in the lower flat. He wasn't amused afterward when he learned that Lloyd's had declined to grant the insurance on his house, once they knew that I was living in it—he wouldn't have got a dollar of compensation for any loss arising out of a riot or any other attack on me. He was even less amused when he remembered the mob that had stormed the house we shared and plastered its front, windows, and doors with anti-Confederation posters. I was not home at the time. My wife and daughter were, and they had an uncomfortable half-hour.

And suppose I could get Peter Cashin to back me? He would almost certainly bring Goodridge, Jackman, Kennedy, Hannon, McCormack, and Butt with him—a total of seven—and that would put us over the top. A lot of people would have been astonished to know that I seriously considered the possibility of getting Cashin on my side, because he above all others was the vehement, boisterous, colourful champion of the theme that the whole thing was simplicity itself: let the Commission of Government get out, out of office and out of Newfoundland, and restore responsible government immediately. In his simplistic thinking, the Commission system never should have come in the first place and should have been kicked out long ago. It was there just to protect the bond-holders. It was there to milk Newfoundland for the benefit of England. He started a weekly broadcast over radio station VOCM in St. John's, a few weeks before the Convention plan was announced, and tens of thousands tuned in faithfully each Saturday night to the stirring tune of "Up the Pond", the tune that the bands play at our annual regatta on Quidi Vidi Lake. Then would come Peter's exciting voice and his outrageously bold declarations against the Commission of Government. It was like old times! (For a good many listeners, it was too much like old times.) But Peter, I felt, was not so much concerned with the detail of the kind of government that would replace the Commission system as he was with getting that system out. He had worked in Western Canada in his youth and lived in Montreal until just before he began his broadcasts. He must surely respect Canada a lot, I thought. Confederation would automatically bring with it the restoration of responsible government, so why shouldn't he support my resolution? There was something else: nobody liked his politics or his political style—that is, nobody in the Responsible Government League. And I had good reason to know that men such as Crosbie, Job, Hickman, and Higgins shared the League's mistrust of Cashin. Peter spoke and voted against my resolution the first time I brought it in, but I didn't give up my effort to win him over.

"They don't like you, Peter," I told him. We were in the lobby of the Newfoundland Hotel, where I contrived to run into him "accidentally" one day, and we sat together and chatted. "They don't like you, and they don't want you. They're not going to tell you that, right now, because they want your support in the Convention. But you'll get it in the neck when the Convention is over! I'm sorry to tell you, Peter, but you're like the label on the bottle, the chimney on the roof—outside." It was precisely what Cashin himself feared in any case. I felt that he had as much use for the League and the others as they had for him, and it made him uneasy. My determination was to get a delegation sent by the Convention to Ottawa, for I was confident that Ottawa would give us the few special terms and conditions, over and above all of the great and good ordinary benefits of Confederation, that we would need to have for Newfoundland.

Peter was tempted, but too ashamed, I fear, to take the step. "You don't have to change your tune," I told him. "You don't have to become a Confederate. In fact, you can declare that you don't think that the terms would be good enough, and you could tell your followers, through the Convention, that you were reserving the right to reject Confederation after you saw the terms." Then I tried to clinch it. "You can tell the people that you're too good a democrat to deny the people the chance to know what terms Canada would be prepared to offer." It was no good, and although from then on we were on reasonably friendly terms, as Crosbie and I were, Peter stuck out to the end against my approaches. I think, if the truth were known, that Cashin saw in my efforts only a dangerous attempt to confuse the issue and leave us stuck with the Commission of Government.*

I didn't tell even Gordon Bradley the number of members that I felt we could count on to support my resolution, nor did I tell the eight or ten supporters that I called together for a caucus one night. They suspected that I didn't have a majority, and their advice was that I should not introduce my resolution until I was sure that I could count on its passage. I disagreed completely with that view. Who could say that we would ever get a majority of the Convention? If we didn't, would we just let the matter drop? I had at least some hope that I would win over the seven or eight votes that I needed; but if not, then at least the issue would have been projected into the Convention and into Newfoundland. I felt intuitively that if I could convince the people that a majority of the Convention Members were absolutely refusing to allow Canada to be asked for the terms and conditions of Confederation, that if the majority refused to allow Confederation as a possible, or at least conceivable, form of government to be raised, then the people would become indignant. They

*He was proud of his participation in the First World War. "Where were you in 1914?" he demanded of me in the course of a speech in the Convention, but he probably felt little satisfaction with the retort that I called across the floor. "I was fourteen years old in 1914, at the end of 1914."

would suspect the motives of the majority, and they would become curious to know what those terms might be. My every instinct told me to fling the issue boldly into the Convention and thus perhaps win the majority I needed or, failing that, to make Confederation an issue that wouldn't lie down in the minds of the people. My supporters fell in line at that caucus, but some of them shook their heads when the vote was finally put and we lost.

Every word of the Convention's debates was broadcast over the state radio system. The Anti-Confederates promptly accused me of having instigated the setting up of microphones around the Convention Chamber. They sneered at the microphones—"Get those things out of this room", "Whose idea was it to put these things here?"—looking at me. I asked them what their objection was to the microphones. Didn't they want the people to hear the discussions? The fact is that I did not even know that the microphones were going to be put in until the moment I walked into the Chamber on opening day and saw them in place, and saw the Broadcasting Corporation's personnel and apparatus stationed in a corner of the room. But if I was in no way responsible for the introduction of the microphones, I was most certainly profoundly happy to see them! From the moment that the Governor, Sir Gordon Macdonald, opened the Convention with a speech, to the last dying moments of the Convention nearly two years later, every word spoken in it was broadcast to the people—every last word.

The Convention normally sat from three o'clock to six o'clock every afternoon, Monday through Friday. The proceedings were carefully recorded on wax discs,* and at nine o'clock that same night, they were put on the air until midnight. I have never heard of anything to equal it for mass coverage by radio in a democratic land. Three hours each night for five nights a week, nothing, absolutely nothing, on the air over the state broadcast system but the words spoken, the actual voices, in the National Convention! In every settlement of the country, there was at least one radio receiving set. In most places, there were half a dozen or a dozen homes with receiving sets, and several dozen, or even hundreds, in the larger places. Radio owners, through the life of the Convention, spent a small Newfoundland fortune on radio batteries in the places—the majority of

*These records are in the possession of the CBC at St. John's. One day, they'll be a precious historic treasure, if they're not already that.

Newfoundland's settlements—that had no electricity. Wind-chargers were bought by the hundred. Every effort within financial and practical means was made to keep those radio sets going the full three hours each night. Every radio owner's house was crowded—the whole adult population of a settlement would be in the home or homes of those who owned radios; and dare anyone speak, dare anyone make any noise entering or leaving to interfere with the engrossed listening of the crowd! There would be quick bursts of laughter at some sally made in the Convention, and more than one listener in the outports marvelled at my thirstiness. "A terrible thirsty man, that Mr. Smallwood," one man would remark. "Yes, he's always calling for a pint of water," the others would agree. Perhaps it was because many of them were not used to the term, or perhaps it was because, in my anger or indignation, I didn't always enunciate the words clearly enough when I rose to my feet and declared, "Mr. Chairman, a point of order!"

The very procedures laid down for the Convention strengthened my case for obtaining Canada's terms. Remember that the Convention had been given two tasks: 1) to examine the state of Newfoundland's economy and, taking into account the effect of the war on that economy, to determine whether or not Newfoundland was now self-supporting; and 2) to recommend to the United Kingdom what forms of government should be submitted to the Newfoundland people in the national referendum that was to follow after the Convention. For the purpose of carrying out the first of these two great purposes, the Convention was divided into ten committees, each of which was to study a particular aspect of the country's affairs: fisheries, agriculture, industries, transportation and communication, public works, public finance, education, public health, and so forth. Most Members of the Convention were appointed to two of these committees. I was appointed to three: education, health and welfare, and transportation and communication. In addition, I attended many of the meetings of the other committees. I felt that while these studies were going on—and it was felt that they would take months to complete—another study could be going on simultaneously. This was the examination of the terms and conditions that Canada would be willing to extend to us.

Once these committees were appointed, I introduced my resolution, on October 28, 1946.

WHEREAS it is desirable that the National Convention and the people of Newfoundland should be fully informed as far as possible of all facts having any bearing upon forms of government that might be submitted to the people in a national referendum; therefore be it

RESOLVED that the appropriate authorities be advised that the Convention desires to inform the Government of Canada of the Convention's wish to learn that Government's attitude on the question of Federal Union of Newfoundland with Canada; and further wishes to ascertain the terms and conditions on the basis of which the Government of Canada consider that such Federal union might be effected; and be it finally

RESOLVED that the Delegation should have no authority whatsoever to negotiate or conclude any agreement or in any manner to bind the Convention or the people of Newfoundland.

Then I launched into my speech.

Our people's struggle to live commenced on the day they first landed here, four centuries and more ago, and has continued to this day. The struggle is more uneven now than it was then, and the people view the future now with more dread than they felt a century ago.

The newer conceptions of what life can be, of what life should be, have widened our horizóns and deepened our knowledge of the great gulf which separates what we have and are from what we feel we should have and be. We have been taught by newspapers, magazines, motion pictures, radios, and visitors something of the higher standards of well-being of the mainland of North America; we have become uncomfortably aware of the low standards of our country; and we are driven irresistibly to wonder whether our attempt to persist in isolation is the root-cause of our condition. We have often felt in the past, when we learned something of the higher standards of the mainland, that such things belonged to another world, that they were not for us. But today we are not so sure that two yardsticks were designed by the Almighty to measure the standards of well-being: one yardstick for the mainland of the continent; another for this Island which lies beside it. Today we are not so sure, not so ready to take it for granted, that we Newfoundlanders are destined to accept much lower standards of life than our neighbours of Canada and the United States. Today we are more disposed to feel that our manhood, our very creation by God, entitles us to standards of life no lower than those of our brothers on the mainland.

Our Newfoundland is known to possess natural wealth of considerable value and variety. Without at all exaggerating their extent, we know that our fisheries are in the front rank of the world's marine wealth. We have considerable forest, water power, and mineral resources. Our Newfoundland people are industrious, hard-working, frugal, ingenious, and sober. The combination of such natural resources and such people should spell a prosperous country enjoying high standards, Western World standards, of living. This combination should spell fine, modern, well-equipped homes; lots of health-giving food; ample clothing; the amenities of modern New World civilization; good roads, good schools, good hospitals, high levels of public and private health; it should spell a vital, prosperous, progressive country.

It has not spelt any such things. Compared with the mainland of North America, we are fifty years, in some things a hundred years, behind the times. We live more poorly, more shabbily, more meanly. Our life is more a struggle. Our struggle is tougher, more naked, more hopeless. In the North American family, Newfoundland bears the reputation of having the lowest standards of life, of being the least progressive and advanced, of the whole family.

We all love this land. It has a charm that warms our hearts, go where we will; a charm, a magic, a mystical tug on our emotion that never dies. With all her faults, we love her.

But a metamorphosis steals over us the moment we cross the border that separates us from other lands. As we leave

Newfoundland, our minds undergo a transformation: we expect, and we take for granted, a higher, a more modern, way of life such as it would have seemed ridiculous or even avaricious to expect at home. And as we return to Newfoundland, we leave that higher standard behind, and our minds undergo a reverse transformation: we have grown so accustomed to our own lower standards and more antiquated methods and old-fashioned conveniences that we readjust ourselves unconsciously to the meaner standards under which we grew up. We are so used to our railway and our coastal boats that we scarcely see them; so used to our settlements, and roads, and homes, and schools, and hospitals and hotels and everything else that we do not even see their inadequacy, their backwardness, their seaminess.

We have grown up in such an atmosphere of struggle, of adversity, of mean times that we are never surprised, never shocked, when we learn that we have one of the highest rates of tuberculosis in the world; one of the highest infant mortality rates in the world; one of the highest maternity mortality rates in the world; one of the highest rates of beriberi and rickets in the world. We take these shocking facts for granted. We take for granted our lower standards, our poverty. We are not indignant about them. We save our indignation for those who publish such facts, for with all our complacency, with all our readiness to receive, to take for granted, and even to justify these things amongst ourselves, we are, strange to say, angry and hurt when these shocking facts become known to the outside world.

We are all very proud of our Newfoundland people. We all admire their strength, their skill, their adaptability, their resourcefulness, their industry, their frugality, their sobriety, and their warm-hearted, simple generosity. We are proud of them; but are we indignant, does our blood boil, when we see the lack of common justice with which they are treated? When we see how they live? When we witness the long, grinding struggle they have? When we see the standards of their life? Have we compassion in our hearts for them? Or are we so engrossed, so absorbed, in our own struggle to live in this country that our social conscience has become toughened, even case-hardened? Has our own hard struggle to realize a modest competence so blinded us that we have little or no tenderness of conscience left to spare for the fate of the tens of thousands of our brothers so very much worse off than ourselves?

Mr. Chairman, in the present and prospective world chaos, with all its terrible variety of uncertainty, it would be cruel and futile, now that the choice is ours, to influence the handful of people who inhabit this small Island to attempt independent national existence. The earnings of our 65,000 families may be enough, in the years ahead, to support them half-decently and at the same time support the public services of a fair-sized municipality. But will those earnings support independent national government on an expanding, or even the present, scale? Except for a few years of this war and a few of the last, our people's earnings never supported them on a scale comparable with North American standards, and never maintained a government even on the pre-war scale of service. Our people never enjoyed a good standard of living, and never were able to yield enough taxes to maintain the government. The difference was made up by borrowing or grants-in-aid.

We can indeed reduce our people's standard of living: we can force them to eat and wear and use and have much less than they have; and we can deliberately lower the level of governmental services. Thus we might manage precariously to maintain independent national status. We can resolutely decide to be poor but proud. But if such a decision is made, it must be made by the 60,000 families who would have to do the sacrificing, not the 5,000 families who are confident of getting along pretty well in any case.

We have, I say, a perfect right to decide that we will turn away from North American standards of public services, and condemn ourselves as a people and government deliberately to long years of struggle to maintain even the little that we have. We may, if we wish, turn our backs upon the North American continent beside which God placed us, and resign ourselves to the meaner outlook and shabbier standards of Europe, 2,000 miles across the ocean. We can do this, or we can face the fact that the very logic of our situation on the surface of the globe impels us to draw close to the progressive outlook and dynamic living standards of this continent.

Our danger, so it seems to me, is that of nursing delusions of grandeur. We remember the stories of small states that valiantly preserved their national independence and developed their own proud cultures, but we tend to overlook the fact that comparison of Newfoundland with them is ludicrous. We are not a nation. We are merely a medium-size municipality, a mere miniature borough of a large city. Dr. Carson, Patrick Morris, and John Kent were sound in the first decades of the nineteenth century when they advocated cutting the apron-strings that bound us to the Government of the United Kingdom; but the same love of Newfoundland, the same Newfoundland patriotism, that inspired their agitation then would now, if they lived, drive them to carry the agitation to its logical conclusion of taking the next step of linking Newfoundland closely to the democratic, developing mainland of the New World. There was indeed a time when tiny states lived gloriously. That time is now ancient European history. We are trying to live in the mid-twentieth-century, post-Hitler New World. We are living in a world in which small countries have less chance than ever before of surviving.

We can, of course, persist in isolation, a dot on the shore of North America, the Funks* of the North American continent, struggling vainly to support ourselves and our greatly expanded public services. Reminded continually by radio, movie, and visitor of greatly higher standards of living across the Gulf, we can shrug incredulously or dope ourselves into the hopeless belief that such things are not for us. By our isolation from the throbbing vitality and expansion of the continent, we have been left far behind in the march of time, the "sport of historic misfortune",† the "Cinderella of the Empire".‡ Our choice now is to continue in blighting isolation or seize the opportunity that may

*Tiny, barren, uninhabited, unpopulated (except for wild sea-birds) islets lying about thirty miles off the northeast coast of Newfoundland.
†F. E. Smith (Lord Birkenhead).
‡Lord Roseberry.

beckon us to the wider horizons and higher standards of unity with the progressive mainland of America.

I am not one of those, if any such there be, who would welcome federal union with Canada at any price. There are prices which I, as a Newfoundlander whose ancestry in this country reaches back for nearly two centuries, am not willing that Newfoundland should pay. I am agreeable to the idea that our country should link itself federally with that great British nation, but I am not agreeable that we should ever be expected to forget that we are Newfoundlanders with a great history and a great tradition of our own. I agree that there may be much to gain from linking our fortunes with that great nation, but I insist that as a self-governing province of the Dominion, we should continue to enjoy the right to our own distinctive culture. I do not deny that once we affiliated with the Canadian federal union, we should in all fairness be expected to extend the scope of our loyalty to embrace the federation as a whole. I do not deny this claim at all, but I insist that as a constituent part of the federation, we should continue to be quite free to hold to our love of our own dear land.

Nor am I one of those, if there be any such, who would welcome union with Canada without regard for the price that the Dominion might be prepared to pay.

I pledge myself to this House and to this country that I will base my ultimate stand in this whole question of Confederation upon the nature of the terms that are laid before the Convention and the country. If the terms are such as clearly to suggest a better Newfoundland for our people, I shall support and maintain them. If they are not of such a nature, I shall oppose them with all the means I can command.

In the price we pay and the price we exact, my only standard of measurement is the welfare of the people. This is my approach to the whole question of federal union with Canada. It is in this spirit that I move this resolution today.

Confederation I will support if it means a lower cost of living for our people. Confederation I will support if it means a higher standard of life for our people. Confederation I will support if it means strength, stability, and security for Newfoundland.

I will support Confederation if it gives us democratic government. I will support Confederation if it rids us of Commission Government. I will support Confederation if it gives us responsible government under conditions that will give responsible government a real chance to succeed. Confederation I will support if it makes us a province enjoying privileges and rights no lower than any other province.

These, then, are the conditions of my support of Confederation: that it must raise our people's standard of living, that it must give Newfoundlanders a better life, that it must give our country stability and security, and that it must give us full, democratic responsible government under circumstances that will ensure its success.

Mr. Chairman, gentlemen, I have given a statement of my faith, but I do not expect members to support this motion for the reasons that impel me to do so.

Members no doubt have a variety of reasons of their own, and their support of this resolution does not at all necessarily imply agreement with mine. There are many cases to be made for submitting and supporting this resolution quite apart from those I have given here today.

In the name of the people of Bonavista Centre and of thousands of other Newfoundlanders throughout this Island, I move this resolution. I believe that this move will lead to a brighter and happier life for our Newfoundland people. If you adopt this resolution, and Canada offers us generous terms, as I believe she will, and Newfoundland decides to shake off her ancient isolation, I believe with all my heart and mind that the people will bless the day this resolution was moved. With God's grace, let us move forward for a brighter and happier Newfoundland.

The roof fell in on me!

The Anti-Confederates tore me to pieces. Harrington made the bald assertion that I had tried to bribe him with a seat in the Senate of Canada. Cashin called me a Quisling, a Judas Iscariot. Others settled for the petty treason charge that I was trying to sell Newfoundland up the St. Lawrence. I had no love of country; I was a traitor; I was a disgrace to Newfoundland. All this stuff of mine was a "plant", a dirty trick to take people's minds away from the noble cause of responsible government. I must be a tool of the Commission of Government or of the British Government—or more likely the Canadian Government. Why should we waste time talking about joining Canada? Canada was no country to join; if we joined anyone, let it be the United States. Canada was hopelessly in debt, burdened with fearsome taxes. Newfoundlanders would be taxed to death if they were foolish enough to join Canada. Their homes would be taxed; their land, their boats, their fishing gear, their everything. The Maritime Provinces wanted to get out of Confederation, especially Nova Scotia.

But the debate that began on Monday, October 28 and ended on Tuesday, November 5 was not entirely one-sided. The Confederates fought back valiantly. I myself had written more than a third of the speeches delivered in favour of my resolution, though that didn't prevent me (such being the way of politics) from poking gentle fun at Eddie Reddy, from Burin East, who delivered, in good style, a well-written speech against my resolution. I congratulated Reddy and, I added, I congratulated the author of his speech, too.

I had, of course, the right of reply to close the debate. I commented on Peter Cashin's holy indignation over my brazen attempt to bribe Michael Harrington with a seat in the Canadian Senate. I suggested playfully that the gallant Major was not so much indignant as jealous and said frankly that as Mr. Harrington was going to get the senatorship, I would have to give Mr. Cashin something else. I told him that I hadn't decided exactly what it would be, but I gave him my promise that, whatever it was, it would carry with it a special uniform consisting of a three-cornered hat and silk pantaloons and stockings, and silver buckles on his shoes.

I did win over two members to my resolution, Leonard Miller of Placentia East and Alfred Watton of Fogo. The vote was as follows:

Supporting my resolution—18

Rev. Lester L. Burry
William J. Keough
Michael J. McCarthy
John T. Spencer
Kenneth McDonald
Daniel Hillier
Samuel F. Vincent
Isaac Newell
Leonard J. Miller
Thomas G. W. Ashbourne
Edgar L. Roberts
Charles H. Ballam
Roland G. Starkes
William J. Banfield
Percy Figary
F. Gordon Bradley
Alfred Watton
Joseph R. Smallwood

Opposing my resolution—25

P. Wellington Crummey
Wilfred Dawe
David I. Jackman
Edward P. Reddy
Albert E. Penney
Albert J. Goodridge
Malcolm Hollett
Colin G. Jones
Thomas Kennedy
John Hannon
Pierce Fudge
Archibald Northcott
Dennis L. Ryan
Joseph Fowler
John J. McCormack
Gordon F. Higgins
Edgar L. Hickman
Frank A. Fogwill
Chesley A. Crosbie
Major Peter J. Cashin
Michael F. Harrington
Albert B. Butt
Edmund C. Craniford
Reuben Vardy
Capt. Charles L. Bailey

Kenneth M. Brown was not present to vote. He sat on the same side of the Chamber as I did, separated from me by Bradley—all members sat in alphabetical order according to the names of their constituencies. Vincent of Bonavista North, I for Bonavista Centre, Bradley for Bonavista East, and then Brown for Bonavista South. Brown, a giant-framed man who towered above everyone else in the Convention, even above Bradley, was making a trenchant speech against my motion, and he was particularly strong in his condemnation of my speech introducing the resolution, which he said made him ashamed as a Newfoundlander. He was a choleric man, and suddenly the members on the opposite side who were watching him noticed that his face turned a much deeper red. He was reaching for the inside pocket of his coat and saying that he had something there that would kill Confederation, when he stopped in the middle of the sentence, swayed, and then crashed his full length onto the floor in front of his desk in the middle space of the Chamber. The Convention was in momentary confusion as those nearest him looked quickly, saw that he was unconscious, and called for a doctor. Quickly an ambulance arrived, and Brown was taken to the General Hospital. He had had a massive cerebral hemorrhage, and it was weeks before he recovered enough to be able to speak a little. Soon after that, he died. Brown's collapse ended the debate for that day, the third day of the debate. Mr. Job did not vote either, and I think that illness was the cause of his absence.

The most popular radio broadcaster in Newfoundland at the time was Donald C. Jamieson, and he was doing a nightly report and commentary on the day's events in the Convention. His very attractive voice and his ready fluency, which have become well known all across Canada since then, made him VOCM's star performer. He began his broadcast on the night of my resolution's defeat with the dramatic words, "Confederation was born and died in the National Convention today." I didn't think so. I had, in fact, when the loss of my resolution was announced, risen in my place and told the Convention that I would be raising the issue again.

I was happy over the whole debate. We Confederates had had by far the better of the discussion: our statement was more clear-cut, more factual, far more powerful in the simple argument that the least the Convention could do, the very least, was to ask Canada for the terms. I thought I knew what the effect of the debate, and of my resolution's defeat, would be on the population. Nothing now, I knew, could keep back discussion of Confederation. It was an issue that wouldn't die. It was a cause that could only go up, provided I had the skill and patience to direct the campaign well.

The Confederate

13

To Battle —Even Literally

The best way I know to win an argument is to start by being right.

Lord Hailsham

The maxim "Nothing avails but perfection" may be spelled "Paralysis."

Winston S. Churchill

A feeble man can see the farms that are fenced and tilled, the houses that are built. The strong man sees the possible houses and farms.

Ralph Waldo Emerson

Every country is renewed out of the unknown ranks and not out of the ranks of those already famous and powerful.

Woodrow Wilson

With my motion proposing an approach to the Canadian Government disposed of, at least for the time being, the Convention continued its discussion of the various reports of the committees as they were tabled. I took an active part in these debates, and I must say that for a few weeks the atmosphere in the Convention was reasonably friendly. I had taken careful note of the Hon. R. B. Job's particular interest, expressed by him on every occasion, in the United States market for frozen fish fillets from Newfoundland. Mr. Job, who represented the East End of St. John's, commanded the respect of us all. He was truly a senior statesman among us, and the one abiding interest he had from first to last was the advancement of Newfoundland's frozen fish industry. His pet belief was that Newfoundland should bargain with the United States, offering American bases in Newfoundland in return for special customs concessions on Newfoundland frozen fish going into the United States. It was useless to argue that we really had no bargaining strength in that matter, as America already had her bases in Newfoundland, and that in any case the United States could not very well give Newfoundland a preferential position over the many other countries, including Canada, with which she did trade and had very close and friendly relations. Mr. Job admitted, of course, that America had the bases already, but he insisted that there should be a quid pro quo. His frequent use of the term *quid pro quo* was the cause of an amusing remark by a Member of the Convention one day. Mr. Job had risen to his feet to make another speech and had just begun to dwell again upon the idea of bargaining with the United States when one delegate groaned aloud, "My God, the quid are struck in again."*

Mr. Job simply couldn't get it out of his head that Newfoundland should somehow or other get special tariff privileges from the United States in return for the military base concessions that that nation en-

*Squid are the favourite bait-fish for cod-fishermen, and they wait impatiently every early summer for the squid to "strike in" to inland waters from the deeper ocean.

joyed on our soil. I decided to talk it over with him, and we met for the purpose. I admitted that it would clearly be of enormous importance to Newfoundland to establish a special relationship, if that were possible, with the United States in the matter of our fish products, but I wondered how that could be done. He answered promptly that the thing was to approach the United States quite frankly with the request. I expressed some doubt as to whether it were possible for such an approach to be made by the Convention. We discussed that aspect of the matter and then agreed that the first step to take was to approach the Commission of Government seeking advice. He asked me bluntly if I would support the idea of approaching the Commission of Government. I answered just as bluntly that I would, indeed, gladly, if he would support my reasonable proposal that we should ask the Government of Canada for the terms and conditions of union with Newfoundland. He asked if I didn't think that it would suffice to ask the Commission of Government for their advice on that matter at the same time that advice was sought on the other question. I agreed and added, "And while we're at it, let's ask the Commission for their advice on the matter of finding out from the United Kingdom what they would be prepared to do for Newfoundland if responsible government were restored." He thought that this was fair, and so we agreed that the Commission should be asked by the National Convention for their advice on three questions: 1) how could an approach be made to the United States with regard to tariff concessions on our fish? 2) how could we find out from the Government of Canada whether and what terms could be offered for a federal union of Newfoundland and Canada? and 3) how could we find out from the British Government what it would be prepared to do to help Newfoundland in the event that we chose a return of responsible government? We discussed the question of who should move and second a resolution in the Convention, and it was agreed that he would move it and that he would ask Gordon F. Higgins to second it. Higgins had seconded my motion, but with a declaration to the Convention that he did not personally believe in Confederation but thought that it was only right that we should get Canada's terms. I asked Mr. Job if he would see Albert Butt and seek his support for the resolution, and he promised to do so. He did, I think, but failed. I confess that I felt half-ashamed about this compact with Mr. Job. I thought I knew precisely what reply the Commission of Government would be obliged to give to the Convention's request, and that reply could only be a rejection of Mr. Job's proposal and at the same time a triumph for mine.

On Tuesday, February 4, 1947, Mr. Job, seconded by Mr. Higgins, moved his resolution asking that the Commission of Government be approached for the following information:

> 1. What steps if any can be taken for establishing improved economic or fiscal relationships between the United States of America and Newfoundland, particularly bearing in mind the present occupation of certain Newfoundland territory and the fact that free entry is given to the United States for its importations into Newfoundland.
>
> 2. What financial or fiscal relationships could be expected between the Government of the United Kingdom and Newfoundland:
>
> 1–Under continuation of Commission Government in its present form;
>
> 2–Under a revised form with elected representatives thereon;*
>
> 3–Under Responsible Government in approximately its previous form;
>
> 4–Under any other suitable form of Government.
>
> 3. What could be a fair and equitable basis for Federal Union of the Dominion of Canada and Newfoundland, or what other fiscal, political or economic arrangements may be possible.

The resolution concluded by saying that "the Convention desires to appoint a committee of its members to confer with His Excellency the Governor-in-Council on ways and means of determining these matters".

The resolution was carried thirty to eight. Those voting against it were Messrs. Hollett, Fudge, Northcott, Butt, Cashin, Harrington, Bailey, and Crummey. The passing of that resolution, which I had helped to draft, was one of the happiest moments I had in the Convention. The committee to see the Commission of Government were Messrs. Job, Crosbie, Higgins, Ashbourne, Newell, Fogwill, and my-

*There were a few, including Mr. Job, who actually thought that the Commission system of British-appointed Commissioners could somehow be made to work better by the addition of some *elected* Commissioners!

self. We saw the Commission of Government at Government House and had a frank discussion about the matters contained in the resolution. As I had expected, the Commission told us that an approach to the Government of the United States by the National Convention was altogether out of the question. The United States was a foreign nation, and approaches had to be on the level of government to government. Everybody on the delegation but Mr. Job could see this, and he was bitterly disappointed. On the matter of what the United Kingdom Government might be willing to do under various circumstances, the answer was simple: ask that Government. The Commission of Government would be glad to make the necessary arrangements for a delegation of the National Convention to meet with the relevant Ministers in London. The same was true of Ottawa. If the National Convention desired to learn anything from the Government of Canada, the proper step was to ask that Government; and again, the Commission of Government would be quite willing to make the necessary arrangements.

Our report was conveyed to the National Convention on Wednesday, February 26, and was thoroughly debated in the hearing of the whole population of Newfoundland and Labrador, thanks to radio. I tried by every legitimate means I could think of to win a majority of the delegates for my second attempt to get a delegation to Ottawa. I cultivated Mr. Cashin assiduously. I felt that he had a sneaking regard for Confederation and for Canada and possibly even for me. I felt, too, that he was beginning privately to weaken in his belief that this whole Convention and my introduction of the Confederation issue were blinds intended to frustrate what he fondly believed was the people of Newfoundland's determination to have responsible government. I continued to have conversations with Ches Crosbie.

On March 1, 1947, resolutions were passed in the Convention for the sending of two delegations: one to London and the other to Ottawa. The delegation to Ottawa was not to leave until after the London delegation had returned and made its report to the National Convention. This proviso had been insisted upon by the advocates of responsible government in the fond hope that the report from London would be so satisfactory as to make the question of a visit to Ottawa purely academic. Vain hope, indeed! The London delegation, consisting of Gordon Bradley as chairman and Messrs. Cashin, Crosbie, Butt, Hollett, Fudge, and Keough, went off on its mission. Bradley and Keough were, to say the least, friendly to Confederation. The other five strongly supported responsible government. The mission to London cleared the air greatly, but it was a sore disappointment to those who hoped that the old British principle, that self-government and financial assistance from Britain simply do not go together, would be abandoned in Newfoundland's favour. If Newfoundland, which had lost responsible government when it ceased to be self-supporting in 1933, needed financial assistance from Britain, then Newfoundland was not ready for self-government; and if it was ready for self-government, then clearly it did not need financial help from England. All this was made abundantly clear to the delegation, and it did not speak well for their knowledge of British history, and the history of Britain's relationships with its colonies and Dominions, that the response surprised and disappointed them.

The delegation that went to Ottawa consisted of Gordon Bradley again, as chairman, and Messrs. Higgins, Ashbourne, Job, Burry, Ballam, and myself. We Confederates suspected that I might not be elected to be a member of the Ottawa delegation, so I suggested that we should give "plumper" votes for me and thereby greatly improve my chances. It worked. Messrs. Crummey and Starkes were elected to be alternates, and when Mr. Job was not able to go, Crummey took his place.

We went to Ottawa by rail, all the way from St. John's, because Bradley wouldn't fly. When we arrived in Ottawa on June 24, it was like going into an oven. It was the hottest summer, they told us, for many years, and the heat was unbelievable. Gordon Bradley especially suffered from it. He wore suits made of normally heavy material for Newfoundland and Stanfield's heavy woollen underwear to his ankles. In Newfoundland, that kind of clothing might be all right on some days of the year, but not in Ottawa in the summer. He suffered every hour, by day and night, for the three months that we were there. He was never more than a few minutes away from the firm and reckless determination to throw the whole thing up and get on the first train back to St. John's. I never saw a man suffer so much from the weather. I got him to buy himself a lightweight suit and summer shorts, and this gave some relief. But it was an experience that he never forgot.

Bradley loved to walk, and I had to walk with him. We walked, it seemed to me, in those three months, hundreds of miles around the streets of Ottawa. I got to know every article in every hardware shop window on Bank Street and Sparks Street, for he was fascinated by any kind of hardware, and we stopped at every window to look. He had precious little belief that we would get Confederation placed on the ballot paper in the forthcoming referendum, and even less belief that Confederation would win if it were on the ballot. The whole expedition appeared to him to be futile, and the terrible heat of the Ottawa summer made it seem even more useless.

Bradley made a fine impression on the Canadians, and I must confess that I was proud to have him as our chairman. The weather made it quite impossible for him to do any work, for he could not get relief even in air-conditioned rooms. Indeed, he almost preferred the heat! He was content to leave the work to me, and this made me more than happy.

Eleven committees were set up, with Canadian and Newfoundland representatives on all of them. Among the Canadian members were C. D. Howe, Frank Bridges, J. L. Ilsley, Lionel Chevrier, and Dr. J. J. McCann from the Canadian Cabinet; Mitchell Sharp, James E. Coyne, and Dr. E. P. Weeks represented the Canadian civil service. I was the only person who was a member of all eleven committees, and I attended every meeting without fail.

We really did not need to be in Ottawa for all of those three months. We would have come back to St. John's thoroughly well informed had we spent only half of that time in Canada. The Canadian Government itself, however, was in a quandary. The Ministers were not sure whether they should give us actual terms of Confederation or merely a sort of general statement of what Confederation would mean to Newfoundland. For a while, there was a definite inclination toward the general statement. I remember so well the day they finally made up their minds on that! Scott Macdonald, who was in Ottawa throughout that period, attended the Cabinet meeting at which the decision was taken. I waited in the vicinity of the East Block for him to emerge from the meeting, and I was overjoyed when at a distance of a hundred yards he held up his hand with thumb and forefinger placed together in the well-known "okay" sign. I had not dared let Bradley know that this matter had been, until that moment, still undecided.

Another awkward fact was an impending by-election in the federal constituency of York-Sunbury in New Brunswick. Frank Bridges, who had befriended me on my first visit to Ottawa, had died in August, and Milton Gregg, V.C., was running as the Liberal candidate. The Government was very much afraid that the question of Newfoundland's possible entry into the union and the nature of the terms that might be offered would be dragged into the election campaign and cause goodness knows what harm both in Canada and Newfoundland. There was a proposal at one moment that a special private rail car or two be placed at the Newfoundland delegation's disposal to travel all the way to the Pacific Coast and back, calling in at the provincial capitals and making a "study" of the working of the federal system. This quite frankly was intended to be a time-consuming device, but luckily it was dropped. We were actually beginning to be bored with Ottawa, even the most ardent of us, when it came time at last for us to return to St. John's.

We did not bring the terms of Confederation back with us, for the very reasons that had made it necessary for us to remain so long in Ottawa continued to exist for some short time after our departure. What we brought back were the "Black Books", which soon became famous in the Convention. The Black Books contained an excellent description of the federal system in Canada and described in detail what the Canadian Government did in and for the several provinces, and would thus do for Newfoundland as a province. The special terms arrived soon afterward through the Governor, who delivered them to the Convention. They were printed in a grey-covered pamphlet, and I promptly christened it the Grey Book. For weeks afterward, all Newfoundland was hearing over the radio of the Black Books and the Grey Book.

But we had not escaped unscathed in Ottawa! Twenty-four days after our arrival in Ottawa, a group of delegates in St. John's telegraphed Bradley demanding that he return at once and call the Convention together again. (It was adjourned, of course, during our absence in Ottawa, as it had been during the absence of the London delegation.) Mr. Bradley replied courteously that we had not yet completed the business that the Convention had sent us to perform and that we would not be returning until this work was done. Not long afterward, an even larger number of the Responsible Government League telegraphed to the Prime Minister of Canada, denouncing us and repudiating us. They sent another telegram to Bradley, and together we worded his reply, denouncing their telegram and their whole attitude as being nothing short of national treachery.

So they were waiting for us when we got back! As soon as the National Convention reopened, with Bradley in the Chair, the attempt was made on him. Mr. Butt had been put up as the spokesman, and he launched into an impeachment of the chairman. Bradley was more than ready for him. He had come into my apartment on Duckworth Street East during lunch, and we had discussed the possibility of this attack. I had typed out a short, curt speech of resignation, and he had this with him as Mr. Butt launched into his attack. In his magnificent voice, Bradley said, "Just a moment, Mr. Butt," and proceeded to read his brief, electrifying speech of resignation. With that, he left the Chair and strode down the centre aisle to the main exit of the Chamber, his black gown ballooning out behind him as he went. The tables were beautifully turned on his would-be attackers, and I couldn't help exclaiming, "Where do we go from here, boys?"

Frankly, I do not know of one single step taken in the National Convention by the opponents of Confederation that was sound, or shrewd, or such as to win the support of our Newfoundland people. They were at no pains at all to conceal their abhorrence of Confederation, their determination to keep Confederation out of discussion and off the ballot paper, and their implacable advocacy of responsible government. They were bound to antagonize countless numbers of people by this attitude, especially when, on every possible occasion, I rubbed in the fact that they were endeavouring to cheat the Newfoundland people out of their right to know the terms of Confederation. Why, I asked repeatedly over the microphone in the Convention, why were they so determined to keep these facts from the people? Were they afraid that the people would learn the truth? The point sank into the minds of many Newfoundlanders.

I think that the greatest weakness of the anti-Confederates in the National Convention was their lack of a leader. They had many leaders, but not one whose leadership they were all prepared to follow. Their cause was thus never given a united front, and they never had united strategy; and their tactics, therefore, were always contradictory.

Their argument about responsible government did have a certain simple strength, however, that carried a lot of conviction to a lot of minds. "Here," they said, "here is the situation: Britain promised us that responsible government would be restored when we were self-supporting again. We are self-supporting, so why don't they keep their promise!"

It was a strong point, but quite untrue. Britain had never said that it would restore responsible government to Newfoundland when the country became self-supporting again. What Britain had promised was that responsible government would be restored, when Newfoundland became self-supporting again, *on request of the Newfoundland people*. It was short-sighted, to say the least, to omit that second vital condition. It was not enough for the Newfoundland people to request it, for the country itself had to be self-supporting. It was not enough for Newfoundland to be self-supporting, for responsible government had to be requested by the Newfoundland people. You couldn't have one without the other, but the ardent advocates of responsible government chose on every occasion to ignore that vital and thoroughly fair and democratic condition imposed by the British Government.

In a speech that I wrote for Bradley at that very time, I put the matter this way. A man says to his young son, "You see that house there? When you're twenty-one, I'll give you that house as a gift if you ask me for it." When the lad is twenty-one, and before he asks for the house, the father says, "Look, I own these three or these four houses. You can have any one of them, if you choose to ask me for it." Among the three or four houses is the one that the father originally promised, and if the son now chooses to ask for that house, he gets it. If, however, he chooses to ask for one of the other houses, he gets that instead. The choice is his own. Where has the father broken his promise? Britain says to Newfoundland, "If you show us that you are self-supporting, and ask us for the restoration of responsible government, or any other rational form of government, we will grant it to you." Where has Britain broken its promise? If Britain refuses to put responsible government on the ballot, then clearly the promise has not been kept. Provided always that responsible government is on the ballot, and that the people have the clear right to ask for its restoration, it is no breach of faith or a broken promise on Britain's part if Newfoundlanders are given the opportunity to ask, not for the return of responsible government alone, but for some other form of government instead, if that should be their will. To this argument, the advocates of responsible government never once chose to make an answer.

When the Convention reassembled some days later under the new chairmanship of John B. McEvoy, K.C., my presentation of the terms of Confederation was soon commenced, and what Newfoundland was now treated to was a sight to behold! In my first resolution calling for the sending of a delegation to Ottawa, I had managed to get the whole idea debated on five different days in the National Convention. For those five days, Newfoundland heard of virtually nothing but Confederation. Now I began again, and the attention and time given to the subject of Confederation on that earlier occasion was trifling compared with what happened this time. The House met at three in the afternoon, commencing on Thursday, November 20. From three to six every afternoon but Saturday and Sunday, and on two nights a week as well, the Convention sat for three hours, with every word being broadcast over the radio. I had the time of my life explaining and expounding Confederation. The Convention sat in Committee of the Whole, a procedure that leaves a great deal of freedom of debate. I explained every point and attempted to answer every question and every debating speech made against Confederation or any point of it. On Thursday and Friday of that week, the Convention's time was given exclusively to my presentation of the terms of union. On the following Monday and Monday night, and on Tuesday, Wednesday, Thursday and Thursday night, and again on Friday—seven days and two nights—nothing was heard but Confederation! On the following Monday, December 1, on Tuesday and Tuesday night, on Wednesday, and on Thursday as well, nothing was heard but Confederation. On Monday, December 8, and on Tuesday, Wednesday, Thursday, and Friday, it was the same thing exactly. On Monday, January 5, following the Christmas recess, and on Tuesday, Wednesday, Thursday, and Friday, it was the same. On Monday, January 12, in the afternoon and at night, and on the Tuesday following in the afternoon and at night, and on Wednesday afternoon and night, it was the same thing precisely! On the night of Thursday, January 15, the debate concluded. For twenty-four days, the terms of union were considered, explained, and debated in the National Convention, with every word going out over the air to the entire population of Newfoundland and Labrador. I piloted the debate throughout those days and nights. When you include the earlier motions and the debates on them, and now the debate on the terms of union, there was a total of thirty-four days in the National Convention when the sole topic of discussion was Confederation with Canada. The opponents of Confederation must have been asleep!

True, I indulged in a little gentle deception. I got the rumour started that I was near collapse; that the strain was simply too great;

that no one person could possibly hold out much longer in carrying the debate on his shoulders in this way. The opponents of Confederation were torn between two emotions: their desire to throttle me and close off the debate; and their fear that the public reaction would be violently against them and for me if they did so. The rumour of my impending collapse encouraged them to do nothing; from their standpoint, it would be far better for me to give up the debate than to be stopped by them. The fact of the matter is that I could have gone on another three months without the least difficulty, for I never enjoyed anything more in my life than those twenty-four days of explaining and championing Confederation.

For the most part, I got on very well personally with the Members of the Convention. There were, admittedly, three or four of them with whom I just couldn't make friends, so strong were their prejudices against my Confederate proposals. I have a strong voice for speech-making, and I was going great guns in a speech one day when Al Penney of Carbonear rose to a point of order, asking the chairman whether there was some way to stop Mr. Smallwood from splitting his eardrums? Nobody else, even those who sat many feet closer to me, seemed to be hurt by my voice—only Mr. Penney. Replying to the point of order, I confessed that I had perhaps a loud voice, but that this was something that I couldn't help—it was part of me. "I can't be blamed for my voice, Mr. Chairman," I protested, "any more than Mr. Penney can be blamed for his nose!" I might have cited his ears, or his gait, or any other natural feature of Mr. Penney's physique, but unfortunately, he had a very large nose. I fear that my innocent comparison started an almost hysterical laugh among the members—and the public, too, when word of Mr. Penney's big nose circulated through the country.

There was another Member who, when sober, was scholarly, friendly, and companionable. When he got drinking, he was another man altogether. He was very strongly opposed to Confederation, and there was much suppressed excitement in the Chamber when Chairman McEvoy was told by an official that Mr.—— (who had been home on a drunken bout for almost a week) wanted to speak to him on the telephone. McEvoy left the Chamber to answer the call. Mr.——announced that he was coming down to the Convention right away to "shoot that traitor Smallwood". McEvoy called the Chief of Police and arranged to have half a dozen police constables stationed around the exterior of the Colonial Building, home of the Convention; but luckily (for me, at least!), I wasn't shot.

Captain Charlie Bailey from Trinity South was loved by all the Members. He was an old sailorman, and he had sailed all around the world. He spiced his speeches with anecdotes of his sailor days: "I was running down to Pernambuco once, Mr. Chairman, when . . . "; "A fellow said to me in Istanbul one time . . . ." He was strongly anti-Confederate, and he was very anxious to warn Newfoundlanders against its dangers! He was completely unfitted to deal in masses of statistics and figures, but loved to do it. One day, after a speech full of figures that nobody could follow, he concluded emphatically, "Well, Mr. Chairman, there you have it! The people can't say I haven't warned them, and all I can say now is them that gets their arses burned needn't complain if they have to sit on the blisters." Another day, he was toiling through some tangled, incomprehensible figures that he said were from Manitoba. He wound up triumphantly, "So there you have it, Mr. Chairman, and all I can say is that the munissikal tax lawrs of Mannertober is a gumshaw!"

One of the Convention's first acts had been to set up a steering committee of ten or twelve members. Bradley and I were members of it, as were Cashin, Hollett, Fudge, Job, and Ashbourne. It was a sort of Cabinet that was supposed to regulate the order of business of the public sessions, but about the only thing I remember clearly about it was the wrestling match between Peter Cashin and myself. John McEvoy, as chairman of the Convention in succession to Bradley, was presiding on this occasion. I sat on his right, Cashin on his left, with the other members ranged around the large table between us. I forget the precise topic that was under discussion, but the first thing I remember happening was that Cashin got into a rage, rushed behind the chairman to me, and struck out with his fist at me. I caught his wrist and so warded the blow off, but Cashin, losing his balance, fell to the floor. I, holding both his wrists, was dragged to the floor with him, and there we both were, now I on top of him, then he on top of me. I continued to hold him by the two wrists and thus prevented him from taking a poke at me.

It all happened so quickly, and so unexpectedly, that the others were taken by surprise; and it was a few minutes before several of them rushed over and hauled us apart. We stood facing each other then. I lit a cigarette and, with both of us still held apart, I said, "Cashin, I'll show you how scared I am of you," and with that blew a mouthful of cigarette smoke into his face. He struggled to get at me, but his friends held him, as mine held me. Malcolm Hollett (or was it Pierce Fudge?) was hit in the face by Cashin's elbow, and became a little weak and was led to a sofa. Tom Ashbourne kept repeating, "How disgraceful, how disgraceful." As he was a loyal friend of mine in the Confederate cause, I assumed that he was condemning Cashin.

The Responsible Government group was scared that when word of the incident got out, they and their cause would suffer. They were certain that I would sue Cashin for assault. They actually felt some affection for me when I didn't say a word about it, and nothing got around about what had happened.

And I didn't do myself or my cause any harm when Cashin was sued in the Supreme Court by some members of the Commission of Government for libel over some raw statements that he had made about them in the Convention—remarks that suggested that they had been bought with their appointments to the Commission. We adjourned the meetings of the Convention for the duration of the trial. Most of us went into the Court to watch Cashin act as his own lawyer and Bob Furlong (now the Chief Justice of Newfoundland) act for the Commissioners. While the jury was out, we all stood around in the large hallway, and I firmly reassured Peter that the jury would give him the verdict. I was right, and the crowd outside on the street cheered Cashin when he went outside. I felt that I had chalked up a point for Confederation by making friends with him.

Never, in all the Convention's life, did I utter a word of public criticism of the Commission of Government—you couldn't have lived in Gander without discovering the high proportion of pro-Commissionites among our people. My task was to keep Bradley from publicly expressing his contempt for it. I would argue to him that we wanted to capture the pro-Commission vote when the referendum came, and he was politician enough to see the point. He often had to gulp to hold back the criticism that he was bursting to voice.

In startling contrast to the thirty-four days we spent discussing Confederation, responsible government was debated for only four days in the National Convention, on January 19 to 22 inclusive. It was on the motion of Gordon Higgins that the Convention recommended to the United Kingdom that responsible government should be placed on the ballot. I supported that motion in a brief speech in which I said that I considered that I would be traitorous to the Newfoundland people if I did not endorse their opportunity to vote for or against responsible government as they chose. The inference was clear, of course: the opponents of Confederation should do likewise!

But they made two mistakes: they didn't vote to place Confederation on the ballot; and their recommendation for responsible government contained the words, "Responsible Government as it existed in 1933." What good use I was to make of those fatal qualifying words, and how the Anti-Confederates must have groaned every time I rubbed their noses in them!

After the Anti-Confederates had for those four days debated the motion to recommend responsible government, I had the last word after all in the National Convention; for on Friday, January 23, 1948, I introduced my motion that the Convention recommend to the British Government that Confederation based on the terms received from Ottawa be placed on the ballot paper in the forthcoming national referendum. This was debated on Friday, and on the following Monday afternoon and night, and the next Tuesday afternoon and night. My motion was, of course, defeated, twenty-nine to sixteen, but the whole Confederation issue had got another three days of country-wide attention. The sixteen who voted to have Confederation placed on the ballot paper were William J. Banfield, Kenneth McDonald, Roland G. Starkes, John T. Spencer, Charles H. Ballam, Percy Figary, S. F. Vincent, Joseph R. Smallwood, Rev. Lester L. Burry, Michael J. McCarthy, Edgar L. Roberts, William J. Keough, Isaac Newell, Thomas G. W. Ashbourne, Daniel Hillier, and F. Gordon Bradley.

Virtually everyone was convinced that the fight was over. Confederation had lost. The Responsible Government people had won. On the ballot paper in the forthcoming referendum, the people would be forced to choose between responsible government as it existed in 1933 and a continuation of Commission Government for a period.

But I never felt so sure of winning as I did the day we were defeated in the National Convention. I had never accepted the Convention itself as being representative of the will and sentiment of the people. I had learned too much about the sentiment of the people while living at Gander. But I knew that it was going to be a fierce fight.

The advocates of responsible government had powerful weapons to use. The overwhelming majority of the businessmen of Water Street and of St. John's generally, and indeed of many parts of the country, feared Confederation and opposed it strongly. The manufacturing interests were powerfully opposed. The ownership and management of the great pulp and papermills at Corner Brook and Grand Falls were not content to be opposed to Confederation, but engaged the services of a well-known firm of chartered accountants in Montreal to prepare a statistical case to show that Newfoundland could not hope to prosper under Confederation if it did come. Nearly all of the well-known names in Newfoundland were opposed to Confederation: Crosbie, Job, Higgins, Hickman, Cashin, and dozens of others. Many prominent and some very powerful ecclesiastics opposed Confederation and took strong steps to make the fact known. All of the newspapers of the Island, with the exception of the *Evening Telegram*, favoured responsible government. The *Telegram*, though taking no strong stand one way or the other, was at least friendly toward Confederation. I think that most of the owners, and the editor, were sympathetic. I do not wish to exaggerate the extent of their sympathy or to suggest that they were convinced Confederates. I think, on the whole, that they mildly preferred Confederation to simple responsible government.

Prominent among the Anti-Confederates were the merchants of St. John's. I had gone to Bishop Feild College with some of them and thus knew them well. "Why are you against Confederation?" I would ask. "It's not going to hurt you. If it helps the people, it's bound to help you. After all, the safest way for you to be prosperous is for your customers to be prosperous—your customers and your customers' customers." It was useless. They were afraid of Eaton's and Simpson's and the other chain stores, for they had nightmares of being put out of business by them. It was futile to point out that in Canadian cities, shopkeepers tried to be in business next door to, or across the street from, the big chain stores. I cited instances of small shops right in the middle of a city block, surrounded by a big chain store, refusing point-blank to sell out to the chain. Our merchants were very conscious of the big mail-order business done by Eaton's and Simpson's in Newfoundland, and they were shocked by the possibility of those chains actually opening stores in competition with them right on Water Street.

And they were afraid of the Canadian income tax—the double tax, as they called it. This was an allusion to the universal practice of taxing the income of a corporation and then taxing the income that the corporation's shareholders received as dividends. In any case, the merchants were doing reasonably well already. Why change? Why take chances? Leave well enough alone! What they never foresaw was the staggering increase in the income of the people, their customers, virtually every dollar of which would chink merrily into the merchants' cashboxes. They didn't dream of the dozens, hundreds, thousands, and millions of dollars that would pour into Newfoundland in an ever-swelling total—payments to the Provincial Government, payments to thousands of federal civil servants, thousands of railroaders and airport workers, thousands of war veterans; payments to the people in the form of family allowances, old age pensions, Canada pensions, unemployment insurance, and hospital insurance, and in a dozen other ways; payments for roads, for housing, for harbours, for post offices, and for a whole host of other necessary and costly services.

The Newfoundland people were—how shall I put it: startled, shocked, angry?—by my assertion during the Convention debates that there were "twenty millionaires along Water Street". "It's not the twenty millionaires on Water Street that we're here to serve, Mr. Chairman, it's the Newfoundland people." "The form of government that's best is the one that's best for the masses of the people—the toiling masses—not just the twenty millionaires." I had a lot of fun contrasting the "twenty millionaires" and the "toiling masses". People tried to add up the names of the twenty. The knowing few didn't have to puzzle over the question. And the knowing few knew, too, that most of the twenty were related by blood, marriage, or business. Whatever the feeling of the "toiling masses" might have been, you didn't have to be a ranting, down-at-heel Socialist to be deeply shocked to realize that in a country of a quarter of a million people, nearly all of them poor, there were as many as twenty millionaires. "Ill fares the land . . ."

Today in Newfoundland, there are ten times as many millionaires. That is a high proportion of a half-million, or somewhat more than a half-million, population; but if there were twice as many millionaires as that in Newfoundland today, it wouldn't represent such a brutal contrast as the one we had in the years before Confederation. The people themselves have now so much more, enjoy so much higher a standard of living, that the contrast is not at all so violent or so startling.

For all that, it is something to "mark, learn and inwardly digest" that 452 years of pre-Confederation history produced twenty millionaires, and less than a quarter of a century of Confederation yielded up 180 more. And it's not only the number that has swollen, for the average millionaire in Newfoundland today is worth many times more than was the average one before Confederation. And there are dozens of other wealthy men whose fortunes don't quite reach the million mark.

It would not be so much a matter for public concern if our millionaires today, making their money and living with their families in a capital-hungry province, instead of investing their money only in the wholesale and retail trade, in amusement centres, in high-rise buildings, and countless other high- and quick-return enterprises, in and out of our own province, were to put large proportions of it into basic productive industries to strengthen the fundamental economy of the province by creating jobs. Even our great basic industry, the fishery, has not attracted locally the capital that it has needed. My administration had to pour many millions of dollars of public money into the fisheries, largely as loans, to make up for the failure of local millionaires, near-millionaires, and other wealthy individuals and companies to do so.

From the standpoint of personalities, the Confederate cause appeared to be generally weak. Mr. Bradley and I were well known by then, and the names of Keough and Newell were at any rate far better known than they had been before the Convention. It turned out later that the Hon. Walter S. Monroe, a former Prime Minister, leaned to Confederation, as did Colonel Sir Leonard C. Outerbridge, Mr. H. B. Clyde Lake, and Mr. A. B. Baird. Still later the fact emerged that two of the Commissioners, Herman W. Quinton and Herbert L. Pottle, preferred Confederation to responsible government. A few other well-known names were to emerge on the side of Confederation. But this was later. Now, with the Convention ending, in terms of personalities the Confederate cause consisted of only Gordon Bradley and me.

But I felt that we had a great ace in the hole. This was a public sentiment favourable to Confederation that existed among the common people in many parts of the Island and in Labrador. The task was to arouse their enthusiasm and their faith in the possibility of success in the coming referendum. This would take an enormous effort and no trifling amount of money.

But first, Confederation itself had to be placed on the ballot paper in the forthcoming referendum. How could we get it there? Mr. Bradley wanted to hurry back to Bonavista. (He was never happy away from there, either as a member of the National Convention or as Secretary of State for Canada, or later as a member of the Senate of Canada.) But I wrote a speech for him to deliver over the radio, and he stayed long enough to do so. Under the rules then existing, I was not permitted to broadcast, but the Confederate cause was lucky indeed to have on its side at least one Newfoundlander who could. Bradley's speech denounced "the twenty-nine dictators" for denying the Newfoundland people the right to vote for, or even against, Confederation in the referendum. It was a rascally thing, I wrote, to cheat the people out of their chance to exercise their own judgement about their own country. But, the speech said, it was not too late. It was not too late, if the people would act and act promptly. "If you think that Confederation should be placed on the ballot paper, so that people can vote for or against it according to their own free and independent will, send instantly your telegrams demanding that Confederation be put on the ballot paper, and your demands will be delivered to the British Government."

The result was electrifying. The telegrams poured into my flat on Duckworth Street East in a rising flood for days. Some contained only one or two names, some a dozen, some a hundred; a few contained several hundreds of names. I rigged up a table in my living room to accommodate volunteers who came every day and night in relays (in fact, they numbered not more than a dozen) to make faithful copies of the telegrams, with every name, for the forthcoming compaign. Every few hours, I gave out a press statement about the progress of the "crusade", and this fanned the fire, of course. In St. John's, a small band of men and women went from door to door seeking signatures to a petition demanding that Confederation be placed on the ballot paper.

In something like a week, I had between 50,000 and 60,000 names, and I called on Governor Macdonald to inform him that I wished to present the telegrams and petitions formally to him at his earliest convenience. He set a time, and we went up in a small group and I made the presentation. He received them gravely and promised to forward them to the Secretary of State for Dominion Affairs in London. A short time later, perhaps a week or so, meeting the Governor's son, Kenneth Macdonald, I asked him if he thought the reply would soon come back from London, and added that the petitions and telegrams must have reached London by now. "Oh, we didn't actually send the telegrams and petitions to London," Macdonald said, and my heart nearly stopped beating. "You didn't send them!"

I exclaimed. "What did you do with them?" And young Macdonald explained that his father had sent a long dispatch to London explaining and describing the telegrams and petitions, the number of names attached, and the widespread character of the territory from which they came. I was unhappy and uneasy. I showed as much, and Macdonald said reassuringly, "Surely you don't think the British Government is going to refuse the request of the petition?" This bucked me up again for a while.

But I had to live through an interminable, intolerable, maddening wait for word from London! When it came, the general manager of the Broadcasting Corporation of Newfoundland, William Galgay, was invited to send someone to Government House to receive the precise wording that he was to have broadcast over the BCN stations. He sent up Richard O'Brien, who was to do the actual broadcasting of the news. Dick O'Brien was my friend, and I asked him to give some kind of sign when he came back to the studio, and he promised to do so. I wanted to avoid the suspense of those few minutes that would elapse between his arrival in the studio from Government House and his actually broadcasting of the fateful news. I was in the corridor as he arrived, and Dick gave me a broad wink that sent my spirits soaring. The announcement said that the British Government did not think that it would be right to deny the Newfoundland people the opportunity to pronounce on the question of Confederation. We had won! Glory hallelujah!

The Confederate

14

Back to the People —Twice

All oppressed people are authorized, whenever they can, to rise and break their fetters.

Henry Clay

If there be fuel prepared, it is hard to tell whence the spark shall come that shall set it on fire.

Francis Bacon

A nation usually renews its youth in its deathbed, and there finds again the spirit that it had gradually lost.

Nietzsche

At the bottom of the tributes paid to democracy is the little man, walking in the little booth, with a little pencil, making a little cross on a little bit of paper,—no amount of rhetoric or voluminous discussion can possibly diminish the overwhelming importance of the point.

Winston S. Churchill

The referendum was set for June 3, 1948. Confederation would be on the ballot along with responsible government and a continuation of the Commission of Government. I now set to work to organize the Confederation campaign. Gordon Bradley was in Bonavista at the time, and I do not now remember whether I succeeded in getting him back to St. John's to attend the meeting on March 26 at which I launched the Newfoundland Confederate Association. I think he was not there. At any rate, there were a hundred or so of us present, in the ballroom of the Newfoundland Hotel. I had arranged for someone to nominate Bradley to be president of the Association and to nominate me for campaign manager. I subsequently appointed Gregory J. Power to be assistant campaign manager. The simple truth of the matter is that the actual running of the campaign from that moment forward was in my hands, and that I had the loyal help of a tiny group: Gregory Power, Philip F. Forsey, Harold Horwood, Irving Fogwill, and a few others.

I was the leader, and the character of dictator so often attributed to me by my opponents after I became Premier—and attributed unjustly—could much more truly have been attributed to me throughout the two Confederate campaigns. Of course, *dictator* is too harsh a word to describe the facts. The cause needed nothing so much as the thinking and work of a strategist and tactician, a coordinator, a band leader, an orchestra conductor—but a conductor with more than the usual authority over the orchestra. This was readily seen, and there was never any argument or dispute about it. The others had no aspirations in the least to take my place, and each was happy to do the part assigned to him. We were joined by a number of enthusiastic and tireless supporters. Irving Fogwill was a tower of strength. Herbert Wells was a volunteer, and so was Jack Oakley. Phil Roche of the Railway was a strong supporter, as were Jack St. John and Claude E. Dawe. Roland Baggs was one of the group. Fred Harris worked like a trojan, and so did Bill Case. Sam Brace and Clarence Hancock were in the group. Jim Duggan was a valued helper. My old Corner Brook friend, Michael Foley, dropped in and volunteered his services. Norman Janes came along and enlisted, and so did Arthur W. Smith. Max Howell, Tom Croucher, Walter Parsons, Charlie Winsor, Ken McBay, and Billie Bond Taylor were all ardent Confederate workers. Bill Frampton, Art Sullivan, Police Sergeant Joe Seaward and his wife, Harry Bishop, Solomon Drodge, Gerry Healey, Ed Wyse, Bill Corbett, Matt Furlong, Tommy Sergeant, Bill Martin, Captain Alf Kean, Captain Bert King, Wes Collins, Armand Lee, and Mrs. James P. Adams, the mother of the present Mayor of St. John's, were great workers. My old school friend Sam Hefferton joined me. Ted Garland was my chauffeur-bodyguard; Rudy Williams and Clarence Harding were competent bodyguards; and Doug Kelsey was a valued driver-bodyguard. Charlie Penney did a very useful piece of work: I sent him to Ontario to seek out Newfoundlanders and get them to sign a joint letter advising their relatives and friends back home to vote for Confederation; this letter I published in our newspaper, the *Confederate*.

I was to decide who should broadcast for us, what every broadcast was to say or not say (I wrote most of the broadcasts), and every word that appeared in our paper was to be written or at any rate controlled by me. I insisted that we had to have a unified story from beginning to end, without contradiction, and following a single theme. My argument, which the others accepted readily, was that so small a group had no chance at all of succeeding if it didn't marshal and use its forces with maximum unity and with concentrated, coordinated effort. This, I think, was the secret of our success. Too many cooks would have spoiled that broth.

We didn't have a dollar to our name, but we had to have an office. I found one behind Bartlett's barber shop at 158 Water Street, a few doors west of the *Evening Telegram* office. Charlie Garland had his office on the second floor in the building across the street, and he and I carried some of his furniture into our new Confederate offices (*offices* is correct, for there were two of them, one inside the other). I was lucky to get Mrs. A. M. Templeman as my secretary-typist, and with great daring I persuaded Gregory Power to leave his family at Dunville and come to St. John's to join me. He was at least as eager to come as I was to have him; and from the moment he arrived, we were inseparable and saw eye to eye at every point of battle. Phil Forsey was teaching at Prince of Wales College and could get in only after school and at night. Harold Horwood, whose interest in the movement fluctuated, would drop in as the spirit moved him. His brother Charlie, who wore a great black beard, took to dropping in at the offices until Harold expostulated one day, "For God's sake, don't you start coming in here or they'll think we're making bombs!" Harold at that time had given up wearing a beard.

I had decided that we had to have a newspaper, so I registered it as the *Confederate* and sought from the *Evening Telegram* a price for which they would print our paper. They gave me a price but, suspecting the truth about our financial condition, insisted that each issue be paid for before being removed from the printing office. I assured them airily that of course it would be paid for and tried to insinuate an indignation I did not feel about their daring to doubt the financial strength of our great Newfoundland Confederate Association.

Phil Forsey paid for the first issue of the *Confederate*. He went to his friend Chesley Handrigan, manager of the Bank of Nova Scotia, and persuaded him to get the bank to discount Forsey's note for several hundreds of dollars. I remember Forsey's asking me anxiously for my assurance that the note would be met by the Association when it fell due, and my assuring him that it would. I really believed it would, for I was sure that we would succeed in raising some funds. I had asked my old friend Ray Petten to become treasurer of our movement, which meant in fact that his was the job of raising our funds, as mine was to spend them. Charlie Garland meanwhile had become secretary-treasurer of the Association, and never a more faithful follower was there.

What excitement when we got out that first issue of the *Confederate*! It and the succeeding installments were beyond doubt the wittiest and most devastatingly effective political propaganda ever to appear, to this day, in a Newfoundland newspaper. Philip Forsey wrote one or two short pieces, as did Harold Horwood, but I think I can say I wrote about 90 per cent and Gregory Power about 10 per cent of all the issues. We made no real effort to sell the paper—that would have limited the circulation severely—so we gave it away and blanketed the country with it each week. (I deeply regret that I do not own a complete set of the *Confederate*.)

One of the greatest features of the *Confederate* was the cartoon in every issue. They were drawn by Jack Boothe, the successful Toronto *Globe and Mail* cartoonist. When I was in Ottawa with the National Convention delegation, I saw his cartoons in the *Globe* and decided that he was exactly the man I wanted to do cartoons for the paper that I intended to publish; so I went down to Toronto see him. I told him what I had in mind, and he good-humouredly agreed to become our official cartoonist. Thereupon I took out a sheaf of papers on which I had drawn very crudely indeed a couple of dozen cartoons of my own devising. I was not, of course, able to get the proper expression or proportion or anything else into these cartoons, just the central idea itself. I had therefore covered each cartoon with written notes describing how I wanted each face to look and so forth. He looked them over and agreed that he saw exactly what I wanted. Indeed he did, for the cartoons were among the greatest ever seen in a political campaign in Canada. Boothe also came up with brilliant cartoons of his own devising. I sent him each issue of the *Confederate*, and he could see the general nature of our argument and was able to base his own cartoons upon it.

I had to decide at the outset what form our campaign should take. There just was not enough time, and the Island was too big and the money too scarce, to allow us to hold a large series of public meetings. In any case, I saw that one public meeting that ended in disorder would do terrible damage to our cause throughout the country. This I had to avoid at all costs. I never held a single meeting in either campaign in any place where I was not sure of getting a great reception; and I held meetings in such places purely for the publicity that they would generate, in order to help to create a bandwagon psychology throughout the Island.

Some perverse instinct led the Anti-Confederates into the very opposite tactic. Don Jamieson and Geoff Stirling tried to hold an Anti-Confederate rally in the Confederate stronghold of Bay Roberts—they were lucky to get out with their skins! Ches Crosbie and Phil Lewis tried their hands at Grand Bank—the local people would hardly let them land on the wharf! Peter Cashin wouldn't believe that Grand Bank was all that favourable to Confederation, but he went there himself and found out. Bert Butt went to Twillingate, and I heard that he had to take refuge underneath the hall.

Our campaign therefore focused chiefly on our newspaper and our broadcasting. I enlisted a small corps of broadcasters, reasonably well-known citizens who were willing to go on the air to make speeches for us. I myself wrote most of the speeches, but obviously not those of Colonel Sir Leonard Outerbridge and one or two others like him. I did insist, however, upon seeing their speeches before they were broadcast. I think that we beat the others badly in broadcasting. I saw to it that every speech was worded with almost elemental simplicity and that it dealt with issues that were elementally simple. I wanted above all to broadcast a message that would be understood and appreciated by the thousands. The other side, on the contrary, broadcast in high falutin' language expressing lofty philosophical concepts which left most people stone cold. It was only when they made impassioned pleas to Newfoundlanders not to sell their country that they really did us some damage.

I adopted the practice of travelling throughout the Island by aircraft. That would be easier to do today than it was then, for my choice of aircraft was rigidly limited. Indeed, there was only one. It was a tiny one-engined affair with floats, and it would be a compliment to it to call it airworthy. It took an interminable length of take-off to get off the water. I carried a public address system on it, and my pilot would land me in a bay, preferably one containing several coves or settlements. After he and I had rigged the loudspeaker onto the wings, I would stand on the pontoon with the microphone and, as I faced the settlement, speak to it from a distance of a few hundred feet or yards. In this way, I could blanket the entire population with my voice. Then we would go up again and head for another settlement or bay, where we went through the same procedure. I suppose that in the course of the two campaigns, I must have flown thousands of miles and spoken many dozens of times to thousands of people in the aggregate. Some of these occasions were remarkable. In Twillingate, I arrived three hours late, but the entire population was waiting for me. Twenty-five men with great sealing guns were crouched on some rocks out in the middle of the harbour, and as we circled Twillingate, I fancied that our small plane was actually shaken by the concussion from those guns. Gunfire was the usual form of approving reception, and I sometimes wonder why I did not contract shell shock.

Captain Eric Blackwood, my pilot, had more nerve than I did, for he knew more surely than I could that the tiny seaplane was really not airworthy. Sometimes, we would taxi for a mile across the water before she could get airborne. I'm sure that we had far more narrow squeaks than I was aware of, but I was all too aware of the narrowest one of all. We were flying southward along the northeast coast to St. John's when we ran into a bank of fog that seemed to extend a dangerously long distance toward the city. Blackwood headed her farther off the coast, over the Atlantic, to get outside the fog, and kept on going south. I asked him anxiously if he thought that the fog went all the way to St. John's, and if it did, where were we going to get into a safe harbour to land? He replied, with much more confidence than he felt, that he was sure we would get into St. John's. But we didn't—the fog blanketed The Narrows, St. John's Harbour, and the town itself. But as God should have it, there was a narrow break in the fog-bank leading in through the cleft in the hilly shore outside Quidi Vidi Cove and Lake, two or three miles east of the Narrows. The rift in the fog was just wide enough for us to fly through for a landing on the lake. It was, as far as I know, the closest shave that I ever had.

It was on one of those flights around the Island—on the northwest coast, I think it was—that my pilot told me the saying that circulated among pilots: "There are old pilots, and there are bold pilots—but there are no old bold pilots." Maybe not, but I have personal knowledge of one or two who have been pretty long-lived.

Tommy Sergeant, an Englishman who was a respected and popular teacher in St. John's, asked to go with me to my meeting in Freshwater, below Carbonear, where George Warren was my chairman. Ted Vincent and Phil Forsey went, too, but Sergeant stole the show. He explained to the audience that he was no great speaker and that he was really in no position to explain the details of the benefits that would flow from Confederation. But if someone happened to have a full page of a newspaper with him, he'd be glad to demonstrate what these benefits were. Someone on the platform passed him a page of a newspaper (arranged beforehand), and Tommy took out his cigarette-lighter. The audience watched attentively as he lit the bottom corner of the sheet and the flame ran up to consume it. Tommy slapped the burning sheet between his hands and put out the fire. In full view of the audience, he rubbed the ashes together between his hands and then with a flourish produced, and held up for all to see, a $10 bill!

"That's all, ladies and gentlemen," he said simply. "It's really quite easy to do, and you should all be able to do it. If you can do this, you don't need Confederation. If you can't, then I can tell you that Confederation is the next best thing!" Uproarious applause! (Eighty per cent of Freshwater voted for Confederation.)

Throughout both campaigns, I had to be virtually our only campaigner around the Island, and to organize and control every last detail of the campaign at headquarters. It involved incredibly long hours for seven days a week, but it gave us a unified control without which there could have been no hope whatsoever of success.

Our opponents were completely lacking in organization and control. They were hampered by several unsound practices and weaknesses almost from the beginning. The Responsible Government League had numerous citizens of high reputation and standing in Newfoundland, but particularly in St. John's. They put on a radio broadcasting campaign and held a few public meetings. Their radio campaign had all the shortcomings of an amateur program. Individual speakers went off on their own tangents, so that it became fairly easy to attack their campaign on grounds of inconsistency, pointing out that whereas one Responsible Government League speaker had said this or that, the other had come on and in effect completely contradicted him. The most capable personal campaigner of them all, Major Peter Cashin, though nominally of the Responsible Government League, was really a soloist who just didn't like choirs and orchestras, and he always made the League nervous when he was around. Yet he had more followers in the country than the whole League put together.

The most serious division of all was caused by Ches Crosbie. He was a very popular figure in Newfoundland, with thousands of personal friends throughout the Island. Many of these were small businessmen, but a sizable number were fishermen, loggers, and precisely the kind of common men and women who were the backbone of our Confederate cause. In short, Ches Crosbie gave us our only real competition. And to make matters worse, at least worse for Confederation, Ches Crosbie was advocating a form of economic understanding or arrangement between Newfoundland and the United States whereby some degree of free trade would exist between the two countries. The Crosbie "Economic Union with the United States Party" told the people of the vast benefits that would flow into Newfoundland if our fish and other products were allowed into the United States duty-free. Geoff Stirling, publisher of the *Sunday Herald*, who with Don Jamieson ran Crosbie's campaign, hurried off to the United States to get a statement from Senator Robert Taft, but the statement that he obtained must have been a severe disappointment to him and his friends. John McEvoy hurried after him to the States and brought back convincing evidence that the New England fishing industry would never stand for duty-free admittance of Newfoundland fishery products into the United States.

Crosbie admitted candidly that this option would not be put on the ballot in the referendum, and that the agreement could be made only after Newfoundland had obtained responsible government. He therefore advocated that responsible government be restored so that Newfoundland could properly approach the United States for some form of economic union. Responsible government was thus presented merely as a means to an end. If you believed in economic union with the United States, you had to vote for responsible government as the only way to get it. It was a powerful argument with many people, and the moment Crosbie announced it, I knew that we were in trouble. I tried to counteract the effect of this campaign by christening it "Comic Union", and indeed thousands of people were calling it that before the campaign ended. Most people knew what *comic* meant, which is more than could be said of *economic*.

I thought deeply about the problem that Mr. Crosbie's crusade was causing us, and I found the answer I needed. I directed that our propaganda should thenceforth lay more emphasis than ever on the fact that while joining Canada as a province would allow us to continue to be British subjects, to fly the Union Jack, and to continue our allegiance to the Throne and Crown, economic union would end in requiring us to strike the flag, forswear our allegiance to the Union Jack, and swear a new oath of allegiance to a foreign land and flag. I went into Long Brothers, the printers, and placed an initial order for 50,000 copies of a small multi-coloured poster to be placed in household windows. It said, "British Union", with a picture of the Union Jack between the two words; and on the second line, in much larger type, was the word "CONFEDERATION!" The sudden appearance of thousands of these in house windows and elsewhere was a striking reminder of the fact that we were British, not American, and that Confederation would allow us to continue to be British subjects. I am sure that it weaned thousands away from the Economic Union movement.

The other side tried in two ways to counter this. First, they printed a poster saying, "CONFEDERATION MEANS FRENCH-CANADIAN UNION". After midnight on a Saturday, they sent a truck around pasting or nailing these posters on fences, electric light poles, and even on people's houses. They plastered the areas in front of the principal churches in St. John's, so that the first thing the church-going crowds would see Sunday morning would be this offensive propaganda. They sent bundles of those posters to some of the outports, and Albert Delaney, of St. George's, received a bundle for distribution in his area. But Albert Delaney, an ardent Confederate and friend of mine, was not of Irish descent, as his name might suggest, but French! Second, the Anti-Confederates pleaded with people: "Don't sell your country"; "Don't let Canada take our forests, minerals, water powers." I ridiculed that argument by trying to picture Canada coming down to Newfoundland, seizing the forests, rivers, and mineralized lands, and making off with them—a sort of burglary. They said the Canadian Government would tax everything in sight—your house, your land, your outhouses, your boats, engines, fishing-gear; your horses, cows, pigs, hens—everything you had; and if you couldn't pay the tax, they'd take the property itself. Yes, there was an old-age pension; but before you got it, you had to mortgage your property to the Canadian Government. Family allowances, in Peter Cashin's words, were "immoral". Yes, they were paid; but as soon as you passed your sixteenth birthday, you had to start paying it all back to the Canadian Government again. Once we got into Confederation, we'd never be able to get out of it. We'd be taxed to death.

In the 1869 General Election, when Confederation had been the principal issue, the Anti-Confederates had had two songs that helped their cause. The first read in part as follows:

Ye brave Newfoundlanders who plough the salt sea,
With hearts like the Eagle so bold and so free,
The time is at hand when we'll have to say
If Confederation will carry the day.

Would you barter the right that your fathers have won?
No! let them descend from father to son.
For a few thousand dollars Canadian gold
Don't let it be said that our birthright was sold.

Men, hurrah for our own native Isle, Newfoundland—
Not a stranger shall hold one inch of her strand;
Her face turns to Britain, her back to the Gulf,
Come near at your peril, Canadian Wolf!

And the second read in part:

Cheer up, my gallant countrymen,
The fight is fought and won.
Confederates are routed,
And beaten two to one.

The people have declared their will,
The people's voice has spoke,
They ne'er will bend to alien laws
Or to a foreign yoke.

So now Confederation
A shameful death has died.
'Tis buried up at Riverhead
Beneath the flowing tide.
And may it never rise again
To bother us, I pray!
Hurrah, my boys, for Liberty,
The Antis gained the day.

The 1948 song caught up very well the fears and prejudices of the Anti-Confederate cause:

THE HERO OF '48

(Sung to the Air of "A Mother's Love")

A fisher boy was leaving and going to Labrador,
Fishing the same old trap-berth where his father fished before,
And as he was leaving his mother, while standing on the quay,
He threw his arms around her neck, and this to her did say:

Chorus

Don't vote Confederation, and that's my prayer to you;
We own the house we live in, likewise the schooner too;
But if you heed Joe Smallwood, and his line of French Patois
You'll be always paying taxes to the men in Ottawa.

But if you heed my warning, when we come sailing home
We'll be loaded to the scuppers, and I'll have no need to roam.
I'll buy a new accordion, and we will dance all night,
And the guy who mentions Canada, he sure will have to fight.

Chorus

From Blanc Sablon to Chidley is owned by Newfoundland—
The rivers, bays, and coastlines, back to the height of land;
We won it in a lawsuit from Quebec years ago,
But now they hope to get it back with the tricks of Schemer Joe.

Chorus

Oh, mother, dearest mother, God guard our fishing room,
It is the best one on the coast from Hebron to Quirpon;
But if Confederation should win on polling day,
The Ghost of Uncle George will rise, and this to you will say:

Chorus

We want no French Canadians, and what we have we'll hold;
It has given us a living, and it's something more than gold;

I thought the French Shore question was settled years ago,
But like the cat that has nine lives, it lives in Schemer Joe.

Chorus

There'd be Frenchmen in their galleons, and Frenchmen in their sloops,
There'd be Frenchmen in their batteaux, all wearing wooden boots;
They'd be full of false politeness, as they'd take our choicest berths;
They'd fly their flag the Fleur de Lis,
Oh, Mother, that's what hurts.

Chorus

The Winsors, and the Barbours, the Blackwoods and the Keans,
The Samsons and the Murphys, the Roberts's and Paynes,
Will all turn over in their graves, if Smallwood wins the day,
Cape Ann's will be forbidden—and we'll wear a French beret.

Chorus

We're a Scotch and English mixture, and the fighting Irish breeds;
We live in peace and harmony, and help each other's needs;
We like our brewis and flippers, and a scattered time a turr,
And we don't want any Frenchmen, with their talk of Mal de mer.

Chorus

So! Mother, dearest mother, don't let them win you over—
On polling day just mark your X for dear old Terra Nova;
Tell Sarah Jane, fish or no fish, I'll have her in the fall,
And Joey's baby bonus in-ter-ests me, not at all.

Chorus

Our life has not been easy, and our fight was hard and long,
But IF we have faith in ourselves, we'll carry right along;
We want no strangers in our crew, let us be on our way,
And mark your X RESPONSIBLE when comes the polling day.

Chorus

Our skies above look brighter, our papermills now hum,
There's iron ore on the Labrador, enough till Kingdom come;
The U.S.A. she wants our fish, the long dark night is o'er,
So don't surrender, Newfoundland, likewise the Labrador.

Chorus

Now, mother, dearest mother, we are Newfoundlanders true,
Our ship is sound from stem to stern, and we can get the crew.
So keep the old flag flying, and keep her off the land,
As loved our fathers so we love, God guard thee Newfoundland.

Author unknown

At least my opponents didn't use the argument of the Antis of

1869: "Your sons will all be conscripted into Canada's army and their bones left to bleach on the desert sands of Canada!" But even without that particular idiocy, there were still dozens of silly arguments that blanketed the country, and I had enormous fun answering them with cartoons and skits in the *Confederate*, on the radio, and in public speeches throughout Newfoundland. Albert B. Perlin was the author of none of these silly arguments, but he was the clever source of every last sensible argument that ever surfaced in the Anti-Confederate campaign. I privately agreed fervently with one of his arguments, that the coming of Confederation would loose a flood of emigration of our people to mainland Canada. This was my personal nightmare, and it moulded and coloured my thinking and policy in the first ten or fifteen years of my premiership – indeed, I haven't lost that fear yet. There was another Anti-Confederate argument: "I'm not against Confederation; I'm only against the way it's being done" – the idea being that we should first restore responsible government and only then approach Canada for the terms of union. That was easy to answer: a General Election of a House of Assembly would inevitably involve large numbers of irrelevant issues, personalities, and non-sequiturs; but a simple secret-ballot referendum confined to direct issues would be a far fairer and more realistic referral of the matter to the people. As for the terms, there was no finality in those in any case; an elected responsible government might obtain better terms, but it would do so after the alternative of Confederation had been accepted.

The case for Confederation I put broadly in these terms: "Commission of Government means security, but no democracy; responsible government means democracy, but no security; Confederation means democracy and security, both." We could expect a reduction in the cost of living. We would share in Canada's great social security program, with family allowances for every child under sixteen; old-age pensions at $30 a month for the husband and an equal amount for the wife, as against $30 a quarter for the two combined; unemployment insurance for those who had no jobs; and vastly improved allowances for our war veterans. In addition, thousands of civil servants would pass over to the Canadian Government services in Newfoundland, at substantially higher pay; and thousands of railroaders, airport employees, and lighthouse-keepers would come under federal employ at much higher pay.

This letter that I published in the *Daily News* over my own name helped our cause substantially:

Editor Daily News,

Dear Sir: The alarm clock (60%)* rang noisily at 7:45. Bill Doakes stirred, then woke up. He threw the bed clothes (40%) off him and the mattress (50%) creaked as he leapt out of bed (50%). Picking up his eye-glasses (65%) from the chair (65%) he put on his slippers and hurried over to the window. He let the blind (50%) slip up with a whirl and pushed the curtain (50%) aside. He saw as he looked through the glass (45%) that it was a fair morning.

Hurrying to the bath (35%) room, he threw off his pyjama (40%) coat and turned on the hot water tap (50%) into the wash basin (35%). First he washed with soap (40%) and then vigorously lathered (40%) up with his shave brush (65%). Adjusting a new blade (50%) to his razor (50%) he soon had the stubborn stubble off. His face felt cool and clean after he had slapped on some after-shave lotion (65%). Throwing the damp towel (40%) down, he hurried back to his room.

Quickly he got into his underwear (40%) hauled on his socks (40%) slipped into his shirt (40%) and reached for his collar (40%). He swore under his breath as the collar-button (40%) slipped, but finally he got it on and tightened his tie (40%). He slipped into his suit (30%) and hurried downstairs. Bill went into the kitchen and warmed himself by the range (50%). While his wife placed two rashers of bacon (6¢ lb.) in the frying-pan (30%) he drank his fruit juice (35%). He ate his corn flakes (50%) and soon was enjoying his bacon. His wife handed him a cup (35%) of tea (10¢ lb.) and he buttered his toast and reached for the marmalade (6¢ lb.). The tea wasn't quite sweet enough, so he added a little sugar (4½¢ lb.). He was finished at last. He struck a match (3/5 of a cent per box) and lit a cigarette ($4.95 lb.).

In the hall he put on his leather windbreaker (45%) his hat (50%) and gloves (45%) and went out the front door. Glancing at the thermometer (50%) to see the temperature, he crossed the cement (35%) walk to the car (20%) and got in. Slipping a stick of chewing gum (65%) between his teeth (false, 40%) he started down the street.

*The rate of the ad valorem customs duty payable by Newfoundlanders on goods imported into the country—and, practically speaking, everything had to be imported.

> It was exactly 8:30 by his watch (60%) as he sat at his desk and took up the morning's *Daily News*. After he had looked over the paper he settled down to the editorial page and read the letters carefully. Then for the first time that morning he spoke. Addressing his stenographer, who already (!) was busily clattering the keys of the typewriter (35%) he said: "I just can't see where they get the idea that Confederation would help us. Why, we'd be taxed to death!

Many Newfoundlanders believed the anti-Confederate propaganda that the Nova Scotians were unhappy in Confederation and wanted to get out. I decided to shatter that propaganda, so I wrote a letter to a large number of prominent Nova Scotians—mayors of cities and towns, heads of universities, and so forth—asking them to write me their answers to this question: "If the people of Nova Scotia were asked, in a secret-ballot referendum, for their choice, would they have their province break away from the Canadian Confederation and become an independent British colony again, or remain a province of Canada?" I do not guarantee the wording of my question, but the sense of it was assuredly as I have stated. I expected to receive a chorus of replies that would knock out the anti-Confederate propaganda based on Nova Scotia's alleged discontent. I was deeply disappointed in the majority of the replies that I received, and I decided to let the matter drop, and to keep it very mum!

Countless stories could be told of that campaign, for it was something the like of which Newfoundland has never seen, before or since. Feelings ran deep and bitter. Churches were split wide open, as were societies, trade unions, and families. Friendships were shattered. Each side accused the other of unspeakable crimes, and the accusations continued to be made long after the issue was settled.

The hatred for me was, in some quarters, frightening—though, in fact, I was never frightened. Perhaps that is because I never went near the places where the hate was strongest. I am reminded of the gentleman who came into the Confederate offices one day and, standing at the counter separating the outer from the inner part of the office, demanded to see me. He was told that I was out campaigning, and he then explained that he and other people of his harbour wanted me to come up to visit them. The place was in invincible responsible government territory, and my friends in the office knew that there was no chance on earth of my going there. They did not say this but explained patiently that one man could not be expected to visit everywhere. He was adamant and continued to insist that I come to their harbour. Again, it was explained that I could not possibly visit every place, and his final remark as he began his retreat was that the people up there wanted me to visit them so they "could drown the bastard!"

Naturally there were some lighter moments. Early in the campaign, Ted Russell, who became a Minister in my Cabinet but whose sense of humour wouldn't let him stay in it, paid his first visit to our Confederate Association offices. In the doorway, he hesitated and asked his companion, "Is this where you look up and down the street to see if anybody you know sees you going in?" When he got inside, he saw me entering one or two coloured pins into a large map of Newfoundland on the wall. It was supposed to show the strengths and weaknesses of our Confederate following—the key word is *supposed.* I had just announced in a full-page advertisement in the daily papers the names of 100 vice-presidents of the Confederate Association. "More vice-presidents?" Russell asked innocently.

Three nights before the first referendum, and again three nights before the second, I held big public meetings in the CLB Armoury in St. John's. There were huge crowds each time. The street outside at the first meeting was a solid jam of thousands who listened to my speech on the loudspeakers. When I came out after the meeting and pressed through the dense crowd, I was punched and pummelled; but a police constable, Bert Tucker, shielded me, and several friends helped. I was pushed and led out into the middle of Harvey Road, where I was lifted bodily up onto the top of a coupe, owned by Kevin McCarthy, who immediately started through the crowd, while I waved cheerfully at them. McCarthy didn't stop until we were hundreds of yards away from the crowd; then I got down and sat in the car beside him. He drove me to the Newfoundland Hotel, where I stayed overnight; and the next morning I started off on my final speaking tour in that campaign, delivering fifty or more speeches in two days around Conception Bay and Trinity Bay.

My movements in the last two days were almost identical in both referendum campaigns. I travelled with a car and a truck, accompanied by two or three friends. Gregory Power was with me on one of these occasions, and Dr. Fred Rowe on the other—at least that's my recollection. The truck was equipped with extremely powerful loudspeaker trumpets on the roof, and inside were the machinery of the loudspeaker system and a large supply of new batteries. The microphone cord from the truck was fifty or sixty feet long. Our procedure was to drive up to a settlement and choose some nearby elevation from which, provided that the wind was in the right direction, I could speak to the entire community. The first stop was Brigus. I spoke for perhaps fifteen or eighteen minutes there, and we then moved on to Cupids, and then on to Clarke's Beach. Clarke's Beach is so spread out that we had to have two "meetings" there. Then on to Coley's Point and Bay Roberts, and on to the Port de Grave area.

There was one part of my speech that I used in every settlement.

> You should have no trouble making your choice on polling day. You have got to make that choice, you know; it's your country, it's where you have to live, and your children and grandchildren after you, as well; and it's in your own hands now to settle your country's future, and your own future, and your children's future. That's what you'll be doing when you walk into the polling booth at eight o'clock tomorrow morning [or the day after tomorrow, as the case might be]. You'll go into the place, and the Deputy Returning Officer will ask you your name. That may surprise you, for of course you know that he already knows your name. But don't mind that—he'll only be following the rules. So you'll tell him your name and he'll write it down, and then he will give you your ballot paper. You'll take that ballot paper into the little private place. It may be nothing more than a corner of the room partitioned off with a bed sheet. No matter. There you'll be all by yourself. There'll be a little table there for you, and a pencil. All you have to do is mark an *X* on the ballot paper. Just one single *X*. Don't put two there, and don't put anything there except that one single *X*. Don't use your own pencil, and don't use a pen—be sure you use the pencil that is provided for you there.
>
> So there you'll be, all by yourself, in that little private space, with the table before you, and the pencil, and the ballot paper in your hand. All you'll have to do is lay the paper on the desk, face up; take the pencil and mark one single *X* on it.

It is so simple! You won't find anybody's name on the ballot paper—not Joe Smallwood's, not Ches Crosbie's, not Peter Cashin's, nobody's. You will not be voting for me, and you'll not be voting to "give Ches a chance".* Don't you bother about me or Ches or anyone else—you bother about yourself tomorrow, and you bother about your family, your children, or your grandchildren. You vote tomorrow to give them a chance! "Give Ches a chance", indeed! And how do you go about giving Ches a chance? By voting for responsible government as it existed in 1933, with all the dole and dole bread. I don't think Ches was on the dole in 1933—he didn't have to eat the dole bread. You had to, or your relatives or friends—but Ches didn't. And if responsible government as it existed in 1933 wins tomorrow, it's not Ches who'll have to go on the dole and eat the dole bread; not likely. You know who will be going on the dole. And that's what you will be voting for if you vote to give Ches a chance. Why should you do it? Have you thought it over? Have you found a good, sensible reason why you should give Ches a chance? Or anyone else except your own family?

Well, there you are, alone in that little polling booth, you and your conscience.

The choice is clear: responsible government as it existed in 1933, or Confederation with Canada. You make a last-minute decision between the two forms of government. You know what responsible government was like in 1933; the depression, the destitution, the dole, the disease. You know all about the tuberculosis and the beriberi. You know all about the brown dole bread. I don't have to remind you of the suffering under responsible government "as it existed in 1933". There may be a few youngsters around who don't remember anything about it—but you do. Even if you weren't on the dole and didn't have to eat the dole bread yourselves, your neighbours did, and you know all about it.

You ask yourself, "Will I mark this *X* for responsible

*The slogan "Give Ches a Chance" was being widely used by Crosbie's Economic Union group.

> government as it existed in 1933?" And you say to yourself, "Yes, I'll do it. I'm no namby-pamby—I'm tough, I am; I took it before, and I can take it again. I starved before, and I'm willing to starve again. I ate dole bread then, and I'm prepared to eat it now. I pulled in the belt in 1933, under responsible government, and I'm willing to pull it in again, and take whatever they hand out to me. I'll vote for responsible government as it existed in 1933!" And with that, before you change your mind, you take the pencil and mark that *X*.
>
> Then you fold up the ballot paper, as they told you to do, and you take it outside into the polling booth, and you push it down through the slot into the ballot box. You give it a couple of taps to make sure that it's gone into the box and can't be hooked out. You want to be sure that your ballot won't be hooked out by someone who is not prepared, as you are, to pull in the belt again. The deed is done! You've made your choice. You walk out of the polling station and make your way down the road to your home.
>
> And as you go down the road, you meet a little boy, or a little girl, coming toward you.
>
> If you have a conscience at all, you'll stop and you'll say, "Little boy (or little girl), I make my apology to you. I have just betrayed you. I have just voted for responsible government as it existed in 1933—the dole, the dole bread, the tuberculosis and the beriberi. I was able to take it; I pulled in my belt—now it's your turn. I don't see why you should get off any more than I did and other children did in 1933—but all the same, I suppose I should make my apology for condemning you in the polling booth today."

I improved on the speech as I went along the shores of Conception and Trinity bays, and I imagine that I reached the ears of 15,000 or 18,000 voters, and the hearts of well over half of them. It would be dangerous to say that it was those voters in Conception Bay and the south side of Trinity Bay that gave Confederation its perilously slender majority on the climactic day, for there were so many parts of Newfoundland of which it can be said that Confederation would have lost without their support: Labrador, White Bay North, the St. Barbe Coast, the great Humber area, Port-au-Port Peninsula, the whole southwest coast. But if it cannot with truth be claimed that the votes won in those two days tipped the balance in favour of Confederation, most certainly it can be said that Confederation couldn't have won without them. Dr. Fred Rowe, Gregory Power, and my driver-bodyguard Ted Garland, who accompanied me throughout the tour, were witnesses to the visible signs in the faces of my audience of what they were going to do tomorrow or the day after in the polling booth.

The words that I have quoted from my speeches were admittedly emotional, intended to appeal to the people's emotions. I cannot deny it—I haven't any desire to deny it. But in fairness to myself, I must add that these words did constitute a relatively small part of my speech in each harbour or cove, the peroration; the rest of the speech dealt very factually with the issues before the people in that fateful referendum.

The speeches ran from fifteen minutes to half an hour, and in a few cases, over half an hour. The larger the town, the longer the speech, of course. I remember reaching Harbour Grace just before dark, and going to the south side and turning the trumpets across the harbour toward the main part of the town. My voice boomed across the water like the sound of doom, and I was told after that it had been heard three miles beyond Harbour Grace! If so, I daresay they heard it better than did the people in Harbour Grace itself; for there, a large number of cars and trucks owned by Anti-Confederates attempted to drown my voice by leaning on their horns all the time I was speaking. It must have been hard on their batteries, but I don't know what success they had in drowning me out. I remember reaching Saddle Hill, Carbonear, about ten o'clock or later that night, and the large crowd that gathered about the sound truck as I held forth. It was close to midnight when we reached Victoria, and I wound up the day's campaigning with a speech that I am sure was heard by every living soul in that widespread town.

Early next morning, we were off "down the shore" from Carbonear to Salmon Cove, Blackhead, and all the way down to Bay de Verde and Grates Cove, and on up the south side of Trinity Bay to Heart's Content late that night. I shall always remember the marvellously enthusiastic crowd in Winterton. We spent the night at Heart's Content, and the next day, which was polling day, I continued up the shore to Whitbourne and made my final speech there. It was then mid-day, and my voice was virtually gone. We drove to Carbonear, the home of my wife's parents; and by the time we arrived, my voice had disappeared so completely that I was not able to make even the faintest audible sound.

I had delivered fifty-six speeches in two and a half days. It was a very emotional tour, and in some places, I could see tears in the eyes of the many who crowded about my car and me. Of course, there were the inevitable few places where I was heard in stony silence. This, with scarcely any variation, is what I did in the last two or two and a half days of the two referendum campaigns; and on both occasions, I delivered almost exactly the same number of speeches in the same places and with the same effect on my voice! The vote, however, was better the second time. The area from Brigus around to Whitbourne included the five present House of Assembly districts of Port de Grave, Harbour Grace, Carbonear, Bay de Verde, and Trinity South. I often think that it was the votes we won thereby that gave us Confederation. But then, I can think of many parts of Newfoundland that gave us Confederation! At all events, we couldn't have had it without them.

I will never forget the stricken countenances of my friends that June night as the count came in from the first referendum: responsible government, 69,400; Confederation, 64,066; Commission of Government, 23,311. They could not understand my satisfaction. They did not see that the run-off had to give us success. I was confident that most of the few thousands who had voted for a continuation of the Commission system would, in the run-off referendum, vote solidly for Confederation and give us our needed majority.

The second referendum was held on July 22. The campaign was a cruel ordeal, but I entered it with unbounded faith in the outcome. Again, the flying about the Island, the broadcasting, the newspaper; and again, but more importantly than ever, the dire need to exercise almost an iron dictatorship over our campaigners. The slightest wrong word might lose us thousands of votes. The feeling was running deeper than ever, and fiercer; and things would be dirtier than before. A man had to have eyes in the back of his head to keep things right.

It was in the second referendum campaign that religious sectarianism made its all-too-obvious and all-too-odious appearance. It was not absent from the first referendum, but it was not until the second that it really ran riot. In the first campaign, and throughout the period leading up to it, I had used every effort I could to keep it from being what so many elections before had been: a sectarian dogfight.

I was painfully aware of what appeared to be the bitter animosity of Archbishop Roche to the whole idea of Confederation with Canada. The evidence of that animosity hadn't appeared, but I was certain that it existed, though I had no notion then of the depth of its bitterness. I was acutely conscious of the precious store placed by His Grace, and indeed by the Roman Catholic Church everywhere else, upon the demanded right of the Church to control their schools; and I was all too aware of the importance of that issue in Newfoundland. A very large part of the cost of operating schools in Newfoundland was borne by the Newfoundland Government, though the Government itself didn't own a solitary school in the country—they were all, without exception, owned by the various religious denominations. These denominations undoubtedly enjoyed more rights and privileges than did their counterparts in any part of Canada; and the Archbishop feared, so I believe, that this system would be gravely imperilled if Confederation with Canada ever came about. Bishop John M. O'Neill was subsequently to tell me that it was not an undermining of the principle of state financing of denominational schools that he had feared about Confederation, but rather the danger that under Confederation, the Government of Newfoundland as a province of Canada would find itself without the money to pay what it had always paid toward the cost of operating church-owned schools. I was terribly conscious of these fears of the Roman Catholic Church in Newfoundland, and I was implacably determined to see that the terms and conditions of Newfoundland's union with Canada would contain absolute protection of the existing rights of the churches to public funds for the operation of their schools. In short, I vowed that the status quo should be maintained in the most unalterable way that could be found and that this should be covered within the actual terms of union. (It was done, in Term 18, which forms part of the very Constitution of Canada today.)

I was aware, too, of the Roman Catholic Church's opposition in principle and in practice to the whole idea of divorce. They were against it in every shape and form, not only for their own people in Newfoundland, but for all people.

In Ottawa, during the three months that the first delegation was there in 1947, I strove strenuously to solve these two problems, for I wanted desperately that the decision of the Newfoundland people,

Roman Catholic and all others, be made on the sheer merits of Confederation itself, without the beclouding effects of sectarian strife. Gordon Bradley had once been Grand Master of the Loyal Orange Association in Newfoundland, and he was a vigorous Protestant. As a matter of fact, he had precious little interest in religion as such—Catholic, Protestant, or any other. He was simply an Orangeman with a strong antipathy to any possibility of domination of Newfoundland by the Roman Catholic Church or any other hierarchy. I understood his feeling very well, for it was almost exactly the way my own father had always felt—and, I daresay, thousands of other Protestants as well. But Bradley was our chairman in Ottawa; and when I discovered to my own disgust that Gordon Higgins, a prominent and respected Roman Catholic, had not called on the Archbishop before we left for Ottawa, and had not called on the Apostolic Delegate to Canada in Ottawa, or indeed made any approaches to anyone or done anything about the problem of denominational schools and divorce, I realized that it was up to me to solve the problem. I talked earnestly to Bradley about it, fighting his resistance, undermining his stubbornness, wearing him down, over a period of five or six weeks in Ottawa. I told him what he had to do: he had to see the Apostolic Delegate and put the problem to him. But Bradley, besides being a prominent Orangeman, was essentially a very shy man who wasn't comfortable meeting prominent people; and indeed, he wasn't used to it.

I kept at him and finally won his half-hearted consent to call on Rome's ambassador to Canada. This happened one night in my room at the Château Laurier; and the minute he consented, I took the phone and called the Apostolic Delegate's house (I had already obtained the telephone number). A male voice answered, and I gave my name and told him that I was speaking for the chairman of the Newfoundland delegation visiting Ottawa to discuss the terms of union. I went on to explain that Mr. Bradley was very anxious (!) to meet with His Grace to discuss two most important matters involved in a union of the two countries. To my surprise, the voice at the other end of the telephone answered, "Yes, of course, Mr. Smallwood. We are well aware of the fact that you and Mr. Bradley and the other delegates are here—you see, I'm a Newfoundlander myself." "You are!" I exclaimed. "What's your name, sir?" "My name is Carew," he told me, and I could hear the suggestion of a smile in his voice. "Will Carew's son!" I exclaimed, and he said yes. He was the Apostolic

Delegate's private secretary.* Father Carew said he was quite sure that the Apostolic Delegate would be happy to meet with Mr. Bradley, and he would call me back in a few minutes. He did, and the appointment was made for noon the following day. Bradley was relieved to know that a Newfoundlander was the Roman prelate's secretary; but by the following morning, he had uncomfortable second thoughts about the idea that he, the former Grand Master of the LOA, should be calling upon a Roman Catholic priest of high rank and status. I kept him in my company that whole forenoon and walked along the street with him the fairly considerable distance to the Archbishop's palace. I walked him to the very door and rang the bell, and it was only when Father Carew welcomed us at the door that I turned away and walked up and down the street waiting for Bradley to re-emerge from the lion's den.

To my astonishment, Bradley came out an hour later all smiles, telling me that the Archbishop was a fine fellow, a real gentleman, and a man who, though a Roman Catholic and an Italian at that (!), was a fine sensible fellow. The Apostolic Delegate had taken him into his den, offered him a drink and a cigar (both of which Bradley always appreciated, though he never took either to excess), and put my friend completely at his ease. They were chatting about everything for ten or fifteen minutes before Bradley got around to the two problems that were tormenting us. He told me that the Archbishop didn't seem to be too much concerned about the divorce matter—his concern was for the financing of their schools. I congratulated Bradley warmly and sincerely, and told him that it was a big thing that he had done and that his name would be remembered for it. I am happy to make the fact known here.

In the weeks that followed, I discussed both matters with the acting Prime Minister, Mr. St. Laurent, and between us we prepared two drafts on schools and divorce for possible inclusion in the terms of union. On our way back by train to Newfoundland, I entrusted copies of these two proposed terms to Gordon Higgins to deliver to Archbishop Roche with a request for his concurrence or suggestions for any change that he might desire. I would deliver copies to the

*Father Carew was stationed subsequently at the Vatican, and all Newfoundlanders swelled with pride when, a few years ago, he was elevated to the rank of Archbishop and took up his duties on the African continent. I had the deep personal pleasure to be his host at a great state banquet that we tendered him when he first returned to St. John's with his new rank. It was a proud night for my old friend, his father, Will Carew.

heads of the other religious bodies in Newfoundland and seek their approval. I was told by Higgins afterward that the Archbishop didn't receive him, and we never did get any authoritative report of his feelings about the draft terms themselves. In any case, the importance of the divorce matter seemed to evaporate; no special term appears in our terms today, and divorce proceeds in Newfoundland much as it does in the rest of Canada. The school clause, with one or two changes, now forms part of our terms of union.

The one thing I wanted, almost above all others, was to keep sectarianism out of the forthcoming battle for votes, but my desire was almost completely frustrated by the events of the first referendum campaign. The Archbishop was implacable in his antagonism, and Roman Catholics in the archdiocese were well aware of his feelings and wishes. A small number of his priests were quite cool to his policy. Father Collins wrote to me from Fox Harbour near Placentia, enclosing a $5 bill toward our campaign fund. He told me in his letter that, though he was a Confederate himself, he had no influence whatsoever among his parishioners, who sincerely equated Confederation with Communism. Father Collins is in Heaven today—and if he isn't, then I don't want to go there myself. Monsignor Dinn of South River in Conception Bay, in the diocese of my friend (but then and for some time afterward my political opponent) Bishop O'Neill, was an outspoken supporter of mine. His answer was blunt when I asked him one day in the lobby of the Newfoundland Hotel, "Will Confederation with Canada hurt the Roman Catholic Church in Newfoundland?" "How can the Church in Newfoundland, which is about one-third of Newfoundland, be hurt by joining a country where nearly 40 per cent are Catholic?" he asked.

St. Patrick's Church in the West End of St. John's (on the original construction of which my grandfather David had worked as a carpenter) published once each quarter a small parish paper called the *Monitor*. Its circulation generally was confined to the parish of St. Patrick's, but a metamorphosis came over it just before the first referendum campaign began. It was greatly enlarged in size, published monthly, and distributed throughout the whole country. Overnight it changed from a small parish quarterly to an all-Newfoundland monthly of many more pages. It took a forthright position against Confederation. On polling day in that first referendum, to the astonishment of everybody, including Roman Catholic people themselves, the nuns and the Christian Brothers flocked to the polls to vote, undoubtedly for responsible government—although I am persuaded that more than one of them jumped the traces and voted for Confederation!

Between the two referendum campaigns, the Newfoundland Grand Lodge of the Loyal Orange Association held their annual convention, which they had been doing around the same time of the year for nearly a century. It was held at Grand Falls. I was told by friends who were there that the Orangemen, who flocked to the convention from most of the 200 Orange Lodges throughout the country, were angry with the position taken, apparently officially, by the Roman Catholic Church in the first referendum. They noted, as indeed one couldn't help doing, that every Roman Catholic electoral constituency in the diocese of Harbour Grace (Bishop O'Neill's) had voted solidly for responsible government. The more overwhelming the Roman Catholic percentage of the people in any District, the more overwhelming was the majority for responsible government. In the archdiocese itself, the only constituency with a Roman Catholic majority that failed to follow the Archbishop was Placentia West. They gave Confederation a small majority. But the Roman Catholic majority there was small, and the people of the southwest coast, regardless of religious denomination, were overwhelmingly in favour of Confederation. Bishop O'Reilly, in Western Newfoundland, didn't follow the Archbishop either. Delegations of young Roman Catholic Confederates called on him officially in Corner Brook and asked for his advice. He told them, frankly and freely, that if their conscience told them to support the Confederation, how could they do otherwise? The bishop's attitude was a great comfort to my dear friend Bill Keough.

The Orange Grand Lodge convention adopted a resolution which Grand Master Chesley Fillier circulated to all the Lodges in these terms:

> Clarke's Beach
> July 16, 1948
>
> Dear Sir and Brother,
>
> As your Grand Master I direct your earnest and loyal attention to the following important resolution adopted at the recent Session of our Provincial Grand Lodge at Grand Falls. It requires your immediate consideration:
>
> "Whereas a referendum on forms of government for Newfoundland was held on the 3rd of June, 1948;

"And Whereas the nature of the campaign waged by the Monitor, the official organ of the Roman Catholic Church, the attitude of its clergymen, the nature of the arguments used by its adherents, and above all, the records of the polls in the various settlements and districts, indicate clearly an attempt to influence the result of the said Referendum upon grounds having no relation to the merits of the various forms of government submitted to the people;

"And Whereas this, in the opinion of this Grand Lodge, constitutes an unwarranted invasion of and an effort to dominate the right of free choice of the individual elector;

"THEREFORE BE IT RESOLVED:

"That this Grand Lodge in regular session assembled condemns such efforts at sectional domination, and warns the Orangemen of Newfoundland of the danger inherent in all such attempts to influence the result, and calls upon them to use every effort to bring such attempts to naught."

I cannot too strongly impress upon each member of our Order the importance of this decision of your Grand Lodge and the necessity for his loyal cooperation.

Yours fraternally,
Chesley Fillier,
Grand Master.

I am far from wanting to attribute the blame for the sectarianism of the second referendum campaign exclusively to the Roman Catholic Church or to Archbishop Roche. The facts that I have stated are true enough; but what I have not stated is true too: that non-Roman Catholics in Newfoundland as late as that, and even later, were not all sweetly reasonable. For generations, sectarian animosities had separated the Protestant two-thirds of our people (a term loosely used to describe all who were not Roman Catholics) from the one-third and had put them at each other's throats. As the political parties sank more into intellectual bankruptcy, losing much of even the pretence at differences of genuine policy, they resorted to shameless personality differences, character assassination, and sectarian strife in election after election. Rightly or wrongly, but no doubt inevitably, the civil service had to reflect the denominational division of the population: one-third of them had to be Roman Catholics; one-third Church of England; one-third nonconformists, including Methodists (now United Churchmen), Salvation Army, Presbyterian, Pentecostal, Jews, Moravians, Christian Scientists, and even those with no professed religion. The House of Assembly itself was supposed to reflect the denominations in the same proportions. Each party would send only Church of England candidates to constituencies that were predominantly Church of England, and so with all the constituencies. The Cabinet was the same. It, too, was supposed to be made up of one-third representation. It was not a law but a powerful convention. There were Protestant candidates who would go about campaigning with cries of "Popery", sneers against "The Papists", "The Romans", or "The Romish Church", and remarks sometimes more vicious. There were Roman Catholic candidates who would, at a public meeting, hold out an orange in one hand and a set of prayer beads in the other and demand, "Which are you going to choose?"

Everything was operated along sectarian lines. The schools, without exception, were denominational: Roman Catholic, Church of England, United Church, Salvation Army, Pentecostal. All athletic activities and organized spectator sports were denominational. There were Roman Catholic fraternal and religious societies, and similar bodies for the others. Companies often employed, almost exclusively, men and women of the same religious denomination as the owners, with little more than token employment given to people of other faiths. The early settlers in Newfoundland had flocked to bays, and coves in those bays, where they would find people of their own religion. White Bay originally was very largely Roman Catholic; Notre Dame Bay was overwhelmingly Church of England and then Methodist; Trinity Bay initially was mostly Church of England. St. Mary's and Placentia bays were overwhelmingly Roman Catholic. Whole settlements would be composed exclusively of people of the one denomination. You could travel the full length of the Shore, St. John's to St. Shotts, and scarcely ever meet a non-Roman Catholic after you passed Petty Harbour. Along the long southwest coast, after you passed Fortune Bay (which did have a small minority of Roman Catholics), the population was all but completely Church of England. All people were conscious of their denomination, and they watched each other's activities narrowly. The civil service was watched keenly, and the railway. Every few years, the Government would compile a private census of the civil service, showing how many persons of each denomination were employed, with what status, and at what salary; and the whole thing would be reduced to percentages, with comparative tables showing the number and percentage of jobs for each denomination, and the total amount of money drawn in the aggregate by each denomination, with percentages. I have in my collection several of these reports compiled in the 1920s. The sectarian spirit saturated all society in Newfoundland.

After about 1900, but particularly after 1908, Roman Catholics in Newfoundland were overwhelmingly Tories or Conservatives, regardless of the changes in name that that party adopted from time to time. The Protestants, almost as overwhelmingly, were Liberals. This was the exact opposite of the situation that had prevailed for the first three-quarters of the century, up to 1900. The Protestant Tory Party led by Sir Robert Thorburn in the General Election of 1885 had brazenly raised the cry, "No truck or trade with Roman Catholics!" And to emphasize their meaning, they didn't put a candidate in even one constituency having a Roman Catholic majority. The Roman Catholic Liberal Party put a candidate in every constituency. The Protestant Tories elected their man in every Protestant constituency, and the Roman Catholic Liberal Party elected their man in every Roman Catholic constituency—they couldn't help doing so, for their men were elected by acclamation. And so the House of Assembly was to meet with two-thirds of the Members, Protestant and Tory, occupying the seats on the Government side, and the one-third Roman Catholic Liberals sitting across from them in opposition. Not a Roman Catholic was in the Cabinet. It was possibly the inevitably climacteric conclusion of decades of savage sectarianism in Newfoundland, but it was also a savagely dangerous moment in Newfoundland history. Roman Catholic Bishop Power called on Prime Minister Thorburn and suggested that the ugly situation be remedied by Thorburn's admitting one or two Members of the Roman Catholic Opposition into the Cabinet. This was done. It is remarkable that a decade and a half later, generally speaking, the Liberal Party had become the party of the Protestants and the Tories had become the party of the Roman Catholics, with a few exceptions on both sides.

In the General Election of 1919, the Protestant Liberal Party under Richard Squires did almost exactly the same thing that the Protestant Tory Party had done in 1885, except that in 1919 the Liberals contested all the seats. They managed to elect only two of their candidates in Roman Catholic seats—Harry J. Brownrigg as the running mate of Squires himself in St. John's West, and James R. Macdonnel in St. George's. Before the House opened, Macdonnel left the Liberal Party and joined the Tories. The House opened with one Roman Catholic sitting on the Government side of the House, and with the Opposition having only one Protestant in their ranks. I myself, sixty-two years later, was the first Liberal after Sir Robert Bond to win a majority of the Roman Catholic seats in Newfoundland—in my second-last election, I won nine of the thirteen seats that had Roman Catholic majorities.

I think that I have said enough here to show that there was truly a long, unhappy history of religious sectarianism in Newfoundland politics, and to explain my own strong desire to keep sectarianism out of the fight for Confederation. It explains, too, the unhappy circumstance that sectarianism did break out in the fight for Confederation. It would probably be quite unjust to put all the blame on one side. Only one who was ignorant of our political history would attempt to do so.*

That second referendum was a gruelling, grinding, savage battle, but it ended gloriously: Confederation, 78,323 (52.34 per cent); responsible government, 71,334 (47.66 per cent). The angels in heaven must have been on our side; for now that we know what Confederation has meant to our people, the thought is not to be borne that Confederation would lose. Defeat for our cause would have been a fatal blow to Newfoundland. Fatal.

I cannot find the words to convey my happiness over our glorious victory. From that December day in 1945 in Montreal to July 22, 1948, for thirty-two months, I had worked day and night to achieve this result. I had known the insuperable obstacles, but I had not accepted them as insuperable.

My friends in Conception Bay hastily organized a celebration of the victory. From the whole area between George's Town and Victoria, cars streamed to the grassy sandbank at the side of the highway, between Bay Roberts and Spaniard's Bay. After my speech and the cheering and excitement, I wanted to get back to St. John's. A few of my friends, with what I thought then and now know was altogether

*Sectarian considerations were not absent from mainland Canadian politics. In Halifax, it was long the unwritten rule that a Roman Catholic Mayor was to be followed by a Protestant. Two MP's were elected by the Halifax constituency—one was always Protestant; the other, Roman Catholic. Other examples were seen in many parts of Canada.

unwarranted anxiety for my safety, arranged to have my car preceded by three or four other cars and followed by as many, full of men armed with stout sticks; for we were to pass through Anti-Confederate territory in the District of Harbour Main. That part of our country had voted quite overwhelmingly against Confederation. Although there was there an old tradition of rambunctious political campaigns, better people never lived, and we passed through the "enemy" territory placidly, in a degree of safety that made the clubs look ridiculous. After a while, the mobile bodyguard turned back rather sheepishly to where it had come from.

The feeling among the Anti-Confederates in St. John's was ugly, and there I really did think that I might be in some physical danger. I got a room in the Newfoundland Hotel and holed up there for the first night, not going back to my home on Kenmont Road until late the following day.

Peter Cashin and his friends decided to hold a great open-air demonstration in Bannerman Park, beside the Colonial Building, to denounce any move to make Newfoundland a province of Canada. No doubt they felt that even at this late date, they might be able to frustrate the Confederates, for Prime Minister Mackenzie King had not yet commented on the outcome of the referendum. The Chief of Police, Llewellyn Strange, managed somehow to dissuade Cashin and his friends from going ahead with their big outdoor demonstration, and perhaps it was a lucky thing that he did; for once you had thousands of outraged Anti-Confederates gathered in Bannerman Park, with the fiery oratory of Peter Cashin to stir them more, who is to say that some, perhaps a large proportion, of the crowd would not have decided to extend their activities throughout the city?

Ottawa was the scene of the next act. A new delegation, this time representing, not the National Convention, which had been dissolved, but rather the Commission of Government, had to be appointed to go to Ottawa to sign the terms of union, after arranging a few desirable changes.

Sir Albert J. Walsh, the Commission of Government's Deputy Chairman, was appointed chairman of the new delegation. He had been a Member of the House of Assembly and Speaker of the House. Walsh had entered the Squires Cabinet but had been defeated in the rout of the Liberal Party in 1932. He had, in quick succession, become a Chief Magistrate, Labour Relations Officer, Member of the Commission of Government in charge of Home Affairs and Education, and then, as Commissioner for Justice and Attorney General, Deputy Chairman of the Commission. He was one of the most surefooted men that I have ever known, and he commanded respect from all who knew him. He was a perfectly magnificent chairman of that second Ottawa delegation. He was deeply respected in Ottawa, particularly by Mr. St. Laurent, as Bradley had been by Mr. King. Bradley was the second member of the new delegation, and the others were Gordon Winter, Philip Gruchy, Ches Crosbie, John McEvoy, and myself. The Canadian delegates were the Rt. Hon. Louis St. Laurent, the Rt. Hon. C. D. Howe, the Hon. Douglas C. Abbott, the Hon. Brooke Claxton, the Hon. James J. McCann, and the Hon. Lester B. Pearson. Bradley and I were the only two who had been members of the earlier Newfoundland delegation. We arrived in Ottawa on October 6, 1948.

It seems to me, even now, incomprehensible that it should have been so, but the fact is that we spent another three months in Ottawa. It was not until December 11 that the terms were finally signed. Frank O'Leary had suggested publicly that the people should accept Confederation, but Cashin had addressed a large meeting in the Star Hall denouncing Confederation. Two days after we arrived in Ottawa, the Responsible Government League held a big rally in the CLB Armoury to put the finishing touches on a petition to the House of Commons in London. The meeting adopted a resolution denying the right of our delegation to commit Newfoundland to Confederation without the holding of a plebiscite. Further to bedevil the picture, Premier Maurice Duplessis of Quebec expressed publicly his belief that the Quebec Government could sue for adjustment of the boundary separating Quebec and Newfoundland. Duplessis announced, too, that he was opposed to Newfoundland's entry into the Confederation.

On November 12, the Responsible Government League's representatives left for London to present the League's petition to the House of Commons. Included were Major F. W. Marshall, Major Peter Cashin, John Higgins, K. C.; and, as though that were not enough, six men who had been Members of the last Legislature before the coming of the Commission of Government issued their writs in the Supreme Court on November 13, claiming that all the procedures of the National Convention and the national referendum were unconstitutional and should be expunged. In short, Confederation should be cancelled! The signing objectors were the Hon. John Currie, the Hon. Frank McNamara, and the Hon. John V. O'Dea, who had been appointive Members of the Upper House; and W. C. Winsor, Harold Mitchell, and Magistrate W. J. Browne,* who had been Members of the elective House of Assembly.

Subsequent events can be chronicled briefly.

November 23: Sir A. P. Herbert presented the Responsible Government League petition to the House of Commons in London, and the League delegates addressed a private all-party meeting in a room in the Parliament Building.

November 26: An all-party motion presented to the House of Commons called for the introduction of a new Bill to replace the Newfoundland Act 1933 (the British Act that set up the Commission of Government system in the first place) and for the restoration of responsible government.

November 30: The League delegates conferred with the Rt. Hon. Philip Noel-Baker, the Secretary of State for Commonwealth Relations.

December 6: The writ issued by the six former Members of the old Legislature was heard by Mr. Justice Dunfield.

December 9: The League delegates arrived back in St. John's, and Mr. Crosbie announced that he would not be signing the terms of union because of his view that the financial provisions were inadequate.

December 10: The League delegates held a public meeting in the CLB Armoury to report on their visit to London, and a resolution was adopted protesting what they called the methods being used to "push" Newfoundland into Confederation and calling on the Governor to stop the signing of the terms at Ottawa. A big parade marched to Government House at eleven o'clock that night, and a delegation presented the resolution to the Government.

December 11: After three months of discussions, the final meeting was held between the Canadian and Newfoundland delegations, and the terms were signed at noon in the Senate Chamber. On the same day, the Governor rejected the demand of the League presented to him the night before.

December 13: Mr. Justice Dunfield threw out the writs of the six former Members of the Legislature.

*He resigned from the magistracy in 1949 and was elected to the House of Commons from St. John's West.

December 14: Albert Walsh, Bradley, and I flew back to St. John's.

December 16: The Responsible Government League sent a letter of reply to the Governor's rejection.

January 1 (1949): The Responsible Government League appealed again for the restoration of an elected House of Assembly.

January 14: The six former members of the old Legislature appealed the judgement of Mr. Justice Dunfield.

January 15: Sir A. P. Herbert circulated a draft of his "Newfoundland Liberation Bill".

January 27: The Speech from the Throne at the opening of the Canadian Parliament announced that provision would be made by legislation for Newfoundland's entry into the Confederation. The Responsible Government League sent a protest to Mr. George Drew, Leader of the Opposition.

January 28: Sir A. P. Herbert's draft bill lost in the draw for a hearing. On the same day, I arrived in Montreal on my way back to Ottawa to hear the Commons debate on the Newfoundland Bill.

February 7: Prime Minister St. Laurent introduced the Bill providing for Newfoundland's entry into the Confederation. I remember that Peter Cashin, too, sat in the gallery and listened to the debate. As the debate proceeded, I sent several notes down to Mr. St. Laurent with information that enabled him to answer some points raised by Mr. Drew.

February 8: The Supreme Court granted leave to the six former Members of the old Legislature to appeal to the Judicial Committee of the Privy Council in London against the judgement of the local Court.

February 9: Ches Crosbie presented his minority report to the Governor.

February 11: The Bill providing for Newfoundland's entry into the Confederation was given final reading in the House of Commons.

February 14: George Drew, Leader of the Opposition, moved an amendment to the Government's motion that an address be sent to the King praying His Majesty to cause the British Parliament to pass the necessary Imperial Legislation providing for Newfoundland's entry into Confederation. Mr. Drew's amendment called for consultation with the nine provinces before Newfoundland should be admitted.

February 15: By a vote of 192 to 12, the House of Commons defeated Mr. Drew's amendment.

February 16: The Newfoundland Bill was passed by the House of Commons 140 to 74. The Progressive Conservative Party and the CCF voted against the Bill.

February 18: Royal assent was given by the Governor General to the Newfoundland Bill.

February 21: The Commission of Government, acting as the Legislature, approved the terms of union.

February 22: The British House of Commons gave first reading to the terms of union.

February 23: Sir A. P. Herbert and thirteen other Members urged the British House of Commons to defer consideration of the terms of union pending the appeal to the Privy Council.

March 2: Sir A. P. Herbert's amendment was rejected by the British Commons by a vote of 217 to 15.

March 9: The British House of Commons gave third reading to the Confederation Bill, without division.

March 12: Lord Semphill announced that he would move for rejection of the Newfoundland Bill when it came before the House of Lords.

March 15: The House of Lords gave second reading to the Newfoundland Bill, and Lord Semphill withdrew his motion.

March 23: The House of Lords gave third reading to the Newfoundland Bill, without amendment.

March 28: The Responsible Government League sent a message to the Speaker of the House of Commons of Canada declaring that they reserved the right at any future time to take such steps as might be required to secede from Canada and to restore Newfoundland's lost sovereignty.

March 31: Just before the stroke of midnight, Newfoundland became a province of Canada.

Why not on April 1? This was the date selected, but I raised strong oral objection at the final joint meeting of the Canadian-Newfoundland delegations. The financial year of Canada, and of all nine Canadian provinces, and of Newfoundland, began and still begins on April 1. Why not, then, have Confederation begin on the first day of the financial year? Because, said I, I didn't want to spend the rest of my life listening to taunts that Confederation had come on All Fools' Day. The Canadians fell in line, and so we became a province a few seconds before the coming of All Fools' Day.

I was bitterly disappointed by Ches Crosbie's refusal to sign the terms. I argued with him that the terms could not properly cover all eventualities, and I was able to quote for him Sir Wilfrid Laurier's dictum, "There is no finality to the Terms of Confederation." I told him that the terms of admission of Nova Scotia, New Brunswick, Prince Edward Island, and the Prairie Provinces, had been amended again and again, always upward for the provinces. The same would happen to our terms. But it was useless; he just wouldn't listen. He packed his bag and went back to St. John's a day or two before the remaining six of us signed the terms. This ceremony moved me deeply. The Canadians sat at one side of the long table in the centre of the Senate Chamber, and we Newfoundlanders at the other. Mr. St. Laurent spoke graciously; and our chairman, Sir Albert Walsh, as always, said just the right words. We took turns going to the head of the table and signing the terms with individual gold-mounted pens which we were asked to keep. (I keep mine proudly locked up.) Then the Canadian band, stationed in the adjoining lobby of the Chamber, played "O Canada", and we stood to attention. I was racked with emotion and couldn't hold my head up for fear my wet eyes would be noticed.

I was clear in my mind on the question of what would be the proper constitutional procedure to transform Newfoundland into a province of Canada. The Newfoundland people themselves had pronounced in favour of Confederation, in a special referendum, and this mandate was far more unmistakable and unavoidable than would have been the victory in a General Election, even of a party whose main proclaimed policy had been Confederation. Constitutionally, therefore, Newfoundland should become a province as quickly as practically possible, by the shortest route; and there should be a complete ending of our status as a colony or dominion. Before the day appointed for the entry of Newfoundland into the Canadian federation arrived, the Governor of Newfoundland, who represented and was answerable to the United Kingdom that had appointed him, and who was Chairman of the Commission of Government, would have to go. The very first step would be the appointment, by the Government of Canada, of a Lieutenant-Governor (a title that I have always disliked, on the ground that he is lieutenant to nobody), and his first duty would be to call on someone to form a Cabinet. As soon as possible, the Prime Minister of Canada would invite a Newfoundlander to become a Member of his Cabinet.

All of this would be preceded by the signing of the terms by Canada and Newfoundland; enactment of the proper legislation and prayer of petition by the Canadian Parliament; enactment of the proper legislation by the Parliament of Newfoundland, which, constitutionally, was the Commission of Government; and, finally, enactment of the proper legislation by the United Kingdom Parliament.

I discussed these points with Mr. Pickersgill and one or two others from time to time. I heard that Mr. St. Laurent had other ideas; that he was thinking along the line of letting the British-appointed Governor of Newfoundland remain in office until he had called for the holding of a General Election and a majority party had been elected, so that he could call upon its leader to form a Cabinet. But that procedure would mean having Britain, through her Governor, virtually ruling a Canadian province, and this I just couldn't see.

I argued the point strongly at a meeting in Brooke Claxton's house one night in a company made up of Claxton, Mr. St. Laurent, John Pickersgill (I think), and Bradley and myself. Claxton supported my view, and at length Mr. St. Laurent, with what I fancied was a trace of reluctance, accepted the view that I had propounded. Or was he just being devil's advocate for the occasion?

I had done some hard thinking about the place of my friend Gordon Bradley in the new system. Certainly, he had to be Newfoundland's Minister in the Canadian Government – we had shaken hands on that in his home at Bonavista. He himself, however, had had second thoughts about that whole matter afterward, in St. John's, and this became the cause of the only personal quarrel we ever had. We were out for a long walk in the northern suburbs of St. John's, and as we came down Robinson's Hill and approached the Feildian athletic field, we turned in and sat in the empty bleachers to continue our discussion. It happened to be one of the few times when, briefly, Bradley was not completely pessimistic about the prospects of success for the Confederation cause. Suddenly, as we sat there, he sprang his surprise. I couldn't become the first Premier of the new province. I wouldn't be acceptable to the people. I didn't have the standing. I was, so I inferred him to be thinking, a nobody. Indeed, I was a nobody; but in spite of that, I had an altogether different opinion from him of my standing with the people. Gordon's plan was this: 1) he should get a knighthood and an Imperial privy councillorship; 2) he should become the first Premier of the province, but he would take me into his Cabinet; and 3) he would, some months later, enter the Canadian Cabinet, and his last act as Premier of Newfoundland would be to recommend me to the Lieutenant-Governor for the premiership.

I could scarcely believe my ears, and my response was prompt and categorical. "Count me out, Gordon. I withdraw. You take it—you carry on the fight for Confederation. You get Confederation, and then you'll deserve your knighthood and Imperial councillorship. You'll have earned the right to be called the Rt. Hon. Sir Gordon Bradley, Prime Minister of Newfoundland, Newfoundland's Minister in the Canadian Government. I'm through."

He was alarmed, and back-tracked quickly, and that was the last I ever heard of those particular ideas.

Now, in Ottawa, I was trying to think of the best place for him. My problem was that Gordon would hate living in Ottawa in any position. He had never had any experience in public administration, nor any ambition to acquire it; he really wasn't interested in the complicated system of Canadian Federal Government, and he had no intention of becoming interested. Yet Newfoundlanders would be watching to see what he got, and they would be mortally offended if he didn't get a good appointment.

It was at lunch at the University Club one day with Jack Pickersgill and Dr. R. A. MacKay that I brought forward my idea. Pickersgill looked somewhat apprehensive as I outlined the problem: that Newfoundlanders would make quick judgement of where they stood in Canadian eyes the moment they saw what office Bradley received. What was coming? Pickersgill must have been wondering: Minister of Justice? Minister of Fisheries?

"Newfoundlanders are more familiar with the titles in the American Government," I remarked. "The two most familiar titles are President and Secretary of State. Cordell Hull, Secretary of State—most people are familiar with that name and title. So I suggest that Secretary of State of Canada would sound dignified and important." Pickersgill, leaning forward, slapped me on the knee and exclaimed, "It's perfect!" And, of course, that is what Bradley became. He wouldn't have been happy in any office in Ottawa, but he was less unhappy there than he would have been anywhere else.

But there was still the problem of getting Prime Minister St. Laurent to see it my way, and I was happy, three nights before we signed the terms on December 11, when, as our conference of that day was ending and we stood about the floor, St. Laurent called Bradley and me to his side. "I think," he said, smiling, "we may assume now at last that the business and constitutional side of our meetings has been completed. Now, perhaps, we may turn to some less ponderous matters. Could you, Gordon, come over to my apartment this evening for a chat?" Bradley assented at once, and the Prime Minister turned to me and said, "Perhaps, Joe, you would come over tomorrow night?" It was the only time I remember his calling me by my first name.

All of Bradley's irrepressible pessimism flooded over him that evening as he prepared for the interview with the Prime Minister. I walked with him from the Château Laurier to St. Laurent's apartment building a few blocks away and left him as he took the elevator up. I had already sold him on the office of Secretary of State and had urged him to name that portfolio in case Mr. St. Laurent should wonder aloud what portfolio might be best for him. I waited back at the hotel for his return, and as he came into my room, I greeted him, "Come in, Secretary of State!" "Secretary of State be damned," he growled, and I saw from his face that I had another problem. "How did you get on?" I asked. "I didn't." "How do you mean?" "The matter just wasn't mentioned," Bradley said in disgust. "St. Laurent didn't mention it?" "Not a word." "And didn't you mention it?" "No, it wasn't my place to mention it"—which, of course, was strictly correct.

"Never mind, Gordon," I tried to reassure him. "I'm going there tomorrow night, and I'll raise it then."

Bradley was silent and moody for a while; and then his voice boomed out, "What did I tell you? Didn't I tell you that we'd be dumped if this thing ever did succeed?" Indeed, he had, many times. I never knew a man in whom there was such contrast of great potential and utter lack of faith in his own destiny.

It was a different story the following evening, the night before we signed the terms. Mr. St. Laurent was gracious—he wasn't capable of being anything else. We talked generalities for a while, and then I tried to pin it down.

"Of course, sir, you'll be taking Gordon Bradley into your Cabinet?" The Prime Minister replied, "But I have no vacancy in my Cabinet." "Yes, I know, sir, but I'm talking of April 1 next year. Surely some Member of your Cabinet is going to die before that—or be appointed to the Senate, or something!" He smiled, appeared to consider for a moment, and then said, "Have you any thoughts as to what portfolio Gordon might fill?" "Yes. Secretary of State." "You think this would please Newfoundland?" (Pickersgill must have talked to him!) "Yes, very much so." There was a short silence, and then I persisted, "May I assume then, sir, that Bradley goes in on Confederation Day?" St. Laurent replied cautiously, "I will endeavour to find a place for Gordon." That was enough for me.

Then he spoke of the Government of the new province-to-be, and I was, to say the least, pleased to notice that he seemed to be taking it for granted that I would be the Premier. He asked me the names of the people that I would propose for my Cabinet, and as I named them, he jotted down their names and asked me to tell him a bit about each one. I named some fine men, and he appeared to be satisfied with my assurance that my fondest hope was that I would be able to get a "Cabal of all the Talents"; that I would work strenuously for a policy of reconciliation; and that above all, I would reject anything resembling a carpetbagger approach to government. It was a very pleasant evening, and I was more impressed than ever by the astute mind and gracious manner of Canada's great leader— "Canada's Sir Robert Bond", as I often called him.

Back at the hotel, Bradley, who had an exaggerated concept of my skill, was waiting with something of my impatience of the night before. I breezed into his room and greeted him with hand outstretched. "The Premier of Newfoundland greets Canada's Secretary of State!" A full account of my meeting with the Prime Minister followed, and Bradley was more cheerful than I had seen him for a long time. The truth of the matter is that he was altogether too conscious in his meeting with Mr. St. Laurent of the greatness of the constitutional and historic position of the prime minister, and too shy in any case to raise a plea for his own advancement. I expect that he needed someone like me to plead his cause.

15

Graduation – The Premiership, That Is

There is no security on this earth; there is only opportunity.
General Douglas MacArthur

A wise man will make more opportunities than he finds.
Francis Bacon

The Prime Minister is the source and arbiter of public policy.
Winston S. Churchill

Blessed is he who has found his work; let him ask no other blessedness.
Thomas Carlyle

Try first thyself, and after call in God;
For to the worker God himself lends aid.
Euripides

Ah, Love! could and I with Fate conspire
To grasp this sorry Scheme of Things entire,
Would not we shatter it to bits—and then
Remould it nearer to the Heart's Desire!
Omar Khayyam

At about eleven o'clock on the morning of April 1, 1949, I took the oath as the Province of Newfoundland's first Premier. (The title for nearly half a century in Newfoundland had been Prime Minister, and it took people quite a while to get used to the word *Premier*.) The ceremony took place at Government House, and the oath was administered to me by the new Lieutenant-Governor, Sir Albert Walsh, whose own oath had been administered to him only minutes before by Colin Gibson, Canada's Secretary of State up to that moment. Gibson then telegraphed his resignation to the Prime Minister in Ottawa, so that Mr. St. Laurent could invite Bradley into his Cabinet to fill that portfolio. Gibson became Minister of Mines and Resources and later was appointed to the bench in Ontario.

I was Newfoundland's first Premier for fifteen years, and when I resigned in 1972, I was the only Premier that Newfoundland had known for thirty-eight years.

It was a bit of a misunderstanding that put Sir Albert Walsh in as our first Lieutenant-Governor and deprived Sir Leonard Outerbridge of the honour. I had been asked to recommend someone for Lieutenant-Governor, and I was ready at once to recommend Sir Leonard. But first I had to know whether he'd accept the office. I called on him at his home, and he agreed readily enough. I was chagrined when I got back to my flat to discover that I had gone tieless to see him. I was wearing clip-on bowties then and had forgotten to put one on. I recommended Sir Leonard to Mr. St. Laurent; but what I didn't know was that, just before the coming of Confederation, Walter Harris, the Prime Minister's parliamentary assistant, had arrived in St. John's and had a conversation with Sir Leonard about the premiership. I was not in the city at the time. Harris got the impression that Sir Leonard, if he became Lieutenant-Governor, would be hesitant as to whom he should send for to become Premier. Sir Leonard called on me at the Colonial Building the day after I was sworn in and told me that this was pure misunderstanding on Walter Harris's part—that he, Outerbridge, had never the slightest doubt that in all constitutional as well as practical propriety, he really had no choice but to send for me. I have never doubted Sir Leonard's word on this or any other matter.

Sir Edward Emerson, the Chief Justice, died a few months after Confederation, and Sir Albert Walsh was promptly appointed in his place on the recommendation of Mr. St. Laurent, who had great respect for him. My recommendation of Sir Leonard Outerbridge as Lieutenant-Governor was now accepted without hesitation. Sir Albert was one of the most exemplary public men that Newfoundland has produced; he was in turn Speaker of the House of Assembly, a Cabinet Minister, a Chief Magistrate, a Commissioner, Lieutenant-Governor, and Chief Justice—a career quite unparallelled in our Newfoundland history.

Only my old friend William J. Carew was present in the room as Sir Albert administered the oath to me. Once I had signed the oath, I informed Walsh that I was ready to present my Cabinet to him to be sworn in. I had previously discussed the names with him, and he had rather demurred over what he thought was the large number of Ministers that I proposed. I insisted, and at length he agreed.

Moments later, Carew ushered my colleagues-to-be into the room. They stood in a semi-circle, and Sir Albert administered the oath to them individually. They kissed the New Testament and then sat one by one at the table and signed their double oath. Sir Albert shook hands all around and withdrew. A photographer was brought in and took a picture of us: the Hon. Leslie R. Curtis, Minister of Justice and Attorney General; the Hon. Herman W. Quinton, Minister of Public Health; the Hon. Dr. Herbert L. Pottle, Minister of Welfare; the Hon. Gordon A. Winter, Minister of Finance; the Hon. William J. Keough, Minister of Natural Resources; the Hon. Michael J. Sinnott, Minister of Public Works; the Hon. Charles H. Ballam, Minister of Labour; the Hon. Samuel J. Hefferton, Minister of Education; the Hon. Philip F. Forsey, Minister of Home Affairs; and the Hon. Joseph R. Smallwood, Premier.

In front of the Parliament Buildings in Ottawa, St. Laurent had organized a fine public welcome for Newfoundland. The Armed Forces paraded, a large number of people gathered, and St. Laurent and his Cabinet colleagues assembled on a specially built platform. St. Laurent and Bradley, who had just been sworn in as Secretary of State, made symbolic incisions with mallet and chisel into the blank shield that had been left under the portico to the handsome centre block of the three buildings. The shields of the other nine provinces, of the Territories, and of Canada itself had all long before been chiselled. Some genius had left a blank shield, and never once during our two three-month visits to Ottawa, and that earlier private one of my own, had I gone through that doorway without looking thoughtfully—and hopefully—at that blank shield. Then St. Laurent spoke, and his words were carried by radio throughout the nation, from St. John's to Victoria.

Telegrams showered in upon me from all across the continent, and every newspaper in Canada published warm words of welcome to us. This, after all, was the first occasion in a long, long time—the only time, I imagine, in this century—that one country had decided, by secret ballot, to abandon its ancient isolation and had deliberately chosen to become part of another country.

I held my first press conference in an adjoining room of Government House, the first of uncounted hundreds there were to be in the next twenty-three years.

Now, indeed, we were a province of Canada. For a dozen years and more to come, our people would still speak of "going to Canada", "coming from Canada", "Canada and Newfoundland" or "Newfoundland and Canada", and "Canadians and Newfoundlanders". These and a dozen other expressions would fall thoughtlessly, but for the most part without malice, from the lips of people whose ancestors had for nearly five centuries belonged to a proud, if poor, independent British colony to whom "those Canadians" or "those Americans" were little more, for all their riches, than johnny-come-latelies.

There were, of course, a few exceptions to the general satisfaction. A few wept. Some flew improvised black flags at half-mast, or draped their front doors and gates with black crepe. Some wore bands of black crepe on their sleeves. There were at least some thousands, on Confederation Day, who felt that Newfoundland had been betrayed, sold out to Canada, and by treacherous Newfoundlanders at that. Newfoundland was "gone", finished. For more than two years they had been educated by insistent propaganda to think thus; and Confederation Day was too early for many of them to concede that the propaganda was false. I had been hated as the arch-fiend in this whole diabolical business, and for years I continued to be that in the eyes of a large, though shrinking, number. The interesting thing is that as people came gradually to accept and even to approve Confederation and its blessings, they seemed, many of them, to forget why they had hated me. They were at last approving Confederation, but they continued to despise the man who had advocated the very thing that they now accepted. It took nearly a quarter of a century from Confederation Day for that feeling to meet its lingering death.

There were Newfoundlanders whose intense Newfoundland nationalism wouldn't allow them to call themselves Canadians. My old friend Bob Furlong, who was a notable collector of Newfoundlandia, as his famous father Martin W. Furlong had been before him, repudiated the title *Canadian* and was never backward in proclaiming himself an unhyphenated Newfoundlander. When Mr. Diefenbaker years later appointed him as Chief Justice of our Supreme Court, he changed not at all in that respect; so I had great fun for myself one year, when the House of Assembly was about to open in the absence of the Lieutenant-Governor, in putting the proper words into the mouth of Chief Justice Furlong, who, as Administrator, was required to read the Speech from the Throne opening the session. I piled it on: "we Canadians", "we Newfoundlanders who are so proud to call ourselves Canadians", "this proud Canada of which Newfoundland now forms a part", and so on and so forth. Bob knew what I was up to, but there was simply nothing that he could do about it. "You devil, you," he said to me afterward, smiling; and I replied innocently, "It was a fine speech, didn't you think, Bob?"

I was forty-eight on Christmas Eve 1948, three months before I was sworn in. I was not a lawyer, or an administrator, or even a businessman. I had never been a Member of a Cabinet or of a legislative body. The only assets I had for the job were 1) prodigious good health, for I have never had a headache or a pain in the stomach or a touch of indigestion in my life to the moment of this writing—indeed, except for the measles and scarlet fever when I was a boy at Bishop Feild College, and an operation for a detached retina in my right eye three or four years ago, I have been offensively healthy from birth to now; 2) equally prodigious physical and mental energy, which someone once called animal strength; 3) a personal knowledge of Newfoundland's geography and history, particularly in the outports, and of Newfoundland and Newfoundlanders, past and present, that was all but unique; 4) the intimate knowledge of governmental and departmental affairs that any smart, interested newspaperman can acquire; and 5) a vaulting ambition for Newfoundland, and a probably inordinate and unreasonable faith in its possibilities.

As I jog my memory hopefully for some other qualifications to be my province's Premier, I brighten at the recollection:

1. I had organized one cooperative society of cod-fishermen and one or two other cooperatives.

2. I had organized half a dozen unions and led one successful strike of seal-hunters.

3. I had originated and conducted one of the most popular of all radio programs.

4. I had written half a dozen books, several of which were published.

5. I had been organizer and editor of the biggest literary enterprise in Newfoundland's history.

6. I had done some farming on Kenmont Road.

7. I had run one of the largest hog-raising establishments in Canada.

On receiving an honorary degree at Waterloo Lutheran University in Ontario, I remarked that it was my presence in Gander, as boss of the piggery, that had started the ball rolling for Confederation. I went on to lay down two indispensable qualifications for premiers of Newfoundland: that they should have served an apprenticeship at cleaning out after pigs—for a knowledge of pigs, two-legged as well as four, was very valuable; and that they should have spent many hours out on our Newfoundland barrens and marshes, picking berries. Frankly, I said, I couldn't see how a man could be fit for the office without those qualifications.

These were qualities to make a good propagandist, but were they the qualities to make a good leader? Who shall say? In the country of the blind, the one-eyed man is king, so they say; and although there were men in my Cabinet then, and ever afterward, who were superior to me in many ways, never was there one more capable or desirous of expending himself with hard work and long hours. As Premier in working fifteen hours a day, seven days a week, I was only following my normal routine, but it sounded fantastic and even outrageous to many people, including some of my colleagues. I went to work at 8:30 each morning and stayed at it until one o'clock in the afternoon. Half an hour did me for lunch, and I worked until six in the evening. Then I went home, undressed, and went to bed and slept for precisely an hour. After a light dinner, I was back in my office by 7:30, and I kept working until one or two o'clock the following morning. I followed that regimen for the first fifteen years of my premiership. Then I relaxed, and after that I rarely worked more than twelve hours on each of the seven days. People marvelled at my capacity for work, but they needn't have. It was as normal for me as the seven-hour day, five-day week is for many people. You inherit longevity, or you don't. I inherited health, strength, and energy, from both sides of my family; so they are no credit to me.

Before forming my first Cabinet at all, I grappled with a problem that I was convinced had dire possibilities. This was the problem of religious sectarianism. Sectarian passions had been aroused, and more than one of my Protestant friends urged me, in effect, to take a course that could only have the effect of keeping them aroused. They said, "You have the Protestants at your back; now keep the Romans in their place!"

I was not without fierce pride in the effort I had made to bring Confederation about, and not without lively appreciation of the fact that my name was bound to go down in Newfoundland's history, perhaps even Canada's. I hadn't started the sectarian propaganda, but I would assuredly run the danger of being blamed for it if I followed the advice that some friends were offering me now. As I said to several of my friends, "A footnote in Canadian history will mention me. It will say, 'Bitter sectarian animosity raged throughout the referendum campaigns, and Smallwood, when he became Premier, allowed these animosities to continue'; or it will say, 'but Smallwood exerted all possible skill to dampen the fires and reconcile the Newfoundland people.' I would rather have the second of these two."

And so, as I had told St. Laurent I would do, I endeavoured to put together a Cabinet that would be representative of the broad denominational divisions of our people. In short, I tried to get strong Roman Catholic representation in my Cabinet. I called first on Bob Furlong, who was then the solicitor to the Roman Catholic Episcopal Corporation, and asked him to join my Cabinet. I told him very frankly that I was trying to build a representative Cabinet, and that I was anxious to help heal the wounds of the referendum. He declined my invitation. I invited Professor Allan Fraser, who was on the staff of Memorial University College, and I could see that he was eager to accept. He asked me to give him a day or two to give me his answer, and when it came, it was no. I asked my old friend and former employer Frank O'Leary to join my Cabinet, and he was most friendly. He had been leader of the Responsible Government League, but when the battle was over, he had called on the Newfoundland people to accept Confederation. He, too, wanted a day or two before giving me his answer. His answer was no. I saw my old friend Leo Murphy, who had once sat in the House of Assembly as a Liberal Member, and he also appeared to be willing to join me. He wanted a day or two to consider the matter, and his answer was no. The day or two wanted by most of them was, I was quite certain, to enable them to consult the Archbishop, and I was sure that the refusals reflected the feeling of His Grace. My first Cabinet thus had but one Roman Catholic in it, my dear friend Bill Keough. If he consulted anyone, it would have been Bishop O'Reilly, whose advice, if he gave it, would have been that Bill should accept.

I talked things over with the Deputy Minister of Education, Dr. G. Alain Frecker.* I got encouragement and advice from Fred Scott, and both men were so civilized and decent that my resolution was strengthened. I stuck stubbornly to my policy of bridging the gulf, as I used to call it, and by sheer goodwill I helped to break down the wall of enmity that had been raised. I felt that one of the most useful means I furnished for the ending, or at any rate the virtual ending, of denominational animosity in politics was to introduce other great issues about which men could quarrel and on which they could have strongly opposed views. I am prouder of nothing more in my career as Premier than I am of my success in this direction.

The general public knew little if anything of these issues at the time. They were fascinated by the in-coming blessings of Confederation, and I personally went from strength to strength as most people gave me all too much credit for these benefits. I had little time to do any philosophizing or reminiscing, but I did wish that some of the giants of other days could be around to see what was happening to their beloved Newfoundland: the Rt. Hon. Sir William Whiteway, the Rt. Hon. Sir Robert Bond, the Rt. Hon. Sir Edward Morris, the Rt. Hon. Sir Richard Squires, Sir Alfred Morine, Sir William Coaker, Archbishop Howley, Sir Wilfred Grenfell—Confederates all.

At the outset of my premiership, I established our method of operating in the Cabinet. I would allow nothing to pass in Cabinet until certain conditions were met. What was desirable was complete unanimity; that is, with not even one Minister dissenting. But with a dozen or more strong-minded men, unanimity was a difficult end to reach, so from the start I adopted the practice, and described it

*He later joined my Cabinet as Minister of Education. He is now, in his retirement, Chancellor of Memorial University.

frankly to my colleagues, of postponing decisions on any matter on which more than one Minister dissented. If only one Minister disagreed, I would ask him, "Do you disagree in conscience, or in any case to the extent that you wouldn't vote for it when the House opens?" Almost always the Minister would give his assurance that he would not oppose the measure in the House. "But even that is not enough," I would remind him. "You may be the very Minister that I will ask to explain and defend the measure in the House. It will not be your measure or mine—it will be the measure of the whole Cabinet, for which every individual Minister is responsible equally with all the others." It was only when the Minister agreed with this position that I ever, in my twenty-three years, allowed any decision to be made in Cabinet.

Not one member of my first Cabinet had ever been a member of a Cabinet under an elective form of government, though of course Pottle and Quinton had been members of the Commission of Government. Curtis had been the law partner of Sir Richard Squires and, when Squires went away on some of his long absences from Newfoundland, the liaison between the Prime Minister and the Cabinet. Thus he had personal experience of the far-reaching authority of a premier. But he had no personal experience of Cabinet procedures, and he was not alone in this. I noticed in the first few weeks that one of my colleagues would gather up his papers and slip out of the meeting half an hour or more before it ended. I was mildly annoyed by this but assumed that he had some important family matter to attend to. At last, one day, as he was gathering his papers to go, I inquired, "Anything wrong at home?" "No, no indeed, Premier." "Are you going to meet someone at the airport, perhaps?" "No." "Then what is the important matter that takes you away from a Cabinet meeting?" The Minister was genuinely surprised. "Nothing," he admitted. "It is only that my business is finished, and I thought I would get back to my office." "But your business isn't finished," I told him. "Oh yes, it is. We dealt with the last of my papers just a few minutes ago, don't you remember?"

So then I had to deliver a little lecture, telling my colleagues in general that they were only incidentally, very incidentally, and possibly very temporarily, Minister of this or Minister of that. Their particular portfolios were not the crucial thing. The crucial thing was their membership in the Cabinet as such. They were not to think of themselves as dukes with their own dukedoms, with all the dukes meeting in conclave, each to get his own particular affairs dealt with. The Minister of Education, for example, was just as responsible in the House and in the eyes of the people for roads and bridges as was the Minister of Public Works; and the Minister of Public Works was just as responsible as the Minister of Justice, except in a purely technical sense, for decisions taken in the Justice Department. In short, my little lecture (which I repeated briefly at many future Cabinet meetings) pointed up the great principles of British Cabinet government: Cabinet solidarity and collective Cabinet responsibility. This meant that no Minister had any right whatsoever to make any public pronouncement on any public problem about which the Cabinet as a whole had not taken a position. I emphasized, too, the fact that no Minister should ever say publicly what he intended to recommend to the Cabinet. Above all, no Cabinet Minister should ever indicate that he had in Cabinet taken a position contrary to the collective decision. I never could see, and still do not see, how Cabinet government can function successfully without strict observance of these time-tested principles and practices.

Even before I became Premier, I had made up my mind on the great single issue that would exist in Newfoundland from the moment it became a province. We could spend the millions in our cash surplus to build roads, bridges, and causeways, and schools, hospitals, and water and sewer systems, and the hundred and one other improvements that we needed so desperately. But every instinct in me rose up in alarm at the idea. By following that course, we would have better roads, schools, and hospitals, more housing, electricity, water and sewer systems, and public libraries than we had ever dreamed of—and still most of our people could be unemployed.

Of course, I used to argue in Cabinet, we could decide to turn Newfoundland into a Canadian stud farm. We could use our money to make Newfoundland a pleasant place for youngsters up to the age of sixteen or seventeen, whereupon they would all leave the province to get the jobs on the mainland that they couldn't get in Newfoundland. But was there any enduring future even in a stud farm? In any case, having been so long a colony of Britain, would we now want to become a colony of Canada? Surely our common-sense told us that the only sane course for us to take was to create jobs: not just jobs building houses and roads, schools and hospitals, electric lighting, and all the rest of it, happy as such development would be; but jobs producing pulp and paper, minerals, cement, building boards, and other products that could be sold for cash. I preached this doctrine in season and out, in Cabinet and out, to the last day I was Premier, and I preach it now.

My colleagues agreed with me almost to a man, almost to the end. They were under powerful pressure from the people to provide the public services that they felt far more vehemently, now that they were Canadians, to be their rightful due. I, too, though not as vividly as many of my colleagues, realized the need for such improvements; but I confess candidly that my mind was so immersed in the greater problem that I never really did share fully their anxious desire for roads and hospitals and electric lights.

It took me a good many years to realize that there was another side to my equation: if it would be futile to make Newfoundland a pleasant place to live in, but there were no jobs, wouldn't it be equally futile to provide the jobs and not the pleasant place in which to live? If the thousands of young men and women then growing up in Newfoundland could have good jobs, what realistic assurance could we have that even then they'd stay in Newfoundland? Wouldn't they go to other parts of Canada where they could get both good jobs and good living conditions? Surely we would have to give them both in Newfoundland if we were going to keep them here.

This theme had been part of my thinking for many years; but now that I was Premier, and largely responsible for Newfoundland's success, it burned itself indelibly into me, almost to the point of obsession. I listened with half an ear to the theme of improvement in the public services, the infrastructure of the new province, but gave my whole soul to the great need.

The drawbacks that we faced on Confederation Day were formidable. We Ministers, the Deputy Ministers, the heads of divisions and sections of Government Departments, the whole civil service, and indeed everybody else in Newfoundland were quite hopelessly ignorant of what natural resources we had. There had always been talk of "our great resources", "our great untapped wealth", and other expressions of our belief (but not our knowledge) that Newfoundland was very rich in natural resources. Perhaps we were, but it was only perhaps. Only the broadest and most generalized geological surveys had been made, with few exceptions, and Newfoundland was almost a complete stranger to the diamond drill. Doubtless the big papermill company at Grand Falls had a shrewd idea of how much pulpwood timber grew on their particular holdings, and doubtless the big

Corner Brook company knew about theirs. But nobody in Newfoundland knew how much timber grew in Newfoundland or in Labrador. Water power? Most of it had been given away, fifty, eighty years before, to anyone who had had the energy to ask. The payment receivable by the Newfoundland Government? A peppercorn here, a peppercorn there, but mostly not even a peppercorn. And for the most part, these resources remained as unproductive as they had been at the Creation.

What precious time I could have saved if I had been able to reach into this pigeonhole or that for authentic data on our resources! I wouldn't have had to waste time going to large mining companies, papermill companies, and power companies around the world to interest them in the development of resources that I didn't know and couldn't prove that we had. We had to start from scratch, and that meant hiring the best technical people we could find anywhere (and that almost invariably was anywhere outside Newfoundland itself) to drill, survey, measure, delineate, and blueprint specific resources. It would take years, and it would take millions of money. One of my regrets is that I didn't crowd on even more sail then, and engage two or three times as many outfits and spend two or three times as much money on that great drive to discover and blueprint the resources. What on earth had all previous governments been about? How was it possible for the Commission of Government, for example, with so many millions of dollars stashed away in a cash surplus, to fail in so obvious a duty to Newfoundland?

It would take years for complete surveys and maps to be made of our forest wealth, our mineral potential, our water resources. It was a heartbreaking delay. Precious time would be lost before actual resource development could begin; but it had to be done, and I got the concurrence of my colleagues in Cabinet in my proposals to employ competent firms in Canada and the United States to do the surveys. One such survey was the biggest of its kind ever done in the world up to that time: an air-borne magnotometer survey of 10,000 square miles of Notre Dame Bay for significant mineralization. Our own Newfoundland scientist at Ottawa, Robert W. Boyle, who had been head of the National Research Council of Canada, had played a notable part in the development of the air-borne magnetometer. That one survey cost us about half a million dollars, but never was money better spent! It has already produced five or six working mines. We spent millions of dollars getting these surveys made, but it was little short of criminal negligence on the part of the Commission of Government to have failed to make those very surveys. I think that they really had little or no faith in the likelihood of such surveys revealing wealth even equal to the cost of making them. I could have saved five or eight years, those first precious years of Confederation, if I had known then what I knew later, after those surveys had been made.

We hadn't the accumulated cash capital in Newfoundland, then, to finance natural resource development, even if there were known resources to develop. The capital would have to come from outside Newfoundland. Newfoundland's own reputation outside was excellent—if you were a partisan of fogs and dogs and codfish. There couldn't have been many spots in North or Central America less likely to occur to the minds of developers and promoters than Newfoundland. It would almost certainly be the last spot to be considered for the site of an industry.

What a proud boast we can make in Newfoundland—that we have led all Canada since 1949 in the rate of increased mineral production. Over $100 million dollars have been spent on mineral exploration, and nearly three-quarters of a billion dollars have been spent on actual mineral development. In the first year of Confederation, our mineral production was $25 million. In my last year as Premier, the production was $349 million. During my term in office, the total value of mineral production was $3½ billion. We have brought some of the world's best-known mining companies to our province.

I have not mentioned the one supreme disadvantage that overshadowed the whole scene in our first years as a province of Canada: the swift approach of world depression. In one country after another, times were worsening and unemployment was beginning to reach alarming proportions. All across Canada, there was worried talk of probable depression that might before long drive Canada back, and the United States too, to the very state of affairs that only the outbreak of the Second War had "remedied". But was there a permanent remedy, men asked? In Newfoundland, the coming of Confederation was almost exactly simultaneous with deepening depression, and we discussed it in Cabinet very earnestly. My mind rebelled against the thought of simple relief or even simple unemployment insurance. My colleagues agreed with my proposal that we should make an attempt, hazardous as it would be, to use both relief and unemployment insurance to finance socially useful projects that would provide jobs for men throughout the whole province.

We appointed Al Vardy as head of a Work Relief Administration, and a fine job he did. The immediate problem was to find specifically those socially useful projects: clearing away stumps and rocks to make local playgrounds in the outports; deepening and damming pools in local brooks to make simple swimming holes for the children; building a bridge here or there; even building a rather elaborate causeway to connect an island to the main shore; improving the road leading to a local graveyard, or church, or school; beautifying the landscape in and around the settlements. We estimated carefully how many days' work each man would need to qualify for the special unemployment insurance that Ottawa was offering us in that first year or two of Confederation. Vardy set up a small but efficient organization in St. John's and got hundreds of local committees operating throughout the province. We spent, of our own money, what appeared to us then to be the fearsome amount of $3 million on the WRA program. That whole experiment (which was soon made almost unnecessary by the outbreak of war in Korea), with all its weaknesses and failures, nevertheless confirmed me in my conviction, which strengthened with the years, that direct cash relief to able-bodied men who had no jobs is essentially insulting and debasing. Organized society cannot turn indifferently away from the sight of women and children going hungry because the bread-winner has no job; but direct cash relief is at best a cowardly answer to the problem. If our modern private enterprise system has no job for a man, then let organized society (the Government) provide him with a job at cash wages and under conditions established by the trade union movement. The real problem then will be that of finding socially useful work that will be efficiently performed. I advocated this theme at federal-provincial conferences held under the auspices of prime ministers St. Laurent, Diefenbaker, Pearson, and Trudeau, so far without much result.

Another drawback, a very serious one indeed, was the probability that our already sparse population of 300,000 would be disastrously reduced by a rush to mainland Canada to get the jobs that didn't exist in Newfoundland. In the twelve months before Confederation Day, 2,500 Newfoundlanders had gone off to Canada, mostly to Ontario, seeking work. In the year before that, another 2,400 had gone—almost 5,000 people lost in two years!

There was no Premier's office the day I took over. Throughout the fifteen years of the Commission of Government, the Chairman of the Commission—the nearest thing to Premier—had been the Governor of Newfoundland, thus fulfilling the dual functions of personal representative of the monarch and executive head of the Government. I couldn't very well use Government House (though there were those who strongly urged me not to allow that fine building to be used as the Lieutenant-Governor's residence), so I had to look around for an office. The suite of offices that had been used by our prime ministers before, in the Court House Building on Water Street, had been absorbed into the Department of Public Works. I chose temporarily the two rooms in the Colonial Building that had been used by the Speaker of the House of Assembly. It was in these very rooms that the steering committee of the National Convention had met, where Peter Cashin and I had our wrestling match and in which our first Ottawa delegation had held its meetings when we were getting ready for our visit to Canada's capital. I asked Gregory Power to be my executive assistant, and Mrs. Templeman continued with me as confidential secretary. She remained with me to the day of my resignation in 1972.

After a few months, I moved into Canada House on Circular Road. This was a large rambling three-storey house in which Sir Michael Cashin and a line of other prominent men had resided. Canada had purchased and furnished it for the High Commissioner, who lived in one end of it and used the other end for offices. Now the Canadian Government leased the whole property, furniture and all, to the Newfoundland Government, and I in turn rented the residential part from the Provincial Government. I was thrilled to move into it, and I saw to it that the building continued to be called Canada House. I continued to live there until Mr. Diefenbaker, after he became Prime Minister of Canada, insisted that I leave. I hung on to the last moment in hopes that he would be misguided enough to have me evicted, for we were in the midst of our feud, and I planned to have the photographers there to see my family and me sitting on the furniture scattered on the sidewalk outside. (I had meanwhile bought the furniture from Ottawa.) Mr. Diefenbaker didn't oblige.

I commenced at Canada House my long-continued practice of seeing anybody who wanted to meet with me. Michael Foley became my reception clerk, and he saw to it that callers took their places in the order of their appearance, as in a barbershop. Merchants, bankers, unemployed, labourers, fishermen, teachers, women looking for houses or flats—it made no difference; it was first come, first served for all. The fact became widely known and understood, and if there was grumbling, it was over the long time that people often had to wait to see me. Even that was forgiven me when it became known that once someone did get in to see me, he could take his time and receive close attention to his problem. I saw tens of thousands of people in this way throughout my twenty-three years. Stories are still told of my making midnight appointments for people to see me, but I recall very few such appointments. Often enough, it was midnight or later when the last visitor for the day succeeded finally in seeing me. When personal friends or Cabinet colleagues remonstrated with me on my willingness to see everybody, my invariable answer was "It's when they stop coming to see me that we should all start to worry."

Miracles we saw every day—we couldn't help seeing them; they were all about us—as the benign air of Confederation breathed over us: the miracle of shopkeepers' shelves and floors filled to overflowing with children's clothes and shoes and bicycles and toys, with women in tens of thousands crowding into the shops; the old men and women, too, all with their Canadian cheques, going in at first with deep-down doubt that they were any good, coming out with armfuls of goods and happy faces; the Confederates glowing, and the Antis quiet but very thoughtful.

And so our poor, downtrodden, backward Newfoundland, "sport of historic misfortune", "Cinderella of the Empire", after countless bludgeonings and bleedings, with her everlasting moratorium on hope, was launched at last upon her astonishing career as a Canadian province, leading swiftly to a degree and quality of advancement that left even the most incorrigible Anti-Confederate abashed and the great majority proud, happy, and grateful.

16

Develop or Perish Is What I Said

Wealth unused might as well not exist.

Aesop

A man willing to work, and unable to find it, is perhaps the saddest sight that fortune's inequality exhibits under this sun.

Thomas Carlyle

The finest poems in the world have been expedients to get bread.

Ralph Waldo Emerson

Wealth is the means, and people are the ends. All our material riches will avail us little if we do not use them to expand the opportunities of our people.

President John F. Kennedy

I worried about the danger of losing our population, and I knew, even before Confederation Day, that somehow I had to inspire the Newfoundland people with new faith in their prospects. I had to persuade them that Newfoundland was a place with a bright future; a place to stay in; a place where a young man could get married, raise a family, and enjoy a good life—that there was no need to go rushing off to Toronto. And so I never lost a chance to speak of the coming glory of Newfoundland, of the bright star that Newfoundland was destined to be in the Canadian crown; though Newfoundland might be one of the have-not provinces now, soon it would be one of the booming parts of Canada. But, I pointed out interminably, with a thousand expressions of reasoning, we had to develop! We had to develop our resources. We had to develop everything we had in Newfoundland and Labrador. The price of failure would be disaster, and so our slogan had to be "Develop or Perish!" Amazingly, my opponents threw that up against me, but I think that most people understood what I meant.

Were we now to become a colony of Canada? Was that to be Confederation's meaning? Was Newfoundland merely or mainly to be a market for merchandise of the other nine provinces? We knew all about being a colony! We had been Britain's "most ancient and loyal Colony". It was at St. John's that the foundation of the British Empire had been laid in 1497. Our progress had been retarded, deliberately impeded, by official British policy. Settlement had been forbidden, and the Royal Navy had even been known to receive orders to go to Newfoundland and demolish every dwelling that had been unlawfully erected—and that meant all of them. It was not to be a Canadian colony that we had given up being a British colony!

Were we to be a Canadian poorhouse? A horde of dependent suppliants, living on Canadian charity? Family allowance payments were coming in every month now, blanketing the whole province, received by every family of the land, rich and poor, high and low, in every nook and cranny of Newfoundland. Old-age pensions were coming in just as regularly, and almost as universally, as the baby bonus. Unemployment insurance payments were pouring in, often giving families more money than the bread-winner had been earning when he had a job. Greatly increased war veterans' payments were pouring in. Thousands of men and women were being taken into the Canadian civil service in Newfoundland, and they were getting more pay than Newfoundland had ever been able to afford. Thousands of employees of the Newfoundland Railway, which was taken over by the Canadian Government at the moment of Confederation and entrusted to the CNR to operate, got sharply increased rates of pay, as did the employees of the railway's fleet of coastal passenger and freight ships. Federal employees in airports, lighthouses, fish-bait depots, federal public buildings, and many other areas began to get much better pay than they had been getting from the Newfoundland Government. The money was pouring in from Ottawa! We had never seen anything like it before. And we knew that it was going to continue pouring in, and that the amount pouring in would get larger, not smaller.

And then we had the cash surplus! This amounted to $45.5 million. We were not free to spend it in any way we wished, for at my suggestion, when we were drafting the terms of union in Ottawa, part of the surplus had been ear-marked for ordinary current-account expenditures. Still, what we were free to spend amounted to two-thirds of the total, and besides that we had certain physical assets that we could turn into cash.

As I have said, I was irrevocably committed to a policy of economic development of the province, and I was happy to be Premier chiefly because of the opportunity it gave me to initiate that development. I put the matter bluntly in the manifesto that I issued at the eve of the first Provincial General Election, held a few weeks after Confederation Day. I titled my statement, "Ahead—or Astern", and it read as follows:

> As a Province of Canada, Newfoundland will be either a glorified "poor-house" with most of her people depending too largely on Family Allowances, Old Age Pensions and other cash payments from the Government of Canada; or else a growing prosperous Province of independent families. We will either be a drag on the rest of Canada, or we will stand on our own feet as a prosperous, progressive Province.
>
> The policy of the Liberal Party is to make New-

> foundland one of the prosperous, progressive Provinces of Canada; a Province able to hold its head up and proud to look the rest of Canada squarely in the eyes. A Province willing and able to help its people to a higher standard of living than they have ever enjoyed before.
>
> Our first great undertaking as a Government will be the development of our country, both Newfoundland and Labrador. We will push vigorously ahead with a policy of searching for natural resources, measuring them, developing them; day and night we will work for this great purpose. We will strain every effort and use all our ability to open up our country and to increase our country's wealth and prosperity.
>
> Newfoundland can not stand still—we must go ahead or go astern. We can go ahead only when we develop our country's natural resources.
>
> The fish in the sea, the minerals in the earth, the water power running to waste, the good earth itself—these are useless to the people if they are not developed.

And then came the signal words:

> We must find out what natural resources we have in our country; we must advertise these resources throughout the world; we must bring new capital in to open up our country and give jobs for our people. Our country will stand or fall according to how far we go to develop our natural resources.

And then the promise:

> Every bit of our strength and energy as a Government will be used in this great work of development.
>
> We will put into this work of developing Newfoundland *the greatest drive that Newfoundland has ever seen.*

Those words were printed in black type. I really meant them.

I took the portfolio of Minister of Economic Development myself, even before the first House of Assembly was elected in May 1949, and before there could be the legislation to authorize the creation of the new Department. I declared in my election campaign speeches, and afterward in the House of Assembly, and at public dinners and the like, that our policy was to develop Newfoundland or perish in the attempt. I'm not sure as I write this that I explained always in my speeches what I meant by "perish", for I didn't suppose an explanation to be needed. It didn't mean that the people would die in the streets and Newfoundland cease to be. It didn't mean some catastrophic blow that would annihilate the province. What it meant was that Newfoundlanders, especially the young ones, would never be willing to stay in a province that didn't give them a chance to work for a good living, a chance to rear families in independence, a chance for those families to enjoy a good life in Newfoundland. They would flock out in far greater numbers than they had been doing before Confederation Day. Those numbers would grow so large as to lead to a veritable stampede of Newfoundlanders to the mainland of Canada. Newfoundland would perish indeed.

There was something else. Never in my life have I, in public or in private or in my own thoughts, taken sole credit for bringing Confederation to Newfoundland. Never once did I refer to myself as "the only living Father of Confederation", and I have invariably shrunk from the term when I have read or heard it. There are many fathers of Newfoundland's Confederation: King, St. Laurent, Pickersgill, Bradley, Petten, Gregory Power, Philip Forsey, to name but a few of them. But I had played a part, a very public part, in bringing Confederation about. In any event, I was now the Premier of the new province, and I thus had double reason for wishing to make Confederation a great success. I had far more than ordinary responsibility to make a successful and happy province, and the way to fulfil my duty was through stimulating economic development. Social development had to come, of course: education, public health, roads, electricity, water and sewer systems, public parks, and other recreational facilities. But all these would amount to nothing in the end if they were not supported by a broadened, deepened, strengthened economic base.

The delay there had to be in obtaining the necessary basic facts about our natural resources was hard to take. It was not in my nature just to wait for the results of the surveys; I had to do something while I was waiting. I felt in my bones that there must be possibilities of economic development that needn't wait for the surveys; but I felt, too, just as positively, the need for expert advice and guidance. I began to look around for it. It was useless to turn to the businessmen of Newfoundland. Most of them were scrambling around, like hen-hawks eyeing a chicken coop, for their share of the millions of family allowances and other cash pouring in from Ottawa. Wholesale, jobbing, retail shops, they were stocking up to the bursting point, telegraphing and telephoning urgently to the mainland for more supplies, and scouring Canada for new agencies. I didn't dare venture my life in that mob of single-minded traders. It would be useless to talk to them about investing money in new industries, so I would have to search outside, and I did.

Donald Nelson had been chairman of the War Production Board of the United States, and I thought that he'd make an excellent director general of economic development. My approaches met no favourable response. Approaches to George Cadbury, of the famous English family, similarly failed. I mentioned the matter to the one man who perhaps in Canada's history was the country's greatest economic developer, the Right Hon. C. D. Howe, and it was from him, through one of his lieutenants, that I heard of Alfred A. Valdmanis. He was highly recommended to me, so the next time I was in Ottawa, in May 1950, I asked Valdmanis to come to see me at the Château Laurier. There my colleague James R. Chalker and I heard his amazing story from Valdmanis himself. He was a Latvian, of medium height and build, with the lithe body of an athlete, a handsome and very intelligent face, and a clarity of expression in English that impressed everyone who met him.

When Latvia got its independence from Russia after the First World War, the powerful patriot, President Ulmanis, in his determination to develop Latvia, introduced a government scheme of adopting 1,000 young men and women for special training to serve the nation. Valdmanis was one of them. To be adopted in the first place, these young people had to pass the most rigorous tests of health, physical and mental stamina, personality, character, and academic prowess; and no failure was forgiven in any part of the training: deportment, social manners, athletic skills, or academic studies. One failure in any of these and out you went! The thousand shrank to a few hundreds, and the hundreds to a score or two, and Valdmanis still remained in the group. The course for him included the study of law, which culminated in his being called to the bar, and finance and economics, culminating in his becoming Minister of Finance of Latvia. With this portfolio, he was responsible for industrial development and economic development generally in Latvia, so that under the authoritarian President Ulmanis, the young Valdmanis became virtually the economic czar of his country. This was the story he told us that night, in what appeared to us to be straightforward terms and tones. A biography of him published in Latvia, a translation of which I read later, seemed to confirm much of the story.

About one thing there was no possibility of doubt: he was brilliant and knowledgeable, and he was convinced there that night that the first step to be taken in Newfoundland was the building of a cement mill. The Newfoundland Industrial Development Board, a body of local businessmen, had considered and rejected the idea of a cement mill, but I had not been impressed by their rejection. Valdmanis's proposal interested me greatly. He was not only willing, but eager to come with me to Newfoundland; and on my return to St. John's, the Cabinet approved my engaging him as our first Director General of Economic Development. From occupying a minor teaching position at Carleton University, doing some work for Mr. Howe's Department of Trade and Commerce, and performing other odd jobs around Ottawa, Valdmanis found that he had moved up to a position of prestige and authority—and a good salary.

From the beginning, because of his imperious manner and rather obviously insincere flattery of my colleagues, each of whom he called "Your Excellency", he was hated by some, tolerated by others, and greatly liked by only a few; but he was respected for his brains and talents by all. I was amused by his obviousness in some things, but I admired him immensely for his seemingly unlimited skills and accomplishments and for his capacity for hard work. He was one of the best tennis players we ever saw in Newfoundland; he was a superb dancer, had a glorious singing voice, was an accomplished musician, spoke half a dozen languages (all with meticulous clarity and perfect grammar, if I can judge by his handling of English). He was a walking encyclopedia on many of the countries of Europe; he knew every industrialist of importance in Western Germany (having been made an economic planner there when Hitler overran Latvia and Valdmanis was carried off to Germany); he was a superior chess player, so some of my chess-playing friends told me; and generally he was one of the most talented men I have ever known. He gave signs of being devoted to me and my ambitions for Newfoundland, worked like a Trojan, and appeared to me to be implacably determined to realize for me my dream of an industrialized new province.

Valdmanis's first step was to prepare the case for starting two separate industrial plants: the cement mill, and a mill using gypsum rock as its main raw material. This factory would make gypsum plaster building board and lath, the latter being the underlay of plastered walls and ceilings. We certainly had, and still have, vast tonnages of high-quality limestone and of gypsum rock, so there was no question that these plants, if they could be built cheaply enough and operated efficiently, should be quite successful. I told Valdmanis to go ahead with his preparations, but wondered in my own mind who would build the two plants and own them when they were ready for operation. I had no thought whatever that the Government should operate them; indeed, I would have greatly preferred it if private enterprise had been willing to build and own the plants in the first place. Valdmanis went off to West Germany and came back with prices on both plants. The fine Braunschweig firm of Miag quoted a price for which they would build and install a 100,000-ton cement mill, and the capable firm of Benno-Schilde gave their quotation on the same services for the gypsum plant. We decided to go ahead with both plants, at Humbermouth near Corner Brook on the West Coast. There are great deposits of limestone at Humbermouth, but the gypsum rock would have to be brought by rail from Flat Bay, beside St. George's, a few miles to the west. This was the beginning of our great drive for industrialization, while we waited for the survey reports on our natural resources.

The two plants were built by us and went into production, and for a short period, they were operated by the Government. I looked about to find private operators who would be willing to buy both plants, but without luck. We did get the Flintkote Corporation of the United States to operate the gypsum board plant for a while; then, when their contract expired and they indicated no wish to renew it, I invited the Lundrigan firm in Corner Brook to put together a Newfoundland company to take over the ownership and operation. This they did, and they continue to this day to operate the plant successfully. We made a similar arrangement for the cement mill. A new company was formed in Newfoundland to buy the mill, and this took in some of the more important local businessmen of Corner Brook, Grand Falls, and St. John's, as well as an important Toronto industrialist to give the company added prestige. Both mills have been operated profitably ever since.

While the machinery for both mills was being manufactured in

Germany, I decided to go there myself, and Valdmanis organized a tour. I took two of my Cabinet colleagues with me, Finance Minister Herman Quinton and Health Minister James Chalker. My old friend Ches Crosbie, though he had refused to the end to support Confederation, was now actively supporting me politically. He wanted to go along at his own expense, and as he was good company, I agreed. That was the first of many visits I made to West Germany in the following years. Valdmanis led us on a very strenuous tour from one city and industrial plant to another: by the end of my last trip, I had visited every industrial city and most of the largest industrial plants in West Germany. Valdmanis arranged a whole series of luncheons and dinners hosted by such industrial giants as Krupp, I. G. Farben, Mannesmann, Voight, Siemens-Schukart, Demag, and numbers of others as well.

In October 1950, Germany still showed on every hand the devastating results of war-time bombing, with vast stretches of most cities and towns reduced to rubble. You would say that not in fifty years to come would the Germans be able to clean up the mess and rebuild their towns and factories. But the very next year, I could see a big improvement; in the third year, the improvement was unbelievable; in the fourth year, one began to believe in miracles again; in the fifth and sixth years, the miracle was all around to be seen. I grew to have boundless respect for the energy of the German people: their neatness, cleanliness, and love of good order. I quickly formed the opinion that Canada should be doing the same thing that the United States and the Soviet Union were doing in Germany then: seeking out all the scientists and highly trained technicians that could be found and bringing them to Canada. Indeed, I began to form a sort of good-natured contempt for my own nation of Canada for its failure to seize what I believed, and still believe, was a golden opportunity to gain twenty or thirty years of progress. Certainly, the few Germans that I was instrumental in bringing to Newfoundland have turned out to be excellent citizens: for the most part, you wouldn't want better.

We had one cloak-and-dagger episode in Germany. The vast Krupp plant in Essen—and it was vast, measuring a full mile along both sides of a broad avenue, and extending back a full mile from both sides of the avenue—had been levelled after the war had ended but was now in process of rebuilding. It was determined to become a great enterprise again, and Valdmanis and I decided that it was well worth going after. Alfred Krupp was still in semi-imprisonment, but he was allowed to have visitors. Valdmanis went to see him every night for several days in succession, coming back to report to me late each night. Krupp appeared to be genuinely interested in the idea of establishing some kind of enterprise in Newfoundland. Later, I attended a meeting of the directors of Krupp at their head office in Essen. They told me that this was, in fact, the first meeting of their full board since the end of the war. We signed an agreement at that meeting to the effect that Krupp would send a small team of highly skilled mineralogists to Newfoundland to take a good look at Steel Mountain, near St. George's on our West Coast, where there was known to be a deposit of manganese. We were to supply tents and cooking and sleeping equipment, and an airplane to put them in there, and they were to provide the skilled personnel. They kept their side of the bargain, and we did too. The prospecting party was caught in the first snow storm of the fall, and we had to leave the equipment in there and be satisfied with getting the men out safely. The conclusion was that the deposit wasn't extensive enough to justify further exploration.

I signed an agreement also with another German industrial giant, I. G. Farben. This provided for the starting of a factory in Newfoundland for the manufacture of a fire-retardant chemical that would be mixed in paint. Nearly all houses in Newfoundland are built of wood, and fires are all too frequent, as they are in wintertime in the Province of Quebec, when perhaps people turn their heat up too high. This factory was to be merely the start of bigger and better plants to come, we were told, but it all came to nothing. Not even the first plant was built, and they never as much as told us why.

I should explain why it was to Germany rather than, say, mainland Canada or the United States or Great Britain that I turned so often in my search for Newfoundland development. It was because of the well-known German ingenuity and skill in industry, the tremendous drive of the Germans, and the fact that their towns and their industries were smashed to pieces. I called it "fishing in troubled waters", and I didn't hesitate to attempt to play on German industrialists' fear of Communist Russia. "When the Russians sweep across Europe," I would tell them cheerfully, "whose throats do you think will be the first to be cut?" Theirs, of course; and that is pretty much what they believed themselves. If only those German industrial leaders had had some capital! What we wanted in Newfoundland was not immigration, but actual industrial plants. We would be happy to have the key personnel come in from Germany to own and run them, and to provide the know-how.

We got a rubber company to build a plant in Newfoundland; a boot and shoe plant; a leather-goods plant; a leather tannery; a leather-clothing plant; a car and truck-battery plant; a cut and sew plant; a particle-board plant; a very large machine-engineering plant. From Austria, we got a woollen-knitwear plant; from England, a chocolate factory. We decided on our own, because of the large stands of birch forest we have on the Island, to build a birch-veneer and plywood plant, and a birch-flooring plant beside it. The plywood and flooring plants imported oak and mahogany logs as well, to enable them to turn out a greater variety of products for sale in Newfoundland and the nearer parts of the mainland of Canada. A substantial amount of the particle board was used as a sub-structure in the plywood plant, which would veneer it with mahogany or birch for sale to furniture factories in Quebec. At Clarenville, two plants had been constructed during the war by a large American company: one to manufacture asphalt for paving; another to do creosoting of railway ties, telephone poles, wharf sticks, and the like. Not long after Confederation Day, these plants closed, and there were two good reasons why we should acquire them: 1) Newfoundland was going to need more asphalt than ever for the program of paving that we had in mind; and 2) we didn't want the loss of jobs that the closure produced. We acquired them, and they became very successful under our management. In the second half of my term of office, we were asked by a Canadian company that had had considerable success in operating small steel mills, producing steel mainly from scrap metals, to back them and several local shareholders in the building of a small steel mill beside St. John's. The local shareholders were three or four of the most successful money-makers we had in the province. It looked like a pretty good bet, and we agreed to back them financially. They got further backing from the Canadian Government, and I must confess that it was a proud moment for me in 1967 when I threw the switch that started Newfoundland's first steel mill going! Employment in the mill rose to about 300 men, but after several changes of ownership, involving the withdrawal of the mainland Canadian firm, the mill, after my retirement, came under the control of a large Canadian steel company. They too pulled out after a few months. Another mainland Canadian company sought and received financial help from us to establish a plant for the manufacture of magnesia from sea water.

Twenty plants were initiated or salvaged in the early drive toward industrialization. Of these, nine are operating today as they did when they were established, two have been converted to a different kind of production, and strenuous efforts are being made to give new life to one other plant. We put a total of about $50 million altogether into those plants; and although, if you look at them from a narrow, orthodox, private enterprise, balance-sheet point of view, over half of them have been losers, the fact is that from the Province's point of view they have, taken as a whole, been a profit-maker. Substantially more than $50 million has gone back into the Province's economy in the form of wages and other disbursements by the industries concerned, and a lot more will go back in. This is the case even before the cost is counted of what would have been incurred by the Treasury for relief to the men and women who otherwise would have been unemployed. I suppose that any normal businessman would throw up his hands at such reasoning, and from the point of view of his own private enterprise, he would be perfectly right.

I remember a brief conversation I once had in the air terminal at Gander with Prince Philip. There was an immense jam of cheering youngsters there from around central Newfoundland to greet the Queen and the Prince. "We have the highest birth rate in North America," I told him. "Our population is growing at a faster rate than anywhere else in Canada." He seemed to take a dim view of that fact, but his response changed quickly when I pointed out that we were only half a million souls in Newfoundland, which didn't make too good a market for industries catering to the Newfoundland market. "When we have a million people in this province, they'll be able to support dozens of factories and other kinds of enterprise that couldn't survive today," and he nodded in agreement.

There was one feature that I didn't like about most natural resource development: the small amount of direct revenue that came from it to the Provincial Treasury. Men got jobs, of course, and that generated revenue to the Treasury, directly and indirectly. But when it was all put together, the Province got, I felt, much too little from the development of its natural wealth. Short of Communism or Socialism, was there nothing that we could do to improve the situation? Then I became aware of the fact that the corporation income tax imposed by the Federal Government did not apply to provincial

Crown Corporations. A Crown Corporation was defined as one that was at least 90 per cent owned by the Provincial Government. So the Newfoundland and Labrador Corporation (NALCO) was born in 1951. It had a paid-up capital of $1 million: $900,000 from the Government, $100,000 from a combination of Wood, Gundy Limited and Wills, Bickle and Company, both of Toronto; and Harriman, Ripley and Company and Cement and General Development Corporation (Sir William Stephenson's organization), Lyttleton B. P. Gould, and Michael Lewin, all of New York. To this Crown Corporation, whose income would not be taxable by Canada, we ceded exploration and development rights in large areas of Labrador and the Island itself. Our hope was that the minority private shareholders would be sufficiently attracted by the prospect of profits to go out and make special efforts to bring development corporations into the province to survey particular areas within the concession, and to proceed with development of anything profitable that they might find. The idea didn't work, and it soon became apparent why. Ten per cent of the profits that might accrue to NALCO, when divided between all the private shareholders, just didn't constitute enough incentive. Sir William Stephenson, whom we appointed chairman, made strenuous efforts, and indeed was successful in bringing large American sub-concessionaires into the province for surveys made at their own expense. We were excited briefly in NALCO (I was a director) by the reports we had of considerable deposits of titanium in the Mealy Mountains of Lake Melville in Labrador.

We soon discovered that the million dollars of capital was little more than a token of the money needed to be spent, but we realized in Cabinet that it was out of the question for us to put up 90 per cent of the many millions that NALCO itself needed to spend. In the end, we decided to "denationalize" NALCO—that is, to sell some of the Government's 90 per cent share-holding, which would of course "un-crown" the corporation. Even that didn't produce the results we wanted, and in the end we sold our shares in NALCO for a handsome profit of about $2 million. It is not without interest to notice that the great Churchill Falls was originally part of the NALCO concession.

I am as firmly convinced as ever that Newfoundland can be the home of numerous industrial plants of many kinds, but this doesn't mean that I have ever, even for a moment, failed to have a lively appreciation of the importance of our natural resources. I have worked too hard and too long to get these resources developed for anyone to be able credibly to charge me with that particular lack of faith. But I was perhaps the first in our Newfoundland history to see, and expatiate upon, one of the greatest of all our natural resources: our physical location in the Atlantic basin, with our several great deep-water, all-weather seaports. It was John Shaheen who led me to that truth, and he was ably supported by Homer White and Roy Furmark. Nobody laughs at me any more when I point to that great natural resource of our province. Properly developed, it will become perhaps our greatest treasure.

As I have said, most of this drive for industrial plants was made while I awaited impatiently the numerous reports on our conventional national resources; but this seems to be an appropriate point at which to summarize the numbers of new jobs that exist now, for the creation of which, directly or indirectly, my policy and I have been responsible in Newfoundland:

Natural resource development (mines, etc.).	3,000
Fish plants, draggers, etc.	9,000
Industrial establishments	3,000
Wholesale and retail trade	23,000
Catering (hotels, restaurants, etc.)	4,000
Roads (garages, service stations, truck and bus-drivers, etc.)	23,000
Transportation and communications (CNR, airports, airlines, telephones, etc.)	6,000
Financial (banks, etc.)	2,000
Doctors, nurses, dentists, hospital workers, municipal workers, federal and provincial civil servants, teachers, etc.	22,000
Miscellaneous.	2,000
	97,000

The total work force in Newfoundland, as this is written, is in the order of 167,000. The rate of unemployment is high this winter of 1973, as it always is in wintertime in Newfoundland—18 per cent.

Just four years after he came with us, the Valdmanis tragedy exploded. It began with a visit that I received from a man for whom I had great respect. He came to see me late one night and asked me if I would take him somewhere or other for a drive in my car—he wanted a very private interview with me and wanted no possible interruption. Besides, he said, it was a very secret matter. This same man had asked me, very tentatively, some weeks before, a question to which I had paid little attention at the time: had Dr. Valdmanis arranged any contributions to the Liberal Party's election funds? I had answered shortly, no. I remembered the question now and decided that I would go for the drive. This is the story he told me. Valdmanis had demanded, and received in cash, sums totalling around half a million dollars from the Miag and Benno-Schilde firms in Germany. These payments had been made to him in periodic amounts, spread over a year or so. They had been paid to the American Express Bank in New York, through a relative of Valdmanis who held his power of attorney. One of the two companies had been approached several times by Valdmanis for additional payments over and above the original amount that he had demanded, and they had agreed to pay; but these amounts were so considerable that the company's officers became angry and then suspicious. Valdmanis had represented himself to both German firms as the personal and confidential representative of the Premier of Newfoundland in his capacity as leader of the Liberal Party. In short, the demand for the money was declared by Valdmanis to come from me, he being nothing more than my messenger. One of the officers of the second company had come to Newfoundland and told the story to my present informant. I turned the car about and went back to my office. I telephoned Gregory Power and asked him to come along quickly to my office. There I got my informant to repeat the story in detail. It was around midnight, and after my informant had taken his departure from the office, I telephoned the Newfoundland Superintendent of the Royal Canadian Mounted Police, D. A. MacKinnon. He was at his home—I think he had just gone to bed—but I told him that it was a matter of the gravest importance and that I really wanted him to come to my office immediately. He was there within a few minutes. I told him the complete story and asked him to take whatever action was required to get to the bottom of it and prove its truth or falsity. After he had gone, Gregory Power, who had taken a suspicious view of Valdmanis all along, refrained from rubbing it in to me. My last word to Superintendent MacKinnon was "Find the money, Superintendent! If you don't find the money, even the Atlantic Ocean won't wash me clean—everyone will believe that the money was truly for me or for the Party. Find it, will you?" He said that he would do his best.

The Superintendent flew later that same morning to RCMP headquarters in Ottawa, and from that point the action was swift. FBI and RCMP specialists examined and photographed all references to the money in the American Express accounts in New York, and got the complete story. Whether or not Valdmanis was blackmailed into doing it, as he subsequently claimed, the fact seems to be that a very large part of the money had been sunk in the bottomless pit of a crazy fish venture in New Brunswick. A huge monstrosity of a concrete fish plant building had been erected by a company that soon afterward failed, and a group in New York acquired it and spent large sums of money on it—Valdmanis's money. With the facts in their possession, the RCMP shadowed Valdmanis day and night, sat with him in the same car on the train from Montreal to the site of the fish plant in New Brunswick, and arrested him at two or three o'clock the following morning, April 24, 1954. The RCMP telephoned me at my home as soon as the arrest had been made and told me that Valdmanis was being brought to St. John's for arraignment. I called the Canadian Press man out of bed and gave him the dramatic news. I informed the House soon after that I had instigated the arrest. Valdmanis himself provided the finishing touch to the evidence against him when he contrived to smuggle a letter out of the penitentiary. It was addressed to a man in Germany, and in it Valdmanis asked him to swear that the money had been for the Liberal Party. The man in Germany sent the letter to the authorities in St. John's—the Department of Justice, I think—and it proved to be quite damning. On September 18, after Valdmanis had pleaded guilty, the Supreme Court sentenced him to a term of four years in the penitentiary. Valdmanis's wife wrote me a very sad letter in which she apologized for Alfred's treatment of me and told me that her husband, before they came to Canada, had sworn that he would get rich by any means within his power. During the short time he was out on bail, Valdmanis telephoned me at my home and pleaded with me to show mercy on him.

This whole business was a shattering experience for me, and I confess that I felt bitter toward Valdmanis. I had defended and praised him. On one occasion, by way of defending him against the all but continuous attacks on him, I went so far as to say that I wouldn't want to continue to be Premier without him. Newfoundland, I said, would one day raise a monument to him.

I could have hushed up the whole thing, and not a word of it need have got out. My original informant would have been quite content to say nothing further if I had decided to bury the matter. I was not for a moment, not even a fleeting moment, tempted to bury it.

This brilliant and tragic man lost his life a year or so ago in an automobile accident in Western Canada. I always felt that he was a product and a victim of the dire events through which he lived in Latvia and war-time Germany.

There's nothing queer about our Joey.

The Chronicle-Herald (Halifax)

17

Dreams That Didn't Come True

How far high failure overleaps the bounds of low success.
Sir Lewis Morris

We have forty million reasons for failure, but not a single excuse.
Rudyard Kipling

There is not a fiercer hell than the failure in a great object.
John Keats

In great attempts it is glorious even to fail.
Longinus

I have been guilty of more failures and policy mistakes than any Premier or Prime Minister in our history. I once began my campaign for re-election—I think it was my third General Election—by making a radio speech in which I recited ten or twelve mistakes and failures of which I had been guilty up to then. I went on to say that I was sorry, but that I couldn't give any undertaking that I would not make many more mistakes if the people re-elected me. I would try not to make the same mistakes, but I felt certain that I would make new ones. If I were to bring that list up to date, it would fill this chapter, and even my strongest opponents would be bored before I finished. The failures of which I am most conscious are these:

1. I had a plan to duplicate in Newfoundland the little town of Rothenburg in Germany. This is a very ancient town, quaint beyond words, where large quantities of attractive toys are made. My thought was that the existence of a replica of this, or possibly some other German town, peopled by Germans who operated hotels, restaurants, taverns, shops, and the like, would attract to Newfoundland each year thousands, or possibly even scores of thousands, of German tourists from the United States and across Canada. I had the same thought exactly about Italy and Spain. It would have cost a good many millions, but I'm still not sure that it wouldn't have been a profitable venture for Newfoundland.

2. I had the idea of lining the first twenty miles of the Trans-Canada Highway eastward from Port-aux-Basques with flowering trees and shrubs that would come into blossom in succession throughout a period of several months each year. This we would advertise as "the longest lovers' lane in the world", and it would have been, I still think, a lively tourist attraction in our province.

3. I intended to find some deserted cove in one of our bays and recreate in it as perfect a replica as possible of a sixteenth or seventeenth-century Newfoundland fishing settlement—the fishermen using the same techniques, dressing much the same, and living as their forefathers had done 200 or 300 years before. They and their

families would live there only through the summer and early autumn fishing season. This too would be a superb tourist attraction for Newfoundland.

4. I deeply regret my failure to institute a really powerful policy of conservation and, what is even more necessary, of promotion of our trout and salmon resources on the Island and Labrador. We did something, but not one-quarter enough. One day, our descendants may condemn us harshly for my failure and the failure of others in this field.

5. I all but completely failed in my program to set up a substantial number of statues and monuments in front of the Confederation Building. My plan envisaged a statue of the American Indian Squantum or Squanta, who had lived in Newfoundland and later, when the Pilgrim Fathers landed on the American continent, had become a Heaven-sent friend to the impractical settlers. It was my intention to ask the United States Government to donate such a statue, and to ask the Italian Government to donate a statue of John Cabot, and the British, French, and Spanish governments to give statues of great nationals of theirs who had played a part in the early history of Newfoundland. I got so far as to obtain the first of these statues, that of the Portuguese Gaspar Corte Real, and I got our own Newfoundland Government sculptor, the young Dutch artist Hans Melis, to do John Cabot and Sir Wilfred Grenfell. I asked him also to do a symbolical early Newfoundland fisherman. Only three statues are there, but I had hoped to have twenty or more.

6. I had a dream, that I often mentioned in public speeches, of a great Newfoundland Polytechnique, which I thought at first we would build at Fort Pepperrell but afterward thought should be put on the height just north of the university itself, thus in a very general kind of way almost forming part of the university, though not doing so in fact. The Polytechnique would absorb the College of Fisheries, Navigation, and Marine Engineering and Electronics, as well as the College of Technology. The students in it would share some of the athletic and other physical facilities of the university.

7. I thought of establishing a School of Law for the university. My idea was that we would build a new Supreme Court building on Memorial campus; we would also endeavour to arrange for the Law Library of the Law Society to be moved into a new building that would house the School of Law. The library would be expanded from time to time.

I wanted a school of Public and Commercial Administration in which students would receive special training for employment in Government Departments and on Government Boards, as well as for participation in the commercial and industrial life of the province.

8. I tried hard, particularly when my friend Joseph McDaniel, Jr., was its director, to persuade the Ford Foundation to put some money into a project to bring students from all around the world to our College of Fisheries. They never did go for it, but I still think that it is a sound plan.

9. I visited the famous Humboldt-Klockner-Deutz plant in Germany and tried to induce them to come to Newfoundland and engage in the manufacture of small air-cooled diesel engines. These were not being produced anywhere in Canada, and for a while, the directors were quite interested. They even sent a research man to Canada, but he reported that the market was not large enough to support a factory.

10. My mouth watered as I went through the great camera plant of Ernst Leitz, manufacturers of the Leica camera, at Wetzlar, Germany, when I saw the army of men and women assembling the cameras. I did succeed in getting them interested in establishing a branch plant in Canada—but they went to Toronto!

11. I failed to institute a policy of making a really great search for salt and oil in Newfoundland. We made what I know now was little more than a half-hearted effort, but Newfoundland might be much better off than it is today had I pushed such a drilling program much harder twenty years ago.

12. I tried with all my might to get the iron ore pelletizing plant put at City of Wabush, and fought the owners straight down the line, resisting the approaches of important intermediaries sent to me by the Wabush Company. I surrendered only when I was convinced that further insistence on my demand would lose the plant for Canada—that they would build it in the United States instead, if they weren't permitted to build it at tidewater. It was one of the most wracking experiences of my life.

13. I failed to get the Bell Island iron mine restarted. I tried hard enough, but the facts were against us. Bell Island ore is very high in phosphorus, and there are not many steel mills left in the world that can use it. I did succeed in getting one large German steel mill to come and look at it, and they were immensely interested. We offered

them virtually outrageous inducements to take it over and to own and operate it. We worked all through the night, until two o'clock the next morning, with the three special representatives of the company who came over from Germany for the purpose of making an agreement. I had with me several of my Cabinet colleagues and a group of lawyers from the Department of Justice. We came to an agreement at last, and all went home to bed. The three Germans took their copy of the agreement back to Germany for the company's approval and confirmation, and it was some time afterward that I learned why the company's board of directors turned it down. The iron ore that they would be getting from Bell Island would replace much of what they were getting from France, and it was put bluntly to them that if they did this, they would not be allowed to sell any of their finished products in France, which was an important market for them.

14. I tried in every way I could to get the heavy-water plant for Newfoundland; but, Heaven be praised, Nova Scotia beat us!

15. One of my strongest efforts made through my premiership was the attempt to establish an aluminum industry based on low-priced electricity. I negotiated for a couple of years or more with American Metals Climax, and they sent team after team to Newfoundland, as we sent team after team to the United States. They surveyed Bay d'Espoir, Bell Island, Marystown, Come by Chance, Stephenville, and other places, for the most suitable site for a big aluminum plant. The ownership and management of the company changed, but whether that had anything to do with their final decision not to go ahead in Newfoundland, I know not.

16. I tried hard to get a plant that would use petroleum coke from Long Harbour and perhaps Come by Chance for the manufacture of graphite electrodes for sale on both sides of the Atlantic. We negotiated with the well-known United States firm of Air Reduction Co. of New York, owners of a number of subsidiaries, but it all came to naught in the end.

17. Perhaps the most outrageous attempt I ever made for Newfoundland's industrial development was to try to bring the German Volkswagen plant to Newfoundland. I went to Germany three different times in that attempt, and my emissary each time was Dr. Alfred Valdmanis. Hitler, as the world knows, promoted "the people's car", which is what *Volkswagen* means. He collected money from virtually every family in Germany to finance the development and production of the car. The German State that had done all this was

now gone, and there was a strongly held theory that the plant and car were no longer "owned" by anyone—in short, that they were just there for the taking! It will be no news to you that I failed to bring the Volkswagen plant to Newfoundland.

18. I failed equally in my attempt to get a Japanese company to assemble their car in Newfoundland for sale across Canada.

19. I had the idea that, to give very necessary practical help to certain industries that we were establishing (cement, gypsum, plaster board, birch plywood and flooring, and particle board), we should have a specially designed ship, to be owned by the Government but operated by efficient ship's-husbands. This ship would have made a vast difference to the economics of an automobile assembly plant in Newfoundland, for by it the cars could be transported up the St. Lawrence to the very heart of the continent.

20. I failed to make a deal with the Government of the Soviet Union for the partial manufacture, and the assembly, of their Yak jet aircraft in Newfoundland, for sale throughout North America and possibly Central and South America.

21. I failed (but perhaps if I had had another year or so in office, I would not have failed) to establish for Newfoundland, at Marystown, a great ship-building project. I did succeed in interesting one of the world's finest ship-owning and operating companies, Pan-Maritime and Maritime Fruit Carriers, based in Haifa, Israel. The company's two joint managing directors, Ya'acov Meridor and Mila Brener, are two of the finest men I have ever known. I actually got them to Marystown, and I took colleagues with me to New York and to Ottawa for conferences with them. They entered into a contract with us to operate and eventually own the Marystown shipyard; but that utility was to be a mere sideline to a great enterprise—the greatest that Canada ever dreamed of—that these two men of vision wanted to create: a shipyard that would build supertankers of up to 225,000 tons. We were negotiating this project when I left office in January 1972. I hadn't been out of office many weeks before my successors announced that the Israeli firm was out of Marystown, and my dream of setting up Canada's largest shipyard at Marystown died. I will always regret deeply the failure of that great concept, and the measure of my regret is this news item that appeared in the March 26, 1973, issue of *Time* magazine:

In the late 1940s, Mila Brener and Ya'acov Meridor

would have seemed the least likely candidates imaginable for the job of rescuing the sinking British shipbuilding industry. Both men were then Zionists fighting British forces in Palestine—the Russian-born Brener as skipper of a blockade-busting refugee ship, the Polish-born Meridor as deputy commander of the bomb-wielding Irgun underground and sometime inmate of British prison camps in Kenya and Eritrea. But last week, Brener and Meridor's little-known Haifa-based firm, Maritime Fruit Carriers, completed placement of roughly $700 million in orders and options for 26 ships—the largest transaction from a single customer in British history.

The order, which included ten supertankers of 260,000- to 330,000-ton carrying capacity, is only part of Maritime's plan to add a lucrative business in hauling oil to its rich slice of world-wide fruit shipping. Altogether, Maritime now has 23 VLCCs (very large crude carriers) under construction throughout the world, including three 265,000-ton monsters being built in the U.S. by Bethlehem Steel Corp. for $235 million.

All of the tankers will be operated by Maritime's newly formed American subsidiary, General Maritime Corp., which will thus become the second U. S. shipper to operate VLCCs. General expects to announce soon the full composition of its board, which already includes Sol Linowitz, former Ambassador to the Organization of American States, and ex-Secretary of the Navy John Chaffee.

As they do with the rest of their fleet of 48 ships, the two Israelis hope to sell 70% to 80% shares in the tankers to other shippers—who, they believe, will be eager to invest. Meridor and Brener expect that the world energy shortage will more than double demand for supertankers over the next decade, and they foresee soaring construction costs for shippers who try to build their own vessels.

Shrewd timing has characterized Maritime's operations since its inception. In 1953, Brener foresaw the need for fast, modern, refrigerated ships known as "reefers." Meridor, a confident entrepreneur and ex-member of Israel's Parliament, was impressed, but the two moved cautiously, acquiring their first reefer in 1960 and building up an "intelligence network"—a staff of 40 researchers who keep track of world shipping needs and who have predicted temporary declines in shipyard activity. The moment to build at relatively low cost came in June 1963, and the partners ordered from Norway four reefers that were fast enough (21 knots) and big enough (400,000 cu. ft.) to deliver twice as much fruit each season as conventional ships. These "core class" reefers—designed by Israeli engineers and largely financed by government-guaranteed loans—eventually grew into an armada that by 1971 totaled 36. All were then leased to Maritime's main competitor, Sweden's Salen, for $500 million. The agreement gives the two firms control of more than half the world's privately owned refrigerated ships.

Maritime did not rest on its reefers. While Brener, now 51, concentrated on operations and planning, Meridor, 59, sniffed out investors, government subsidies and tax loopholes. The pair also perfected the cost-cutting construction techniques that they learned while assembling their reefer fleet. Today, Meridor estimates, they save from 5% to 25% on the cost of every ship by not going into details like "the color of plastic on the walls of the captain's cabin." Last year Maritime netted profits of $13 million on revenues of $82 million.

The two Israelis could be in a predicament if, for any reason, demand for their ships suddenly declines. Maritime has built its flotilla on a thin money base: only $102 million of equity in a fleet that will soon be worth roughly $1.7 billion. Typically, Maritime covers the down payment on a ship out of government subsidy, leases the vessel while it is still being built, and takes out a mortgage loan to cover the remaining construction costs, with the lease as security.

Meridor and Brener see nothing but smooth sailing ahead. They point out that Maritime has long-term charter contracts that will bring in $2 billion over the next 14 years. The two middle-aged guerrillas also predict that peace will soon come to the Middle East—and that in a few years, even Arab nations will be leasing Maritime's tankers.

22. I didn't really fail to get expansion of the new oil refinery at

Come by Chance, for the time for expansion had not arrived until after my resignation as Premier. But I talked the matter over many times with John Shaheen, and his remarkably able lieutenants Homer White and Roy Furmark, and I passed the information over to my colleagues: the Come by Chance refinery was to be doubled in size, and even then was to keep on going until it reached 600,000 barrels a day. The development of the great port of Come by Chance, including the presence of the three-quarter-mile-long pier, would inevitably attract other development. And my dream of half a dozen satellite towns within twenty or thirty miles of Come by Chance, with an aggregate population of 50,000 at least, will still come true if John Shaheen can get his way.

23. Then there was the orange juice plan! The incredibly rich Captain Ludwig of California spent close to $15 million to establish great orange groves in Chiriqui Province in the Republic of Panama. I visited the orange groves on three occasions, taking with me on my final visit Mr. Dick Winter of St. John's, a young businessman who is up to his chin in the bottling business. Once a fortnight, throughout the year, a Golden Eagle oil tanker departs from the Panama seaport of Colón for Holyrood, thirty miles from St. John's. My thought was the essence of simplicity: the large steel drums of frozen orange-juice concentrate would be put into refrigerated compartments on the tankers, delivered to Holyrood, taken to a plant where the juice would be thawed out, and put in bottles or cans for delivery to the customers. It would have made orange juice incomparably more plentiful, and very much cheaper, than milk in Newfoundland. It was a good idea, and it would have succeeded but for the fact that Ludwig's whole vast scheme collapsed in utter failure and all those millions of dollars were lost. It seems that the Panama groves could not produce the uniform quality of orange juice that could sell consistently. I was a disappointed man over this particular failure, for I had pictured generous supplies of low-cost orange juice becoming available throughout Newfoundland and Labrador.

Failures: twenty-three in twenty-three years. It wouldn't be too bad if that were the whole story. But these twenty-three aren't even 10 per cent of the total; they are only the most serious ones. There are those in Newfoundland who would paint a far more damaging—and sinister—picture. There's no room for doubt; I must be placed at the head of the list. I am guilty of more failures and mistakes than Alderdice, Monroe, Squires, Morris, and Bond, the other elected prime ministers before me in this century, all put together.

18

– *And Some That Did*

All growth is a leap in the dark, a spontaneous, unpremeditated act without benefit of experience.

Henry Miller

I prefer the errors of enthusiasm to the indifference of wisdom.

Thomas Carlyle

It is not the going out of port, but the coming in, that determines the success of a voyage.

Henry Ward Beecher

There were more than 1,200 different settled communities in Newfoundland on the day that I became Premier. Hundreds of them were tiny coves with fewer than fifty families. There weren't a dozen places with as many as 8,000 souls. Virtually all of the places in Newfoundland and Labrador stretched along the 6,000 miles of deeply indented coastline, and you could count on the fingers of your two hands the places that were out of sight and sound of the Atlantic Ocean. You could reach perhaps 300 of them by road. For the rest, the sea was the only roadway; or you could walk through the trees, over the barrens and bogs, trying always to keep the sea in sight most of the time. There was one small seaplane on the Island—the one that I had used while campaigning for Confederation—and there were lots of places that you could get into by her. But the great majority of the communities were physically as isolated, as remote, as they had been centuries before.

The price that people paid for this isolation was a heavy one. It had been growing more difficult for little places to get a share of the pitifully small number of teachers (only 2,400) who were formally qualified to teach. The proportion of one-room schools with uncertified teachers condemned tens of thousands of Newfoundland's youngsters to a state of education little better than illiteracy. Trained nurses had become difficult to find; doctors, all but impossible. It was not easy for the sick to be in a cove of fifty or even a hundred families with no doctor or nurse and no hospital nearer than fifty or a hundred miles—or even two hundred miles—with rough seas or rough, roadless country between. Lumsden, for example, lies north of Bonavista Bay on the other side of Cape Freels. On a fair day, a fisherman's small motor-driven fishing boat would take a patient in an hour to the cottage hospital at Brookfield. On days when the Atlantic was very angry around Cape Freels, they didn't take sick patients by boat; they carried them by hand on improvised stretchers over the bogs and marshes, through the stunted spruce, over or around the rocks and boulders, the eighteen miles to the hospital at

24. As premier, J. R. S. averaged five hours a night, seven nights a week, at work in this chair at his home.

25. Reading to four of his grandchildren – Jane, Dale, Lorraine, and Joey II

26. Plenty of help to turn a first sod

27. Campaigning

28. Lunch break on the campaign trail with Prime Minister St. Laurent

29. With Queen Elizabeth II at Gander

30. Greeting Mrs. Eleanor Roosevelt

31. John Diefenbaker and Lord Thomson of Fleet

32. Lunching with Premier Kosygin at Grand Falls

33. With Justice Minister Trudeau and Prime Minister Pearson

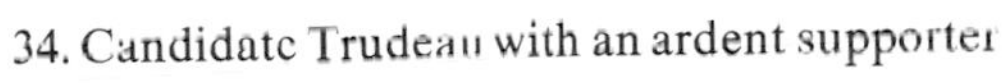

34. Candidate Trudeau with an ardent supporter

35. Moscow, here we come!

36. Comparing notes with Fidel Castro, May, 1973

Brookfield. Twelve men would have to go—three teams of four-man stretcher-bearers taking turns carrying the patient. That was no picnic on days when the weather was so tempestuous that you couldn't go by water. No wonder people came out and kissed the road that I punched through to Lumsden!

This curse of isolation had darkened Newfoundland for generations. It had created, and time had strengthened, psychological barriers between settlement and settlement, bay and bay, coast and coast. Only a road across the full breadth of the Island, linked to a network of regional highways and local tributary roads, would bind our people together and make them one.

It took us fifteen years to build the great paved Newfoundland section of the Trans-Canada Highway, and Canada paid $92 million of the $120 million that it cost to put there. (Our province's share, $28 million, came to more than Newfoundland had spent on roads in the fifty years before Confederation.) Over 12,000 men got jobs building the road, and they drew $28 million in wages.

We had built and rebuilt more than 5,000 miles of roads between the time I became Premier and January 18, 1972, when I resigned. This included the 300-mile highway from Deer Lake to St. Anthony, opening up the great northwest coast of the Island, the part of Newfoundland that Canon Richards aptly called the Forgotten Coast. All the settlements of the great Notre Dame Bay had to be linked, except for the islands—and even some of these have been linked by causeway. The project included a highway from Gambo all the way along the north side of Bonavista Bay to Cape Freels, and from there all the way to Gander Bay, and thence back to the Trans-Canada Highway at Gander. It involved building "the Road to the Isles" from Lewisporte to Twillingate on New World Island. The whole south side of Trinity Bay had to have its cowpath widened and straightened, resurfaced, and much of it paved. The road around Conception Bay had to be similarly improved, and long stretches built or rebuilt from Carbonear to Grates Cove, where it connected with the Trinity South highway. The great coast south of St. John's, on the way to Trepassey, and on to St. Shotts, was all but completely without a highway. There had been a branch railroad along that shore, but it had fallen victim to the economy drives forced on the Government in the early 1930s by the sheer weight of poverty and debt. There were sections of the alleged highway where, for eight and ten miles, the only visible sign of a road was the former railway roadbed, with the trees and bushes crowding in on both sides and leaving a space so narrow that only one car could pass over it at a time. If a car came toward you, there was no alternative but for one of you to back up for miles, until you came to a place where both cars could pass. It was one of the great adventures left in eastern North America, to go the ninety-six miles from St. John's to Trepassey. Today it is a very good highway, much of it paved.

The network includes a road on the east side of Placentia Bay that connects at St. Shotts with that other highway, making now a great road circuit from there back to St. John's. And the great Burin Peninsula, and the long west side of Placentia Bay, and the great Fortune Bay, and the wonderfully beautiful Port-au-Port Peninsula, and the incredibly beautiful Bay of Islands, and that part of Newfoundland which is one of the most breath-taking beauty spots of the North American continent, Bonne Bay—all are linked by road; not always the smoothest or straightest paved highways, but at all events *roads*, enabling people to go almost anywhere in Newfoundland by car or bus. We even connected the northern half of Newfoundland to the southern half by building a highway across the middle of the Island in a straight line from Bishops Falls to the head of Bay d'Espoir.

Can there be another part of North America where, in twenty-three years, so vast an improvement has been made in road transportation in terms of mileage built, the proportion of the population that has been rescued from isolation and made, for the first time in centuries, one people! If Confederation with Canada had accomplished nothing else in Newfoundland, it would be the great miracle in our nearly five centuries of history. We spent over $500 million to build these roads, and nearly one-fifth of that immense sum came directly from Ottawa. The rest of it, though it came out of Newfoundland's own Treasury, must surely be credited to Canada as well.

Dozens, maybe hundreds, of times in public speeches that I made while opening new schools, hospitals, or roads, I used to pose a problem for my audience. "Our needs for roads"—or for schools, or hospitals, or electric lighting, or municipal improvements, as the case may be on each occasion—"are appalling, frightening." And then I would describe the needs, not only of the area where I was speaking, but of others all about the province. "It would be possible to get these roads if we had nothing else to build but roads; if we could spend the bulk of our money to satisfy these needs. We could do it in the next ten years, possibly eight or even seven years—if that's all we had to do."

And then, of course, would come the punch-line. "But if we give the people the roads they need, and use up our money doing it, what will happen to people's health when the hospitals are not built, and the clinics, and the nursing stations? What will the children's fate be if we don't build the schools?" That wasn't just rhetoric or the weasel words of a deceiving politician. It was a severely truthful and realistic description of Newfoundland's problem. People who had done without so much for so long before Confederation, and didn't seem to miss these amenities then, now clamoured and agitated, with increasing insistence everywhere, for instant roads, instant paving, instant snow-clearing in the winter, instant hospitals, instant schools, instant electricity, instant water and sewer systems, instant paving of local community roads, and instant everything else. No sooner had a road been built, and the people of settlement after settlement connected to it, and no sooner had people bought trucks, pick-ups, and cars, than they set up a determined demand for snow clearing in the winter. And after snow clearing had been introduced, and the dust nuisance and wear and tear on their vehicles were costing them discomfort and money, the quick demand was for paving. But that demand would occupy only part of people's minds and time—they never seemed to lack the energy to demand all the other things as well; and of course, they wanted them yesterday.

I took this province-wide clamour for improvement to be the greatest compliment that anyone had ever paid me; for I had for years, before Confederation and after, saturated Newfoundland with my propaganda for better things for our people. I had used whatever skill I possessed to plant the "spark of divine discontent"; and, of course, above everything else, it was the greatest compliment of all to Confederation. I don't think that people gave much thought to the costs, or to the source of the money, or to the size of the public debt, or to the proportion of the money spent that came from Ottawa. Every cove and harbour in the province, hearing on the radio or seeing on television the improvements in this bay or that, wanted the factories or mills, the hospitals or clinics, the schools or roads, the water and sewer systems, and the electric lights that other places were getting. Each individual settlement that didn't get these things had a sort of unspoken feeling that it was the only place in the province not getting them!

There were 9,022 passenger cars in 1949 and 104,873 in 1972. There were 4,443 trucks in 1949 and 22,559 in 1972. There were 110 trailers in 1949 and 10,891 in 1972. There were 18,438 driver's licences in 1949 and 180,000 in 1972. The Government's revenue from motor vehicle and driver's licences was $337,095 in 1949 and $6,490,861 in 1972.

All oil companies in Newfoundland employed 500 persons in 1949 and over 3,000 in 1972. Close to 25,000 persons find employment today in Newfoundland, driving trucks, buses, and taxis, and working in gas and service stations and garages. That's an increase of 20,000 jobs resulting from the road program—and, of course, from Confederation.

Over 800 settled communities have been connected to this network of roads—the most powerful thrust against physical isolation, as radio, electricity, and television were the most overwhelming blow struck at psychological remoteness.

In the first year of Confederation, there were 18,590 income tax returns, and 111,698 in 1969. The total income declared was $57 million in 1950 and $675 million in 1969. The income tax paid was $4½ million in 1950 and $92 million in 1969. Capital and repair expenditure on buildings rose from $32 million in 1949 to $800 million in 1970. Sales of gasoline went from 5½ million gallons to 61 million gallons by 1970.

On Confederation Day, we had 66,000 dwellings—today, it's just short of 100,000. Precisely one-half (50.3 per cent) of them had electric light in 1949, and today the proportion is over 97 per cent. In the twenty years before Confederation, a total of $66 million had been spent to build houses and do major repairs. In the twenty years after Confederation, the figure was $551 million. It's close to three-quarters of a billion by now.

In 1949, we had fifty-one hotels, motels, tourist homes, and cabins, with a total of 740 beds. Now there are 232 such establishments, with 3,300 beds. Tourists spent $2½ million in 1949; in 1971, they spent $77 million. There were 133 restaurants and snackbars in 1949; in 1970, there were over 700, giving jobs to over 2,000 persons.

Telephones have increased in number from 16,295 in 1949 to 141,000 today; telephone employees from 810 to 1800; their wages from $1.3 million a year to $12 million. About $120 million of new capital has been spent to give Newfoundland an efficient telephone system.

There were only twenty-two places in the province on Confederation Day that had even the most elementary form of municipal or local government. Today, there are 274, and they have a combined population of 422,000, as against the 85,000 within municipalities in 1949. Total revenue of the municipalities in 1949 was $1 million a year. Today, it is $34 million. Their combined assets in 1949 were worth $2½ million. Today, the value is $160 million. There were only eight places in the new province that had water and sewer services in 1949: St. John's, Harbour Grace, Carbonear, Placentia, Heart's Content, Grand Falls, Corner Brook, and Buchans. There are ninety-eight places now with water and/or sewer services.

Since Confederation, Newfoundlanders have spent $1 billion dollars on the purchase of automobiles. The rate of increase in car sales has been much greater than in any other province.

Wage rates have risen perhaps more precipitately than elsewhere in Canada since 1949. These examples may show the revolution in Newfoundland:

	1949	1972
Plumber	$.71	$4.55 -4.90
Electrician	.90	4.23 -4.73
Motor mechanic	.70	3.30
Municipal labourer	.70	2.57
Municipal truck driver	.75	2.77
Male clerk	$44 /week	$131 /week
Papermill labourer	1.00	3.85
Woods labourer	.68	2.54
Papermill machine-tender	—	6.56
Mine mucker	.92	3.18
Railway section-man	.86	3.00
Railway blacksmith	1.22	4.30
Railway despatcher	$355 /month	$950 /month
Coastal boat seaman	$155 /month	$485 /month

Just over 137,000 children received the family allowance in 1949, to a total of $7¼ million. In 1971, there were 209,000 children, and they received $17 million. In the twenty-three years from 1949 to 1971, Newfoundland's children received a grand total of $332 million!

In the last year before Confederation, there were 2,999 old-age pensioners in Newfoundland. To be eligible, the recipient must have passed his seventy-fifth birthday, and if his wife had passed her seventy-fifth birthday as well, he might receive the pension. The pension was $30 each quarter for the couple, or $120 a year. If a man had no wife, the pension was $18 a quarter. People didn't automatically receive the pension even when they qualified by age and need—it depended upon the amount of money available for distribution. Many an old man began to receive the pension when he was nearer eighty. He would get his application in, and then wait for some other pensioner to die.

Overnight, with Confederation, came a pension of $30 *a month* for a man and another $30 a month for his wife, at age seventy—a jump from $120 a year to $720. The amount has been going up ever since, and the age going down: the pension is at a minimum of $100 a month or $2,400 a year for a couple, and the eligible age is sixty-five. From Confederation Day to the end of 1971, by which time the number of pensioners had risen to over 32,000, the total amount that had been received by them was $351 million.

The two amounts, family allowances and old-age pensions, totalled $683 million. In the same period, if there had been no Confederation, that figure would have amounted to about $10 million. The difference between the two amounts (over half a billion dollars) brought comfort and ease of mind to tens of thousands of people—and millions of dollars of profit to Newfoundland shopkeepers and merchants.

And there were Canada's generous payments under the Veterans' Charter; the scores of millions received in Newfoundland in unemployment insurance; the other scores of millions of additional income received by railroaders, coastal boat crews, airport workers; the further scores of millions from higher salary scales of thousands of federal employees; and at least a dozen other new sources of income from Ottawa.

Put it all together, and deduct from the total the amount that Ottawa got back from various sources of federal revenue in Newfoundland, direct and indirect, and the net result of it all was that Newfoundlanders were better off by a figure that ran into the *billions*.

I get particular pleasure remembering the phenomenal rise of Eastern Provincial Airways, which is now the third largest airline in Canada and still growing. I became acquainted with it when it had one small plane, the one in which I campaigned for Confederation.

As Premier, I persuaded my Cabinet to back EPA with loans amounting to a total of $5 or $6 million, and I took the initiative in bringing about the absorption of Maritime Central Airways by EPA. This involved my conversations with both airlines and the Newfoundland Government's advancing the money that had to change hands. Today, as I write early in 1973, EPA has nine magnificent passenger planes worth $20 million and is expecting to add two Boeing 737 jets, at a cost of over $6 million each, bringing the value of its aircraft to a total of $32 million. The airline has over 500 employees who receive a total of $5 million in wages. EPA in 1972 carried 380,000 passengers into, out of, and within Newfoundland, the three Maritime Provinces, and the Province of Quebec, and it expects to carry 500,000 passengers in 1973.

I foresaw the phenomenal increase in the numbers of cars, buses, trucks, and other gasoline-driven vehicles that would inevitably follow the construction of roads, and I became determined that Newfoundland should have its own oil refinery. I tried to get Imperial Oil, Irving Oil, British American Oil, and others to start an oil refinery, and offered concessions as an inducement. None of them was interested, until I negotiated with a man who wasn't operating in Canada at all. This was John Shaheen, of New York, who was then the most important shareholder of Ultramar of England, who in turn controlled Golden Eagle Oil. He agreed to build a small refinery at Holyrood, on Conception Bay, and in return we agreed that the Government would purchase from that refinery all its petroleum product needs for a period of twenty years. The prices were to be set by the wholesale tank-car prices obtaining in Nova Scotia from time to time. The arrangement has worked well, and the refinery has doubled its production since its early start. It was this transaction that brought Shaheen into Newfoundland and led to the building of the enormous oil refinery at Come by Chance. I'll have more to say about that later.

I had been hearing for years of the hydro-electric power potential of Bay d'Espoir, at the head of Fortune Bay. I gathered together whatever reports there were in existence, including the report of a survey that Bowaters had in their possession. In addition to that, we had a new survey made; and as a result of it all, we became convinced that about a million horsepower could be produced. But we had to have customers for the power! That was the rub, as I soon found out. The smallest development there could be, to be economically sound, would turn out 70,000 horsepower; but where were we going to find customers for that much power? It sounds like the last word in the ridiculous, now, to ask the question; but it didn't sound a bit ridiculous then. If a papermill were built, it would consume about 30,000 horsepower. The United Towns Electric Company agreed to take 10,000 horsepower. The two big paper companies at Corner Brook and Grand Falls agreed to take 20,000 horsepower each, but not together: one agreed, but then the other wouldn't; then the second agreed, but the first one pulled out. We just couldn't get the consumption up to 70,000. We had given BRINCO the rights to Bay d'Espoir, and the company tried hard to get the project going. The killer was the cost of the long transmission line, but we agreed to build the line and charge BRINCO nothing for it until after the enterprise had begun to make money. Even that didn't do the trick. Great oaks do truly from little acorns grow, for today Bay d'Espoir is producing 600,000 horsepower of electricity; we have built a great transmission line from end to end of the Island, with important branch-lines as well; we have spent a total of $270 million to do it, including an ambitious program of rural electrification. Several thousand men worked for several years on the construction and installations.

I have never, since the coming of Confederation, had abundant enthusiasm for Newfoundland's farming possibilities, as far as root crops and grains are concerned. But I became convinced that we could become entirely self-supporting in the production of eggs, broilers, and other poultry products. I became equally convinced—not surprisingly!—that we could become even better than self-supporting in the production of pork. And of course, if we could, then we should! Well, we are self-supporting in eggs. Indeed, we have even exported eggs to the mainland of Canada. We have come up from a production of fewer than a million dozen eggs a year to a figure close to eight or nine million dozen; and we are increasing our broiler production steadily.

I was particularly keen that we should build a pork production program, and we did. We are far, far short of being self-supporting in it, but the raising of hogs has increased markedly.

These programs required, between them, the establishment of at least five enterprises that didn't exist before I began: an animal and poultry feed mill (there wasn't one in the province), a very modern hog-breeding establishment, a hog and cattle abattoir, a poultry-processing plant, and an egg-grading and processing plant. It cost quite a few dollars, but we now have all five of them in operation—each of them the first of its kind in Newfoundland.

The Marystown shipyard! Here my feelings are a mixture of satisfaction and disappointment. I am satisfied because it is a magnificent shipyard, with a magnificent general manager, John Rannie (who built the *Queen Elizabeth* in Scotland), that is giving jobs and new skills to Newfoundlanders. I am disappointed because for reasons that leave me bitter, I didn't get the huge expansion of the shipyard into one that would build big ships of up to a quarter of a million tons. The shipyard also is a subject on which I must express a word of cordial commendation to my successor, Premier Frank Moores. He has brought in a magnificent program whereby the Government will build draggers for the deep-sea fishery and rent (or sell) them to the various fish plants that may need them. I am chagrined that I didn't think of doing it.

Mention of fish plants reminds me of the considerable satisfaction I got from bringing to Newfoundland a fine Canadian company, National Sea Products of Halifax, to reactivate and considerably enlarge the Ross-Steers plant in St. John's.

I have often said that God must have had Newfoundland in mind when He saw to it that airplanes were invented. But there had to be airports or, at the very least, landing strips, if Newfoundland was to share amply in the blessing of aviation. My preliminary program was for the building of landing strips at St. Anthony, Springdale, Fogo Island, the Bonavista area, the Burin Peninsula area, the Bay d'Espoir area, a suitable spot along the southwest Coast, one at Port au Choix, on the Northwest Coast, and at least two in Southern Labrador. We have new air strips now at Winterland, Port au Choix, Springdale, and Bonavista.

"All work and no play makes Jack a dull boy," so they say; so we instituted, first, a program of building parks and camping and picnic sites across the province. We must surely lead all of Canada in the sharp increase in the number of such attractions. As I retired from public life, I could (and did!) point with happy pride to the forty-six parks and 1,335 camping and picnic sites that had been created since Confederation Day. Last year, more than 1,753,000 people enjoyed these recreation areas. Thousands of them were tourists who visited our province from all across Canada and the United States and other countries too.

Of course, tourists couldn't be expected to depend exclusively on public parks for overnight accommodation. I myself had done so long before, in New York City, so I knew that this would be a shaky foundation for a tourist industry. They had to have hotels; and after negotiating with one hotel chain after another without success, I did at last prevail upon John Adams to operate a chain of Holiday Inns if the Government built them. We built splendid Holiday Inn hotels in St. John's, Clarenville, Grand Falls, and Corner Brook. We also got the Holiday Inn people to take over management of a hotel that had been built at Port-aux-Basques under Government guarantee but was failing badly. The five hotels have flourished, and they are now paying back to the Government around $1 million a year. I don't know what would have happened to our tourist industry if we hadn't built those hotels.

We had to come to the financial rescue of a group that was working hard to get a big new skating and hockey rink for St. John's; but having undertaken to do so for St. John's, being primarily "Her Majesty's Outport Government", we had to do at least as much to help eager groups to get rinks in their communities. In fact, we did more for them; and as I left office in 1972, I had the comfortable knowledge that we had helped to provide rinks at Harbour Grace, Clarenville, Bonavista, St. Anthony, Port-aux-Basques, Channel, Lewisporte, Gander, Bell Island, Happy Valley, Baie Verte, and Springdale, and that others were under construction or about to commence construction.

But all of this—roads, schools, airports, parks, hotels, skating rinks, and the rest—would be futile, a very dead loss, if the health of the people were not looked after; and with men such as my friend and colleague Dr. James M. McGrath, and his close associate and departmental colleague the incomparable Dr. Leonard Miller, there to inspire, lead, guide, and goad us, there was little chance that I would overlook the matter. We built new hospitals at Carbonear, Fogo Island, Gander, Grand Falls, Baie Verte, St. Anthony, Happy Valley, and Labrador City (both in Labrador), Corner Brook, Stephenville Crossing, Channel—Port-aux-Basques, Burgeo, and Harbour Bretton; and nursing stations at Trepassey and several other places. We made major enlargements and improvements to the General Hospital at St. John's and to outport hospitals at Old Perlican, Brookfield, Corner Brook, Grand Bank, and Placentia.

And the Children's Health Centre! This surely must be one of the most glorious achievements of Confederation. Certainly, it represents a battle royal that I had to fight. It seemed to me that the whole medical profession, with two or three exceptions, was opposed. Even the medical men in our own Department of Health were opposed. Almost to a man, they wanted a wing added to the General Hospital to look after the children. One man was my immovable advisor and inspiration, my Party colleague in the House, the popular pediatrician Dr. Clifford Joy, Member for Harbour Main. He, with great patience and skill, educated me about children's hospitals. When I wanted advice from outside the province, he gave me, first, the name of the famous Dr. Charles Janeway of the great Children's Hospital at Boston and then the names of the great pediatricians who were running children's hospitals across Canada, as well as the name of the chief officer of the Canadian pediatricians' body. I wrote to all of them, asking whether they would advise a new wing to the General Hospital or a separate children's hospital? I asked Dr. Janeway if he would come down to St. John's to look over the situation. That magnanimous man sacrificed his Christmas vacation to come to untropical Newfoundland and spend a week with me. He talked to the doctors, particularly those of the Department of Health; he looked at the large building at Fort Pepperrell that the Americans had used as a hospital and that was now lying empty and idle. He advised me strongly to have a separate children's hospital, and he gave me the name of Sir Alan Moncrieff, head of the famous Children's Hospital in London and Britain's most distinguished pediatrician. I went over to London to see Sir Alan, and put the whole question before him. Without hesitation, he advised me to go for the separate children's hospital. So I was well armed when I brought the matter for the decision of my Cabinet! I was glad that my dear friend McGrath had backed me.

And so we got our Janeway Children's Health Centre in St. John's, and a pearl of great price it is. I invited Dr. Janeway himself to come down on August 9, 1966, to open the magnificent new hospital. It has 280 beds and cost $7 million. There are 140 doctors on the medical staff or otherwise closely associated with the hospital. Other hospital staff amount to 640 persons. To the end of last year, 35,800 children had been admitted for treatment in the hospital, and there were in addition 173,000 out-patients and emergency visits. It was the first Government hospital in Newfoundland whose management we decided to place under a Board of Directors consisting of able, public-spirited private citizens, appointed by us. The Hon. Campbell Macpherson, former Lieutenant-Governor, was the first chairman of the board, and he couldn't have given the task more loving care if it had been his own personal property! Mr. James J. Green, Q.C., former Leader of the Opposition, has, I am happy to see, taken on the heavy duties of chairman since April 1, 1972.

I have had only one disappointment in connection with the Janeway Centre. I reminded my Cabinet that children from all over the province would be referred to the Janeway, and that the parents of these children, especially the mothers, would not be very happy to have their children in a hospital so far away from them as to make visiting too expensive for them. I suggested that we erect beside the hospital a simple, though well-built, hotel type of residence where the mothers could board and do their own simple cooking, all at the lowest possible price. The Cabinet so ordered, and the buildings were erected and equipped. To my surprise and chagrin, I discovered, years afterward, that the buildings were not in fact being used for that purpose, but for the accommodation of members of the hospital staff! I realize the need for that latter kind of accommodation, but I have never been happy over this particular development.

I cannot leave the subject of public health without at least a reference to my Children's Health Plan. This, which was entirely my own personal idea, I had no difficulty whatever in getting my Cabinet to adopt. Under it, all the children of the province were to have free hospital care. We brought it into effect in 1957, and in 1958 we expanded the scheme to include free doctor's care for all children under sixteen while they were in hospital. We were the only province in Canada to have such a plan. It was well before the National Hospital plan was instituted by the Government of Canada, and even longer before Medicare was brought in for the whole of Canada. We were unique.

I think that without excessive immodesty I may boast of Newfoundland's record in developing the arts. We have certainly led the whole of Canada, if not in absolute terms, then most certainly in the rate of acceleration. We restored the Newfoundland Museum, which had, to their shame, been vandalized by the insensitive Commission of Government. We put a splendid new army, navy, and air museum in the Confederation Building, devoting the whole of the top floor of the tower to the purpose. We built a magnificent new art gallery in the Arts and Cultural Centre in St. John's. We instituted an annual arts and letters contest that has, with its exhibition and cash awards, been a very distinct encouragement to the swelling number concerned with the cultural side of life.

Long years before I became Premier, I had resolved that if I ever found myself in a position of authority, I would give Newfoundland an archives enterprise. I had done too much historical research not to know Newfoundland's dire need for such a facility. I am proud and happy with our splendid Provincial Archives in the Colonial Building, where Burnham Gill (whose New England forebears came to Newfoundland nearly 200 years ago) and his skilled staff are giving Newfoundland rare service.

Joining with the rest of Canada to celebrate Canada's 100th birthday, we built the superb Arts and Culture Centre beside Memorial University. The theatre of this building is reputed to be among the three best in the whole of Canada. The building cost about $7 million to erect and equip. We also joined with the Lundrigan and Bowater firms to build a magnificent Arts and Culture Centre at Corner Brook. A surprising feature of that centre was a large indoor swimming pool, and it has turned out to be one of the most favoured spots in the whole of western Newfoundland.

I went to Expo '67, where I joined the millions who admired the two beautiful Czechoslovakian exhibition buildings, and a lot of other buildings as well. I hungered and thirsted after them, and I pulled every string I knew how to pull to obtain some of them. I did get the Czechoslovakian buildings, and most of the equipment in them, and the Yugoslav building as well. Mayor Jean Drapeau of Montreal hated to see them go and exerted all his famous guile to get me to release them back to him, but I stood firm. I had them taken apart, piece by piece, with tender loving care, loaded carefully aboard a ship, and brought to Newfoundland. I had them re-erected, one Czechoslovakian building at Grand Falls, the second at Gander, and the Yugoslavian building at Grand Bank. They had to be winterized and heated, and in other respects improved, and I will never forget the day I opened the big indoor swimming pool that we installed in the building at Gander. Five arts and culture centres in a small province that would surely have committed to the mental hospital anyone who had had the gall, twenty years before, to suggest the starting of even one in poor Newfoundland. Could we afford the $10 million that we spent to give Newfoundlanders those five beautiful centres of art and culture? Rather ask: could we have afforded not to do so!

Some of these accomplishments of Confederation are very great indeed, but none of them is the greatest. The greatest is the disappearance forever of the old benumbing sense of inferiority that had Newfoundlanders in its grip for so long. We have a new sense of pride and confidence. Bigness of concept frightens us no longer. Where we gasped at the thought of a million dollars as the cost of a project, we are mostly unconcerned about the costs of projects that run to ten, fifty, a hundred, two hundred, ten hundred millions.

It can be done, it must be done: so, simply, Newfoundlanders now demand, and will never again be willing to do without, constant, unending development and advance.

I tried, in the long years before Confederation, to propagandize our people into that frame of mind, that habit of thought; but never did I think that I would live to see it become a fact of life in Newfoundland.

And this is Confederation's greatest glory.

"Now I lay me down to sleep!"

The Moncton Daily Times

19

So You Don't Believe in Miracles

If anybody calls
Say I am designing St. Paul's.

E. C. Bentley

In revolutions men fall and rise. Long before this war is over, much as you hear me praised now, you may hear me cursed and insulted.

General W. T. Sherman

Perhaps the craziest thing that happened in Newfoundland was Sir William Whiteway's decision in 1880 to build a railroad across the Island, 600 miles from St. John's to Port-aux-Basques. The whole population of the country then was under 200,000. Not a soul lived in any part of the route of the proposed railway—nothing but caribou, small game, birds, and trout.

The total revenue of the Government was under $2 million a year—but it was going to cost the total revenue of the Government for six years to build it: $11½ million. His opponents said that Whiteway was insane or, worse, a traitor to Newfoundland. He was going to plunge Newfoundland into irretrievable bankruptcy. And for what? For a railway that would run nowhere and serve no one!

Perhaps our decision to create a university in Newfoundland was just as crazy, but if the results are as favourable to Newfoundland as were those of the railway, it may turn out to be just the crazy sort of thing that's good for us.

They thought the railway would cost about $12 million to build. By the time Confederation arrived, it had cost over $50 million. So with our university. We knew that it was going to cost about $12 million—extraordinary coincidence—but as with the railway, the cost has escalated to an amount that will be over $100 million not long after this book appears.

To create Memorial University was virtually our first decision after Confederation. I had been advocating it for several years and had no difficulty at all in obtaining the ready support of my colleagues; they were as keen on it as I. We already had a small junior college—Memorial University College—that had been built, just after the close of the First World War, as one of the two memorials to our war dead. By 1950, it had grown to accommodate 300 students per term.

In 1972, our university had 6,960 full-time undergraduates, 1,545 part-time students on campus and 1,722 off campus, with 621 full-time graduate students—10,848 in all. In the present year, the total enrolment is expected to be 12,000, making Memorial the seventeenth in size, by student enrolment, among the sixty-four degree-granting institutions of Canada. The total budget for 1972 was $23 million; it is $27 million for 1973. From 1962 to 1972, Memorial had a total of 7,093 graduates.

On Confederation Day 1949, there were not 250 university graduates in the whole of Newfoundland, except for a handful of medical doctors and lawyers. Memorial, every year now, graduates far more Newfoundlanders than the number of graduates that Newfoundland had altogether throughout her entire pre-Confederation history.

One of the greatest joys that I have known was that of introducing for Memorial what was Canada's only project for giving free tuition to all students. We began by making tuition free for the fourth, third, and second years, with the intention of adding the first-year students as time advanced and as we could afford the cost. Then, in addition, we paid an allowance, which I insisted on calling salary, to the students in the third, fourth, and fifth years. This was a modest monthly amount of $50 for those whose homes were in or near St. John's and $100 for those outside. Our plan here, too, was to pay the salary to the whole of the student body in the course of time. We were the only university in Canada, or, I think, the United States, where this plan was in effect. We were intensely proud of it, for our belief was then, and mine is now, that the welfare of Newfoundland requires that every young man or woman capable of benefiting adequately from it should be entitled, by right, to an education of the best quality available. I wouldn't limit that principle to Newfoundland, either.

Alexei Kosygin, Premier of the Soviet Union, applauded me heartily when I told him of our program, but he told me that I was wrong in saying that we were the only university in North America with free tuition and salaries. He had just come to Newfoundland from Cuba, and he told me that Fidel Castro had introduced the same plan into the universities there.

The spirit was willing, but the flesh – our Treasury – was weak. We had to modify the plan and postpone extension. The plan has been largely wiped out since my retirement from public life.

The frightening cost of medical education had more than a little to do with the decision to modify the free tuition and salaries program. I brought the great medical leader, Lord Brain, from England to advise us on the question of establishing a medical college at the university. He and a number of other authoritative voices advocated its establishment, and we went forward with the plan, at pretty shattering cost. The first medical doctors were graduated from Memorial in 1973. For a long, lonely time the only supporter I had for my proposal to start the medical college was Dr. Gordon Thomas, chief of the Grenfell Hospital at St. Anthony.

In an attempt to solve at least partially the problem of a serious falling-off in the supply of medical doctors, before the Medical College was started, we had introduced a Newfoundland Government scheme of subsidizing the education of Newfoundland students in medicine and dentistry in universities outside Newfoundland. I think that it was the only such scheme in Canada. Some 304 young Newfoundlanders embraced the plan and entered Memorial for their pre-medical or dental training. They had to agree in advance that upon graduation and internship, they would serve in Newfoundland for at least three years and go where the Government wished them to go. If they failed to complete these conditions, so it was agreed, they would have to pay back the Government's outlay on them. By this scheme, we managed to get 124 doctors* and thirty-five dentists† for Newfoundland. Over a period of eleven years, we paid out about $2,000 and then $2,500 to each student yearly, for a total cost of $2½ million for the whole program.

Our College of Engineering has been an outstanding success, too, and our first engineers will graduate next year.

It is stunning to remember that the Newfoundland Government's total expenditure on all forms of education in the last year before Confederation was one-ninth of what we are spending on the university alone this year!

Such comparisons are numerous. School buses carrying tens of thousands of students more than 3 million miles a year are costing the Government exactly twice as much as all education cost us in 1949.

On the day I became Premier, we had 2,424 teachers in the new province, and they received $2 million in salaries—an average of $862 a year. Today, we have 7,200 teachers, and their salaries came last year to roughly $59 million—an average of about $8,200 per teacher.

*Of whom seventy-three are now practising in the province and fifteen are taking postgraduate courses before returning to Newfoundland.
†Of whom fourteen are still in training.

In my first year as Premier, the Government spent $3 million on education—in my last year, the figure was $135 million.

I don't know whether I am slightly less, or slightly more, proud of our College of Fisheries, Navigation, and Marine Engineering and Electronics than I am of our university. The College, which Dr. D. L. Cooper and Dr. William F. Hampton helped me to establish and Dr. Ray Barrett has carried to such a superb success, is incomparably the best institution of its kind in the Western Hemisphere. Perhaps only Japan and the Soviet Union have better colleges of this kind. The faculty have been brought from all around the world and some of the students, too, though the overwhelming majority are Newfoundlanders. Since I opened it in January 1964, 25,522 students have registered at the college. Dr. Barrett tells me that they expect to have a registration of 4,000 students this year. It is costing the Government three and a half times as much each year to operate this one college as all education cost us in the first year of Confederation—$13.8 million.

In technical and trade education, our leap forward exceeded anything of its kind that has happened anywhere else in Canada! We were the first province to seize hold of the Canadian Government's offer of generous help to establish new trade schools. We built seventeen of them before I resigned, and the magnificent College of Technology. These nineteen schools have cost us $40 million to build and equip. In 1972, they employed over 600 teachers and instructors, with construction of several of the newer schools not quite complete; the total student body was 19,000. Since we built them, 62,000 students have passed through them. These students received cash allowances of $1½ million last year and a total of over $15 million since the program began.

One of the things that appealed strongly to me was that these nineteen institutions were not all in St. John's. Two of them were, but there was one at Bell Island, two in the populous Conception Bay, one in Trinity Bay, one in Bonavista Bay, three in Notre Dame Bay, one in White Bay, one in Labrador, one in Bay of Islands, one in St. George's Bay, two in Placentia Bay, and one each at Gander, Grand Falls, and Port-aux-Basques. Newfoundlanders who have not been home for years will rub their eyes if they read this!

I was particularly happy with the program of scholarships and bursaries that we brought in. The Government are paying these each year to nearly 1,500 students in all parts of the province. I myself have signed thousands of the handsomely printed certificates going to the students. I could have had a good replica of my signature made, but that would have spoiled the immense enjoyment of personally signing each individual certificate and looking at the amount, ranging from $100 to $700, the name of the student, and the town or settlement to which the award was going. The millions of dollars that we have paid out in these scholarships and bursaries must surely be one of the finest investments of public money ever made in our province.

As one who has travelled in every nook and cranny of our province, I marvel at the almost unbelievable number of young Newfoundlanders from all our coasts, bays, and coves, including much of Labrador, who have gone through these special new centres of learning: 30,000 through the university, 25,000 through the College of Fisheries, 62,000 through the College of Technology and trade schools–117,000 altogether, all but a small number doing so in the past ten or twelve years! What thrills me is not the total number alone, but the universal character of their geographical distribution. Almost every cove and small bay within the big bays has had one or more of its young men and women studying in these very modern schools: the sons and daughters of the rich and the poor, of the high and the low; the most complete, intimate, social intermixture of the youth of Newfoundland and Labrador ever to take place, indeed the only such intermixture ever known in our part of the world. This is an island where, until just a few years ago, there were thousands who had never in their lives been farther away than a dozen or twenty miles from their native coves, and then for only a few hours at a time. The ease, indeed the inevitability, of getting to know each other and each other's home coast or bay: the exchange of information and ideas, and the intellectual cross-fertilization that results from this amazing admixture–this leaves you shaken if you have grown up in the old Newfoundland, and gives you more absolute confidence in Newfoundland's future than you ever had before.

Before I leave the subject of our university, I want to give some account of my efforts to find the right man for its Chancellor. I went to see Lord Beaverbrook in New Brunswick and asked him to accept the appointment. I knew that he was already the extraordinarily generous Chancellor of the University of New Brunswick, but I reminded him, when he mentioned it, that there was no law or rule to prevent a man from being chancellor of two universities at the same time. It didn't work, but he gave me the names of three men that I might approach: wealthy men, for of course he knew precisely the kind of qualifications I had in mind for the man who should occupy the office. They were Frank Ross, then the Lieutenant-Governor of British Columbia (the stepfather of the Hon. John Turner), Garfield Weston, and Izaak Walton Killam. Only one of these three names appealed to me, Garfield Weston. Ross I didn't think to have enough wealth. Killam I dismissed instantly in my own mind–I didn't like the name! It was the one most serious blunder I made in connection with our university. Beaverbrook told me that Killam was very wealthy, that he had no particular cause to espouse just about then, and that he should be ripe to accept this honour from Canada's new province. He died soon after, and the Canadian Government collected tens of millions of dollars in estate duties from his fortune. His estimable widow bought the Brooklyn Dodgers as a pastime, and at the last account I heard she had donated $10 million to Dalhousie University at Halifax. I hang my head in shame every time I remember my stupid failure to invite Mr. Killam to become Chancellor.

Garfield Weston I approached in London. He used the top floor of the famous Fortnum and Mason building, which he owned, as an apartment, and it was there that we had our chat. I was startled by his frankness in discussing his business affairs in Britain, Europe, and of course Canada. He had become the third largest vendor of food-stuffs in the world, coming after the vast Unilever empire and the immense Nestlés, but he was determined not to stand still. I tried hard to use him as the link between his vast fortune and the needs of Memorial. He was sympathetic to my invitation but didn't accept it. He told me frankly that he wanted nothing ornamental; in effect, that he was a plain man of business who loved the effort and joy of building an industrial-commercial empire. He had declined Winston Churchill's offer of a seat in the House of Lords. "What would I want with being a Lord?" he asked me. "And furthermore, when I die only my oldest son could inherit the title" (This was before life-time peerages were introduced) "and why should I agree to a system that would set up that kind of difference between my oldest son and his brothers and sisters?" Mr. Weston assured me that although he wouldn't accept the chancellorship, he wouldn't forget Memorial. I think that Memorial may benefit yet from my pleasant conversation with this great Canadian.

The man we got for Chancellor was Lord Rothermere, the great

English publisher and an important shareholder in the pulp and paper mill in Grand Falls. His health didn't allow him to continue in office many years, but Memorial benefited to the extent of about three-quarters of a million dollars at his hands. As Rothermere's successor I chose a Canadian and another great publisher, Roy Thomson. I made my approach to Thomson when he was the owner of a mere 100 daily newspapers around the world—not the 150 or 160 that he owns now. Roy accepted my invitation with alacrity, for he was pleased with it. With the disarming frankness that endears him to people everywhere, he told me that it would help him to get the seat in the House of Lords that he so badly and openly wanted. I never knew a man to be so eager for anything—even the premiership of Newfoundland—as Roy Thomson was for that peerage. He became Lord Thomson of Fleet, and he came back and forth to Newfoundland several times as Chancellor of Memorial, travelling economy class on the big jets across the Atlantic. Roy gave Memorial $500,000, not the $5 million that I asked him for. I wanted it for the Medical College that we were proposing to build, and I offered to have the college named after him. "You have had many honours, Roy," I said, "but this will make you one of the few men living in the world with a medical college called after him." "It's too much, Joe," Thomson demolished my suggestion. "You're aiming too high." And that was it; but at least there is the students' centre at Memorial by which Lord Thomson is remembered affectionately. Who knows? He may remember his first great honour, and Memorial may benefit even more at his hands.

At Thomson's resignation from the chancellorship, I looked about the world for another rich man, and one of the first to come to mind was the ambassador of the United States to the Court of St. James in England, Walter Annenberg. Annenberg was not only a very rich man, but like Rothermere and Thomson, he was a great publisher; and I thought that the position might appeal to him. So I went to London and proffered the honour, but he turned it down. He was already connected with educational institutions in the United States and didn't feel like taking on any more. So the line of succession was broken—I couldn't find another newspaper publisher rich enough to ask. By then, I had come to think, and my colleagues in Cabinet had come to think, that the time had arrived to look for other qualities than material wealth. We appointed our former colleague, Dr. G. Alain Frecker, to the post. He is the first native son to be Chancellor of Memorial, and there is no living Newfoundlander more widely respected than he.

Can there have been many university functions to equal the one that we had to launch Memorial's new campus in 1961? I invited Mrs. Eleanor Roosevelt to come and open it. She was the special personal representative of President John F. Kennedy for the occasion, and arrived at St. John's airport in a stylish American Government jet. The Prime Minister of Canada, Mr. Diefenbaker, was there for the Government of Canada, and the Duke of Devonshire came for the British Government. I invited the president of every university in Canada to attend, and chartered a large plane to pick them up at airports all the way from British Columbia to Halifax. We had presidents of universities in the United Kingdom and the United States—indeed, so large a gathering of university presidents from around the world must have been a rare event. I brought the famous military band from Kingston, Jamaica, in their Zouave uniforms, and the superb girls' band from Nova Scotia and a military band from the Canadian Army, and the Shriners' Band from Halifax, and other bands too. From all around the world, I invited distinguished Newfoundlanders—native sons who had become prominent in England, Australia, the United States, across Canada, and in other countries—to come home as Newfoundland's guests for the happy event. I took a chance on having an important part of the celebration outdoors—a big chance to take, for unfavourable weather would have ruined it. This was nothing less than the biggest parade ever held in Newfoundland's history! I brought students into St. John's from all parts of Newfoundland and from Labrador, and they marched in contingents, proudly carrying banners denoting their school. There were 14,000 of them, and all those distinguished visitors sat on benches along Elizabeth Avenue and took the salute as the big parade of Newfoundland youth marched past. Nothing like this whole affair had ever been seen in Newfoundland before, or anywhere else in Canada, I'm sure. It started Memorial off in real style on their new campus. I was often asked why I organized so grand an opening of the new campus. The answer was easy: Newfoundland is an island, at the end of the line in Canada; when you're in St. John's, you're physically closer to London, England, than you are to Winnipeg and closer to Warsaw than you are to Vancouver. If Memorial was to be the success we intended, then it would have to attract faculty members of outstanding, even distinguished, quality; and I was determined that the Government would do everything that it was capable of doing to give our university a genuine air and reputation of distinction. It assuredly has that reputation today.

We built and rebuilt 1,000 schools while I was Premier, and the number of students rose from 68,000 to over 150,000. We racked our brains to think of useful things to do to make our schools more attractive and efficient, our teachers more secure and happy with their profession. We instituted a check-off for the Newfoundland Teachers' Association to enable them to build their membership. This was a system whereby the members' monthly dues were deducted from the teachers' cheques each month and passed on to the Association. This scheme rapidly increased the membership, until today close to 100 per cent of Newfoundland's teachers belong to the Association. The teachers of our province are now a proud segment of our population, and their organization is financially independent, progressive, and powerful, possessing a strong sense of professional mission.

Our far-reaching program for education has cost us many fortunes. In the twenty years before Confederation Day, the Government of Newfoundland spent a total of $32 million on education in Newfoundland. In the first twenty years after Confederation Day, we spent $502 million. In my last year in office, we spent nearly three times as much on education as had been spent in the 452 years before Confederation. The grand total amount of money spent on education in Newfoundland after Confederation Day is now rapidly approaching the $1 billion mark.

If Confederation had done nothing for Newfoundland but to make possible this one revolution, it would have to be hailed as one of the greatest blessings ever to descend upon Newfoundland's people.

The law gave the Government the right and duty to appoint the University's President. The first President was Dr. A. G. Hatcher. Next came Dr. Raymond Gushue, one of our most successful non-elective public men of this century. His management of the university in its early years was careful and sound, though I disagreed strongly with his view of the number of students it ought to have. In a public speech, he mentioned the figure "around 2,000" as ideal. A fortnight or two later, in a public speech, without referring to his remark, I said that I could see no limit to the number—indeed, why shouldn't our university serve 8,000 or 10,000 young Newfoundlanders? No one should attempt to fix an arbitrary maximum number, I said. A month or two afterward, Dr. Gushue made another public speech and repeated his figure of around 2,000. A few weeks following that, I spoke strongly of the Government's policy and intention to limit the enrolment only by the amount of funds that could be made available. I repeated my statement that the figure should be 8,000 or 10,000, or even more! Dr. Gushue made one final attempt, in a public speech, and after that he subsided. The general public was amused by the oratorical contest.

When Dr. Gushue decided to retire from the Presidency in 1966, I looked around for a successor. I tried to get Dr. Norman MacKenzie. I tried to get Dr. McTaggart-Cowan of the University of British Columbia, and also in British Columbia I tried to get Dr. Gordon Schrum. In England, I asked R. A. Butler, the ex-Chancellor of the Exchequer, but he became head of one of the Colleges at Oxford. Then I went after Sir Douglas Logan, head of London University. We had a very pleasant chat, but it was no shattering surprise when he declined the honour. He made some valuable suggestions of other names. I tried to get the President of the University of Bristol, and Alan Bullock, who wouldn't leave St. Catherine's College of Oxford to come to St. John's. I asked Sir James Cook of Exeter and Sir Edward Mayfair. In the United States, I made a strenuous effort to get Barbara Ward (Lady Jackson) and had several conversations on the telephone with her. Her husband, Sir Henry Jackson, the distinguished economist and economic advisor to the Government of India and several other governments, I tried to persuade to become economic advisor to the Newfoundland Government. Both he and Lady Jackson declined. The great Canadian-born economist John Kenneth Galbraith, of Harvard, helped me in my negotiations with Lady Jackson,* and subsequently I persuaded him to come to St. John's and take a leading part in an amusing Thinkers' Conference which some of Canada's most distinguished persons attended. Then, while he was in St. John's, I invited him to become President of Memorial. But he also declined.

*When I had the idea of naming our new Children's Hospital after the widow of President John F. Kennedy, or after her little girl, Caroline, I telephoned to Mr. Galbraith in Switzerland, where he was escorting her and her children on a skiing trip, and asked him to intervene with her on my behalf. She didn't accept either suggestion, and I was impressed by her reason for rejecting the proposal concerning her daughter: that it was difficult enough to have her children grow up in a normal atmosphere without naming hospitals after them!

In the event, I captured the medical doctor Stephen Taylor, then a life-peer. Lord Taylor had had a remarkable career as a practising physician, as an assistant editor of the *Lancet*, as a Labour Member of Parliament, then as a Junior Minister in the Labour Government. It was he who had been asked by the Saskatchewan Government to go to that province to settle the grievous medical doctors' strike; he accepted and succeeded—with a little swearing and profanity, I understand. To meet him I went, with my colleague the Minister of Education, the Hon. H. R. V. Earle, to Harlow, the new satellite city outside London, which he had played a great part in creating. In fact, his full title was Lord Taylor of Harlow. He scarcely believed my words when I invited him to become President of Memorial, but it dawned on him after a while that I wasn't joking at all. Perhaps the appearance of the handsome, dignified Minister of Education helped to convince him. The upshot of it all was that, as he and Lady Taylor (a distinguished medical doctor and public administrator in her own right) were due to visit the United States soon, he agreed that they would accept the Newfoundland Government's invitation to visit St. John's. They both took my invitation more seriously when they saw the big new campus of Memorial; and in the end, he agreed to serve.

Before he actually did so, I called him several times on the telephone to London. In one of those conversations, he called me Joey, then hastened to apologize for the familiarity. In so doing, he said that he hoped that I would call him Stephen. In reply, I told him that I wouldn't think of calling him Stephen—I would call him Stevie. I made it an unofficial condition of his appointment that he would retain his seat in the House of Lords, and I told him why: I wanted him to put in an occasional appearance in the Lords and make a speech, so that from time to time someone seeking to see him at Memorial could be told, "I'm sorry, but Lord Taylor is in the House of Lords just at present. He'll be back next week." And I told Taylor of another reason: I wanted to be able to telephone him at the House of Lords sometime and get him out of the Chamber and start my conversation, "Is that you, Stevie? This is the Prime Minister of Newfoundland speaking." He enjoyed the fun, and so Memorial got the only live Lord in captivity among all the universities of the Western Hemisphere. He has such a violent temper that I consider it to be one of my great personal achievements that I didn't lose mine with him and thus start the most unholy row ever seen or heard in St. John's.*

"But *really* Mr. Smallwood, I kept this knucklehead in after classes and he demands time-and-a-half!"

The Edmonton Journal

*Lord Taylor was to relinquish the presidency in August 1973, and the *Evening Telegram* generously editorialized on May 25, 1973: "Lord Taylor is going and the man who brought him here, Joey Smallwood, whom even his detractors must concede was the university's greatest benefactor, is no longer around to push forward with the great dream for Memorial. Instead the clear-eyed dollar conscious Conservative pragmatists could be planning to embalm the university in economic formaldehyde."

20

Shall Might Be Right?

With all their faults, trade-unions have done more for humanity than any other organization of men that ever existed. They have done more for decency, for honesty, for education, for the betterment of the race, for the developing of character in man, than any other association of men.

Clarence S. Darrow

The safety of the people is the highest law.

The Twelve Tables, 450 B.C.

Nonviolence is the first article of my faith. It is also the last article of my creed.

Mohandas Gandhi

Let there be no strife, I pray thee, between me and thee . . . for we be brethren.

Genesis 13:8

The strife is o'er, the battle done.

Francis Pott

If the International Woodworkers of America (the IWA) had invaded Newfoundland in 1890 to organize the workers who were building the Hall's Bay railway it might or might not have been a good thing. In the fascinating piece he wrote for my *Book of Newfoundland* on the building of the Newfoundland Railway, Alfred R. Penney tells why.

> There were 1,500 men employed. Wages were $1 a day of ten hours. Ten miles were completed by the end of the year. There were no bunkhouses in those days. When a man got a job he was given a roll of felt and a few nails. He and a friend cut a few poles for a frame and built a tar-paper shack. Cooking utensils and food could be purchased at reasonable cost from the contractor at construction headquarters. This consisted of a number of large canvas tents with wooden floors for accommodation of the engineers, supervisors, blacksmiths and timekeepers as well as for the storage of supplies, equipment, and feed for horses.
>
> After the day's work was over the men cooked their suppers over open fires. It was quite a sight in the fall of the year to see the cooking fires of a thousand men spread along five to ten miles of railway grade. There was no work on Sunday and the day was spent mending clothes and boots, baking bread in iron bake pots by the side of an open fire for the week ahead. There was not as much frying of damper-dogs on a shovel as is sometimes alleged; but it was done, and a round top shovel can in a pinch make a very good frying pan. . . . It was primitive, but it was a way of life.

That's how our railway was built across the Island, but when Lord Northcliffe's new pulp and papermill was built at Grand Falls fifteen or sixteen years later, he did at least provide tar-paper shacks for the loggers—the men didn't have to provide their own. He provided cooks and cookees—the food was rough, but the men didn't have to cook it themselves. The bunks had spruce and fir boughs for mattresses—I suspect that the men would have had to find these for themselves. It was all pretty crude, but an improvement over railroad-building.

And you could earn cash wages in the logging camps! For a fisherman who had had a poor season out on the coast, or one who had had a good season but wanted some cash (which he was unlikely to get for his fish), it was, they felt, a glorious and altogether unprecedented and unexpected chance to use their spare time in fall and winter to earn a few dollars. Competition for the jobs was fierce. His Lordship could have had ten times as many men any day of the cutting and driving seasons. So it was, and so it continued, right up to the end of the First World War and for quite some time afterward.

Then Joe Thompson emerged. He was a pulpwood cutter from Green Bay, and he organized the first union of loggers in the country. It grew rapidly, and soon it had just about every logger in its membership. Perhaps it grew too big too fast, or perhaps Joe Thompson himself was hardly big enough to prevent what happened; for two of his Western organizers, Pierce Fudge of Corner Brook and Charlie Tulk of Deer Lake, broke away from the union and formed new unions of their own. There must have been close to 20,000 men in the three unions; but to an unhappy extent, they were more at each other's throats, for a while, than they were at the throats of the paper companies.

Then came the Woods Labour Board. This was wisely set up by the Commission of Government, under the chairmanship of Ray Gushue, a cool-headed lawyer whose real talent lay less in law than in being chairman of bodies that would almost certainly have foundered without his kind of competent leadership. Representatives of the three unions and the Fishermen's Protective Union (a few of whose members were loggers), and the heads of the two big paper companies constituted the Board. There was a full-time secretary. The Board's job was to bring worker and employer together in meetings at which the details of contracts would be worked out—wages, accommodation and board, and the hundred and one aspects of life and work in the camps and on the rivers. These meetings were held regularly, and the results were impressive. Wages rose year after year, conditions in the camps improved steadily, and the old hands in the woods were unstinting in their praise of the unions and of Joe Thompson and the other leaders. There simply isn't any room to doubt that, by comparison with the 1920s, the logger's position was enormously improved. By comparison with the camps in Quebec, our loggers were well off. It would be difficult to compare their standard with that of the Nova Scotia and New Brunswick loggers, for the conditions in those two provinces were, for the most part, quite different. Farmer-held woodlots were the source of much of the pulpwood and saw-logs used in Nova Scotia and New Brunswick. Ontario was better, admittedly; but what was there in Ontario that wasn't? You had to go all the way across the continent to British Columbia to find the loggers' heaven, but there again you were in another world: a world in which one tree felled commonly yielded as much wood as did fifty to a hundred of our small spruce and fir trees in Newfoundland. One tree in British Columbia might be worth hundreds of dollars by the time the main products and all the side products had been extracted from it. Indeed, the mere offal or waste of such trees would form a large part of the source of pulpwood fibre for the pulp and papermills. In Newfoundland, it was a rare tree in the pulpwood forests that yielded anything more than pulpwood fibre.

The loggers' unions in Newfoundland were not militant enough. They weren't fierce enough. But they *had* produced fine results for the men, and they were continuing to do so. None of the four unions was affiliated with the Newfoundland Federation of Labour, let alone any international body or national Canadian body: they were simply local Newfoundland unions of loggers, led by simple but sincere men, who were perhaps a trifle, or more than a trifle, mild in their attitude toward the employers. They were sitting ducks for any militant and competent mainland outside union that decided to invade the province. The first such union to show any interest in the loggers was the big Brotherhood of Carpenters and Joiners, which has a department that organizes men in the logging industry. They are competent, but not fierce. They made approaches to Joe Thompson and the other leaders of the local unions, and I suspect that some little progress was being made in the talks when the barracuda IWA came on the scene in 1956, leap-frogging across Quebec, New Brunswick, and Nova Scotia into Newfoundland. Undoubtedly they had their eye on those loggers: not the 20,000 there had been, but the

12,000 to 15,000 there were then, thanks to the abandonment of the axe and hand-operated bucksaw in favour of the small one-man power saw.

The IWA was beyond comparison the ablest, most experienced union that Newfoundland has ever seen to this day. They were veterans of countless savage battles fought with the great woods industry companies of the Pacific Coast in Canada and the United States. They had learned all the skills of labour warfare. They were hard-bitten and tough, and skilled in ways and to a degree that had never even been suspected by Newfoundlanders. There was a strong suspicion that some of the IWA leadership in Canada was Communist, but perhaps that was only the rather inevitable epithet that would in any case be used against a militant union. H. Landon Ladd, the man sent into Newfoundland to lead the IWA campaign to capture Newfoundland's loggers, was one of the most capable and apparently one of the straightest trade union leaders ever to set foot on Newfoundland's soil. He was a hard worker, an inspiring speaker, even an orator. One or two of his lieutenants, however, were "poor white trash".

Like everyone else, I knew that the IWA had arrived in Newfoundland and was holding meetings in the logging camps, mostly at night or on Sundays, when the men were at leisure. What of it? There was nothing unlawful or wrong about that. And there was nothing wrong in the union's steady recruitment of new members. There was nothing at all alarming about the rapid growth of its membership, every man of whom had to come from the existing local unions. There was nothing unlawful or wrong in any sense or degree about the union's applying to the Department of Labour for certification as the loggers' sole bargaining agent to negotiate with the paper companies. It had indisputably won over the majority of the men—virtually all of the younger men joined, and some of the older. And it was entirely proper that the union should be certified and that, after certification, it should approach the companies to negotiate the new labour contract. Wisely, the IWA's demands upon the company were not outrageous, or even extravagant. But it was not altogether surprising that the companies rejected the IWA's demands; nor was it surprising that the arbitration board appointed by the Department of Labour on request, as the law prescribed, reported favourably on the IWA's demands.

All was very right and proper. Nothing was unlawful; there was no impropriety; everything was done according to Hoyle. I had no feelings whatsoever about the matter, and said nothing publicly and little privately. It was very much a matter to be settled by the loggers themselves, through the union of their own choice, in negotiation with their employers. If then, or for the next four or five weeks, I had expressed a word in public, it would have been one of warm sympathy with the loggers and the union. That was in the fall of 1958, and my own sentiments in the affair were those that would be felt by any trade unionist in the province.

After the paper companies had refused to accept the recommendations of the arbitration board, the next step could only be disastrous surrender and retreat by the IWA—or a decision to stand and fight, to call the men out on strike. This is what the union did, on December 31, 1958.

From that moment, the IWA did nothing right. Virtually every move it made was wrong, most of them palpably illegal and some of them unbearably so. For what the union started on December 31 was not a strike, but a war; and not an ordinary labour war, but a blitzkrieg. Its policy was "Hit the enemy—hit him with all you've got, crush him, beat him down into the earth, never mind if it's legal or illegal; if violence must be used, use it; never mind if a little blood is spilled here and there. Just win the war!"

There were in actual fact only a few hundred men still in the logging camps on the day the strike was called, but the IWA publicly ordered them to stay where they were. The strikers ate the company's food and used the company's camps and facilities, and its tractors and trucks; and the IWA introduced on that very day a system of mass picketing the like of which, for size and lawlessness, law-abiding Newfoundland had never witnessed. The companies had built their own private roads leading up to their camps from the public highways. The picketing at first consisted of throwing large relays of picketers at the junction of these private company roads and the public highways, to prevent physically anyone—and they meant anyone!—from going up those private roads. That was the first stage. Next, the union began to take physical possession of the *public* highways, to prevent company trucks from passing back and forth along the Queen's Highway and later to prevent privately owned trucks from hauling pulpwood over the same highways. So far, the lawlessness consisted only of the union's enforcing its will by the presence of sheer numbers of picketers; but after a week or two, it began to change. Picketers were not content to order truck-drivers to turn about and go back, but began to seize the trucks and throw their loads of pulpwood into the ditches. Some of the truck-drivers were physically assaulted.

The strike, which had been going on for several weeks by now, was beginning to heat up. The five or six trade unions that operated the mill at Grand Falls, in central Newfoundland, where most of the strike activity was going on, were very much opposed to the lawlessness of the IWA. There was not the slightest possibility of the millworkers joining with the IWA; indeed, a lot of bitterness was developing between the millworkers and striking loggers. The IWA was determined to stop the flow of pulpwood to the mill, so that the mill would be forced to shut down. Landon Ladd was seen on television by thousands, pointing jubilantly at the sky and reminding everyone that the sun was getting stronger every day, so that soon pulpwood couldn't be hauled out of the forests.

I still hadn't said a word publicly, nor had anyone in the Government, though our minds were being forced by events to turn against the IWA. Then on January 12, I took my first step, a mild one. In collaboration with Leslie Curtis, the Attorney General, I prepared a statement that he subsequently issued, both verbally and in the form of printed leaflets, thousands of which were distributed to the picket lines. It said simply, calmly, and mildly, that the Queen's subjects had no right to obstruct the public highways, had no right to prevent other people from using the public highways, and had no right to interfere with the free passage of traffic over the public highways; and that by doing so, they were putting themselves outside the law, becoming outlaws, and making themselves liable to the penalties of the law. Curtis said:

> My advice to you therefore is: don't break the law. Don't let anyone persuade you to break the law. Don't attempt to block any roads. Don't attempt to attack men in the camps or the camps themselves. Don't attempt to attack your fellow-men at all. If anyone asks you to do any of these things, ask him or them: Why me? Why don't you do it? If he or they won't do it themselves, there's a reason. Don't let them make you the goat. What they ask is probably unlawful. Be honest to yourselves, your wives and children. Obey the law. Keep out of jail.

It was a sane appeal for peace on the public highways. It didn't discuss the strike in any way, or the issues of the strike. We were perhaps slow to issue this necessary statement. Certainly, as the Government, we could do no less.

I have said that everything was lawful and proper up to the very day that the strike began, but that is not precisely true. In December, the Grand Falls company had secured a court injunction restricting the use of company roads and property. This was after IWA officials were alleged to have broken the locks on the company's gates. The main resort to force and violence, however, did not come until January 5, when pickets forcibly stopped contractor Frank Burt at Badger. On the Point Leamington Highway, trucks were forcibly stopped and the pulpwood dumped on the roadside. The RCMP ordered the picketers to clear the pulpwood away, and they obeyed. On January 8, the RCMP escorted woods operators through picket lines that had been offering mass force against them.

Then a split occurred between the local mill unions at Grand Falls and those in the mill at Corner Brook, the latter supporting the IWA. The Newfoundland Federation of Labour backed the IWA. By January 18, feelings were running so high that the RCMP trebled the number of men they had in that part of Newfoundland. There were a few convictions of IWA officers or picketers for relatively minor offences that could be proved in court. Fifteen picketers were arrested on the Point Leamington Road on January 20. On January 21, I announced that the Welfare Department would give relief to approximately 5,000 union men who had not been in the camps on the day the strike was called, but that no relief would be offered to the men who were and had remained. On January 30, the IWA predicted that all cutting of pulpwood for the Corner Brook mill would stop in a few days. Union after union throughout the province took its stand in support of the IWA. On February 3, I said publicly, "I am keeping a daily and hourly watch on the situation." On February 6, British unions announced that they were supporting the IWA. On February 7, Ladd explained that he didn't expect that the British unions would refuse to unload a ship due there with a load of Newfoundland paper, but only that the unions would protest the situation to the ship's owners with a view to holding further shipments. Meanwhile, various raids had been made on the Grand Falls and Corner Brook logging camps by IWA picketers. Feeling was now running dangerously high.

On February 7, a turn came in the situation when a mob of IWA men descended upon two central Newfoundland logging camps between two o'clock and three o'clock in the morning. With four-foot cudgels, they smashed everything in sight and drove the non-striking loggers out into the snow, in weather that was well below zero. One man was knocked unconscious, others were struck repeatedly, and a number were forced out doors without even being allowed to put on their boots. In one of the two camps, that of Bob Budgell, seventeen of the forty-three loggers refused to leave. The others joined with those from the camp of Burt Matthews and fled through the woods. The RCMP arrested 104 IWA strikers who were suspected of having taken part in the raids. Other strikers and picketers in other parts of the province were arrested almost daily on charges of violence, physical assault, raids on working camps, and the like. I was sickened by the reports of Newfoundland workers assaulting each other.

On February 9, I announced that in three days I would speak for half an hour on all television and radio stations in the province; I gave no hint of the nature of the broadcast, except to say that it would concern the strike. The IWA intensified the struggle. They brought picketers distances of hundreds of miles to man the picket lines. They even recruited wives of the striking loggers. In Botwood, on February 9, when Harry Thompson, president of the Longshoremen's Union there, led fifteen carloads of union men in an attempt to cross the loggers' picket line, forty-five women maintained the line. The men, declining to force their way through the ranks of the women, turned back. On February 11, I released the names of three IWA men who had sent me a telegram announcing that the IWA strikers were going to march on the jail in Grand Falls to rescue strikers who had been sentenced to short terms for violence on the picket lines.

In my speech on the night of February 12, I spent the first quarter-hour laying the heaviest possible emphasis on the life and death need of the loggers to have a powerful union to protect and advance their interests. In the second half of my talk, I said that the IWA strike had failed and that the IWA itself was a failure in Newfoundland. In my opinion, the union was a menace to Newfoundland, and it should go. I advised the loggers to get rid of the IWA and to form themselves into a new union. If they did, within the next week, all camps could be operating at full blast; and within a fortnight, a new working agreement could be signed with the two paper companies.

> I am absolutely sure and certain [I said] that our loggers must have a strong union to protect their interest and help them forward in the battle of life. It would be madness or suicide for our loggers to be without a strong union—it is not enough for them to have a union, the union must be strong, it must be honest, it must be honourable, and it must be independent of the employers. It would be better to have no union at all than to have one that was only a company stooge.
>
> If it were not for the loggers of Newfoundland we probably would not have Confederation today, and our people would have been forced to do without the great blessings of Confederation. All Newfoundland owes you a great debt of gratitude for the noble part you played, often right in your camps, on the day the Referendum was held, in that glorious fight for Confederation. Confederation can never be a complete success, as long as there is discontent and unhappiness among loggers, their wives and children. We cannot have a happy and prosperous Province if the loggers and their wives and families are unhappy and suffering under a sense of injustice.
>
> Now after this new loggers' union is formed, and they hold their first convention, they can decide for themselves whether they want to have some kind of connection with the Fishermen's Federation, with the Newfoundland Federation of Labour, with the Canadian Labour Congress, or any other congress, or any other federation, or any other organization.

Then I made the loggers an offer: I would vacate the Premier's office for one week, go to Grand Falls, and there help them to form a new union for all loggers. Max Lane, General Secretary of the Newfoundland Federation of Fishermen, had acceded to my request that he help in the formation of the new union. If the loggers of Newfoundland or other Newfoundlanders agreed with what I was saying, they could do so by sending me a telegram next morning.

The result was astonishing. A teleprinter in the Premier's office began to transmit messages at 8.50 the next morning and continued throughout the day without cease. The telephone began to ring the moment I stopped speaking and continued for days. Thousands of loggers telegraphed me, as well as housewives, fishermen, clergymen, doctors, and labour leaders; those who telegraphed their dissent were outnumbered, by actual count, 20 to 1. Newsmen sat around the teleprinter all day and checked the results. The favourable messages showed 4,007 in my support and 218 opposed. Max Lane was swamped with telephone calls and messages.

The Opposition Party issued a statement describing my action as "courageous". William Breen, president of the Longshoremen's Protective Union in St. John's, issued a statement of strong support for my suggestion that the IWA get out of Newfoundland. "These proposals by the Premier make sense and I feel that the loggers will follow him." Every newspaper in Newfoundland, without a single exception, supported the position I took. The heads of all the religious denominations did the same, and I was showered with assurances of agreement and support from them. As it turned out, there was more unanimity among the Newfoundland people in opposition to the IWA than on any issue in Newfoundland from the Second World War to the present day.

But not outside Newfoundland! The Canadian Labour Congress denounced me hip and thigh, and organized an extraordinarily loud chorus of denunciation from union presidents ,and executives from coast to coast. They did more: they organized powerful protests from the United States labour movement, from the British labour movement, and from the International Labor Organization at Geneva. They started a fund that was supposed to amount to at least a million dollars to help the IWA fight in Newfoundland. I was a fascist, anti-union, and anti-labour, they told the world. They tried to get Lester B. Pearson, leader of the Liberal Party in opposition at Ottawa, to read me out of the Liberal Party; but I had a powerful advocate at court in the person of Jack Pickersgill, and on March 17 the Newfoundland Liberal MP's publicly declared their support of my actions.

The countless telegrams of protest from unions across Canada didn't impress me. I was too familiar with the way that particular machine works. I knew too much to think that a telegram saying that "this union strongly condemned" a particular action meant that the 1,200 or 3,000 or 7,000 members of that union had met, considered the question, and then voted to adopt the resolution. Rather, I could imagine the resolutions and telegrams being written in the publicity department of the CLC or by the international headquarters of the unions, and distributed to the local bodies for automatic adoption.

In any event, they weren't the Legislature or Government of Newfoundland, and they weren't the people of Newfoundland. Never in my life have I been surer of the rightness of my stand. Violence just could not be permitted. Lawlessness could not be countenanced. No union, no corporation, no church, no group of any kind, could be permitted to take the law into its own hands and defy the law of the land. If the IWA succeeded, the real harm would be the lesson their success would teach all unions: that violence and lawlessness were a sure and certain means of victory. The IWA would have enormous prestige and power. It would be the tutor to the trade union movement in Newfoundland, which would have profound respect for its teacher. For Newfoundland's sake, this couldn't be allowed to happen. "The Government will resign if it cannot maintain law and order," I told the House on March 11.

I went to Grand Falls on February 25, accompanied by Max Lane and a young lawyer, William G. Adams, who subsequently served in the House of Assembly and then as Mayor of St. John's. Leaders of the six or seven trade unions in and around Grand Falls gave me one of the most cordial receptions of my life, as did the whole population. Men poured into Grand Falls from every point of the compass to attend my meeting, coming distances of up to 100 miles. Some even came in over the ice that separated their island from the mainland of Newfoundland, and others skated in!

Two days before I held my meeting, eight of the eleven member unions of the Grand Falls—Gander District Labour Council withdrew in a body in support of the proposed new union, and the Council collapsed. On the platform with me in the Grand Falls Town Hall at the big loggers' meeting on February 28 were officers of the eight local unions, and they volunteered to assist loggers to fill out their application forms for membership. In the first two days, close to 2,400 men joined the new union, the Newfoundland Brotherhood of Woods Workers. That was three times as many men as had voted to call the strike in the first place. The strike was now sixty-two days old. On March 3, Landon Ladd, John McCool, and G. Hall entered an action against me in the Supreme Court for defamation of character that they alleged I had uttered in my radio speech, and claimed $300,000 damages from me. (They didn't get it!) The membership of the NBWW grew rapidly and under the leadership of Max Lane, who had been elected provisional president, began negotiations with the paper companies for a union contract.

I advised the Lieutenant-Governor to call a special session of the House of Assembly, and there I proposed the adoption of legislation that would decertify the IWA in Newfoundland. This would deprive the union of the monopoly it had obtained to represent the loggers in negotiations with the paper companies. While the IWA had certification, the companies had no choice, under the law, but to negotiate with it. Once the IWA was decertified, the companies would not be obliged to deal with it, but might do so if they chose. Decertification did not mean that the IWA would be outlawed or be barred from negotiating with the companies—only that the union couldn't insist on it.

The House of Assembly was unanimous. Every member spoke in strong support of my actions and those of my administration and in support of the proposed legislation. Opposition Leader Malcolm Hollett declared stoutly that, had he been Premier, he would have done exactly what I had done. He declared, "Any government, sir, which neglected to put a stop to this threatened emergency and actual emergency would not be worth its salt. We on this side of the House would not be worth our salt if we did not get after the Government and tell them to do something about it. That is the reason, sir, we supported this legislation. There was an emergency and there was violence."

I myself pointed up the situation.

> Forty-eight days of violence and lawlessness; three to four weeks' unlawful occupation of the camps. On the fifteenth day of February the I.W.A. picketers refused, by offering physical force, to permit the inspectors and officials of the A.N.D. Company to go up into the Millertown Camps and inspect them and see what condition they were in. I don't mean that those pickets stood there and said in all politeness, in a decent way as Newfoundlanders will: "Excuse me, sir, but I suppose you did know that we have a strike on and you know that we don't like to see people going up into the camps." Is that the kind of peaceful picketing they did? For forty-eight days and nights: lawlessness and violence; forty-eight days' unlawful possession of the camps, the theft of tens of thousands of dollars' worth of food and other property, seizure of trucks, the seizure of pulpwood; gangs of pickets sitting on the wood and daring

anyone to touch it or load it; unlawful possession of A.N.D. Company gates leading from the Queen's Highway up the private roads to the camps; raiding the camps in separate raids of men numbering from 100 to 300 each raid at two and three and four o'clock in the morning; violence, lawlessness and bloodshed for forty-eight days and nights before I even opened my mouth, before I did or said a thing: forty-eight days.

And what did I do then? On the forty-eighth day I went on the radio and made a speech to the loggers telling them that in my opinion the strike had failed and could not succeed; the I.W.A. had failed and could not succeed; that they had been misled by the I.W.A.; that they, in my opinion, should get rid of the I.W.A. and send them packing; but that they could not do without a union; they still had to have a union, and if they followed my advice they would form a new union; and if they wanted my help to do it I would be glad to offer help.

That is what I did. That was my intervention. That is the only intervention I made; nothing else. Mr. Diefenbaker thinks that I aggravated the strike. The heat was indeed on me for twelve days to intervene. Who put the heat on me? Let me tell the House. First and foremost, Mr. Jodoin, the labour leader of Canada. He telephoned me from Ottawa and asked me to intervene. He was the first. Then he came to see me at the hotel in Ottawa when I went up to see the Prime Minister. Who else asked me to intervene? The Canadian Labour Congress through Mr. Chafe, who came to see me and asked me to intervene. Who else? The President of the Newfoundland Federation of Labour. Who else? Scores of telegrams showered on me—written by the I.W.A., because they all had the same phraseology but signed by picket lines demanding that I intervene; and when I said only that I was observing the situation, keeping careful watch on it by the day and by the hour (the House may remember the phrase) they then changed the propaganda line and began sending me telegrams saying: "Never mind watching, now we want you to act." This went on, starting about a fortnight before I did at last intervene—forty-eight days after the strike began, forty-eight

> days of lawlessness and violence. Yet I aggravated it, according to Mr. Diefenbaker, who does not think there is any need of a Royal Commission to find out the facts. He is sure that he knows the truth.

Mr. Diefenbaker's rejection of my request for a Royal Commission was in reply to a telegram I had sent him on March 13:

> In the interest of peace order and good government of Canada and to protect the good name of the R.C.M.P. the Government of Newfoundland invites the Government of Canada to set up at once a public enquiry under a Supreme Court judge from outside Newfoundland to investigate the acts of lawlessness and violence which have taken place in central Newfoundland since the strike of the loggers began on December thirty-first for the purpose of ascertaining the facts and assessing the responsibility. The Government of Newfoundland would extend every facility and assistance to such a commission in its enquiry.

Diefenbaker refused to appoint the enquiry.

But I am slightly ahead of my story. The House unanimously, in an altogether unprecedented *standing* vote, passed the law decertifying the IWA in Newfoundland. On March 9, the new union opened contract talks with the Grand Falls paper company.

March 10 brought the most savage riot in Newfoundland's history. It was at Badger, a few miles from Grand Falls, where a large number of picketers had been brought together from places as far distant as 200 miles. The inadequate RCMP force in central Newfoundland had been reinforced by members of the Newfoundland Constabulary of St. John's. As the combined force of seventy-one, unarmed except for their ordinary night-sticks, marched down Badger's main street that night, the big crowd of pickets opened ranks to let the police pass through and then closed in again. The police marched some distance and then turned back and retraced their steps. Again, the picketers drew back to both sides of the road; but as the policemen marched through, the attack began. Some picketers held three- and four-foot clubs, birch sticks; a few wielded bottles and axes. One club hit St. John's constable William Moss between the eyes, and he was felled to the ground like a log, unconscious. He was rushed to the hospital at Grand Falls, where an emergency operation was performed. He died just before three o'clock on the morning of March 12. Newfoundland was aghast. A body of 400 men, mostly war veterans, escorted the body of the slain policeman from the hospital to the train that was en route to St. John's. As they did, at Windsor, an angry mob of Grand Falls and Windsor union men threw rocks through the windows of IWA headquarters. An RCMP contingent kept the surging crowd from getting into the building.

St. John's was virtually without a police force, and the Newfoundland Superintendent of the RCMP, Arthur Parsons, advised Attorney General Leslie Curtis that in his opinion the RCMP forces in Newfoundland were not large enough to maintain law and order in the central part of the Island. He wanted reinforcements. Following the advice of Parsons, the Attorney General telephoned Davie Fulton, Canada's Attorney General, asking that reinforcements be sent from the mainland at once. Parsons made his own direct approach to the Commissioner of the RCMP, Leonard Nicholson. The RCMP had no choice in the matter, for it was clearly covered in a contract signed by the Federal Government and the Province on June 12, 1957. Clause thirteen said:

> Where in the opinion of the Attorney General of the Province an emergency exists within the Province requiring additional members of the force to assist in dealing with such emergency, Canada shall, at the request of the Attorney General of the Province, increase the strength of the division as requested if, in the opinion of the Attorney General of Canada, having regard to other duties and responsibilities of the force, such increase is possible.

In Fulton's opinion, the Newfoundland Attorney General's request to him and Superintendent Parsons' request to Chief Commissioner Nicholson were justified, and he so argued in the Diefenbaker Cabinet Diefenbaker rejected the proposal. The RCMP reinforcements, who were actually on their way by airplane to Newfoundland, were grounded at Moncton and ordered to return, and Chief Commissioner Nicholson promptly resigned his position, to the mortification of the Canadian Government and the anger of the Canadian people. Other high officers of the RCMP were dissuaded by Nicholson from resigning too—he didn't want to hurt the famous force. There was surprise that Fulton didn't resign from the Government.

On March 3, 1959, Attorney General Curtis entered an action in the Exchequer Court against the Canadian Government for breach of the contract under which we had the services of the RCMP. In the next chapter, I describe the outcome of this action.

Across Canada, there had been an almost complete lack of understanding of the issues surrounding the IWA strike, and I had been painted in the newspapers and on television as an anti-unionist, virtually a tool of the paper companies, and an enemy of poor loggers who were trying to break the chains of slavery by which the paper companies had bound them. The media hadn't the faintest idea of the tremendous forward strides that the loggers had made under the leadership of the four local Newfoundland unions, and they simply didn't know that camp conditions were better in Newfoundland than they were in any part of Eastern Canada. But now, overnight, the climate changed. Many of Canada's greatest newspapers came down firmly on my side. Said the Montreal *Daily Star*:

> Parliamentary debate on the Newfoundland strike crisis has been astonishing. The mishandling of the problem by both the Conservatives and Liberals is almost incredible. The only rational explanation that leaps to the mind is that the party leaders have been scared by the pressure campaign laid on by the C.L.C.

The Toronto *Globe and Mail* stated:

> Justice Minister Fulton did not improve his case for refusing R.C.M.P. reinforcements to Newfoundland by his press conference statements last night. He told the Commons that sending reinforcements "might act only as provocation to further incidents of violence and defiance." The Provinces must be alarmed to think that capricious interpretation of this clause, after the event requiring its fulfillment, can deny a Province urgently needed help. The Dominion's Provincial relations may be permanently harmed by this assumption of a jurisdiction Ottawa has no right to take.

The *Halifax Herald* noted, "The Newfoundland loggers dispute now has advanced, or rather deteriorated, into a stage of law-breaking and violence that cannot be tolerated." The *Gazette* of Montreal gave us full editorial support in our effort to oust the IWA and voiced firm approval of my intervention in the dispute. The *Calgary Herald* published its support of the Newfoundland Legislature's stand against the IWA, and the Regina *Leader-Post* denounced Diefenbaker for refusing RCMP reinforcements for Newfoundland.

The *Financial Times* said:

> It had to come sooner or later, the moment of truth in Canadian labour relations and labour legislation. The fact that it could not go on much longer the way it had been going had become obvious to everybody. Everybody, that is, except those who still think in terms of a labour vote which dare not be antagonized.

I began to receive hundreds, then thousands, of letters and telegrams from all the provinces, almost unanimously supporting my stand. I wasn't happy to hear from company executives, Chambers of Commerce, and other representatives of industry; but I was very happy to hear from many men who were loyal trade unionists and opposed to the use of force and violence in trade disputes.

In Newfoundland itself, public opinion was more nearly unanimous than I had ever known it to be. Even the members of Newfoundland's trade unions supported the stand I was taking against the IWA, although some of their officers did not.

The rest is quickly told. The IWA closed its offices at Windsor and moved to Deer Lake, vowing that it would never leave Newfoundland and would win the strike yet. After a few months, the union quietly disappeared from the province. The new union signed contracts with the two paper companies, or their representatives. The Brotherhood of Carpenters and Joiners, which had quietly kept at least a toe in Newfoundland all along, now launched a campaign among the new union's officers and members to win them over. I was glad to see this and did whatever I could to help bring about the absorption by the Carpenters of the union that I had helped to form. Today, every logger in the province is a member of the Carpenters, which has done excellent work to carry on, and substantially improve upon, the accomplishments of the four old unions that existed before the IWA invasion.

It will be a long time before anything more than mere casual violence is used in labour disputes again in Newfoundland.

21

In This Corner —John Diefenbaker

The definition of injustice is no other than the not performance of covenant.

Thomas Hobbes

In a really just cause the weak conquer the strong.

Sophocles

Fair play's a jewel.

Sir Walter Scott

Bargain like a gypsy, but pay like a gentleman.

Hungarian proverb

John G. Diefenbaker became Prime Minister of Canada in 1957. Although in that election Newfoundland gave him only two of its seven MP's, I had reason to believe that he would have a kindly feeling for me; for in the course of our brief acquaintance, I had performed no less than four favours for him. One was not so much a favour, perhaps, as a friendly gesture: I was the very first Newfoundlander to greet him the first time he set foot in our province. I happened to be at Torbay Airport, just outside St. John's, when he arrived. I was expecting Jack Pickersgill on the same plane, so I was standing at the foot of the ramp when Diefenbaker, then a candidate for the prime ministry of Canada, came down it. His Tory friends who were waiting to greet him were inside the terminal building, so I shook his hand and expressed a cordial welcome. On another occasion, I attended a St. John's Rotary Club meeting at which Diefenbaker was the special guest and speaker of the day. As I chatted with the Tory leader before his speech, I suggested that he ask the audience to sing one or two of our Newfoundland ballads, which he later did. Then, when he was introduced, I stood applauding, and looked suggestively around the room until everyone else was on his feet as well—and standing ovations have never been a Newfoundland practice. The third favour was requested by Diefenbaker himself, just after he became Prime Minister. There was a medical doctor who had been elected Tory MP in Ontario. The new Prime Minister wanted him in Ottawa, but the doctor had to find a locum tenens, and he knew whom he wanted—a medical doctor who worked for the Newfoundland Government. Diefenbaker telephoned me in St. John's and asked me if I would release the man to go to Ontario. I arranged it. The fourth favour also was initiated by Diefenbaker. He himself was away in London, but his staff telephoned me on his behalf. A federal-provincial conference was coming up at Ottawa. Would I oblige Mr. Diefenbaker at its opening by standing and, on behalf of the premiers, speaking a few words of welcome to him? I thought it a peculiar request and wondered why I should be the one to do it. I realized that the other premiers would be surprised, but I agreed. Four favours for Diefenbaker—would they add up to Diefenbaker's friendliness to me? I found out, the hard way, that they did not.

The really big dispute with Diefenbaker, the one that probably started the decline in his popularity in Canada, was over Term 29. For half a dozen years, *Term 29* was among the best-known phrases in Canada. I doubt that the people of Canada ever understood what it really meant and signified—even a majority of the Members of Parliament never understood the true nature of the argument. But if they didn't understand, they were at least sympathetic to Newfoundland and became increasingly impatient with Mr. Diefenbaker for his obdurate refusal to show a generous spirit to Newfoundland.

When we Newfoundlanders negotiated with the Government of Canada to find terms and conditions under which the two separate countries might unite federally into one, it was clear that the union, if it could be brought about, would be good—better than good, excellent—for the great majority of Newfoundlanders. Canada's famed family allowances, old-age pensions, Veterans' Charter, and all the rest of its social security system would go far indeed toward blunting the sharp edge of social poverty in Newfoundland. In return, Canada would greatly expand its trade with Newfoundland, and this forecast has been handsomely borne out since Confederation. Everyone would benefit from Confederation—everyone, that is, but the Government of the new province. As we negotiated in Ottawa, we couldn't see much more than poverty, or even bankruptcy, for the Newfoundland Government under Confederation.

A people who would be much better off headed by a government that would be near bankruptcy: such was the contrast that seemed to make Confederation unworkable. This was the major problem that Canada's seven Cabinet Ministers, under the chairmanship of Mr. St. Laurent, and the seven Newfoundland representatives, led by Gordon Bradley and later Sir Albert Walsh, wrestled with for months in Ottawa. The solution of this problem was the *sine qua non* of making the deal. Robert A. MacKay for the Canadians and I for the Newfoundlanders sweated over it for days on end.* At the end of

*When I say sweated, I mean it literally as well as figuratively. We two were locked up all day in a room in the East Block of Parliament Buildings, without air conditioning, in the heat of July and August. I usually stripped to the waist—and still sweated in that oven.

each day, our notes and attempted drafts would be gathered up and burned. MacKay would report back to the Canadian Treasury experts and to Mr. St. Laurent, and I to my colleagues. Finally, we found the solution.

To compensate for the revenue lost to the Newfoundland Government as an immediate result of the disappearance of the Newfoundland customs tariff, excise taxes and excise duties, and numerous other sources of revenue that it had possessed, there was substituted in Term 29 an annual grant from the Government of Canada. This was called the Transition Grant, because it was meant to tide the new Government over the transitional period, which we assumed would be about eight years. Within those eight years, the new Government would have a chance to develop all possible sources of provincial revenue—sales taxes, much higher gasoline taxes, increased royalties, and anything else that they might find. It was clear that the Newfoundland Government would have to impose taxes that would be as heavy as the people could reasonably bear; after all, other "have not" provinces would be watching. The amount of the Transition Grant would be a constant $8 million a year for the first three years and would then be progressively reduced for the remaining five years.

Would this be enough to support the activities of the Newfoundland Government? Really, we didn't know and couldn't make much of a guess at it. The Canadian Treasury and Bank of Canada experts, and we ourselves in the Newfoundland delegation, made determined efforts to estimate the probable revenue of the new Government. We simply couldn't tell whether the tax income of the Government, plus the Transition Grant, plus other normal and ordinary payments from Ottawa, would be enough to enable the Government to carry on its responsibilities as laid down in the British North America Act. We didn't know for sure, but we had an uneasy feeling that the total income from all sources wouldn't be enough, particularly after the Transition Grant had ceased. In Term 29, we were confident that we had the solution: it provided for a full-scale review of the province's finances before the eight years were up and for recommendations about the aid that might continue to be necessary.

Quite frankly, it was a confession by the two teams of negotiators representing Canada and Newfoundland that they couldn't, at that stage, make final terms of Confederation for the two countries. We could do most of it; we could cover an enormous part of the field, duly sign the terms, and get them put through the constitutional processes that would make them binding. One part we couldn't do ourselves, but we did make provision for that very thing to be done that would complete the terms of union. That is what Term 29 was. It read:

> *Provision for financial review:* In view of the difficulty ["impossibility" is what we really meant] of predicting with sufficient accuracy the financial consequences to Newfoundland of becoming a Province of Canada, the Government of Canada will appoint a Royal Commission within eight years of the date of Union, to review the financial position of the Province of Newfoundland, and to recommend the form and scale of additional financial assistance, if any, that may be required by the Government of the Province of Newfoundland to enable it to continue the public services at the levels and standards reached subsequent to the date of Union, without resorting to taxation more burdensome, having regard to capacity to pay, than that obtaining generally in the region comprising the Maritime Provinces of Nova Scotia, New Brunswick, and Prince Edward Island.

Without that clause, there would have been no Confederation. Even with it, Chesley Crosbie refused to sign the terms of union; without it, Bradley and I and all the others in the Newfoundland delegation would have refused to sign. In a sense, Term 29 was the most important clause in the terms. It was stupid, if not dishonest, to argue in effect, as a few did, that this term was only a piece of deceit or bluff on the part of Canada to entice Newfoundland into Confederation. Either Canada meant what it said, with the full honest intention of living up to the literal and moral obligation implied in the term, and would feel bound in honour faithfully to carry out the findings of the Royal Commission which, in this term, it undertook to appoint; or else the terms of union were nothing more than a cheap shell-game on the part of the Canadian Government and the Canadian Parliament. There was no human possibility of doubting Mr. St. Laurent's honour in the matter: he would have died rather than deny the moral obligation created by Canada's signing of Term 29. The weakness of the clause lay in the fact that Mr. St. Laurent might not be the Prime Minister of Canada when the Royal Commission was appointed or, even more vital, when the Royal Commission reported. And as it turned out, of course, John Diefenbaker was the Prime Minister on that fatal day.

We imposed our sales tax—people cheerfully paid their "three cents for Joey"—and our grievously heavy gasoline tax, and other taxes to enable the Government to take back temporarily from Newfoundlanders some of the blessings of Confederation. We raised the levels and standards of public services as much as we could with the money we had, for it was to be for the continuation of those levels and standards that the Royal Commission would be recommending the scale of payments we would be receiving after the eighth year. We had to keep a sharp eye on the burden of taxation in the three neighbouring provinces; for obviously the Royal Commission would not recommend a scale of payments to enable us to maintain high levels and standards of public services without taxing our people at least as heavily as the Maritimers were being taxed. There was, however, an important saving grace: the burden of taxation in Newfoundland and in the Maritimes would not be a simple comparison of dollar for dollar. Rather, Newfoundland's capacity to pay taxes, compared with the Maritimes' capacity to pay, would be the real basis for evaluation.

The Royal Commission would be everything. Our fate would be in their hands, and we had to prepare our case more thoroughly than we had ever done anything before. Late in 1953, we appointed our own Newfoundland Royal Commission to do this before the federal Royal Commission was appointed. Philip J. Lewis, Q.C., was its chairman, with Albert B. Perlin, Gerald S. Doyle (who died before its work was finished), and Philip Gruchy (who had signed the terms of union with the rest of us in Ottawa) as commissioners and Douglas Hunt, Q.C., as its secretary. The Commission retained Carl Goldenberg, the prominent labour lawyer; James Thompson, the province's special Public Accounts advisor; and Donald Armstrong and his very able wife as chief economic advisors. Our Royal Commission sat for nearly four years, from January 1954 to April 1957, and rarely, if ever, in Canadian history has any body of men performed so faithfully and competently. Thanks to them, Newfoundland was ready for the Royal Commission that was appointed by Ottawa in the fall of 1957. Its members were Chief Justice John B. McNair of New Brunswick, economist John Deutsch, and our own Chief Justice, Sir Albert J. Walsh.

In agonies of impatience, we waited for the recommendations of the McNair Commission. Would they give us the $15 million we asked for? They wouldn't, and they didn't. Their report, delivered on July 25, 1958, recommended that the Transition Grant, which had declined annually until it was now only a shadow of itself, be raised to $8 million to the year 1962, and that the same amount be paid annually "thereafter". It was a bitter disappointment for all Newfoundlanders, quite literally all. We hadn't been able to raise the level and standards of our public services to be fit for a Canadian province, for we just hadn't had the money to do it. We could, of course, have raised them by going in debt for it, but that would have undermined the new province's credit. Yet it was to enable us to "continue" those very levels and standards, as they existed when the McNair Royal Commission reviewed them, that the Commission was to recommend the amount that we should get for the future. It was truly a dilemma out of which there was no way but generosity on Canada's part. The inadequacy of $8 million a year was appallingly obvious; so I asked the House, and the House agreed unanimously, to adopt a resolution asking Ottawa to make us an interim payment while we argued the larger question. Diefenbaker did nothing.

I find embarrassing difficulty in describing the quick succession of events from this point on. Richard Gwyn has told it graphically, and thanks to his generosity, and that of his publishers, I give the story in his words:

> In January, 1959, Smallwood once again put on the mantle of supplicant: he called on Diefenbaker in Ottawa and pleaded with him to increase the Term 29 settlement to the original $15 million proposed by the provincial commission. Diefenbaker's reply was noncommittal. Two months later, at Smallwood's behest, Pickersgill made a personal call on Diefenbaker carrying with him a message from Pearson. If the McNair Commission award of $8 million a year in perpetuity was accepted without change, Pearson would rise in the Commons to praise Diefenbaker for his statesmanship. Again the Prime Minister's answer was inscrutable.
>
> When the announcement was finally made, its timing caught Smallwood by surprise. It came on March 25, just six days before the tenth anniversary of Confederation. Diefenbaker's opening remarks made it clear that the coincidence would not be a happy one.

"Both governments," he said, "have entertained serious reservations concerning the basis of the conclusions reached by the Commission." He agreed to Newfoundland's request for periodic reviews, "since it would be quite inappropriate to endeavour to provide for a fixed amount payable annually over a period of unlimited duration." For that reason, the $8 million a year would be paid only until 1962 when "Newfoundland's position can be considered in the light of the general methods of providing financial assistance to the provinces." The payment of special amounts to Newfoundland up to 1962, Diefenbaker concluded, "will be in final and irrevocable settlement of . . . the contractual obligations of the union consummated in 1949."

Across the floor, Pickersgill leaned forward to listen. At first he was angry, then, as the phrase "final and irrevocable" rolled out, he hid a smile of delight. He leaned forward to whisper to Pearson, who rose to denounce Diefenbaker's declaration as "quite unwarranted." Pickersgill then hurried out of the Chamber to call Smallwood in St. John's. After a quick conference, each man set out to fire the first shots of a counter-barrage.

Mystifyingly, Diefenbaker had staked out all the low ground for himself. The most succinct comment on his performance came from the Toronto *Globe and Mail*, which called his statement a "classic example of how to do the right thing in the wrong way at the wrong time." The explanation for his first blunder—his use of so provocative a phrase as "final and irrevocable"—was simple, if incredible. Diefenbaker had never read the statement before he delivered it in the House. It had been drafted by the Finance Department, and handed to him by Finance Minister Donald Fleming just before he spoke. As the Prime Minister later ruefully told a cabinet minister: "I knew it was wrong the moment I said it." As for his unhappy choice of timing, Diefenbaker was so out of touch with Newfoundland sentiment, and cared so little for it, that neither of the two Newfoundland Conservative MP's, Minister without Portfolio Bill Browne, and Jim McGrath, was consulted about the date, or even forewarned that the announcement would be made. Instead, they heard the news by chance, over a car radio while on their way to a meeting outside St. John's.

"I am only one among twenty-two members of the cabinet and I can't ram my opinions down their throats," said the hapless Browne when he was finally cornered by reporters. McGrath, younger and less equable, flew to Ottawa, demanded an interview with Diefenbaker, and was treated to a half hour of vintage, finger-stabbing Diefenbaker fury. It was directed at Smallwood, who by now had taken off in full, unstoppable flight.

In the spring of 1959, Diefenbaker stood at the height of his dominion over Commons and country. Two months earlier, a Gallup Poll had shown that fifty-seven per cent of Canadians were ready to vote for him at the next election. But even The Chief was powerless in a debate in which he was cast as Scrooge and Smallwood as Tiny Tim. Smallwood inflicted on Diefenbaker his first major setback since taking office. By August, when Smallwood had completed his work, only forty-seven per cent of voters considered themselves Diefenbaker supporters. For good measure, Smallwood also used the Term 29 issue to destroy the Newfoundland Conservatives so thoroughly that the party took a decade to recover.

On the day of the announcement itself, Pickersgill issued a press statement calling it "an act of bad faith unequalled in the history of Canada." Smallwood was more moderate. He drove hurriedly from his farm to the CJON TV station, and there delivered an eight-minute address: "This is a sad day for Newfoundland, for our hospitals, for our schools, our rural electrification programs, our water and sewerage systems, and the other endless needs of our people. The last thing anyone on earth would guess would be that Mr. Diefenbaker or anyone else would put a time limit on Term 29."

The next day he stepped up the pace with a gesture in the grand style. To "mark the unspeakable betrayal of Newfoundland," he ordered three days of official mourning. All over the city, flags hung at half mast; the doors of government buildings were draped in black crepe* On March 27,

*In fact, broad bands of crepe hung from eave to ground on most public buildings. (J.R.S.)

Memorial University students marched through the streets of St. John's bearing placards: "A Modern Judas Has Betrayed Us", "Secede", and "Diefenbaker, Thief and Faker". In the vanguard was the college band, playing "The Dead March from Saul". Dressed in a black coat and Homburg as "suitable for the occasion", Smallwood met them on the steps of the legislature.* "The rest of Canada is ready to rise up in rebellion against Mr. Diefenbaker's betrayal of Newfoundland", he bellowed. "The entire responsibility rests with Mr. Diefenbaker".† That night the students burned the Prime Minister in effigy.

At the Confederation anniversary dinner three days later, Smallwood was confident enough to mock his distant opponent: "I now make this offer," he told the guests, "if Mr. Diefenbaker will treat Newfoundland fairly and give us a fair deal, I'll resign Tuesday when the House opens." The magnanimity of the offer, and the likelihood of its being accepted, were reduced by his next sally: "I suppose Mr. Diefenbaker is nursing a grudge against me because I kept him out of five seats."

Ottawa, in fact, was already eager for a truce. Smallwood's imaginative histrionics, coupled with sympathetic articles about conditions in Newfoundland after ten years of union, had inspired genuine sympathy for the province. Almost no one understood Term 29; almost everyone believed that little Newfoundland was being hard done by. Letters of protest, particularly from fellow have-nots in the Maritimes and on the prairies, poured into MP's' offices. On a CBC "National Business" telecast, Diefenbaker soothingly regretted "any misunderstandings that may have arisen," and promised "consideration" of a compromise settlement. Asked if he would meet with Smallwood, the Prime Minister replied: "I am ready at all times to meet with anyone who has a case to present."

Smallwood had no intention of letting his arch-foe off so easily. He intended to repay injury with insult. And the more he talked about Term 29, the less he needed to say about the loggers' strike, an issue which had already

* The students telephoned to my office asking me to join them. (J. R. S.)
†They were attacking Canada. I pleaded with them to attack not Canada, but Mr. Diefenbaker. (J. R. S.)

aroused bitter feelings between himself and Ottawa.

Confident that the Canadian public was behind him, Smallwood unleashed his full fury against the federal Conservatives. He launched a suit against Ottawa in the Exchequer Court for "breach of contract" on the issue of RCMP reinforcements, and a week later followed it with another suit to protest Ottawa's "unwarranted, impertinent interference" in attempting to place federal nominees on the St. John's Housing Authority, a body seventy-five per cent financed by Ottawa.* When Public Works Minister Howard Green ventured to explain that this contretemps had come about because of Smallwood's failure to answer his mail, the Premier snapped back: "I didn't answer because I didn't want to offend the old fellow." Told of this, Green replied, "The man's impossible." In the meantime, work was halted on a five-hundred-acre, federal-provincial housing project in St. John's.

When Ottawa tried to reply in kind, Smallwood rolled effortlessly with the punches. After he was ordered to vacate Canada House (formerly the residence of Canadian High Commissioners and therefore federal-provincial property), Smallwood deliberately procrastinated in the hope, as he later explained, "they would kick me out. Then I would have had to put my luggage and furniture on the sidewalk, got my wife, children, and grandchildren to sit on it and arranged, shall we say, for some photographers to drop by." The Diefenbaker Government managed to avoid the trap, but in retaliation it stopped all repairs and repainting, so that the Premier for a time lived in the shabbiest mansion in St. John's.

So far, Smallwood had fired all his ammunition from long range. In a stroke of inspiration and daring, he now announced he would march on Ottawa. The whole country waited in fascination. For Smallwood, it meant a sortie into the heart of enemy territory, and his first star part on the national stage. Outwardly cocky, Smallwood was conscious of the risk he was taking. On the flight up from St.

*Since when did Ottawa have or even claim to have the right to put its own nominees on purely provincial boards, even if 100 per cent of the funds came from Ottawa? (J. R. S.)

John's he rushed off the plane at each stop to snatch up the latest newspapers and to pace nervously around the terminal.

The rustic demagogue from the outports arrived at Ottawa's Union Station on April 8. A dense crowd of reporters, many of them primed with hostile questions, surrounded him as soon as he reached the platform. Soon the questions died and pencils raced across notebooks: "Even the Prime Minister can't bully me. He can kill me, but he can't bully me. We are just a poor little province trying to be modest, well-behaved little Canadians—but when you tread on a worm—it will turn." He lashed out at Browne as "the biggest slum landlord in St. John's." (The next day he retreated from the threat of a libel suit and described Browne instead as "a lawyer and for many years he collected rents, and maybe for himself, for some of the worst slums in the city.") Reporters bobbing in his wake, he then set off with Pickersgill to the Château Laurier.

That evening he took on four veteran Press Gallery reporters on the half-hour national television program "Press Conference." Between them, the journalists spoke perhaps three minutes. As one later explained to his caustic colleagues, "We were hypnotized." Smallwood was unstoppable. When one reporter was brash enough to correct his pronunciation of heinous as "haynous" to "heenous," Smallwood rapped back smartly by working "haynous" into his next three sentences. Making Diefenbaker's action on Term 29 sound like the worst insult to Newfoundland since Cabot sailed past without stopping, Smallwood stormed on: "Newfoundland's life is at stake. Term 29 must remain in force as long as water runs wet and grass grows green. . . . We put our faith in the people of Canada to see to it that justice is done to Newfoundland." The program pre-empted the first half-hour of the Stanley Cup finals; the CBC received fewer than a dozen complaints.

Not since the Confederation battles had Smallwood had such a good time. To Canadians, he had become a latter-day Pied Piper. As guest speaker at a meeting of the Ottawa Canadian Club the next day, he attracted the largest audience in the chapter's history. He needed barely five minutes to win the businessmen, civil servants, and diplomats over to his side. Confederation, he said, was "God's greatest gift to Newfoundland." But, "I am trying, under some difficulty these days to be a Canadian." Once the Term 29 issue was settled, he went on, flashing a broad grin, "Canada will be able to resume its glorious role of ten years of completely ignoring Newfoundland." When he had finished, bow tie askew and sweat pouring down his face, the audience gave him a standing ovation.

He ended his march of triumph with a full-scale press conference. He had nothing new to say, other than that: "If Mr. Diefenbaker maintains his present stand, then I'm going to fight him till the end—his end, not mine." The conference began at 3:00 p.m., and ended at five-fifteen. It had been the longest and best attended in the history of the Ottawa Press Gallery.

"He could sell Santa Claus a razor," wrote Clark Davey of the *Globe and Mail*, once Smallwood had departed. Charles Lynch of Southam News Services called it: "A display of virtuosity seldom matched in Ottawa." For two days Smallwood had held the nation spellbound, revelling in the publicity and in his role as underdog. As the Minister of Agriculture, Alvin Hamilton, commented astutely: "Joey's out to destroy Diefenbaker's image as the protector of the little guy, and he's damn smart." Insofar as he could, Smallwood had accomplished this.

In his own way and in his own style, Smallwood had done much at Ottawa. He had sold Newfoundland's case to the Canadian public. He had also sold his own. He left Ottawa as an accredited national character, a kind of Harry Truman with style. From then onwards, the nickname "Joey" appeared in headlines without any other identification, a status Smallwood, ironically, shares only with "Dief" among contemporary Canadian politicians.*

Thus wrote Richard Gwyn, competently and with his unvarying fairness. I would add this: that at no point would I allow the issue to

*From *Smallwood: the Unlikely Revolutionary* by Richard Gwyn, pp. 189-96. Reprinted by permission of The Canadian Publishers, McClelland and Stewart Limited, Toronto.

degenerate into a Newfoundland attack upon Canada. That was my determined purpose, next only to pressing Newfoundland's claim. Canada was not to blame, but only Diefenbaker.

The Tory Party in Newfoundland was reduced to a sickness of indecision and disagreement by Diefenbaker's extraordinary stand. They were just as eager as we to get a good deal for Newfoundland—and we both knew that the people were as one in the matter. James D. Higgins and Augustus M. Duffy broke from their party and formed the United Newfoundland Party. They sat apart from their former colleagues in the Chamber. I pleaded with the House for unanimous support of my resolution condemning Diefenbaker's violation of our rights; and I told the Assembly frankly that if there wasn't unanimous support for the resolution, I would have no choice but to advise the Lieutenant-Governor to dissolve the Legislature and call a General Election. Malcolm Hollett and Rex Renouf rejected my appeal, and the election was held. We didn't oppose the two United Newfoundland Party candidates, and they were elected over the Tories. I ran against Malcolm Hollett in St. John's West and won the seat with a popular vote of two to one. I continued my crusade for the honouring of Term 29 and against its despoiler, John Diefenbaker. Public sentiment in Canada was running strongly in our favour, and Diefenbaker's behaviour in Newfoundland in this issue, as in the IWA dispute, lost him droves of his supporters across the nation. My crusade succeeded, but it took the defeat of the Diefenbaker forces and the return to power of the Liberal Party under Lester B. Pearson to clinch the matter. In May 1965, Pearson and Pickersgill argued eloquently in the House of Commons that the $8 million grant should be paid to Newfoundland indefinitely, and Parliament adopted the legislation that made it so.

I had quite a time of it getting Mr. Diefenbaker to come down to St. John's for the opening by Mrs. Eleanor Roosevelt of our magnificent new Memorial University campus in October 1961. I phoned him several times, and he kept evading, saying neither yes nor no. I tried to enlist the help of some of his staff by telephone. At last one day, Diefenbaker said quite frankly on the telephone, "You want to get me down there to make a victim of me." I was sincerely shocked and told him so. "You're our country's Prime Minister, and we are good Canadians down here. You come, Mr. Diefenbaker, and I guarantee you right now that you'll get as good a reception as you ever had anywhere in Canada." "Do you mean that?" he asked. I assured him vigorously that I did. He said that all right, he'd come. He was as good as his word, and I was as good as mine. I had an immense crowd to greet him at the airport. At Government House, where we met immediately after the public reception, I grinned at him and asked him, "What did you think of our reception?" He liked it, and I suggested that he and I slip away into another room for a private talk. We did so; and knowing that he was fairly deaf, I drew my chair up close to him, so that our very knees touched. Then, leaning forward and speaking louder than usual, I put several points to him. In short, I proposed that we make a bargain. I wanted him to recognize our claim for the greater part of Fort Pepperrell, in St. John's, which the Americans were giving up. My claim was that it should, all of it, fall to us, as it had been ours in the first place, before Confederation and before the war. He had earlier asked me to drop our case against him in the Exchequer Court on the breach of the RCMP contract. We would drop that case, I told him, if he would agree to our having Fort Pepperrell, or at any rate, the greater part of it. He agreed, and we shook hands on it and came smiling out of the room to join the guests. That night, our great banquet was certainly one of the most distinguished gatherings ever seen in Canada, and Diefenbaker was at his best. I sent him afterward a remarkable series of photographs taken of him while he was telling a joke.

But weeks slipped by, and there was still no action on Fort Pepperrell. At last, I telephoned Diefenbaker in Ottawa, and to my absolute astonishment, he denied that we had made a bargain. I decided there and then that I would stand no more of this nonsense. I wrote a statement describing our meeting at Government House, our bargain, and our shaking hands on it. I pulled no punches. I had 100 copies of the statement made and took them to Ottawa. I phoned his office and told them that it was most urgent for me to see the Prime Minister, and the appointment was soon made. With scarcely any words of introduction, I handed Diefenbaker a copy of my statement and told him that on leaving his office it was my intention to call a press conference and issue the statement. He darted a look at me and then read the statement. He laid it on his desk and said, "You wouldn't actually issue this?" "I would and I will," I told him, "if you don't keep the bargain we shook hands on in St. John's." His response was quick and sure. It was to tell one of his secretaries to get Douglas Harkness to come along right away. The secretary told him that Harkness, the Minister of National Defence, was at the moment attending a Cabinet meeting. "Never mind that," Diefenbaker ordered. "Get him here." We sat silently while we waited for Harkness. When he arrived, Diefenbaker went out to meet him, leaving me alone in his office. In about three minutes, they came in together, Harkness and I shook hands, and Diefenbaker told me that Harkness would "fix things up" to my satisfaction. I thanked him, and Harkness and I went off to his office. He had one or two of his staff brought in, they produced a large blueprint of Fort Pepperrell, and I traced my finger the length of a brook that runs through it. "We'll be fair with you," I told him. "We'll take everything west of the brook, and you can have everything east of it." Harkness agreed promptly, and we both initialled the plan, after I had run my pen along the bank of the brook. (I still have the plan.) Later, we came to mutual agreement to reverse the division, giving Newfoundland everything east of the brook, including the big hospital building, numerous industrial buildings, and many fine residential buildings as well.

I had one other spat with Mr. Diefenbaker before he went out of office. He was evidently anxious to appoint a Tory as Lieutenant-Governor of the province. The widely respected Campbell Macpherson was already Lieutenant-Governor, but this didn't appear to worry Mr. Diefenbaker. Macpherson and his wife were virtually ordered out onto the streets, as he told me on the telephone. I was sincerely aghast. The Lieutenant-Governor is the personal representative of the monarch, and in Newfoundland he has always been regarded with great respect for that reason. It was, I declared publicly, a pretty scurvy way for Ottawa to treat the Queen's personal representative. I announced that the Newfoundland Government, the owners of Government House, had invited Mr. and Mrs. Macpherson to continue living in it as long as they wanted to—for years, if they wished—as guests of the Newfoundland Government. I added that if Mr. Diefenbaker persisted in his contemptible conduct, his appointee to the office could live in his own home or at a boarding house. In no time, Mr. Macpherson got a telephone call from Ottawa almost pleading with him to stay on for another couple of months or so.

In the federal election of 1962, I went all out to help defeat Mr. Diefenbaker, and we won six of the seven seats. There was yet another General Election in the following year, and I worked even harder, with even more success, for we got all seven seats. I have never been able to understand why Mr. Diefenbaker was so cranky and ungenerous to Newfoundland, unless it was the fact that when he swept Canada, almost from stem to stern, Newfoundland stood out and gave him only two of its seven seats. Perhaps he never forgave us for that. For myself, I was genuinely anxious to cooperate with Diefenbaker, and I made no bones of it until he drove me to oppose him. I had privately, and in my own intimate circle, welcomed the election of a Tory Government in Ottawa. My reason: I had come to understand that there were thousands of Anti-Confederate Newfoundlanders who would not be reconciled to Confederation or to Canada until their Tory Party took office. And so, in fact, it turned out to be. The last lingering opposition to Confederation in Newfoundland vanished like the wind after Diefenbaker's great sweep of 1957.

When Joey turns 'em they *stay* turned.

The Chronicle-Herald (Halifax)

22

Heart's Desire

With all my heart, and a piece of my liver.

Jonathan Swift

Ideas won't keep. Something must be done about them.

Alfred North Whitehead

First a new theory is attacked as absurd; then it is admitted to be true, but obvious and insignificant; finally it is seen to be so important that its adversaries claim that they themselves discovered it.

William James

John Christopher Doyle was thirty-seven years old in 1953, the first time he came to see me at my office. I had never seen or heard of him before, and little did I imagine, that day, the great part he was destined to play in our province's development. He was born in the United States of Canadian parentage, and so was a Canadian citizen by law, though most of his life was spent out of Canada. Doyle was educated in the United States and in France, was a graduate mining engineer, and had served in the American Army in the Second World War, with service in North Africa, Sicily, and Italy. He had the rank of Captain, and his work for the Army was mainly in an engineer landing brigade, re-establishment of fuel services in the Mediterranean area, and counter-espionage, in which his remarkable linguistic talent came in very useful.

He came to ask me if his company, Canadian Javelin, of Montreal, could have a mineral concession in Labrador.

I knew just the area to give him. Our predecessors, the Commission of Government, years before, had given to the Labrador Mining and Exploration Company (which was, largely, Jules R. Timmins) exclusive exploration rights of a vast portion of Labrador—10,000 square miles, in fact. They were required to drop large slices of their concession at intervals; and one of the first things we had to decide in my administration was whether we would agree to that company's request for a deferment of the date of the first shedding. They had been concentrating on their iron ore project around the Knob Lake area and had not had much time to explore the larger part of their concession. We gave them the deferment, but the time had finally come when they were obliged to release a large part of their total area. Here they experienced some difficulty. Labrador was indifferently mapped, and the company was in a poor position to lay down the precise lines of the area they would abandon. They used one shore of large Wabush Lake, retaining the land to the north of the shoreline and passing back the southerly portion to the Government. Low-grade iron ore was known to exist on both sides of that rather haphazard dividing line. But the 35 per cent iron content of the Wa-

37. Initialling the agreement with BRINCO for the development of Churchill Falls, 1953

(above) 38. That Labrador road – Premier Jean-Jacques Bertrand has his doubts

(right) 39. J. R. S. with his first great-grandchild, Natasha, at Churchill Falls, where she was born

(centre right) 41. J.R.S. counts the bringing of John M. Shaheen to Newfoundland among his greatest triumphs

(*far right*) 42. The launching of the 31,000-ton *Joseph R. Smallwood*, built by Swan Hunter Shipbuilders, at Newcastle-on-Tyne, July 1972

40. Signing the agreements for the oil refinery at Come by Chance

43. It's been a good life

bush Lake ore appeared economically worthless compared with the 50 per cent or better in the Knob Lake area, where a minimum of 300,000,000 tons of ore was confidently believed to exist.

Doyle wanted a concession in Labrador? All right, see what he could make of the apparently useless Wabush Lake territory! I took the matter to Cabinet, we passed the necessary order, and Doyle went off with his concession of several thousand square miles of allegedly mineralized territory.

But Doyle had ideas that had not occurred to anyone else in Labrador. The ore around Wabush Lake was very friable—it was something like coarse salt that you could let run through your fingers—and his experience in the coal industry in the United States, where he had been a coal salesman, and in Alberta, where with Sir Harold Mitchell* he had owned a producing coal mine, had suggested to him that much the same sort of thing could be done with that friable ore of Wabush as he had seen done with coal: it could be compressed into pellets or briquettes. But first the ore had to be beneficiated to 60 or 70 per cent iron. It was a billion-dollar idea; and as far as I know, Doyle was for a time the only man in Labrador to think of it.

Fourteen million dollars and five years later, not to speak of interminable troubles, corporate attacks on him, and endless calumniation that would have plowed most men under, Doyle and his company won their great victory, the signing of the agreements with the Pickands Mather group for development of a large new mine. He had brought the E. J. Longyear firm from the United States to drill a quarter of a million feet of holes into his Wabush Lake concession. He had engaged the American engineering firm of Ford, Bacon and Davis, the engineers Behre-Dolbear, and the Battelle Memorial Institute, besides other institutions whose reputations were respected throughout the mining world, to the service of his Wabush venture. He proved the existence of well over a billion tons of ore, the technical feasibility of upgrading the ore to 66 per cent or better by the Humphrey Spiral system of beneficiation, and the profitability of the whole scheme. There are four companies in Cleveland, Ohio, that specialize in iron ore production: M. A. Hanna, Pickands Mather, Ogilbay Norton, and Cleveland-Cliffs Iron Company. Doyle nego-

*I met Mitchell afterward at his home in Jamaica. He had been a Member of Parliament in Britain and stood high in the Tory Party. He was a close friend of Winston Churchill, and it was at Sir Harold's home, Prospect, that I had my third meeting with Churchill, who was Mitchell's guest. Mitchell spoke highly of Doyle.

tiated with three of them. He couldn't very well talk with the Hanna Company, for the Labrador Mining and Exploration Company was negotiating with this group about the development of *their* Wabush Lake deposits. In turn, sometimes singly and otherwise conjointly, Doyle negotiated with Pickands, Cleveland, and Ogilbay. He was trying to get one of them to develop the mine field by putting together a consortium of steel mills that would become the customers for the beneficiated, pelletized ore; it was necessary to pull in a group of mills because no single steel mill would want to take the whole output of so large a mine. This is what Timmins' people had done at Knob Lake in forming the Iron Ore Company of Canada. That group, when added to the group of steel mills brought together to develop Wabush Lake, constitutes today perhaps the largest group of steel mills operating iron mines anywhere in the world.

The Wabush group with whom Doyle for Javelin made his agreement consists of Youngstown Sheet and Tube, Pittsburgh Steel, Inland Steel, Italsider of Italy (the Italian state steel industry), and two of Canada's large steel mills, Dominion Foundries and Steel, and Steel Company of Canada, all led by Pickands Mather of Cleveland. That group have put over $300 million into the development of the mine and town at City of Wabush, and they are producing 6 million tons of iron ore a year. The Wabush enterprise is now the largest source of income of Doyle's Javelin Company. The whole story is a tribute to the imagination and dogged courage of John C. Doyle. I was privy throughout to the facts of the machinations, plots and counterplots, and insidious attacks on Doyle and his company, and of negotiations that seemed never to end. More than once, urgent appeals were made to me to intercede with Doyle on behalf of one company or another. Once, the chief executive officer of one of the great iron ore companies telephoned to me from Cleveland asking if I would see him should he come down in the company's jet. I told him that I was going to Montreal in any case and that he could meet me there. What I did not tell him when we met was that I knew from Doyle that this was the very company with which he hoped to make his final deal. He did make it with them.

Doyle did more than promote the great Wabush development, for undoubtedly one of the reasons that induced the Iron Ore Company of Canada to move to the part of the Wabush Lake area that had not been abandoned to the Government (the Iron Ore Company being the tenant of the Labrador Mining and Exploration Company) was

Doyle's demonstration of the presence of such vast tonnages of ore in the area and the realization, no longer confined to Doyle, that 35 per cent ore beneficiated up to 66 or 67 per cent and pelletized would be cheaper to produce, easier to sell, and more profitable. And so we have the remarkable situation of two groups of great steel mills operating two separate mines in two separate cities three miles apart in the heart of the great Labrador Peninsula: two very fine towns, Labrador City and City of Wabush (both of which I named), producing nearly 20 million tons between them every year and supporting a total population of over 16,000.

A tense moment was produced for me by that rivalry, but one that was not without its humour too. A 365-mile railway had been built from Seven Islands, in the Province of Quebec on the north shore of the Gulf of St. Lawrence, northward through Quebec and into Labrador to Knob Lake. This was a common carrier. The trouble came when a tributary railway had to be built roughly two-thirds of the way along the line, at Mile 224, and extending about forty-one miles westward to the site of the two new mines at Labrador City and City of Wabush, neither of which in fact existed at the time. Both companies wanted to build the railway, and one of them was determined to build its own line if a joint line couldn't be agreed on. The Wabush Mine group certainly didn't want that vital link with the main railway to the shipping port to be owned by their rivals, the Iron Ore Company of Canada, which might be said already to control the main railway. This, they feared, would make them the absolute prisoners of their rivals. Indeed, they told me emphatically, they would drop out of the picture altogether if they couldn't build and own their own railway; and they pointed out that they would be happy to have that tributary line become a common carrier. In that case, each company would own or control its own railway, and both would be protected by the common carrier feature. The Iron Ore Company were just as eager to be the owner of the new line.

I had very great respect and admiration for all of the pioneers of the Labrador Mining and Exploration Company and the Iron Ore Company, particularly Jules Timmins, Bill Durrell, and George Humphrey (who later became Secretary of the Treasury at Washington). I was not willing for a moment to see them hurt, for I felt very strongly that they were good for our province. But I was equally determined, as far as I was able, to protect the Wabush Mine group. I agreed cheerfully with the Iron Ore Company's suggestion, later, that the two companies should build and operate one town between them; and I have never been able to understand the strong disinclination of the Wabush Mine group to do so. But on the question of the new railway, I was adamant, and it was in that spirit that I accepted the invitation of the Iron Ore Company to fly to Montreal in the company's jet to meet with the directors for a discussion of the railway problem. They had rented a huge suite in the Queen Elizabeth Hotel in Montreal, and there we had a sumptuous luncheon in a private dining room before a word of business was spoken. When we got down to business, they pointed out with great earnestness their desire to build and operate the railway. We discussed the matter, back and forth, and then I tossed my bombshell among them.

"What makes me very curious about this whole thing," I told them innocently, "is the obvious anxiety of each of you to own the railway, and the obvious unwillingness of each of you to let the other fellow own it. I think I have the solution: neither one of you shall build or own the railway. We'll build and own it and run it!" There was a deadly silence. I think it was my friend Bill Durrell, one of the finest men that ever lived, who broke the silence. "We?" he queried tentatively. "Yes, we—the Newfoundland Government. In fact, the more I think of it, the more I like it. It would probably be a profitable operation, and why shouldn't the Newfoundland Government make something more than just taxes out of these two iron mines?" I never saw such instant conversion. The two companies quickly agreed on the very thing that I wanted: one railway built and owned by the two rival companies together, and not two parallel lines. I can say without hesitation that this was the only occasion in nearly a quarter of a century of experience with the Labrador Mining and Exploration and the Iron Ore companies that I saw any evidence whatsoever of what I might call small-mindedness or narrow selfishness on the part of these fine concerns.

Doyle didn't sublet the whole of the Javelin iron ore deposits around Wabush Lake but retained for the 20,000 shareholders of his company a great deposit at Julienne Lake, ten or twelve miles away from City of Wabush. He did the same thorough job of drilling and blueprinting that deposit as he had done on the other. He also built a road to it, the longest road in Labrador at the time. I have sat in at conferences that he has held in England, Germany, and Japan in an effort to bring about the development of the Julienne Lake deposit, so I know how hard he has worked and is still working to get that one going, too.

Meanwhile, Doyle turned his mind to the realization of what was for him a highly desirable goal and for me one of the dreams of my life: the building of what had become known in Newfoundland as "the third mill". The first was the great pulp and paper mill built at Grand Falls for Lord Northcliffe and his brother Lord Rothermere under the leadership of the Rt. Hon. Sir Robert Bond, back around 1905. The second mill was erected in 1923 at Corner Brook under the leadership of the Rt. Hon. Sir Richard Squires. The towns of Grand Falls and Corner Brook are monuments to these two Liberal prime ministers. I used to say in speeches in and out of the House that pulp and paper were words to be found only in the Liberal vocabulary in Newfoundland, but that was intended more in fun than anything else. Certainly, I had the driving ambition to build the third, and the fourth, papermills in Newfoundland. Through NALCO, which Canadian Javelin had acquired, Doyle had enough pulpwood forest growth in the Lake Melville area of Labrador to support a mill, and he now proposed that the Government back him financially to build it. That was how the Corner Brook mill had been built: in 1923, the British Government, through the Trade Facilities Board, had guaranteed $10 million and the Newfoundland Government another $10 million of the $25 million that it cost to build the mill. The British Government had taken a first mortgage on the whole enterprise, leaving the Newfoundland Government holding the second mortgage.

As long ago as 1950, I had launched my campaign to get the third mill. At that time, I was told by Beland Honderich, then the financial editor (today the president and publisher) of the Toronto *Daily Star*, of a very interesting outfit in New York called the International Basic Economy Corporation. IBEC, as it is usually called, is owned by Governor Nelson Rockefeller, and from its inception he has intended it to be a sort of catalyst for the development of the basic resources of underdeveloped countries. IBEC has done quite remarkable things to develop agriculture, forests, and fisheries in Brazil and a number of Central American countries. Indeed, I believe that the Rockefeller interests have invested many millions of dollars in this development. When I saw their representatives at the IBEC offices in Rockefeller Center (the time that my black friend Frank Crosswaithe drove me there), I hoped that they'd invest some money in Newfoundland. They wouldn't, but at least they were willing, for a fee, to put their organization behind a study of some of our resources. Three men came to Newfoundland in that study: Jack Maddigan, a director of IBEC and head of the engineering firm of Maddigan-Hyland, which had built the great Triborough Bridge across the Hudson River and had played a major part in designing the Mulberry facility to enable the troops invading Europe to make a landing from their ships; Richardson Wood, who conducted one of the many investigations that I have had made of our fishing industry;* and Dr. Tracey Martin, a hydro-electric engineer, who made for us what I believe was the first engineering survey ever made of the Muskrat Falls on the lower Churchill in Labrador. Maddigan spent many hours in my company, and he had numerous ideas of how a new pulp and paper mill could be made practicable. The report of this team condemned the idea of building on Lake Melville (as Doyle had preferred) and recommended instead that the mill be built at Bay d'Espoir, to which the wood, or possibly the pulp, would be brought by ships.

I must confess that as the years passed, my determination to build a third and a fourth mill increased as one concern after another failed to come through with a firm commitment to build. Over the years, I negotiated vigorously with companies on both sides of the Atlantic: Hudson Pulp and Paper Company of New York, Kreuger Pulp and Paper Company of Quebec, The Brown Company, Parsons and Whittemore (Carl Landegger), Champion Paper Company of the United States, Crown Zellerbach of California, Snia Viscosa of Italy, United of Finland, Boise Cascade of the United States, Whippany Paper Board Company of New Jersey, *The Saturday Evening Post's* papermill company, and the vast magazine-printing firm of Cuneo of Chicago, to name but some of them. Negotiations with several of these companies occupied a year or more each. Some involved my travelling repeatedly to meet with their officials, and some involved their chiefs' coming privately to see me in St. John's. The Royal Commission on Forestry, which we had appointed under the chairmanship of General Howard Kennedy, reported that there was enough pulpwood growing on the Island of Newfoundland to support a third mill and recommended strongly that the mill should be built and operated jointly by the two pulp and papermill companies already operating in Newfoundland—Anglo-Newfoundland Development Company at Grand Falls and Bowater (New-

*One of Wood's ideas was that the fish, before being shipped to market, should be treated chemically so as to make it smell of some fruit—oranges or bananas, for instance!

foundland) Pulp and Paper Mills at Corner Brook. Subsequently, I made strong personal appeals to Lord Rothermere and Sir Eric Bowater, but nothing came of them. Albert Martin, vice-president and general manager of Bowaters of Corner Brook, was keen on the idea; but at a meeting I held with the Bowater directors in London, the idea was rejected without hesitation.

The vast Crown Zellerbach organization seemed for a time to be our best bet for the third mill, and I will never be able to describe my disappointment when the company turned back its option on the pulpwood forest of Sandwich Bay in Labrador and the forest area not otherwise committed on the Island of Newfoundland. That was a body blow indeed, and it came in the very midst of the IWA warfare.

Given all these failed attempts to establish the third mill, I welcomed John Doyle's approach, and the Government decided that it was willing to back him strongly. Doyle's studies had convinced him that the mill should make the kind of paper that is used to give a surface lining to corrugated paperboard, used increasingly in the world for packaging goods of all kinds. I went with him to Stockholm, where he became greatly interested in the DeFibrator process. Doyle flew plane-load after plane-load of Labrador pulpwood to Sweden for tests under the DeFibrator system and for research by the Swedish forest service. I went with him to Vienna to meet with Wilfrid Heinzel, who was to market the mill's output in Europe. The railways and trucking companies in Europe require a higher standard of quality in paperboard packages to reduce the amount of breakage; and Doyle's idea was that his mill should cater to the European market with a superior quality of linerboard paper, similar to the Swedish standard. He believed this would create and maintain a bigger and more profitable market, and this belief was strongly supported by Heinzel, who is one of the largest independent marketers of paper products on the continent of Europe. In Eastern Europe, Heinzel represents such great papermills as International Paper, MacMillan Bloedel, and Union Camp. As I visited those places and sat in on conferences, sometimes accompanied by Cabinet colleagues, I reported back in minute detail to my Cabinet.

Doyle's plan was to build a mill that would produce 1,000 tons of linerboard paper every day, but to have the mill designed to an actual capacity of 1,200 tons a day. The great paper machine was to be almost the largest in the world. He planned to increase the size of the mill to 1,800 tons a day and ultimately 2,500 tons a day. He would make it the largest such mill in the world.

As I have mentioned, Doyle's first thought was to build the mill on Lake Melville, a large inland sea inside Hamilton Inlet, close to the wood supply. He abandoned that idea when it became apparent that, as Lake Melville would be closed to navigation for five or six months of the year, vast warehouses would have to be built to store the production of those months. Interest charges would add further to the cost. Doyle then had studies made of a mill operation at Sandwich Bay, out on the open Labrador shore, where only the drifting Arctic ice would present a problem of navigation. A light railway would bring the wood from Lake Melville to the mill. He abandoned that idea and then concentrated his studies on Forteau, on the Labrador side of the Strait of Belle Isle. This would be open to navigation for most of the year, and the plan was to bring the pulpwood south from Lake Melville to the mill by pipeline, a distance of nearly 200 miles. The Canadian Bechtel Company and other concerns were confident that such a pipeline would be practical. In the end, Doyle decided, on the basis of all the studies, that the mill should be built at Stephenville on Newfoundland's West Coast.

The great advantage of Stephenville was that ample land was available, a harbour was there, and all the infrastructure of a comfortable town already existed, so that it would be easier to obtain and hold competent staff to manage and operate the mill. The principal disadvantage of this site was the distance of the source of the pulpwood supply from the mill. Doyle planned at first to place a chipping mill on Lake Melville to convert the pulpwood logs to chips; these would be blown or otherwise conveyed aboard two large ships, each running to 90,000 tons. He was worried about the possibility that one of the ships might be wrecked and leave the mill without sufficient supply. Final studies of the economics convinced him that the sound course was to build the chipping mill beside the papermill in Stephenville and to bring the round pulpwood in a fleet of much smaller ships. He had the further insurance that should something happen to interrupt the flow of wood from Labrador, recourse could be had in such an emergency to temporary supplies of softwood from neighbouring provinces of Canada and of some hardwoods, principally birch, from the Island itself.

This decision was a bitter disappointment to the residents of Happy Valley on Lake Melville, and I took Doyle and his managers there with me for a great meeting with the people. Some 1,200 men jammed the hall, and it seemed for a while that I might not get out of the building safely. I have held hundreds of meetings in my life, but that was probably the most exciting. The newspaper reporters and radio men who were there agreed that it was one of the greatest accomplishments of my life—winning over what was at first a violently antagonistic audience.

The original concept of a 1,000-ton mill would cost $72 million. The wood chipping plant would cost an additional $4 million. Development of the forest, building woods roads, and acquiring wood harvest equipment would cost another $14 million. Docks and shipping facilities would cost a further $10 million. That was a total of $100 million. Working capital would amount to $10 million, and the ships would cost $27 million. The whole project, according to the careful engineering estimates of the mill's designers, E. and B. Cowan of Montreal, who have engineered numerous pulp and papermills, would thus cost $137 million. An amount of about $5 million, which Ottawa was to have contributed, failed to materialize. The new concern that swept across Canada to prevent pollution cost the enterprise an additional $6 million. An amount of $4 million was added to the cost by the withdrawal of the Greyhound Leasing Corporation and by subsequent changes in location plans. Another $4 million was added to the cost when 3,000 tons of steel had to be added to the mill because of the earthquake hazard that was afterward found to exist in the area. These totalled nearly $20 million of overrun, but the overrun came within the estimated overall cost of $137 million.

In December 1970, in connection with a bond issue that we were about to sell, a conference was convened in St. John's by our Department of Finance to explain to the underwriters and the banks what our needs were. John Doyle appeared before that meeting and gave the figure of $140 million as the total cost of the enterprise to completion. In the summer of the following year, our auditors, Peat, Marwick and Mitchell; the mill's designers, E. and B. Cowan; and D. D. Dick, the engineering firm that the Newfoundland Government had engaged to be our eyes and ears throughout the construction of the mill, all agreed on their carefully estimated cost of completing the mill to the point where production would begin. Their figure was $139½ million, almost identical with Doyle's estimate of the year before.

The financing of the enterprise was to be provided by eight or nine of the largest banks in Great Britain, led by the famous Lazard Brothers banking firm. They would lend $42 million on the joint guarantee of the British Government (through the Export Credits Guarantee Department) and the Newfoundland Government; and $17 million would be provided by German banks on the guarantee of the Newfoundland Government. The Newfoundland Government subsequently guaranteed two further loans of $2¼ million in New York and $31 million in Germany.

I am, of course, unaware of the facts of the enterprise since my retirement from the premiership on January 18, 1972. As of that date, 66 per cent of the mill had been completed, and it was drawing rapidly to the point of completion. It was in fact being completed at the rate of 6 per cent a month and was to be ready to start production by the end of July 1972. By January 18, 1972, 98 per cent of all machinery, equipment, and materials for the mills was on the construction site.

On the day that I resigned, $104 million had been expended on the whole project, and in addition to that an unspent amount of $31 million had just been borrowed in Germany, making a total of $135 million. Javelin on its own had borrowed $3½ million for woodlands equipment, bringing the whole cost to approximately $138½ million. To that point, the Government's obligation in the whole enterprise was $59 million, plus $2½ million, plus $31 million, for a total of $92½ million. This left the Javelin concern with a total investment of $47¾ million.

Premier Moores' administration, which succeeded mine, decided a few weeks after taking office to nationalize the whole papermill enterprise, which they did promptly. As I write these words, in March 1973, the Government has been the owner and manager of the mill for a year. The mill was not completed by the end of July 1972, or even by the end of December. At this writing, the run-in of the mill is proceeding, and it should be operating smoothly by the early summer of 1973, almost a year late. I am under the disadvantage of not having the official figures, but my understanding is that the enterprise will cost $225 million—about $85 million more than it was to cost on the date that I left office. The new administration has continued to retain the services of Peat, Marwick and Mitchell, the chartered accountants, and the D. D. Dick engineers that my administration engaged. It has entered into agreements with a small Massachusetts company to market the output of the mill.

I wish with all my heart for the success of this great enterprise.

23

Churchill Falls

Ye have heard of the patience of Job.

James 5:11

My ambition to develop Churchill Falls was born one day in 1926 at the Cecil Hotel on the Strand in London. I was in Sir Patrick McGrath's room, and he was telling me about the work he was doing for the Newfoundland Government's case in the Labrador boundary dispute. The case was to come soon before the Judicial Committee of the Privy Council at Westminster. The Province of Quebec, too, was hard at work gathering material for the hearing. Sir Patrick waxed eloquent on the magnificent Grand Falls of Labrador, subsequently known as Hamilton Falls and then ultimately as Churchill Falls.*

Later, back in St. John's, I attended a lecture that McGrath gave on the Falls and read everything that I could find about the mighty cataract. It was one of my deepest convictions, when I became Premier, that the Falls must be developed. It was almost a compulsion with me, and the compulsion was intensified in 1950, when I flew in narrowing circles above the Falls in the Jules Timmins plane that was taking me for my first visit to his mining camp at Knob Lake. Winston Churchill was later to say of them, "These horses must be harnessed," and that is how I felt myself.

A few days after my second flight over the Falls, in 1952, I was in London, and I took up Lord Beaverbrook's standing offer to get me in to see Winston Churchill at Number 10 Downing Street. Leslie Curtis, Minister of Justice in my administration, went with me to the Prime Minister's office-home at three in the afternoon of August 14. He waited in an anteroom until, our meeting being near an end, I told Churchill of Curtis's presence outside. He immediately brought Curtis in, and they chatted for a moment. Curtis has never forgotten the thrill of his encounter with the great man.

Churchill met me at the door of the Council Chamber, where all British Cabinets meet and which he used as his office. In his left hand, he held a very tall glass nearly full of a liquid that I did not suspect to be lemonade, and between two fingers of the same hand,

*To avoid confusion I use the name Churchill Falls for most references in this chapter.

he held a long cigar. He extended his right hand to me in a warm handclasp and, still holding me by the hand, led me to a chair beside his own at the Council table. He asked if I would have a drink, and I said, "Thank you, sir, no." "You'll have a cigar?" "No, sir, but if you don't mind, I'll smoke a cigarette." He grunted but held out a lighter as I put one between my lips. I thanked him for his kindness in receiving me and pressed on to tell him that I was anxious to draw his attention to the vast riches of Labrador. "Labrador, Prime Minister," I told him earnestly, "is the Alaska of the western shores of North America. Labrador is the great northeastern corner of the continent, as Alaska is the northwestern. It is a vast storehouse of natural wealth, all of it undeveloped, lying idle and unused." I had brought with me a large map of Labrador. I unrolled the map and opened it on the Cabinet table, and we both leaned over it as I traced with my finger the different parts and their reputed resources. Here was the vast iron ore field in western Labrador. Here were the great timber stands of Lake Melville and of Sandwich Bay. And here, I said triumphantly, as I traced the mighty Hamilton River upstream from its mouth in Lake Melville, was one of the great rivers of the American continent. And here—my finger stopped—were the majestic Hamilton Falls, higher than Niagara, with enough water plunging over them every five minutes to fill twenty-eight football fields to a depth of ten feet, or to fill all the bath-tubs in Newfoundland every six seconds, or a lake three miles by three miles, ten feet deep, every hour.

"This is an empire in itself, sir," I insisted, "and it's British: it's part of Newfoundland, and Newfoundland is Britain's most ancient and loyal colony, even now that we are a province of Canada. What's needed to develop this great wealth is precisely the kind of pioneering skill that British enterprise has, with which so many of the far-off places of the earth have been developed. Why, sir, there's more experience and skill of that kind in the City of London than there is anywhere else on earth. I want it for Labrador."

Then I sprang my idea on him. This was altogether too big a project for any single company in Britain, even the largest; what I wanted was a great syndicate of companies—industrial, mining, electrical, and financial.

"I'm thinking of something like the old East India Company, or the Hudson's Bay Company—a big syndicate of all the commercial talents to launch a vast program of what you might have to call industrial colonization. It's not a moment too soon, if Labrador is to be developed by Britain's skill. Already the Americans are about to take control of the great iron ore fields. Can't we see to it that the rest of Labrador is looked after by British interests?"

Beaverbrook had told me that Churchill was a bit deaf (though he wasn't as deaf then as he became later), so I had raised my voice and spoken very distinctly, and I knew that he hadn't missed a syllable. He seemed to be listening with rapt attention, making little sounds in his throat that I took to be murmurs of approval. When I finished, we both sat down again, and he made his pronouncement. "It is a great imperial concept." And then he growled, "And I don't mean Imperialist."

"A great imperial concept!" I asked if I could quote him publicly to that effect, and he said that indeed I might. I was to make good use of the term in the days that followed, for it was indeed a benign blessing of my whole plan from the great Prime Minister of England. Then Churchill considered the matter. I waited. "Why shouldn't this development be carried out by the Government?" he asked. I was taken aback. "Which Government?" I asked, and he was silent. Then he said, "I suppose it's best done by private enterprise," and I told him that I agreed entirely. Radicalism from a Tory; conservatism from a Socialist! It was a theme that would come up again before construction started at the Falls.

Curtis and I had not been back at the Savoy Hotel for more than a few minutes when I received a telephone call from Lord Leathers, Churchill's close Cabinet colleague. The Prime Minister had called him, he explained, and asked him to get in touch with me and offer his services and be a constant liaison between the Prime Minister and me. He suggested that he come over to see me at the hotel, but I told him no, that I'd rather go to see him. The next day, Curtis and I went to his offices near the Admiralty. One of the first things Lord Leathers told us was that these were the offices Churchill had used during the war. He showed us Churchill's map room, and the single cot on which he slept whenever he spent the night there; and he told us many a tale of his own experiences with Churchill. Well before the Second War, he had invited Churchill to become a director of several of his companies—Leathers was a major shipping magnate and industrialist—and he recounted the amusement of the other directors as Churchill, utterly ignoring the business of the meeting, repeatedly expressed his views on German rearmament, the horrors of

Nazism, and the dire need for Britain to prepare against the coming war.

A few days after my meeting with Lord Leathers, the head office of the Federated British Industries asked me to speak to a group of English industrialists and financiers, and I promptly agreed. The Federated British Industries was the British equivalent of the Canadian (or American) Manufacturers' Association, and I was more than glad of the chance to tell my story to nearly a hundred of the industrial and financial leaders of Great Britain. They published my speech as a pamphlet and circulated it widely. I told them generally the same things that I had told Churchill but added that there was scarcely any limit to the size of the area that we would be willing to give a great syndicate of British companies in Labrador; and that we would also give a lesser amount of land on the Island of Newfoundland itself. "Thirty thousand square miles; forty thousand, fifty thousand—we'll give an area as big as England herself."

But, said I, we would give it, not for a game preserve, not for a park, not for holding against a hazy future time. We would insist on imposing two main conditions: first, certain large minimum amounts of money would have to be spent on surveys to map, blueprint, and spell out the nature and size of the various resources; and second, so as to speed up the process of survey and investigation, so many miles of the concession would have to be shed every five years or so. The syndicate would have the right, virtually forever, to develop anything they found—there would be nothing niggardly in the amount of territory that they could have indefinitely for actual development. What we were determined to avoid was the syndicate's just sitting on their concession. I gathered that my talk made a strong impression, and a good one.

Then I held what newsmen told me was the biggest press conference in England since the end of the Second World War. Again, in language more appropriate to journalists than to Prime Ministers and bankers, I described the vastness of Labrador, the Hamilton River and Falls, the great airport at Goose Bay, the 365-mile railway that was to be built from the shore of the Gulf of St. Lawrence to the heart of Labrador at Knob Lake. I lingered on the awesome wonder of the Falls and added that the concession that we were prepared to cede to British industry would be the largest real estate deal of the present century. The pencils raced. I concluded by saying that the Newfoundland Government would want something more out of all this development than merely the revenue it would get from taxes of general application. We would want a reasonable share of the profits—something off the top before taxes were paid at all, whether federal or provincial.

One newsman asked me what company I thought would be most likely to receive the concession? I told him that there was no company in England big enough. It would have to be a syndicate of many of the largest industrial, commercial, and financial concerns of the country.

Who was going to form this syndicate? That I didn't know, I replied. That was the nub of the whole thing. What I needed above all else was some good British individual or organization that would put the syndicate together, lead it, and see it through to a successful conclusion.

That day and the next, the British press and radio rang with the story. Churchill's "great imperial concept" was played up heavily, as was my description of my proposal as "the biggest real estate deal of the century". An extraordinary thing happened. I seemed to have touched a nerve of the British people, a sympathetic one. Britain had bled itself white in the war against Hitler, and its people were down in their spirits. Here was a vast and imaginative scheme that might, as I had remarked at the press conference, be a means of restoring Britain's greatness. At any rate, there was one who was prepared to gamble on it! I was bombarded by telephone calls, letters, and telegrams. People in all parts of Britain wanted to help. Doctors and nurses volunteered to go to Labrador, as did engineers, tradesmen, journalists, and civil servants. I returned with sincere thanks the cheques and money orders that began to pour in to me at the Savoy Hotel from people who thought that I was seeking money for the development. At an unearthly hour of the morning, the telephone rang in my room—it was an Englishman somewhere in South Africa calling to volunteer his services for Labrador.

It was all very encouraging, but where was the one company that would spearhead the whole thing, that would put the syndicate together? Newsmen telephoned every day asking if I had found the right company or men yet, and I was obliged to say no.

Curtis and I moved on to the continent to keep appointments previously made with several large industrial concerns that we were trying to interest in other developments in our province. Then, on September 12, a friend telephoned from London to give me the glad news that the famous House of Rothschild was about to make a public statement that it would investigate my project. A fortnight later, on September 26, back in London, I received a letter from Rothschilds indicating the company's positive interest and inviting us to lunch on September 30. Sir Eric Bowater, who took a lively interest in my campaign, had talked with Anthony de Rothschild, who was his banker, and I think that I may owe his memory a real debt for his part in the whole affair.

The lunch at Rothschilds was my first visit to the famous offices. We were met at the door by an official who led us to the Partners' Room. Here was the very room in which incidents famous in modern British history had occurred: the decision to finance Disraeli's purchase of the Suez Canal shares for the British Government; the financing of the Battle of Waterloo; perhaps—should I say it?—some connection with the Jameson Raid in South Africa. Countless great industrial and financial projects around the world had been initiated and discussed in this room; and it looked like it! Here, where Anthony de Rothschild, head of the English House, sat, was the very desk which his predecessors had used. Here, where his nephew Edmund sat, predecessor partners of the family had worked. I wondered if the very carpet on the floor had been there all through the years; it seemed worn enough to have been. The whole place looked like a room out of Dickens, as did the adjoining room, where senior officials of the company were bent over their desks. I could see them, for there were windows in the intervening wall. It was clear that the visit to this particular room was to be purely social, for after a few moments the blind was drawn to cut us off from the adjoining room, sherry was produced, and we talked amiably for some time about inconsequential things. Then Anthony de Rothschild led the way out through the hallway with its many paintings of members of the family reaching back a couple of hundred years. One of them showed the crowded Chamber of the House of Commons, with Lionel Nathan de Rothschild, the first orthodox Jew ever to be elected to that august body, standing in his proper place at the foot of the Treasury table, being presented to the House. We passed more family portraits and went up one flight of stairs to the dining room, which was just opposite the small room where, for many decades, the House of Rothschild each work-day had fixed the world price of gold. Several of the senior directors of the House were there having a sherry before the meal, and there too was Lord Bessborough, a relation by marriage of the de Rothschilds, who had been Governor General of Canada. They asked me to sit at the head of the table, and of course I resisted politely until I was told that this was the practice in that room. (Winston Churchill had sat there more than once.)

After the meal, Anthony de Rothschild took my place. Now that we were getting down to business, the only man in the room I feared at all was Anthony. I saw him as a stern head of a mighty financial empire—cool, unimpressed, a little sceptical of the whole business. I set out to impress and win him over. Edmund, who later succeeded him, was amused when I told him my impression of his uncle. He said that Anthony was a dear, delightful man, not a bit hard or stern at all. I replied drily that Anthony had very successfully concealed those qualities from me. There was no doubt about the interest of that group that day, for they allowed me to break a firm rule of the dining room: the immemorial practice was to be out of the room and back to work by 2:00 p.m., but it was 3:00 p.m. before we left that day. I knew my job was done when Anthony asked the simple question, "Do you wish us to put this thing together for you?" I replied, "Yes, yes by all means."

It was a day that changed Newfoundland's history, and I was happy to tell Churchill so at seven o'clock that evening at Number 10 Downing Street. He listened with satisfaction to my report. My colleague Edward Spencer was with me, and Churchill greeted him warmly. Churchill asked me if I had read his latest book. I hadn't and was lucky enough to admit it, for he sent out for a copy which he inscribed and autographed for me. We talked briefly about his books, and he remarked that the only money that he had ever made was from his writing.

We went back to Newfoundland, and the work quickly took shape. Peter Hobbs, one of the top officers of Rothschilds, came to St. John's for talks. Then came a lanky London lawyer, Hilary Scott, from the famous law firm with the improbable name of Slaughter and May. He and Leslie Curtis and his lawyers in the Justice Department, and Dr. Fred Rowe, the Minister of Mines, Agriculture, and Resources, and his officials conferred for days to get agreement on the innumerable points of a contract and the proper wording for a statute that I was to bring to the House of Assembly. There were very few angry words; but when there were, the matter was referred to me and I, from my Olympian height (even before there was an eighth floor of the Confederation Building!), straightened out the problem.

Indeed, from the moment I had first talked with Churchill, there had been only one real hitch in the discussions. Rothschilds were trying to get a project that they could induce very great British concerns to join. That was understandable, but during a visit to London, there came a moment when I feared that the deal was becoming a wee bit too one-sided. Prime Minister St. Laurent and Jack Pickersgill also were in London at that time, so I went to them and put the facts before them. I got kindly and useful advice from both. I saw Lord Leathers and told him of my difficulty, and I had the impression later that he had intervened. At all events, the difficulty disappeared without a sound, and all was well again. Finally, the agreement between the House of Rothschild and the Newfoundland Government was signed. I brought the legislation before the House, and it was passed on March 31, 1953.

So the British Newfoundland Corporation (BRINCO) was born. The syndicate of giants that the Rothschilds put together was possibly the greatest of its kind that the world had seen. If that sounds exaggerated, see who they were!

> Merchant Bankers: N. M. Rothschild and Sons, Robert Benson-Lonsdale, Morgan Grenfell, Kleinwort and Sons, M. Samuel (chiefs in the titanic Shell Oil), Hambro's Bank, J. Henry Schroeder.
>
> Insurance Companies: Prudential (the famous British "Pru"), Alliance Assurance.
>
> Mining Companies: Anglo-American Corporation of South Africa, Rio Tinto, British South Africa Corporation, Powell Duffryn, British Metal Corporation, B.I.S.C. (Ore), Sogemines of Belgium, Frobisher Ltd. of Canada.
>
> Industrial Concerns: English Electric, British Insulated Callenders, Imperial Chemical Industries, Bowater Corporation of North America, Anglo-Newfoundland Development Company.
>
> Other Companies: William Baird, Odhams (the great publishing house), C. T. Bowring and Company (Newfoundland, England, the United States, and other lands).

Later, the Bank of Montreal and The Royal Bank of Canada were brought in. The crowning touch, I thought, was when the Suez Canal Company bought into BRINCO.

In the aggregate, those companies controlled resources with a value of not less than $20 billion.

As they had done with Sir Robert Bond's Grand Falls papermill project and Sir Richard Squires's Corner Brook papermill project, the Opposition spoke out vehemently against the BRINCO project; and one of them remarked wittily that not BRINCO, but BUNCO, was the right name for the whole scheme. They didn't vote against it, however—principally, I think, because I dared them to. I appealed to them to be consistent and vote now, as their predecessors had, against any program for the development of Newfoundland!

The great crusade was launched. Geologists, forestry experts, hydro-electric engineers went to work on the Island of Newfoundland and also, mainly, in Labrador. They spent millions on surveys and explorations. They discovered a fine copper-lead deposit at Whalesback in Newfoundland, a whole uranium field in the Monkey Hill part of Labrador, and a potentially very big copper deposit within a fairly comfortable distance of Churchill Falls itself. Up to 1972, BRINCO, its subsidiary BRINEX (Exploration), and a number of outside American and Canadian mining companies with whom they had entered into prospecting deals, spent $13 million prospecting in Newfoundland and Labrador—$8 million more than their original contract with us required them to do.

A man has only so much energy to put into anything, and so much time, and so it has been with BRINCO. The company has done a respectable amount of prospecting and exploring for minerals, but the eye of the cyclone has been aimed at Churchill Falls. Hard-bitten bankers and insurance companies were certainly not going to pour hundreds of millions into the development of the Falls on the basis of somebody's guess of the amount of power that could be developed there, the cost of doing it, and the prospect of a profit. The estimate had to be precise indeed, and that called for a mighty effort of man and machine.

BRINCO spent $17 million proving the power capability of the watershed at the Upper Churchill, and that was gamble enough, in all conscience. But it had spent a total of $150 million by the time a firm contract was signed with Hydro-Quebec. If that wasn't courage and faith in an idea, I don't know what is.

Suppose the power of Churchill Falls *could* be developed at a feasible cost and that an attractive profit could be made? Who would buy it? Where was the customer? All kinds of ideas floated through our own minds in the Government. What about using it to smelt Labrador's iron ore into steel? That alone would use up millions of horsepower, though not all of the more than 5 million horsepower that we were confident the Upper Churchill would produce. But who would smelt the iron ore? Who would put up the hundreds of millions of additional capital to install the smelting facility? And where would the steel be sold? The United States, Canadian, German, and Italian steel mills that were financing Labrador's iron ore production were doing so to secure raw material for already existing steel mills. They were scarcely likely to sabotage their own operations by making steel in Labrador! A possible pulp and papermill at Lake Melville was very much in our minds, but that would use up little more than 70,000 horsepower. What might the consumption of power amount to on the Island of Newfoundland itself if Labrador's power could be moved there—a million horsepower? Even that much consumption in Newfoundland would be too little to justify the development of Churchill Falls.

In the mind of A. W. Southam, BRINCO's president, and in the minds of the de Rothschilds, a great theme was developing. Indeed, it was more than developing: they were discussing it with the United Kingdom Government. This was nothing less than the construction of a huge plant at the mouth of the Hamilton River, a little upstream from Goose Airport, for the manufacture of fuel rods to be used in atomic energy plants. The cold water of the river, having produced the electric power, could be used as a coolant in the plant. The British Government decided in the end that instead of depending upon another country, even Canada, for the supply of these rods, it would be nationally wiser for Britain to bring in the raw material and make its own. That idea went down the drain for what was then the foreseeable future.

Then came a very exciting turn in 1962: the mighty Consolidated Edison of New York was interested! It would buy, if the price were right, large amounts of Hamilton Falls power for delivery to New York State. That was when I made the prophecy that got so much attention: the Labrador power would one day be lighting the streets and running the subways of New York. Consolidated Edison's plan interested me greatly, for I had actually seen a somewhat similar establishment in Western Germany. It was a plan to use Labrador power, in the low-consumption time of New York's electric day, to pump a great volume of water from the Hudson River up to a reservoir to be created on top of the Palisades. When the peak consumption hours arrived in New York, this water would be allowed to fall back into the river in a mighty flood that would create the electricity to meet the state's needs.

But how was the power to be got to the Hudson River? By what geographical route? It was all very well to say that it would be moved by direct current and converted, at the receiving end, to alternating current; but what would be the actual physical route of the great transmission line? Robert H. Winters, who became chief of BRINCO and of the Churchill Falls Power Corporation in 1963, was convinced that the transmission line would have to follow an overland route. This meant going through the Province of Quebec to the U.S. border and then down through New England to New York. This was fair enough, provided that an acceptable arrangement could be made with the Government of Quebec for the route through its territory.

And there was the rub. Quebec, under the premiership of Jean Lesage and the dynamics of René Lévesque, had not the least intention of allowing a company to do any such thing. Its determination was all the firmer when the Government suddenly, with scarcely an hour's warning, nationalized virtually all power production and transmission in Quebec.

Property and civil rights, under Canada's written constitution, are of exclusive provincial jurisdiction. Accordingly, Quebec would be within its rights to forbid the use of its soil for a transmission line. Bob Winters and Jean Lesage had been colleagues in Mr. St. Laurent's Cabinet. Because of the personal friendship of the two men, there was confidence in BRINCO circles that Winters would win Lesage over to a reasonable approach. Winters put himself into very close touch with Lesage, but from beginning to end, his conversations with me were an unmistakable reflection of the ups and downs of his negotiations. There were times when Winters was in despair and times when he was quite hopeful. On several occasions, he told me that he was tempted to throw in his hand. Once, he was so close to it that Lesage himself telephoned me and said, "Bob mustn't get out. He mustn't."

It became perfectly obvious to me, and to my colleagues in Cabinet, that Quebec was taking an altogether selfish view. The Government believed, in the first place, that Newfoundland was a usurper in

Labrador; that Labrador rightfully belonged to Quebec. At any rate, it professed to believe this. I daresay there are many in Quebec who believe it to this moment, though I would find it hard to believe that any knowledgeable Quebecker holds that view today. In the second place, Quebec was implacably set upon using Labrador power for its own purposes. Labrador power, Quebec was convinced, couldn't be used within Labrador, and couldn't be used anywhere unless it passed first through Quebec. Where did that leave Newfoundland? It left us at the mercy of Quebec. Our people's heritage could be developed only if Quebec consented, and it would consent only if it got its own way.

All this became quite apparent, even publicly apparent, with the result that from coast to coast in Canada there was lively sympathy for Newfoundland's predicament and hearty condemnation of Quebec's selfishness. Even within the Province of Quebec itself, there was some of the same feeling. It will come as a surprise to some people that the whole concept of the so-called Anglo-Saxon Route originated, as far as we were concerned, in engineering circles in Quebec. The explanation is simple: engineers everywhere are a sort of universal community of their own; they keep few things secret from each other, and some engineers in Quebec were disgusted by their own province's narrow-minded approach to a vast engineering project for Labrador.

The Anglo-Saxon Route (a name which I deprecated from the moment I heard it) involved conveying the power from the Falls roughly southward through Labrador to the north side of the Strait of Belle Isle, thence underwater the eleven miles across the strait to the northern tip of Newfoundland, thence by land down the full length of Newfoundland's West Coast to Port-aux-Basques, thence underwater across the Cabot Strait to Cape Breton Island, and so by land across Nova Scotia and New Brunswick to the American border. Canada was to hear much of the Anglo-Saxon Route in the next two or three years.

On a visit I made to Stockholm early in 1964, I went to see some of the top directors of the ASEA Corporation for their ideas on long-distance underwater transmission of power. They told me that it was being done quite successfully in several places: the sixty miles from the mainland of Sweden to the Island of Gottland; from England to France, each way; from the Mediterranean island of Sardinia to the mainland of Italy. Indeed, at that very time, such a line was being built between the north and south islands of New Zealand. They told me that they were familiar with the Hamilton Falls project, for they were doing business with various power concerns in Canada. I showed them the proposed Anglo-Saxon Route, and they said that they saw no particular reason why it couldn't be done. They gave me the names of two highly reputable companies in England that were experts in that kind of power transmission; and the next day in London, I sought out Preece, Cardew, and Ryder. The firm was willing to make a careful study of the route; and, subject to the approval of my Cabinet, I engaged it there and then.

The company went to work with a will, and the work was concentrated on the two straits, Belle Isle and Cabot. Under command of an experienced master mariner, a ship was sent to make careful surveys of the precise nature of the sea bed, depth of water, and the general contour of the bottom. Icebergs would be the principal danger in both straits, particularly in Belle Isle. The bergs come into the strait at its eastern or outer entrance, and they normally move slowly through the strait until they bring up on the bottom. This causes them to break into pieces, and the pieces continue to float westward. The shallowest part of the strait, west of the entrance, ends before it reaches the place where the power cables would be laid from Labrador to northern Newfoundland. At that point, any bergs that had travelled that far westward would float freely past the cables. As an added precaution, however, trenches would have to be gouged out along the bottom and the cables buried in them. This would be necessary particularly near the shore on both sides of the strait. The cables would be well protected by being encased in several layers of different materials, and the whole of each cable would be enclosed within a very hard steel shield.

The water in Cabot Strait is much deeper, the bottom is quite sandy, and there would be virtually no risk of damage by icebergs. There would be danger, in both straits, from the operations of fish draggers or trawlers that might fish close to the cables; but Preece, Cardew, and Ryder suggested that this danger could be eliminated by the provision of lines of warning buoys, well lit and electronically activated. Also, there was the danger that corrosion from salt-water spray would attack the land section of the transmission lines along Newfoundland's East Coast, but this was not an insuperable problem. It seemed that the Anglo-Saxon Route was feasible.

Now commenced an extraordinary, tortuous series of manoeuvrings. My personal diaries set them forth baldly:

1964

February 18. Stockholm. Edmund de Rothschild phoned me here from Montreal in anguished tones. He is greatly worried about the situation. Told me Bob Winters coming to London. I saw ASEA directors. Arrived London. Winters arrived 10 p.m. from New York City. Came to see me at Savoy. Curtis and I and Winters talked until 1 a.m. He urged me to see Lesage and try to persuade him.

February 21. St. John's. Winters phoned from London. I tried phone Lesage—out of town.

February 24. Lesage phoned. We will meet Montreal Sunday.

March 1, Sunday. Montreal. Queen Elizabeth. Lesage came 12:15 my suite. We lunched and talked 'til 3 o'clock. He wants:

1. BRINCO out.
2. Quebec and Newfoundland jointly to develop Churchill Falls.
3. The border to be changed—in Quebec's favour of course.
4. Newfoundland to absorb 4,000 Quebeckers in construction of Churchill project.
5. Quebec materials to be used.

Told him No!

There was another point that I didn't note in my diary. Lesage insisted that the power from Churchill Falls would have to be delivered on the Quebec side of Point A. Point A was his euphemism for the Labrador boundary, and his reason for wanting the power delivered to Hydro-Quebec, the province's publicly owned hydro system, was to enable the actual sale of the Churchill power to be made on Quebec soil. At that time, the Federal Government was paying to the government of a province in which the power was sold, one-half of the federal corporation income tax collected from the profits made in the sale. This meant that, under Lesage's arrangement, income which in all conscience belonged to Newfoundland would go instead to Quebec!

March 3. St. John's. de Rothschild phoned from London and I told him Lesage situation. Invited Greene [Opposition Leader] and Browne [his Chief Lieutenant in the House] in and I briefed them on Lesage. Bob Winters phoned 2:30.

March 8. Montreal. Met Bob W., Sir Mark Turner. W. had just come from seeing Lesage. W. said Lesage had now agreed drop every condition except border and on that he merely wants my word that something will be done afterwards.

March 19. Lesage phoned noon. I talked to W. in Jamaica.

March 31. Quebec City. Conference of Premiers. Lévesque [the present leader of the Parti Québécois, then the most important Minister in Lesage's Cabinet] and I discussed Hamilton Falls. He thinks we should nationalize.

April 1. Lesage, Lévesque, Curtis and I met privately and discussed boundary and Hamilton. "Discussion" consisted almost wholly of our listening to them. Dinner that night by Lesage. To all of us and to my surprise he spoke openly about the boundary and Hamilton. I phoned Bob W. and told him of these things.

April 13. I made public announcement that no deal had been made on boundary. Lesage issued statement confirming me. Talked to Bob W.

April 22. W. and I talked on phone. Perhaps looking better.

April 29. W. announced Hamilton off for one year. I phoned him tonight and strongly suggested we approach the Governor of Maine.

May 11. Phoned W. and told him I wanted Preece, Cardew and Ryder hired by BRINCO. Made statement in House in response to Lévesque.

May 12. Tried reach Governor of Maine.

May 14. Got Governor of Maine, had chat: told Winters.

May 20. Phoned W. again re P., C., & Ryder.

May 23. Winters wired and wrote. Lane [of Preece, Cardew and Ryder] has agreed to do a thorough report for BRINCO.

June 2. Phoned W. Told him who had made the estimates of "Anglo-Saxon" route—he surprised.

June 15. Montreal. George Hobbs, Wally Read, Don McParland and I had dinner. Bob W. arrived from Boston. Lane over from London, dined with us. We discussed "Anglo-Saxon" route.

June 16. Winters, Lane, Hobbs and I discussed "Anglo-Saxon" route.

July 23. Ottawa. Bob W. phoned me—speaks of resigning as chairman of BRINCO. I urged him not.

July 30. W. phoned. Told him of my idea to announce publicly our desire that he hold everything 'til Preece, Cardew, Ryder report.

August 4. Cabinet approved my telegram to Bob W. and my statement.

August 6. W. asked me to wait 'til after the Brinco meeting of Sept. 2. I agreed.

August 12. Had Greene and Browne in and briefed them.

October 4. Lane and Miller [of Preece, Cardew and Ryder] and George Hobbs to my house for talk.

October 21. London. [Eric] Kierans [a Member of Lesage's Cabinet] had issued statement on Churchill Falls. Papers phoned me. I asked: "Who is Kierans?"!

November 4. London. Lane tells me report won't be ready 'til end of month. Lunched at Rothschild's and reported.

November 9. St. John's. Talked on phone to J. W. P[ickersgill] on Hamilton.

November 16. Two men from Dillon, Read (incl. Peter Flanigan*) in my house all afternoon on Hamilton.

November 24. New York City. Lane and Miller, George Hobbs and I in my suite. Then to Dillon, Read 'til 3 p.m. and lunch. Seems to be the case that "A.-S." route OK but it means nationalization.

November 25. Lane, Miller, Hobbs, I all day at Dillon, Read's.

November 26. Montreal. Curtis, Hobbs, Pushie and I lunched with Bob W. Told him of favourable P., Car., R. report. Press conference 4 p.m. Lesage issued statement. I replied, exposing his March 1st demands. Flurry of calls and telephones in all this.

November 27. Montreal. Lesage made a much more moderate statement.

December 12. Toronto. Lane, Miller, Hobbs, J. D. Fraser† and I in long huddle 'til 10 p.m.

December 14. Toronto. Meeting in Rio-Algom office. Bob W., de Rothschild, Turner, Mulholland, Young (of Morgan, Stanley), Bechtel-Acres man, etc., etc., and Curtis, Hobbs, Fraser, Lane, Miller and I—19 in all. All appeared to be much impressed. I phoned Webster (New England Electric System) who was at Washington.

If much of this sounds chaotic, it is largely because it was. I think it quite likely that Lesage was being pushed hard by Lévesque. They definitely wanted us to cut BRINCO out of the picture and Newfoundland to nationalize the Churchill project. They gave me figures of their own compilation to convince me that we would profit more from nationalization than through development by BRINCO. I gave the figures to BRINCO, without revealing their source, and asked for a reply. I was convinced that if we nationalized the project and en-

*He is now a highly placed member of President Nixon's White House staff.

†I had engaged this brilliant chartered accountant to do analytic work for us and generally to advise us on anything involving figures—profits, taxes, and so on.

tered into the partnership with Quebec, Newfoundland would truly get the rotten end of the stick. I was convinced that Quebec would show neither scruple nor conscience in its treatment of Newfoundland—that we would be victimized at every turn.

The Dillon, Read proposals were fascinating. That great firm had been very closely associated with large hydro-power developments on the West Coast of the United States and elsewhere, and I received from Peter Flanigan and his associates in Dillon, Read quite an education in that field. Their proposals were based on the Anglo-Saxon Route. They wouldn't have objected to the Quebec route, but they knew Quebec's stand—that it simply wasn't going to permit passage through the province of a transmission line that it didn't own; it wasn't going to allow power to pass through the province unless Quebec owned it. The Dillon, Read idea was that from the American border down to New York, a publicly owned transmission system would be built. This would be free of all American taxes, so that the money for the whole project could be raised at a very low rate indeed. They would have financed for us the Newfoundland Government's construction of the whole Hamilton Falls project, as well as the cost of our constructing the transmission line by the Anglo-Saxon Route all the way from the Falls to the American border. The power would thus be publicly generated and publicly transmitted all the way from the powerhouse to the wholesale consumers in New England and New York, who would buy it from the publicly owned transmission line. I had Peter Flanigan and his business associates meet with various members of my Cabinet, usually at my home, and I had them meet my whole Cabinet, in formal session, once or twice.

Why wouldn't I fall in line with the proposal to nationalize? I wouldn't as long as there was a reasonable alternative. It was not merely because some members of the Royal Family, and Winston Churchill, and other great personages in England were shareholders in BRINCO, though obviously that was no insignificant aspect. Rather, it was because it would represent a vile piece of treachery on Newfoundland's part. I had gone to England asking help and had offered the British this opportunity, and they had spent many millions working up the project. If we were to nationalize BRINCO now, the English-speaking world would denounce our conduct, and rightly. I felt that financial circles on both sides of the Atlantic would never trust Newfoundland again; that Newfoundland's name would stink in the nostrils of business people everywhere. I was convinced that never again would we be able to induce an industrial or commercial concern to take us seriously.

There was one possible justification for nationalization: the failure of BRINCO to perform. But we had to give the group every possible chance to perform, and all possible help.

I continue quotations from my diaries:

1965

February 1. Boston. Dinner tonight with N. England Electric Power people—Webster, Knapp, Moore, Boston-Edison President, Bob Winters, Hobbs, Pushie. Not good. Looks like something close to 4 mills U.S. 11 to 1 a.m. after dinner. All our crowd in my room, joined by Lane just arriving from London.

February 2. Boston. All forenoon 'til 4 p.m., conference of private enterprise power companies. I spoke on Hamilton. Lane answered questions. Governor Hoff of Vermont spoke at lunch.

February 4. St. John's. Announced change of Hamilton to Churchill [I had been to the funeral of Churchill in London, Edmund de Rothschild taking me in his car to the lying in state at Westminster. He was deeply affected, and so was I. I told him that I thought that the least Newfoundland could do to honour Churchill's name was to call our great falls and river after him.]

February 5. de Rothschild delighted when I told him on phone.

February 22. Bob W. back in Montreal from London. Very gloomy—thinks almost impossible raise the capital in U.S. He still argues the Quebec route.

February 24. At Cabinet. Bob W. phoned. I said we're now thinking of just developing enough power for ourselves. Greene and Browne in for lunch and I briefed them.

February 25. Ottawa. Went over whole ground with J. W. P[ickersgill].

February 26. Ottawa. Pearson's house. J. W. P. and Walter Gordon [Canada's Minister of Finance]. We discussed Churchill. L.B.P. and W.G. both said Canada anxious to get the development. After dinner J.W.P. came with me and we heard the whole Dillon, Read proposal from Christie of that firm.

February 27. Home. Cabinet meeting. Had Christie and George Hobbs in. We went over whole idea. At 1 a.m. (11:30 in Toronto) I phoned Bob W. and asked him come down next week for talks. Agreed.

March 10. Cabinet. Bob W. present and George Hobbs, J. D. Fraser, Gordon Pushie. In House I made a statement on Churchill and introduced Winters, who spoke.

March 11. On phone tonight I asked Bob W. to sound Lesage on a joint Quebec-Newfoundland survey of the headwaters and rivers that are separated by the East-West Labrador–Quebec border, with view to joint development. [These rivers, which flow through Quebec and empty into the Gulf of St. Lawrence, have their headwaters across the boundary in Labrador.]

March 21. Sunday. Had Members of H. of A. up, 3–7:30 to meet Lane and Miller for briefing.

March 24. Bob W. phoned. He is to speak on phone tomorrow a.m. to Lesage.

March 29. W. phoned me a report from Toronto.

April 27. London. Bob W. phoned from Montreal. Seems that Lesage has made another unfortunate statement.

April 28. Home. Winters shattered by Lesage's double-talk and says he wouldn't disagree now if we nationalized.

April 30. Talked to de Rothschild in London and told him we had practically decided to nationalize.

May 1. Phoned J. W. P. in Ottawa.

May 2. Winters phoned twice from Toronto. Read me a letter he had sent to Hydro-Quebec.

May 3. Ottawa. Dinner with J.W.P. and Bob Bryce [then Deputy Minister of Finance]. Lesage was having dinner with L.B.P[earson.]

May 4. Lunch with L.B.P. J.W.P. with me. I updated Pearson. Press conference afterwards. I explained the new approach. In Montreal Lesage exploded in print, because Canadian Press had circulated an absolutely incorrect report of conference. I phoned Lesage and corrected.

May 5. Home. Series of phone calls J.W.P. and Bob W.

May 6. Peter Flanigan, Christie and Stacy of Dillon, Read, and Connolle, went over with me their technique for nationalization.

May 7. Dillon, Read people in office and then I took them in Cabinet. They then flew to Montreal to meet L.B.P. and W. Gordon tomorrow morning.

May 8. Peter Flanigan phoned from Montreal–They'd had a good meeting with L.B.P.

May 11. Lesage on CBC announced that a change in the boundary must be a condition of the Falls development.

May 12. I announced No, not a chance. Called Bob W. and told him what Lesage had said. He's disgusted and discouraged.

May 13. W. phoned tonight that he has a deal with Hydro-Quebec, but is it along agreed lines? He said Yes. Will Lesage impose the boundary change condition he announced recently? W. thinks not. I'm very suspicious.

May 14. Pushie phoned from Montreal and read out Bob W.'s letter to me. Sounds like a sell-out. Lesage said in his House that he may soon be meeting me.

May 15. Pushie delivered W.'s letter to me which represents a perfect double-X. Tonight I had J.W.P., Curtis and F.W.R[owe] over to dinner and we went all over the ground. It ended in my dictating over the phone to Miss Duff a letter to W.

May 16. Sent the letter to W. special delivery.

May 17. At Cabinet I tabled both letters. Agreed that I write asking for detailed projections of both ideas. D. C. line and Hydro-Quebec buying at Point A. W. phoned me tonight—he's received my letter. Says he negotiated right up to last Friday on the March 10 agreement. He agreed send me the projections after I told him of them.

May 18. Lesage phoned me tonight. Conciliatory. Wants meet me secretly after his Cabinet meeting Wednesday next week. Says Winters today was very discouraged.

May 20. Fraser phoned from Montreal.

May 22. Hobbs up to House and we went over whole situation.

May 23. J.W.P. phoned and I updated him.

May 25. Cabinet. Hobbs, Read, Frank Newbury, Wilf Garland, Fraser, Pushie—we reviewed and discussed.

May 26. Maurice Sauvé [a Minister from the Province of Quebec in Pearson's Cabinet] phoned from Q. City and I suspect that he was speaking from Lesage's office. Coming to see me couple of days time.

May 27. Lesage phoned. He wants the headwaters of his rivers. We're to meet Mon. 7th.

May 28. Sauvé came and spent the night at my home. We talked 'til 1 a.m., after he had helped in the opening of the new Anglican regional high school on the highway near Bay Roberts.

June 1. Bob Winters and Vollmers of Morgan, Stanley and I talked 4 to 7 p.m.

June 2. Winters in. I asked Ministers in. I phoned Lesage and suggested a swap of rights—his headwaters in Labrador for our transmission rights in S.E. Quebec.

June 5. Fraser in to report on his visit to BRINCO in Montreal.

June 7. Montreal. Lesage and Jean Lessard came 8.30 a.m. to my room 'til 10.45. Apparently we agreed on everything. I flew to Ottawa and saw L.B.P. He and J.W.P. delighted. I reminded Pearson of his promise to vacate federal tax on power and he agreed. J.W.P. and I afterwards drafted letters to L.B.P. and we took it to him at 8 p.m. and after we had all made a few improvements in it L.B.P. agreed and I signed it.

June 8. Montreal. At 8.45 I phoned Lesage and read him my letter to Pearson. He was satisfied and told me his Cabinet last night had approved letter of intent to BRINCO. This was to be delivered this a.m. to BRINCO by Hydro-Quebec and it was. Richard Nixon and John Shaheen came to my room in the hotel and chatted.

June 9. Chatted with Lesage on phone.

June 10. Lesage called me. Also Bob W.

June 11. BRINCO and Hamilton Falls Power Corp. boards met and approved deal with Hydro-Quebec.

August 19. W. phoned. I talked to Lesage—possibly there'll be agreement on 2.25 mills average rate.

August 27. W. phoned—thinks the agreement about done.

September 16. W. phoned. Consolidated Edison willing to give Hydro-Quebec the letter of intent, as I told Lesage I would suggest. Bob is quite evidently anxious to get into the election. He'll go for the P.M'ship. I told him if Q. will give our letter of intention Tuesday or Wednesday it will force him to get in.

September 17. W. phoned. He's made up his mind to jump in. I urged him not to announce or let Lesage know 'til letter of intent received from Q.

September 19. Many visitors at house all day. John Crosbie over—he wants to be a candidate.

October 7. McParland to lunch. I broached tunnel scheme.

October 31. W. phoned. Apparently deal OK.

November 9. W. elected. His majority 17,300. I told him he'd replace L.B.P. when P. retires.

November 14. W. phoned from N.Y.C. where he was to see Forbes of Con. Ed.

November 23. W. phoned—"pretty close now!"

December 15. W. phoned to say he hasn't resigned from BRINCO, at least not yet publicly.

December 18. W. phoned—he announced his resignation in case Diefenbaker attacks him.

December 22. W. announced that Churchill will start in the new year but this radio report turned out to be false alarm. I called W. Just sloppy reporting, he says.

1966

January 4. Nassau, Bahamas. I had cable from W. saying Thursday meeting in N.Y.C. with himself, Henry Borden, Val Duncan and other BRINCO directors has been called off.

January 6. Montreal. W. told me that Con. Ed. would today probably sign letter of intent, but with the 9 months "reservation." I told him that if there's any danger of losing this year we would be back to consideration of nationalization. He said that that's what he had told them.

January 7. Val Duncan phoned to "pay his respects." Said the meeting with Con. Ed. in N.Y. yesterday was not so good. He and Henry Borden may come next Wednesday for a talk.

January 12. Ottawa. Borden, Duncan, McParland in a.m. and for lunch. Position is that Con. Ed.'s letter of intent to Hydro-Quebec is full of ifs and ands—"as full of holes as a colander is" Borden said. They propose to accept this and try get the holes plugged one by one through the year, but meanwhile to get the preliminary start made. I said the time was beginning to get precious—we wouldn't be willing to wait many weeks—the thing just has got to get going this year, even if we have to nationalize, which we don't prefer.

January 28. Henry Borden phoned.

February 4. McParland phoned—C.F. may be very near.

February 25. Borden phoned—BRINCO deal almost ready.

February 27. McParland came by jet and lunched with me. He and Curtis read over the Quebec draft letter of intent.

March 16. McParland phoned to report. Val Duncan phoned report from N.Y.C.

March 22. I had the 5 bank managers and Arthur R. Lundrigan in for lunch and briefed them.

April 18. Pushie phoned from Montreal. Updated. Seems that Hydro-Quebec ready to go, but if not BRINCO will go without them. At any rate for time being.

April 29. Borden phoned—coming next Friday. We had some hard words.

May 6. Borden, McParland in. Until [Quebec] election over there is not to be a word. In July I am to turn sod.

June 6. Borden phoned and we discussed in the light of results of Quebec election. [The Union Nationale Party had defeated Lesage's Liberals.]

June 9. McParland phoned from Montreal re political situation Quebec.

June 28. McP. phoned—news not so good. Johnson did call on Hydro-Quebec yesterday but gave no word.

July 7. McParland phoned—Johnson may slow OK to Hydro-Quebec.

July 20. McP. phoned—Says Johnson seems to have cast the die in his own mind.

July 22. McP. phoned—he, Borden and Duncan meeting me in Dorval tomorrow.

July 23. Dorval. Met above. Told me that Daniel Johnson adviser had met them and demanded that they produce from a Canadian bank a guarantee of one hundred million dollars. They refused but did agree give one before contract is signed. Meanwhile it was only yesterday that the French translation of the draft letter of intent was delivered to Johnson.

August 8. McP. phoned saying that the deal was now on Quebec Cabinet agenda.

August 17. McP. phoned—says good.

August 30. McP. phoned—D. Johnson today changed his time—but not I think his mind—on Churchill.

September 12. Cabinet at my request passed order that on 23rd we'll ask Ottawa to declare the Churchill to be in the national interest if by then Quebec has not agreed. J.W.P. to lunch—told him, and he phoned Ottawa to tell them. John Turner in to lunch.

This was a new turn. Although property and civil rights are of exclusively provincial jurisdiction, there is an overriding principle that allows the Government of Canada to declare something to be in the national interest, and in that case the federal authority is paramount. I proposed to my colleagues in Cabinet that we ask Prime Minister Pearson to declare the development of Churchill Falls to be in the national interest, but I wasn't fooling myself, or my colleagues. How safe would a transmission line built through Quebec by BRINCO be in that case? For most of its distance, it would go through wild, uninhabited wilderness. A well-placed bomb here and there would put the line out of commission for days at a time, and BRINCO could be led an un-merry chase restoring the destruction as fast as the bombs could be placed. Not for a moment did I suppose that designation of the project as national would be a solution of itself. The threat might, however, be more effectual than the reality. It was much like our repeated threat to nationalize.

September 13. Told McP. of our order and he said he'd get word to Johnson.

September 17. J.W.P. phoned—says Quebec Cabinet split.

September 18. George Hobbs, Newbury 10 12. Borden, Duncan, McParland 12-3—stayed to lunch.

September 21. Conference telephone call from Borden, Duncan, McParland.

September 23. J.W.P. called asking be updated.

September 28. McP. phoned—Q. Cabinet met yesterday and today and tonight. He thinks green light. I wrote my letter to L.B.P. I read it over phone to J.W.P.—he thinks it's just right. Hope I don't have to send it.

Next day, I flew to Montreal and at the Holiday Inn three unhappy men met me—Borden, Duncan, and McParland. They knew that I was bringing the letter to the Prime Minister. Indeed, I let them read it in confidence. They pleaded with me not to deliver it; they gave me the details of Johnson's Cabinet meeting, and delivered a message that Johnson had sent me through them, asking me to wait until October 6. I appeared to consider the request and said I hoped they wouldn't mind if I went into the next room of the suite to be alone. It wasn't very long before McParland came in and added his personal plea to me to wait. I went back into the other room and agreed. After they left, I phoned Pickersgill in Ottawa and told him.

A week later, I left for Tokyo for an important meeting with large Japanese interests. I was in Bangkok when McParland sent me the glad news. Quebec was signing! My comment, which the news services sent around the world, was in two words, "Glory hallelujah!" Cables of congratulation poured in on me from everywhere.

Back in Newfoundland, there was another fuss. The president of Hydro-Quebec, Jean Lessard, made a public statement to the effect that all the workers, and virtually everything else, for the Churchill Falls development were to come from Quebec. I denounced his statement as a tissue of falsehood, and Daniel Johnson hastily issued a public statement agreeing completely with me and condemning Lessard. In November, McParland and I went for a drive out of St. John's, and we went over the whole ground of labour, purchases, supplies, and the like. I issued a statement on the matter, and it was reassuring to our people. Toward the end of November, Donald Gordon came in to see me on his first visit as the new head of Churchill Falls. He came to St. John's regularly to see me until his death, and we formed a strong friendship.

That was quite a year, 1966—but it wasn't until July 10th, 1968, nearly two years later, that Premier Daniel Johnson telephoned me to say that they were signing the Churchill deal on the following day and that he would be announcing it the following night or the next morning! But it was not until May 14, 1969, yet another year later, that the final signing of the Churchill documents took place at Montreal! I had been at it since August 14, 1952—seventeen years!

Alexei Kosygin, Premier of the Soviet Union, and I once argued warmly about the comparative size of the Churchill Falls development. I claimed that at 10 million horsepower, or perhaps 11 million, Churchill was the biggest on earth. He claimed that a development they had in the Soviet Union was bigger. He had his slide rule out making calculations, but in the end I think that it turned out that we were talking about two different things. I was talking about one single river or one single watershed, and he was talking about a complex of rivers.

It will cost $950 million to develop the 7 million horsepower of the Upper Churchill. Already the Upper Churchill is producing 2½ million horsepower. In 1974, it will be producing 5½ million, and in 1975 the full 7 million. That will be a whole year ahead of schedule—a remarkable fact in itself.

The Lower Churchill, including the Muskrat Falls, will turn out more than 3 million additional horsepower, but it will cost over $700 million to do it, for of course money is far more expensive to buy today than it was when the Upper Churchill contracts were signed in 1969. If the Upper Churchill contracts had to be made today, the cost of the project would run far beyond $950 million.

BRINCO has between 21,000 and 22,000 shareholders, the majority being Canadian. The capital structure of the power development is complicated, but it may be enough to say that a bond issue of $500 million, the biggest of its kind ever attempted in the United States, was successful, and 15 per cent of the money came from Canada. (That $500 million U.S. was worth $540 million Canadian at the time.) A second issue, Series B, of $50 million was raised in Canada. The total Canadian subscription was therefore $65 million. Canadian banks made a ten-year $150 million loan available to the company, but probably no more than a third of that will in fact be used. It was the biggest bank loan ever arranged in Canada. A general mortgage bond issue of $100 million was made by Hydro-Quebec. The Newfoundland Government, when I was Premier, put $10 million into the Churchill Falls Power Corporation.

What is Newfoundland going to get out of the Churchill development in cash revenue? The value of the return from the Upper Churchill will average between $15 million and $16 million a year. During the forty-year contract with Hydro-Quebec, Newfoundland will receive over $600 million from the Upper Churchill. The Corporation relieves the Government completely of the burden of providing, building or maintaining roads, hospitals, police services, the fire department, and the airport. The Lower Churchill deal has not been negotiated as this is written, but undoubtedly that will add substantially to the Government's revenue. As it stands at this writing, the Government will receive a royalty of fifty cents per horsepower for the electricity sold; 8 per cent of the profits of the company taken off the top, before taxes, which is the equivalent, I believe, of 11 per cent after taxes; and half of the taxes the company will pay to the Government of Canada. The Government of Canada has agreed to pass back to the Newfoundland Government all but about 5 per cent of their take each year, and the Newfoundland Government has agreed, as one of the inducements to get the project going, to return each year approximately one-half of this payment to the company from which it came in the first place. About 36 per cent of the Company's income will go to the Newfoundland Treasury. Twenty-one thousand Newfoundlanders have found work on the great project and they have received $121 million in wages. There is a beautifully constructed town at the site and this will remain. Construction at the Lower Churchill will provide jobs for many thousands of Newfoundlanders over a period of five or six years and will mean hundreds of millions of additional dollars for the Newfoundland Treasury.

B. C. Gardiner, Greville Smith, and A. W. Southam were the three pioneering heads of the company. Other distinguished men have played their part in Canada: Robert Winters, Donald McParland, and Henry Borden. Donald Gordon, Robert D. Mulholland, and Sir Val Duncan also made valuable contributions.

In 1969, William David Mulholland (who is unrelated to Robert Mulholland) became chief executive of BRINCO. He was not new to the project, for as a high-ranking officer of the great financial House of Morgan, Stanley in New York, who are the project's principal bankers, he started working on the BRINCO project in 1958. An American by birth and upbringing, Mulholland has adapted wholly to the Canadian scene and is undoubtedly today one of the great industrial leaders of Canada.

Four of the great names of BRINCO and Churchill Falls are no longer living: B. C. Gardiner, Robert Winters, Donald Gordon, and Donald McParland. They all died in the same year, 1969. McParland lost his life when a company jet crashed into the side of Smallwood Mine near Labrador City. Eric Lambert and John Lethbridge, two of the company's most valued officers, died with him.

The one supremely great name in the whole BRINCO–Churchill Falls saga is Rothschild: the House of Rothschild in general, and Edmund de Rothschild in particular. Never was a project, from its first inception, the beneficiary of such endless care and dedication as that given to it by that modest, patriotic Englishman. Once only did I know him to be discouraged. That was when he was in Montreal and learned of the Quebec demand that Newfoundland nationalize Churchill Falls, and subsequently telephoned to me in London. Otherwise, his courage and cheerful dedication never faltered.

My own special satisfaction from the Churchill miracle was the birth at Churchill Falls, on March 29, 1970, of my first great-grandchild, Natasha; and of course there was the thrill of having Smallwood Lake named after me. Smallwood Lake is the principal water storehouse for the Churchill Falls hydro-electric power development, and is the third-largest man-made lake in the world. As I write, the Lake is not yet filled, but eventually it will cover an area of 2,200 square miles – larger than Prince Edward Island. Only Volta Lake in Ghana and V. I. Lenin Lake in the U.S.S.R. are larger.

24

Almost Drowned in a Sea of Oil

Whatsoever thy hand findeth to do, do it with thy might; for there is no work, nor device, nor knowledge, nor wisdom in the grave.

Ecclesiastes 9:10

It is my belief that every man has the divine right to work. If he cannot find work in private industry, it is the duty of the government to create work.

U.S. Senator Ernest Lundeen

We had good reason to be confident in John M. Shaheen when he came to us in 1966 with his proposal to build a big new oil refinery at Come by Chance. He had performed admirably, and kept every syllable of his word, in the one other relationship we had with him: the construction of the small oil refinery at Holyrood. We were assured that we were dealing with a man who was both honourable and able.

I had had inquiries made about Shaheen, and it was clear that he was an outstanding American of excellent repute. He'd had a very distinguished career indeed in the Office of Strategic Services (the famous OSS of General "Wild Bill" Donovan), and he had served in both the European and Pacific theatres in the Second World War. He holds the Silver Star of the United States Navy and the Legion of Merit of the United States Air Force. It was Shaheen, in 1948, who attempted to establish Puerto Rico's first oil refinery. He had established the Golden Eagle Refining Company of Panama, the Golden Eagle Refining Company of California, and the Golden Eagle Refining Company of Canada, with refineries in each of them. He had subsequently merged his Golden Eagle companies with the Ultramar Company of England and become that fine company's principal shareholder. He had become head of the Macmillan Ring-Free Oil Company, which refines a broad range of motor oils and lubricants as well as asphalts, naphthas, heating oils, and jet fuels. I found out that after attending the University of Illinois and the University of Chicago, Shaheen had served as assistant commissioner with the banking department of the State of Illinois. He was (and is) the owner of a small chain of radio broadcasting stations, and he had (and still has) a number of other business interests. Above all, he is a man of simply enormous energy and had great successes in assembling teams of men who were almost as able and hard-working as himself.

What Shaheen had in mind made sense. It was a plan to use Newfoundland as a sort of oil-refining anchorage for the United States on one side of the Atlantic basin and for Europe on the other. Crude oil would be brought to this big anchorage and, after being refined into jet fuel, gasoline, and other derivatives, would be taken to market on both sides of the Atlantic.

The very heart of the idea was so simple, and so sound, that it required genius to see it: to make use of the great deep-water seaport of Come by Chance, where vast oil tankers, the biggest then in the world or likely to come, could steam in from the oil-producing lands with an enormous volume of crude oil, at the great savings that such bulk transportation generates. Smaller ships of 30,000 or 40,000 tons would ferry the finished products to the relatively shallow harbours of North America and Europe. It was and remains as simple and sound as most of the great ideas of modern industry.

The oil refinery was to refine 100,000 barrels each day of the year, and it would be one of Canada's largest. But what use would this be to Newfoundland? We'd get work for perhaps 2,000 to 3,000 men during the actual construction of refinery and wharf, and then we'd get the smaller permanent employment in and around the refinery and port afterward.

I told Shaheen that it wouldn't pay Newfoundland to commit a substantial slice of its credit to the project if that's all there was to it, and he agreed promptly. But the 100,000 barrels was a mere beginning: the refinery was to expand in a couple of stages to 600,000 barrels a day. That would bring the permanent employment in and around the refinery, and around the port itself, to more than 1,000 well-paid jobs. But even then, would it be enough? Perhaps not, but there was an ace in the hole. This was the likelihood of the creation of a petrochemical industry based on the availability of ample supplies of raw materials from the refinery.

Putting it all together, even if it took ten to fifteen years to accomplish, it would be a brilliant addition to the province's economy, and it would give Come by Chance a status in the world that could only attract other industries to strengthen and enhance the province still further.

Shaheen was very frank with us. "I can't compete with those islands to the south of you [Puerto Rico, for example] because the refineries down there have all kinds of advantages that Newfoundland hasn't got." The principal advantage that the Caribbean Islands had was the freedom from taxes they could give to refineries establishing there.

There was a solution, and Newfoundland itself, soon after I became Premier, had discovered it and made good use of it. This was the technique of the Crown Corporation, which was exempt from federal taxation. I had brought about the organization of a number of these Crown Corporations in Newfoundland. The shipyard at Marystown was owned by one such body, as was the big new fish plant, also at Marystown, that was being run by Atlantic Fisheries, which in turn was owned by Atlantic Sugar of Toronto. A Crown Corporation had built and owned an animal and poultry feed mill, the first such mill in Newfoundland, and it was being run by the Robin Hood flour and feed people of Montreal. Newfoundland and Labrador Corporation—NALCO—was a little different from the others, in that the Crown initially owned only 90 per cent of it, with the other 10 per cent shared among several private companies.

There was one special feature about several of our Crown Corporations. This was an arrangement whereby the Government would create a Crown Corporation, enter into an agreement with a private company to manage it, and at the same time, from its inception, give to that company an option to buy all the shares of the corporation at some point in the future, after the cost of the enterprise had been paid off. The feed mill and the big new fish plant at Marystown were examples of this procedure. We called it the Robin Hood Technique, for we had first worked it out in our negotiations with the milling company of that name.

I saw that we could apply the same principle to the proposed refinery at Come by Chance. A Crown Corporation would build and own it from the start, but Shaheen's organization would superintend the design and construction of the refinery and manage the enterprise. This would mean that Shaheen's able and experienced team would obtain the firm commitments for the continuing supply of the crude oil and, of supreme importance, would get firm commitments from reliable consumers for the output of the refinery. Shaheen would borrow the money, or most of it, to build the refinery, and he would pay off the debt out of its operating profits. After he had paid off the full cost of the refinery, he would have the right to buy the establishment from the Government for $10 million plus a perpetual share of its profits to the Crown.

We made no bones about it at all: it was a device, lawful and proper, that we were already employing in a number of fields, to give a new enterprise a chance to survive and prosper by exempting it from federal taxation until its heavy borrowings were paid off.

I myself, as Premier and as Minister of Economic Development, undertook to negotiate the broad terms with Shaheen and his chief lieutenants, Homer White and Roy M. Furmark. Periodically, I reported to Cabinet the progress of our negotiations. When these were sufficiently well advanced, I appointed a committee of Cabinet—T. Alex Hickman (Minister of Justice), John C. Crosbie (Minister of Health), and Clyde Wells (Minister without portfolio), all of them lawyers—to draft the actual agreement that we were to sign with the Shaheen people. This involved our setting up a Crown Corporation to own the refinery and another Crown Corporation to operate it.

The enterprise proposed by Shaheen would cost more money to create than any enterprise had ever cost on the Island proper. Churchill Falls and the two great iron ore developments in Labrador were bigger, but the Come by Chance refinery and subsidiary aspects of it would cost about three times as much to create as the two great papermill enterprises at Grand Falls and Corner Brook. What we were talking about was a project that would cost close to $200 million, as follows:

Fixed-price construction contract for refinery	$155 million
Work done prior to making of construction contract	5 "
Working capital required	10 "
Deep-water dock and tanker handling facilities	20 "
Total	$190 million

(In the event, the grand total cost of the project has gone a little over $200 million.)

How was this immense sum to be raised? Shaheen was to provide the working capital. The Newfoundland Government would enable Shaheen to obtain $30 million of it by means of a bond issue that he would sell and the Government would guarantee. We hoped that the Government of Canada would provide about $20 million for the big wharf at Come by Chance on a user-fee basis, which meant only that the refinery itself would reimburse the Government of Canada over a considerable period by paying for the use of it. The balance of the money Shaheen was to obtain himself by means of bank loans to be guaranteed by the Government of the country in which the money was obtained, but none of it by the Newfoundland Government.

Shaheen discovered that the English were eager to back the project, as were the Germans and the French. In all three countries, there are programs to help exports of goods from job-giving industries. The British have their Export Credit Guarantee Department of the Treasury (the modern equivalent of their Trade Facilities Board, which had financed the big papermill at Corner Brook just after the First World War). Under this plan, if the banks are willing to lend money to an enterprise starting up somewhere in the world, and the machinery and other materials going into it are purchased from British industry, the ECGD may guarantee the banks that they will get their money safely back, with interest in the interim. The ECGD, before actually agreeing to give the guarantee, makes its own investigation of the proposed enterprise; for, of course, if all else fails the British Treasury has to foot the bills. The banks, too, investigate the realistic prospects of the proposed enterprise; though here, I should think, they leave it mostly to the financial house that is putting the financial scheme together. (In this case, it was the house of Kleinwort, Benson.) The British Parliament has given the ECGD authority to guarantee amounts totalling billions of dollars, and there can be no doubt that this credit-guarantee plan has done more than any other single device to keep British industry going since the end of the Second World War.

Almost exactly the same kind of system operates in Germany and in France, and indeed in other countries of Europe. Any sound industrial or commercial enterprise wishing to start up in any dependable country in the world can get these credits from the banks, guaranteed by the Government, provided that the organization makes a commitment to purchase substantial values of machinery and other materials from the country guaranteeing the loan.

Despite the interest and opportunity, Shaheen found that it was hard going, Roy Furmark negotiated with a consortium of European companies headed by the great Thyssen corporation of Germany, and including Brown Boveri and Sulzer Brothers of Switzerland, Waagner Biro of Austria, and the French Compagnie Métallique de Provence. The American firm of Ralph M. Parsons would do the design engineering if a deal were made with the European group. The negotiations with the Europeans were carried on in Europe and the United States. The Europeans' prices were not attractive, however, and the Shaheen group renewed its negotiations in England. These renewed talks were very successful, for suddenly, with scarcely half a day's notice, we all hurried out to the Paris airport to board planes to

London. In a few days, a satisfactory agreement was reached with the British; and with the television cameras recording the moment for history, we signed the documents on March 16, 1969. Procon (Great Britain) Ltd., the resident British representatives of the American oil refinery construction group owned by Universal Oil Products of Chicago, gave an acceptable firm contract price to supply all machinery and materials, convey them to Come by Chance, and erect and assemble the refinery ready to be put into production.

So far, there hadn't been any serious problems, though there were the intolerable delays and dislocations always to be found in initiating big projects. But now trouble set in, and the source of it was the mainland of Canada. They didn't like the Crown Corporation feature of the project. Who were "they"? They, I was convinced, were the large oil companies of Canada, virtually all of which have United States parents. The oil companies must surely be the roughest big business giants in the world. If they are not, I'd hate to meet the ones that are! A great hue and cry was raised against the fact that the Newfoundland Government, through its own wholly owned Crown Corporation, was building, owning, and—through the Shaheen organization—going to run a large oil refinery. You'd think, if you didn't know better (and very few knew better), that there was something at least faintly, if not openly, corrupt about the idea of a Crown Corporation oil refinery—as though the Government of Canada itself didn't have a number of Crown Corporations; as though other governments in Canada didn't have them; as though Newfoundland for years hadn't had a number of Crown Corporations. True, we intended the oil refinery to be sold to the Shaheen organization for $10 million, but that would happen only after John Shaheen had paid us back our $30 million bond issue and paid off, too, the tens of millions of dollars that he himself had borrowed in England for the building of the refinery.

The Newfoundland Government and people stood to gain enormously from the enterprise. We would get 5 per cent of the profits of the refinery, taken off the top, before payment of taxes, forever, as long as the refinery lasted. Ten million dollars and 5 per cent of the profit—at what cost to the Government? Thirty million dollars cash that we invested in the enterprise in the form of mortgage bonds, which we did in lieu of the original proposal to guarantee that amount. Shaheen himself would have found the money to build the refinery; Shaheen would have put together the experienced skills needed to design the refinery, make certain of economic contracts for the supply of the crude oil, provide the sure and certain profitable markets for the output of the refinery, and generally do everything that a Government normally is incapable of doing, in the free enterprise system of society, to make a financial success of the whole enterprise. The pity of it was that there weren't ten Shaheens, ten Come by Chances, or ten such opportunities for the Newfoundland Government to raise the standard of living for Newfoundlanders. But that is not how the project was presented to the Canadian people!

Perhaps at the urging of competitive oil companies, the Federal Government examined the Come by Chance project and announced a sudden change in policy: henceforth, in cases where it was provided at the outset that a Crown Corporation subsequently would be purchased by private enterprise, the Corporation would not be entitled to tax immunity. This was a tremendous blow, and it jeopardized our entire project. Fortunately, however, and to its credit, the Federal Government soon recovered its balance and, perhaps with a slight sense of shame, softened considerably the new policy. It announced that taxation of such corporations still would not be abated, but it would be temporarily deferred. This qualification undoubtedly helped our particular enterprise; but the fact remained that in one stroke, Ottawa had destroyed a sensible device whereby underdeveloped provinces could attract industry to their domain.

The Come by Chance refinery project quickly developed into a political issue, involving not the Opposition, but Members from within our own ranks. Our agreement with John Shaheen required the Newfoundland Government to give its formal guarantee of a $30 million bond issue which the Shaheen organization was to float as part of the financing of the project. The tight-money situation was extremely bad throughout North America; the Province had its own need to float direct bond issues; and although Shaheen was well able to float his issue on our guarantee, we were strongly disinclined to allow him to do so. We very much feared that the money market, already precarious, would be further upset by his proposed activity in it. He well understood the situation, but pointed out urgently to us that our refusal to allow him to get his $30 million could delay the start of construction, and thus the beginning of production, by a year, or possibly more. Such a delay might very seriously endanger the long catalogue of arrangements, agreements, and contracts that he had been obliged to make in various parts of the world to ensure the economic and financial soundness of the project.

Shaheen himself suggested a solution that would at least temporarily solve the problem: the Government would lend him in cash $5 million of the $30 million as "bridge" money that would be sufficient to continue the administrative and engineering services of the project in unbroken process. To me and most of my colleagues in Cabinet, this seemed an eminently sensible solution, and we gave him the money. But two of our colleagues, John Crosbie and Clyde Wells, came to me privately, while the House was in session and a federal by-election in process, and told me that they couldn't live with the "bridge" money decision and intended to resign from the Cabinet. I was astonished. The oil refinery project itself was big, in all conscience; but its bigness was not the main thing about it. The main thing was the virtual certainty that the refinery would become the catalyst of tremendous industrial development at Come by Chance. Shaheen was determined to increase the projected 100,000 barrels a day to 600,000. The presence of a large oil refinery facility was bound to attract an expanding petrochemical industry to the port. The superb harbour of Come by Chance, one of the few really great deep-water harbours on the Atlantic coast of North America, would rapidly become one of our most important assets. Come by Chance would grow quickly as the centre of a large group of towns surrounding it, not equalling St. John's, but ranking second to the capital in population and importance. It was ludicrous to suggest that we should risk the loss of all this for the sake of a trifling $5 million (trifling in the context of the entire scheme), given as a temporary advance to the Shaheen organization and to be repaid promptly after the $30 million bond issue had been floated.

There were several occasions during my premiership when being Premier could only vanish into utter insignificance for me if I wasn't to accomplish a great purpose that lay at hand. Come by Chance was one such issue. I pleaded with Crosbie and Wells not to leave the Cabinet. There had been no word from either of them, or from me, suggesting anything more than that they would leave the Cabinet. My assumption, if I had thought of it, would have been that they would merely take their places among the backbenchers on our side of the House in company with the Members of the Party who were not Cabinet Ministers but who supported the Government and kept it in office. We talked several times in the next day or so, and at one point I felt that Crosbie was about to change his mind. Wells didn't waver. He kept reminding Crosbie that they had made their decision together, and he was able to steel Crosbie's will to resign. To everyone's surprise, both men crossed the floor of the Chamber and sat a few feet away from the official Opposition, facing their former colleagues.

I have always suspected that the issue of the $5 million advance was not the real reason behind this move. Wells, I think, simply wanted to get back to his fast-growing, money-making law practice in Corner Brook, and the Come by Chance deal was as good an excuse as he could think of. Crosbie, with his inherited wealth, didn't need to go back into the private practice of law; indeed, his ambitions were altogether different from those of Wells. Crosbie came to me in the first place, asking if I would have him as a Liberal candidate and then if I would make him a Cabinet Minister, with the sole object of seizing my job at the first opportunity. Perhaps he did not regard opposition to the Come by Chance project as being in itself a sufficient springboard to the premiership, but at least it singled him out for the special attention that his nature craved.

One of the minor annoyances in the refinery project was the stubborn opposition to it of Canada's Minister of Public Works, Arthur Laing. He was for years, even before the oil refinery project was mentioned, a consistent wet blanket in Cabinet when any Newfoundland matter came up; but never was his negative attitude to our province as apparent as when the proposal was made that Ottawa provide the big wharf for Come by Chance. Even after $20 million had been spent on the project and another $20 million had been committed, he affected to believe that it was all nonsense: there wasn't going to be a refinery, so why build a wharf? The millions continued to pour into Come by Chance—no matter, he didn't believe that there was serious intention to build a refinery. When over $25 million had been invested in Come by Chance, he still doubted us and sent people to England to do some detective work. His men interrogated factory managers all over England where the component parts of the refinery were being made: were those parts really for a refinery being built at Come by Chance, Newfoundland? And when at long last he could no longer dispute the facts, he wouldn't let the wharf be built commercially but sent a chill down the backs of the developers of Come by Chance by ordering that it be built by the Department of Public Works itself. No wonder the wharf cost millions more than it should have!

Eventually, all these problems were ironed out, and the Come by Chance dream began to be a reality. After my resignation as Premier in January 1972, the new administration, to the credit of Premier Moores, made an abrupt about-face, took John Shaheen to its breast, and praised him to the skies when he took the second of the series of steps that he and I had planned together—that of putting in a facility to refine another 300,000 barrels a day above and beyond the initial 100,000 capacity. When this expansion is installed, Shaheen will have brought about an investment of $500 million at Come by Chance; and that is only a start, for I'm confident that it will lead to the investment of another half-billion dollars in the community. The refinery, at a capacity of 400,000 barrels a day, will be the largest in all Canada. Even John Crosbie has had to praise the project.

Bringing John Shaheen and his team of fine men to Newfoundland was one of my proudest triumphs. I have negotiated with many industrial and financial leaders, and Shaheen is among the top half-dozen of them. If he isn't the quintessence of the famed American drive, then I would marvel to meet the real thing! Awake and asleep, everywhere, all the time, his wonderfully quick and fertile mind works on the project he has in hand. But no dour, repellent money-grabber is he, but rather full of fun and wit and laughter. This third-generation American brings to bear on every endeavour his brilliant Americanized Lebanese traditional trading skill; but never have I suspected that his arguments are deceitful, or tawdry, or narrowly selfish. I have seen President Nixon's respect and affection for Shaheen; and at conferences and other functions and in many conversations in London and New York, Montreal and Paris, I have witnessed the obvious respect with which he is regarded by some of the best in the land. It has angered me to see him slandered by little men for little partisan purposes. Of course it was to make money for himself that Shaheen came to Newfoundland. But wasn't it the same desire that brought Bowaters, Lord Northcliffe and Lord Rothermere, the American Smelting and Refining Company, and all the great steel mill companies that make up the two big iron ore enterprises in Labrador? Didn't they come to make money for themselves? Of course they did—and so did the Rothschilds and Rio-Algom-Zinc and the score of other great concerns associated with them. But they have not come only to Newfoundland—and if there is a province in Canada where they and others like them have not come, then all you can hear in that province are moans of unhappiness. Throughout the whole of the Third World of undeveloped lands, the same importunate cry goes up for money-making companies and individuals to come and develop them. After all, it's that or Communism.

Before I was twenty, I had written to the English economist, John A. Hobson, asking him to suggest a remedy for Newfoundland's benumbing problem: lack of development capital. The moment I became Premier, I couldn't wait to go outside Newfoundland for the development capital that we didn't have ourselves. And, as I retorted when I was "accused" of "consorting" with rich companies and men, what would they have me do: go to the poorhouses, the soup kitchens, and the bread lines looking for the hundreds of millions of dollars needed to develop Newfoundland and create jobs for Newfoundlanders? Often I said in speeches that I would welcome development capital from any part of the world "this side of the iron curtain"; and after a while, I amended that by dropping any reference to the iron curtain, for I wanted to get the Soviet Union to come to Newfoundland with a plant to manufacture or at least to assemble their famous Yak passenger plane. I didn't care, and no Newfoundland Premier (or Nova Scotia, New Brunswick, or Prince Edward Island Premier) should care two straws where the capital comes from to develop his province. It would be pleasant indeed if the needed capital could come from within one's own province, or from some other part of Canada. But if it isn't there, the Provincial Government's slogan should be "Whosoever will, may come."

There isn't the slightest doubt that Canada's four Atlantic Provinces are still miles and years behind the rest of Canada. These four provinces have made real progress in the last quarter of a century; but the gap today is wider and deeper between them and the rest of Canada than it was before. The Atlantic Provinces are farther behind or below the Canadian average than they were twenty-five years ago. At a federal-provincial conference in Ottawa, I once quoted Abraham Lincoln's dictum that "this nation cannot endure half free and half slave" and said that Canada could not be the great, harmonious, and happy nation we wanted it to be while nearly half the provinces were lagging badly behind the others, and the discrepancy was becoming more acute all the time. I said then, and on many other occasions, that if Confederation didn't mean Parliament's using its sovereign power to deploy the economic strength and wealth of the nation to raise the standards of the underdeveloped provinces, then Confederation was meaningless. The underdeveloped provinces mustn't be just "colonies" or mere "markets" for the rest of Canada. Will Ottawa ever have the imagination, and the courage, to break the mould which has patterned a Canada of crass provincial inequality? Mention the idea of the underdeveloped provinces being permitted easier credit in times of tight money, and a look of distaste comes over Ottawa's face. Mention the idea of tax-free bonds for the underdeveloped provinces, and Ottawa's only answer is a palpable inaccuracy—namely, that in the United States, where that financial device is so widely used, it is going out of fashion. Let an underdeveloped province make use of the Crown Corporation technique to get development, and all hell breaks loose. The policy of reducing so-called regional disparity boils down, in the end, to a half-hearted willingness to dole out money for road paving, water and sewer systems, schools, and hospitals. After dealing with four prime ministers of Canada for twenty-three years, I am convinced that with the exception of a few brave souls, nobody in Ottawa has the slightest belief in the likelihood, or even the possibility, of the four Atlantic Provinces ever being much more than mere markets or colonies for the rest of Canada. They won't admit this; they'll deny it with vehemence, sarcasm, wit, indignation, and in a variety of other ways, for of course they can't possibly admit it—except in action.

Someday there may come to Canada a government that will brush aside all weasel thoughts of the Atlantic Provinces as Canada's poorhouse; one that will attack the problem with nerve, employing for an experimental period of ten or twenty years the devices that have been condemned in the past, and others that it will think up, to get these four provinces thirty or forty years ahead in the space of a decade or two.

25

Far Side of the Moon —and I'm Going Again

This country, with its institutions, belongs to the people who inhabit it. Whenever they shall grow weary of the existing government they can exercise their constitutional right of amending it, or their revolutionary right to dismember or overthrow it.

Abraham Lincoln

I have been over into the future and it works.

Lincoln Steffens

Russia is a riddle wrapped in a mystery inside an enigma.

Winston S. Churchill

The export of revolution is nonsense. Every country makes its own revolution if it wants to, and if it does not want to, there will be no revolution.

Joseph Stalin

The old order changeth, yielding place to the new; And God fulfills himself in many ways.

Alfred, Lord Tennyson

Desolate was the day for me when the great California pulp and papermill company, Crown-Zellerbach, dropped its option on the huge timber resources of Sandwich Bay in Labrador. I had worked hard to bring Crown-Zellerbach into Newfoundland to build my heart's desire, Newfoundland's third pulp and papermill, and the company's abandonment of the project was a crushing blow.

And then John Shaheen came to me and said simply, "Premier, give me the same chance you gave Crown-Zellerbach!" Given my boundless respect for Shaheen, I was not inclined to scoff at his request; but I couldn't help reminding him that although he was undoubtedly an authority on oil, his knowledge of pulp and paper left a lot to be desired. He admitted it cheerfully, but reminded me that you could know a lot about eggs without being a hen. "I know where to get men who know the pulp and paper business," he said. And, anyway, did I know "a better hole to go to"? as Bruce Bairnsfather asked in his World War I cartoon.

I didn't, and the Cabinet had no hesitation in transferring to Shaheen's Newfoundland Pulp and Chemical Company the concessions that Crown-Zellerbach had dropped. When the House of Assembly debated the matter, with Shaheen sitting in the distinguished visitors' gallery, I told the Legislature frankly that we were giving Shaheen the chance to give us that third mill partly because nobody else was showing the slightest interest in doing it. John Shaheen put his team to work, and within a year or two he had lined up twenty or more United States publishers of daily newspapers to join him in the papermill project. These publishers between them would absorb a high proportion of the newsprint to be produced at Come by Chance, at the head of Placentia Bay.

One day, Shaheen told me that he had established a negotiating connection with the large United Paper Company in Finland; he hoped to persuade the company to join him in building and operating the mill. He had chosen United because of Finland's geographical similarity to Newfoundland, and because of the company's skill in operating such a mill. The negotiations went on and on, and then in April 1965, Shaheen telephoned from New York to tell me that he was ready for the signing of tentative agreements with the Finns. Would I join him in Helsinki, where he would bring his lawyer from New York? A group of his executives were already in Helsinki, and would I take the next plane? I landed in Helsinki and was in my hotel room no more than a few minutes when there came a tapping at my door. I opened it, and John Shaheen's lawyer stood there with hand outstretched. His name was Richard M. Nixon—like myself, a politician.

I was charmed at once by him, as thousands have been in personal encounters with him. Shaheen led us into a round of meetings at Helsinki and in other parts of Finland, and it was at a gathering in a small industrial town that I first saw the extraordinary effect that a simple speech by Richard Nixon could have in a small gathering. We were at the home of the head of the Finnish papermill company, a hard-bitten business executive whose father had been a famous soldier of Finland, General Waldheim. (It was at this same gathering that I met Paavo Nurmi, the famous runner.) I was asked to speak, but it was Richard Nixon who, by his friendly words about Finland, brought tears to the eyes of those industrialists and businessmen. Again and again in the next year or two, I was to see the surprisingly favourable effect of Nixon's personality on small groups. I spoke twice afterward at gatherings where he was the principal speaker: at a luncheon of American newspaper publishers that John Shaheen had organized in New York, and at a luncheon of the full board of directors of the Bank of Montreal. It was the same everywhere—Nixon seems to be another man altogether in smaller gatherings. In this respect, he reminded me a little of Lester B. Pearson, who always was at his worst in large meetings.

As our business in Finland drew to a close, Nixon said to me, "Have you ever been to Russia, Joe?" I hadn't, but he had. As Vice-President of the United States, he had visited Moscow; and in the famous "kitchen debate", he and Nikita Khrushchev had argued to the fascinated interest of millions who saw and heard it on television throughout the world. It was no distance from Finland to Leningrad, and after John Shaheen had got the necessary visas for us from the Russian Embassy in Helsinki, we all boarded the train for Leningrad. Before we reached the birthplace of the Soviet Revolution,

Nixon suggested that it might be as well if we took the Moscow express from Leningrad and went the whole way. Between trains at Leningrad, I wandered off by myself in the neighbourhood beside the railway terminal, wishing that there was someone of whom I could ask whether this was the very railway station into which Lenin had come from Sweden and Finland in 1917. I wandered a little too far, and in panic I hurried back to the railway station to join the others in boarding the Moscow express. After a while, a girl came gushingly up to me and said in good English, "Is it true that Mr. Nixon is on board? Are you a member of his party?" I admitted that Mr Nixon was on board, but John Shaheen, with his OSS experience, was highly suspicious. He had known of too many nice-looking, apparently harmless women who had been successful spies. He made it his business to see that nobody got near Nixon's compartment in the car. I twitted Shaheen about it once or twice, but he only smiled and held his peace.

We got into Moscow at eight o'clock next morning, and there began instantly a hectic round of experiences that stretched late into the day and then ended late at night with an escapade that echoed around the world. Nixon was given an Intourist interpreter-guide, an able woman in her business; and I was given another. Mine spoke, she told me, eleven languages; she had gone to countless conferences around Europe and North Africa, and she held the rank of Colonel. She was pleasant enough, and certainly highly intelligent. The two of them never let Nixon or me out of their sight for a moment throughout the day. We went to Red Square, Lenin's tomb (I was excited to see that it is built of what I am sure is Labradorite, a beautiful building stone that we have in Labrador), the Kremlin Museum, the GUM department stores, the unequalled Moscow underground railway, a popular restaurant, the incredibly wonderful Bolshoi Theatre (where we saw a superb performance of "Swan Lake"), and the Moscow University skyscraper, where we had the first of our two Moscow adventures.

Driving past a huge open-air swimming pool (we could scarcely see the hundreds of swimmers in the thick vapour that rose from the heated water into the cold Moscow air), we reached the university and were whisked almost to the top floor, where the Vice-Rector greeted us. He had fifty or sixty students with him, and we were accompanied by our whole party and the contingent of newspapermen. The Vice-Rector delivered a short speech of welcome, and if I ever heard a better speech of insulting invective cloaked in polite phrases, it was the one that Nixon delivered in reply. They were so glad to welcome the two visitors, the Vice-Rector told us through the interpreter, especially Mr. Nixon. The United States was such a great country, and in the Soviet Union they were so anxious for friendship between the two peoples. But there were some things that were difficult to understand about America! Perhaps Mr. Nixon could explain? The John Birch Society? The Ku Klux Klan? How was it possible for the President of their country to be assassinated? And so on and so on. Sitting next to Nixon, I was able to lean back in my chair and observe him. His neck turned deep red above his collar, but his reply was calm and careful. The Soviet Union was such a great land, said Nixon, and the American people were so anxious for friendship with the people of the Soviet Union. He regretted, as one American, that he was not able to give the Vice-Rector the particular information he wanted about America. But while he was at it, he thought it would be an excellent opportunity to get the answers to some things that were puzzling Americans. What happened to Khrushchev? What happened to Beria? and so forth.

I made a feeble attempt, in my short speech, to defuse the bomb. I was a Canadian, I told them. Canada, though geographically the second-largest land mass of the earth, was by comparison with the Soviet Union and the United States a very small place indeed. But there we were, destined to be living between two great giants. Which of the two giants was the greater? We didn't know and we didn't want to know, for it would cost mankind too much blood to find out. But as a peace lover, and an admirer of both giants, might I venture to suggest a move that would possibly strengthen the understanding of each giant for the other? My suggestion was this: let the two men, Richard Nixon and Nikita Khrushchev, visit each other's country and stand for office again–Khrushchev running for President of the United States; Nixon for Premier of the Soviet Union. I still think my proposal was worthy of at least a fleeting smile, but I regret to say that it was met with stony silence. The thaw hadn't come then in the cold war.

That night, we had our big adventure: the search for Khrushchev. Nixon was quite anxious to meet him; not for any particular reason, but merely to shake his hand and renew acquaintances. Off and on through the day, he had remarked quietly in asides to me that he wished he could find some way to meet with Khrushchev, but he guessed that any effort would be blocked. But the chance came! We had come back from the Bolshoi and were gathered, six or seven of us, at a table in the hotel dining room. It was well past ten o'clock. A messenger came to the table and asked for me, and told me that a Mr. David Levy was out in the lobby wanting to see me. "Ask him to come in," I said. Levy was the Canadian Broadcasting Corporation's resident correspondent in Moscow, and I had often heard his voice. He came in with a portable recording machine slung over his shoulder and at my invitation drew up a chair beside me. He wanted to record an interview with me to send back to the CBC. We chatted, and I asked him about Khrushchev—would he know where he could be found? "Yes, of course. He has an apartment in a large apartment block. As a matter of fact, it is on the same street, a few yards away, as the Canadian Embassy." This was exciting! I turned to Richard Nixon and whispered the news. "Do you think he'd take us there?" Nixon asked. I turned to Levy and whispered the question. "Sure," he said promptly. He told me that he spoke Russian pretty fluently, and so we cooked up our scheme.

I spoke up for all the table to hear, saying that Mr. Levy wanted to do interviews with Mr. Nixon and me and we were going outside for the purpose. When we reached the lobby, we followed Levy out to the sidewalk and climbed into a somewhat run-down taxicab to go to Levy's apartment. This, if reported, would be natural enough: the CBC man was merely taking us there to record the interviews. The apartment was in a building containing the apartments of a number of other North American journalists, and we chatted with Mrs. Levy and her husband for fifteen or twenty minutes, long enough to "record the interviews"—that is, long enough for Levy to telephone for another taxi to pick us up at the front corner of the building. The three of us piled into the taxi, and it hurtled at breakneck speed (only in Milan have I seen taxis go faster) to the Canadian Embassy. We were going there to pay our respects! We did, indeed, sign our names in the book in the lobby of the Embassy, a little after eleven o'clock, and then we strolled nonchalantly along the sidewalk to the main entrance of the apartment block.

In the small lobby, two women sat underneath a large portrait of Lenin. One, who must have been close to seventy, looked and sounded a very battle-axe. She was dressed in a long padded coat, and she was stern and unyielding. The other was younger, close to forty, and friendlier. Levy explained in Russian that this was the former Vice-President of the United States, Mr. Nixon, an "old friend" of Khrushchev, and he wished to meet the former Premier for a moment to shake hands and greet him. This perhaps sounded reasonable enough to the younger woman, and she looked expectantly at her companion. But the battle-axe said sternly, "He can't be seen." Levy persisted: such discourtesy couldn't be shown to a great public man of the United States! No matter. Levy resorted to threats: he would report this unseemly attitude to the highest authorities. This helped. There was a brief conversation between the two women, and the young one went off, ostensibly and perhaps actually, to Khrushchev's apartment.

While we waited, I tried to engage the battle-axe in conversation. Pointing to the portrait of Lenin, I asked, "Did you know him?" Translation and a headshake. "Did you ever hear him speak?" A headshake. "Did you ever see him in the flesh?" No. So I wondered where she had been all her life. It was like being in Virginia while Washington was living and never laying an eye on him, or Gandhi in India, or Kemal Pasha Atatürk in Turkey.

But now the younger one returned and reported that Khrushchev was not in his apartment. He was, she said, in his dacha—the small house he had in the Moscow countryside. It was disappointing, but Nixon borrowed some paper from Levy and wrote a note:

> Dear Mr. and Mrs. Khrushchev: I had so hoped that I might have the pleasure of greeting you both on this brief visit to Moscow, so that two men out of office might exchange some reminiscence of former times. I hope that we may have the pleasure to meet again some day. Sincerely yours, Richard M. Nixon.

It was after midnight when we got back to the hotel.*

*In Newfoundland in 1967, it fell to my lot, representing Prime Minister Pearson and Foreign Minister Paul Martin, to go to Gander to greet Alexei Kosygin, Khrushchev's successor as Premier of the Soviet Union. He was on his way from Cuba to Paris, where he was to meet General de Gaulle, and he stopped over at Gander for five or six hours. I spent three or four hours with him, and in the course of the conversation I mentioned Richard Nixon's name and told him of our attempt to meet with Khrushchev. Kosygin didn't smile—evidently he didn't think it funny. His only remark was "A bad man," referring to Mr. Nixon. I never did let Nixon know of his remark, and I tell it now only after the establishment of apparently cordial relations between the two men. No doubt Mr. Kosygin has changed his mind about the man who is now the friend of Mao Tse-tung.

As we drove back to the hotel that night, Nixon asked me if I thought I would like to go to China. I said yes, much more that I had wanted to go to Moscow. I asked him if he had been there himself, and he admitted that he had not but that he would very much like to do so. "Then why don't you?" I asked. "Americans are not allowed by our government to go to China," Nixon explained. "How do they stop you?" "The State Department forbids it. They just won't give permission." "Do you mean to say that you, a former Vice-President of the United States, and a man who came within a hair's breadth of becoming President—in fact, the coming President of the United States—are not permitted to visit China?" "That's the size of it," Mr. Nixon admitted, smiling. Then he added, "There is one way for an American to get permission to visit China—he can go in his purely professional capacity." "Such as what?" "Well, such as legal counsel."

I pondered this a moment. "You mean to say that if someone wanted you to go to China as a lawyer you could go?" "That's it, exactly." Then Nixon said with mock seriousness, "You wouldn't go to China without a lawyer, would you?" In horror, I exclaimed, "Not on your life! I wouldn't dream of it." "Have you decided on a lawyer?" "I have, indeed." "Who?" "You, if you'll go."

And so, there and then, nearly two years before he became President of the United States, Richard Nixon and I made our bargain to go together to China—I as the Premier of the great and important Province of Newfoundland; he as my efficient legal counsel.

But it was not to be. We simply couldn't find a time that was mutually convenient to make the trip. I had my duties to perform, and he had his: he was building the nation-wide organization that was to win him his Party's nomination for the American Presidency. We would, both of us, get to China, but not together.

The next time I saw Nixon was in Paris, when John Shaheen took me to meet him and his family, Mrs. Nixon and their two delightful daughters, Tricia and Julie. A famous American lawyer resident in Europe* was with Nixon when we joined him, and after a few minutes Mrs. Nixon and the girls went out to do the town, leaving the four of us alone. Nixon asked his two American friends in turn to

*He had only three clients—Aristotle Onassis, John Paul Getty, John M. Shaheen—so he managed to stay off the dole.

give him their thoughts about his problem of winning the Republican nomination. They did so at some length; and while Nixon questioned them closely on the points that they raised, I sat with fascinated interest and listened. Then he turned to me and said, "What are your thoughts?" I protested in alarm that I had no thoughts—that I didn't understand American politics and it would be impertinent of me to express an opinion. "That be hanged," he retorted pleasantly. "A politician is a politician, and I know you're a good one. Come on, let's have it." So I gave him my views.

"You happen to be," I told him, "the only person that I have ever heard giving what appeared to be a level-headed justification of the American war in Vietnam. And, I can tell you, 'almost thou persuadest me'. But all the world is against the war in Vietnam, and my guess is that before too long most Americans will be against it, too. In short, when you become President, you'd better put an end to that war before it puts an end to you. [It hadn't, up to that point, put an end to President Johnson.]

"You can't all of a sudden reverse yourself, but you certainly can stop making public statements about the war—you can cease advocating it. I know that you can't remain completely silent about it—it's too hot an issue in America, and it's going to get hotter. But what you can do is to wait for the right moment and then say categorically, and for everybody's sake really mean it, that as President of the United States, you will bring that war to an end."

Nixon didn't agree with the main contentions of his two American friends, and he didn't give any indication at all of agreement, or for that matter disagreement, with what I said. I was subsequently at a small reception that he gave some friends in his apartment in New York, and I had a chance to remind him briefly of my advice to him in Paris. He only smiled back.

And then he was elected President of the United States and, through his friend Shaheen, sent me an invitation to come to his inauguration. I was the only Canadian Premier there; and although I didn't feel that the panoply and excitement of the day equalled the greater occasions, such as the Queen's coronation in London, I nevertheless felt the awesome power of America. Next morning, Mr. Nixon did me the incredible honour of including me among the small number of friends whom he invited to the White House. After we had wandered about that particular section of the White House and heard young David Eisenhower make a neat, happy little speech, we guests formed a double line down through which the President and Mrs. Nixon strolled. He smiled at this friend, nodded to another, shook hands with some, and quite evidently was as happy as they were. Then he spotted me, came over, and put both arms around my shoulders and gave me, not a Russian, but an American bear-hug. I had time to remark sotto voce, "I guess our trip to China is off now." He grinned but said nothing.

In 1972, short weeks after I had retired from the Premiership, I had the mournful experience, in my apartment in Florida, of watching on television Mr. Nixon's departure from Washington, his arrival in Peking, and all those other unbelievable, impossible scenes in the mighty capital of China. Here were two of the most powerful and most ideologically opposed men on earth actually shaking hands in sight of hundreds of millions of people around the world; and here was Richard Nixon sitting in Mao Tse-tung's book-lined den, chatting amiably, and Mao Tse-tung probably cracking a joke or two in their conversation! I was happy for mankind (how pompous can you get?) but sad for myself. My heart yearned to be in Peking, and the more the television showed us of the Great Wall, the Forbidden City, the mighty T'ien-an-men Square, the Gate of Heavenly Peace, the tombs of the Ming emperors, and other wonders of China, the more my determination grew to get there, even if I had to walk.

The first step was made easy for me when a large United States industrial corporation commissioned me to go to China. The next was more difficult: getting the visa. I was in London, doing literary research, when Canada's High Commissioner gave me a warm introduction to the Embassy of the People's Republic of China. They were cordial enough at the Embassy, and I spent the best part of a couple of hours with them, explaining carefully the kinds of things that I wanted to see in China: mainly their communes or countryside cooperatives; and, of course, the usual tourist attractions as well. I had hoped that the visa would come through from Peking while I was still in London, but I was actually back in Florida three weeks or more before it came. Then, my heart singing, I was off, not by slow boat, but by fast jet, to China.

Canton, Peking, Hangchow, Shanghai, Nanking, and then back to Peking: I felt like John Cabot and Marco Polo rolled in one. Before I got to China, I felt rather as a man would feel going to the far side of the moon. But that's not how I felt when I got there and saw thousands of Chinese men, women, and children, and talked with hundreds of them. I think that they must be the nicest people that I have ever gone among, second only to our own Newfoundland people, of course! I saw more smiling faces, a greater absence of gloominess, a more relaxed look on people's faces, than in any other large country that I have visited. Here, with overwhelming obviousness, are no cowed, frightened, apprehensive people; but men and women who work hard, love their country, have ineffable faith in it, and share the feeling that they're building China into a land far greater than they have known. As for the children, they are quite irresistible.

Immediately after arriving in Peking, I sent a cable:

> President Nixon, White House, Washington, U.S.A.
> You got here before me but better late than never
> Joseph R. Smallwood

to which the President wrote me a pleasant reply.

The Chinese International Travel Service looked after me from the moment I set foot in China until I left three weeks later. The English-speaking guide who met me in Canton with a chauffeur-driven car took me about the famous city of 2 million people, and it was here that I saw the vast swimming pools surrounded by the large amphitheatre. I had the luck to go to the pools when some swimming contests were on, and I was one of the very few non-Chinese people among the tens of thousands who were there. Seeing me take snapshots, the officials sent someone over to invite me to move to a spot where I could more easily do so. There was smiling, unaffected friendliness on all sides as I watched droves of well-built young Chinese swimmers meet in contest after contest.

In the beautiful park beside the famous West Lake in Hangchow,* I was interested to see the California redwood tree that had been planted only a few months earlier by President Nixon, and another tree planted by our own Canadian Foreign Minister, Mitchell Sharp, who had been there several weeks before. In the city of Hangchow, too, I saw the huge coloured portrait of Dr. Norman Bethune, our Canadian medical man who is such a hero in China and whose memory is kept fresh by a poem that Mao Tse-tung wrote about him.

*Without doubt, said Marco Polo in 1271, "the grandest and the best city in the world." It is 1,400 years old.

In the metropolis of Shanghai, with its great harbour at the mouth of the mighty Yangtze River, I was shown the park where the Europeans and Americans relaxed with their wives and children in those days when they dominated China—the very park that had contained the sign at the gate: "Dogs and Chinese not admitted." It was in Shanghai that I was taken to one of the Children's Palaces, to which thousands of school boys and girls come through the year, mostly after school hours, to learn all kinds of things that the schools don't teach them: how to play various musical instruments, to assemble radio receiving sets, to perform acupuncture, to put on plays, and a hundred other interesting and, I'm sure, useful things. I was expected at the Palace, and a group of children met me outside. There was a blackboard with a welcome to me in Chinese, with my name in that language, so they gleefully told me. A small boy took me by one hand, a small girl by the other, and they never let me go (except to clap hands) until we had toured the whole of the large building. In every room, something different was going on; and as I entered, the children stood and clapped to welcome me. In one room, there was a full orchestra of children playing ancient Chinese musical instruments—one of the most entrancing orchestras I have ever heard. In a second room was another orchestra made up entirely of accordions; and in a third, there was yet another orchestra made up exclusively of violins. And there were playlets with those youngsters earnestly portraying scenes from their revolution—the revolution that had made the Children's Palaces possible. There are ten of these palaces in Shanghai alone, but the tens of thousands of children who get the chance to learn special skills in them are only a token number of all Shanghai's youthful population. The Chinese have cleverly got over that difficulty by having all the children who do enjoy the special opportunity of the Palaces go back to their own schools and become instructors of the other children.

A personal friend of mine for years past has been a collector of Chinese carved ivory, and in spite of myself, I became interested in ivory, though not a collector of it. In one of the suburbs of Shanghai, I was taken to a factory where 700 men and women, nearly all of them young, were carving ivory and jade. I noticed half a dozen quite elderly men among them, and I soon learned the story. This ancient Chinese art had all but died out before the revolution succeeded in 1949. Under Communism, it has been revived, so that where there were only about eighty skilled carvers in the whole of

China by 1949, now there were several factories employing thousands of them.

Nanking I remember for one very dramatic feature: the people have planted trees, millions of them, along both sides of the avenues and streets of the city; not just one row of trees down each side of the street, but two and three rows, and even four, so that on some streets there are eight rows of leafy trees! This, they told me, makes for coolness in the hot weather of the Chinese summer. It is staggering to consider the incredible expenditure of human effort involved in gathering and planting those millions of trees. In this, as in scores of other things that I saw, I realized what magnificent achievements are possible when the inherent strength and vigour of a whole people are released by some mighty event, such as a great war or a great revolution.

In the commune that I visited outside Nanking, where about 30,000 people were banded together, I saw something that equals, in its way, the building of the pyramids of Egypt or parallels even the building of the Great Wall of China. This commune extends along the shore of the Yangtze River for twenty-five or thirty miles and stretches back from the river for about ten or twelve miles. Close to the river, to a width of about a mile, the land is quite low-lying, but then it rises precipitously to a height of seventy or eighty feet and extends into a broad plateau. Water—precious, life-giving water—is the vital need of the land in the summer when the crops are coming to fruition, and the Yangtze can supply as much as the peasants can use. So they have dug four great parallel ditches, miles apart, across the mile-wide lowland to the foot of the steep bank. I saw one of them and marvelled. It is, remember, a mile long. It is fifteen feet wide at the bottom, seventy-five feet at the top, and about ten feet deep. The water runs into it from the Yangtze, and at the foot of the inner bank, electric pumps drive the water up the seventy or eighty feet to the top. There it flows into concrete culverts which lead off for miles, for the length of the commune, and side ditches carry it to the crops. *The ditch was dug by hand. Men, women, and children dug it. It was started and finished in twenty days.*

I was told of a case of 480 members of a brigade (village) in a commune planting 100,000 fruit trees in their spare time. Another brigade dug a huge irrigation canal 340 kilometers long in nine months. During one winter, 450 peasants dredged and drained a river 164 kilometers long to provide electric power and water for irrigation. In another commune, thirty miles of irrigation canal were dug by 50,000 peasants and soldiers in eighteen days and nights.

And so, almost literally, I stumbled on the secret of Mao Tse-tung's success in China. Everybody who could read or write, socialist or capitalist or anything else, knew that whatever conceivable chance Communism might have in the lands where private enterprise had brought the economy to an extraordinarily high standard of productivity, and where there was a mountainous quantity of accumulated capital, there was not a chance in this world of Communism being made to work in a land such as China, with no accumulation of capital whatsoever. This was the common knowledge of all readers and thinkers—except Mao Tse-tung. He knew what Abraham Lincoln knew: that labour is the mother of all capital. If that is so, then China, with its 800 million dedicated, hopeful, patriotic people, with its sense of national purpose, has in a way more capital than the United States itself.

I saw so much evidence of miracle works done without big accumulations of capital. There was the huge two-tier bridge across the Yangtze from Nanking. The Japanese, when they had occupied Nanking, and the Americans when they were there helping Chiang Kai-shek, and the Russians while they were still helping Mao Tse-tung, all without exception declared that it would not be practical to build a bridge there. The Chinese did it! Seven thousand men used a million tons of cement and over a million tons of steel in building the bridge between 1960 and 1969, when it was finished. The bridge proper is 1,577 meters long. Ten-thousand-ton ships can pass beneath its spans. Ninety trains cross over it every day. I had never walked across the Yangtze, but when I saw the bridge, I decided to do so; so I got them to drive me across the full length of the bridge, got out, and walked back to Nanking—and I didn't get my feet wet!

The Tung Ching people's commune (the name means *bronze well*) was one of three that I visited. The land was cursed before 1949, part of China's sorrow. Year after year, horrifying, death-dealing floods washed the very seed out of the ground and took thousands of lives; and year after year, in the very same years, scorching drought burned what crops had managed to survive the flood. That was the life of the area for thousands of years. The productivity of that land, acre for acre, peasant for peasant, was scarcely worth the trouble of counting it. Now the dams that the people have built to store the flood water and the irrigation ditches that they have dug, together with other innovations, have raised the productivity of that land from 150 kilograms per mu in 1949 to 600 last year. The people appear almost ashamed of that figure when they tell of far higher yields in certain other communes, and they are determined to catch up. Before the commune was formed, there was no electricity, no farm mechanization whatsoever, no damming of water, no irrigation, not one hospital, not even one middle school. Now 70 per cent of all households have electricity. Every house in the commune has rediffusion radio. In 1949, there were three primary schools with 300 students; today, there are twenty-six primary schools with 4,500 students and five middle schools with 700 students. There's a hospital now, with free medicine since 1969; each work team has one "barefoot" doctor and each brigade one clinic. Before liberation, they told me, 80 per cent of all the people forty years old and over were illiterate. There is no illiteracy any more, except among the very old.

Tung Ching has a forge and a somewhat primitive machine shop where the people repair such farm machinery as they have (they haven't a quarter yet of what they need). They even make new parts for their machinery. They have a flour mill, a rice mill, a feed mill for animal and poultry feeds, a sugar mill, and an oil mill. And I, who as a boy had marvelled at our unbelievably long Rope Walk in St. John's where the cordage was made for our fisheries, wondered even more at the rope walk of the Tung Ching People's Commune. It consists of two men, who walk back and forth, back and forth, over a 500-foot stretch—a literal rope walk—making cordage for the commune. When I returned from China, I described this particular commune as a little "paradise on earth" and told of what the peasants were producing there: corn, wheat, rice, sugar, rape seed, soy beans, peanuts, sesame, sweet potatoes, lotus, pears, apples, watermelons, oranges, peaches, beans, jute, cotton—much of it on the 5,000 mu of land that they have reclaimed. I was captivated by the way some newspapers treated my allusion: the headlines had me describing China as a paradise on earth!

Although the revolution came to its great success in 1949, it was not until 1958 that the system of People's Communes was brought into operation. Now there are 26,000 of them, each commune being made up of a population ranging from 10,000 to 60,000. About 20 million city and town dwellers have been moved to the countryside, many of them having specialized skills that have become very useful to the communes in which they now live. The most successful of all the People's Communes in China is that at the Tachai Village; at any rate, it is the one that has been given most national publicity, and nearly 5 million people have visited it from all parts of China, thousands of them going on foot for many hundreds of miles, reminding us of faithful Muslims going to Mecca.

All the tourists go to the famous Tea Commune up the narrow valley outside Hangchow, and it is certainly worth a visit. Outside Peking, I visited another commune where they raise pigs and keep poultry. My heart sank as I saw their hog and poultry establishments. They have a lot to learn about pig-breeding and raising, and perhaps even more about poultry. Mr. Trudeau and Mr. Sharp could do much worse than to offer Mao Tse-tung the help of Canadian specialists in these fields, for Canada is far advanced in them. I formed the ambition, when I was in China, to go back and spend much more time in some of the communes, and perhaps that ambition will be realized.

Friends hearing me extol the People's Communes in China, and seeing hundreds of slides of pictures I took of them, have asked me curiously if I think that they are an example to be followed everywhere. Horrors, no! Farms in Europe and North America are eons ahead of China, and North American farmers particularly have developed to a high pitch their own systems of producers' cooperatives. But India? All of Southeast Asia? Africa? South and Central America and the West Indies? I think so. The Chinese communes, if you allow for obvious necessary modifications and adaptations in each separate land, may well be the model for the future for these countries.

My tour had been organized for me in such a way as to enable me to be in Peking for the October 1 celebrations. The Chinese people that I met were amused when I reminded them that I, too, had led a revolution: that mine would be very roughly equivalent to someone leading a revolution in Taiwan for the purpose of uniting Taiwan with mainland China; that our revolution had been successful; and that I had "taken over the Government" precisely six months, to the very day, before the Chinese revolution had succeeded and Mao Tse-tung had "taken over the Government" of China. I didn't hesitate to remind them that our birthdays were only two days apart—Mao's on December 26, mine on December 24. They understood well enough my hope that I would see Mao Tse-tung at the Gate of Heavenly Peace, at T'ien-an-men Square, but warned me that he probably wouldn't appear that year. I had determined to go back to Peking in any event, and happy I am that I did.

I saw all the great sights. My very hotel, the Hsin Chiao, was one of the complex of buildings that formed the foreign compound of foreign embassies in Peking that had been under siege in the Boxer Uprising in 1900, the year of my birth. In this hotel had stayed Edgar Snow, author of the prestigious *Red Star Over China* and Chairman Mao's personal friend, and Han Suyin, author of *A Many Splendoured Thing*.

I visited the Forbidden City. It covers 180 acres with its 9,999½ rooms in hundreds of buildings; it housed the emperors from 1421, 76 years before John Cabot sailed to Newfoundland, until 1911, eleven years after I was born. I saw the Great Hall of the People, where Chou En-lai entertained President Nixon at the great state banquet. It covers 171,000 square meters and has thirty elevators. The hundreds of rooms are carpeted, and I saw one carpet that weighed over three tons. The main hall holds 10,000 people, and it can accommodate 5,000 at a meal. The Great Hall was built in ten months.

And of course the Great Wall! I went to the very part of it where Mr. and Mrs. Nixon had gone, but I walked three times as far along it as they did and twice as far as the Japanese Premier Tanaka did a few days before me! So, in one respect at least, I outdid the President of the United States and the Premier of Japan! My amiable Chinese interpreter-guide, Huang Chih-cheng, who went with me everywhere I visited in China, had to stop for a rest every now and then, and told me that I was a monster of energy.

I saw the Ming Dynasty tombs. The Emperor Cho Li Juen built his own tomb, and he needed 30,000 men working every day for six years, and they used materials from all over China. The cases of jewelled crowns, golden bowls, and quantities of gold ingots that were on exhibition in the palatial subterranean tombs were not replicas, but the actual, original, priceless objects themselves. Of course, I had myself photographed standing under the trunk of the same concrete elephant near the Ming Tombs beneath which Mrs. Nixon had been photographed before me.

And then there was the unforgettable October 1! Millions of happy Chinese crowded the public parks and the Summer Palace (where that foolish woman, the Empress Dowager Tzu Hsi, spent the nation's navy money to build a big marble ship at the shore of the lake). My regular guide was accompanied that day by three or four other important English-speaking officials, and I knew that something was up. I had, of course, said that I would love to meet Chou En-lai, though I realized that there was no chance of my meeting Chairman Mao. I was given no assurances whatsoever, and it was the only time that I found my Chinese friends inscrutable. But they knew what they were doing! I was alert enough to notice their surreptitious looks at their watches from time to time, so I followed them obediently from one place to another until we arrived at a great hall not far from T'ien-an-men Square. I think they left a man stationed outside, and he was to give the signal, for suddenly they urged me up and out of the building. There I met Chou En-lai and Chiang Ching, the brilliant wife of Chairman Mao; Vice-Premier Lee Chien Nen; Marshal Yet Chieng-ying, Chairman of the Military Commission; Lee Teh Sung, Director of the Political Department of the Army; Prince Norodom Sihanouk, Chief of State of Cambodia (in exile) and Bin Nu, his Prime Minister! Charming and very human I found them all. But you can imagine how chagrined I was afterward to discover that the lady I had met was the famous Chiang Ching—I hadn't realized who she was! As a matter of fact, most of my attention was for the very recognizable and very handsome Chou En-lai. He had both personality and charm in a degree that I have rarely met in public men throughout my life. Perhaps Louis St. Laurent would most nearly resemble Chou in this respect.

Later, I had an hour's chat with the scholarly Kuo Mo-jo, Vice-President of the People's National Congress of 1,700 representatives of the people. He is China's leading poet and historian, and President of the Chinese Academy of Sciences. He was eighty years old, but looked and sounded like man in his late sixties. The President of the Congress was eighty-two!

I travelled about 5,000 miles by jet, propeller aircraft, train, and car, was given several dinners, and made several speeches. From the moment that I entered China to the day before I left, I hadn't spent a cent on hotels, meals, air fares, trains, taxis, or anything else. It was not until just before I departed from Peking that I was presented with the pleasantly modest bill that covered all expenses of my long visit. In Europe, it would have amounted to at least $1,600; in the United States, $3,000. They charged me around $600.

No unemployment, no inflation, no crime, no prostitution, no drug addiction, no alcoholism—what a land!

26

The Politics of It All

Politics and philosophy are alike. Socrates neither set out benches for his students, nor sat on a platform, nor set hours for his lectures. He was philosophizing all the time—while he was joking, while he was drinking, while he was soldiering, whenever he met you on the street, and at the end when he was in prison and drinking the poison. He was the first to show that all your life, all the time, in everything you do, whatever you are doing, is the time for philosophy. And so also it is of politics.

Plutarch

My first word must be one of warning: if you are a political leader in Newfoundland, don't win too many General Elections!

Your opponents won't like it if you beat them once. They will dislike you heartily if you beat them twice. They will begin to hate you if you beat them three times. Their hate will intensify if you beat them four times. It will begin to master them if you beat them five times. If you're smart, you'll drop out before the sixth General Election approaches, for by then you may be in real danger. It will be perilous in the extreme for you if you engage them in a seventh joust. When, at last, the other side does get into office, your opponents will spend at least their first year there acting like an Opposition, still trying to put you down.

So you will have to choose: will you win election after election, stay in office, and try to realize your ambitions for the province; or will you call it quits after three or four elections, drop out, and enjoy what's left of your life and retain at least a remnant of your good name?

I battled in seventeen elections in the twenty-six years, 1946-1971: my own election to the National Convention, the two referendum election campaigns, seven provincial General Elections, and seven federal General Elections. I was the leader of our cause in sixteen of those seventeen appeals to the electorate, for we made no distinction whatsoever between federal and provincial elections in Newfoundland, and I performed precisely the same function in both. For a hundred years in Newfoundland, the leader of a political party exercised an authority that disappeared in mainland Canada long ago. It was the leader of the party who personally selected and appointed every individual candidate of the party in each election. It was the leader who selected and appointed the person to be the party's collector of campaign funds, although I was probably the first party leader in Newfoundland to decline personally to handle the funds when collected. I followed the normal Newfoundland practice and selected every candidate in every constituency in every provincial General Election while I was leader. With two exceptions, I selected and appointed every federal candidate of our Party in the first seven federal General Elections in Newfoundland. Sir Richard Squires, Lord Morris, Sir Robert Bond, and Sir William Whiteway had all done precisely the same in their time, and the Tory leaders did it too, before and after Confederation. Unless he was a fool, the leader would seek advice and guidance in most of the constituencies; in some of them, his own knowledge would be so extensive and sure that he could act without consulting anyone. In all elections before Confederation, it was the leader of the party who issued *his* manifesto: "my manifesto", "my policy", "my program", and so forth. (I have quite a number of these manifestoes in my collection.) I wrote and issued manifestoes, too, but I presented them as "our" manifesto and "our" policy or program.

My political opponents always spoke of the wonderful organization of the Liberal Party in Newfoundland. They appeared to believe that we were organized down to the last square inch of the province. You'd think, to hear them, that we were a marvel of efficient organization. Well, we weren't. Our organization was imperfect—so imperfect that it didn't even exist! True, we had the Liberal Association, but that was a paper tiger if ever there was one. We had the Young Liberal Association, and that was a tissue-paper tiger. They both existed in little more than name. The Women's Liberal Association had some reality in St. John's and in Corner Brook, and they had to be taken seriously; in both cities, the women were ardent, dedicated, efficient campaigners. But they were the only organized Liberal Party we had. Lady Squires, widow of Sir Richard, was the first president of the St. John's group; she was succeeded by Mrs. Philip J. Lewis, and the current leader is Mrs. Mark Badcock, known fondly to all of us as Alma. I have often said that it was the women's vote that gave us Confederation, and I am bound to add that it was the women's vote that gave me the premiership every time I won it.

When Confederation came, there was no Liberal Party in Newfoundland, and no other party either. In 1934, the two existing political parties had disappeared along with the House of Assembly and elected Government. They, too, had been merely groups of elected Members in the House, with not even the vestigial remains of a political organization in the country. Coaker's FPU, which was a union not a political party, and not tightly or efficiently organized in any case, would support the Coaker candidates along the northeast coast. But the FPU had virtually disappeared even before the House of Assembly was dissolved in 1934. From 1934 to 1949—fifteen years—there had been not even a sign or token of a political party anywhere in Newfoundland.

The first thing I decided to do after taking the oath as Premier was to found and organize a Liberal Party. I could have done this easily and cheaply by emulating Sir Richard Squires; in 1919, he had held the famous "cock-loft" meeting to form his Liberal Reform Party. The meeting took place in the unused attic of his *Daily Star* newspaper building, and Squires invited fifty or sixty friends to attend, a few of them undoubtedly Liberals of the old school. They adopted a resolution constituting the Liberal Reform Party and making Mr. Squires its leader. And thus was born the party which claimed the mantle of the old Bond-Whiteway-Kent-Shea-Carson Liberal Party. I don't suppose that meeting cost Squires more than a hundred dollars. I might, at little more expense, have splurged as Walter S. Monroe did a few years later: through his friends, he organized a public meeting in the old Casino Theatre. The CLB brass band was hired for the night, the speeches were eloquent, and a resolution was adopted asking Mr. Monroe if he would please become the leader. John T. Meaney, who organized the whole thing, told me about it years afterward. He was behind the platform, his eyes on the audience and his ear to the telephone receiver, giving Mr. Monroe at his home a running account of the meeting and then telling him when he should hurry to the theatre to receive the tumultuous greeting of the carefully selected audience.

I chose otherwise. I invited 1,200 or 1,400 men and women to come into St. John's to form, or re-form, the Liberal Party of Newfoundland and Labrador. We chartered a train to cross Newfoundland from Port-aux-Basques, taking delegates aboard from every sizable place across the Island. Others poured into St. John's by regular trains, truck, bus, and a few by private car. For three days, we met in the big CLB Armoury; and there, after speeches by Bradley and me, we constituted the Liberal Party. Nominations were asked from the floor for the positions of leader of the Party federally and leader of the Party provincially. Bradley was elected to the former and I to the latter, both unanimously, by acclamation, amid scenes of indescribable emotion. We then split up the big meeting into many smaller ones, so that I could tell the individual constituencies who their candidate was to be. In one instance, a staunch Confederate and Liberal had loaded his own dump truck with ten or twelve of his friends who had promised to vote for him as the District's candidate. In that very District, I had chosen one of my Cabinet colleagues to be the candidate, and the truck owner afterward uttered the rueful but historical statement, "But for a trick of fate, today I'd be the 'onable 'arvey!"

My first administration took office on April 1, 1949, and the provincial General Election came on May 27. Years before, under Premier Alderdice, the House had been reduced to twenty-eight Members, and so it was in this General Election and the one that followed. In the event, twenty-two Liberals were elected, five Tories (Progressive Conservatives), and one Independent—Peter Cashin, for Ferryland. I offered myself to the constituency of Bonavista North, where the Tory candidate was the well-known and very popular Jim Way. Jim told everybody with a wink that "somebody has to oppose 'im, you see, brother—and the Tories are paying my expenses anyway". Jim made it abundantly clear that he had no intention of "losing his vote", which no Newfoundlander likes to do; so he was going to vote for Smallwood, too. The vote was Smallwood, 4,215; Way, 637. I received unanimous electoral support in twenty or more individual settlements, though I had spent only two days in the whole constituency.

One month to the day after that election, in the first federal General Election in which Newfoundland took part, Newfoundland sent Bradley and four other Liberals to the House of Commons, as against two Tory candidates. The two Tories elected were William J. Browne (St. John's West) and Gordon F. Higgins (St. John's East). Higgins had been a member of the first National Convention delegation to Ottawa. My Confederate friend Thomas G. W. Ashbourne was elected for Grand Falls-White Bay-Labrador—he, too, had been a member of the first Ottawa delegation. My Confederate friend Captain Leonard T. Stick was elected for Trinity-Conception. The present Senator Chesley W. Carter was elected by Burin-Burgeo. W. R. Kent was sent to the Commons by Humber-St. George's-St. Barbe.

Twenty-two to six provincially, five to two federally—not bad. Much better was to come.

I called a General Election for November 26, 1951, to get the people's endorsement of my "Develop or Perish" philosophy and program. This time, the Liberals got twenty-three and the Opposition five. Three of our Liberal candidates were elected by acclamation.

On October 10, 1953, the second federal General Election was held. This time Gordon Bradley was not a candidate, as he had accepted appointment to the Canadian Senate. His place in Bonavista-Twillingate was taken by my friend John W. Pickersgill. He won the seat by a vote of 10,072 to his opponent's 2,564. We won all seven seats in that election! Even the two St. John's seats came with us. Our candidate in St. John's East was Professor Allan Fraser, and he opposed Gordon Higgins. I didn't think that he could beat Higgins, and my secret wish was fulfilled when, to everyone's surprise, Peter Cashin entered the ring as an Independent. He took enough votes from Higgins to give Fraser the victory. People wondered what had induced Peter to run.

Three years later on October 2, 1956, we held our third provincial General Election, and by then we had restored the thirty-six seats that composed the House before the economics of Premier Alderdice. We won thirty-two, the Tories four. In Bonavista North, I was given 3,429 votes to my opponent's 258, though again I was able to be in the constituency for only two days. Four Liberal candidates were elected by acclamation that year. The four Tories came exclusively from St. John's constituencies.

On June 10, 1957, the third federal General Election sent five Liberals to the Commons and two Tories. Pickersgill that time drew 9,158 votes to J. C. Pinsent's 1,347. The two St. John's seats elected Browne and James A. McGrath.

The fourth federal election was March 31, 1958, when again five Liberals and two Tories were elected. Pickersgill took 13,670 votes to his opponent's 4,323.

The year after that, on August 29, 1959, we held our fourth provincial General Election, and the Tory Party was badly split. The Liberals elected thirty-one, the Tories three, and the new United Newfoundland Party two. These two were John R. O'Dea, St. John's South; and A. M. Duffy, St. John's Centre, who had broken away from the Tory Party on the issue of Mr. Diefenbaker's attitude to Newfoundland on Term 29. The Tory leader, Malcolm Hollett, had represented St. John's West in the previous House. In conversation with him on a visit to Churchill Falls in Labrador, I had pleaded with him to leave the Tory Party on the Term 29 issue, about which he felt much as I did, but he had refused to do so. I told him then that if he wouldn't, I would run personally against him in his constituency, and he shrugged and said, "You'll defeat me if you do." I ran against him in St. John's West and received 4,243 votes to his 2,221—a two-to-one majority over him. I was inwardly happy when Diefenbaker afterward arranged the appointment of Malcolm Hollett to the Senate, from which he has now retired to enjoy the eventide of a long and interesting life.

On June 18, 1962, the fifth federal election put six Liberals in Parliament and one Tory. Young Richard Cashin, whom I had with great delight selected as our candidate, defeated the veteran campaigner Browne by twenty-four votes.* Pickersgill that time received 11,530 votes to his opponent's 3,846.

Five months later, November 19, 1962, we held our fifth provincial General Election. We had increased the membership in the House to forty-two. We won thirty-four; the Tories won seven, their high-water mark after Confederation; and there was one Independent. In Bonavista North, I received 3,195 votes to my opponent's 742, after spending one day in the constituency. Three Liberals were elected by acclamation.

The very next year, on April 8, 1963, the sixth federal General Election was held, and we sent seven Liberals to the House of Commons. I spent a lot of my time in that election advising Joseph P. O'Keefe, our candidate in St. John's East, where I was exceedingly anxious to see the defeat of the sitting Tory Member James McGrath. McGrath had failed to take a stand against Diefenbaker on the Term 29 issue. O'Keefe got in with 14,768 votes to McGrath's 13,191. Pickersgill had two opponents in Bonavista-Twillingate, and the vote was Pickersgill, 11,748; G. J. Eveleigh, 2,448; and W. H. David, 1,943. It was the second time that the Liberals had a clean sweep of Newfoundland in a federal election.

There was another federal General Election, the seventh, on September 8, 1965. Again, we sent seven Liberals to the House of Commons, making it the third time in seven elections that we had done

*In a public meeting at Corner Brook, I had great fun with Browne's candidacy in St. John's West. "Browne is going to lose," I told the audience. "Billy Browne is going down!" I repeated it. "Billy Browne is going down!" and some in the audience took it up. Then I had the whole audience reciting it again and again, "Billy Browne is going down!" ending in a great roar of delighted applause. Dear, delightful days of election campaigns!

so. McGrath didn't run against O'Keefe in St. John's East that time, but the war-scarred veteran William J. Browne resigned his seat in the House of Assembly to run, in spite of my friendly warning to him that he'd be going once too often to the well. The vote was O'Keefe, 16,182; Browne, 11,894. Pickersgill won again, for the sixth time, with 10,113 votes to Captain W. Moss's 3,687.

And then we came to September 8, 1966, the sixth provincial General Election. We won thirty-nine seats to the Tories' three. The three Tory Members elected were Gerald F. Ottenheimer in St. John's East, A. J. Murphy in St. John's Centre, and Thomas V. Hickey in St. John's East Extern. We were truly then "Her Majesty's Outport Government"! Three Liberals were elected by acclamation.

I ran this time in Humber West, the western half of the great Humber area that has Corner Brook as its heartland. I had two reasons for running there. One was the fact that Sir Richard Squires had represented it in the House of Assembly, with substantial help from me at the time (as I have related elsewhere): I took great inward satisfaction from representing another of the seats that Squires had represented, the first being St. John's West. My second reason was that I was anxious to help in the defeat of a man who subsequently became a dear friend, one for whom I continue to have great respect – Dr. Noel Murphy, now the able Mayor of Corner Brook. He was then the misplaced leader of the Tory Party and was running for re-election in Humber East. I thought that it would be too bad, in his case, to run against him in his own constituency; so I looked about for a promising candidate to oppose him. I chose the young lawyer Clyde Wells, who afterward told the province publicly that I had almost literally dragged him into the House of Assembly. If Dr. Murphy's defeat was the initial cause of his joining the Liberal Party and becoming my colleague in Cabinet, then that fact gives me some satisfaction, at least, over his defeat and Mr. Wells's victory. My own opponent was a popular Labour leader, C. J. Normore, but I was able to defeat him by 4,431 to 2,162 – better than two to one. I spent all of a week in the constituency. Again, we won three seats by acclamation.

It was a remarkable showing, to win six provincial General Elections in a row and seven federal General Elections during the same time. But I was not too elated. Indeed, the night of the 1966 election, after the results were all in, I made the public statement that I hoped that this would be my last General Election. I meant every syllable of it, and it would have been my last but for certain events that were to follow soon after.

By 1968, I had two firm resolves: I would get the Come by Chance oil refinery, and I would get out of politics.

But I couldn't go and leave our Party in the dangerously unorganized state in which it still was, after more than a century, and after nearly a quarter of a century of my leadership. I decided that my last gift to the Liberal Party would be the formation of a real "grass roots" organization of the Liberals throughout the province: to get the Party placed formally in the hands of what Abraham Lincoln called the common people.

I called a great conference to be held at Grand Falls in September 1968. Over 1,400 men and women poured into it from all around the province, and there we formed the Liberal Association and adopted a constitution which would come into effect only after I had called two other great meetings: at Clarenville for eastern Newfoundland and at Corner Brook for western. About 1,400 came to the Clarenville meeting and slightly more than that number to the one at Corner Brook. Allowing for overlapping, I am confident that nearly 3,500 individual Liberals came to form the Association.

Despite his actions since his resignation from the Cabinet, John Crosbie negotiated privately with me for his admission to the three big meetings. I agreed that it would be proper for him to attend, provided that he gave a written undertaking to support the Liberal Party, which of course he couldn't do while sitting in opposition to the Liberal Government. He claimed the right to oppose the Liberal Government on any particular matter, and I agreed that he and all Liberals should have this right. He wrote the letter, crossed the floor again, and took his place among the Liberal backbenchers. Wells refused to give any undertaking; and although he went to Grand Falls while the conference was on and tried to be admitted, he was barred.

Subsequently, I got the Come by Chance project through the House, we gave the Shaheen company the $5 million of "bridge" capital, and there was no interruption in the progress of the big project.

On my second resolution, to quit politics, I soon took action: I wrote to the president of the Association, John Mahoney, asking him to call a special leadership convention at which I would tender my resignation as leader of the Liberal Party and the Convention would elect a new leader. In the meantime, incredibly, Crosbie had announced that he was going to run for the leadership! I loved the Party too much, and was too profoundly grateful to it for its endless support, to turn my back on the danger of Crosbie's seizing the leadership. It had been my intention, which was widely understood, that soon after resigning as leader of the Party, I would tender my resignation to the Governor as the Premier and recommend to him that he send for the newly elected leader of the Party and invite him to form a new administration. If Crosbie succeeded in winning the leadership, I would be bound in honour, if not by constitution or by law, to follow the same procedure; but the one thing I could not see in Newfoundland was any wisdom in John Crosbie's becoming Premier. I knew that Crosbie was a very hard worker and had great determination; and as I expected, he set out to win to his cause the delegates who would be attending the leadership convention. It was a great effort, greater by far than anything that had ever been seen in Newfoundland and, beyond all comparison, more expensive.

I soon concluded that my close friend and confidant, Fred Rowe, who had announced his own candidacy for the leadership, didn't have the financial strength or organizing personnel to beat Crosbie. For years, it had been common knowledge in Newfoundland that I was hoping to see Rowe succeed me in the leadership of our Party. I had moved him from one Department to another in the Government. In succession he was Minister of Welfare, of Highways, of Mines, Agriculture, and Resources, of Education, and of Finance, all as part of a deliberate plan to let him become more familiar with the workings of Government than any man in our history. He was honoured and respected universally in the province, but he didn't have John Crosbie's grim industry or money. Fred and I talked it over and agreed that he would withdraw, that I would run, and that he would use all his strength to support me. I announced this accordingly.

One day, about three weeks before the convention, Alex Hickman slipped upstairs from his office to mine to tell me that he thought he'd throw his hat into the ring. I pitied his innocence and told him, "Alex, you can't be serious. It's too late. It's a fight between Crosbie and me, and you'd only get hurt." He was determined and soon after resigned from the Cabinet.

The leadership convention, held in the big sports arena in St. John's on October 30 and November 1, was possibly the most dramatic event of its kind held anywhere in Canada for many years. The convention voted as follows: Randy Joyce, 13; Alex Hickman, 187;

John C. Crosbie, 440; and Joseph R. Smallwood, 1,070.

When the House opened again, Crosbie crossed the floor for the third time and took his place on the Opposition side. There he was joined by Wells and by Hickman, who had now decided to join the Tory Party, though in fact he didn't actually join them for some little time after, with Crosbie following suit.

I was still determined to quit politics, but it had become evident that I would have to lead the Party through another General Election. I talked it over with a few of my closer colleagues and spelled out the plan that I had formed. This was to resign the premiership as soon as I could decently do so following the General Election. But before resigning as Premier, I would ask for another leadership convention, so that in resigning as leader of the Party and enabling the Party to elect a new leader, I would have someone that I could recommend to the Governor to form a new administration and become Premier. I did consider carefully an alternative plan. This was to resign the premiership before the General Election. In that case, I would resign as Premier first and then subsequently, at a convention, resign the leadership. Meanwhile, upon resigning as Premier, I would recommend the name of the most likely successor, and he would become Premier. He would soon afterward run for the leadership of the Party in the second convention, and the prestige of the premiership would more than likely get him the leadership. I soon discovered that this course would cause violent objection and disruption in the Party, and I dropped it. I would have to go through with the election.

My judgement had been wrong when I decided at the beginning of the 1968 federal General Election not to play my customary part. I will never know what difference there might have been in the outcome, had I continued what had been my normal practice up to then; but I will always believe that we would have won not one but at least four of the seven constituencies. But if my judgement was wrong in the federal election of 1968, it was atrociously so in the seventh and last provincial General Election in which I led the Liberal Party in October 1971. It was atrociously wrong because I simply didn't lead it at all. My error was in not laughing at those who informed me that I no longer enjoyed the support of the Newfoundland people. John Crosbie's brother, Andrew, who had organized and led John's unsuccessful campaign for the leadership of our Party, took over the management of the Liberal Party's election campaign. I allowed myself to be kept in the background. I saw it happening, and foolishly I didn't object. Andrew, in his own printing plant, produced a superbly printed piece of literature containing uniform pictures of the forty-two Liberal candidates. I appeared among them, as just one of them, and no more: same size, same format as the other forty-one. When I objected mildly to Andrew, he had my picture printed larger than the others; but he counterbalanced it by printing his own picture also on an enlarged scale in the same publication. The principal movie that he had made for TV showed all of the Liberal candidates walking up to the camera, one by one, and he had me as one of them, but no more. I said nothing. I was being suppressed, and instead of sweeping Andrew and his whole outfit aside, and taking over the leadership of the campaign, as I had done on sixteen previous occasions, I allowed myself to be pushed into the background. My reason? My reason was my inner belief that the people would stand by me anyway and give us our seventeenth victory.

They almost did.

Nobody won the election of October 28, 1971. The result:

Liberal	*Tory*
Labrador North	Grand Falls
Labrador South	Lewisporte
White Bay North	Gander
White Bay South	Carbonear
Green Bay	Harbour Main
Twillingate	Harbour Main
Fogo	St. John's North
Bonavista North	St. John's West
Bonavista South	St. John's South
Trinity North	St. John's Centre
Trinity South	St. John's East
Bay de Verde	St. John's East Extern
Harbour Grace	Ferryland
Port de Grave	St. Mary's
Bell Island	Burin
Placentia East	Burgeo-La Poile
Placentia West	St. George's
Fortune Bay	Port-au-Port
Hermitage	Humber West
St. Barbe North	Humber East
	St. Barbe South (almost)
20	20 (21 ?)

But forty-two Members were supposed to be elected to the House of Assembly. The forty-first was Thomas Burgess. He had been elected as a Liberal in the General Election of 1966, but had crossed the floor and sat in the House as an Independent. He was organizer in Labrador West for the Steelworkers' Union, and he had formed a new party called the Labrador Party. It had run three candidates, all of them in Labrador. Only he had won.

The forty-second Member should have been elected from St. Barbe South, but here one of the most absurd situations had developed during the recounting of the ballots: the Deputy Returning Officer in one of the booths, that of Sally's Cove, Mrs. Olive Payne, had actually burned all the ballots as soon as she finished counting them. This fact came out during the recount in the Supreme Court.

So here we were in a stalemate. Neither Party had won; neither had lost. It was a virtual tie.

But five of the constituencies that we had lost were lost with a grand total of 384 votes in the aggregate! A mere 200 more votes for the Liberal candidates in the five constituencies, and 180 fewer for the Tory candidates, would have elected twenty-four Liberals to sixteen Tories. As against that, the Liberals had won Bay de Verde with the slender majority of twenty-one votes.

Such narrow margins had not been known in Newfoundland for a long time, and it was perfectly obvious to everyone but the Tories, who clamoured for my immediate resignation, that recounts had to take place in five constituencies at our request, and probably one at theirs. The law provided for it, and the applications were made.

In the meantime, from the moment the results were known on election night, Burgess began one of the strangest series of manoeuvrings, twistings, and turnings in our political history. I have known some strange goings-on in our Newfoundland politics in more than half a century of active observation, but never anything resembling the Burgess affair. He began by announcing cheerfully to the province and the world that he was now the king-maker; he was cock-of-the-walk, the man in the saddle, the holder of the balance of power, the arbiter of the situation. John Crosbie on television the night of the election made an open appeal to "old palsy-walsy Burgess".

John Doyle chanced to be in Labrador City with his private jet during the election, and Burgess sought and got a free ride to Deer Lake on it. From Deer Lake, he got a free ride to St. John's on Arthur

R. Lundrigan's private jet. In an interview with a Montreal newspaper reporter, Burgess declared that he had been offered $1 million for his support. He didn't say who made the offer or on whose behalf it was made; but he clearly wanted the world to applaud his contempt for a million dollars. On arrival in St. John's, he telephoned to me suggesting that I might wish to see him, and I said that he might wish to drop over to my office in the Confederation Building. It so happened that I was bound away somewhere by helicopter that morning, but I kept the helicopter waiting until I had seen Burgess. He came to me from having seen Frank Moores, the leader of the Tory Party, and John Crosbie, minutes before. He told me so and asked me if I wanted his support. I said that it must be pretty obvious that I would welcome it, for it would break the impasse. What would he get for his support? he asked. I told him that I could offer him a seat in the Cabinet. He wanted to know what portfolio. Could he be Minister of Labrador Affairs? I told him that we already had someone in that portfolio, Melvin Woodward, the newly elected Liberal Member for Labrador North. I said that I would think more about the question of portfolio and let him know.

I talked to Woodward on the telephone about it. He was adamantly opposed to giving up the portfolio in favour of Burgess. I asked Woodward if he would object to my admitting Burgess to my Cabinet as, say, Minister of Mines, Agriculture and Resources. Woodward loyally agreed. I told Burgess this, and he said he was pleased. Then Burgess put a temporary end to all conjecture about his intentions by publicly announcing that he was going to support the Tories under Mr. Moores.

I made a speech on television, saying that I had no desire to remain in office if I lacked the support of a majority in the House.

The recounts went forward, and in the five constituencies where they took place, there was no change.

This meant that we were still tied at twenty-twenty, with Burgess saying that he would support the Tories and St. Barbe in the balance. If the Court ruled, as we requested, that the election there be declared null and void, we had no doubt whatsoever that we would win the consequent by-election. The question was would the election in St. Barbe be declared invalid? The precedents in the Supreme Court of Canada clearly pointed to its invalidity, but many people were startled when Chief Justice Furlong declared from the bench that he didn't recognize judgements made by the Supreme Court of Canada prior to our Confederation in 1949. John Turner, then Canada's Minister of Justice, quite frankly refused to believe me when I told him on the telephone of Furlong's declaration.

All these events took place over a period of several weeks. On November 12, Moores and Burgess met, and Burgess announced that he had entered into "a sort of coalition" with the Tories. It was on the next day that Furlong announced that he didn't recognize Canadian Supreme Court judgements made before we became a province.

The chronology is worth noting:

December 6: The executive committee of the Liberal Association announced that the leadership convention that I had requested would be held on February 4 and 5.

December 13: The Supreme Court rejected a petition made for the Tory Party that Mr. Maynard, their candidate, be certified as the elected Member for St. Barbe South.

January 5: The Liberal Party's lawyers petitioned the Supreme Court to have the St. Barbe South election declared null and void. The Court promised an early decision.

January 11: The Supreme Court rejected the Liberal Party's request and in effect declared the Tory candidate elected in St. Barbe South.

January 13: Mr. Moores was quoted in the press as saying that Burgess was still supporting the Tories. On that day, I announced my decision to resign. This would automatically end my administration's term of office.

January 17: Burgess publicly renounced the Tories and declared that he was remaining an Independent.

January 18: I resigned the premiership and recommended to the Lieutenant Governor that he invite Mr. Moores to form a new administration.

January 21: An extraordinary thing happened: Augustus Oldford, the Liberal Member, resigned his Fortune Bay seat in the House of Assembly! He had been a magistrate at Grand Falls, and a few months before had accepted with alacrity my invitation to join my Cabinet and be a Liberal Party candidate in the coming election. He had won a good victory in Fortune Bay. Now, suddenly, the Liberal Party's ranks were reduced by one. I was in Florida when I heard the startling news of Mr. Oldford's resignation, though not from him, and I called him on the telephone to ask if it was true. I cannot say that he hung up on me. I know that the line suddenly went dead, and

I was not able to get him back on the telephone. Mr. Oldford was put back on the Grand Falls bench by the new Government.

January 24: The Party arithmetic was restored when Hugh Shea, who had been elected by St. John's South, left the Tory caucus to sit as an Independent Tory.

January 26: In a speech at Memorial University, Burgess declared that he had been promised a Cabinet seat by the Tories.

January 31: Burgess and Shea both announced, though separately, that they were joining the Liberal Party.

While I was vacationing in Florida between December 20 and January 4, I had received a telephone call from Tom Burgess—he was at Gainesville, in the same state, staying with his brother. Would I see him? I agreed to meet him at the terminal of Tampa Airport. He came there with his brother, a former Roman Catholic priest from Ireland who was now, he told me, on the staff of the University of Florida. I was a little surprised that Burgess had brought his brother with him, but suggested that he go ahead and tell me what he had on his mind. What he had on his mind was apparently clear enough: he wanted to clear out from the Tories and throw in his lot with us. I was not enthusiastic, for I didn't have much faith left in Tom Burgess at that point. I told him, however, that if he would issue a categorical statement of his intention, and make it very public, I would accept him. Would he get the seat in the Cabinet? I told him yes. Was it an actual fact that I was going to resign the leadership of the Party? Yes, I had already taken steps to have a leadership convention called by John Mahoney. Then he startled me. Could he run for the leadership of the Party? I recovered quickly and told him what was obvious anyway: that if he entered my Cabinet and won restored membership in the Liberal Party, he certainly could run for the leadership, provided he got the requisite number of proposers at the convention. Would I support him in his bid for the leadership? I told him that I doubted that I would support anyone but that I would certainly support my elected successor in the leadership, whoever he might be. Could he get some funds to finance his bid for the leadership? I couldn't help asking him jokingly, "What about that million dollars you were offered and turned down?" He grinned, and so did his brother. That was the only reference to funds. After a couple of hours' conversation, we parted on the understanding that we would meet again in a day or so, with Burgess thinking the matter over in the meantime.

I have no knowledge of whom he contacted between our first and second meetings in Florida. He told me, however, at our second meeting, which was held at the terminal of Clearwater Airport, again with his brother in attendance, that he had decided to come back into the Party and to accept the seat in my Cabinet. He asked me to write a statement for him to issue, and I promised to do so. When I had it done, I telephoned to him at Gainesville and asked him to get paper and pencil to take it down in his own handwriting—I didn't want him to have it in mine. The statement said that in the few weeks he had been associated with the Tories, he had lost all faith in them—that they were split and divided, warring with each other; that they were not one party, but several. (He had told me this himself.) He had been elected originally as a Liberal in Labrador West, but as everyone knew, he had quarrelled with me and sat across the floor of the House. Now that Smallwood had announced his decision to retire, however, and had called a leadership convention for the purpose, he saw no reason why he should not rejoin the Liberal Party, and so forth. He said he was happy with the statement, that it summed up his feelings exactly. I told him that I was returning in a day to St. John's—I went back on January 4—and suggested that he hurry back, too. He said he was going back in a couple of days from then. I told him that it was essential for him to issue his statement before the verdict on St. Barbe South came down from the Supreme Court. If he made his move after the Court verdict, assuming it to be favourable to us, then he would have every appearance of just climbing on the bandwagon. He agreed and said that he would certainly issue it before that happened.

Back in St. John's, I discovered that he and his family had lingered another week in Florida and were spending nearly a week in Montreal as well, as the guest of the man who had financed their trip to Florida. In a telephone conversation with him, I suggested that he should issue his statement in Montreal. He said no, he couldn't do that, for he had to confer with his Party in Labrador City. "You'd better get back there, then," I told him, "if you're going to make your decision known ahead of the St. Barbe decision." He telephoned me from Labrador City the day of his meeting with his committee there and told me that he would issue the statement as soon as his meeting was over that night. He rang me after midnight to say that he had decided to go to Happy Valley to meet with his committee there. I was suspicious, of course, and asked him what he was up to. He was evasive, but told me that the meeting at Happy Valley would be a mere formality and that he would issue the statement by ten o'clock that night.

Later that same day, Frank Moores issued a blistering attack on Burgess, announcing that Burgess was about to throw in his lot with the Liberals and run for the Liberal leadership. I heard nothing from Burgess that night from Happy Valley; but after two o'clock the following morning, I had a phone call from Gerry Corbai, a news reporter at radio station VOCM, asking me for my comment on a piece of news that he had. The news was that Burgess had telephoned to him a statement denying Frank Moores' allegation and reaffirming his support of the Tory Party. Corbai told me that he had said to Burgess, "What kind of a game are you playing, Tom? You're about to join the Liberals, and here you are denying it." "I'm not about to join the Liberals, and I never said I was," Burgess had retorted. "Whom are you trying to kid?" Corbai had asked. "Why, you told me yourself!" "Yes, I guess you must be thinking that I'm a lying son-of-a-bitch," Burgess had replied. Corbai told me he had taped the interview, and he played it back for me. Burgess later asked Corbai if he had Frank Moores' home telephone number. When Corbai said he did, Burgess asked him if he would ring Moores and tell him that he, Burgess, wanted to speak with him. Corbai did so, and Burgess spoke with Moores. Corbai called me back a little later to give me that latest development. As a newsman he was eager, of course, to be in on all the play and to get all the comments he could from me.

It was no overwhelming surprise to me when, a week or two afterward, Burgess suddenly announced that he could stand the Tories no longer and was rejoining the Liberal Party! He actually sat with us on our side of the House in that one-day session that followed on Wednesday, March 1. He ran for the leadership of the Liberal Party and met with a crushing rejection, and he was badly defeated in Labrador West in the General Election that followed soon after. I had made one public statement a week or two after the October 28 General Election, while the Party stood twenty to twenty and Burgess was telling the world that he had Newfoundland by the tail: "All Newfoundlanders should be on their knees praying that their fate will not for a moment be in the hands of Tom Burgess."

In December 1971, I had been told some sombre news by a friend of mine who was in close touch with the Tory Party: that one of the Liberal MHA's was going to join the Tories. I didn't believe it. But after I had resigned as Premier, while I was in Florida, I thought about it and decided that it would be sound practice if I telephoned to a number of our newly elected Members. One of them was my friend Bill Saunders, Member for Bay de Verde. He had told me rather bitterly a few weeks before that he had gone heavily in to debt in his October election campaign; he felt that the Party should be able to look after his election debts if it could afford to give Tom Burgess and his family a trip to Florida and Montreal. I telephoned to Saunders at Carbonear on the night of February 26 and told him that the Party had not paid a cent of the cost of the Burgess vacation—that this had been paid by an individual who lived in St. John's. I had not forgotten his debt problem, I told him, and as I was returning to St. John's the following day, Tuesday, I would have $2,000 for him and an equal amount a couple of weeks later. He'd get half of his sessional indemnity on Wednesday, as we all would. Would that take care of the situation? Yes, he told me. He also told me that he wasn't feeling well. When I suggested that on Wednesday morning he could drive over to St. John's with me in my car, and that I could give him the first $2,000 on the way over, he expressed some doubt that he'd be able to make it to the House on Wednesday. He went on to say, "I hope you don't have any doubt about my loyalty to the Party or to you? I will never let you down—you can bet your life on that."

After we hung up, I spoke on the telephone with Edward Roberts, the new leader of the Party, and told him of my conversation with Saunders. Roberts said that he would go over to Carbonear the following day, Tuesday, and have a talk with Saunders. He did so, and Saunders gave him positive assurance of his continued loyalty to the Party and to him. He wouldn't be well enough to get to the House next day, but he could be counted on for a little later in the session. Roberts so reported to me and to the House next day—all Newfoundland heard it over TV and radio. On the Friday before the House met, Roberts held a Party caucus at the Laurier Club. The House standing at the time was Liberal 21, Tories 20, Fortune Bay vacant. He remarked that as the Liberals were a majority of the House, all they had to do was hold the line steady. "It would take only one of us to put us down." Saunders, in the full hearing of the caucus, declared his loyalty. Privately to Roberts, he said he was hard up.

On Monday night, February 28, Saunders told me earnestly on

the telephone that his loyalty to the Party must not be doubted. On Tuesday afternoon, he told Edward Roberts the same thing. But though we were not aware of it until the night of Wednesday, March 1, when I spoke with him on Monday night, and Roberts did so on Tuesday, Saunders had already resigned.*

When the House opened on Wednesday, March 1, the Liberal Opposition had a majority of its membership, with one seeming Opposition Member (Saunders) absent. The Government were apparently a minority of the House. The standing was Liberals 20 actually present in the House, Tories 20 (including the Speaker). But not for long! The House met at three o'clock in the afternoon, the Speech from the Throne was read and the speeches made about it, and the House adjourned by about five o'clock in the afternoon.

At eight o'clock that night, Mr. Moores went to Government House and presented the Lieutenant-Governor with William Saunders' letter of resignation from the House of Assembly; the letter was dated Monday, February 28. This gave Mr. Moores the constitutional right to ask the Lieutenant-Governor for a dissolution of the one-day General Assembly and the holding of a new General Election.

I dearly loved being a Member of the House of Assembly, and it is quite possible that I created an all-time Newfoundland record for faithful attendance in the Chamber. I was physically present and in my seat at least 99 per cent of the time the House sat from 1949 to 1972. From the moment the sitting began at three o'clock until the closing moment, whether it was at six o'clock or eleven or midnight, I was in my place, marvelling often over the transparent eagerness of so many Members to seize any excuse, or to make one, to get outside the Chamber. Not a word was spoken that I did not hear. I might be reading Cabinet papers or other documents, or signing letters, but one ear was unfailingly open for every word uttered. Even when I chatted with Leslie Curtis, who sat beside me throughout the twenty-three years, I kept one ear open for every word of every speech. It was a mistake, but I couldn't help it. My colleagues and supporters in the House soon fell into the habit of leaving things to

*If Saunders had attended one more session of the House, he would have been entitled to a pension; by resigning his seat, he forfeited the pension forever. He forfeited also the $10,000 sessional indemnity that he would have received (as we all did) for attending that single two-hour session on the Wednesday following.

me—points of order, challenges to Opposition speakers, parliamentary procedures; everything but the order of business, which was always the responsibility of Curtis as leader of the House. I was always puzzled by the apparently complete indifference of Ministers and private Members where parliamentary practice, precedent, and principle were concerned.

I enjoyed the House, and particularly any fun there was. I tried my own hand at making some fun, and I found the humourless William J. Browne the perfect foil. He was known to be a most ardent anti-Communist, and I had wondered idly what his position had been when, as a Minister in the Diefenbaker Cabinet, he had acquiesced in the decision to trade with Red China by selling them wheat. When he returned to provincial politics and our own House, I twitted him on it. "I wish I had been there, hiding in a closet, to watch the Hon. Member's face. It must have been quite a struggle in his mind. Would he starve the Communists, or make a little profit out of them? He was something like the girl plucking the petals off the flower: 'He loves me, he loves me not'. Can't you picture him there, Mr. Speaker? So at last, to settle the matter, our brave anti-Communist fingered the buttons on his coat: 'eeny, meeny, myney—MAO'. And Mao got his wheat."

Another time, Browne, on orders of the day, asked if I had any comment to make on a statement made by Albert Martin, general manager of the Bowater Paper Mill at Corner Brook, who had quoted someone in England to some effect about something or other. I stood up and managed a look of surprise as I remarked that Browne was asking me to comment on his allegation of what Martin was alleged to have said about what somebody else had said over in England? "He can't be serious, Mr. Speaker. I'm willing to comment when I have it from the horse's mouth—not the other end of him!" Browne's own colleagues, who never did feel at ease in the presence of his stern Cromwellian face and voice, leaned back in their seats out of Browne's sight to smile delightedly.

The Tory Party in Newfoundland had eight leaders during my leadership of the Liberals: H. G. R. Mews, John G. Higgins, Malcolm Hollett, James J. Greene, Dr. Noel Murphy, Gerald Ottenheimer, Anthony Murphy, and Frank D. Moores.

There were five Lieutenant-Governors: Sir Albert Walsh, Sir Leonard Outerbridge, Campbell Macpherson, Fabian O'Dea, and E. John A. Harnum.

We had three Chief Justices: Sir Edward Emerson, Sir Albert Walsh, and Robert S. Furlong.

Canada had four Governors General: Field Marshal Viscount Alexander, Vincent Massey, General Georges Vanier, and Roland Michener.

Canada had four Prime Ministers: Louis S. St. Laurent, John G. Diefenbaker, Lester B. Pearson, and Pierre Elliott Trudeau.

The other nine provinces had thirty-eight premiers: in British Columbia, Johnson and Bennett; in Alberta, Manning, Strom, and Lougheed; in Saskatchewan, Douglas, Lloyd, Thatcher, and Blakeney; in Manitoba, Campbell, Roblin, Weir, and Schreyer; in Ontario, Kennedy, Frost, Robarts, and Davis; in Quebec, Duplessis, Sauvé, Barrette, Lesage, Johnson, Bertrand, and Bourassa; in New Brunswick, McNair, Flemming, Robichaud, and Hatfield; in Nova Scotia, Macdonald, Connolly, Hicks, Stanfield, Smith, and Regan; and in Prince Edward Island, Jones, Shaw, Matheson, and Campbell. Thirty-two of them are no longer in office. Nine of them are no longer living.

When I became Premier of Newfoundland, I was the first to hold the position (formerly called Prime Minister) in fifteen years. There were many Newfoundlanders that day who had never known another Prime Minister. When I resigned in 1972, I was the only Premier or Prime Minister that 90 per cent or more of the people had ever known. In fact, I was then the only Premier that Newfoundland had known in thirty-eight years. My misfortune as a politician was that there was no other Premier with whom Newfoundlanders could compare me. They could compare me with perfection, but that was a comparison in which I could only lose.

I won six provincial General Elections in twenty-three years. A wag said, "It took the Tory Party and the Supreme Court to topple him in the seventh."

27

*And Now to Conclude and Finish**

In Ionian times, Ephesus was famous for its sanctuary of the goddess Artemis, continuing the local tradition of the worship of the Anatolian mother goddess. Dating back to the eighth century B.C., the sanctuary was repeatedly rebuilt, the most famous occasion being after 365 B.C., when Herostratus set fire to it *as the only way he could devise of immortalizing his memory*. It was after this gratuitously-caused reconstruction that it came to be numbered among the seven wonders of the world.

Andrew Mango

I hate the man who builds his name on ruins of another's fame.

John Gay

*The final verse of many Newfoundland ballads starts with these words.

Some of my Cabinet colleagues and other friends often told me that they just couldn't see me quitting politics. I wouldn't be able to give up the exercise of power, they thought; the opportunity to make decisions, to influence and often determine the shape of Newfoundland's future. And they were sure that I'd miss the House of Assembly too much to give it up.

They were quite wrong. I was anxious, years before I got out, to do so; and almost the only concern I had about getting out was that, like a deep-sea diver coming up too quickly from the depths, I might get "the bends" and have to be put into some kind of decompression chamber. After working fifteen or sixteen hours a day, seven days a week, for a quarter of a century, would I be bored to death? It was imperative, I knew, to keep busy; not just at "make work", but doing something that I sincerely believed to be worthwhile.

I've got back to my reading since retiring from politics, and I've read more than 200 books since my resignation to the moment of this writing—over twenty of them on China. A mile-long procession of unread books beckons compellingly.

I've been out of politics fourteen months, and I haven't had a pang of regret over it. I've spent six weeks in England, Scotland, Ireland, and the Channel Islands, doing research for this book and other books that I hope to write; and I spent a few weeks travelling across Europe, from Beirut to Munich, so that my wife and I might have our first real holiday together in a quarter of a century. I had three weeks in China and one week in Cuba. The rest of the time was given to the writing of this book, and I've worked an average of ten hours a day, every day of the week.

There's not been even one year since I was born without conflict in some part of the world. We've had seventy-two years of wars, revolutions, revolts, assassinations; of the rise and fall of ideological thrones, the disappearance of ancient empires and dynasties and the rise of new ones; of sweeping and often bewildering changes in arts and letters, religion, morals, mores; in science, industry, communications and travel, in government and education and medicine. I have been ship-mate through the seventy-two most revolutionary years in human history.

I am proud, probably inordinately so, of the part I was able to take in the grand drama of Confederation, and happy with the results. I know that in spite of my numerous flaws of character, and weaknesses and inconsistencies of personality (and that's no hypocrisy), I have been the willing instrument for pointing my countrymen to a great destiny. We may not yet be come to the land of Canaan, but assuredly we have left the land of Pharaoh.

I've lived many lives, and they have been exciting, every one. I have piled up experiences as some men pile up money. I've had countless failures, made countless friends and countless enemies—enough enemies to know the truth of the Chinese saying, "He that hath a thousand friends hath not a friend to spare, and he that hath one enemy will find him everywhere."

I have known sixty-nine premiers and prime ministers: Canada, five; Canadian provinces, forty-four; England, three; Australia, two; Jamaica, two; Newfoundland, six; Antigua, one; Barbados, one; Soviet Union, one; Germany, two; China, one; India, one; Cuba, one; Rumania, one. The last Premier I spoke with was Fidel Castro. Twenty-four of the sixty-nine are no longer living.

I've had one full-length book written about me by Richard Gwyn, and a small one edited by James R. Thoms. Julian Biggs made a full-length movie of me—*Little Fellow from Gambo*—for the CBC and the National Film Board (it hasn't been shown on television yet).

I have frighteningly good health, almost undiminished energy, a good yearly income, eleven grandchildren, and two great-grandchildren. Ten Canadian universities appear to have recognized in me a very learned scholar—it must be so, or they surely wouldn't have made me a doctor.* Wherever I run into Canadians, in any province or any country, they recognize me and shake my hand and say nice things.

I notice in myself a slow ebb of the strength of a lifetime's emotion about the Union Jack, almost exactly balanced by an ever-growing love of our Canadian national flag. But I love Britain and almost everything British.

*Acadia, British Columbia, Dalhousie, New Brunswick, Victoria, McGill, Waterloo Lutheran, Windsor, Prince Edward Island, Memorial.

Now I'm free to travel wherever I want to go, up to the limit of my means. I'm going to travel the Mississippi River and the Amazon, the Nile and the Ganges and the Yangtze, and the Mackenzie, and maybe write my first travel book. And I'm going to indulge my growing interest in archeology. That means going to the Indus Valley, and Iraq, and Palestine, and the best of the Inca, Aztec, and Maya ruins in Central and South America; and that magic valley in East Africa where perhaps true man first walked on our earth. And maybe they'll let me look at the archeological treasures of China, for one of my pressing ambitions is to go back to that vast and wonderful land and, if the fates decree, get a glimpse of the greatest practising revolutionary in man's history.

I feel Albania and Cuba calling, and Samarkand and Tashkent, and Bokhara. I want to visit the King Ranch in Texas and the even bigger million-acre Gang Ranch in northern British Columbia.

I referred to my income. This is it:

Canada Pension	$ 675.72
Old Age Pension	1,200.00
Pension as Premier and Member of House of Assembly	9,226.60
Golden Eagle service station payments	16,910.00
	$28,012.32

Twenty-eight thousand dollars a year! Even when income tax comes off it, a handsome and adequate income. If I didn't have to part with a substantial slice of it for interest on a large bank loan that I obtained to buy BRINCO shares, as I advised all Newfoundlanders to do (not borrow, but buy!), I wouldn't spend it all every year, and I'd be better able to indulge a grandfather's (and a great-grandfather's) instinct to ease the way of younger ones. I work to pay off the bank, so as to have only the income tax to put a hole in my income. I work to become solvent again.

I'd say that I was to be envied if I didn't remember Lord Beaverbrook's comment to a man who was interviewing him on the CBC. "You're to be envied, Lord Beaverbrook," he said. Beaverbrook replied drily, "Nobody of seventy-two is to be envied." Still, I cheer up when I remember that he lived to be eighty-four and that I am related by blood to a small army of people to whom eighty was a synonym for youthfulness.

My experiences and memories can be listed as follows:

> Wounds: the Valdmanis affair, the resignations of Herbert Pottle and Gregory Power, the defection of Beaton Abbott,* death of Lord Beaverbrook.
>
> Gladness: First child, first grandchild, first great-grandchild. My election to the National Convention as a Confederate. My first election as Premier, and my sixth. Churchill Falls. First honorary degree. Receiving 33rd degree, Masonic. Come by Chance. New campus of Memorial University. Children's Hospital. Arts and culture centres. Trans-Canada Highway. Mothers' allowance. Student aid. First meeting with Churchill. Smallwood Lake. Motor vessel *Joseph R. Smallwood.*
>
> Emotion: Churchill's speech, "Where Now are the Years that the Locusts Have Eaten." *Ode to Newfoundland* played on the great organ of Notre Dame Cathedral. Playing of *Greensleeves* at Mackenzie King's funeral procession. First speech of Eugene V. Debs after his release from prison. Jane Cowl as Juliet in *Romeo and Juliet*. General Bramwell Booth at Central Hall, Westminster. With my grandchildren seeing, by television, the first men on the moon. Meeting Chou En-lai. Visiting Tyre, Sidon, Baalbeck, Persepolis. Donald Creighton's *The Old Chieftain*. Trudeau winning the leadership of the Liberal Party. Signing the terms of Confederation.
>
> Elation: Listening to Liszt's Second Hungarian Rhapsody in Budapest. On the platform with Billy Graham in Ottawa. Hearing Wilhelm von Hoogstraten conduct *Overture of 1812* in Central Park, New York. The Scheherazade in Paris. Coronation of Queen Elizabeth II.

I've known the most interesting Newfoundlanders of the twentieth century: Sir Robert Bond, Sir Edward (Lord) Morris, Sir Richard Squires, Sir William Coaker, Dr. Arthur Barnes, Sir Michael Cashin, Sir John Crosbie, Sir John Bennett, Sir Patrick McGrath, Sir Alfred

*My friendship with Power and Abbott has been re-established.

Morine, John Murray Anderson, and Captain Bob Bartlett.

I remember with lively pride some of the able Newfoundlanders that I brought into public office:

Leslie R. Curtis	Beaton J. Abbott
Philip J. Lewis	George Warren
Dr. Frederick W. Rowe	Harold G. Starkes
William J. Keough	Edward Roberts
James R. Chalker	Gerald I. Hill
Melvin Woodward	John T. Cheeseman
Herman W. Quinton	Gregory J. Power
Dr. Hubert Kitchen	Dr. G. A. Frecker
Captain Uriah Strickland	Dr. Noel Murphy
William R. Callahan	John Mahoney
Dr. James M. McGrath	C. Max Lane
Edward S. Spencer	John Nolan
Aidan Maloney	Philip F. Forsey
Charles H. Ballam	Captain Earle Winsor

I took an energetic part in getting a lot of industrial development capital put into the province, including:

Electrical, fisheries, etc.	$ 500,000,000
Oil	500,000,000
Mining	1,000,000,000
BRINCO	1,000,000,000

That four billion capital invested in Newfoundland in the quarter-century after Confederation is as much as in the 452 years before. As much? Four times as much!

If I sought a family crest, I'd insist on having a pig in it. It was keeping pigs that kept me in Gander. If I hadn't been in Gander, there might conceivably have been no Confederation.

If I had advice to give to my successors in power, and to my fellow-Newfoundlanders, it would concern the ever-present danger that threatens to destroy Newfoundland. We are so far removed from the corridors of power, so far from the massed population and power of Canada, so far from the main Canadian market, so much out of the minds of Canada's principal captains of industry and finance, that we could easily be wasted down the drain. It will require our most stubborn determination to defeat the force of megalopolis. Never say die! Never give in! Turn a deaf ear to the timid and faithless. And then at last, if the very fates do defeat us, go down, not with a whimper, but defiantly to the end. With that spirit there will be no going down.

I'd like to have said of me what Kingsley Martin imagined Sir William Beveridge might say: "I ruled over an empire in which the concrete never set."

Another scalp for his political collection.

The Moncton Daily Times

28

Omnium Gatherum

I doubt if there have been, in the whole of Canadian history, half a dozen political partnerships so harmonious or so enduring as that I enjoyed with J. R. Smallwood. I honour him as one of the makers of Canada; I admire, and did my best to share, his unflagging determination to serve the people of Newfoundland, to improve their welfare and, above all, the opportunities for the young; I have an awesome respect for his political genius; and I have an abiding affection for him as a man and a friend. It is a privilege, on his retirement, to join in a tribute to the greatest Newfoundlander.

John W. Pickersgill

One thing I want to add—and nobody is in a position to contradict me, for I have sat in the Cabinet since its very first meeting. For twenty years I have been a close student of the Smallwood approach to the art of the possible . . . which is politics. Joseph Roberts Smallwood has never forced his will upon any Cabinet. Instead, more than once, he has set aside a proposal upon which he had set his heart, not because the consensus of Cabinet was against it but because one man only was strongly opposed.

William J. Keough

All my life, I've been privileged to meet and know fascinating people. To say what I'd like to about so many of them would make this book twice as long as it is, but I'd like to mention at least a few of them:

King George VI
Queen Elizabeth
Prince Philip
Winston Churchill
Eamon De Valera
Mackenzie King
Chou En-lai
General Franco
Louis S. St. Laurent
Prince Sihanouk
Lester B. Pearson
Alexei Kosygin
C. D. Howe
Dr. de Oliveira Salazar
Richard Nixon
Harry Boland
Big Bill Heywood
Clarence Darrow
John Alcock
Arthur W. Brown
Bertrand Russell
Upton Sinclair
Arthur Henderson
James Maxton
Eleanor Roosevelt
Pandit Nehru
Willy Brandt
General Bramwell Booth
Pope Pius XII
Robert F. Kennedy
John M. Shaheen
Edmund de Rothschild
Field Marshal Montgomery
Paavo Nurmi
Gene Tunney
Fiorello La Guardia
Norman Thomas
Plutarco Elias Calles
Sir Alexander Bustamante
Norman Manley
Luis Múñoz Marín
John C. Doyle
Jules R. Timmins
Enrico Caruso
Count Ilya Tolstoy
Maria Callas
Philip Snowden
Lord Beaverbrook
Crown Prince Akihito
René Lévesque
Polly Moran
Marie Dressler
General George C. Marshall
Astronaut Gene Cernan
Astronaut Wally Schirra
Ali Khan

M. James Boylen
Dr. Billy Graham
Chiang Ching
Sir Sydney Olivier
Aristotle Onassis
Queen Salote of Tonga
Roy Chapman Andrews
W. A. C. ("Wacky") Bennett
Rabbi Stephen Wise
Fidel Castro
Will Durant
E. Haldeman-Julius
Lincoln Steffens
Jim Larkin
Anastas Mikoyan
Baron Guy de Rothschild
Harold Macmillan
Sir Alec Douglas-Home
John Haynes Holmes
Arthur Fiedler
Field Marshal Earl Alexander

* * *

Roughly half-way in my career as Premier, I collapsed in helpless silent laughter one night as I listened to Robert Stanfield on the radio from Nova Scotia. There had been an election in that province that day, and when the results of the poll were known, Stanfield expressed his satisfaction over the result: the Tories had scored a big advance—they were now the Opposition to the Liberal Government! (The CCF, with a handful of members, had been the Opposition. I'm not sure that the Tories had had even one man in the Nova Scotia House.) But he who laughs last laughs best. It wasn't long before the Tories had a majority and Bob Stanfield was Premier. Years afterward, I told him how unutterably funny I had thought his modest boast was that night.

* * *

Having walked across Newfoundland by the railway track in 1925, I was determined to be the first to drive a car across the Island, which I did in 1958 in a four-wheel-drive Land Rover. I didn't relinquish the wheel for the 565 miles between St. John's and Port-aux-Basques.

* * *

On June 24, 1964, Professor Hugh Lilly and John Snow, in diving suits, walked on the ocean floor on the Grand Banks and deposited bronze plaques announcing Newfoundland's possession of the area.

My administration paid most of the cost of the expedition.

* * *

Brendan Bracken—Lord Bracken, then—once came to Lord Beaverbrook's apartment on Arlington Street in London. It was nearly midnight, and I noticed that Bracken scarcely spoke during the half-hour he was there. Beaverbrook did the talking. Bracken sipped a small drink and finally left without a word. "He's dying," said Beaverbrook to me. "He's got cancer of the throat." Bracken died within the next three weeks.

* * *

Not long after the Profumo scandal broke out in England, it became known that John Diefenbaker had had his portrait painted for him by Dr. Stephen Ward, who had committed suicide after his part in the scandal became known. I didn't feel like laughing at Diefenbaker's discomfiture—I just kept quiet and hoped that my own "connection" with the scandal wouldn't get out. I had been introduced to a beautiful, charming, and wealthy housewife in London whose hobby was collecting antique English mahogany furniture and an interest in interior decoration generally. She had the mistaken idea that I wanted to buy some of the stuff; I didn't, I was just interested in looking at it. She called for me in her car at the Savoy Hotel and took me to several antique dealers around London. We lunched together, and I accompanied her as she picked up her two small children at their private school; then she drove me back to the hotel. She was the former Valerie Hobson (England's talented motion-picture actress) and Profumo's wife. She is one of the most gracious ladies I ever met. The world applauded her loyalty to her husband when he got himself into such desperate trouble.

* * *

General Franco's eyes glistened as I showed him enlarged photographs of big tuna, weighing from 500 to 600 pounds, that had been caught in Newfoundland. As a sportsman and fisherman, Franco was excited by the size of our Newfoundland tuna, many times larger than those he was accustomed to catching in the Mediterranean. I invited him to come to Newfoundland to try our fishing, though I knew that there was no likelihood whatever that he could accept. Nevertheless, I sent him a specially printed fishing license. I had been invited by Franco to be his guest in Spain, and the tour included visits to Madrid, Toledo, Granada, Málaga, and Algeciras.

* * *

In London, I had a brief chat with Sir Stafford Cripps after he had addressed a crowded pro-Loyalist meeting at Kingsway Mission on Southampton Row. My sympathies were wholly with the Loyalists, and I never dreamed that the day would come when I'd chat with Franco.

* * *

I threw away thousands of dollars by failing to spend a dollar or two to buy a couple of Newfoundland postage stamps that had been overprinted for the de Pinedo flight across the Atlantic from Trepassey. I was covering the flight for the United Press Newfoundland correspondent, John T. Meaney; and my old employer, William J. O'Neill, who had become private secretary to the Postmaster General, was in Trepassey to deliver a small bag of airmail letters to de Pinedo. He had a few of the specially printed stamps with him in case anybody in Trepassey wanted to buy. Nobody did, including me. Eventually, the de Pinedo airmail stamps went up in value to $25,000 each.

* * *

I don't know if it's a record, but I once had two honorary degrees conferred on me in one day. The first was at Dalhousie University in Halifax; the second, at the University of New Brunswick in Fredericton. The ceremonies were only an hour or so apart, so a friend who owned a private plane flew me from Halifax to Fredericton. I was met at the airport by Brigadier Michael Wardell and Lady Jean Campbell, Lord Beaverbrook's granddaughter—she was daughter of the premier Duke of Scotland, head of the Campbell clan. The academic procession had already started, but I was able to catch up to take my place beside the great cartoonist, David Low, who also was made a doctor of laws, honoris causa.

* * *

In New Delhi, India, I bought a beautiful, hand-carved ivory crucifix with the intention of giving it to Archbishop Skinner when I got back to St. John's. But when I unpacked it in my home in Newfoundland House on Roache's Line, I changed my mind. "He's got a crucifix," I told myself, "I'll keep this." And did. Some of my Protestant friends are surprised when they see it for the first time on the mantel in my library.

* * *

In Rome, my Cabinet colleague Gregory Power and I drove in an open horse-drawn tourist carriage along Rome streets, enjoying immoderately the absurd values of Italian paper money—with a few dollars' worth, you could paper a room. An impish thought flashed through my mind. Back home in Newfoundland, the Opposition never ceased to complain because we were spending the cash surplus that we had inherited three or four years before, at the coming of Confederation. Suppose, I said, we started throwing out handfuls of these low-value Italian lire bank-notes on both sides of the carriage, and that dozens, then hundreds, of pedestrians started scampering after them, and the police moved in and arrested us and took us to the police station, and there it got out, in the newspapers and on the international wire services, that the Premier and Minister of Finance of Newfoundland were in Rome throwing away handfuls of money. Back in Newfoundland, people would exclaim in despair, "My God, they're over there throwing away the last of our surplus!"

* * *

I happened to be in Gander when Anastas Mikoyan was there on his way to Cuba. We met and walked back and forth on the tarmac while he waited for his Ilyushin plane to be refuelled. At his invitation, I had a look inside the plane and was surprised to see how lacking in spit and polish it was.

* * *

Reference to Gander reminds me of a pleasant chat I had with Ali Khan, who happened to be passing through there. Wasn't he one of the husbands of the beautiful Rita Hayworth? Ali and I were photographed together—but I'd rather that it had been with Rita.

* * *

Once, Canada's great rodeo champion, Herman Linder, on his own ranch in the foothills of Alberta, demonstrated for me the roping of a yearling by lariat from horseback, while I took movies. At my invitation, Linder came down to Newfoundland, and his cattleman's eyes sparkled as he saw some of our wild native grasses and the ubiquitous supply of fresh drinking water for cattle. He told me that he had never seen anywhere wild grass growing in such profusion as on our Newfoundland barrens.

* * *

It was a very beautiful day when I opened the new Bonavista North highway. Big crowds of happy people poured into the area from all over the bay, and for the first time at such an event, the music of church bells added to the excitement and celebration.

When I opened the highway to Lumsden, people were overjoyed by the event. One small boy went up to a truck-driver and, holding out a silver coin, asked earnestly for "fifty cents' worth" of drive on the new road.

* * *

I had nearly two hours' conversation in his office in Washington with the Attorney General of the United States, Robert Kennedy. Proudly, he introduced me to his huge, handsome Newfoundland dog, who went pretty well everywhere with him.

I was impressed by the very real depth and strength of Kennedy's personality.

* * *

In Oberammergau, Germany, at the restaurant of Alois Lang, who played the part of Christ in the Passion Play, Johannes Lerch gave us his superb imitation of Hitler. He was more like Hitler than Hitler! Lerch was owner of Miag, of Brunswick, West Germany, the firm that manufactured the Humbermouth cement mill for the Newfoundland Government. He had been an opponent of Hitler and a personal friend of Pope Pius XII.

* * *

Bishop John M. O'Neill and I were among the guests at Government House when Princess Elizabeth and her husband, the Duke of Edinburgh, visited Newfoundland. The Bishop asked me what I was doing about a Liberal candidate for the Harbour Main district in the forthcoming General Election, and I told him that I didn't know but would appreciate having his advice. He suggested that after the royal couple's departure that afternoon, I might run over to his home (the Episcopal palace) at Harbour Grace to talk it over. I did, and the two of us chatted until we got hungry. Then the bishop and I went into the kitchen and fried some ham and eggs and made tea and toast, and had a fine meal in his den upstairs. Then we agreed that Philip J. Lewis would be an excellent candidate. He was, and he became a tower of strength in my Cabinet for years afterward.

* * *

Britain's Secretary of State for Commonwealth Affairs, Lord Douglas-Home (who dropped the "Lord" to become a more democratic "Sir" and briefly Prime Minister of Britain), visited Newfoundland and drove to Roache's Line to the cattle-farm of my son-in-law Edward Russell to examine the bunker silo, the first in Newfoundland. There, ensilaged-green grass was stored for self-feeding cattle. Home, the owner of a large herd of beef cattle in Scotland, was much interested in the self-feed aspect of the silo.

* * *

A poignant event was my opportunity to speak at the unveiling of a plaque to Newfoundland's dead at the military cemetery of Beaumont Hamel in France. Present for the occasion was a large contingent of Newfoundland soldiers of the Canadian Army stationed in Germany.

* * *

The English have an interesting practice at large banquets: men change places so that they can chat with others around the room. At the big dinner that Beaverbrook gave for the four premiers of the Atlantic Provinces in the Dorchester Hotel, I saw this work to perfection; Herbert Morrison, the famous Labour Party man, slipped into a chair at the head table, opposite Beaverbrook. "What do you think, Max?" he asked Beaverbrook. "Do you think I should take it?" "Take it," advised Beaverbrook. Take what?—a seat in the House of Lords. He took it.

* * *

I sat and chatted with Winston Churchill in Prospect, Sir Harold Mitchell's beautiful and striking home at Ocho Rios in Jamaica, and he showed me the painting he was then doing of Mitchell's private beach, where he, Churchill, went swimming in the nude each day. The painting was one of a series of his paintings that later appeared on a set of Christmas cards.

* * *

Driving from Toledo to Granada, I was curious about the rows of soldiers I saw standing in the ditch along both sides of the road. They stood at attention, rifles slung over their shoulders, several hundred feet apart and in staggered formation, so that no two soldiers were directly opposite each other. The lines of these soldiers stretched for a distance of thirty or forty miles. We stopped at a roadside inn for a light lunch before reaching Granada and thereby missed seeing the reason for all those soldiers or guardsmen: namely, General Franco, who was proceeding back along that very road to his castle. He was on his way home from a partridge-shooting expedition, and the soldiers were there for his protection against possible assassination.

In my two meetings with him, I found Franco a surprisingly pleasant and relaxed dictator. It took an effort to remember the detestation that I had felt for him at the time of the fascist revolution in Spain.

* * *

Sir Robert Bond, the last of the Edwardians in Newfoundland politics, was stately, gracious, handsome, and a beautiful speaker. But he couldn't bear to be interrupted, and I was sitting in the gallery on the occasion when he turned the tables. Phil Moore, Sir Michael Cashin's co-Member of the House for Ferryland, had often driven Bond almost to distraction by his interruptions; but Sir Robert was waiting for him this time. "The Hon. Member reminds me of the story of Sandy, the Highland Scot, who was salmon fishing one day when the mosquitoes were very bothersome. They kept getting inside his kilt and biting him. Sandy, in his determination to keep on fishing, ignored the mosquitoes as long as he could, but his patience gave out; and, lifting his kilt high"—Bond lifted his coat-tail—"he turned his back to the mosquitoes"—Bond turned his back to Moore—"and said 'Now bite, you little beggars, bite!'"

* * *

Ernie MacFarland had almost as much fun getting me made Chief Big Water (Atlantic Ocean) of the Blood Tribe of the Blackfoot Indians as I did in getting the beautiful feather head-dress. Chief Shot on Both Sides performed the ceremony.

* * *

In West Berlin, I was received by the famous Lord Mayor, Willy Brandt. It was exciting being escorted by screeching motorcycles through Berlin's streets to City Hall. I met Brandt afterward in Tokyo, when he was West Germany's Foreign Minister, and we had a fine chat at the Okura Hotel.

* * *

The day after he was elected Premier of Jamaica, and the day before he was sworn in, Norman Manley came to the Myrtle Bank Hotel to have breakfast and a chat with me. Business people that I knew in Kingston were frightened: they thought Manley was a Communist, and if he did win the election, they'd get out of Jamaica quickly. He laughed when I told him, and as he was interested in a possible federation of the British West Indies, he wanted me to tell him about our federal union with Canada.

* * *

At a roadhouse-restaurant a few miles outside Nice in southern France, I met Aristotle Onassis and his companion, the great and famous singing genius, Maria Callas. Onassis was interested in the prospective Churchill Falls project in Labrador, which had not at that time been given a green light. He asked me to let him know when the deal was signed, so that he could buy BRINCO shares, and I later remembered to cable him the news.

* * *

I saw a book about Canada, back in 1951, and it had a reference to me, so I bought it. And, vanity of vanities, I have bought ever since each new book that has been published about Canada and includes references to me. The collection now occupies about four feet of bookshelf space and is still expanding—and my vanity with it.

* * *

When I was Lord Beaverbrook's house guest at Montego Bay in Jamaica, I got him talking about Churchill one night after dinner. Beaverbrook was the only man who served in both the War Cabinet of Lloyd George in World War I and the Cabinet of Churchill in World War II—the inner war council of each man. I asked him, "Do you consider Churchill to be an authentic great man?" "Oh, yes," he replied without hesitation, "a really great man." "Was Lloyd George a great man?" "He was," said Beaverbrook emphatically. "Which of the two was the greater man?" "Lloyd George, without a doubt!" And he spelled out the reasons: Lloyd George was a far greater orator, a far greater peacetime leader, and a greater war leader; Lloyd George had to fight his way every inch to introduce the innovations of the first war—the tank, the ships' convoy system, centralized war production, and all the rest. Churchill could begin where Lloyd George had left off, and he had the enormous benefit of the pioneering that Lloyd George had had to fight to perform.

* * *

At Staffelstein, West Germany, Dr. Arthur Seigheim, owner of the

Seigheim timber concessions in Lake Melville, Labrador (which we eventually cancelled for non-performance), entertained us at his *Schloss*. He had an entire ballet company come from Munich to perform under floodlights on the lawn. This was followed by a brilliant fireworks display that ended with an immense replica of Hamilton (now Churchill) Falls, running water and all.

* * *

In Bonn, West Germany, Tommy Davis, former Premier of Saskatchewan and future Canadian Ambassador to Japan but then Canada's High Commissioner, gave me a dinner; and the British High Commissioner to West Germany, Sir Ivone Kirkpatrick, was a guest. He had been British Ambassador to Italy and was the author of a fine autobiography. At this dinner, he gave us his unsurpassable imitation of Winston Churchill. He was so like the man himself that it was uncanny.

* * *

Dr. Salazar came downstairs to the main entrance to his ancient castle outside Lisbon to greet me and escort me upstairs to his office. Hello, I thought, this is scarcely the way for a dictator to act! But it was as a scholar and a college professor that I saw him in the next hour as we talked about Europe and the world. Men are often very different in fact from their public image.

It was on this particular visit to Portugal (which has been so close to Newfoundland for the past 500 years) that I became, in the words of Canadian newspaper headlines, "Sir Joey". That is, the Portuguese Government, in a dignified though informal ceremony in the stately old Foreign Affairs building, with the British Ambassador present, made me an officer of the Order of Prince Henry the Navigator—with medals, sash, and all. I wore it then and at the banquet that followed, and at the great convocation of Coimbra University. There I wore also the magnificent scarlet gown of a Doctor of Letters of Memorial University; and the famous cartographer Armand Cortesao, also a doctor of Memorial, and I walked together in the procession. (Privately, I felt that Gambo was well up in the world that day.)

* * *

Wit in the House of Assembly: Philip Moore, Sir Michael Cashin's colleague in the two-man Ferryland District, interrupted W. F. Coaker, who was speaking from the Opposition side of the House, and in so doing mentioned the leader of the Liberal Party, Sir Robert Bond. "The Hon. Member tells us of the Leader of the Opposition in my District, Mr. Speaker. Let me tell him this: the Leader of the Liberal Party has no followers in my District! Those who used to support him have turned his photograph in to the wall." "Yes," flashed Coaker, "because they can't look an honest man in the face!"

* * *

At lunch one day in my private dining room in the Confederation Building, I had an idea. I immediately telephoned Chesley A. Pippy and said, "I want a million dollars from you, Ches." "What for?" he asked. "To buy land around Memorial University to allow for expansion." "When do you want it?" "Oh, spread over a period of years will be fine." "All right, you've got it." "Thanks, Ches—and we'll call it Pippy Park." Which we did. It was the quickest million dollars the Newfoundland Government got in a long time.

* * *

Arthur Fiedler, leader of the Boston Pops orchestra, came with his wife for a brief vacation in St. John's. I heard on the radio that he was in the city, so I telephoned him and introduced myself. I told him that I was flying next day to Labrador and invited them along. On the bank of Churchill Falls, in the BRINCO guest house, the whole party of us sang Newfoundland ballads to Fiedler's hand-waving accompaniment.

* * *

When I walked across Newfoundland, there weren't more than half a dozen motor-driven section-men's cars, and in every case, the engine had to be bought by the section foreman, with or without the help of his crew. I helped pump the hand-driven cars for many a mile but came to the conclusion that I'd rather walk!

* * *

I was present in Cabot Tower, on Signal Hill in St. John's, in 1926, when the first wireless telephone conversation was carried on across the Atlantic. I, like the others, was breathless with awe at the strength and clarity of the voices.

* * *

Eamon De Valera, President of the Irish Free State, was eighty years old when I met him in Phoenix Park in Dublin. He surprised me with his knowledge of Newfoundland—of the loss of responsible government in 1934, of the Commission of Government, of our becoming part of Canada. When I'd been with him twenty minutes, his secretary came in and passed him a note. He waved her away and continued our talk. Twenty minutes later, she was in again, and again he waved her away. Twenty minutes again, and again he sent her back. On her fourth entry, he thanked me for the visit, and I took the hint. I thought his was an excellent arrangement.

* * *

I met John King, the American multi-millionaire natural resources developer, at the blast-off of Apollo IX and invited him to take a look at our province's resources. He telephoned me a few months later and told me that he was flying to Newfoundland to see me. He was to reach my home on Roache's Line at ten o'clock on a Sunday morning. Instead, he arrived at seven o'clock, accompanied by the astronaut, Wally Schirra, and one or two others. After the greetings, I invited them to have some breakfast, and they accepted with alacrity. "We have no cook, and my wife is still asleep," I told them, but they agreed cheerfully that we should all pile in and make our own breakfast. So into the kitchen I led them—only to run into the unspeakable humiliation of finding the kitchen sink piled high with unwashed dishes. We had had friends in the night before, and they'd had a midnight meal. So now King, Schirra, and his friends helped me to clean up the mess. Wally Schirra starred as a dish-washer, but King was magnificent at the scrambled eggs.

* * *

On the fiftieth anniversary of Suvla Bay, in Gallipoli—in company with Sir Leonard Outerbridge and a small group of Newfoundland veterans of Gallipoli—I visited the battlefield to lay wreaths on the graves of fallen Newfoundlanders. I had known personally some of the men whose graves I visited and had read of the deaths of others.

* * *

I asked Lord Beaverbrook to tell me what was the single most dramatic moment he had known in Churchill's Cabinet, and he had a prompt answer. "I went with Churchill to Paris when he made the extraordinary offer of joint and merged citizenship of the French and British, to try to keep France in the war. There came the awful decision of what to do about the French fleet when France was overrun by the Germans—to sink it, and probably incur the hatred of the French, or let it fall into the hands of the enemy. We debated it in Cabinet till past midnight and couldn't agree. Then we decided to leave it absolutely to Churchill's personal decision, and the Ministers left and went home. I went out into the garden with Churchill, and we walked about a while without talking. Then I put my hand on his shoulder and said, 'Good-night, Winnie,' and left him quite alone to make the decision."

* * *

On the occasion of Beaverbrook's banquet for the four premiers of the Atlantic Provinces, I sat at Beaverbrook's left, with Prime Minister Harold Macmillan on my left, and Robert Stanfield sat at Beaverbrook's right, with Churchill on his right. I was envious of Stanfield's wonderful chance to spend nearly two hours sitting beside Churchill and chatting with him, until Beaverbrook remarked to me afterward at his flat, "Did you see Bob Stanfield talking to Churchill? Churchill didn't hear a bloody word—he's just about stone-deaf!" Churchill had had several strokes by then, and he quite noticeably dragged his leg as he shuffled into the Dorchester and went through our receiving line.

* * *

There was but one automobile in Corner Brook, indeed in the whole of western Newfoundland, when I first lived there in 1923: that of the paper company's manager, John Stadler. The first taxi was owned by my friend George Seabright.

* * *

When I was trying to entice the gargantuan American conglomerate, Litton Industries of California, into Newfoundland, I was invited to have breakfast with its leader, Roy Ash. We had a fine talk. Today, Ash, as Director of the Budget, is one of the two or three most powerful men in the American Government after the President. There are now three men in Washington with more than a nodding acquaintance with Newfoundland: the President, Ash, and Peter Flanigan, who is one of the key members of the President's staff.

* * *

One of the most interesting of my experiences the first time I went industry-hunting in West Germany occurred at the opera at Frankfurt-am-Main. Between acts, the floodlights turned on me in the gallery front seat, and I was introduced to the audience as Neufundland's Minister President. I bowed to the ovation. I was, in fact, the first leader of any government to visit West Germany after the war.

* * *

Thrill of a lifetime: Sir Leonard C. Outerbridge and I walked up the great centre aisle of Notre Dame Cathedral in Paris, preceded by ten specially caparisoned priests who had met us at the door, followed by a small contingent of Newfoundlanders, as the great organ filled the air with the *Ode to Newfoundland*. I was there to unveil a plaque affixed to a large pillar in honour of the Royal Newfoundland Regiment that fought in France in the First World War.

* * *

A Morris Government supporter was praising the Government and the Prime Minister for all that they had accomplished. This was too much for W. F. Coaker, who called out, "What have they done? Never mind the generalities—tell us what they've done!" The Morris supporter managed to think of one or two things, including the Long

Bridge connecting the north and south sides of St. John's. "The Long Bridge," snorted Coaker. "Long bridge! Why, I could piss halfway across it!" The startled Speaker expostulated, "The Hon. Member is out of order!" "Yes, and if I wasn't, I'd piss all the way across it!"

"Me retire – who'd hold all this up!"

The Chronicle-Herald (Halifax)

Appendices

Appendix One

A. MY BLOOD RELATIONS

Not one person in a million can give you a realistic idea of the numbers of people with whom he has, or has had, blood relationship. For almost every living person, the number is almost infinite. The female members of the family—aunts, grand-aunts, cousins, sisters—that married, changed their names; but their children are blood relations, of course, generation after generation.

Here are the surnames of my blood relations, so far as I have been able to discover them, mostly with the help of Robert Mutch:

Abbott, Acorn, Adams, Affleck, Allan, Almond, Anderson, Antle, Auld, Avery.

Baird, Balderston, Barker, Barrett, Bears, Beer, Bell, Bernard, Berrigan, Bishop, Blake, Bockman, Boisner, Boswall, Boucher, Boulter, Bovyer, Boyle, Brehaut, Brown, Bryan, Bryenton, Burnett, Burns, Bursey.

Callbeck, Cameron, Campbell, Carr, Carter, Carver, Chandler, Chapman, Chasse, Chipman, Chirichiello, Clark, Coady, Coffin, Coiley, Colella, Collins, Constantine, Cook, Cooper, Cormier, Corso, Costain, Costello, Coulson, Coulton, Crampton, Craswell, Cross, Currie, Curtis.

Dagg, Darrach, Dauncey, Dawson, Dempsey, Dick, Dicon, Dillon, Doran, Dornan, Douglas, Down, Drake, Drover, Druken, Duncan, Dunne.

Eldershaw, Emery, Enman, Ennis, Enos, Erikson, Ernewein, Ernst.

Fach, Fairclough, Farquharson, Farrant, Ferguson, Fillmore, Fisher, Flack, Foggin, Follett, Foy, Fraser, Frizzle.

Gamberg, Gamble, Gay, Gillispie, Glotch, Glover, Goodell, Graham, Green, Greigg, Gullison, Gulliver.

Haddon, Hamlyn, Hanniford, Hardy, Harkness, Harty, Harvey, Haslam, Heartz, Heaton, Hebb, Hessian, Higgins, Higgs, Hillcox, Hiscock, Horne, Horton, Hosford, Howard, Howath, Howie, Huggan, Hutcheson.

Ings, Inman.

Jack, Jackson, Jamieson, Jardine, Jay, Jenkins, Johnston, Jones.

Kaas, Kaufman, Keating, Keizer, Kelly, Kielly, King, Kramer.

Laird, Laishley, Lambert, Lawson, Leard, Leduc, Leitch, LeRoux, Livingstone, Long, Lowther, Lund, Lyons.

MacArthur, MacCabe, MacCallum, MacCollester, MacCollum, MacDonald, Macdonald, MacEachern, MacEwen, MacFadyen, McGrath, MacGregor, Machnig, MacInnis, MacKay, MacKechnie, MacKendrick, MacKenzie, Mackie, MacKinley, MacLaughlen, MacLeod, MacMillan, MacPhail, MacQuarrie, MacRae, MacRobie, Maher, Marshall, Martin, Mason, Matheson, Mayo, Meek, Metcalf, Middleton, Miller, Monnahan, Morrow, Murphy, Murray, Mutch, Muttart.

Nelson, Niland.

Pahl, Pangborn, Passmore, Paul, Pepin, Peterkin, Picco, Pickard, Pickering, Pidgeon, Pippy, Pound, Powell, Power, Prior, Profitt, Prowse, Purdie, Pushee.

Ralph, Ramsay, Reardon, Regular, Reid, Richards, Richardson, Robinson, Rodd, Ross, Russell.

Samson, Sanders, Sanderson, Sanson, Scholtz, Schurman, Scott, Sharpe, Shay, Shepardson, Skeans, Skelching, Smith, Snow, Sorensen, Sorenson, Stagman, Stairs, Stansfield, Stead, Stedman, Stephano, Stewart, Stout, Strong, Sullivan, Swan, Sweet.

Tanton, Tayman, Thicke, Thompson, Tiers, Tringale, Tucker, Turner.

Vanderstine, Vessey, Vickerson, Vincent.

Waldock, Walker, Walsh, Ward, Watts, Webb, Webber, Weeks, Westaway, Wheeler, White, Whiteway, Wilson, Wiseman, Wood, Woodside.

Young, Younker.

B. WE'RE A LONG-LIVED LOT

It would appear to be the case that my family are a long-lived tribe. Here is a partial list, and an encouraging one it is for a man of seventy-two.

Age	*Born*	*Died*	
111	1775	1886	Graham, Mrs. Donald (née Catherine Brown), my great-great-grand-aunt

108			Ford, Mrs. John (née Younker)
106			Crampton
102	1857	1959	Auld, George
102	1828	1930	Mutch, Solomon
101			Younker, George
99	1860	1959	Bovyer, Rhoda Jane
98			Younker, Joseph
97	1860	1957	Abbott, Mrs. George (née Moore)
97	1873	1970	Marshall, Herbert
97			Purdie, Mrs. (Dr.) (née Brown)
96	1862	1958	Dagg, Mrs. Elisha (née MacMillan), British Columbia
96	1866	1962	MacLeod, Gaven
95	1816	1911	Farquharson, James, Jr.
95	1876	1971	Putnam, Mrs. E. C. (née Vickerson), Massachusetts
95	1878		Dauncey, Mrs. Russell (née Coffin), Alberta
94	1835	1929	MacLeod, Mrs. James (née Sanders)
94			Younker, Oliver
94	1834	1928	MacLauchlan, Mrs. John (née Rodd)
94	1879	L.	Kielly, Mrs. George Herbert (née Wheeler)
94	1871	1965	Bishop, Philip Sanders
94	1877	1971	Harty, Mrs. Alex (née White)
94	1819	1913	Kielly, Robert
94	1849	1943	Marshall, Robert, Jr.
94	1858	1952	Marshall, Louis
94	1853	1947	Duncan, Mrs. R. A. (née Mason)
93	1785	1878	Smallwood, John, my great-grand-uncle
93	1870	1963	Farquharson, Charles A., Alberta
92	1821	1915	Duncan, Mrs. John (née Lawson)
92	1881	L.	Sanders, James Robert
92	1881	L.	Bovyer, Beatrice
92	1862	1954	MacQuarrie, W. Alexander
92	1852	1944	Mutch, Francis
92	1871	1963	Meek, William C.
92	1881	L.	Meek, Reagh
92	1869	1961	Bovyer, Dr. Nelson
92	1875	1967	Brown, C. Alexander
91	1836	1927	Smallwood, John B.
91	1881	1972	Smallwood, John Holman
91	1882	L.	MacMillan, Ephraim
91	1845	1936	Lawson, John, Sr.

91	1799	1890	Smallwood, Mrs. James (née Brown), my great-grandmother
91	1840	1931	Marshall, Jane
91	1881	1972	Brown, Mrs. Frank (née MacKay)
91	1872	1963	Brown, Aubrey
91			Brown, William
91	1854	1945	Brown, Ebenezer
91	1882	L.	Stout, Mrs. Frank (née Vickerson), Massachusetts
91	1858	1950	Auld, Charles H.
90	1868	1958	White, Mrs. James D. (née Farquharson)
90	1808	1898	Woodside, Mrs. John (née Pickering)
90	1852	1942	Woodside, John
90	1863	1953	Miller, James A.
90	1874	1964	Farquharson, Gertrude
90	1875	1965	Meek, Leonard
89	1839	1928	David Smallwood, my grandfather
89	1815	1904	Farquharson, Harriett
89	1879	1968	Sanders, Margaret Rosella
89	1868	1957	Bishop, Calvin D.
89	1878	1967	Cantello, Mrs. James (née MacLeod)
89	1884	L.	MacLean, Henry B., British Columbia
89	1778	1867	Brown, Mrs. John (née Lawson), my great-great-grandmother
89	1855	1944	Miller, Benjamin
89	1846	1935	Inman, William Henry
89	1857	1946	Matheson, Mrs. Ronald (née Farquharson
89	1847	1936	Mutch, Anna, British Columbia
89	1861	1950	Currie, Mrs. Hugh (née Clark)
89	1884	L.	Boulter, Mrs. Neil (née Schurman)
89	1877	1966	MacGregor, Alexander
89			Brown, James
89	1866	1946	Brown, Stephen
89	1882	1971	Brown, Ira
88	1885	L.	Strong, Mrs. William (née Haddon), California
88	1882	1970	MacLean, Archibald, Western Canada
88	1799	1887	Farquharson, John, Sr., Prince Edward Island

88	1798	1886	Power, Mrs. Martin (née Marshall)
88	1828	1916	Farquharson, Benjamin, New Brunswick
88	1818	1906	Farquharson, William ("Black Bill") Jr.
88	1868	1956	Farquharson, Frank C.
88	1880	1968	Farquharson, Ernest W.
88	1878	1966	Brown, Hammond
88	1885	L.	Ralph, Mrs. W. M. (née Mutch)
87	1886	L.	Matheson, Walter
87	1837	1924	Sanders, Robert
87	1876	1963	MacMillan, Edmund
87	1870	1957	Bovyer, John M., British Columbia
87			MacLean, Mrs. Alex (née Douglas)
87	1816	1903	Auld, David
87	1800	1887	Leard, Samuel, Jr.
87	1837	1924	Smallwood, Mrs. John (née Farquharson)
87	1873	1960	Smallwood, Mrs. (Dr.) Frederick (née Farquharson)
87	1861	1948	Farquharson, Mrs. John T. (née Mutch), British Columbia
87	1874	1961	Howard, Lea
87	1886	L.	Schurman, Rev. Grover, California
87	1883	1970	Barnett, Mrs. George (née Vincent)
87	1878	1965	Bell, Mrs. Cole (née Marshall)
87	1886	L.	Mutch, William W.
87	1886	L.	Davis, Mrs. O. O. (née MacMillan), Alberta
87			Wiseman, Mrs. Saidy (née Devanna)
86	1817	1903	MacGregor, Mrs. John (née Farquharson)
86	1830	1916	Gillespie, Mrs. John (née Young)
86	1833	1919	Wheeler, Mrs. John (née Sanders)
86	1885	1971	Sanders, Violet Matilda
86	1815	1901	Inman, Mrs. William (née Farquharson)
86	1820	1906	Mutch, William
86	1837	1923	Leard, Thomas H.
86	1841	1927	Mutch, Benjamin
86	1874	1960	Woodside, William
86	1881	1967	White, Russell
86	1887	L.	Shepardson, Mrs. R. J. (née Mutch)

86	1886	1972	Stewart, Mrs. Frank (née Mutch)
86	1887	L.	MacInnis, Mrs. William (née Mutch)
85	1888	L.	Barrett, Mrs. Golding (née Smallwood)
85	1888	L.	Prowse, Hon. T. W. L.
85	1873	1958	Smallwood, Dr. Frederick
85	1839	1924	Miller, Mrs. Samuel (née Lawson)
85	1802	1887	Brown, William
85	1860	1945	Douglas, Mrs. George (née Marshall)
85	1854	1939	Brown, Mrs. William (née Kielly)
85	1888	L.	Currie, Walter
85	1879	1964	Clark, Russell
85			Devanna, Richard, printer
85			Devanna, Richard, jeweller
84	1827	1911	Farquharson, Henry
84	1833	1917	Smallwood, Charles
84	1791	1875	Farquharson, James
84	1795	1879	Mutch, Mrs. James, Sr. (née Farquharson)
84	1833	1917	Farquharson, James, Prince Edward Island
84	1816	1900	Mutch, Robert
84	1818	1902	Auld, David
84	1847	1931	Farquharson, James R. ("Jim Bill")
84	1876	1960	MacMillan, Mrs. W. M. (née Farquharson)
84	1860	1944	Mutch, Edwin
84	1874	1958	Stewart, Mrs. Charles P. (née Mutch)
84	1889	L.	Wood, Mrs. James (née Farquharson)
84	1889	L.	Allan, Mrs. Thomas (née Bovyer)
84	1889	L.	MacQuarrie, Rev. Waldron
84	1889	L.	Turner, John
84	1889	L.	Peterkin, Mrs. L. (née Mutch), Western Canada
84	1885	1969	Jack, Mrs. George (née Mutch), Western Canada
84	1871	1955	Hutcheson, Mrs. F. G. (née Coffin)
84	1889	L.	Goodell, Mrs. John (née Duncan), Montana
84	1889	L.	Ings, Lloyd
84			Smallwood, Charles William, my father
83	1880	1963	Smallwood, Mrs. Charles W. (née Devanna), my mother

83	1821	1904	Smallwood, David, New Brunswick
83	1828	1911	Smallwood, William, my grand-uncle
83	1885	1968	Smallwood, Percy L.
83	1814	1897	Douglas, Mrs. William Lawson (née Smallwood)
83	1890	L.	Gillis, Mrs. Malcolm (née Smallwood)
83	1876	1959	MacEachern, William Smallwood, Prince Edward Island
83	1890	L.	Haddon, John, California
83	1874	1957	Wheeler, John Louis
83	1821	1904	Pickering, Alexander
83	1798	1881	MacGregor, Mrs. James (née Brown)
83	1816	1899	Brown, David
83	1834	1917	Mutch, Francis
83	1834	1917	Brown, Isabel
83	1865	1948	Abbott, George
83	1852	1935	Mutch, David
83	1857	1940	Clark, James Mutch
83	1890	L.	Glotch, Mrs. Stanley (née Brown)
83	1887	1970	Wood, Mrs. Alex (née Mutch)
83	1887	1970	Barker, Mrs. Gordon (née Mutch)
83	1881	1964	Farquharson, Seymour
83	1875	1958	MacFarlane, Mrs. John (née Miller)
83	1890	L.	Martin, Ella, Columbia
82	1820	1902	Gambert, Charles, my great-grandfather
82	1842	1924	Sanders, James
82	1877	1959	Sanders, David John
82	1876	1958	Reid, Mrs. Stephen (née Bishop)
82	1881	1963	Prowse, Herbert T.
82	1885	1967	Higgs, Mrs. Verne (née Farquharson), Nova Scotia
82	1885	1967	Douglas, MacLeod
82	1826	1908	Farquharson, John Jr.
82	1830	1912	Ings, Mrs. Robert (née Mutch)
82	1873	1955	Pangborn, Mrs. William (née Kielly)
82	1871	1953	Mason, Herbert
82	1855	1937	White, Mrs. William C. (née Emery)
82	1891	L.	Bovyer, Frank
82	1891	1973	Inman, Leitch
81	1819	1900	Smallwood, William, Newcastle, N.B.
81	1868	1949	Smallwood, Mrs. Frederick (née Hyde)
81	1863	1945	Smallwood, Henry

81	1863	1944	Carson, Mrs. Mark (née Young)
81	1879	1960	Bovyer, Wilfred
81	1819	1900	Clark, Mrs. Nathan (née Leard)
81	1843	1924	Leard, Archibald
81	1852	1933	Leard, Matthew R.
81	1849	1930	Farquharson, Samson
81	1874	1955	Jardine, Mrs. Arthur (née Farquharson)
81	1834	1915	Clark, Mrs. Haviland (née Smallwood)
81	1861	1942	Haddon, Mrs. John (née Mutch)
81	1868	1949	Antle, Mrs. (Rev.) John (née Mutch)*
81		L.	Smallwood, Roy Dawson
81	1892	L.	Younglove, Mrs. Ralph (née Haddon), California
81	1891	L.	Jones, Mrs. Cecil B. (née Kielly)
81	1876	1957	Mutch, Robert Everett
81	1892	L.	Thicke, Mrs. Claude (née Mutch)
81	1884	1965	Stanley, Mrs. Arthur (née Mutch)
81	1890	1971	Mutch, Thorley
81	1891	1972	Ings, Earle
81	1892	L.	Glover, Mrs. Robert (née Mooreside)
80	1893	L.	Woodside, Willa
80	1893	L.	Christiansen, Mrs. John (née Mutch)
80			MacMillan, Frances
80			MacMillan, Millicent
80	1866	1946	Ings, Cyrus
80	1883	1962	Woodside, Preston
80	1892	L.	Marshall, Mrs. Walter (née Douglas)
80	1887	1967	Martin, Edwin
80	1891	1971	Mutch, Percy
80	1893	L.	Mutch, Hazel
80	1893	L.	Bishop, John T.
80	1883	1963	Pickard, Mrs. Alfred (née White)
80	1892	L.	Mutch, Courtland
80	1821	1901	MacEwen, Mrs. William H. (née Farquharson)
80	1826	1906	Clark, Mrs. George (née Mutch)
80	1834	1914	Woodside, Andrew
80	1849	1929	Inman, Mrs. James (née Inman)
80	1866	1945	Farquharson, Albert H.

*The Rev. John Antle, a native of Brigus, Newfoundland, was the famous missionary on the British Columbia coast. He was called "the Grenfell of the Pacific Coast".

80	1868	1948	MacMillan, Mrs. Ernest (née Abbott)
80	1856	1935	Coffin, Mrs. Robert (née Mutch)
80	1865	1945	Mutch, Ernest F.
80	1871	1950	MacMillan, Blair
80	1796	1875	Smallwood, William, Prince Edward Island
80	1812	1891	Bovyer, Mrs. John J. (née Farquharson)
80	1871	L.	Sanders, James
80	1873	1953	Sanders, George
80	1755	1835	Higgins, Mrs. Cornelius (née Lawson)
80	1801	1881	Leard, John
80			Devanna, Frederick James
80	1863		Auld, Walter
80			Devanna, Charles

C. SOME OF US HAVE DONE VERY WELL

Here follow the names of some of my blood relations who have made something a little more than usual of their lives in Canada and the United States. The great majority of the persons in the list originated in Prince Edward Island. Robert Mutch is adding to the list every week.

1870		Abbott, Waldron, Commissioner of Public Works, Nebraska
		Auld, Dr. J. William, medical doctor
1863		Auld, Walter, who after returning from the Klondike contracted his first and only marriage at the age of 80
		Auld, Dr. Benson, medical doctor, Halifax, Nova Scotia
		Auld, Walter, head of the Prince Edward Island telephone system
		Bishop, Rev. Harvey, Presbyterian Minister, Montreal
		Blake, D. F., Mayor, High River, Alberta
1900	L.	Bovyer, Harold F., merchant, Neutral Bay, Australia
1869	1961	Bovyer, Dr. Nelson, medical doctor
1912	L.	Callbeck, Lorne, author of *Cradle of Confederation*; research scientist
1922	L.	Campbell, Bert, lawyer
1879		Clark, Hon. Russell, merchant, for many years member of the Prince Edward Island House of

		Assembly, Minister without portfolio in the Liberal administration of the Hon. Walter Jones
1910	L.	Clark, Hon. Keir, Minister in the Liberal administration of the Hon. Walter Jones, Minister of Education in the Liberal administration of the Hon. Alex Matheson, Minister of Health in the Liberal administration of the Hon. Alex Campbell
1888	L.	Currie, Walter, ex-Deputy Minister in the Prince Edward Island Government
		Douglas, MacLeod, merchant
1913	L.	Douglas, Howard, wholesale merchant
1927	1969	Douglas, Wallace, wholesale merchant
		Drake, Dr. Lawson, professor of biology, University of Prince Edward Island
1792	1824	Farquharson, William J., Jr., exporter of produce to Newfoundland; died on board his own vessel, the *William and Ann*, on her fatal voyage from Trepassey, Newfoundland, December 12, 1824, when all hands were lost
1799	1887	Farquharson, John, exporter of produce to Newfoundland, named the district where he lived, Mermaid, after his schooner
1825	1894	Farquharson, H. W., wholesale merchant
1834	1903	Farquharson, the Hon. Donald, Premier of Prince Edward Island, 1898-1901; MP for Queen's from 1902 until his death; Liberal Member of Prince Edward Island House of Assembly from 1876; director of Merchants' Bank; wholesale merchant; ship-owner, trading to Britain, Newfoundland, and West Indies; my grandfather David's second cousin
1880	1954	Farquharson, Dr. Howard, medical doctor, Alberta
1863	1935	Farquharson, Richard, wholesale merchant
1942	L.	Frizzell, Dr. Haldane, Halifax, Nova Scotia
1929	L.	Frizzell, Dr. Robert L., Los Angeles, California
1934	L.	Harkness, K. Blair, lawyer, son of the Hon. Douglas Harkness, Calgary
1860	1922	Ings, Hope S., inventor of potato picker
		Kelly, Dr. Hammond, chief of P.E.I. Government veterinarians
		Kelly, Dr. Blair, veterinarian

1901	L.	Kielly, Wendell, historian and genealogist
		Kielly, Harry, author and historian
1860	1911	Kielly, Charles, Superintendent of Schools, Prince Edward Island
		Lawson, Captain David, master mariner, settler in 1770, my great-great-great-great-grandfather
1800	1883	Lawson, Cornelius, master ship-builder, Perth Amboy, New Jersey.
		Lawson, the Hon. John, Solicitor General of Prince Edward Island in 1829
1815	1895	Lawson, Alexander, owner-editor of the *Herald*, Yarmouth, Nova Scotia
		Lawson, Henry, editor of the *B.C. Colonist*, sometime editor of the *Patriot*, Charlottetown, Prince Edward Island
		Lawson, Rev. Stephen, sometime newspaper publisher
		Lawson, Dr. G. C., Quebec City
		Lawson, Miss L. E., missionary in China
		Lawson, Miss Mary, missionary in Western Canada
1838	1877	Lawson, Dr. Frank, medical doctor, St. Paul, Minnesota
		Lawson, John L., editor of the Chicago *Record Herald*, associate of Colonel Theodore Roosevelt
		Leitch, Lieut.-Col. Roy, officer, Serbian Army, World War I
1884	L.	MacLean, Henry B., originator of the MacLean system of writing
1889	L.	MacQuarrie, Rev. Waldron, United Church Minister
1933	L.	MacQuarrie, Ian, Doctor of Philosophy, University of Prince Edward Island
		Miller, the Hon. Cecil, Speaker of the Prince Edward Island House of Assembly, ex-minister of Natural Resources in the Liberal administration of the Hon. Alex Campbell
		Miller, Dr. A. F., Medical Superintendent, Sanatorium, Nova Scotia
		Moore, Rev. Albert, Methodist Minister, Dorchester, Massachusetts
1828	1930	Mutch, Solomon, wholesale merchant in Newfoundland, where he lived a number of years

		and where he founded the first cannery; his son, Ernest, married Sir Frederick Carter's daughter Josephine
1834	1917	Mutch, Francis, hotel-owner
1860	1944	Mutch, Edwin, Canadian army soldier in Riel Rebellion
1868	1890	Mutch, Dr. Percy, medical doctor
1874	1946	Mutch, John, wholesale merchant, Nova Scotia
1876	1957	Mutch, R. Everett, wholesale merchant, president of Northumberland Ferries, Ltd.
1901	L.	Mutch, J. Robert, genealogist, author *Genealogy of the Mutch Family*
1911	L.	Mutch, Walter, professor, Bible Institute, Western Canada
1934	L.	Mutch, R. Lloyd, professor, Mohawk College, Hamilton, Ontario
1932	L.	Mutch, Earnest A., vice-principal, Vocational Institute, Charlottetown
1937	L.	Mutch, George, professor, Technical College, Kentville, Nova Scotia
		Pahl, Denis, professor, St. Mary's College, Winona, Wisconsin.
1897	L.	Pickering, Mrs. Wilfred; with her husband and her sister, Vivian Woodside, operated "Green Gables House", Prince Edward Island
1858	1925	Prowse, Lemuel, Member of the Prince Edward Island House of Assembly, Liberal MP for Queen's County
1862	1930	Prowse, Benjamin C., Member of the Canadian Senate
1874	1937	Prowse, Lieut.-Col. Waldron, Canadian Army, World War I
1888	L.	Prowse, Hon. T. William L., Member of the Prince Edward Island House of Assembly, Mayor of Charlottetown, Lieutenant-Governor of Prince Edward Island, 1950-1958
1914	L.	Prowse, Dr. Lemuel, Chairman of the Prince Edward Island Hospital Commission
1913	L.	Rogers, General Allison W., honorary aide-de-camp to the Governor General
1886	L.	Schurman, Rev. Grover, Baptist Minister, Los Angeles, California
1785	1878	Smallwood, John, exporter of farm produce to Newfoundland

1794	1863	Smallwood, James, exporter of farm produce to Newfoundland
1796	1875	Smallwood, William, shipyard-owner and master ship-builder
1812	1890	Smallwood, Rev. Frederick, Methodist Minister
		Smallwood, Joseph Cornelius, manufacturer of oat and wheat meals
1839	1928	Smallwood, David, merchant, boot and shoe manufacturer, Newfoundland
1833	1859	Smallwood, James C., merchant
		Smallwood, inventor of Smallwood shingle machine
1855	1928	Smallwood, K. C., Charles R., lawyer
		Smallwood, Dr. George W., dentist
		Smallwood, Dr. Frederick, dentist
		Smallwood, C. W., inventor of a potato digger
		Smallwood, Col. Kenneth, with Canadian Forces presently in West Germany
	L.	Smallwood, Clifford, MP
	L.	Smallwood, John, President, Queen's Liberal Association, Charlottetown, Prince Edward Island
		Stead, J. C., inventor of the Stead circulating generator for steam boilers
1885	1955	Turner, Percy, ex-Mayor of Charlottetown, Prince Edward Island
1926	1972	Turner, Dr. William, cardiologist and director of internal medicine, Moncton, New Brunswick
		White, Gordon, ex-deputy minister, Prince Edward Island
1912	L.	Whitehead, Mrs. Harry (née Mutch), owner of Prince Edward Island's largest outdoor movie theatre
1911	L.	Woodside, Elton, farmer; owned his own small plane and known as "the flying farmer"
	L.	Woodside, Rev. Russell, United Church Minister, Bathurst, New Brunswick
		Woodside, Dr. Donald, dentist

Appendix Two

SMALLWOOD – PICKERSGILL CONVERSATION, MAY 31, 1971

In 1971, the Canadian Historical Association held its annual meeting at Memorial University in St. John's. The Hon. John W. Pickersgill and the Hon. Joseph R. Smallwood were invited to appear before the Association on May 31, 1971, and to engage in a conversation about Newfoundland and Confederation. This is a transcript of their talk.

SMALLWOOD: Mr. Chairman, I understand that Mr. Pickersgill and I are to talk about Confederation, Newfoundland's part in Confederation, the story of how we came to be a Province. And he can tell an awful lot about it, and I hope he does, and I can tell a lot. And between us, I think, we can tell most of the story, perhaps not all.

I suppose in one sense it began here in Newfoundland, in St. John's, in fact, but most of it happened in Ottawa. Here it began, I think, in a walk, in one of many walks that Gordon Bradley and I had around Quidi Vidi Lake. Down to the east of us here there's a large lake, I think a mile, two miles long—Quidi Vidi. And Bradley was a terrible walker, I mean he was a wonderful walker as we would say here: he was a man who loved to walk. And I walked three million miles with him in Ottawa to keep him there. When we went to Ottawa, if I hadn't been willing to walk all over Ottawa—after me came Charlie Granger and the late Senator Petten—if we hadn't walked Gordon Bradley in Ottawa, he wouldn't have stayed there, and there probably wouldn't have been any Confederation. But he was a great fellow for walking, and he and I would go for long walks. He was Solicitor General in the administration of Sir Richard Squires, and it was about 1925 or '26.

We would talk about the desperate condition Newfoundland was in, and had been in ever since the end of the First War and up to then, seven or eight or nine years. The prospects looked terribly bleak: unemployment, the worst possible kind of unemployment, and no money to relieve the unemployed, the destitute; the country in debt, heavily in debt, and the prospects looked—well, she didn't seem to have any prospects, really. We agreed on this. He was Solicitor General, a member of the Cabinet, and we would talk as two partisans, as partisans of that Party, and wonder what was going to happen. We agreed on one thing—that it was a pretty hopeless prospect. There didn't seem to be any hope at all for Newfoundland, none, just completely hopeless. And then he would say in that enormously powerful voice—he had one of the finest voices of any man that ever lived; he was a magnificent orator and a man of great physical stature—he announced that there was only one hope for Newfoundland. "What's that?" He said, "Confederation with Canada." I said, "You're crazy!" He said, "No. The only hope." I said, "Why do you say that?" "Well," he said, "that's a great country. That's a country; I've been full of admiration of that country ever since I studied law at Dalhousie University." I said, "Gordon, what's Canada got that we haven't got?" He said, "Are you crazy?" "What has she got?" He said, "She's a great country; she's one of the world's great countries; she's a country that's going to get somewhere; she's going places—I hate to use that term—she's going to get somewhere. We should link up with her. It's the only hope we've got."

Well, I didn't believe it; I didn't agree; I didn't see it. Now, frankly, at that point, I didn't know anything about Canada. The only part of Canada I'd ever been in in my life was Sydney, Halifax, and Saint John . . . I'd worked in Halifax as a reporter on the *Halifax Herald* and I'd gone on to Boston and then New York and on the way back stopped over at Saint John. That's all I knew of Canada—Sydney, Halifax, and Saint John. I wasn't terribly impressed. In Halifax, there used to come into the office every night, every weekday night, a man whose name I've never been able to remember, but he was a poet and a scholar and a very famous man in Nova Scotia. Every night he'd come into the *Halifax Herald* office, and a crowd of cronies would gather there, and they'd gossip about Nova Scotia and what had happened and what a calamity Confederation had been for Nova Scotia. They would recite the names of the industries they had had and the rate of growth in Nova Scotia and how Confederation had killed their industries. Then they'd point to New Brunswick and make out a worse case. This wasn't prepossessing. So I couldn't understand Gordon talking that way. But I did make a mental note that one day I would make one of my, for me, in my own mind, famous studies. I've done that sort of thing all my life. You know, throw myself for maybe three months or six months into a study, make millions of notes. I would make a study of the thing; I promised myself I would make a study of Confederation.

And the first time I began the making of that study, I ran into Mr. Pickersgill. I landed in Ottawa with a view to talking to the various Ministers and Deputy Ministers and heads of divisions to find out just how the Government of Canada functioned. And landing there, I went up to see the Prime Minister. But the Prime Minister was in Paris at the time, I think he was in Paris, somewhere in Europe.

PICKERSGILL: He was in Paris at the peace conference.

SMALLWOOD: At the peace conference. What peace? What conference?

PICKERSGILL: The peace with Italy.

SMALLWOOD: Oh, that one. And Mr. St. Laurent was acting Prime Minister, and I went up to see him. And the man who met me was the Prime Minister's executive assistant and boss, Mr. Pickersgill. And that's where it all began. So, Jack, you know that part better than I do.

PICKERSGILL: Well, it really began a long time before that, you know (*laughter and applause*). We had a grand design, we older Canadians—and I refer to my first native province, Ontario, when I say that—that would encompass the whole of British North America. . . . That was in 1864, and we did get two Newfoundlanders to come to the Quebec Conference, and a real effort was made before Confederation, the original Confederation, and just afterward to get Newfoundland into Confederation and there was a couple of other, what my children would call abortions, in between. The last one was in . . .

SMALLWOOD: Why would your children call it that?

PICKERSGILL: Well, of course you know, the permissive society.

The last one was in 1932, when before the Commission of Government was established, a final overture was made to Canada; and I regret to say that it wasn't very well received. But I formed the opinion at that time, and I think quite a lot of Canadians did, of my age, that we had made a very great mistake. But I think when the need, from Canada's point of view, to have Newfoundland as a part of Canada really became apparent to a lot of Canadians—I don't mean the majority of ordinary people who don't normally think much about these things, but I mean the people who do think about the future of the country, who do think about public life and so on—was at the beginning of the war. . . . If you look at the speech that Mr. Mackenzie King made in Parliament of September 1939, there are two references in it to Newfoundland, in both of which he said substantially this: "that next to the defence of the soil of Canada, the most important interest of Canada in the war was the defence of Newfoundland." And I think that.

SMALLWOOD: Did you write that?

PICKERSGILL: Yes, I did. Modesty would have prevented me saying so, but thank you (*loud laughter*).

SMALLWOOD: And he didn't tell me to ask.

PICKERSGILL: But I remember the time of the destroyer bases deal in 1940 that our Government and our Prime Minister showed very little interest in any of the details of that arrangement except with respect to the bases in Newfoundland. And all these things are in *The Mackenzie King Record*. . . . Every reference to Newfoundland that I can find in Mr. King's diary is in that book.

SMALLWOOD: That's all there were?

PICKERSGILL: That's all there were. That is perhaps very significant, because you will remember that many a time when you were in Ottawa, you worried about how enthusiastic Mr. King really was; and I know that there were grave doubts in the minds of nearly all, well, I think all the Ministers in Ottawa. Not about the desirability of having Newfoundland as a part of Canada, but about the viability of fitting Newfoundland into the federal-provincial picture in Canada; because at the time the negotiations took place with Mr. Smallwood, at the time he came to Ottawa, in fact, we were in the midst of very difficult negotiations after the war with the provinces about federal-provincial financial relations. And we had got a pattern more or less worked out into which the more you studied it, the more clear it became Newfoundland could not fit, because there was no way that you could give a financial deal to Newfoundland which would make a provincial government sound that the others wouldn't have thought to be extravagant. With hindsight, we can see it wouldn't have mattered very much. But at that time, prudent men—and there were prudent men in those days—had some doubts about the Government of Canada being a great tax-collecting agency for provincial politicians providently to spend. That was one of the problems. I think you know it was the central problem.

SMALLWOOD. It was awful; it really was quite awful. I thought that, God in heaven, if Newfoundland wanted to join Canada, if that should happen, if that should turn out to be the case (and there was a lot of doubt about that), but if it should turn out to be the case that Newfoundland wanted to join Canada, for God's sake, Canada would throw her arms wide open and welcome us, wouldn't they? I thought. But they wouldn't, no, they wouldn't. I went up to Ottawa—before going up, I had gone out and got myself elected, with the help of the voters, in Bonavista Bay, which later Mr. Pickersgill represented in Parliament. I had gone out and advocated union with Canada, way out on the end of a big, long limb. And got elected with a big majority, as a Confederate. And now before the Convention opened (this is the thing I had been elected to, along with forty-four others), before it met, I decided to go up to Ottawa as a Confederate, as one who was committed to Confederation if we could get acceptable terms, and find out, in Ottawa, how it would work if we did become a province. And I expected to have a warm welcome in Ottawa.

If the plague had descended on them, I don't think they would have been any more scared. They were scared. They were really scared; I was almost an untouchable. They appointed Frank Bridges, who was the Minister of Fisheries—he was a New Brunswick Minister—they appointed him to meet me and to organize for me meetings I would have with various people. And he did. He organized meetings for me with half a dozen Ministers and Deputy Ministers. And also with Mr. Solon Low, who was then the leader of the Social Credit Party and with Mr. Coldwell, who was then the leader of the CCF, and with John Bracken, the leader of the Tory Party. They arranged meetings for me with those men and with the Ministers. With the Ministers and Deputies, especially, I wanted to find out if we became a province of Canada, what would the Department of Fisheries do for Newfoundland? . . . What would other Ministers, other departments, do? What would Newfoundland get out of it? This is a very practical question. It was then no use going to the Newfoundland people and saying, "Look, vote for union with Canada" without showing them what Newfoundland and they in it were going to get out of Confederation. We were 350,000 people; a big country now, half a million. But we were 350,000 people and as proud as Lucifer, and as cocky and independent as any little group of people ever was in North America. Most people in Newfoundland thought they'd be condescending to let Canada join Newfoundland. I'm not exaggerating very much, not very much. People in Newfoundland were innocent enough and lacking, sufficiently lacking, in information about Canada to feel that Newfoundland would be doing an awfully big thing to join Canada. The feeling in Canada at the time [was] "Oh, those poor bastards. They're half-starved. Let's take them in and feed them." If the Newfoundland people had known how the ordinary Canadian . . . really felt about it, there wouldn't have been a chance in hell of the Newfoundland people in a majority voting to join Canada. And they thought they were doing Canada a great favour; it was a great mark of respect that we were showing Canada to agree to join her. And we only barely agreed then, 51-49; 51 per cent said let's join, and 49 per cent said no. And the 49 who said no felt that the 51 were all savage, brutal traitors. All of us were just utter traitors, to sell out, sell Newfoundland up the river (that means the St. Lawrence River), to give up our birthright, to give up our birthright and surrender and give in, and throw in our lot with another country. When the showdown came, there were only 51 per cent who could be persuaded, and I put great emphasis on the word *persuaded*, to do that.

So when I went up there, innocently . . . I landed in Ottawa expecting the red carpet out, expecting that I'd get a wonderful reception, I'd be a hero. I'd been elected down in Newfoundland to go to the National Convention as a Confederate.

PICKERSGILL: At least I knew that.

SMALLWOOD: Mr. Pickersgill is about the only man in Canada who did know. I was going up there expecting a big reception in Ottawa. Well, they were scared stiff. I never saw such a timid crowd. It was my first experience with Canadian politicians. I was not impressed. I sat in the House of Commons and no Minister could get up, or anybody else, without reading out a speech. God in heaven, he called in someone and dictated it, had it typed up, and stood up in the House and read it out. No one ever reads a speech down here. We might or might not have a note or two [as a reminder], . . . but read out a speech! And the stuffiest nonsense that was ever, ever read in a House, and they reading it out! I never ran into such timidity, such prudence, in my life, before or since! I've been in the Commons at Westminster, and they don't do that. They only do that at Ottawa. . . . Prudence and timidity all the way around. And scared to death of me! And then I discovered why.

There were two reasons. One was that a lot of people weren't a bit interested in the idea of Newfoundland joining Canada, and a lot of people who would more or less favour it were scared stiff that in Newfoundland people might think that Ottawa was trying to influence them, influence Newfoundlanders, trying to psychologize them, try to pressure them; that they were so eager to get us that they would use influence to get us in. If they'd only known! I tell you, it was the . . . first of many disappointments, the first big disappointment I ever had with Ottawa, where I expected a warm hearty welcome, and [that people would] enter into the thing with me [and] say "Now, if you join, we'll do this, and if you join, we'll do that." This is what I expected. I got nothing.

The only warm reception I got was from Solon Low; he was very warm about it, and he told me what to do if we became a province, about our natural resources: "Don't let Ottawa get their fists on your natural resources!" He was very keen on that . . . John Bracken used to raise Palomino ponies, and he had a farm fifteen or twenty miles from Ottawa, and Gordon Bradley and I went down there night after night. And we'd sit out in the front porch of his house, and talk and talk and talk. He was very friendly. And Jack Pickersgill. A Liberal, a Social Crediter, and a Tory. Coldwell was nice and friendly, very civilized, very decent, but I don't think he took it very seriously. But the one man who really took an interest was Jack Pickersgill. And I think that quite literally if he hadn't, I doubt if we'd be a province tonight. I doubt it; I really do.

PICKERSGILL: Well, I think this exaggeration calls for an intervention on my part. I like to think that at one or two points, things I did and said . . . may have had some influence. But if I had to pick the one Canadian without whom there would not have been Confederation, it would be Louis St. Laurent. . . . In your article, in your book, on Confederation, you say you had a very few minutes with Mr. St. Laurent that first time in 1946. And you had more than a few minutes with me; you talked to me for over an hour while you were waiting for him. When I say you talked to me, it's true, I listened. Mr. St. Laurent told me right afterward that he was very greatly impressed by you; but he had that Gallic reserve, and he didn't show these things much until he really sized someone up thoroughly. But there is no doubt that Mr. St. Laurent, more than any other living Canadian, was the man who really did the job in the negotiations and also the man who persuaded the Canadian people it was a good thing. And there was one other man in the Government who is not with us, Brooke Claxton. He was convinced from the outset and enthusiastic from the outset. But there weren't many others.

Mr. King had an almost pathological fear that if anything was done that indicated we were trying to influence the Newfoundlanders, the effect would be the exact opposite. I'm sure Mr. King thought that—well, I know he did, because he recorded it in secret. And he would have had no motive for doing it if he hadn't really felt it. I know he felt that Canada without Newfoundland—or perhaps I should put it the opposite way—he had feared that Newfoundland might fall into the hands of the United States and be an Alaska on the east, like the Alaska on the west; and he believed that Canada wouldn't have had room to breathe if that had happened, and so did I.

And I must say that before I knew Newfoundland, it wasn't any great sentimental attraction to Newfoundland. It was a kind of feeling of the destiny of Canada that pushed me into my enthusiasm for it. But I think we found out a little later, not during your first visit, because it hadn't percolated into the public mind until after the referenda, that you meant business. But once that was clear, there was an extraordinary wave that went across Canada, of interest and enthusiasm.

SMALLWOOD: There was a Gallup poll.

PICKERSGILL: Yes.

SMALLWOOD: So the Gallup poll did show what you're saying.

PICKERSGILL: Yes, oh yes, and the curious thing was the farther west you went, the more intense the feeling was.

SMALLWOOD: Do you know why? The reason was that—the Royal Canadian Navy was made up of Westerners, wasn't it, in the main?

PICKERSGILL: Yes.

SMALLWOOD: Well, people who had never laid their eyes on the sea landed here in the Royal Canadian Navy and sailed in and out of this seaport. Everyone, you'll admit, in the Navy was from the West. They got to like Newfoundland.

PICKERSGILL: I know, because I went through Canada with Mr. St. Laurent. In the campaign of 1949, I was the head of his office at that time, and you know I went with him to keep him in touch with the Government. Of course, I didn't take any part in politics. There were two things he talked about in that campaign that caught fire, and only two. One was Newfoundland, which was already accomplished by that time, the union. The other was NATO. All the domestic things, people weren't really interested in [; but they were interested in] those two things, almost everywhere, and it was a very surprising thing. . . . Because I think it was the first time Canadians began to escape a little from this introspection which perhaps Mr. King had reflected and maybe even encouraged a little.

SMALLWOOD: Jack, when the Convention was elected and met, the National Convention, we got a resolution through. . . . I wrote out the resolution, passed it into the secretary of the Convention, and it was debated and carried. . . . This resolution was carried, that Ottawa would be asked to receive the delegation from the National Convention, which would go up there to Ottawa to ascertain whether or not fair and equitable terms of a federal union with Canada existed, and we went up to Ottawa. We spent three months there—three months—seven of us. Mr. Bradley was the chairman. He was afterward Senator Bradley. He was the man I walked around Quidi Vidi with. And we were there for three months. Do you remember, ... I had one contact who used to keep me fairly well in the picture, Scott Macdonald. Scott Macdonald was Canada's High Commissioner in Newfoundland. From here, he went as ambassador to Brazil and from Brazil as ambassador to Austria. But here he was High Commissioner, and he went up to Ottawa, and he spent the three months there with us and kept in close touch with me.... He was the only means I had of knowing what was going on, because you didn't tell me, no one told me what was happening privately in the Canadian Cabinet. And I've often wondered about that—we have never really had time to sit down—every time we've been sitting down, it's been to talk of something else. But now that we're here (*laughter*): for those three months, were they kidding us along? I know there was a by-election in York-Sunbury in New Brunswick, and they didn't dare, they said, let the terms that they proposed to give us become known before that by-election was over as it might affect the result of the by-election. Milton Gregg was the candidate, I think.

PICKERSGILL: That's right.

SMALLWOOD: My friend Frank Bridges died.

PICKERSGILL: Yes, that's right.

SMALLWOOD: Milton Gregg was brought into the Cabinet, and now he was running for election. They had to wait. They even suggested that they'd provide us with a train—the seven of us—and send us right across Canada, right to British Columbia, to the capitals of all the provinces west of Ottawa. We'd go and study Confederation in those capitals, which I suspected at the time was just sort of delaying action, because I knew the importance of the by-election. But we were there for three months. Why was that?

... Mr. Pearson was the under-Secretary of State for External Affairs, and he was a sort of spokesman for the Canadian Government, the administration, with the press. And he'd hold a weekly press conference where he was not supposed to be quoted—he was the unnamed source. And he gave this interview, as one of the reporters from the press gallery who was present told me; ... and in this press conference, he told them, "Really, this delegation that are up here from Newfoundland are not going to get any terms. We wouldn't give them the terms and conditions of union. They're just here making a study of Confederation." In other words, he described our mission of seven men from the National Convention for three months in terms that would fit my earlier visit—I was up there alone to try to make [a] study of ... Confederation [and] what it means—and this is what we were there for! ... That nearly wrecked everything.

... Darcy O'Donnell was the only reporter in Ottawa that Gordon Bradley trusted. He didn't believe a word that anyone else wrote but Darcy

O'Donnell. . . . Darcy O'Donnell had this story that he published, he wrote it, that the unnamed source had said this delegation were merely up there to make a study of Confederation; and when Bradley read that, he blasphemed. He said, "Do you see that?" with his thundering, great voice. I had already seen it, and I had taken precautions. I wish I could tell you about that, but I won't. It is almost too good to tell.

This went on for three months, and then finally there came a Cabinet meeting in Ottawa where the showdown came. And I waited down in front of Centre Block, down by the far end of the East Block, and I walked up and down to see Scott Macdonald come out. He was at the meeting, the Cabinet meeting—maybe you were there.

PICKERSGILL: No, I wasn't there.

SMALLWOOD: Well, this was the meeting of the Canadian Cabinet—we were there then about two and one-half months—the meeting of the Canadian Cabinet at which they decided they were not going to send us back empty handed but that rather they would give us actual terms and conditions of the union, and I walked up and down there for two hours. I didn't dare tell Gordon Bradley, because he was so fed up with the heat of Ottawa that he would have gone home at short notice anyhow. This is when I had to walk with him for miles every night to keep him happy, and he had the darkest suspicions of what was up, that we were not going to get terms. And I remember the National Convention was adjourned. We had been elected—seven of us—to go to Ottawa and ascertain what equitable terms we could get, and we were there two and one-half months, and we had no terms—none. In the meantime, they were meeting back here in St. John's and holding public meetings and almost public demonstrations. They were sending telegrams to the Prime Minister, to the Governor General of Canada—anyone they could think of, they sent telegrams—denouncing us and demanding that we come back. They paraded down to Government House to the Governor and demanded that he reassemble the National Convention. We up there trying to get terms, and no sign of any terms, and Bradley beginning to suspect this! Well, [there was] this meeting, finally, of the Cabinet, which decided, "We'll give them terms."

PICKERSGILL: Well, I've always thought that a lot turned on that by-election: that if the Government had not won the by-election, very much more handsomely than they ever thought they were going to, . . . the faction in the Cabinet [that] didn't want to give any terms might have prevailed. To my knowledge, there were two points of view in the Cabinet. There were a lot of people who didn't have any. As you know, in Cabinets there are usually three groups.

SMALLWOOD: Not in our Cabinet!

PICKERSGILL: Well, you know, some of them are more articulate than others. In all Cabinets, there are the timid ones, who don't say anything, and sometimes one wonders if they think much. There are the prudent ones, and there are the bold ones, and there were certainly three or four people in that

Cabinet who were determined not to let you go back without terms.

SMALLWOOD: Mr. Pearson, Mr. St. Laurent . . .

PICKERSGILL: Pearson . . . no, he wasn't in the Cabinet, but he was very much on that side, notwithstanding what he said that day.

SMALLWOOD: How was Mr. Ilsley from Nova Scotia?

PICKERSGILL: Mr. Ilsley? Mr. Ilsley was filled with fear about the financial problem. He didn't see how, having fought so hard to keep the provincial share of the tax take from being what he regarded as exaggerated; he was afraid the whole structure that had been built up would be sunk. I think that he was a very powerful Minister. Mr. King himself I think never really showed his hand, as any wise Prime Minister does in circumstances like that, because once he showed his hand, what's the use of the rest of them talking about it?

C. D. Howe was all for it from the start.

SMALLWOOD: Was he?

PICKERSGILL: Oh, yes.

SMALLWOOD: He was the counterbalance to Ilsley?

PICKERSGILL: I don't think he ever articulated his reasons for it, but he just thought it was a good idea. It may be, you know, that C. D. Howe knew a little more about Labrador than anybody else did. This could have had some influence. But I think it was just his generally constructive disposition. But I would be inclined to think that it would have been very hard to get terms if the Government had lost that by-election, if they felt that here was something that might sink them in the next election, and also might not work in Newfoundland, and they wouldn't have taken the chance, that having got this triumph, I think then, and there is no doubt whatever that you were kept there for the three months because of that by-election. The whole thing would have been resolved much earlier, and I always believed you would have got terms.

SMALLWOOD: Well, I'll never forget when Scott Macdonald came from that meeting. . . . I was walking up and down, and I looked just to try to see how he was walking, if he looked encouraged or discouraged, because he was a great Confederate. Half-way down, he put up his hand like that. My heart leaped. We had it, this was it! And up to then, that was two and a half months, just about (I had it in my diary; I kept a diary). It was absolutely terrific. . . . I could stop kidding Gordon; I could be quite frank with him. I didn't have to buoy him up. I didn't even have to walk so much with him.

There were a couple of serious problems. Here in Newfoundland, you remember, Jack, we had . . . until quite recently we had . . . a school system probably quite different from anything in all of Canada. There were two great moral questions that would divide the people, that would sink anything, if they weren't handled right.

PICKERSGILL: You forget, there was the third one: there was margarine. It was very serious.

SMALLWOOD: . . . It was so serious that when the terms of union were being debated in the House of Commons, Mr. Drew, the Leader of the Opposition, got up and denounced the term in the terms of union which allowed Newfoundland to continue manufacturing margarine. We had a plant, we still have it, manufacturing margarine. We had no dairy industry, and butter was expensive. And margarine—we had lots of raw material for margarine. If you know what it's made of, you'll know what I mean—oil, marine oil, largely, not entirely. . . . It was important to us to continue the manufacture of margarine. . . . Drew got up and objected strenuously to this business of allowing Newfoundland to manufacture margarine, and he said it destroys Confederation. He said goods are supposed to pass freely from province to province, and this stops it. And the Prime Minister, Mr. St. Laurent, said, "Not so. If you look at it, you will find that the Constitution says that goods shall pass free. It doesn't say that they shall pass freely." And then he pointed out the difference. To pass free means to pass free of duty, free of tax, free of imports, but it doesn't mean to pass freely. Then he pointed out the examples. I remember his telling of a friend of his from Quebec who had called on him at his apartment in Ottawa just a week or two before and brought him a bottle of wine as a present, a gift. And he said to him, "Where did the wine come from?" He said, "Oh, Montreal." "Did you bring it with you?" He said, "I did." "And you crossed the border into Ontario?" He said, "Yes." "You know," he said, "you've broken the law, and you've made me an accomplice to your crime. It's against the law of Canada to bring wine from one province to another. A government may import it, but not an individual. . . ."

But the two big things were education—the school system—and divorce. And either was almost enough to wreck it. We had a terrific task. It involved Gordon Bradley going to call on the Papal Delegate in Ottawa, and he didn't want to do it. Gordon Bradley, for all his tremendous vigour and force, was a very shy man. He hated to meet anyone new, he was terribly shy, he really was. And the idea of going and meeting . . . the Papal, the Apostolic delegate, in Ottawa [bothered him a lot]. And I had the work of the world to get him to do it. He did, but I had to go with him. I walked along the road with him from the Château Laurier right up to the door, and I made sure he went in. And I waited till he came out, and he came out raving about the Archbishop. He said he was one of the finest men he ever met. He told me how the Archbishop shook hands with him and offered him a cigar and a drink, and they sat down . . . and chattered away. And before he knew it, he was unburdening himself to the Archbishop and telling him . . . his problems, political problems. . . . The Archbishop said to him, "You know, our Church wouldn't want anything by way of rights, school rights, in Newfoundland more than the Protestant schools get in Quebec. The same rights; that's all." I thought [this] was very, very encouraging. Now on divorce, he didn't seem to be all that excited. But we brought back with us . . . two terms that were not in the terms of union; they were privately written, and I brought them back to submit to the church authorities, which I did. These were proposed terms under which the school systems—the right that the churches had in education and [which] they have had for three-quarters of a century, by law, in Newfoundland—. . . would be entrenched in the terms of union. And they are entrenched. There's nothing in it about divorce, but this question of schools was written as Term 17. And it's still the basic law of this province, although in fact since then the denominations are rapidly coming together to form an integrated school system. But at that time, twenty-five years ago, it would have torpedoed Confederation completely. There was no chance of it.

PICKERSGILL: Do you think now we ought to get on to the campaigns on the referenda?

SMALLWOOD: All right.

PICKERSGILL: That's your story.

SMALLWOOD: The convention met, I think, for about eighteen months. The convention was announced by Mr. Attlee . . . in the House of Commons and in the House of Lords by Lord Addison. . . . They made the announcement the same day in both Houses, that the people of Newfoundland were to be given an opportunity to decide for themselves what form of government they would have for the future. And the way they were to do it was in a secret ballot referendum in which all electors—well, there were no electors, because there hadn't been any electors for eighteen years, . . . but the citizens—would be entitled to vote. . . . On the ballot paper, there would be no names of people, but only forms of government. And the form that would get the majority would be the form that would be brought into effect. This referendum would be preceded by the election of a National Convention, not a constituent assembly, you see, because the Convention was not to make a constitution. It was to meet for two purposes: 1) to examine the economy of the country; and 2) bearing in mind the extent to which the condition of the economy had been made by the war—in other words, how permanent is it, how transitory is it—bearing that in mind, and based on it, to recommend to the United Kingdom Government the forms of government that would be placed on the ballot paper in the referendum to follow.

So we met for eighteen months and talked forms of government. The Convention met at 3 every day to 6. And every word was recorded on discs; they didn't have tapes in those days. And these discs exist now. Every word spoken from 3 to 6, three hours a day, would be broadcast that night from 9 to midnight. And every living soul on the Island listened, unless he was dying. . . . There never was anything like it anywhere. For eighteen months, the entire population crowded to the nearest house that had a radio. Radios then in Newfoundland, 80 per cent of them, were battery operated; there was no electricity. There is now.

PICKERSGILL: A result of Confederation.

SMALLWOOD: And people had to conserve their batteries. So crowds would go to the nearest house, ten, twelve, fifteen, eighteen, twenty, thirty people, crowded into the kitchen. You could hear a pin drop; . . . they just listened intently to every word for eighteen months, five nights a week, from 9 to midnight.

PICKERSGILL: Well, you did have a few recesses.

SMALLWOOD: Yes, it wasn't continual eighteen months.

PICKERSGILL: There were those three months in Ottawa.

SMALLWOOD: There were three months in Ottawa, and there were the Christmas holidays. But extending over a period of eighteen months. And it was an absolutely tremendous exercise in popular education.

Now, what had to be done was to get the Convention to agree to send a delegation to Ottawa. The Anti-Confederates who were a majority were absolutely adamant. No! Absolutely not! They were going to bully England into giving us far more generous help than the Commission of Government had been giving. And there was another group that wanted to go to the United States. So there were three ideas. Peter Cashin, Major Cashin, wanted to force the English Government to give generous help to Newfoundland, restore responsible government and give generous help, forgetting or refusing to face the fact that in the British system, in British history, responsible government and dependence don't go together. One excludes the other. . . . [If you were a colony in the British Commonwealth,] you were entitled to responsible government only if you were self-supporting financially. If you had to have help, support from England, you couldn't have responsible government. But he wanted responsible government and help from England, which flew in the very face of the whole British concept, which would have required a complete revolution in their thinking. Another group wanted to link up with the United States. The United States is a very rich country, and there are probably far more Newfoundland people living [at] this moment in the United States than there are in Canada, if you exclude Newfoundland. And they were very rich. They'd been here during the war; they'd built great military bases. So had Canada. But Canada, a relatively poor country, had built bases economically; America just spent money as though it were going out of fashion. It was incredible; it was unbelievable, the way they spent money. That impresses people, did you ever notice?

And so there were the three points of view. There were the Confederates. We were a minority. And the idea was to send a delegation to Washington. Now I knew that the Commission of Government would never permit this. I knew, too, that the United States Government wouldn't receive a delegation of people who were not a government. To send a delegation to London, this made sense. The British Government had arranged for the election of this Convention to be followed by a referendum; the British government couldn't say, "No. We won't receive a delegation." They had to. The big question mark was would Ottawa? They could, but would they? So I brought my resolution in; I was all but massacred. It was defeated hopelessly. It was in that debate that I got my title "Judas Iscariot"—a bit of plagiarism—and "quisling", "traitor", and so on. It was hopelessly defeated. I had to bring it in again. But now, instead of a frontal attack, [I sidled] up to it: bring in three resolutions which look fair; let's leave no stone unturned. Let's look at everything; let's be big about this thing. So I wrote the three resolutions, and I got some people in the convention who were reasonable—[like] the late Hon. R. B. Job, who had been a member of the Upper House when we had had an Upper House, years before. He was a fish exporter, frozen fish, and he was terribly keen on getting the United States as a market for our fish. He wanted a quid pro quo. The quid was "let our fish [into the United States] free". The quo was the bases that the Americans had here in Newfoundland. . . .

So I got him to introduce [the] resolution that the Convention would appoint a delegation to go to Washington. And then another one that we would appoint a delegation to go to London, to Westminster. And a third one, which was fair, you see, that we'd have one to go to Ottawa. I moved that one. So all three were passed. But there was a fourth one, that we would appoint a delegation to go to call on His Excellency, the Governor, and ask him to make the arrangements. So we called on the Governor—I was one of the delegation from the Convention—. . . and the Governor said, "Yes, certainly. . . . This is very practical, except the one to Washington," he said. "Of course, you can't go to Washington. Anything you want to ask Washington, write it out and we'll send it forward to our ambassador (that's the United Kingdom ambassador) in Washington, and we'll get some answers for you." That sounded so completely reasonable that somehow, by a miracle, when we went back to the Convention, the Convention accepted it. "But," he said, "in the meantime, we will ascertain if the British Government will receive a delegation, and we will ascertain if the Canadian Government will." So we went back to the Convention with our report that two enquiries were to be made at once, if they would receive delegations in London and Ottawa, and as to the third, to Washington, no delegation could go as we were not a government. But any enquiries we had to make would be written out and His Excellency would send them to His Excellency the Ambassador. They had to be content with that. Now, the people who wanted the delegation to Washington wouldn't believe that Government House would refuse to permit a delegation to go to Washington. But I wrote the thing, and I got some support for it and spoke for it and supported it, and it passed. . . . So the delegation went over to London, headed by Mr. Bradley, who was by now the Chairman of the National Convention. He led the delegation, seven of them, to London. It was right after the war, not long after the war; England was still rationed, accommodation was terribly scarce and short—two or three of the delegates complained bitterly over the lack of proper accommodation. After all, they were virtually pleni-potentiaries of a sovereign state, whose status was in suspension, admittedly, but . . . They met Lord Addison and others, and they talked for several days, and they were told politely but very, very unmistakably, "Look, you people in Newfoundland, if you desire to have the Commission of Government continued, you can do so. All you have to do is vote for it in the referendum. And if you want to return to responsible government, you're quite free to do it. Quite free. But if you do it, you'll be on your own. Because responsible government and financial assistance from the United Kingdom do not go together. They never did. Doubtful if they ever will. And in any case, we can't afford it. We're getting help; we need help, and we're not able to give help." So they came back from London bitterly, bitterly disappointed because they went over—well, not all of them; Gordon Bradley didn't think so, and William Keough . . . didn't think so either—but the others appeared to think that the British Government were going to give big financial subsidies to Newfoundland under full responsible government. They were terribly disappointed. . . . By the way, they were so sure they were going to get help from England that they added a rider to my resolution about a delegation to Ottawa: that the delegation to Ottawa should not go until after the return of the delegation from London—of course, bringing back the bacon! They didn't bring back the bacon; and we went to Ottawa and spent three months there, the first time.

Now after that we came back, and the Convention was opened. I piloted the terms of union through the Convention for about six weeks, maybe eight weeks, every day, nothing but Confederation. And broadcast every night for three hours. The people of Newfoundland had no chance to listen to anything but advocacy and explanation of Confederation for those three months.

PICKERSGILL: It's a wonder they ever took it.

SMALLWOOD: The opponents, they loved it. They loved it; they did love it—believe me, they did. It's hard to believe. The opponents of Confederation would walk out; they'd leave me without a quorum. But being an old-time broadcaster, I would keep up a running description of what was happening into the microphone. Say, "Well now, ladies and gentlemen, the opponents of . . . the Anti-Confederates are walking out . . . there's another one gone, there's another . . . there's one more. Now they've left me without a quorum, so I have to wait till they begin sauntering back again." And I would give a description of it, and they got ashamed after a while to do that because they couldn't do it anonymously. When the debate was finally over, we had the resolution that Confederation be put on the ballot paper. It got sixteen votes to 28. . . . We all voted to put responsible government on the ballot paper. Our argument all the time was that there should be no limit. Anything that anybody would move in the Convention to be put on, should be put on. The people of the country in the referendum ought not to be cheated out of a chance to vote for anything they want, even vote against it.

I used to say, "Look, give the people a chance to vote against Confederation. Put it on the ballot paper. Let them decide! What right have we got to deprive them of the chance to vote for it or against it. Put anything on." So we voted to put responsible government on, and that was a unanimous vote. We argued that Commission of Government should be put on. And it was, but Confederation was not. So the Convention dissolved with two forms of government recommended unanimously and Confederation was rejected.

Now what? We made an appeal to the Newfoundland people to flood St. John's with telegrams and petitions. One broadcast; one. And they flooded us with telegrams all over the country demanding that Confederation be placed on the ballot paper. So the people could vote for or against it, put it on the ballot paper for the referendum.

I got up a magnificent procession to Government House and delivered the petitions and telegrams to the Governor for forwarding to Downing Street or to the Dominions office. Then we sat back and waited. We waited several weeks, I think, two or three weeks, I forget the exact period, it's on record . . . when back came the reply. The reply came to the Governor; the Governor's secretary telephoned to the Newfoundland Broadcasting Corporation, the predecessor of the CBC, the Newfoundland Government Broadcasting System—telephoned to them to send a man up. A man went up, Mr. Dick O'Brien, and the Governor recorded a speech in which he read out the telegram received from the Dominions Office. Dick O'Brien, who was a Confederate . . . I was there waiting in the studio, and Dick gave a wink that nearly dislocated his eye, it was such a beautiful wink and I knew it was all right, I didn't have to wait to hear it. But I did; I waited. And they broadcast the telegram from the Dominions Office that it would not be fair to leave Confederation off the ballot paper. It would not be fair. There's no better way that it could possibly have been put. It would not be fair. And so it was put on the ballot paper. And then the campaign started. This is a long introduction to . . .

PICKERSGILL: But the campaign itself, I gathered—I wasn't here and I didn't follow it very closely, but I gathered . . . the first campaign, the campaign when the three choices were before the people, was a relatively mild and civilized one. It was the second campaign that was somewhat more animated. I think your recollections of both would be worth a great deal more than anything I can say about this period of time, of waiting, that was going on on the mainland.

SMALLWOOD: Here, during those eighteen months, I had automatically or otherwise become the leader of the Confederate idea. And everyone who was a Confederate sort of looked to me to lead the cause. I was willing to lead it, eager and happy to lead it. And being an old newspaperman and an old radio broadcaster, I thought I knew something about persuasion of the public. And so—and no one else in our crowd did know very much, if anything about it—so they were quite happy to leave it to me. So I wrote every speech that was delivered; it didn't matter who delivered it, I wrote every speech. And it was always a speech looking for a voice. And every meeting that was held, every plane that was used, every word that was printed, passed through my hands. The result was that there was never one word that contradicted another. This was terribly, terribly important because the Anti-Confederates—there were two groups, two separate groups of Anti-Confederates—were contradicting each other on the air, on the radio, and ... within each group were people contradicting each other. So you had a terrible weakness of presentation. Whereas with us, it was unified and it was strong ... I went myself personally and did most of the campaigning in a small plane. That small plane was a little one-engine thing, she wasn't very good, she wasn't air-worthy, really. She was a seaplane, and she took about a mile and a half or two miles to get off the water. And I would take a P.A. system, and we'd land in some bay or an arm of the sea—maybe three or four or five or eight settlements right along in a row, separated by ten or twelve miles. We'd land and I'd get down on the pontoon and the pilot would help me—just one crewman, a crew of one and myself—he'd help me to set up the trumpets, turn on the battery, and I'd speak. And slowly we'd move down the Arm, opposite each individual settlement, and speak from the water. There was no ... no symbolism was intended. It was the only practical way to do it. Entirely a matter of practicality. In other places, I would land in a harbour big enough. Twillingate which was Mr. Pickersgill's constituency in the House of Commons for twelve years ...

PICKERSGILL: Fourteen.

SMALLWOOD: In Twillingate, I circled around and around and around until everybody gathered. They didn't know quite when I was arriving, so when the little plane drummed around and around, everybody came, coming down to the waterfront. There were, I think, twenty-five men out on that rock in the middle of the harbour. Twenty-five men in a row. And they had sealing guns.

PICKERSGILL: I'll never forget the first time I saw them. It was also at Twillingate.

SMALLWOOD: The first time he saw them, he also heard them, and he jumped three feet. Standing jump. An athletic record. ... They would put about five fingers of powder, rammed down in the muzzle. These were muzzle loaders and flint and steel, mostly. Old sealing guns from Poole, Poole guns, brought out here a hundred years ago, and eighty, seventy, sixty years ago. ... The first man would hold it up and he'd fire. ... And the next man would fire, and the next, and the next. ... By the time the twenty-fifth had fired, the [first] fellow had rammed down more powder, and he'd fire. And it was a fast round after round of these. I tell you, believe it or not, the concussion we'd feel in that little plane up in the air! ...

We'd land and taxi in to the wharf . . . and climb ashore. They had four or five trucks, they had a band, they had other gunners in some trucks, and they took me aboard the truck and we went slowly up through the main street to a square. The entire population [was there. I] set up the P.A. system and I talked.

This went on for six or eight weeks, and I covered most of the Island, carefully avoiding the places that were very hostile. [I] didn't go near them, because if I had and I'd got beaten up or got a bad reception or a rowdy meeting . . . the news would have been spread throughout the country. So by avoiding such things, going only where I was going to get the big, rousing reception . . . this was the great crusade, you see. The people were hearing nothing but unanimous support for Confederation. People do like to get on bandwagons. And when it was all over, I think [after] some six or eight weeks of campaigning . . . nobody had won. So by arrangement, announced previously before it all began, the low man was dropped from the ballot paper, which was Commission of Government.

Then we knew we had it. Anyone who had voted for Commission of Government after all that—eighteen months of National Convention, six or eight weeks of a campaign, and [they'd] still voted for Commission of Government—[was] certainly not going to vote for responsible government. Any people in Newfoundland who wanted to keep the non-elected, English-appointed Commission of Government that had been here for sixteen, seventeen years . . . would certainly not vote for responsible government; they'd vote for Confederation, the security and the safety of Confederation. And in the second referendum, which lasted another six weeks, that's what happened. We nipped in; we just barely made it. We got 51 point something, and they got 48 point something against Confederation.

But that was a rough one; that campaign was really rough. . . . I had to have a bodyguard, a bodyguard of men, who would meet me at the door of my house and fall in beside me—I've only seen it in gangster pictures; that's the only time I ever saw it—they'd fall in on both sides of me, and when I'd come out of my house, they'd fall in behind me. Three men, two on the side and one behind me to the car, across the sidewalk, aboard the car. They'd sit on both sides of me in the car, and one in front, and the driver would start up, get down to the Confederate headquarters, and the same thing in reverse. Wherever we went, bodyguards; and in spite of the bodyguards, I did get beaten up a few times. . . . This was quite a hot campaign.

PICKERSGILL: And you won a smashing victory. And I think perhaps I should tell again the story that's been told a good many times—modestly by me—about that victory. When the radio reported it, I was still in bed in Ottawa. They said it was 50—well, roughly 51—per cent, a little over and a little under 49. I went to the office early. I got hold of Gordon Robertson, who is now the Secretary to the Cabinet. Mr. King used to call me usually at ten o'clock in the morning because I never guaranteed to be at the office before ten. Sometimes I sneaked in earlier to get things prepared, and I certainly did that morning. And I said to Gordon Robertson, "I would like you to tell me the percentage of the popular vote that Mackenzie King got in every election from 1921 on."

SMALLWOOD: In his own seat?

PICKERSGILL: No, the whole of Canada. What percentage voted Liberal, what percentage voted Tory, and what percentage voted for the various other parties? All I was concerned about was what percentage had voted for Mackenzie King's candidates. I knew pretty well what it would be; I knew that he had never got a clear majority [of the popular vote] in any election except one. . . . The only one he got over 50 per cent was in 1940, in the wartime election. And then it was about 52, barely 52. And he called me at ten o'clock, and he said, "Pickersgill, what did you think of this vote in Newfoundland?" I said, "Mr. King, it's a triumph; it's a great triumph. Overwhelming!" I said, "Do you realize that a higher percentage of people voted for Confederation than ever voted for you? Except 1940, and it's almost exactly the same as 1940?" There was quite a long pause. And then he said, "Is that true, Pickersgill? Have you worked that out?" I said, "Oh, yes. I can send you the figures, Mr. King." "Well," he said, "that puts a different light on it."

Well, I wouldn't like to think that I was all that bright. I knew that after the first campaign, when responsible government had come first, Confederation second, and Commission of Government third, I knew it was going to be very close. So did Mr. King. And he began to talk, not to me, because I think he had somewhat lost confidence in my judgement, I was too much of a partisan of Confederation. But he began to talk to other people about what a clear verdict would be. I forget the exact words.

SMALLWOOD: "If the Newfoundland people . . . should express their wish for Confederation beyond not the possibility of doubt but beyond misunderstanding." It had to be unmistakable.

PICKERSGILL: Yes, it had to be unmistakable. And one day, I was having lunch with Mr. St. Laurent and Brooke Claxton at the Rideau Club, and Mr. St. Laurent started talking about what a clear verdict, an unmistakable verdict, would be. And I knew that Mr. King had been talking to him. And I knew that Mr. St. Laurent was an advocate and that he was trying to find some kind of argument. And he turned to me, and he said, "What do you think about that?" And I said, "Under the British system, a clear and unmistakable verdict in a vote is half the votes cast, plus one."

I think maybe that incident that morning may have been the most important but one I ever had to do with Confederation. The one other was the night after your victory, when you came back to Ottawa, when you were discussing the financial terms and before the famous Term 29 had evolved, and when somebody was looking for some way of reconciling the existing federal-provincial tax arrangements with the terms of union. . . . These were the final terms that were to be presented to Parliament; and at that stage, Mr. St. Laurent said to me one morning (they'd sat till midnight the night before), . . . "I really don't think, I don't think we're going to be able to reach an agreement." He said, "I just don't . . . this thing seems to me to be insuperable." And I said—and I remember it very clearly; it was perhaps somewhat impudent of me, but I said—"You know, Mr. St. Laurent, if you are responsible for bringing about this union, it will be the greatest thing you will ever do as Prime Minister. If you fail, no matter what else you do, you will have been a failure as Prime Minister and a failure to Canada." I knew Mr. St. Laurent really much better than I knew Mr. King, and I understood much better how his mind worked. I know that made an impression. I know he really believed it himself. I don't think it would have much impression if I'd just said it. But I think it helped a little at one of the hardest moments.

SMALLWOOD: Well, you underestimate your influence, Jack, on Mr. King and Mr. St. Laurent. Would it be profitable to discuss for a moment the question of the mechanics of our becoming a province, the discussion there was on that, and the difference of opinion? In Mr. Claxton's house, you were there that night, Mr. St. Laurent was there, Gordon Bradley and I, and I don't remember anyone else. . . . Now everything had been settled, the referendum had been held, the final terms had been drawn, they were to be submitted to the United Kingdom Parliament as an amendment to the BNA Act, and they were to be debated and adopted by Parliament at Ottawa; everything was settled now, it was final, completely final, and the practical question arose of just how would Newfoundland become a Province. [Mr. St. Laurent] put the argument that the Commission of Government should remain. Now, we were to become a province, remember, according to the terms, just before the stroke of midnight, March 31. That was 1949. . . . And he said, "There should be held a General Election in Newfoundland, and a Legislature come into existence, and then a Lieutenant-Governor appointed. And the Lieutenant-Governor would call on the leader of the victorious party to form an administration." And I argued that that was wrong, it was quite wrong, because I couldn't see how Newfoundland could become a province of Canada just before the stroke of midnight on March 31 and continue for some time, maybe six weeks or eight weeks, under the United Kingdom Government-appointed Commission of Government—under a Governor who had been appointed in the United Kingdom, not a Lieutenant-Governor. [Newfoundland would] be and not be a Canadian province. Well, he said, "How would you have it?" I said, "It's clear; it's quite clear. Just before the stroke of midnight on March 31, we become a province and following that, the next morning, as early as decent the next morning, the Lieutenant-Governor, the new Lieutenant-Governor, is sworn in. In the meantime, the Governor has retired and gone back to England. The Commission of Government has gone back to England. And Newfoundland is there with a Governor who is the Chief Justice. That's the law in Newfoundland: in the absence of the Governor, the Chief Justice becomes administrator. And so he is the Governor-acting, the administrator, for several hours. And on the morning of April 1, the new Lieutenant-Governor is sworn in. And he calls on someone immediately to form an administration." And I remember that I told him who it was that the new Lieutenant-Governor should call on. And there was really no argument about that. If he was to call on anyone, there was only one he could call on in the circumstances. The victorious cause was Confederation, there had been a leader of that cause, and he was the obvious one to become Premier. I'm not sure that there that night Mr. St. Laurent fell in line and agreed. But he did fall in line, and he did agree.

PICKERSGILL: No, he didn't fall in line that night. He did accept your view about the Governor, right there and then. I remember that very well, because that seemed conclusive, that these people who had been appointed by another government, and a Governor appointed from England, could not continue in any capacity in a Canadian province, that . . . there was a regular procedure for appointing a Lieutenant-Governor, and that could be followed without any difficulty. But he was not convinced that a regularly constituted Cabinet should be formed. And for some days after that, there was a discussion about a provisional government which would be selected from a number of prominent people. . . . I know there were a lot of things and you probably didn't hear about a lot of these things, because they were discussed by him and by Brooke Claxton and by Walter Harris, who had a pretty prominent part in all these things, and by me. But his feeling was that if we selected a politician who intended to go on being a politician, as the Premier, we were rigging the elections. This idea perhaps bothered him more than it would have bothered some other people.

SMALLWOOD: You mean the Opposition up there? You're not referring to anyone down here?

PICKERSGILL: Oh, no. But the more we looked at this, and I know this discussion went on for nearly a week, Brooke Claxton thought it was nonsense right from the start . . . we knew, as you had said that night, we knew who it was who had won the battle for Confederation, who'd been the leader; we knew there were in fact two leaders, yourself and Gordon Bradley, we knew that . . . there had to be a Minister from Newfoundland if Confederation was to be a success, and that was quite a problem too, finding a portfolio to give . . .

SMALLWOOD: Did you talk about that?

PICKERSGILL: Yes. The other question was settled first. After several days, it became perfectly clear that the only thing to do was to assume that the Confederate cause was the nearest thing to a political party there was, that they happened also to be Liberals perhaps was a happy accident, but an accident. But the next question was the question about having a Cabinet Minister at Ottawa.

SMALLWOOD: Well, on that, I have very clear recollection, because Bradley and I had made a pact. We'd shaken hands on it in his home in Bonavista. And he said he wouldn't be found dead in the Newfoundland House of Assembly again. He wanted nothing to do with it. But I said, "Gordon, there will be two great offices of state if we become a province. Newfoundland's Minister in the Government of Canada and Newfoundland's Premier." I said, "Of course, you're the senior; you take your choice." And he said he wouldn't be found dead in Newfoundland politics. "Well," I said, "Mr. Minister, I congratulate you." And I said, "I'll take the premiership, which is what I want. I wouldn't be found dead in Ottawa." And I meant that then, as I do now. So we parted on that, and I knew what he wanted.

Now, Bradley had been out of public life for twenty-odd years, and he had rather hibernated down in Bonavista. Small town. He loved it down there: he loved the sea; he loved the smell and the sound of the Atlantic Ocean. And although he wanted to be a Minister in the Government of Canada, he didn't really look forward to living in Ottawa. But you couldn't be a Minister if you didn't. They should do something about that, you know. As we drew nearer the end of the negotiations, the question of portfolio [arose], what portfolio for Gordon Bradley? Well, here in Newfoundland, up to that time, the great offices that were known were Prime Minister of England, Prime Minister of Canada, President of the United States, and Secretary of State. You remember Cordell Hull? Secretary of State. A great office, a great title. Next to the President, virtually.

PICKERSGILL: Remember, I was Secretary of State twice.

SMALLWOOD: This was before Mr. Pickersgill was a Minister at all. And we met one day, Mr. Pickersgill and I, in the University Club. . . . We went in there and had lunch. And we discussed the question of a portfolio for Gordon Bradley. And I know that Mr. Pickersgill was thinking that I had some elaborate great portfolio in mind for Mr. Bradley; that maybe Mr. Bradley had the same thing in mind for himself. And I said, "Look, the office that he should have is so evident that it doesn't really need argument—the one great office (now I knew that, excuse me, there wasn't an awful lot to do in that office; I mean, back then; I don't know what it's like now). If we were going to be a province, every Newfoundlander was going to be watching: 'Are they going to downgrade us? Are they going to treat us with dignity? Are they going to take us seriously?' " Any little sign there had been at any time—Mr. St. Laurent was so conscious of that, and so were you, that we had to be treated with respect. After all, we were only a handful of people, but we were very proud, stiff-necked people, you know, sinfully proud. You'd be surprised if you hang around long enough to find out how proud we really are down here. You may wonder what we have to be proud of. We could tell you that if we had time.

PICKERSGILL: Don't start on that.

SMALLWOOD: No. And he said, after I had this build-up, he said, "Yes?" I said, "Secretary of State." And I remember he leaned forward, and he slapped me on the knee. He said, "That's exactly it." . . . That was a couple of weeks before we signed the terms of union; and . . . two nights before we signed, that day, as the conference broke up, Mr. St. Laurent said to Mr. Bradley, "Mr. Bradley, could you come over to my apartment tonight, and we'll have a chat." Mr. Bradley said, "Yes, of course, sir." So he went over. And I walked over with him . . . and waited downstairs until he came down. And he came down blaspheming. I said, "What have you got?" He said, "Nothing!" He let out a roar. "Nothing!" "What do you mean, nothing?" I said, "What portfolio?" He said, "No portfolio!" I said, "Of course you're joking." "No," he said, "he didn't mention it." I said, "Well, you asked him, of course?" "No," he said, "I wouldn't mention it." And Mr. Bradley was that kind of man. He wouldn't mention it. He went there to get his portfolio. And he was furious. I said, "Well, all right, forget it, forget it!"

Now, Mr. St. Laurent had said to me, "Joe," he said, "maybe you'd come over tomorrow night." . . . I went over the second night, . . . and we talked about the first Newfoundland Cabinet. He'd had his misgivings and asked me did I have any good men that might join my Cabinet. And I gave him the names of various people, and I described each one, and I think he was impressed. He said, "That will be a very good Cabinet." Now, that having been settled, I was to be asked to form a Cabinet the day of Confederation, just after the stroke of midnight, a few hours later. After that was settled, . . . I said, "Prime Minister, now the question of our Cabinet Minister. That, I take it, is Mr. Bradley?" "Well," he said, "Mr. Bradley is a fine man, and a very prominent and well-respected man, and a professional man, a lawyer and so forth, and I would welcome him in my Cabinet." "Well," I said, "that's fine, that's fine. I take it then that I will be sworn in around ten o'clock on the morning of April 1, and around the same time he'll be sworn in as Canadian Cabinet Minister." "Well," he said, "I have no vacancy. No vacancy." And I said, "Sir, I mean on the first of April. This is the tenth of December. On the first of April, he'd be sworn in, wouldn't he?" "Well," he said, "quite frankly I have no vacancy in the Cabinet." "Sir," I said, "there is a Senate and there are ambassadorships." Didn't he appoint Mr. MacKinnon, a Minister of Trade, to be an ambassador somewhere?

PICKERSGILL: No, he appointed him to the Senate.

SMALLWOOD: That wasn't the vacancy. It was Colin Gibson.

PICKERSGILL: No, I can tell you all about that.

SMALLWOOD: But anyway, anyway, let me just . . . You tell me, but let me finish this part that I know, which was this. I said, "Sir, you know you can't have a Premier without a Minister. You must have a Minister in the Cabinet, mustn't you?" And I said, "If Mr. Bradley is the man, surely some way will be found to put him in the Cabinet the same day I become Premier!" Now I knew that Bradley would have apoplexy, he'd have a fit, if he didn't. He said, "Well, yes," he said, "I suppose that could be done." I said, "Thank you, sir, thank you very much." And when I came back, dancing on air, Bradley was waiting for me. I said, "You're Secretary of State. Shake hands." And he was. Now tell me the inside story.

PICKERSGILL: Well, what really happened after that was, in fact, a little that had happened before; because you'll remember after that discussion in the University Club, I had been applying my mind to the mechanics of doing something about this, and I had spoken to Mr. St. Laurent, and he was still very reluctant to commit himself in any way, and I think wisely so. I think he didn't want any rumours to get around about this position so long in advance. But I said, "It's perfectly apparent to me..." This was right after the terms of union were signed, sometime between then and Christmas—we had several talks about it. I said, "It's perfectly apparent to me that Mr. MacKinnon has no intention of being a candidate in the next election to the House of Commons. I happen to know because of conversations he had in my presence with Mackenzie King that he is very anxious to go to the Senate." I said, "Mr. MacKinnon is an exceedingly accommodating man, and he is an exceedingly patriotic man." And he was too. And I said, "I feel perfectly sure that if you asked him, he would resign his portfolio," which was not Secretary of State...

SMALLWOOD: Trade and Commerce, wasn't it?

PICKERSGILL: ... Yes, I believe it was. He would resign his portfolio, and some arrangement could be made to have another switch. It turned out to be Colin Gibson, who had been Secretary of State. He would take the portfolio of Mr. MacKinnon, and Mr. Bradley could become Secretary of State. And after quite a lot of discussion and so on, this was the course that he decided that he would like to follow, and he saw Mr. MacKinnon, who was not merely acquiescent but very pleased. And then suitable letters were written, and the whole transaction was arranged. It was long before the first of April.

SMALLWOOD: Jack, Colin Gibson came down here before the first of April to swear in the new Lieutenant-Governor, and he was Secretary of State on the same day Mr. Bradley became Secretary. They didn't overlap then, did they?

PICKERSGILL: No.

SMALLWOOD: It was an hour and a half difference in time.

PICKERSGILL: That's right. Oh yes, that was all arranged too. As Secretary of State, he was here present for the swearing-in of the Lieutenant-Governor, which was done, of course, by the Chief Justice of Newfoundland. And then he telegraphed his resignation to Ottawa, or he had left it behind... for greater certainty, I think, he had already left it behind. The other changes were made immediately afterward, and Mr. Bradley was sworn in as the Secretary of State, and then there was that great ceremony on Parliament Hill where Mr. St. Laurent and Mr. Bradley climbed up the ladder and started to carve the coat-of-arms of Newfoundland on the plaque that the architect had conveniently provided in 1920 when the new Parliament Buildings were designed.

SMALLWOOD: Every time we'd go in the building, if there was anyone with me, I'd point to the blank shield [and say], "This is our shield." And on that day, Mr. St. Laurent and Bradley both, didn't they both tap . . . with the chisel and hammer?

PICKERSGILL: Oh, yes. They were both up there together on the platform. I've got a picture of it somewhere.

SMALLWOOD: So have I. It's a good picture. Well, that's at least an outline of the story, isn't it?

PICKERSGILL: I think so.

SMALLWOOD: Not much more, though.

PICKERSGILL: Oh, no, there's . . . I think we can go on till about three in the morning, but I doubt if the audience could take it.

Prolonged applause.

Appendix Three

"NOTHING VENTURED, NOTHING GAINED"

I approached many companies in an effort to get them to establish in Newfoundland, and negotiated with them to that end. Here is a partial list of them.

Canadian

Falconbridge Nickel
Canada Cement
B. C. Packers
Canadian Fishing Co.
National Sea Products
M. J. Boylen Engineering
Algoma Steel
Steel Co. of Canada
Dofasco
Dosco
Imperial Oil
Irving Oil
British American Oil
Toronto Elevators
Atlantic Sugar
Kruger Pulp and Paper
Philips
Atco
Bow Valley
Levy Industries
Pan American Petroleum
Hollinger Gold Mines
O'Brien Gold
McIntyre Porcupine
George Weston

Frobisher
Canadian Johns-Manville
Leitch Gold Mines
Sklar Manufacturing

United Kingdom

English Electric
Ross Group
Unilever
Ultramar Oil
Rothschilds
Powell Duffryn
Llewellyn, Guerett & Llewellyn
British Insulated Cables
John White
Jaeger
British Oxygen
Bellrock Gypsum
British Firestone
Dunlop
Lilly and Skinner
Dolcis Shoes
Barrett Shoes

Finland

United Paper

Sweden

Siporex

Israel

Maritime Fruit

Italy

Snia Viscosa
Olivetti

Belgium

Société Générale de Belgique

France

Schneider, Creusot

Switzerland

Ciba
Brown, Boverie

Japan

Yawata Steel
Fuigi Steel
Taiyo Fisheries
Ataka
Sumitomo
Mitsuibishi

Germany

Krupp
I. G. Farben
Siemens Schukart
Humbolt-Klockner-Deutz
Stinnes
Thyssen
Miag
Mannesmann
Voight
Ernst Leitz
Demag

United States

American Smelting & Refining
Boise-Cascade
Brown Co.
Kaiser Aluminum
Reynolds Metals
Harvey Aluminum
American Metals—Climax
Litton Industries
M. A. Hanna
Pickands Mather
Cleveland Cliffs
Koppers Corp.
Shaheen National Resources
W. R. Grace
United States Plywood
John Fox
Union Bag & Camp

Crown-Zellerbach
Champion Paper
Cuneo Press
Hudson Paper
Parsons & Whittemore
Whippany Paper
Booth Fisheries
Union Carbide
Vita Foods
Lone Star Cement
O'Donnel-Usen
Flintkote
Katy Industries
Hooker Chemicals
American Zinc, Lead & Smelters
New Jersey Zinc
Tenneco Oil
Patino Mining
Texas Gulf Sulphur
National Lead
Stauffer Chemicals
International Basic Economy Corporation

Index